Studien zum ausländischen und internationalen Privatrecht

451

Herausgegeben vom

Max-Planck-Institut für ausländisches und internationales Privatrecht

Direktoren:

Holger Fleischer, Ralf Michaels und Reinhard Zimmermann

Jan Jakob Bornheim

# Property Rights and Bijuralism

## Can a Framework for an Efficient Interaction of Common Law and Civil Law Be an Alternative to Uniform Law?

Mohr Siebeck

*Jan Jakob Bornheim*, born 1984; read North American Studies, Economics, and Law at the Free University Berlin and the University of Cologne; LLM at the University of Toronto; clerkship at the Regional Court Bonn, including a secondment to the Supreme Court of the United Kingdom; Lecturer at the University of Essex, then the University of Canterbury (NZ).
orcid.org/0000-0003-0598-4646

Zugl.: Köln, Univ., Diss. 2016.

ISBN 978-3-16-159168-6 / eISBN 978-3-16-159169-3
DOI 10.1628/978-3-16-159169-3

ISSN 0720-1141 / eISSN 2568-7441
(Studien zum ausländischen und internationalen Privatrecht)

The Deutsche Nationalbibliothek lists this publication in the Deutsche Nationalbibliographie; detailed bibliographic data are available at *http://dnb.dnb.de*.



The book was printed on non-aging paper by Gulde Druck in Tübingen, and bound by Buchbinderei Nädele in Nehren.

Printed in Germany.

*für Hans Georg Bornheim*

# Preface

The following book discusses the interaction of different provincial systems of property law within a federal state. It was accepted by the Faculty of Law of the University of Cologne as a dissertation for the degree of *doctor iuris* in July 2016. The discussion of secured transaction law in § 12 B and C and § 14 B–D, as well as the discussion of Canadian insolvency law in § 16 A–C is partially based on my dissertation for the degree of Master of Laws at the University of Toronto. The relevant sections have been updated before submitting the dissertation for the doctoral degree. The book, including these sections, has been again revised for publication. In particular, the proposals by the Working Group of the Canadian Conference on Personal Property Security Law, and the 2019 secured transaction law reform in Saskatchewan as well as the decision by the Canadian Supreme Court in *Moore v Sweet* have been included, together with any other updates in case law and legal scholarship to the extent available in New Zealand.

Given that a significant part of the book discusses Canadian law, the citations follow the Canadian Guide to Uniform Legal Citation to ensure that the material can be cited as consistently as possible.

I am grateful to Professor Dr Heinz-Peter Mansel for the support and supervision during my years as a student and graduate student at the University of Cologne. I would also like to thank Professor Klaus Peter Berger for examining my thesis.

My studies in Canada, which have led to this book, have been supported by the generous financial support of the Lüderitz Stiftung and the Westhaus-Stiftung.

I am thankful to the editors of the series *Studien zum ausländischen und internationalen Privatrecht* for including my book in the publication programme, as well as their editorial team for all the helpful suggestions and corrections. Mrs Liss Bornheim has helped me by proofreading the book, for which I am very grateful.

Christchurch, March 2020 *Jan Jakob Bornheim*

# Overview

# Table of Contents

# Table of Abbreviations

| | |
|---|---|
| A | Atlantic Reports |
| ABCA | Court of Appeal of Alberta |
| ABQB | Court of Queen's Bench of Alberta |
| AC | Law Reports, House of Lords, Judicial Committee of the Privy Council and Peerage Cases |
| AcP | Archiv für civilistische Praxis |
| Adel L Rev | Adelaide Law Review |
| Advocates' Q | Advocates' Quarterly |
| AJ No | Alberta Judgments |
| AJ | Acta Juridica |
| Ala L Rev | Alabama Law Review |
| Alb L Rev | Albany Law Review |
| All ER | All England Law Reports |
| All ER Rep | All England Law Reports Reprint |
| Alta | Alberta |
| Alta L Rev | Alberta Law Review |
| Alta LR | Alberta Law Reports |
| Am Bankr LJ | American Bankruptcy Law Journal |
| Am Econ Rev | American Economic Review |
| Am J Comp L | American Journal of Comparative Law |
| Am J Legal Hist | American Journal of Legal History |
| Ann Rev Insolvency L | Annual Review of Insolvency Law |
| App Cas | Law Reports, Appeal Cases |
| App Ct | Appellate Court |
| AR | Alberta Reports |
| art | article |
| arts | articles |
| Ass | Assizes |
| ATR | Australasian Tax Reports |
| Austral Prop LJ | Australian Property Law Journal |
| Bank & Fin L Rev | Banking & Finance Law Review |
| Bankr | Bankruptcy Court |
| BC | British Columbia |
| BCC | British Company Cases |
| BCCA | Court of Appeal of British Columbia |
| BCJ No | British Columbia Judgments |
| BCLR | British Columbia Law Reports |
| BCR | British Columbia Reports |

| | |
|---|---|
| BCSC | Supreme Court of British Columbia |
| Beav | Beavan's Rolls Court Reports |
| BGB | Bürgerliches Gesetzbuch |
| BGH | Bundesgerichtshof |
| BGHZ | Entscheidungen des Bundesgerichtshof in Zivilsachen |
| BIA | Bankruptcy and Insolvency Act |
| BLR | Business Law Reports |
| Boston UL Rev | Boston University Law Review |
| BR | Bankruptcy Reporter; Quebec Official Reports, King's Bench |
| Brit J of Can Stud | British Journal of Canadian Studies |
| Brit YB Int'l L | British Yearbook of International Law |
| Burr | Burrow's King's Bench Reports |
| BYU L Rev | Brigham Young University Law Review |
| C de D | Cahiers de droit |
| CA Civ | Court of Appeal (Civil Division) |
| CA Crim | Court of Appeal in Criminal Cases |
| CA | Cour d'appel; Court of Appeal; Quebec Official Reports, Court of Appeal |
| Cal | California |
| Cal L Rev | California Law Review |
| Cal Rptr | West's California Reporter |
| Can | Canada |
| Can Bar Rev | Canadian Bar Review |
| Can Historical R | Canadian Historical Review |
| Can J Econ | Canadian Journal of Economics |
| Can JL & Juris | Canadian Journal of Law and Jurisprudence |
| CanLII | Canadian Legal Information Institute |
| Car II | Charles II |
| CarswellNS | Carswell Nova Scotia |
| CarswellOnt | Carswell Ontario |
| CBLJ | Canadian Business Law Journal |
| CBR | Canadian Bankruptcy Reports |
| CcBC | Code civil du Bas-Canada |
| CCLA | Civil Code of Louisana |
| CCPPSL | Canadian Conference on Personal Property Security Law |
| CcQ | Code civil du Québec |
| CCSM | Continuing Consolidation of the Statutes of Manitoba |
| cf | confer |
| Ch App | Court of Appeal in Chancery |
| Ch Cas | Cases in Chancery |
| Ch D | Chancery Division; Law Reports, Chancery Division |
| Ch | Court of Chancery; Law Reports, Chancery Division |
| Cir | Circuit |
| CJCCL | Canadian Journal of Comparative and Contemporary Law |
| CLJ | Cambridge Law Journal |
| CLR | Commonwealth Law Reports |
| CM | Cour municipale |

| | |
|---|---|
| Co Ct | County Court |
| Co Rep | Coke's King's Bench Reports |
| Col L Rev | Columbia Law Review |
| Com Pl | Court of Common Pleas |
| Comm L Bull | Commonwealth Law Bulletin |
| Comm L World Rev | Common Law World Review |
| Conn | Connecticut |
| Conn App | Connecticut Appellate Reports |
| Conveyancer | The Conveyancer and Property Lawyer Journal |
| Cornell L Rev | Cornell Law Review |
| Cornell LQ | Cornell Law Quarterly |
| Cowp | Cowper's King's Bench Reports |
| CPP | Canada Pension Plan |
| CQ | Cour du Québec |
| CS | Quebec Official Reports, Superior Court |
| Ct App | Court of Appeals |
| Ct Civ App | Court of Civil Appeals |
| Ct Exch | Court of Exchequer |
| Ct Sess, In H | Inner House, Court of Session |
| Cth | Commonwealth of Australia |
| Curr Legal Probs | Current Legal Problems |
| | |
| D | District Court |
| De GF & J | De Gex, Fisher & Jones' Chancery Reports |
| DeCITA | Derecho del Comercio Internacional - Temas y Actualidades |
| Del | Delaware |
| Denn LJ | Denning Law Journal |
| Dist | District |
| DLR | Dominion Law Reports |
| DNotZ | Deutsche Notar-Zeitschrift |
| Duke LJ | Duke Law Journal |
| | |
| E & A | Court of Error & Appeal |
| e.g. | for example |
| ECJ | European Court of Justice |
| Econ J | Economic Journal |
| ED | Eastern District |
| Edin L Rev | Edinburgh Law Review |
| edn | edition |
| Edw I | Edward I |
| EIA | Employment Insurance Act |
| El & Bl | Ellis and Blackburn |
| Eliz I | Elizabeth I |
| Engl and W | England and Wales |
| ER | English Reports |
| ETPJ | Estates Trusts & Pensions Journal |
| ETR | Estates and Trust Reports |
| EU | European Union |

| | |
|---|---|
| Eur Econ Rev | European Economic Review |
| Eur LJ | European Law Journal |
| Eur Rev Priv L | European Review of Private Law |
| EWCA Civ | Court of Appeal of England and Wales, Civil Division |
| Exch Ch | Exchequer Chamber |
| f | following (singular) |
| F | Federal Reporter |
| FCA | Federal Court of Appeal |
| Fed TD | Federal Court (Trial Division) |
| ff | following (plural) |
| Fla | Florida |
| FSupp | Federal Supplement |
| Ga L Rev | Georgia Law Review |
| GB | Great Britain |
| Gen Div | Ontario Court (General Division) |
| Geo III | George III |
| Geo IV | George IV |
| Geo V | George V |
| H & M | Hemming & Miller's Chancery Reports |
| Harv L Rev | Harvard Law Review |
| Hastings Int'l & Comp L Rev | Hastings International and Comparative Law Review |
| Hastings LJ | Hastings Law Journal |
| HBl | Henry Blackstone's Common Pleas Reports |
| HCA | High Court of Australia |
| HCJ | High Court of Justice |
| HL Cas | Clark & Finnelly's House of Lords Reports New Series |
| HL | House of Lords |
| Hofstra L Rev | Hofstra Law Review |
| How | Howard's Supreme Court Reports |
| ibid | in the same place |
| IBRD | International Bank for Reconstruction and Development |
| ICLQ | International and Comparative Law Quarterly |
| i.e. | that is |
| Ill | Illinois |
| Int | International |
| Int'l Rev L & Econ | International Review of Law and Economics |
| Iow L Rev | Iowa Law Review |
| ITA | Income Tax Act |
| J Comp L | Journal of Comparative Law |
| J Comp Leg Int'l L | Journal of Comparative Legislation and International Law |
| J Econ Lit | Journal of Economic Literature |
| J Econ Th | Journal of Economic Theory |
| J Equ | Journal of Equity |
| J Fin | Journal of Finance |

| | |
|---|---|
| J Financial Econ | Journal of Financial Economics |
| J Leg An | Journal of Legal Analysis |
| J Legal Stud | Journal of Legal Studies |
| J Pol Econ | Journal of Political Economy |
| J Priv Int'l L | Journal of Private International Law |
| Jb Dogm | Jahrbücher für die Dogmatik des heutigen römischen und deutschen Privatrechts |
| Jher Jb | Jherings Jahrbücher für die Dogmatik des bürgerlichen Rechts |
| JL & Econ | Journal of Law and Economics |
| JQ No | Jugements Québec |
| JRNS | Juridical Review New Series |
| Jurist | The Jurist |
| JZ | Juristenzeitung |
| | |
| KB | Court of King's Bench |
| Ky | Kentucky |
| | |
| La | Louisisana |
| La L Rev | Louisiana Law Review |
| LARCC | Loi sur l'application de la réforme du Code civil |
| Law & Hist R | Law and History Review |
| LC | Lower Canada |
| LCJ | Lower Canada Jurist |
| Liv L Rev | Liverpool Law Review |
| Lloyd's Rep | Lloyd's Reports |
| LMCLQ | Lloyd's Maritime and Commercial Law Quarterly |
| Loy L Rev | Loyola Law Review |
| LPA | Law of Property Act |
| LQR | Law Quarterly Review |
| LR Ch App | Law Reports, Chancery Appeal Cases |
| LR Ex D | Law Reports, Exchequer Division |
| LRCP | Law Reports, Common Pleas |
| LRQB | Law Reports, Queen's Bench |
| LS | Legal Studies |
| LT | Law Times Reports |
| LTVM | Loi sur le transfert de valeurs mobilières et l'obtention de titres intermédiés |
| LVM | Loi sur les valeurs mobilières |
| | |
| M | Macpherson's Session Cases |
| Mal L Rev | Malaya Law Review |
| Man | Manitoba |
| McGill LJ | McGill Law Journal |
| Mich L Rev | Michigan Law Review |
| Minn | Minnesota; Minnesota Reports |
| MJ No | Manitoba Judgements |
| MMP | Monatshefte für Mathematik und Physik |
| Mo | Missouri |

| | |
|---|---|
| Mo L Rev | Missouri Law Review |
| Modern L Rev | Modern Law Review |
| Monash UL Rev | Monash University Law Review |
| Moo PCNS | Moore's Privy Council Cases, New Series |
| MüKo-BGB | Münchener Kommentar zum Bürgerlichen Gesetzbuch |
| My & K | Mylne & Keen's Chancery Reports |
| | |
| NB | New Brunswick |
| NCL Rev | North Carolina Law Review |
| NE | North Eastern Reporter |
| Neb | Nebraska; Nebraska Reports |
| Nethl Int'l L Rev | Netherlands International Law Review |
| NJ | New Jersey; New Jersey Reports |
| NJW | Neue Juristische Wochenschrift |
| NL | Newfoundland and Labrador |
| Notre Dame L Rev | Notre Dame Law Review |
| NPC | New Property Cases |
| NS | Nova Scotia |
| NSCA | Court of Appeal of Nova Scotia |
| NSR | Nova Scotia Reports |
| NSSC | Supreme Court of Nova Scotia |
| NSW | New South Wales |
| NSWSC | Supreme Court of New South Wales |
| Nw J Int'l L & Bus | Northwestern Journal of International Law & Business |
| NW | North Western Reporter |
| NWT | Northwest Territories |
| NY | New York; New York Reports |
| NYUL Rev | New York University Law Review |
| NZ | New Zealand |
| NZL Rev | New Zealand Law Review |
| NZLR | New Zealand Law Reports |
| | |
| Ohio St LJ | Ohio State Law Journal |
| OHLJ | Osgoode Hall Law Journal |
| OJ No | Ontario Judgments |
| OJ | Official Journal of the European Union |
| Okla L Rev | Oklahoma Law Review |
| ONCA | Court of Appeal of Ontario |
| ONSC | Superior Court of Ontario |
| Ont | Ontario |
| OR | Ontario Reports |
| Ore | Oregon |
| Ottawa L Rev | Ottawa Law Review |
| Oxford J Legal Stud | Oxford Journal of Legal Studies |
| | |
| P | Law Reports, Probate; Pacific Reporter |
| para | paragraph |
| paras | paragraphs |
| PC | Judicial Committee of the Privy Council |

| | |
|---|---|
| PEI | Prince Edward Island |
| Penn St J L & Int'l Aff | Penn State Journal of Law & International Affairs |
| PMSI | purchase-money security interest |
| PPSA | Personal Property Securities Act; Personal Property Security Act |
| PPSAC | Personal Property Security Act Cases |
| Prov Ct | Provincial Court |
| QB | Court of Queen's Bench; Law Report, Queen's Bench |
| QB (AD) | Court of Queen's Bench, Appellate Division; Law Reports, Queen's Bench Division |
| QBD | Queen's Bench Division |
| QCCA | Court of Appeal of Québec |
| QCCQ | Cour du Québec |
| QLR | Quebec Law Reports |
| Quart J Econ | Quarterly Journal of Economics |
| Queb | Québec |
| R du B | Revue du Barreau |
| R du D | Revue du droit |
| R du N | Revue du notariat |
| RabelsZ | Rabels Zeitschrift für ausländisches und internationales Privatrecht |
| RCLF | Revue de la common law en français |
| RDF | Recueil de droit de la famille |
| RDI | Recueil de droit immobilier |
| RDJ | Revue de droit judiciaire |
| Rev dr int dr comp | Revue de droit international et de droit comparé |
| Rev Econ St | Review of Economic Studies |
| Rev Int Dr Comp | Revue internationale de droit comparé |
| RGD | Revue générale de droit |
| Riv dir int priv proc | Rivista di diritto internazionale privato e processuale |
| RJQ | Receuil juridique du Québec |
| RJT | Revue juridique Thémis |
| RL | Revue Legale, New Series |
| RLR | Restitution Law Review |
| RPR | Real Property Reports |
| RSA | Revised Statutes of Alberta |
| RSBC | Revised Statutes of British Columbia |
| RSC | Revised Statutes of Canada |
| RSO | Revised Statutes of Ontario |
| RSPEI | Revised Statutes of Prince Edward Island |
| RSQ | Revised Statutes of Québec |
| RSY | Revised Statutes of Yukon |
| RTD | Revue trimestrielle de droit civil |
| s | section |
| S Cal L Rev | Southern California Law Review |
| Sask | Saskatchewan |

| | |
|---|---|
| Sask L Rev | Saskatchewan Law Review |
| Sask R | Saskatchewan Reports |
| SC | Supreme Court; Session Cases; Statutes of Canada |
| SC (HL) | Session Cases, House of Lords |
| SC (TD) | Supreme Court, Trial Division, |
| SCC | Supreme Court of Canada |
| Scot | Scotland |
| SCR | Canada Law Reports, Supreme Court; Supreme Court Reports |
| SCt | West Supreme Court Reporter |
| SDHI | Studia et Documenta Historiae et Iuris |
| Sel Cas T King | Select Cases in Chancery tempore King |
| SGA | Sale of Goods Act |
| Sing L Rev | Singapore Law Review |
| SJZ | Süddeutsche Juristen-Zeitung |
| SKCA | Court of Appeal of Saskatchewan |
| SKQB | Court of Queen's Bench of Saskatchewan |
| SLT | Scots Law Times |
| SNB | Statutes of New Brunswick |
| SNL | Statutes of Newfoundland and Labrador |
| SNS | Statutes of Nova Scotia |
| SNWT | Statutes of the Northwest Territories |
| SO | Statutes of Ontario |
| So | Southern Reporter |
| Soc Th & Pract | Social Theory and Practice |
| SQ | Statutes of Québec |
| ss | sections |
| SS | Statutes of Saskatchewan |
| St Ch | Star Chamber |
| STA | Securities Transfer Act |
| Stan L Rev | Stanford Law Review |
| STC | Simon's Tax Cases |
| Stu KB | Stuart's Lower Canada King's Bench Appeal Cases |
| Suffolk UL Rev | Suffolk University Law Review |
| SUL Rev | Southern University Law Review |
| Sup Ct J | Superior Court of Justice |
| Sup Ct L Rev | Supreme Court Law Review |
| Sup Ct | Supreme Court; Cour superieure |
| SW | South Western Reporter |
| Swans | Swanston's Chancery Reports |
| Sydney L Rev | Sydney Law Review |
| T & T | Trusts & Trustees |
| Tex | Texas |
| Tex L Rev | Texas Law Review |
| TIGA | Torts (Interference with Goods) Act |
| Tul L Rev | Tulane Law Review |

| | |
|---|---|
| U Chicago L Rev | University of Chicago Law Review |
| U Det LJ | University of Detroit Law Journal |
| U Ill L Rev | University of Illinois Law Review |
| U Pa J Int'l Econ L | University of Pennsylvania Journal of International Economic Law |
| U Pa J Int'l L | University of Pennsylvania Journal of International Law |
| U Pa L Rev | University of Pennsylvania Law Review |
| UBCL Rev | University of British Columbia Law Review |
| UC | Upper Canada |
| UC Davis L Rev | University of California at Davis Law Review |
| UCE & A | Grant's Error and Appeal Reports |
| UCLA L Rev | University of California at Los Angeles Law Review |
| UCQB | Upper Canada Queen's Bench Reports |
| UK | United Kingdom |
| UKHL | House of Lords |
| UKPC | Judicial Committee of the Privy Council |
| UKSC | Supreme Court of the United Kingdom |
| Unif Comm Code LJ | Uniform Commercial Code Law Journal |
| Unif L Rev | Uniform Law Review |
| UNSWLJ | University of New South Wales Law Journal |
| US | Supreme Court of the United States; United States Supreme Court Reports |
| USA | United States of America |
| USC | United States Code |
| Utah L Rev | Utah Law Review |
| UTLJ | University of Toronto Law Journal |
| UWAL Rev | University of Western Australia Law Review |
| | |
| Va | Virginia |
| Va L Rev | Virginia Law Review |
| Vand L Rev | Vanderbilt Law Review |
| Ves Sen | Vesey Senior's Chancery Reports |
| Vict | Victoria |
| | |
| WA | Western Australia |
| WASC | Supreme Court of Western Australia |
| Wash & Lee L Rev | Washington and Lee Law Review |
| WB | World Bank |
| WD | Western District |
| WL | Westlaw US |
| WLR | Weekly Law Reports |
| WWR | Western Weekly Reports |
| | |
| Yale LJ | Yale Law Journal |
| | |
| ZEuP | Zeitschrift für Europäisches Privatrecht |
| ZHR | Zeitschrift für Handelsrecht |
| ZVglRWiss | Zeitschrift für Vergleichende Rechtswissenschaft |

# Introduction

"There are topics of conversation more popular in public houses than the finer points of the equitable doctrine of the constructive trust."

*Attorney General's Reference (No1 of 1985)*, [1986] QB 491 at 506 (CA Crim), Lord Lane

## A. The Problem

The incidents of property rights are manifold. Someone deeming herself the owner of something may be surprised to find out what she can or cannot do with that something. This book is not concerned with the variety of factual rights her ownership entails. This is not because it is arguably misleading to talk of the concept of ownership when speaking about the Common Law. Rather, the aim of this book is a different one. This book is concerned with how assets somebody deems herself the owner of – "property" – can be subjected to satisfy others against whom she undertook a promise or who for another reason claim to be entitled to demand some type of performance from her. These others are her "creditors."

The incidents of property and the way in which one's property is being made available to creditors differ between jurisdictions. One important way in which the property-creditor link is modified is the use of property as a security for an obligation. The framework governing this use of property as a means of security is secured transactions law. As a subset of property law, secured transactions law can differ significantly between legal systems. Within the European Union, that has led to the calls for a uniform European secured transactions law.[1] The United Nations Commission on International Trade Law (UN-

[1] See particularly the work of the working group on a Draft Common Frame of Reference: Ulrich Drobnig & Ole Böger, eds, *Proprietary Security in Movable Assets* (Principles of European Law, Berlin: Sellier-de Gruyter, 2015); Christian von Bar, Eric Clive & Hans Schulte-Nölke, eds, *Principles, Definitions and Model Rules of European Private Law: Draft Common Frame of Reference (Outline Edition)* (München: Sellier, 2009) at 447–99. For an argument for a European secured transaction law see e.g. Boudewijn Bouckaert, "Divergences of the Law on Securities: A Law and Economics Approach" in: Ulrich Drobnig, Henricus J Snijders & Eric-Jan Zippro, eds, *Divergences of Property Law: An Obstacle to the Internal Market?* (Berlin: Sellier, 2006) 175; Ulrich Drobnig, Henk J Snijders & Eric-Jan

CITRAL) has also continued its work. While it initially only published a legislative guide, it has now published a Model Law for Secured Transactions.[2] The desirability of a uniform secured transactions law is not universally accepted.[3] The example of Canadian law shows that it is possible to accept divergent property law systems and – consequently – different secured transactions law systems within one union.

Using the Canadian experience with bijuralism, this book analyses the differences in the notion of property rights in movable property between Common

---

Zippro, "Divergences of Property Law: An Obstacle to the Internal Market" in: Drobnig, Snijders & Zippro, eds, *Divergences of Property Law,* this note, 3; Horst Eidenmüller & Eva-Maria Kieninger, eds, *The Future of Secured Credit in Europe* (European Company and Financial Law Review Special Series, Berlin: Walter de Gruyter, 2008); Eva-Maria Kieninger, "Die Zukunft des deutschen und europäischen Mobiliarkreditsicherungsrechts" (2008) 208:2–3 AcP 182; Eva-Maria Kieninger, "European Regulation of Security Rights" in: Drobnig, Snijders & Zippro, eds, *Divergences of Property Law,* this note, 165; Eva-Maria Kieninger, *Mobiliarsicherheiten im Europäischen Binnenmarkt* (Baden-Baden: Nomos, 1996); Willem Rank, "Harmonisation of National Security Rights" in: Drobnig, Snijders & Zippro, eds, *Divergences of Property Law,* this note, 201; Wulf-Henning Roth, "Secured Credit and the Internal Market: The Fundamental Freedoms and the EU's Mandate for Legislation" in: Horst Eidenmüller & Eva-Maria Kieninger, eds, *The Future of Secured Credit in Europe* (Berlin: Walter de Gruyter, 2008) 36; Henk J Snijders, "Access to Civil Securities and Free Competition in the EU: A Plea for One European Security Right in Movables" in: Drobnig, Snijders & Zippro, eds, *Divergences of Property Law,* this note, 153. For an analysis of secured transactions law harmonization see Moritz Brinkmann, *Kreditsicherheiten an beweglichen Sachen und Forderungen: Eine materiell-, insolvenz- und kollisionsrechtliche Studie des Rechts der Mobiliarsicherheiten vor dem Hintergrund internationaler und europäischer Entwicklungen* (Jus Privatum, Tübingen: Mohr Siebeck, 2011) at 468–87 and Gerard McCormack, *Secured Credit and the Harmonisation of Law: The UNCITRAL Experience* (Cheltenham: Edward Elgar, 2011).

[2] UNCITRAL, *Model Law on Secured Transactions*, (UNCITRAL) <https://uncitral.un.org/en/texts/securityinterests/modellaw/secured_transactions> accessed 20 September 2019

[3] Critical voices include Martin Boodman, "The Myth of Harmonization of Laws" (1991) 39:4 Am J Comp L 699; Martin Boodman & Roderick A Macdonald, "How Far is Article 9 of the Uniform Commercial Code Exportable?: A Return to Sources" (1996) 27:2 CBLJ 249; Ronald J Daniels, "Should Provinces Compete?: The Case for a Competitive Corporate Market" (1991) 36:1 McGill LJ 130; Nuria de La Peña, "Challenges in Implementing Secured Transactions Reform in Latin America" in: Frederique Dahan & John Simpson, eds, *Secured Transactions Reform and Access to Credit* (Cheltenham: Edward Elgar, 2009) 236; Roderick A Macdonald, "In Praise of the Hypothecary Charge" (2007) 7–8 DeCITA 287; Alan Schwartz & Robert E Scott, "The Political Economy of Private Legislatures" (1995) 143:3 U Pa L Rev 595. For an example of an unsuccessful partial harmonization in the United Kingdom see Anja Fenge, "Englisches Kreditsicherungsrecht versus schottisches Sachenrecht: Sharp v Thomson" (1999) 98 ZVglRWiss 410 and George L Gretton, "Reception Without Integration?: Floating Charges and Mixed Systems" (2003) 78:1–2 Tul L Rev 307 on *Sharp v Thomson,* [1997] SLT 636 (HL).

Law and Civil Law, and how transsystemic legislation can cope with these differences. One focus of the book lies in an examination of the difference between the absolute notion of property and its vindication in Civil Law on the one hand and the relative property concept and proprietary restitution as a means of vindication in the Common Law on the other hand. Herein lies the meaning of the introductory quote: the finer points of the equitable doctrine of the constructive trust might be unpopular topics in the public houses of England, but the doctrine itself plays a fundamental role in Common Law property.

This book also shows how the differences between Common Law and Civil Law property law continue to shape secured transactions law. It addresses the law-and-economics suggestion that a Common Law legal system is inherently "better law" by showing that the alleged benefits of the Common Law system are not intrinsically linked to what defines Common Law or Civil Law property. While there is an inherent friction in the retention of two property law sub-systems under the umbrella of one transsystemic jurisdiction, I argue that a complete uniformity of property law would be a radical levelling of the legal culture of either Common Law or Civil Law, or both. Instead, divergent property laws are better addressed in the areas where competing property interests from different property law systems interact. These areas are the conflict of laws and insolvency law.

## B. Outline

The *first part* of this book sets the stage for the analysis of the interaction of property, secured transaction, and insolvency within the framework of Canadian bijuralism. Condensed to its most basic meaning, the term "bijuralism" refers to the co-existence of two legal systems under one roof.[4] In the case of this book, Canada is used as an example of such co-existence. The *first chapter* will thus trace the history of Canadian private law. Because modern Canada is at least institutionally a child of British imperialism, it is particularly the retention of Civil Law in Québec that is of interest. After all, most British colonies have a legal system based on the laws of England, be it the United States, Australia, New Zealand, or most of Canada. The chapter will thus look at the reasons for and the means of retaining Québec's Civilian heritage. The *second chapter* will then look at the modern meaning of "bijuralism." The *third* and final introductory chapter will lay the groundwork for the methodological and theoretical approach I take in this book: the economic analysis of the law. It will trace the development of the economic analysis of the law, the method, and its implication for the retention of legal systems and bijuralism.

---

[4] Marie-Claude Gaudreault, "Canadian Legislative Bijuralism: An Expression of Legal Duality" (2006) 32:2 Comm L Bull 205 at 205.

*Part two* of this book is dedicated to property law. *Chapters four* and *five* give an overview of the substantive notion of property in Common Law and Civil Law. Alas, the scope of these chapters is limited. One very important restriction is that I am only concerned with movable and personal property ("chattel"). The selection could easily be explained as a pragmatic one: this book is long enough as it is without the inclusion of immovable and real property. However, I have two substantive reasons for my selection of movable over immovable property.

First, movable property – by virtue of its movability – is more likely than immovable property to cross the boundaries of legal system. Also, a debtor is more likely to own movable property in different jurisdictions than she is to own immovable property in different jurisdictions. Co-ordination problems between legal systems are thus more likely to occur regarding movable property.

Second, this book is concerned with the impact of property law on economic development. Businesses are more likely to use movable property rather than immovable property as collateral. Thus, the law of movable property is a more appropriate subject of study than the law of immovable property. Nevertheless, this study will show that it is not always possible to explain notions of movable property law without reference to immovable property law. The two are not totally separate areas of law.

Another restriction on the scope of my analysis of property law is that I am not concerned with how the holder of a property right can use her property. Rather, the goal is to place property rights into what the Civilian knows as the notion of "gage commun." Property is only looked at to the extent of securing obligations. However, for this purpose, it is important to consider how something becomes one's property and how one retains this property.

The next two chapters, *chapters six* and *seven,* look at modifications of property law by equity and trust law, and the relationship of both the Common Law and the Civil Law notions of trust and property law. *Chapter eight* presents theoretical accounts for property: why do we have property law, why is it the way it is, and how should it be? Finally, *chapters nine* and *ten* are concerned with a peculiarity of Common Law property: proprietary restitution. Proprietary restitution as such is unknown to Civil Law, but in Common Law, proprietary restitution re-distributes property and thus affects the gage commun. These chapters will thus try to integrate the notion of proprietary restitution with a theory of property.

The *third part* of the book concerns secured transactions law. First, I look at the economic theories behind secured transaction law in *chapter eleven.* Then, *chapters twelve through fourteen* are concerned with the substantive secured transaction law in Canada's two legal systems. *Chapter twelve* looks at secured transaction law in the Common Law provinces. Property law and secured transaction law have a more uneasy relationship in those provinces. Thus, the relationship between secured transaction law and property law merits its own chapter: *chapter 13. Chapter 14* looks at secured transaction law in Québec's Civil Law.

*Part four* looks at the interaction of federal law and provincial law. *Chapter 15* presents security interest created by federal law. These present an interesting object of study because Canadian federal law creates certain security interests without there being a specific frame of reference in which these security interests operate. There is no general federal private law. These security interests depend on their complementary relationship with the general private law systems of the Canadian provinces. *Chapter 16* concerns the treatment of property rights in insolvency. As far as this book is concerned, insolvency is where property rights are most important. It is here where property rights secure the debt. A federal insolvency law that operates on property rights created by divergent legal systems must ensure that the notion of distributional fairness underlying its insolvency regime operates equally on property rights from each legal system. An insolvency framework that realizes this goal addresses concerns that might otherwise lead to the abolishment of one legal system, sometimes euphemistically referred to as "harmonization."

*Part five* concerns a different vector of co-ordination than part four: conflict of laws. Obviously, there is more potential of friction between divergent legal systems than between legal systems with a great degree of uniformity regarding property law. Certain conflict of laws rules can minimize this conflict. *Chapter 17* looks at international property law, including international trust law. *Chapter 18* looks at international secured transactions law. *Chapter 19* looks at the treatment of international proprietary restitution law.

## C. A Note on Terminology

A note on terminology is necessary. When I use the term "Common Law" (capitalized) I mean the legal system that derives from the laws of England. Common Law includes all laws of England, whether they derive from the Court of Chancery or another royal court. If the reader reads the term "common law," on the other hand, this can have two meanings. I could – and in most cases I will – be referring to those laws of England that were not applied by the Court of Chancery, and rules that were later based on those rules. In this sense, "common law" is the opposite of "equity." Confusingly, the word "law" can act as a synonym for "common law" in this sense. If "law" is used to mean "common law," it will usually be preceded by the preposition "at."[5] In a few rare cases "common law" is supposed to mean the general law of the land, as opposed to

[5] Andrew S Burrows, "We Do This at Common Law but That in Equity" (2002) 22:1 Oxford J Legal Stud 1.

the peculiar law of a region, a tribe, or a certain class or estate. An example of such a usage would be the sentence "The 'Coutumes de Paris' formed the common law of New France." In such cases the fact that the second, rarer meaning is intended is made clear either by the context or by an explicit statement to that effect.

Just like "common law," the term "equity" can be ambiguous. Once again, in most cases, "equity" will refer to legal rules that were developed in the Court of Chancery or developed from such rules. In a few rare instances, mostly when discussing topical legal writing that itself used the term in such a fashion, "equity" has been used to refer to the concept of discretionary law – that is, some form of leeway in the application of hard-and-fast legal rules granted to judges.

The capitalized term "Civil Law" refers to a legal system that derives its legal rules mostly from Roman law. The non-capitalized "civil law," on the other hand, distinguishes private law from public law and criminal law. One of the advantages of Civil Law over Common Law is that it commands its own adjective. The capitalized adjective "Civilian" thus denotes that the legal concept is one belonging to the Civil Law rather than the Common Law. The occasionally-used adjective "civilian," on the other hand, refers to the concept of civil society. It is most likely used in this book when referring to a civilian government rather than the military government of British colonies.

Apart from these terminological notes, it will also be necessary to discuss the meaning of the words "right," "remedy," and "legal event." These, however, are more appropriately the subject of a discussion rather than mere definition. The discussion takes place in a later chapter of this book.[6]

[6] See Part II: § 9 C.III.2.b), "Counter-Argument".

Part I

# The Analytical Framework of Bijuralism

## § 1 The History of Civil Law in Québec

The continuing existence of two legal systems on Canadian territory – and thus of Canadian bijuralism itself – is a function of history.[1] To understand why the Civil Law persists in Canada, and how it interacted with the Common Law after the British conquest, it is useful to examine the legal history of French Canada. Furthermore, this helps us to understand the role of the Civil Law in the cultural identity of French Canadians.

The development of the private law in the former French possessions in North America is also a function of the changing constitutional frameworks of these territories. It is thus helpful to begin this chapter with a short overview of the history of territorial changes in these territories.

The territory of New France included all French possessions in continental North America. Initially, it was divided into five provinces: Canada, Acadia, Hudson Bay, Newfoundland, and Louisiana. After the end of the Spanish War of Succession, France ceded Acadia, Hudson Bay, and Newfoundland to Britain. At the same time, the colony of Île Royale was established as a successor to Acadia. There thus remained three French possessions in North America: Canada, Louisiana, and Île Royale.

The colony of Île Royale corresponds to modern-day Cape Breton Island, the northern part of Nova Scotia. Its territory ceased to have its own legal system when it became part of Nova Scotia after the Seven Years War. As a further consequence of the Seven Years War, the French province of Canada became the British province of Québec[2] and Louisiana became Spanish. In 1794, the province of Québec was split into two pieces by the *Constitutional Act, 1791*:[3] Lower Canada and Upper Canada. The former was the Francophone province along the banks of the Saint-Lawrence, the latter was the Anglophone province along the Great Lakes. In 1841, both provinces were united into the United

---

[1] See e.g. Marie-Claude Gaudreault, "Canadian Legislative Bijuralism: An Expression of Legal Duality" (2006) 32:2 Comm L Bull 205 at 206.

[2] By virtue of the *Act for making more effectual Provision for the Government of the Province of Quebec in North America,* 14 Geo III, c 83 [*Quebec Act*].

[3] *Clergy Endowments (Canada) Act, 1791,* 31 Geo III, c 31.

Province of Canada, only to be split again into Ontario and Québec with the coming into force of the *Constitution Act, 1867,*[4] which established the Dominion of Canada as one unified kingdom.

Just like in most parts of France, the customary law of Paris was the law of the land in the French North American possessions. The Coutume de Paris was thus in force in pre-conquest Canada[5] and Louisiana.[6] In Canada, the Coutume de Paris was introduced in 1640.[7]

Louisiana had its own administration, seperate from the French province then called Canada, as of 1712.[8] As in Québec, the Coutume de Paris, along with royal ordinances, were the law of the land in Louisiana until the end of the Seven Years War.[9]

## A. The Conquest of Québec

When the city of Québec was taken in 1759 in the Battle of the Plains of Abraham, in the articles of capitulation, it was stipulated as follows:

> "Que Les habitans soient Conservés dans La possession de leurs maisons, biens, effets et privileges.
> Accordé en mettant les armes Bas."[10]

The wording of this article of capitulation is interesting to compare with s 92(13) *Constitution Act, 1867* – the modern constitutional provision which

---

[4] *An Act for the Union of Canada, Nova Scotia, and New Brunswick, and the Government thereof; and for Purposes connected therewith, 1867,* 30 & 31 Vict, c 3 [*Constitution Act*].

[5] See Mario Dion, "Evolution of Legal Systems: Bijuralism and International Trade" in: Canada, Department of Justice, ed, *The Harmonization of Federal Legislation with the Québec Civil Law and Canadian Bijuralism* (Ottawa: Canada, Department of Justice, 1997) at 41; Gaudreault, *supra* note 1 at 206; Michel Morin, "Introduction historique au droit civil québécois" in: Louise Bélanger-Hardy & Aline Grenon, eds, *Éléments de common law et aperçu comparatif du droit civil québécois* (Scarborough, Ont: Carswell, 1997) 59 at 62; William Tetley, "Mixed Jurisdictions: Common Law vs. Civil Law (Codified and Uncodified)" (1999) 4 Unif L Rev 591–620, 877–907 at 606.

[6] See Tetley, preceding note at 608.

[7] Richard C Harris, *The Seigneurial System in Early Canada: A Geographical Study,* Paperback (Kingston: McGill-Queen's University Press, 1984) at 21.

[8] HW Fontenot, "The Louisiana Judicial System and the Fusion of Cultures" (2003) 63:4 La L Rev 1149 at 1149.

[9] *Ibid* at 1149–51; Vernon V Palmer, "French Connection and the Spanish Perception: Historical Debates and Contemporary Evaluation of French Influence on Louisiana Civil Law" (2003) 63:4 La L Rev 1067 at 1068; John R Trahan, "The Continuing Influence of le Droit civil and el Derecho Civil in the Private Law of Louisiana" (2003) 63:4 La L Rev 1019 at 1021.

[10] Adam Shortt & Arthur G Doughty, eds, *Documents Relating to the Constitutional History of Canada, 1759–1791,* 2[d] edn (Ottawa: J de la Taché, 1918) at 2.

places "property and civil rights in the province," *i.e.* private law,[11] within the realm of provincial jurisdiction. Section 92(13) *Constitution Act, 1867* considers private law as a matter of property and civil rights, the retention of which by the Canadiens was asked for by Lt. de Ramzay in the capitulation.

In 1760, James Murray, at that point military commander of Québec City, issued a proclamation of intent: "Le Roy veut maintenir les Communautés, et les Particuliers, dans tous leurs Biens, dans leurs Loix et Coutumes [...]."[12] However this proclamation was not legally binding for the occupants.[13] When Montréal fell, the articles of capitulation included the following demand:

> "Les francois et Canadiens Continüeront d'Estre Gouvernés Suivant La Coutume de Paris et les Loix et Usages Etablis pour ce pays; Et Ils ne pouront Estre Assujettis à d'Autres Impots qu'a Ceux qui Estoient Etablis sous la domination françoise."[14]

General Amherst's reply referred to his earlier statement: "Ils deviennent Sujets du Roy."[15] This answer meant that the British Crown reserved its right to introduce English law in its new territory.[16]

This attitude can be explained. Lawson identifies a spirit in England at the time of the conquest which was shaped by the accomplishments of the Glorious Revolution and an orthodox legal practice which created an oblivious attitude towards the specific challenges of trying to integrate a whole new society with its particular legal system into the Empire.[17] Furthermore, British policy towards Québec was mostly determined by trying to establish a stable military in the province,[18] not civilian governance. The Home Office in Britain lacked a vision for the civilian future of Québec, and had no policy for the integration of the Canadien society into the British Empire. The Secretary of State for the Southern Department – the minister responsible for Britain's colonial possessions in North America – George Montagu-Dunk, Earl of Halifax, was unsure what shape the civilian government in Québec should take and his proposal for its constitution was an amalgam of the differing advice he received.[19] Halifax,

---

[11] See e.g. André Morel, "Harmonizing Federal Legislation with the Civil Code of Québec: Why and Wherefore?" in: Canada, Department of Justice, ed, *Harmonization I, supra* note 5, 1 at 1.

[12] Arthur G Doughty, "Appendix B" in: Arthur G Doughty, ed, *Report of the Public Archives for the Year 1918* (Ottawa: J de la Taché, 1920) 32 at 48.

[13] Michel Morin, "Les changements de régimes juridiques consécutifs à la Conquête de 1760" (1997) 57 R du B 689 at 689–90 [Morin, "Changements"].

[14] Shortt & Doughty, *supra* note 10 at 20.

[15] *Ibid* at 20.

[16] Morin, "Changements", *supra* note 13 at 690.

[17] Philip Lawson, *The Imperial Challenge: Quebec and Britain in the Age of the American Revolution* (Kingston: McGill-Queen's University Press, 1989) at 25 [Lawson, *Challenge*].

[18] *Ibid* at 32.

[19] *Ibid* at 36.

however, had a strong opinion about the superiority of English law and that thought it inconceivable that British subjects should be subordinate to anything but the law of England.[20] Indeed, the Royal Proclamation of 1763, dated from October 7, 1763, immediately after the Treaty of Paris, called for the introduction of Common Law in Québec: "We have also given power to the said Governors, [...] to make, constitute, and ordain Laws, Statutes, and Ordinances [...] as near as may be agreeable to the Laws of England."[21]

Governor James Murray and the colonial council passed just such an ordinance on September 17, 1764. As Riddell points out,[22] it is notable that the ordinance was passed more than 18 months after the signing of the Treaty of Paris, which gave the Canadiens 18 months to emigrate if they chose to do so.[23] This indicates that the British government was aware of the importance of the Civil Law for the Canadiens, and the potential negative impact an introduction of English law might have on the attitude of the French population towards their new country. By postponing the introduction of English law, the British government prevented the introduction of English law having any impact on the Canadiens' decision whether or not to remain in British Québec.

The ordinance established a Court of King's Bench in the province that was to hear civil law suits "agreeable to the Laws of England,"[24] and a Court of Common Pleas that was to hear civil suits

> "agreable to Equity, having regard nevertheless to the Laws of England, as far as the Circumstances and present Situation of Things will admit, until such Time as proper Ordinances for the Information of the People can be established by the Governor and Council, agreeable to the laws of England."[25]

Furthermore, the ordinance included a provision governing inter-temporal conflicts of law, where all suits brought by Canadiens where "the Cause of Action arose before the first Day of October [1764]"[26] were to be governed by French Law. Any suit exceeding the sum of £10 could be brought before either court; for any suit below, justices of the peace were competent.[27]

Due to the fact that justices of the peace had to swear an oath that amounted to a rejection of the Catholic faith, the judges could not be recruited from the

---

[20] *Ibid* at 36.

[21] Shortt & Doughty, *supra* note 10 at 165.

[22] William R Riddell, "The First Court of Chancery in Canada" (1922) 2 Boston UL Rev 231 at 233.

[23] Shortt & Doughty, *supra* note 10 at 100.

[24] Arthur G Doughty, ed, *Report of the Work of the Public Archives for the Year 1913* (Ottawa: J de la Taché, 1914) at 47 [Doughty, *Report 1913*].

[25] *Ibid* at 47.

[26] *Ibid* at 47.

[27] Morin, "Changements", *supra* note 13 at 695–96.

pool of Canadien lawyers. As a result, the judges were overwhelmingly English, usually had no legal training whatsoever, and decided arbitrarily.[28] Virtually all plaintiffs before the Court of Common Pleas were Canadiens;[29] consequently, the Court commonly applied French law,[30] as is evidenced by the evaluation of the legal system of Québec by Governor Murray's successor, Guy Carleton, later Baron Dorchester.[31] Canadien lawyers were only allowed to practise before the Court of Common Pleas.[32]

The future Attorney-General of Québec, Francis Maseres, pointed out that the law at the time of the conquest remained in force until replaced by new laws that had to be decided upon by the legislative body of the province.[33] Carleton, in a letter to the southern secretary, William Petty, Earl of Shelburne, wrote about the future of the law of Québec. He pointed out that the Canadiens submitted to the Crown under the condition that their law remained in force, and that the French law had a claim to be just and equitable, just like the English law.[34] However, in Carleton's view – while he did not condone this outcome – the ordinance from September 17, 1764 had already completely overturned French law.[35] His Attorney-General took the opposite view because of the fact that the ordinance had been an order-in-council, not an act of the King-in-Parliament or an act of the legislative assembly of Québec. The latter was planned for and provided for in the Royal Proclamation but never called.[36]

An anonymous report also considered the introduction of English law to be void.[37] It put forward three arguments. First, the Canadiens retained their property, so no English law changing the content of these well-acquired property rights could be imposed without an act of a legislature.[38] Second, even if the Canadiens could be stripped of their well-acquired property rights by the Imperial government, the governor's commission from the king still required him

---

[28] Jacques L'Heureux, "L'organisation judiciaire au Québec de 1764 à 1774" (1970) 1 RGD 266 at 313–16; Morin, "Changements", *supra* note 13 at 696–97.

[29] Morin, "Changements", *supra* note 13 at 697.

[30] L'Heureux, *supra* note 28 at 292.

[31] WPM Kennedy & Gustave Lanctôt, eds, *Reports on the Laws of Quebec, 1767–1770* (Ottawa: FA Acland, 1931) at 64, cited as in L'Heureux, *supra* note 28 at 292.

[32] Doughty, *Report 1913, supra* note 24 at 47; Morin, "Changements", *supra* note 13 at 696.

[33] Shortt & Doughty, *supra* note 10 at 261–63.

[34] *Ibid* at 288–89.

[35] *Ibid* at 288–89.

[36] See Lawson, *Challenge, supra* note 17 at 25–59.

[37] William Hey, (attributed), "A View of the Civil Government and Administration of Justice in the Province of Canada While It Was Subject to the Crown of France" (1857) 1 LCJ 1 at 39–48.

[38] *Ibid* at 39–40.

to have the consent of both the council and an assembly when acting legislatively. An assembly did not endorse the ordinance dating September 17, 1764.[39] These two arguments thus resembled Maseres' argument. Third, the author argued, the introduction of an alien system of laws on the Canadien population required a promulgation of the entire body of law, *i.e.* a word-for-word recantation of the law.[40] The same was not necessary in the Anglophone colonies because they were settled by Englishmen.[41]

Whatever the legal argument about the legality of the repeal, Carleton's view that the French law was no longer in force has been endorsed by modern scholars,[42] albeit not unequivocally,[43] and more importantly, it is this view from which legal politics proceeded in the province. After the ordinance, the Canadiens appealed to the King to restore the French law.[44] In order to remedy the situation, Carleton drafted an ordinance to reinstate the French law,[45] which never passed.[46] The British Lord Chancellor had advised the King in Privy Council that a change of the laws of Québec – *i.e.* a return to French law – required an act of the Imperial Parliament. This advice in turn triggered the resignation of the entire Imperial cabinet;[47] the restoration of French law was delayed for another eight years.[48]

## B. The Introduction of Equity in Québec

In the previous subsection, I have described the legal and judiciary system immediately after the conquest. While the British administration of Québec retained French law, it was no longer formally binding, having been given the lowly rank of "equitable" law. Yet the period after the Proclamation also saw the introduction of a genuine court of Equity, where Equity had the same meaning as in English law: a different body of law, separate from the common law. The Court of Common Pleas was not a court of Equity, even though the ordinance made reference to equitable principles.[49] Instead, a separate Court of

---

[39] *Ibid* at 42–43.

[40] *Ibid* at 45–46.

[41] *Ibid* at 46–47.

[42] Morin, "Changements", *supra* note 13 at 697.

[43] *Ibid* at 697, note 40.

[44] Shortt & Doughty, *supra* note 10 at 223–26, 419–21.

[45] Shortt & Doughty, *supra* note 10 at 292–94.

[46] Morin, "Changements", *supra* note 13 at 697.

[47] Lawson, *Challenge, supra* note 17 at 82–83; Morin, "Changements", *supra* note 13 at 698.

[48] Lawson, *Challenge, supra* note 17 at 83.

[49] Riddell, *supra* note 22 at 234.

Chancery needed to be established in order for Equity to be present in the province.

Under the ancient laws of England, courts were not established by an act of the legislature, but rather derived their legitimacy from the Crown, the original source of all justice.[50] According to common law principles, the Courts of Chancery, in turn, derived their jurisdiction from the Chancellor, who in the colonial possessions was the keeper of the Great Seal, *i.e.* the governor. The legal principle that the Keeper of the Great Seal exercised the role of Chancellor was an ancient common law principle, but it was also put into statutory form.[51] In other words, a Court of Chancery as a court of Equity could be established based on the authority of the governor alone. Based on this principle, the province of Nova Scotia had both Courts of Law as well as a Court of Chancery.

The Nova Scotia example was followed and a Court of Chancery for the British province of Québec was established by the Governor-in-Council on November 8, 1764.[52] Later, such an ad-hoc creation of a Court of Chancery was no longer considered to be possible. This was noted by the Chief Justice of Upper Canada in 1846, interestingly without making reference to the equitable court in Québec:

> "That there was in fact no court of equity before 1837, in Upper Canada, is very notorious. It was well known that in the British West India Islands and some other ancient British possessions there were Courts of Equity exercising their authority on no other foundation than that the Governor was by Common Law, Chancellor, in virtue of his custody of the Great Seal."[53]

The Court of Chancery created further diversity in the laws of Québec, as the Court of Common Pleas would apply the French law as equitable law, the Court of King's Bench the English common law (as opposed to Equity), and the Court of Chancery English Equity. This was acknowledged by Carleton, who wrote:

> "A few disputes have already appeared where the England Law gives to one what by the Canadian Law would belong to another; A case of this sort, not easy to determine, lies at present in Chancery. If decided for the Canadian … the uniformity of the Courts of Justice thereby will be still further destroyed, Chancery reversing the Judgments of the Supreme Court as that Court reverses those of the Common Pleas."[54]

---

[50] William Blackstone, *Of the Rights of Persons,* 1st edn (Commentaries on the Laws of England, vol 1, Oxford: Clarendon Press, 1765–1769) at 257.

[51] *Act declaring the Authority of the Lord Keeper of the Great Seal and the Lord Chancellor of England to be one, 1562,* 4 Eliz I, c 18.

[52] Riddell, *supra* note 22 at 234–35.

[53] *Simpson v Smyth* (1846), 1 UCE & A 9 at 66, Robinson CJ.

[54] Shortt & Doughty, *supra* note 10 at 289–90.

It should be noted that by "reversed" Carleton means that the legal principle was reversed by the Court, not that one court was in an appellate relation to the other.[55]

## C. The *Quebec Act*

The Royal Proclamation of 1763 had been criticized even in Britain itself by prominent jurists such as William Murray, Earl of Mansfield, who was at that time Lord Chief Justice of the King's Bench.[56] The subordination of Canadiens under the English law was also criticized by Governor Murray in a letter to the Home Office.[57]

In 1771, the power of the justices of the peace to make judgments in matters relating to property was removed by an ordinance, and all matters of a value below £12 were to be heard before the Court of Common Pleas.[58] As noted above, this court often decided based on French law.

Later, the retention of Civil Law was internally and statutorily enshrined in the *Quebec Act*. The *Quebec Act* pursued the goal of integrating the Canadiens into the British Empire and keeping them satisfied the ultimate objective being to secure their loyalty in the upcoming struggle in British North America.[59] When the province of Québec was split into Upper and Lower Canada in 1791 in order to accommodate the influx of Loyalists from the seceding southern colonies, the *Constitutional Act, 1791* provided that the Civil Law was to remain in force in Lower Canada (modern Québec), and Common Law was to be in force in Upper Canada (modern Ontario), where most Loyalist settlers stayed.

Keeping the civil law of the Canadiens intact relates to the concept in British colonialism that the governance of the colonists by the British Empire was based on the consent of the colonists.[60] Variations in the common law were not unknown, neither within Britain, nor in the colonies.[61] Because the law was not uniform within the British Empire, and was rather an expression of the particular "legal culture" of the parochial people, the leap to having a completely different legal system in the province of Québec was not as big as one might

---

[55] Riddell, *supra* note 22 at 238.

[56] See Lawson, *Challenge, supra* note 17 at 58.

[57] Morin, "Changements", *supra* note 13 at 696.

[58] See Shortt & Doughty, *supra* note 10 at 401–2.

[59] See principally Reginald Coupland, *The Quebec Act: A Study in Statesmanship* (Oxford: Clarendon Press, 1925), passim.

[60] See on this idea Jack Greene, "By Their Laws Shall Ye Know Them: Law and Identity in Colonial British America" (2002) 33:2 *The Journal of Interdisciplinary History* 247 at 253.

[61] *Ibid* at 253.

think at first. The particularity of Québec was due to the degree of difference. Neither was Québec the first non-Common Law jurisdiction, nor the first Francophone territory in the Empire. Rather, it was simply more populated, with stronger civic institutions than any other colony conquered by the British.[62] It thus follows that the degree of differentness in the legal system was higher as well, and the province was to have its own legal system. Civil Law has remained a source of national identity in Québec ever since.[63]

However, the approach of the British conquerors has not been viewed positively by all. For Kolish, the *Quebec Act* cannot be seen as a recognition of the rights of the Canadien people; rather it is an expression of a long-term assimilation strategy. She asks: "Pourquoi établir un double régime juridique, sinon pour protéger les intérêts des anciens sujets pendant la période d'assimilation (on espérait sans doute que cette période serait plutôt courte)?"[64]

## D. The Abolition of the Seigneurial System

One of the more interesting features of the French law in the British province of Québec was the system of land tenure. It was also here where Civilian heritage and English legal principles worked hand in hand to create a genuine Québec law. The following paragraphs deal with the land tenure in Québec and how it turned into the modern system of outright allodial land ownership. While the law of immovable property is in principle outside the scope of this book, it is in this area where the modern Civilian concept of absolute ownership became established in Québec, thus breaking ground for the codification of property law in the *Code civil du Bas-Canada*.[65] In the context of Scots law, Reid argues that abolition of feudalism must come before a codification of property law,[66] presumably because feudal structures of ownership stand in the way of a coherent property law. As we will see, this applies to the development

---

[62] Philip Lawson, "A Perspective on British History and the Treatment of Québec" (1990) 3 *Journal of Historical Sociology* 253 at 263.

[63] See Evelyn Kolish, *Nationalismes et conflits de droit: Le débat du droit privé au Québec, 1760–1840* (Cahiers du Québec Collection Histoire, LaSalle, Québec: Hurtubise HMH, 1994).

[64] *Ibid* at 45–46.

[65] *Code civil du Bas-Canada,* 29 Vict, c 41 [*CcBC*]. See Sylvio Normand, "La codification de 1866: Contexte et impact" in: H P Glenn, ed, *Droit québécois et droit français: Communauté, autonomie, concordance* (Cowansville, Québec: Éditions Yvon Blais, 1993) 43 at 55.

[66] Kenneth GC Reid, "Property Law: Sources and Doctrine" in: Kenneth G Reid & Reinhard Zimmermann, eds, *A History of Private Law in Scotland* (Oxford: Oxford University Press, 2000) 185 at 190.

of property law in Québec as well. First, the seigneurial system was abolished, then codification began.

## E. Extent of the Seigneurial System and Feudalism

In the time of New France, the province of Canada was divided into seigneuries. This division was a semi-feudal land tenure system.[67] It was only semi-feudal because it did not entail military service and the seigneur was not discretionary in his powers towards his subordinates.[68] The feudal aspect was the chain of title from top to bottom. The king was the original seigneur, and while New France was a proprietary company, the Company of France held the land in fiefdom.[69] The Company was a seigneur in its own right insofar as it granted land to its own concessionaires, who again granted land.[70] It is the latter category of concessionaires which is usually meant when one uses the term seigneur.[71] All of New France was to be held in such feudal title.[72]

Apart from simple *seigneuries*, there were also higher – noble – fiefdoms that could be awarded, although nowadays the only remaining title of nobility in Québec that can be traced back to the seigneurial system is the title of "Baron de Longueuil," in the Le Moyne family.[73] Incidentally, the first Baron of Longueuil, Charles le Moyne de Longueuil, was brother to both Pierre Le Moyne d'Iberville, founder of Louisiana, and Jean-Baptiste Le Moyne, Sieur de Bienville, founder of New Orleans. It should be noted that there appear to be other titles of nobility associated with territory in Canada, but they belong to the

---

[67] See for a characterization of the system as "feudal" Harris, *supra* note 7 at 3. Cf. Jean-Pierre Wallot, "Le régime seigneurial et son abolition au Canada" (1969) 50:4 Can Historical R 367 at 368.

[68] Marcel Trudel, *The Seigneurial Regime* (Canadian Historical Association Booklets, Ottawa: Canadian Historical Association, 1963) at 17.

[69] Harris, *supra* note 7 at 3–4.

[70] *Ibid* viii.

[71] As it is meant when we encounter who is arguably the most famous, albeit fictional, and certainly no longer legally such, seigneur: "Athanase Tallard was the only limit, under God and the law, to the priest's authority in Saint-Marc. Since the days of the early French colonization, the Tallards had been seigneurs. For more than two hundred years social opinion in Saint-Marc had depended not only on the parish priest, but also on whoever happened to be head of the Tallard family. Most of their seigniory had been broken up during the latter half of the nineteenth century and they collected no more rents." *ibid* viii; Hugh MacLennan, *Two Solitudes* (Toronto: Macmillan, 1945) at 8.

[72] See Harris, *supra* note 7 at 3.

[73] George E Cokayne, *Complete Peerage of England, Scotland, Ireland, Great Britain and the United Kingdom* (London: G Bell & Sons, 1893) at 137.

peerage of the United Kingdom and are not derived from a Canadien feudal title.[74]

There was no substiantal difference between land held in a barony and land held in a *seigneurie simple*.[75] In fact, the seigneurie of Longueuil had originated as an *arrière-fief* – that is, the *Seigneur* of Longueuil held the land from another *seigneur*, although he later became a *seigneur* in his own right.[76]

## *I. The Seigneur*

The *Seigneurs* were not necessarily nobles.[77] A *seigneur* did not have the exclusive right of enjoyment of the land. He was obliged to concede land to the censitaires.[78] For himself, he had the domain, his own proper land, and the *domain indirecte*, land that was currently not held by *censitaires* but reserved for that purpose.[79] The *seigneur* received a nominal tax from the people who he granted the land to, called *cens* (the term from which the word *censitaires* is derived). The *seigneur* could collect a tax if the *censitaire* sold the land. He also had a right of *retrait* if the censitaire sold the land under value. In that event, the seigneur had 40 days to acquire the land himself.[80] If the *seigneur* died, the eldest son, the new *seigneur*, inherited half the *seigneurie* and the manor; the remainder was divided between the other offspring, the *coseigneurs*.[81] This was a consequence of the law of succession under the *Coutume de Paris*.[82] If a seigneur wanted to regain title to the entire *seigneurie* from his *coseigneurs*, he had to get the consent of his coseigneurs and had to formally try to sell the entire *seigneurie* in a type of public auction by offering it for sale for three weeks in a row after mass, and bidding for the entire *seigneurie* himself. Since he already owned half of it, he would only have to pay the other half, provided he outbid all other interested parties.[83]

## *II. The Censitaires*

The *censitaires* received their small fief for personal enjoyment. Additionally, all censitaires together held the "common" for pasture.[84] The *censitaires* were

---

[74] See e.g. *ibid* at 409.
[75] Harris, *supra* note 7 at 21.
[76] *Ibid* at 39.
[77] Trudel, *supra* note 68 at 10.
[78] *Ibid* at 7–8.
[79] *Ibid* at 8.
[80] *Ibid* at 12.
[81] Harris, *supra* note 7 at 46; Trudel, *supra* note 68 at 11.
[82] Harris, *supra* note 7 at 46.
[83] *Ibid* at 50.
[84] Trudel, *supra* note 68 at 9.

not considered to be the owners of the fief they held title to.[85] If a *censitaire* died, all his offspring, whether male or female, received equal share of his tenure.[86]

### *III. The Seigneurial System and the Civil Law on Immovables*

While the *Coutume de Paris* defined property at a basic level, they did not provide a specific framework for the seigneurial system.[87] Free, or "allodial," land was not unknown under old French law,[88] but it was rather rare.[89] Instead, most land was held under seigneurial title, and the land-holder was never considered to be the owner of the land.[90] However, there was a certain tension between the seigneurial system and the Civil Law as codified in the *coutumes*. Seigneurial title was seen as a modification of the ownership right, not an ownership right in itself.[91] This meant that almost nobody was the owner of any immovable property because the vast majority of land in France was held under seigneurial title. Immovables could be charged with a hypothec by anyone who could alienate the property.[92]

### *IV. The Seigneurial System After the Conquest*

The capitulation of the French troops did not end the seigneurial system and we find evidence of seigneurial land grants under British military rule.[93] An order-in-council dated from November 6, 1764 kept the French law on land in place until August 10, 1765.[94] In a letter dated July 2, 1771 the king instructed

---

[85] *Ibid* at 11.

[86] *Ibid* at 11.

[87] Harris, *supra* note 7 at 21.

[88] Charles Giraud, "Précis de l'ancien droit coutumier français: Deuxième article" (1852) 13 *Bibliothèque de l'École des chartes* 1 at 16; Mary A Quinn, "Pratiques et théories de la coutume: Allodialité et conflits de droits dans la seigneurie de L'Isle-sous-Montréal au XVIIIe siècle" [1986] *Études rurales* 71 at 75–76.

[89] Jean-François Noël, "Seigneurie et propriété urbaine sous l'Ancien Régime: Autour de la maison de Bertrand d'Argentré à Vitre" (1991) 38 *Revue d'histoire moderne et contemporaine* 177 at 185.

[90] *Ibid* at 185.

[91] Giraud, "Précis de l'ancien droit coutumier français", *supra* note 88 at 4.

[92] Charles Giraud, "Précis de l'ancien droit coutumier français: Trosième et dernier article" (1852) 13 *Bibliothèque de l'École des chartes* 407 at 438.

[93] Maurice Séguin, "Le régime seigneurial au pays de Québec: 1760–1854" (1947) 1 *Revue d'histoire de l'Amérique française* 382 at 382 [Séguin, "Régime seigneurial I"].

[94] Doughty, *Report 1913, supra* note 24 at 53.

Carleton to continue granting land under the seigneurial system.[95] The *Quebec Act*[96] confirmed that the seigneurial system would stay in place.[97]

### *V. Abolishment of the Seigneurial System*

The seigneurial system, with its inflexible land division, constituted a significant impediment to the further growth of the Canadien population, which rose from 65 000 settlers in 1760 to 650 000 in 1850.[98] A first crack in the seigneurial system was a law by the Imperial Parliament, the *British North America (Trade and Lands) Act*[99] that allowed *seigneurs* to convert their domain indirecte in return for an indemnity to pay to the Crown. The act was not widely used because the seigneurial system was beneficial for the seigneurs and the act did not allow the *censitaires* to receive free land.[100] However, the few English *seigneurs* were interested in converting their land because it would allow them to attract new English immigrants.[101] In 1825, a second Imperial law, the *British North America (Seignorial Rights) Act,*[102] granted the same rights to the *censitaires*. Section viii *British North America (Seignorial Rights) Act* provided that the land converted from the seigneurial system, held in "free and common soccage," was to be governed by the laws of England, but

> "provided nevertheless, that nothing [therein] contained shall extend to prevent His Majesty, with the Advice and Consent of the Legislative Council and Assembly of the Province of Lower Canada, from making and enacting any such Laws or Statutes as may be necessary for the better adapting the beforementioned Rules of the Law of England, or any of them, to the local Circumstances and Condition of the said Province of Lower Canada, and the Inhabitants thereof."

The Imperial law was met with fierce resistance in the popularly elected legislative assembly of Lower Canada because of its introduction of English law – the very reason for which it was applauded in the appointed legislative council of said province.[103] The Imperial Parliament gave both legislative bodies the

---

[95] Shortt & Doughty, *supra* note 10 at 422–23.

[96] See Part I: § 1 C, "The Quebec Act".

[97] Séguin, "Régime seigneurial I", *supra* note 93 at 383.

[98] Wallot, *supra* note 67 at 379–80.

[99] *Act to Regulate the Trade of the Provinces of Lower and Upper Canada, and for Other Purposes Relating to the Said Provinces,* 3 Geo IV, c 119.

[100] Séguin, "Régime seigneurial I", *supra* note 93 at 391.

[101] Cf. *ibid* at 389.

[102] *Act to Provide for the Extinction of Feudal and Seignioral Rights and Burthens on Lands held Titre de Fief and Titre de Cens, in the Province of Lower Canada; and for the gradual Conversion of those Tenures into the Tenure of Free and Common Soccage; and for other Purposes relating to the said Province,* 6 Geo IV, c 59.

[103] Séguin, "Régime seigneurial I", *supra* note 93 at 396.

joint power to replace the English law with French law, but given the diametrically opposed standpoints of both bodies, a compromise was never reached.[104]

Furthermore, it was initially unclear to what extent English law applied – more precisely, whether the entire (real) property law had been replaced by or had even been English law since the conquest or whether the English law only applied to the extent expressly provided in the *British North America (Seignorial Rights) Act.*[105] The case law was ambivalent. In 1830, the Court of Appeal of Lower Canada in *Patterson c McCallum*[106] held that an 1816 deed constituting a hypothec was ineffective because it did not validly create a mortgage under English law. In 1857 in *Wilcox c Wilcox,*[107] the appellate division of the Court of Queen's Bench, under Chief Justice Lafontaine – who as Premier of Canada East prepared the complete abolition of the seigneurial system – held that the English law was only introduced partially, as regards free tenure, and not comprehensively. Justice Duval noted that a comprehensive introduction of the English Common Law property law would have required the continued establishment of courts with equitable jurisdiction:

> "The Common law courts of England require the assistance of a Court of Equity. In many cases they cannot afford the relief that is required. Take for instance, trust-deeds, marriage settlements, estates-tail, the statute do donis, the statute of uses, the administration of minor's property and the care of his person, a bill of discovery, demands to compel specific performance; in all these cases a Court of Equity alone can give the relief the party desires."[108]

After a change in the public opinion,[109] the seigneurial system was finally abolished on December 18, 1854 by the *Seigniorial Act, 1854.*[110] The *seigneurs* could no longer levy the *cens* from the *censitaires*, but they kept their domain. Since the fiction that the Crown owned the land as first *seigneur* was abolished by the act as well, the *seigneurs* were then the owners of the land, and the *censitaires* were given the option to purchase or rent the land from the seigneurs.[111]

The abolition of the seigneurial system was not brought about by a revolution, as it had been the case in France. Rather, it was the result of the legislative

---

[104] *Ibid* at 396.

[105] John EC Brierley, "The Co-Existence of Legal Systems in Quebec: «Free and Common Socage» in Canada's «pays de droit civil»" (1979) 20 C de D 277 passim.

[106] (1830), Stu KB 429 (LC CA).

[107] (1857), 2 LCJ 1 (QB (AD)).

[108] *Ibid* at 28, Duval J.

[109] See Wallot, *supra* note 67 at 388–89 in particular.

[110] *Act for the Abolition of Feudal Rights and Duties in Lower Canada, 1854,* 18 Vict, c 3.

[111] Madeleine Cantin Cumyn, "Le droit privé des biens: À l'enseigne de la continuité" in: Glenn, ed, *Droit québécois et droit français, supra* note 65, 375 at 377.

process with lobbying by the population, a gradual repeal introducing English elements of land tenure, and then a comprehensive repeal. It is reasonable to assume that the acceptance of free land tenure by the Canadiens was facilitated by the advantages they could see in the English system of free tenure. Even though in the latter system title to real estate is subject to the Crown's dominion, the example of English law helped to change Québec law to a system in which the land holder had absolute dominion and outright ownership of the land, without the intermediary of a seigneur. The introduction of free tenure in Québec differed from the Anglo-Canadian law in precisely this aspect: when introducing free tenure, the Crown renounced its imminent domain.[112]

### *VI. Legacy of the Seigneurial System*

One of the results of the seigneurial system was the shape of the border between Upper and Lower Canada (Ontario and Québec). For most of its run, the Ottawa River defines the border between Québec and Ontario. But in Québec's southeast corner, instead of following the Ottawa River, the province extends south of the Ottawa River, forming the small triangle of Vaudreuil-Soulanges. This was the westernmost land held under the seigneurial system. Furthermore, within the modern territory of Québec, the seigneurial communities did not attract English settlers,[113] who settled either in Upper Canada or in the the Eastern Townships of Québec, outside of the seigneuries. The property law framework thus contributed to the ethnic identity of the Canadiens.[114]

## F. United Canada, Codification, and Confederation

### *I. The Durham Report*

Shortly after the ascension of Queen Victoria to the throne – and thus before the abolition of seigneurial tenure in Lower Canada – rebellion broke out in the Canadian provinces of Upper and Lower Canada in 1837. Both uprisings were quickly quashed by British troops stationed in the provinces. However, the Queen, on the advice of the Imperial Government, concluded that the governance of the Canadian provinces needed be reviewed.[115] John George Lamb-

---

[112] *Ibid* at 377.

[113] See Maurice Séguin, "Le régime seigneurial au pays de Québec: 1760–1854" (1948) 1 *Revue d'histoire de l'Amérique française* 519 at 520; Séguin, "Régime seigneurial I", *supra* note 93 at 384–85, 388; Wallot, *supra* note 67 at 384–85.

[114] Trudel, *supra* note 68 at 19–20.

[115] See Roger K Ward, "Bijuralism as an Assimilation Tool: Lord Durham's Assessment of the Louisiana Legal System" (2003) 63:4 La L Rev 1127 at 1129.

ton, Earl of Durham, was appointed Governor-General of British North America. His mission was to analyse the cause of the uprising and make suggestions as to how prevent future unrest.[116] Lord Durham presented his findings February 1839.[117] Lord Durham concluded that the cause of unrest was to be found in the animosity between the French and the English population of Lower Canada:[118]

> "I expected to find a contest between a government and a people: I found two nations waning in the bosom of a single state: I found a struggle, not of principles, but of races; and I perceived that it would be idle to attempt any amelioration of laws or institutions until we could first succeed in terminating the deadly animosity that now separates the inhabitants of Lower Canada into the hostile divisions of French and English."[119]

In general, Lord Durham advocated an assimilation and Anglicization of the French population.[120] Lord Durham regarded the Civil Law of Lower Canada as one of the impediments to development.[121] The old property law which led to an ever-increasing sub-division of the tenured land between the censitaires rendered the land unproductive in Lord Durham's view.[122]

To remedy the situation, Lord Durham wanted to achieve an assimilation of the Canadien population. However, rather than forceful, swift assimilation, he advocated a slow assimilation process that was to take several generations.[123] The main mechanism by which assimilation was to be achieved was the unification of Lower and Upper Canada into one province, the United Province of Canada, in which the English population would represent the majority.[124] In this united province, Common Law and Civil Law were to co-exist and compete with each other, leading to a gradual extinction of the – in Durham's

---

[116] *Ibid* at 1129.

[117] *Ibid* at 1130. A scholarly edited version of the Report was published in 1912 in three volumes, the second of which contains the substantive report, see John George Lambton Earl of Durham, *Lord Durham's Report on the Affairs of British North America,* ed by Charles Prestwood Lucas (Oxford: Clarendon Press, 1912), vol 3; John George Lambton Earl of Durham, *Lord Durham's Report on the Affairs of British North America,* ed by Charles Prestwood Lucas (Oxford: Clarendon Press, 1912), vol 2; John George Lambton Earl of Durham, *Lord Durham's Report on the Affairs of British North America,* ed by Charles Prestwood Lucas (Oxford: Clarendon Press, 1912), vol 1.

[118] Ward, *supra* note 115 at 1130.

[119] Durham, *Lord Durham's Report on the Affairs of British North America, supra* note 117, at 16.

[120] Ward, *supra* note 115 at 1130.

[121] *Ibid* at 1136.

[122] *Ibid* at 1137.

[123] *Ibid* at 1140.

[124] Durham, *Lord Durham's Report on the Affairs of British North America, supra* note 117, at 299.

view – inferior Civil Law.[125] Lord Durham considered Louisiana – and the retention of Civil Law as the foundation of its private law – as an example of how to achieve the gradual assimilation of a French population in an English country.[126] The two Canadian provinces were united under the *Act of Union, 1840*[127] in 1841. This is considered to be the beginning of Canadian bijuralism because it was at this time that Common and Civil Law would co-exist within one over-arching jurisdiction: the entire Canadian polity.[128]

### *II. The Codification of 1866*

In 1857, the parliament of the United Province of Canada passed the *Codification Act.*[129] The act provided for the appointment of three law commissioners who were charged with preparing a codification of the Civil Law in force in former Lower Canada. Just like in France, the law commissioners were selected from the pool of legal practitioners rather than from academia.[130] The commission started its project two years later, in 1859, and published a number of reports from 1861 to 1865.[131] The *CcBC* entered into force on August 1, 1866, eleven months before the unification of all British North American provinces with the exception of Newfoundland (a process known as "Confederation").

The re-affirmation of the Civil Law of Québec as its own body of law in an overwhelmingly Common Law Canadian Confederation was one of the motives behind codification.[132] In fact, the Civil Law at that time was considered to be one of the defining characteristics of Canadien identity.[133] The project of a Civil Code served as a link to Canada's French past.[134]

---

[125] Ward, *supra* note 115 at 1141.

[126] *Ibid* at 1143.

[127] *An Act to reunite the Provinces of Upper and Lower Canada, and for the Government of Canada, 1840,* 3 & 4 Vict, c 35.

[128] France Allard, "The Supreme Court of Canada and Its Impact on the Expression of Bijuralism" in: Canada, Department of Justice, ed, *The Harmonization of Federal Legislation with the Civil Law of the Province of Quebec and Canadian Bijuralism: Second Publication* (Ottawa: Canada, Department of Justice, 2001) 1 at 2.

[129] *An Act to provide for the Codification of the Laws of Lower Canada relative to Civil matters and Procedure,* 20 Vict, c 43.

[130] Louise Langevin & Denise Pratte, "Du Code civil du Bas-Canada au nouveau Code civil du Québec: L'influence de la codification française" in: Glenn, ed, *Droit québécois et droit français, supra* note 65, 63 at 67.

[131] John EC Brierley, "Quebec's Civil Law Codification: Viewed and Reviewed" (1968) 14:4 McGill LJ 521 at 523 [Brierley, "Codification"].

[132] *Ibid* at 527–29.

[133] Normand, "La codification de 1866", *supra* note 65 at 59.

[134] *Ibid* at 60.

However, Confederation cannot have been what gave rise to the idea of codification: the codification movement started well before Confederation. Codification was already put forward in 1846,[135] while the idea of Confederation was not born until 1858[136] and only gained momentum once the North won the Civil War in the United States, threatening to annex Canada. Confederation was only achieved by the *Constitution Act, 1867,* which established the Dominion of Canada, including Upper Canada (Ontario), Lower Canada (Québec), New Brunswick, Nova Scotia, and, entering shortly after Confederation, Prince Edward Island.

It is notable that in the context of Confederation, the idea of using the Civil Law codification in Québec as a boilerplate for a unique and uniform Canadian legal identity was brought forward. A legal system based on Québec's Civil Law was seen as a means of distinguishing Canada from its southern (Common Law) neighbour.[137] In the end, this idea was not pursued. Instead, the *Constitution Act, 1867* only provided for a fusion of the private law of the different Common Law jurisdictions (*i.e.* all initial provinces except Québec).[138] Even this limited fusion never took place.

Normand argues that the codification of 1866 was the last step in a process of legal modernization happening in Lower Canada at that time. He points to the abolition of seigneurial tenure in Lower Canada as one example.[139] Furthermore, institutional factors were at play as well. The unification of Upper and Lower Canada under one parliament resulted in a consolidation of existing laws, which were collected and published in a bilingual edition.[140] A number of law schools and faculties were established in the 1850s.[141] Codification was pursued in New York, and advocated in Great Britain by Bentham.[142] The codification addressed problems such as the diversity of legal sources,[143] the need for bilingual legislation,[144] and a skeletonization of the Civil Law in Québec, which was cut off from the law of France and did not provide any basis for dynamic evolution.[145]

---

135 Brierley, "Codification", *supra* note 131 at 530.
136 *Ibid* at 529.
137 *Ibid* at 530.
138 *Constitution Act, supra* note 4, s 94.
139 Normand, "La codification de 1866", *supra* note 65 at 55.
140 *Ibid* at 55.
141 *Ibid* at 56–57.
142 *Ibid* at 58.
143 Brierley, "Codification", *supra* note 131 at 534–35.
144 *Ibid* at 535–38.
145 *Ibid* at 538–40.

### *III. The Code civil du Bas-Canada as a Code*

Codification, as a concept, needs to be distinguished from revision and consolidation.

> "*Revision* is the presentation of statute law as is stands at any particular moment in time; the statutes are reprinted in the order of their original enactment, with the parts repealed (either expressly or by implication) expunged from the text. […]
> *Consolidation* of statutory materials amounts to their re-classification, not by order of time but by order of subject matter. It too involves the excision of repealed and the retention of living statutory materials (and in this respect resembles revision)."[146]

Based on this definition, Brierley draws a number of parallels between consolidation and the process of codification pursued in Québec. First, the Code was meant to unify the existing law in one text. Second, the procedure was the same one used for consolidation – that is, simple proclamation under the authority of a statute (rather than legislative enactment). Third, insofar as explicitly or impliedly stated, the new code would abrogate the law in force.[147] One interesting feature of the *CcBC* is that it declared the old common law (in the sense of *droit commun*) of the province to be of interpretative help.[148] This, rather than the autonomy of the new code from the old common law, was a marked departure from the approach taken in French legal codification.[149]

The decidedly "codal" characteristic of the *CcBC* was its approach to the expression and scope of legal rules. A rule in the code, and the entire code, was supposed to be a broad statement of the leading legal principle, which could encompass a number of details. These details were not to be elaborated on by the code itself but by judges and jurists.[150]

## G. The *Code civil du Québec*

### *I. Institutional History*

In 1955, the National Assembly of Québec passed the *Loi concernant la révision du Code civil,*[151] which created the framework for a modernization of the *CcBC.* The law provided for the creation of an Office de révision du Code

---

[146] *Ibid* at 555 [emphasis in original].
[147] *Ibid* at 556.
[148] *CcBC, supra* note 65, s 2613.
[149] Brierley, "Codification", *supra* note 131 at 556–57; Langevin & Pratte, *supra* note 130 at 65.
[150] See Brierley, "Codification", *supra* note 131 at 562; Langevin & Pratte, *supra* note 130 at 80.
[151] *Loi concernant la révision du Code civil,* SQ 1954–1955, c 47.

civil. The office started its work in 1965 under the leadership of Crépeau.[152] Forty different commissions worked on drafting rules in different subject areas and solicited replies from the municipal and international legal communities on their proposals.[153] The office as a whole then combined the individual commissions' works into a draft code. The office presented its draft code in 1977.[154] Contrary to the initial plan, the proposal was not submitted to the Assembly for legislative action. The Québec government claimed that given the scope of the project of modernizing the entire code, further study of the political, social, legal and administrative impact of the project was necessary before a proposal could be submitted for parliamentary approval.[155]

## *II. Scope of the Project*

Unlike the 1866 codification project, the new *Code civil du Québec*[156] was aimed at a modernization of the law, not merely a restatement of the existing law. While the code was supposed to preserve Québec's Civilian heritage,[157] its goal was also to bring private law in line with the values of modern Québec society.[158] The new *CcQ* was not based on the idea of enshrining an eternal idea of justice but on the idea of an expression of the will of the Québec people at that time. Crépeau expressed this goal as follows:

"Le Code civil doit traduire aussi fidèlement que possible les conceptions morales, sociales et économiques de son temps. Le Code civil doit énoncer ce qu'un peuple estime devoir être le juste et le bien dans les relations civiles, reconnaissant en cela que, d'une part, l'ordre juridique ne sera toujours que le pâle reflet de l'ordre moral, que, d'autre part, le Code civil ne peut plus être conçu, ainsi qu'à la suite de Bonaparte on l'a si longtemps cru, comme l'affirmation de la Justice éternelle ou l'incarnation de la Raison naturelle, mais bien, plus humblement, et plus justement, comme l'expression d'une certaine conception de la justice, notion alors temporelle, relative, variable, qui consacre dans le concert des réalités sociale,

---

[152] Rainer Becker, *Die Fiducie von Québec und der Trust: Ein Vergleich mit verschiedenen Modellen fiduziarischer Rechtsfiguren im Civil Law* (Tübingen: Mohr Siebeck, 2007) at 148.

[153] See AS Hartkamp, "Civil Code Revision in Quebec" (1977) 24 Nethl Int'l L Rev 614 at 614.

[154] The reports were published as Paul-André Crépeau, ed, *Rapport sur le code civil du Québec* (Québec: Éditeur officiel, 1978), vol 1 and Paul-André Crépeau, ed, *Rapport sur le code civil du Québec* (Québec: Éditeur officiel, 1978), vol 2. See also Becker, *supra* note 152 at 148–49.

[155] Langevin & Pratte, *supra* note 130 at 69.

[156] *Code civil du Québec,* SQ 1991, c 64.

[157] Becker, *supra* note 152 at 149.

[158] Langevin & Pratte, *supra* note 130 at 66.

une certain façon de penser, une certaine manière de vivre à une époque précise de l'histoire d'un peuple."[159]

Both the preservation of Civilian heritage and the idea of being an expression of contemporary sovereignty were not seen as contradictory. Rather, the *CcQ* was meant to bring Civilian concepts in line with a modern human-rights based system of law.[160]

### *III. The Code civil du Québec as a Code*

The *CcQ* is codal in its ambition to lay down general rules that govern the entirety of private law relations.[161] What it might be lacking in detail it is supposed to contain in general principle, so that any legal question can be answered based on a principle derived from the Code.[162] Arguably, with its improved structure and more logical and coherent presentation of its rules, the *CcQ* is even more codal than both the *CcBC* and the Code Napoléon.[163] I do not intend to hide the fact that there are critics of the new *CcQ*,[164] but a complete analysis of the entire *CcQ* is outside the scope of this book. I will analyse the code's coherence, intelligibility, and its faithfulness to Civilian heritage as regards property law and secured transactions law later in this book.

## H. The Place of Civil Law in Québec

This overview of the Civil Law in Québec shows three things. First, the Civil Law in Québec was under constant threat of being replaced by English law in the first 100 years after the conquest, starting with the *Proclamation*, which set the goal of abolishing the French law and introducing the Common Law. Then, the courts applied English law and even introduced equity in its formal sense. Even after the French law was reaffirmed in the *Quebec Act*,[165] its renaissance

---

[159] Paul-André Crépeau, "Les lendemains de la réforme du code civil" (1981) 59 Can Bar Rev 625 at 626 [Crépeau, "Lendemains"].

[160] Langevin & Pratte, *supra* note 130 at 74.

[161] *Ibid* at 80. On the general nature of codification see also Marie J Longtin, "Le style civiliste et la loi" in: Nicholas Kasirer, ed, *Le droit civil: avant tout un style?* (Montréal: Éditions Thémis, 2003) 185.

[162] Langevin & Pratte, *supra* note 130 at 79–80.

[163] The coherent structure of the new code is praised by John EC Brierley, "The Renewal of Quebec's Distinct Legal Culture: The New Civil Code of Quebec" (1992) 42:4 UTLJ 484 at 491.

[164] See Pierre Legrand, "Bureaucrats at Play: The New Quebec Civil Code" (1995) 10 Brit J of Can Stud 52; Pierre Legrand, "Civil Law Codification in Quebec: A Case of Decivilianization" (1993) 1 ZEuP 574; Pierre Legrand, "Comparative Contraventions" (2005) 50 McGill LJ 669.

[165] *Quebec Act, supra* note 2.

was ignored in the conversion of seigneurial land into free land. Second, the government never succeeded in a comprehensive introduction of the English law. Third, this failure is due to a continued resistance of the Canadiens against the introduction of English law. Crépeau has described the importance of the Civil Law for the cultural identity of Québecers in the following words:

> "Si ces réflexions devaient trouver un écho favorable, alors comme M. le juge Mignault, je n'aurais plus « aucune crainte quant à l'avenir de notre droit civil. » Bien au contraire, il en résulterait, sur cette terre canadienne, une vigoureuse et rayonnante renaissance du droit civil qui constitue, ne l'oublions jamais, autant que les vieilles et nobles pierres de nos églises et de nos manoirs, l'un des plus beaux monuments, l'un des joyaux de notre patrimoine culturel."[166]

[166] Crépeau, "Lendemains", *supra* note 159 at 637.

# § 2 Bijuralism and Mixed Legal Systems

## A. Terminology

### *I. Bijuralism*

The term "bijuralism" is used to describe the co-existence of two different legal systems within one jurisdiction.[1] An obvious example for this scenario is the realm of Canadian federal jurisdiction, which has to make reference to at least two legal systems, the Anglo-Canadian Common Law system used in Common Law Canada and the law of Québec. Bijuralism means that the Canadian federal legislature must address two different audiences when legislating. Its law must pertain equally to the Anglo-Canadian law as well as to Québec law.[2] This is because the recognition of Québec Civil Law in federal legislation is an expression of Québec's status within confederation.[3]

### *II. Mixed Legal Systems*

The term "mixed legal system" is most often used to describe jurisdictions whose legal system is based on the Civil Law but has been partly influenced by the Common Law.[4] As such, Québec and Louisiana (or in Europe, Scotland[5]) are included. These mixed jurisdictions are a result of British imperialism.[6] Of course, the principle in itself is open to generalization. Mixed legal system need not have Common and Civil Law heritage. It just seems that empirically, that is the most common mix, and certainly the one with which this book is concerned. The British connection is also important insofar as it led to

---

[1] Marie-Claude Gaudreault, "Canadian Legislative Bijuralism: An Expression of Legal Duality" (2006) 32:2 Comm L Bull 205 at 205.

[2] See e.g. *ibid* at 205.

[3] Albert Breton & Michael J Trebilcock, "Introduction" in: Albert Breton & Michael J Trebilcock, eds, *Bijuralism: An Economic Approach* (Aldershot: Ashgate, 2006) 1 at 1.

[4] Robin Evans-Jones, "Receptions of Law: Mixed Legal Systems and the Myth of the Genius of Scots Private Law" (1998) 114 LQR 228 at 228; William Tetley, "Mixed Jurisdictions: Common Law vs. Civil Law (Codified and Uncodified)" (1999) 4 Unif L Rev 591–620, 877–907 at 592.

[5] Tetley, preceding note at 592–93.

[6] Kenneth GC Reid, "The Idea of a Mixed Legal System" (2003) 78:1–2 Tul L Rev 5 at 8 [Reid, "Idea"].

an institutional connection between the legal systems of the former British Empire which have a Civilian heritage.[7] Thus, henceforth the term "mixed legal system" shall refer to a system of Common and Civil Law pedigree. Tetley points out that there is a prominent specific difference between the two groups of members of the class of mixed legal systems. That is, that the Civil Law heritage in Québec and Louisiana is expressed in civil codes, while in Scotland or South Africa it is not.[8]

A possible criticism against the use of the term "mixed legal system" is the argument that in fact, all legal systems borrow from each other.[9] Reid, however, identifies a particular development pattern in mixed jurisdictions as regards the reception of legal concepts in a mixed legal system. First, there is the event of the arrival of a legal concept derived from the lending system. For Civilian-heritage mixed legal systems like Québec, the lending system is the Common Law. This arrival can either be sudden (by way of legislative enactment for instance), or gradually by way of what Reid calls "legal osmosis."[10] Second, the receiving legal system reacts – be it positively or negatively – to this reception. Third comes the process of assimilation. In the fourth step the foreign legal concept is reassembled and fully integrated into the borrowing legal system.[11]

Reid lists the reception of the trust in Scotland and Québec as examples of such a process of reception in a mixed legal system.[12] This book will look at the reception of the trust in Québec later as well.[13] Tentatively, I would also argue that the reception of the secured transactions framework in Québec from the Common Law provinces is an example of typical mixed legal system reception, particularly as regards step four of Reid's framework of reception. This reception process will be looked at in more detail in the part of this book on the substantive secured transactions law in the Canadian provinces.

## B. Bijuralism in Action

There are two vectors of bijuralism in action. First, there is the interaction between the two component legal systems – Common Law and Civil Law – and second, there is the influence of the two component legal systems on a third legal system: federal law.

---

[7] See *ibid* passim.

[8] Tetley, *supra* note 4 at 593.

[9] Evans-Jones, *supra* note 4 at 228; Tetley, *supra* note 4 at 597–98.

[10] Reid, "Idea", *supra* note 6 at 28.

[11] *Ibid* at 28.

[12] *Ibid* at 29–33.

[13] See Part II: § 7, "The Civil Law Trust".

*I. The First Vector of Interaction: Common Law and Civil Law*

The first vector of interaction concerns the interaction between the component legal systems; it is horizontal. This interaction can be one of the factors that lead to the creation of a mixed legal system. The close interaction of two legal systems within one overarching framework is conducive for the reception of legal concepts from one legal system in the other system.[14] If we look at the potential cross-pollination of the two legal systems within the Canadian federal framework, we find that the 19th century saw a period of predominant influence of the Common Law on Civil Law rules.[15] For instance, in *Canadian Pacific Railway Co v Robinson,*[16] the Supreme Court of Canada refused to award emotional damages in an action governed by the *Code civil du Bas-Canada*[17] because this would have created a discrepancy between Civil Law and Common Law. In cases involving the interpretation of wills, Common Law rules on the interpretation of wills were applied because the concept of freedom of inheritance was received in a process of osmosis from English law.[18] If Civil Law principles were accepted by a Canadian court in a Common Law action, it was usually by way of English courts referring to French courts, and never through direct reception of Québec law.[19]

Allard identifies the misunderstanding of the codal nature as one of the reasons why non-Civilian judges often introduced Common Law reasoning into judgments in Civil Law actions.[20] In *Quebec Railway, Light, Heat and Power Co v Vandry,*[21] Lord Sumner in a judgment of the Privy Council held that the *CcBC* is foremost a statute. Presumably, Lord Summer pointed this out based on the Common Law presumption that a statute, a legislative encroachment on the Common Law, must be given a narrow interpretation. Lord Summer then

---

[14] See Albert Breton & Anne Des Ormeaux, "Coevolution as an Influence in the Development of Legal Systems" in: Breton & Trebilcock, eds, *Bijuralism, supra* note 3, 125.

[15] See France Allard, "The Supreme Court of Canada and Its Impact on the Expression of Bijuralism" in: Canada, Department of Justice, ed, *The Harmonization of Federal Legislation with the Civil Law of the Province of Quebec and Canadian Bijuralism: Second Publication* (Ottawa: Canada, Department of Justice, 2001) 1 at 3–6 [Allard, "Expression"] from where I have taken the examples used in the following text, and Loius Lavallée, "Bijuralism in the Supreme Court of Canada Judgments Since the Enactment of the Civil Code of Québec" in: Canada, Department of Justice, ed, *Harmonization II,* this note, 1 at 1.

[16] (1887), 14 SCR 105.

[17] *Code civil du Bas-Canada,* 29 Vict, c 41 [*CcBC*].

[18] Allard, "Expression", *supra* note 15 at 4.

[19] *Ibid* at 5; HP Glenn, "Le droit comparé et la Cour suprême du Canada" in: John E Brierley, H P Glenn & Ethel Groffier, eds, *Mélanges Louis-Philippe Pigeon* (Montréal: Wilson & Lafleur, 1989) 197 at 207.

[20] Allard, "Expression", *supra* note 15 at 7.

[21] [1920] AC 662 (Can PC).

proceeded to refuse to assign authoritative weight to French decisions. He reasoned that the *Code Napoléon* was enacted after the connection between Québec and France had already been severed.[22] The Privy Council's treatment of the *CcBC* as an ordinary statute was adopted by the Supreme Court of Canada.[23]

For Allard, this treatment of the Civil Law *CcBC* created two problems. First, it denied the *CcBC* its rightful status as the expression of the general law of Québec. Second, it assumed that the legislature in Québec used a Common Law style of expression when legislating in the private law realm.[24] In a sense, this amounts to a refusal of Common Law judges to accept democratic supremacy over the law. If the code is rightfully seen as the expression of the general outlines of the private law rather than an encroachment on judge-made law, the law becomes the primary product of the elected assembly rather than a product of judicial law-making. The cases referenced by Allard, and, in turn, those on which the Privy Council relied, show that the Privy Council and the Supreme Court of Canada rejected the idea of supremacy of a general law made by the legislature over judge-made law.

As we would expect it to happen, the Common Law-style reasoning and treatment of the *CcBC* was not accepted or shared by Civilian-trained judges. Allard points out that the Common Law-based rejection of emotional damages in *Canadian Pacific Railway Co v Robinson* was subsequently ignored or at least circumvented by Québec courts.[25] It is worth pointing out that the approach adopted by the Québec courts did not consist of an outright refusal to follow precedent. Rather, the provisions of the code were given a wide scope.[26] Thus, it was the affirmation of a very Civilian principle – the generality of the code – that was used as the pivotal point for overcoming decisions considered to be wrong precedent by Québec courts.

Civilian lawyers were concerned about the influence of the Common Law on Québec's legal system.[27] Institutionally, some authors suggested that private law cases stemming from Québec should be dealt with by a separate chamber

---

[22] *Ibid* at 671, relying on the Privy Council Judgments in *McArthur v Dominion Cartridge Co* (1904), [1905] AC 72 (Can PC) and *Maclaren v Attorney-General for Quebec,* [1914] AC 258 at 270 (Can PC).

[23] Allard, "Expression", *supra* note 15 at 7–8. Allard points to *Town of Montreal West v Hough* (1930), [1931] SCR 113.

[24] Allard, "Expression", *supra* note 15 at 8.

[25] *Ibid* at 14.

[26] *Ibid* at 14.

[27] See Pierre-Basile Mignault, "Les rapports entre le droit civil et la 'common law' au Canada, specialement dans la province de Québec" (1932) 11:4 R du D 201. Cf. Jean-Louis Baudouin, "L'interprétation du Code civil québécois par la Cour suprême du Canada" (1975) 53 Can Bar Rev 715.

of the Supreme Court.[28] In the latter half of the 20th century, the Supreme Court of Canada started to recognize the conceptual independence of Québec's Civil Law.[29] One example connected to the subject of this book is the decision of the Supreme Court in *Royal Trust Co v Tucker.*[30] The decision involved the question of the nature of right of ownership of a trustee of a trust established according to then-applicable Québec law. The history of the trust in Québec will be discussed in more detail in a later chapter of this book.[31] For the purpose of the present analysis, it suffices to say that the relevant provisions of the *CcBC*[32] provided that property be transferred to the trustee *(fiduciaires),*[33] while at the same the trustee was deemed to be the administrator of the property.[34] The trust of the Common Law world operates with a concept of split ownership (*i.e.* legal and equitable title), which we will analyse in more detail later as well.[35] This concept was not embraced explicitly by the *CcBC* provisions. Given the Court's application of Common Law principles in wills cases, and its refusal to accept the *CcBC* as the primary source of the common law of Québec, one could have expected the Supreme Court to characterize the trustee's interest under the *CcBC* along similar lines. However, the Supreme Court refused to extend the import of Common Law concepts into the Civil Law.

> "[The] enactment of arts. 981a et seq. did not have the effect of introducing in Quebec the English distinction between legal title and beneficial ownership, a sort of dual ownership, and a concept foreign to Quebec law under which ownership is indivisible and vested in a single individual. [...] English law is relevant only in so far as it is compatible with arts. 981a et seq. of the Civil Code."[36]

The re-affirmation of the conceptual autonomy of Québec's Civil Law *vis-à-vis* the Common Law naturally leads to the question whether there can be fruitful mutual cross-pollination between the two legal systems. In other words, is there a middle ground between complete conceptual separation – a type of legal two solitudes akin to the cultural two solitudes describing the ostensible lack of communication between English- and French-speaking Canada – and superiority of one legal system over the other? Bijuralism analysed along the first vector thus becomes a question whether both component legal systems can be considered to demonstrate examples of successful reception in Reid's mixed legal system analysis.

---

[28] See Baudouin, preceding note at 715.

[29] See Allard, "Expression", *supra* note 15 at 16–19.

[30] [1982] 1 SCR 250 [*Royal Trust*].

[31] See Part II: § 7, "The Civil Law Trust".

[32] Namely *CcBC, supra* note 17, ss 981 ff.

[33] *Ibid,* s 981a.

[34] *Ibid,* s 981b.

[35] See Part II: § 6, "Equitable Property Rights".

[36] *Royal Trust, supra* note 30 at 261, Beetz J [references ommited].

In the realm of property rights, two modern examples of reciprocal impact come to mind, which will be the topic of this book. First, there is the influence modern secured transactions legislation in the Common Law provinces have had on Québec secured transaction law. While in Allard's view there are not many examples in which the Civil Law has exercised significant influence on the Common Law,[37] our second example *is* just such a case. This second example is more difficult to outline than the secured transaction law example. This second example concerns the reception of unjust enrichment principles in the Common Law. The question that shall be addressed is to what extent a parallel can be drawn between the Civilian concept of a vindication of property rights and what is referred to as "proprietary restitution" – the recognition of equitable property rights as an ostensible remedy to what seems to be a case of unjust enrichment. It is straightforward to make the claim that the no basis-approach of modern unjust enrichment law in Canadian Common Law was received from Civil Law. But the question just formulated is somewhat more difficult to examine. In particular, we will examine to which degree Common Law is at a crossroads in Reid's successful reception test.

### *II. The Second Vector: Federal Law and Provincial Law*

The second vector of interaction concerns the process by which the component legal systems interact with and shape the overarching third legal system; it is vertical. Applied to the Canadian example, the second vector of interaction concerns the interaction of provincial and federal private law. As regards this level of interaction, Canadian law has undergone an evolution. We will track this evolution in the following sub-sections.

#### *1. The Concept of a Federal Common Law*

Section 101 *Constitution Act, 1867*[38] provides that the federal Parliament may establish courts for the administration of the "laws of Canada." This was initially construed to mean that any subject matter falling within the realm of federal legislation was governed in its entirety by federal law.[39] This would have required a general federal private law because subject matters falling within the realm of federal jurisdiction include bankruptcy and insolvency law[40] and banking law,[41] areas which necessarily make reference to private law

[37] Allard, "Expression", *supra* note 15 at 19–21.

[38] *An Act for the Union of Canada, Nova Scotia, and New Brunswick, and the Government thereof; and for Purposes connected therewith, 1867,* 30 & 31 Vict, c 3 [*Constitution Act*].

[39] Cf. Allard, "Expression", *supra* note 15 at 23.

[40] *Constitution Act, supra* note 38, s 91(21).

[41] *Ibid,* s 91(15).

concepts. In principle, general private law falls within the realm of provincial jurisdiction by virtue of s 92(13) *Constitution Act, 1867.*[42]

In the initial understanding, federal law could draw on provincial law to fill any gaps in federal statutes. However, this was a form of incorporation by way of static reference. Once a concept stemming from provincial private law would be incorporated into federal regulation, it would become disconnected from provincial law, and its continued development would have been a subject of federal law only.[43] Such a concept of a general federal law common law would have led to a uniform application of any federal statute throughout the entire Dominion.[44]

*2. The Complimentary Relationship of Federal and Provincial Law*

The concept of a general federal private law was rejected by the Supreme Court of Canada in *Quebec North Shore Paper v Canadian Pacific Ltd,*[45] *McNamara Construction et al v The Queen*[46] and *R v Thomas Fuller Construction Co (1958) Ltd et al.*[47] Federal common law does exist, but in limited subject areas (*i.e.* maritime law, aboriginal title, and matters relating to the Crown in right of Canada).[48] Thus, provincial law governs a subject matter that falls within the realm of provincial legislation, even though it appears in the context of a federal rule.[49] This, in turn, means that provincial law governs questions of property, even when they appear in the context of the application of the federal *Bankruptcy and Insolvency Act.*[50]

The Supreme Court of Canada has confirmed the complementarity of provincial private law in bankruptcy matters a number of times.[51] Recently, the Supreme Court in *Re Giffen* reasoned that:

[42] On the delineation of provincial and federal jurisdiction see Jacob S Ziegel, "Harmonization of Private Laws in Federal Systems of Government: Canada, the USA, and Australia" in: Ross Cranston, ed, *Making Commercial Law: Essays in Honour of Roy Goode* (Oxford: Clarendon Press, 1997) 131 at 137–40.

[43] Cf. Allard, "Expression", *supra* note 15 at 23.

[44] Identifying this as one of the goals of the establishment of the Supreme Court of Canada, Lavallée, *supra* note 15 at 1. See also Aline Grenon, "Le bijuridisme canadien à la croisée des chemins?: Réflexions sur l'incidence de l'article 8.1 de la Loi d'interprétation" (2011) 56:4 McGill LJ 775 at 780 [Grenon, "Croisée des chemins"].

[45] (1976), [1977] 2 SCR 1054.

[46] [1977] 2 SCR 654.

[47] (1979), [1980] 1 SCR 695. See Allard, "Expression", *supra* note 15 at 22.

[48] Allard, "Expression", *supra* note 15 at 22.

[49] *Ibid* at 23–24.

[50] *Bankruptcy and Insolvency Act,* RSC 1985, c B-3 [*BIA*].

[51] See Allard, "Expression", *supra* note 15 at 25. See also *Robinson v Countrywide Factors Ltd* (1977), [1978] 1 SCR 753 and *Deputy Minister of Revenue (Québec) v Rainville,* [1980] 1 SCR 35.

"Even though bankruptcy is clearly a federal matter, and even though it has been established that the federal Parliament alone can determine distribution priorities, the BIA is dependent on provincial property and civil rights legislation in order to inform the terms of the BIA and the rights of the parties involved in the bankruptcy."[52]

The Court held that it was provincial law that "defines the rights of the parties involved in a bankruptcy."[53]

### *3. The Interpretation Act*

In 2001, federal Parliament enacted the *Federal Law-Civil Law Harmonization Act, No. 1.* The act added a new section 8.1 to the s 8.1 *Interpretation Act.*[54] The section reads as follows:

"Both the common law and the civil law are equally authoritative and recognized sources of the law of property and civil rights in Canada and, unless otherwise provided by law, if in interpreting an enactment it is necessary to refer to a province's rules, principles or concepts forming part of the law of property and civil rights, reference must be made to the rules, principles and concepts in force in the province at the time the enactment is being applied."

"Le droit civil et la common law font pareillement autorité et sont tous deux sources de droit en matière de propriété et de droits civils au Canada et, s'il est nécessaire de recourir à des règles, principes ou notions appartenant au domaine de la propriété et des droits civils en vue d'assurer l'application d'un texte dans une province, il faut, sauf règle de droit s'y opposant, avoir recours aux règles, principes et notions en vigueur dans cette province au moment de l'application du texte."

This section re-affirms that federal legislation is based on Civil Law as well as on Common Law.[55] It also entails a rejection of the uniform application of federal laws throughout the entire Dominion.[56] Grenon argues that the provision furthermore amounts to a farewell to the supremacy of the traditional canon of statutory interpretation.[57] According to this canon, the interpretation of a certain phrase in a statutory text entailed four steps: first, grammatical interpretation; second, systemic interpretation; third, teleological interpretation; and fourth, historical interpretation.[58]

---

[52] *Re Giffen,* [1998] 1 SCR 91 at para 64 [*Giffen*], Iacobucci J, referring to *Husky Oil Operations Ltd v Minister of National Revenue,* [1995] 3 SCR 453 and Jacob S Ziegel, "Personal Property Security and Bankruptcy: There Is No War!" (1993) 72:1 Can Bar Rev 44 at 50.

[53] *Giffen,* preceding note at para 63, Iacobucci J.

[54] *Interpretation Act,* RSC 1985, c I-21.

[55] Grenon, "Croisée des chemins", *supra* note 44 at 779.

[56] Cf. *ibid* at 780, 795–96 with examples.

[57] *Ibid* at 781.

[58] *Re Rizzo & Rizzo Shoes Ltd,* [1998] 1 SCR 27 at para 21, Iacobucci J, referring to Elmer A Driedger, *The Construction of Statutes,* 2[d] edn (Toronto: Butterworths, 1983) at 87.

*a) Accepting Diversity*

Since the enactment of s 8.1 *Interpretation Act,* a number of cases involving the interaction of provincial and federal law have reached the Supreme Court that are relevant to the subject matter of this book. *DIMS Construction inc (Syndic de) v Québec (Procureur général)*[59] revolved around s 97(3) *BIA.*[60] Section 97(3) *BIA* provides that creditors of a bankrupt debtor who are also debtors of the bankrupt can set off their claims against their debts. To the extent that a debt can be set off, this amounts to a full realization of the creditor's claim. The rule thus creates an exception to the *pro rata* scheme of distribution in bankruptcy, whereby each claim is reduced to a certain percentage in order to satisfy all the bankrupt's creditors. At the same time, the extent of this exception depends on the rules of set off, which are a provincial matter. This means that creditors whose right to set-off is governed by the private law of a Common Law jurisdiction which recognizes a so-called "equitable right to set-off" might be better off than creditors who have no such right to set-off under the private law of Québec. In other words, the extent of the exception from the *pro rata* distribution scheme is a function of the applicable provincial law. The Supreme Court held that this alone does not warrant the introduction of equitable set-off in Québec. The differential treatment is provided for in the *BIA* and is a function of its complementary relationship with provincial law.[61]

*b) The Notion of Property in Federal Law*

In *Saulnier v Royal Bank of Canada,*[62] the Court had to decide whether a fishing licence granted by the Crown falls within the scope of "property" under the *BIA.*[63] The Court held that the definition in s 2 *BIA* was wider than the definition of property in Common Law (and at common law) of "property," as it was Parliament's intention to bring as many assets as possible into the *pro rata* distribution scheme.[64]

*c) The Notion of Security Interest in Federal Law*

In *Caisse populaire Desjardins de l'Est de Drummond v Canada,*[65] a Caisse populaire Desjardins bank extended credit to a debtor. The debtor deposited monies with the bank which – according to an agreement between the bank and

---

[59] 2005 SCC 52.

[60] *BIA, supra* note 50.

[61] *DIMS Construction inc (Syndic de) v Québec (Procureur général), supra* note 59 at paras 63–65, Deschamps J.

[62] *Saulnier v Royal Bank of Canada,* 2008 SCC 58 [*Saulnier*].

[63] *BIA, supra* note 50, s 2.

[64] *Saulnier, supra* note 62 at paras 44–49, Binnie J.

[65] 2009 SCC 29 [*Drummond*].

the debtor – were not withdrawable and could only be used as a security for the benefit of the bank. Bank and debtor also agreed that the bank could withhold repayment of the monies until the credit was repaid, which thus gave the bank a right to set-off the credit contract claims against the debtor's claims from the account. The debtor failed to make interest payments to the bank as well as certain salary deductions for its employees due to the Crown as tax under the *Income Tax Act.* Even where such deductions are not made, the *ITA* provides that a "deemed trust" is imposed on the debtor's property and any property held by a secured creditor.[66] On this basis, the Crown ordered the bank to pay the amount owing to the Crown from the proceeds of the term deposit, which the Crown said was subject to its deemed trust.

Due to the "deemed trust" framework of the *ITA,* the case revolved around the question whether the bank was a secured creditor – who could be subjected to the deemed trust – or whether it merely had an ordinary right to set-off its credit claims against the accounts debts. It is difficult to conceptualize the bank's right to set-off as a security interest in the bank account because it is difficult to view the bank having an interest in its indebtedness.[67] The majority of the Supreme Court of Canada, in an opinion written by Rothstein J, held that because the *ITA* contains a definition of security interest in s 224(1.3) *ITA,* the question whether or not the property was subject to a security interest and thus the bank's status as a secured creditor did not depend on the characterization of the interest in provincial law.[68] Rather, according to the broad functional definition of "security interest," the issue was to be determined by reference to the *ITA* alone: the bank fell under the act's definition of a secured creditor.

Neither *Saulnier* nor *Drummond* made any reference to s 8.1 *Interpretation Act.* Grenon believes this to be due to the Supreme Court's tendency to ensure a uniform application of federal laws throughout the Dominion.[69] Furthermore, she attributes a lack of reference to s 8.1 *Interpretation Act* to the "unijural" background of the writing judges.[70] However, the latter explanation ignores the fact that in both cases the Supreme Court did not simply adopt a Common Law based interpretation, but gave the statutes a meaning that could not be found in Common Law. It is thus hardly an example of a Common Law-only interpretation.

---

[66] *Income Tax Act,* RSC 1985, c 1 (5th Supp.), s 227(4.1).

[67] Roderick J Wood, "Journey to the Outer Limits of Secured Transactions Law" (2010) 48:3 CBLJ 482 at 490–93.

[68] *Drummond, supra* note 65 at para 10, Rothstein J.

[69] Grenon, "Croisée des chemins", *supra* note 44 at 811.

[70] *Ibid* at 811.

### d) Competing Property Rights in Federal Law

In *Bank of Montreal v Innovation Credit Union*[71] and *Royal Bank of Canada v Radius Credit Union Ltd,*[72] the Supreme Court made explicit use of s 8.1 *Interpretation Act.* The cases involved security interests created under s 427 *Bank Act.*[73] Section 427 *Bank Act* creates a security interest scheme that operates in parallel with provincial secured transaction law (although it is limited in its personal scope). The *Bank Act* does not include a provision that governs a priority contest between a provincial security interest granted before the *Bank Act* security interest is created. Rather, s 427(2) *Bank Act* provides that the lending bank receives "the same rights and powers as if the bank had acquired a warehouse receipt or bill of lading in which that property was described." Under s 435(2) *Bank Act,* the effect of taking such an instrument is that the bank has all the rights enjoyed by the owner of the property.[74] Thus, the Court concluded, the question of priority between the *Bank Act* secured creditor and the creditor of a provincial security interest becomes a question of provincial property law: namely, how does provincial property law resolve the priority competition between the purchaser of the property and a provincial security interest?[75] I will discuss the cases in detail below.[76]

---

[71] 2010 SCC 47 [*Innovation Credit*].

[72] 2010 SCC 48.

[73] *Bank Act,* SC 1991, c 46.

[74] *Bank of Montreal v Hall,* [1990] 1 SCR 121.

[75] *Innovation Credit, supra* note 71 at para 31, Charron J.

[76] See Part IV: § 15 A.V.1, "Common Law: Nemo Dat".

# § 3 Law and Economics

In this book, I will repeatedly look at an economic analysis of property law and secured transactions law. There is an inherent and undeniable relationship between property law (particularly secured transaction law) and the economy. Property law provides the framework within which commercial transactions take place. Secured credit is the "engine of economic growth."[1] Unavailability of secured transaction law spurs economic growth.[2] However, secured transactions cannot be created by virtue of contract alone. Secured transactions are dependent on a property law supporting it.[3] These ideas will be elaborated on in more detail later, particularly when looking at the economic analysis of property law[4] and the economic analysis of secured transactions law.[5] Being concerned with resource allocation, a law and economic analysis lends itself to those areas of the law which effect the resource allocation by assigning property rights to market participants. This description of law particularly applies to property law, secured transactions law, and insolvency law.[6]

So far, I have claimed *that* law influences economic performance. The later chapters will present theories on *why and how* law does so. For the present purpose, it suffices to say that if one accepts the premise of a relationship between property law (including secured transactions law) and economic performance then the "legal origin theory" raises a challenge to the retention of a Civil Law system. Within the law-and-development writing, we find the "legal origin" writers, who posit that Common Law systems intrinsically show a better economic development than societies that base their legal system on the Civil Law. If the legal origin theory were true in its broad form and purpose of

---

[1] Neil B Cohen, "Internationalizing the Law of Secured Credit: Perspectives from the US Experience" (1999) 20:3 U Pa J Int'l Econ L 423 at 428. See also Moritz Brinkmann, *Kreditsicherheiten an beweglichen Sachen und Forderungen: Eine materiell-, insolvenz- und kollisionsrechtliche Studie des Rechts der Mobiliarsicherheiten vor dem Hintergrund internationaler und europäischer Entwicklungen* (Jus Privatum, Tübingen: Mohr Siebeck, 2011) at 1.

[2] Heywood Fleisig, *The Power of Collateral* (Public Policy for the Private Sector, Washington, DC: World Bank, 1995).

[3] Cohen, *supra* note 1 at 430.

[4] See Part II: § 8 C, "The Economic Analysis of Property Law".

[5] See Part III: § 11, "The Law and Economics of Secured Transactions".

[6] Brinkmann, *supra* note 1 at 68.

secured transaction law consists of providing an efficient framework than it would seem better to abolish Civil Law and replace it with a Common Law set of rules.

This suggestion does run into a number of obstacles. First, secured transaction law is deeply intertwined with property law, which in itself is intertwined with the remainder of private law. Thus, it is not easily possible to simply replace a Civil Law secured transactions law with a Common Law secured transactions law. Second, it might be that the retention of Civil Law serves more purposes than a simple economic goal.

Both these obstacles could be overcome if one would focus more on what exactly the mechanisms are with which "the Common Law" achieves its supposed superiority and to what extent these mechanisms can be integrated into a Civilian system of private law. Instead of wholesale replacement, the adoption of certain legal mechanisms, coming from Common Law, would present an alternative to a blunt call for the adoption of Common Law over Civil Law. It might even be possible to show that in certain instances, substantive rules of a Civil Law origin fare better in an economic analysis of the law.

If Common Law and Civil Law are to be retained side by side, differences will remain. To prevent these differences from creating too much friction in economic performance, it is necessary to co-ordinate the two legal systems. As far as the subject matter of this book – *i.e.* property law and secured transactions law – is concerned, I argue that such co-ordination can take place on the level of insolvency law and on the level of conflict of laws.

To prepare for an analysis of property law along the lines just presented, I introduce the economic analysis of the law in this chapter. I first trace the intellectual history of law and economics within legal scholarship; thus, in this chapter's first section, I give an overview of approaches to law as an object of intellectual inquiry. In the second section, I look in more detail at the economic analysis of law. Having laid the foundations for an economic analysis of the law, I look at the "legal origin theory" in section three.

## A. Law's Autonomy(?)

On the one end of the spectrum, we find the schools of thought that consider law to be a discrete object of study and intellectual inquiry. On the other end of the spectrum are schools of thought such as legal realism and law and economics, which consider law to be the object of study of other social sciences. We could call the approaches found at the former end of the spectrum "autonomous" or "internal" approaches to law. Another term is legal "formalism." I predominantly use the last term, for no other reason than style.

In contrast to the internal approach, law and economics takes a wider approach to legal scholarship. This approach is based on the premise that the answer to a question of law cannot be resolved by internal reasoning alone. Broadly understood, law and economics rejects the view that the law can be one coherent system from which the answer to all legal questions can be deduced. Thus, law and economics not only posits that the question "How should the law be?" is one that cannot be answered by reference to law alone, but it posits that the question "What is the law?" cannot be answered by reference to law alone because the process of legal reasoning is necessarily indeterminate. This section traces the development of this idea. I should note that the ambition of this book is not to be a contribution to legal theory. I do not mean to advance one legal theory over another. Rather, legal formalism, realism, and law and economics are presented to better understand the different conceptions of property law and secured transactions law later in the book, particularly as regards the economic theories of secured transactions law.

*I. Formalism*

"Formalism" as a legal theory stands in contrast to an economic analysis of the law. Regarding terminology, I should note that "formalism" could be considered an almost derogatory term.[7] At the same time, jurists defending law's autonomy embrace the term.[8] I use the term "formalism" without any negative connotation.

Legal formalism takes an internal perspective to the law. Law is seen as a coherent system, a discrete object of study. Law itself is considered to be governed by certain principles that can be the object of scientific study,[9] similar to the way rules of nature are the object of natural sciences. Law as a discipline is considered to be a closed system and formal logic can be used to arrive at legal conclusions.[10] Legal formalism was the prevalent school of legal scholarship in the 19th century throughout the Western world.

Formalism was very much connected with legal thought in 19th century continental Europe. Starting with the works by Savigny,[11] German legal scholars in the 19th century tried to elaborate the basic conceptions of Roman law into

---

[7] Weinrib calls it a term of "opprobrium," see Ernest J Weinrib, *The Idea of Private Law,* 2d edn (Oxford: Oxford University Press, 2012) at 22.

[8] Weinrib continues by stating that "formalism, properly understood and stripped of the encrustations of hostile polemics, embodies a profound and inescapable truth about law's inner coherence," *ibid* at 22–23.

[9] Hanoch Dagan, "The Realist Conception of Law" (2007) 57 UTLJ 607 at 611 [Dagan, "Realist Conception"].

[10] *Ibid* at 611.

[11] Savigny gave a description of his legal theory in his early work, see Friedrich C von Savigny, *Vom Beruf unserer Zeit für Gesetzgebung und Rechtswissenschaft* (Heidelberg: Mohr, 1814).

a gapless, coherent system.[12] Legal rules and the entire legal system was conceptually based on the "will theory." The will theory posited that the private law was best explained as being based on the notion that the law should protect the rights of legal persons, which meant helping them realize their will. It should be restrained only as necessary to permit others to do the same.[13]

The German approach was received both in the British Empire and the United States. Kennedy points to the British jurist Austin and his *Lectures on Jurisprudence*[14] as a "manifesto of 'classical legal thought' for the common-law world."[15] In the United States, classical legal thought is most closely associated with Langdell.[16] In the Common Law variety of classical legal thought, the right content of the law can be synthesized from cases. Principles can be derived from cases, and these principles provide solutions for future cases. Cases not matching up with an identified principle should be discarded as wrongly decided.[17] Posner calls Langdell's approach to law

> "a form of Platonism; just as Plato had regarded particular chairs as manifestations of or approximations to the concept of a chair, Langdell regarded particular decisions on contract law as manifestations of or approximations to the legal concept of contract."[18]

The distinction between legal formalism and an external perspective on law should not be mistaken being identical to the distinction between a naturalist conception of the law and legal positivism. Proponents of a natural law conception of the law posit that there is a necessary content of the law that can be deduced by an appeal to reason or to morals. Kantianism is essentially a legal theory based on the appeal to reason.[19] Positivists draw a strong distinction between law as it is and law as it should be. Proponents of the latter include

---

[12] Duncan Kennedy, "Two Globalizations of Law & Legal Thought: 1850–1968" (2002) 36:3 Suffolk UL Rev 631 at 638.

[13] *Ibid* at 637.

[14] John Austin, *Lectures on Jurisprudence: The Philosophy of Positive Law,* ed by Robert Campbell, 4th edn (London: J Murray, 1873), vol 1 and John Austin, *Lectures on Jurisprudence: The Philosophy of Positive Law,* ed by Robert Campbell, 4th edn (London: J Murray, 1873), vol 2.

[15] Kennedy, *supra* note 12 at 639.

[16] See Kristoffel Grechenig & Martin Gelter, "The Transatlantic Divergence in Legal Thought: American Law and Economics vs. German Doctrinalism" (2008) 31:1 Hastings Int'l & Comp L Rev 295 at 309–10; Richard A Posner, "The Decline of Law as an Autonomous Discipline: 1962–1987" (1987) 100:4 Harv L Rev 761 at 762 [Posner, "Decline"].

[17] Grechenig & Gelter, preceding note at 310.

[18] Posner, "Decline", *supra* note 16 at 762.

[19] Immanuel Kant, "Grundlegung zur Metaphysik der Sitten" in: Immanuel Kant, *Werke,* ed by Wilhelm Weischedel, 3rd ed (Darmstadt 1971), vol 4, 58 and Immanuel Kant, "Metaphysik der Sitten: Rechtslehre" in: Kant, *Werke,* this note, 306.

Kelsen and Hart.[20] The debate between natural law proponents and legal positivists was one of the great legal controversies of the 20th century. It includes the Hart-Fuller debate,[21] the Hart-Dworkin debate,[22] and Radbruch's criticism of Kelsen's positivism.[23] At the heart of these debates was the question whether morality and law are separate or whether morality or reason is the source of law's binding power. For the present overview, it suffices to say that while naturalists must necessarily take an autonomous view of the law, positivists can also do so. This form of positivism can be called "formal positivism."

Formal positivism focuses on the content of legal rules and judgments. Legal scholarship contributes to the working of the law by means of "[smoothing] its inconsistencies by advancing the understanding of its inherent structure and system."[24] Pursuing external values by means of law is seen as the prerogative of the legislature.[25] Judges are supposed to act solely in the exercise of legislative will.[26] Legal positivism is understood as a strict separation of positive law on the one hand and substantive justification for these norms on the other. Legal scholarship is only concerned with the former.[27] Hart, the positivist, argued that legal rules are determinate, and thus challenged the legal realists' attack on legal formalism.

Formalism has by no means gone out of fashion in legal thought. In his modern manifesto for the autonomy of law, Weinrib tries to address the perception that

> "law is not an autonomous body of learning, that law cannot be separated from politics, that the law's concepts are not to be taken seriously in their own right, and that private law is not distinct from other modes of legal ordering."[28]

He continues to outline his autonomous perception of the law:

> "The alternative approach treats private law as an internally intelligible phenomenon by drawing on what is salient in juristic experience and by trying to make sense of legal thinking and discourse in their own terms."[29]

---

[20] HLA Hart, "Positivism and the Separation of Law and Morals" (1958) 71:4 Harv L Rev 593; Hans Kelsen, *Reine Rechtslehre,* 2d edn (Wien: Franz Deuticke, 1960).

[21] See Hart, "Positivism and the Separation of Law and Morals", preceding note and Lon L Fuller, "Positivism and Fidelity to Law: A Reply to Professor Hart" (1958) 71:4 Harv L Rev 630.

[22] See Keith Culver, "Leaving the Hart-Dworkin Debate" (2001) 51:4 UTLJ 367.

[23] Gustav Radbruch, "Gesetzliches Unrecht und übergesetzliches Recht" [1946] SJZ 105.

[24] Grechenig & Gelter, *supra* note 16 at 297.

[25] See Christian Kirchner, "The Difficult Reception of Law and Economics in Germany" (1991) 11:3 Int'l Rev L & Econ 277 at 284–85.

[26] *Ibid* at 284.

[27] Grechenig & Gelter, *supra* note 16 at 303.

[28] Weinrib, *The Idea of Private Law, supra* note 7 at 2.

[29] *Ibid* at 2–3.

### *II. Utilitarianism*

Even while formalism became the predominant theory of the law, an opposing theory developed: "utilitarianism." Utilitarianism is a school of legal thought connected with Bentham. Unlike formalism, it posits that law can only be understood by reference to an extrinsic goal. Bentham posited that law must follow the "principle of utility."[30]

> "By the principle of utility is meant that principle which approves or disapproves of every action whatsoever, according to the tendency which it approves or disapproves to augment or diminish the happiness of the party whose interest is in question: or, what is the same thing in other words, to promote or to oppose that happiness. I say of every action whatsoever; and therefore not only of every action of a private individual, but of every measure of government."[31]

In his works on law and utility, Bentham was primarily concerned with crime. However, his insistence on a cost-benefit analysis of law making turned out to be a universal principle that need not be restricted to criminal law.[32]

### *III. Realism*

Another school of legal theory that stands in contrast to legal formalism is legal realism. Certain ideas in legal realism can be considered to be precursors to the economic analysis of the law. Thus we take a look at legal realism in this subsection.

#### *1. Holmes*

Early legal realism is most often connected with American jurist and judge Oliver Wendell Holmes. Holmes advocated a view of the law that was less concerned with the abstract principles of the law. He claimed "the prophecies of what the courts will do in fact, and nothing more pretentious, are what I mean by the law."[33] Inherent in this statement is a refusal to accept that synthesized principles of prior case law are the object of legal study. Rather, legal study can be concerned with any factor that would influence a court's decision.

Holmes was a member of the Supreme Court, but his approach was not shared by the majority of the bench. Grechenig and Gelter point us to the Supreme Court's decision in *Lochner v New York*[34] as a typical example of decision-making at that time. Socially progressive legislation was deemed to be

---

[30] Jeremy Bentham, *Introduction to the Principles of Morals and Legislation,* 1st edn (London: T Payne & Sons, 1789) xxi; Grechenig & Gelter, *supra* note 16 at 320.

[31] Bentham, preceding note ii.

[32] Richard A Posner, "Bentham's Influence on the Law and Economics Movement" (1998) 51:1 Curr Legal Probs 425 at 433–36.

[33] Oliver W Holmes, "The Path of the Law" (1897) 10:8 Harv L Rev 457 at 461.

[34] *Lochner v New York,* 198 US 45, 25 SCt 539 (1908).

unconstitutional because in a process of formal deduction, the legislation was held to breach legal principles not explicitly included in the constitution.[35] An impact-analysis was not part of the Court's reasoning; rather, the Court based its decision on a formal deduction of legal principles deemed valid and binding.

Holmes' view gained more traction in legal writing. The developing school of legal realism rejected the notion that there was an inherently right answer to legal questions and that this one answer could be found by means of applying logical reasoning and legal methodology on a set of pre-existing rules.[36] The indeterminacy of the law on the basis of pre-existing materials became the cornerstone of the American legal realist movement.[37] Legal realism was concerned with the effects of legal decision-making. As regards the focus on the effects of law, legal realism followed in the footsteps of utilitarianism.[38]

### 2. The Realist Challenge to Formalism

#### a) Law's Indeterminacy

The realist approach to law challenges the formalist notion because, as a legal realist would argue, law is indeterminate.[39] Hart disagreed with this notion. He maintained that the indeterminacy claim did not present a great challenge to an internal view of the law. He argued that legal rules "are determinate enough at the centre to supply standards of correct judicial decisions."[40] The realist critique of the internal perspective considers indeterminacy to be not only a question of the interpretation and application of identifiable and identified legal rules, but also a result of the "multiplicity of doctrinal materials."[41]

Legal realists maintain that legal actors cannot free themselves from external influences. In this regard, realism differs from formalism.[42] Formalists argue that it is possible to imagine a lawyer free from all external influences. Proponents of the internal position on law claim that a judge with superior analytical qualities can find the correct outcome of any "hard case" by deducing it from the basic principles of the legal system.[43]

---

[35] Grechenig & Gelter, *supra* note 16 at 312–13.

[36] John Dewey, "Logical Method and Law" (1914) 10 Cornell LQ 17. See Grechenig & Gelter, *supra* note 16 at 314.

[37] Grechenig & Gelter, *supra* note 16 at 304, note 33.

[38] *Ibid* at 321.

[39] Dagan, "Realist Conception", *supra* note 9 at 612–13.

[40] HLA Hart, *The Concept of Law,* 2[d] edn (Oxford: Clarendon Press, 1997) at 145.

[41] Dagan, "Realist Conception", *supra* note 9 at 614.

[42] Regarding the formalist position see e.g. Weinrib, *The Idea of Private Law, supra* note 7 at 15: "[The] attribution of self-understanding to the law draws attention to the personal self-effacement of those who participate in the elucidation of law from within."

[43] See Ronald M Dworkin, "Hard Cases" (1975) 88:6 Harv L Rev 1057 at 1083: "We might therefore do well to consider how a philosophical judge might develop, in appropriate

The external influences on legal actors, and thus on law, is not necessarily seen as problematic by legal realists. Rather, what is considered to be problematic is the legitimising effect of law: law's coercive power gives effect to whatever external motifs a legal actor has. Thus, the external motif needs to be out in the open rather than be hidden behind a cloak of legal formalism and a claim of determinacy, so the argument goes.[44]

*b) The Incompleteness Theorem*

The indeterminacy attack is often founded on the limitation of human language.[45] Language is imprecise, and law is expressed in language. Therefore law is imprecise. But the idea that law is indeterminate can also derive some support from formal logic. In 1931, German mathematician and logician Gödel published his first paper on the so-called "incompleteness theorem."[46] The incompleteness theorem posits that any system of formal logic cannot be both consistent and complete. In particular, for any consistent, formal theory that proves certain basic truths, there is a statement that is true, but not provable in the theory.[47] The incompleteness theorem poses a significant challenge to legal formalism. It has only become the subject of study by legal theorists fairly recently.[48]

Applying the incompleteness theorem to law requires one to define law as a system of formal logic. Classical mathematics operated with a simple "reality check" of truth. Theorems of Euclidian geometry were held to be true if they could be shown to apply to reality. However, in modern mathematics, mathematical statements are understood as abstract statements, and they are true within their system "consistent with all other axioms and proven and provable

---

cases, theories of what legislative purpose and legal principles require. We shall find that he would construct these theories in the same manner as a philosophical referee would construct the character of a game. I have invented, for this purpose, a lawyer of superhuman skill, learning, patience and acumen, whom I shall call Hercules."

[44] Dagan, "Realist Conception", *supra* note 9 at 626–28.

[45] Cf. Mark R Brown & Andrew C Greenberg, "On Formally Undecidable Propositions of Law: Legal Indeterminacy and the Implications of Metamathematics" (1992) 43:6 Hastings LJ 1439 at 1440.

[46] Kurt Gödel, "Über formal unentscheidbare Sätze der Principia Mathematica und verwandter Systeme I" (1931) 38:1 MMP 173.

[47] A short retracing of Gödel's theorem can be found in John M Rogers & Robert E Molzon, "Some Lessons About the Law from Self-Referential Problems in Mathematics" (1992) 90:5 Mich L Rev 992 at 995–96.

[48] See Brown & Greenberg, *supra* note 45; Anthony D'Amato, "Can Legislatures Constrain Judicial Interpretation of Statutes?" (1989) 75:3 Va L Rev 561; Rogers & Molzon, preceding note.

theorems."[49] Law could also be seen as a consistent system of legal rules.[50] In this formal conception of law, inconsistent decisions are wrong decisions. This is very much a description of the formal position towards law. Furthermore, put this way, law is very different from how Holmes defined it.[51] If law were nothing more than what the courts do, there could be no wrong or inconsistent decisions; rather, there would be no claim of consistency. Consequently, Holmes' definition of law was attacked by legal formalists.[52] Hart argued that the claim that law is nothing but a prediction of what courts will do could not apply to the court's statement of a legal rule; rather, a court's statement of a legal rule would be the "formulation of rules genuinely regarded by the courts from the *internal point of view* as a standard of correct decision."[53]

Applying Gödel's incompleteness theorem on a system of formal logic requires that this system be self-descriptive. "Self-descriptive" means that the description of what law is is done by legal rules, not external rules. Put differently, self-descriptivism means that a legal system has an *internal* test to decide whether a given proposition forms a rule of law. Formalists hold this to be the case. Hart calls legal rules capable of being descriptive "secondary rules."[54] Kelsen posits there is one (imaginary) rule: the *Grundnorm.*[55] These rules form the basis of law's self-descriptive capability. Following these theories, it is therefore theoretically possible to apply Gödel's theorem on law. However, a proof of law's indeterminacy appears elusive for the simple fact that even if one were to formalize the law as a complete system of formal logic, such a system would be infinitely more complex than arithmetic.[56] The corresponding proof of the incompleteness theorem for law would thus be a much larger task than proving the incompleteness of arithmetic. In a way, the legal realist trying to deliver the fatal blow to legal formalism by way of retracing the incompleteness theorem in law would be a "legal Marxist." Just as a follower of Marx would first need to perfect the capitalist system to prepare the Communist revolution, the revolutionary legal realist would need to perfect the formal construction of law in order to deconstruct it completely. So far, applications of the incompleteness theorem in have been made in discrete areas of the law and

---

[49] Rogers & Molzon, *supra* note 47 at 998.

[50] Ronald M Dworkin, *Taking Rights Seriously* (Cambridge, Mass: Harvard University Press, 1978) at 283: "A proposition of law may be asserted as true if it is more consistent with the theory of law that best justifies settled law than the contrary proposition of law."

[51] See Part I: § 3 A.III.1, "Holmes".

[52] Hart, *The Concept of Law, supra* note 40 at 141–47.

[53] *Ibid* at 147 [emphasis added].

[54] *Ibid* at 79–99.

[55] Kelsen, *supra* note 20 at 196–200.

[56] Brown & Greenberg, *supra* note 45 at 1472–74.

have demonstrated the incompleteness of law as a system of logic.[57] Nevertheless, proof of incompleteness is not a proof of futility of formalism, or in other words, "Gödel's Theorem, however, is not a tool of nihilism."[58] Just like the proof of incompleteness of arithmetic has not led to the abandonment of algebra as a useful discipline, it cannot be said that legal formalism is useless, because

> "[a]ny sufficiently expressive formal system must contain undecidable propositions. Identifying such undecidable propositions in a constitutional or other legal system cannot undermine that system, since any legal system must contain rules that cannot be determined to be the law or not to be the law."[59]

### *3. Consequences of a Realist Approach*

#### *a) Taking Extrinsic Factors into Account*

If, as legal realism posits, law is not intrinsically determinate, the lawyer must look to external sources to answer legal questions. This applies to both rule making as well as to deciding cases. Looking beyond the law is thus a legacy of legal realism.[60] Legal realism requires the use of scientific methods to guide the evolution of law and law's normative goals.[61]

#### *b) The Role of Law in Legal Realism*

Embracing legal realism does not mean to merge law with other disciplines altogether. There is a *raison d'être* for law as a discrete discipline.[62] Dagan identifies "conventional features of adjudication, notably its contextual focus and its dialogic character"[63] as an important constraint. Such constraints prevent a descent into arbitrariness in law-making and adjudication. Formalism and realism can coexist if we take formalism to be the coherent application of the specific legal methodology which will arrive at the moment of indeterminacy. Doctrine is not worthless, but describes the law as far as it can be described. Doctrine understood in this way is the toolkit that allows us to arrive at the moment of indeterminacy.

---

[57] See *ibid* at 1474–80.

[58] *Ibid* at 1487.

[59] Rogers & Molzon, *supra* note 47 at 1022.

[60] Grechenig & Gelter, *supra* note 16 at 317.

[61] Dagan, "Realist Conception", *supra* note 9 at 638.

[62] Dagan claims that there are "distinctly legal features that may, at least at times, adequately address the concern about collapsing law into politics." *ibid* at 637, note 142.

[63] *Ibid* at 638.

*c) Adjudication is Law-Making*

As we have seen, legal realism is a legal theory which espouses the indeterminacy of law. Because law is indeterminate, there is one important terminological consequence: *adjudicating is law-making.* Arguably, the only distinction between: first, parties of a contract; second, a judge; and third, parliament, is the scope of binding force the choice of a certain path has. All three actors are engaged in law making.

*IV. Law and Economics*

*1. From Legal Realism to the Economic Analysis of Law*

As discussed above, legal realism is based on the idea that law is not a closed system. Eventually, legal questions are indeterminate without reference to extrinsic guidance. One approach seeking this extrinsic guidance is the law-and-economics approach.

During the first half of the 20th century, an economic approach to law was found in specific areas of law, most notably competition law.[64] This changed at the beginning of the second half of the century. There is some indication that the fledgling law-and-economics school of legal scholarship was triggered by institutional factors and influenced by legal realism – namely the arrival of legal realists at the University of Chicago, where the law-and-economics movement started.[65] One contribution of legal realism was the notion that legal scholarship needed be open to the social sciences. This created an environment open to the reception of economics into legal scholarship.[66] The ambition of law and economics became bigger and other areas of the law were included in the economic analysis.

*2. Coase's Contribution*

In 1960, Coase published his seminal article on "The Problem of Social Cost."[67] The article used the area of nuisance law to posit a broad principle. Nuisance law describes cases in which a first party claims that the second party

---

[64] Richard A Posner, *Economic Analysis of Law,* 7th edn (New York: Aspen Publishers, 2007) at 23; Michael J Trebilcock, "The Lessons and Limits of Law and Economics" in: Pierre Noreau, ed, *Dans le regard d'autre - In the Eye of the Beholder* (Montréal: Éditions Thémis, 2007) 113 at 116.

[65] See Edmund W Kitch, "The Fire of Truth: A Remembrance of Law and Economics at Chicago, 1932–1970" (1983) 26:1 JL & Econ 163 at 165.

[66] *Ibid* at 165.

[67] Ronald H Coase, "The Problem of Social Cost" (1960) 3 JL & Econ 1. Another important article on the economic analysis of tort law published at that time was Guido Calabresi, "Some Thoughts on Risk Distribution and the Law of Torts" (1961) 70:4 Yale LJ 499. See Posner, *Economic Analysis of Law, supra* note 64 at 23.

violates her property rights by emitting nuisance that affects the first party's property. One case looked at by Coase was the English case of *Sturges v Bridgman.*[68] In that case, a doctor had moved onto a property next to a small sweets factory. The noises from the sweets shop disrupted the doctor's use of the land. The Court of Appeal held that the noises constituted a nuisance and that the doctor was entitled to an injunction. Substantively, the case stands for the principle that the fact that "the plaintiff came to the nuisance" does not constitute a defence against nuisance.[69] Coase argued that it did not matter how the Court had decided the case as long as both parties could rely on the enforcement of their rights. This legal certainty would allow the parties to bargain for their best settlement.[70]

The fact that Coase chose nuisance law as the subject of his economic analysis of the law is perhaps no coincidence. Nuisance law involves a "paradigmatic conflict."[71] It lends itself to an economic analysis for a number of reasons: the measure of damages in nuisance assigns economic value to property;

---

[68] (1879), 11 Ch D 852 (CA).

[69] *Sturges* is perhaps now best known for Lord Denning's rejection of its principle in a later case where the nuisance was a local cricket field and neighbouring residents "came to the nuisance." See *Miller v Jackson,* [1977] QB 966, [1977] 3 WLR 20 (CA Civ), Lord Denning MR: "In summertime village cricket is the delight of everyone. Nearly every village has its own cricket field where the young men play and the old men watch. In the village of Lintz in County Durham they have their own ground, where they have played these last 70 years. They tend it well. The wicket area is well rolled and mown. The outfield is kept short. It has a good club house for the players and seats for the onlookers. The village team play there on Saturdays and Sundays. They belong to a league, competing with the neighbouring villages. On other evenings after work they practise while the light lasts. Yet now after these 70 years a judge of the High Court has ordered that they must not play there any more. He has issued an injunction to stop them. He has done it at the instance of a newcomer who is no lover of cricket. This newcomer has built, or has had built for him, a house on the edge of the cricket ground which four years ago was a field where cattle grazed. The animals did not mind the cricket. But now this adjoining field has been turned into a housing estate. The newcomer bought one of the houses on the edge of the cricket ground. No doubt the open space was a selling point. Now he complains that when a batsman hits a six the ball has been known to land in his garden or on or near his house. His wife has got so upset about it that they always go out at week-ends. They do not go into the garden when cricket is being played. They say that this is intolerable. So they asked the judge to stop the cricket being played. And the judge, much against his will, has felt that he must order the cricket to be stopped: with the consequence, I suppose, that the Lintz Cricket Club will disappear. The cricket ground will be turned to some other use. I expect for more houses or a factory. The young men will turn to other things instead of cricket. The whole village will be much the poorer. And all this because of a newcomer who has just bought a house there next to the cricket ground."

[70] Coase, *supra* note 67 at 9–10.

[71] Jeff L Lewin, "Boomer and the American Law of Nuisance: Past, Present, and Future" (1989–1990) 54 Alb L Rev 189 at 237.

nuisance law involves property rights, its economic analysis does not engender hostility from lawyers who might have more qualms about the application of economic principles to more evidently value-based law such as family law; and finally, defences against nuisance such as "coming to the nuisance," or alleged hypersensitivity prove as illustrative examples on how to assign monetary value to human behaviour and preferences.[72]

Coase's article was highly influential in legal scholarship. It established principles of economic analysis of the law. It introduced the idea that there was an inherent economic logic to an area of the law, more specifically an area of property law, namely nuisance. Basing law on an economic rationale was generalized by later writers.[73] Based on Coase's work, other law-and-economics scholars expanded on the economic analysis of property disputes.[74] The "Coase theorem" posits that where two parties lay competing claims to property rights, it does not matter which party obtains legal victory. As long as transactions costs are sufficiently low, the parties will bargain, and the party which obtains a higher value from its property claim will obtain use of the disputed resource.[75] In other words, parties will maximize the common welfare with negotiations. A further important theorem derived from the Coase theorem takes into account that in the real word, transaction costs are not zero. Because transaction costs are not zero, the law should assign property rights to the party which is set to derive a higher welfare. This is sometimes referred to as the "Hobbes theorem."[76]

*Boomer v Atlantic Cement Co*[77] may serve as an example of how a Coasean analysis influenced legal decision-making. The case involved a *Sturges v Bridgman*-type nuisance claim. The Court granted the injunction. However, it held that the defendant could elect to pay damages instead and continue with the nuisance. By anticipating the bargaining process and assigning a monetary value to the nuisance, the court thus minimized transaction costs, and applied the Hobbes theorem.

---

[72] *Ibid* at 238.

[73] See Posner, *Economic Analysis of Law, supra* note 64 at 24.

[74] See e.g. Guido Calabresi & AD Melamed, "Property Rules, Liability Rules, and Inalienability: One View of the Cathedral" (1972) 85:6 Harv L Rev 1089, expanding on the importance of law for bargaining.

[75] Harold Demsetz, "Toward a Theory of Property Rights" (1967) 57:2 Am Econ Rev 347 at 348; Leslie Rosenthal, "Economic Efficiency, Nuisance, and Sewage: New Lessons from Attorney-General v Council of the Borough of Birmingham" (2007) 36:1 J Legal Stud 27 at 28.

[76] Rosenthal, preceding note at 36.

[77] 26 NY2[d] 219 (1970).

## B. Economic Analysis of Law

### *I. Positive and Normative Economic Analysis of Law*

To what degree law and economics is a successor to the legal realism movement is a matter of debate.[78] They both share the idea that legal reasoning by means of logical deduction is undesirable, and even impossible because the process of interpretation is necessarily indeterminate.[79] In order to understand the relationship between legal realism and law and economics it is important to distinguish the two sides of economic analysis of the law: positive and normative analysis.

The positive, or descriptive, analysis of the law tries to explain how the working of the law can be described in economic terms and why the law is the way it is. A controversial version of this positive account is the thesis that the Common Law has an inherent tendency towards the development of economically efficient legal rules. The legal origin theory is a similarly descriptive account.

Normative economic analysis tries to determine what desirable law-making is.[80] It thus tries to provide an extrinsic mechanism to solve the problem of indeterminacy of legal reasoning. It owes its concern with welfare maximization to utilitarianism.[81] A focus on welfare maximization allowed economics to become normative rather than merely descriptive. By providing a normative dimension to economic analysis, welfare maximization also allows law and economics to make normative statements.[82] Law and economics is not only concerned with describing how law influences economic behaviour, but it also posits a normative goal to which law, law-making, and decision-making should adhere.

### *II. The Normative Analysis of the Law*

#### *1. Welfare and Efficiency*

The economic analysis of the law, standing on the shoulder of legal realism and utilitarianism, posits that welfare maximization should be the purpose of

---

[78] See Grechenig & Gelter, *supra* note 16 at 317–18.

[79] *Ibid* at 318.

[80] Trebilcock, *supra* note 64 at 133.

[81] Grechenig & Gelter, *supra* note 16 at 323.

[82] Posner, "Bentham's Influence on the Law and Economics Movement", *supra* note 32 at 437.

law.[83] What, then, in law, is welfare?[84] To provide a sharp contrast to utilitarianism, Posner originally argued that only wealth should be measured.[85] He still maintains that happiness is neither an appropriate goal, nor is it everybody's paramount objective.[86] An obvious problem with the concept of "utility" concerns its quantifiability. Utility cannot be measured in cardinal numbers. One cannot assign a numeric value of "2" to one state of happiness of a person, and a numeric value of "3" to a different state. Rather, utility can only be expressed in ordinal numbers. In other words: while different states of individual utility can be brought in a certain order, they can not be assigned relative or absolute values.[87]

Notwithstanding the problems involved in measuring utility, modern law and economics takes a broader perspective and considers the maximization of social welfare, comprehensively understood, rather than wealth to be the normative goal of law.[88] There is still a functional relationship between social welfare and individual welfare.[89]

Apart from the intrinsic problems of measuring utility, Posner also attacks utilitarianism for two further reasons. First, he argues that utilitarianism does not treat people as individuals, rather only as contributors to the maximum welfare. Posner gives the example of the "utility monster," "whose capacity for sadistic pleasure so far exceeds the capacity of his victims to experience pain that utility is maximized by allowing him to commit rape and murder."[90]

Second, Posner argues that utilitarianism has no boundary principle and thus does not allow one to distinguish between welfare maximization which restricts the benefits to members of its own society on the one hand, and welfare maximization that also benefits outsiders on the other hand.[91] In other words, Posner criticizes utilitarianism for taking a universal rather than a nationalist approach.

---

[83] Brinkmann, *supra* note 1 at 70.

[84] Cf. *M'Alister or Donoghue v Stevenson* (1931), [1932] AC 562 at 580 (HL), Lord Atkin.

[85] Grechenig & Gelter, *supra* note 16 at 334; Richard A Posner, "The Ethical and Political Basis of the Efficiency Norm in Common Law Adjudication" (1980) 8:3 Hofstra L Rev 487 [Posner, "Efficiency Norm"]; Richard A Posner, "The Value of Wealth: A Comment on Dworkin and Kronman" (1980) 9:2 J Legal Stud 243; Richard A Posner, "Utilitarianism, Economics, and Legal Theory" (1979) 8:1 J Legal Stud 103.

[86] Posner, *Economic Analysis of Law, supra* note 64 at 11–12.

[87] Horst Eidenmüller, *Effizienz als Rechtsprinzip: Möglichkeiten und Grenzen der ökonomischen Analyse des Rechts* (Tübingen: Mohr Siebeck, 1995) at 43–46.

[88] Grechenig & Gelter, *supra* note 16 at 334.

[89] Eidenmüller, *supra* note 87 at 47.

[90] Posner, *Economic Analysis of Law, supra* note 64 at 12.

[91] *Ibid* at 12.

As regards the second point, Posner does not address why welfare maximization should exclude outsiders. From an analytical standpoint, it might be argued that it is futile to base legal reasoning on the potential impact on outsiders because the legal system is restricted to the members of a certain society, and thus has no force to be binding on outsiders. It is possible that this is Posner's argument, and as such it is a pragmatic limitation of economic analysis, rather than a normative statement.

As regards the first point, this appears to be an extrinsic limitation on welfare analysis. There is no internal reason why the utility monster should not be taken into account in welfare analysis. Rather, such a limitation would need to come from a reason- or moral-based theory of law. The example thus shows that the economic analysis of law cannot be an exhaustive theory of law.

Accepting this extrinsic limitation of welfare analysis, welfare maximization is analysed by reference to voluntary transactions.[92] Understood in this way, welfare maximization is measured in terms of "efficiency." Measures of efficiency are essentially measures of how close a certain state of things is to welfare maximization. A change increases efficiency if it increases welfare.[93] This raises the question of how exactly efficiency is measured. In the next subsection, I look at two measures of efficiency.

### 2. *Measures of Efficiency*

#### a) *Pareto Efficiency*

The first measure of efficiency is referred to as Pareto efficiency, named after economist Vilfredo Pareto. A change is considered to be Pareto efficient if at least one individual is better off while no-one is worse off. Transactions are Pareto efficient if each party to the transaction receives something that it values more than the item it gives away.[94] This measure of efficiency runs into problems regarding attributional sets of rules such as property law. Given that property law is concerned with assigning rights to a pre-existing number of goods, any change in property law necessarily takes something away from somebody. There is thus always at least one person worse off. If one compares any one property law rule to an alternative rule, one must necessarily conclude that the property law rule is Pareto inefficient.[95]

---

[92] *Ibid* at 12.

[93] See *ibid* at 11 "As this example shows, the term 'efficiency,' when used as in this book to denote that allocation of resources in which value is maximized, has limitations as an ethical criterion of social decisionmaking [sic!]."

[94] Posner, "Efficiency Norm", *supra* note 85 at 489; Trebilcock, *supra* note 64 at 133.

[95] Brinkmann, *supra* note 1 at 70; Eidenmüller, *supra* note 87 at 48–50; Grechenig & Gelter, *supra* note 16 at 334; Posner, *Economic Analysis of Law, supra* note 64 at 12–13; Steven L Schwarcz, "The Easy Case for the Priority of Secured Claims in Bankruptcy" (1997) 47:3 Duke LJ 425 at 481.

Schwartz argues that a secured transactions regime can be Pareto efficient if one assumes that unsecured creditors – the class of creditors worse off by admitting secured transactions – will be fully compensated by charging higher interests rates. He does concede that in reality, not all unsecured creditors will be sophisticated enough to do so.[96] The efficiency of secured transactions law will be discussed in greater detail later in this book.[97]

### *b) Kaldor-Hicks Efficiency*

In contrast to Pareto efficiency, Kaldor-Hicks efficiency is achieved not if no-one is worse off, but if the accrued benefits of the better-off class outweigh the losses of the worse-off class.[98] Such a state can be called "potential Pareto efficiency," because the better-off side could theoretically reimburse the worse-off side and still retain a benefit.[99] This is a more realistic measurement of efficiency as it is more likely to be achievable in the real word. Posner's wealth criterion is essentially an application of the Kaldor-Hicks criterion,[100] using money as a proxy for the measurement of well-being and as a potential means of effecting the reimbursement.

### *III. The Positive Analysis of the Law*

As indicated above,[101] a positive or descriptive economic analysis of law is concerned with explaining why law is the way it is. At the same time, the variety of a positive economic analysis that is the subject of this book – the legal origin theory – extends this ambition by making comparative statements about different legal systems. It does so by combining a positive analysis towards each individual legal system and relating the positive analysis with a normative goal: the ability of each legal system to achieve maximum welfare is compared, and as a result a descriptive account of why one legal system fares better than another is offered: a theory. Given the normative goal of welfare maximization, this theory entails recommendations. Starting point for such a theory is the positive economic analysis of law.

---

[96] Alan Schwartz, "Security Interests and Bankruptcy Priorities: A Review of Current Theories" (1981) 10:1 J Legal Stud 1 at 2, note 7.

[97] See Part III: § 11, "The Law and Economics of Secured Transactions".

[98] The criterion is named after its two developers John R Hicks, "The Foundations of Welfare Economics" (1939) 49:196 Econ J 696 and Nicholas Kaldor, "Welfare Propositions of Economics and Interpersonal Comparisons of Utility" (1939) 49:195 Econ J 549. See on its application in law Eidenmüller, *supra* note 87 at 51; Posner, "Efficiency Norm", *supra* note 85 at 491; Trebilcock, *supra* note 64 at 133.

[99] Posner, "Efficiency Norm", *supra* note 85 at 491.

[100] Eidenmüller, *supra* note 87 at 54.

[101] Part I: § 3 B.I, "Positive and Normative Economic Analysis of Law".

*1. The Two Steps of Positive Economic Analysis of Law*

A descriptive economic analysis of the law uses the scientific method. The Oxford English Dictionary defines the scientific method as "a method or procedure that has characterized natural science since the 17th century, consisting in systematic observation, measurement, and experiment, and the formulation, testing, and modification of hypotheses."[102] In other words, the scientific method consists of a two-step approach. First, real-life events are recorded as data. Second, a theory that accounts for why the data is the way it is formulated. A theory is valid if and so long as it is not contradicted by the data. These two steps are found in economic analysis of law as well.

As regards the first step, it is not self-apparent what the recorded data should be. The student of mechanics can easily record data such as mass, speed, acceleration, etc. The student of law and economics must first circumscribe the object of study. The object of study is partly a function of the normative goal of law and economics: welfare maximization. As part of the broader discipline of economics, there is a well-developed toolkit for measuring welfare – that is, by measuring proxies such as gross domestic product, transaction size, etc. Harder to measure is the other side of the equation – namely the law-specific part.

*2. Turning Law Into Numbers*

Siems distinguishes six ways in which law can be analysed numerically.[103] The first approach consists of a simple count of key metrics: lawyers, cases, laws, and words. This is often done in socio-legal research.[104] This approach does not posit any relationship between one type of metric and another type of metric. For example, two metrics counted in this approach could be number of laws and number judges in a variety of jurisdictions. This approach does not yet posit any type of nexus between the number of laws and the number of judges in a certain jurisdiction. A problem inherent in this approach is the definition of a metric. Siems points to Posner's classification of English barristers as falling into the same class as judges in the United States as one example of a controversial definition of a metric.[105]

The second approach is the benchmarking approach.[106] In this approach, legal rules are being benchmarked. Legal rules pertaining to a specific subject

---

[102] *Oxford English Dictionary,* 3rd edn, sv scientific method.

[103] Mathias M Siems, "Measuring the Immeasurable: How to Turn Law into Numbers" in: Michael Faure & Jan M Smits, eds, *Does Law Matter?: On Law and Economic Growth* (Cambridge: Intersentia, 2011) 115.

[104] *Ibid* at 116.

[105] Richard A Posner, *Law and Legal Theory in England and America* (Oxford: Clarendon Press, 1997) at 22; Siems, "Measuring the Immeasurable", *supra* note 103 at 117.

[106] Siems, "Measuring the Immeasurable", *supra* note 103 at 117–19.

are categorized and subcategorized. Then, a number of jurisdictions are analysed with the object of determining whether each individual jurisdiction does or does not have a rule pertaining to one of the subcategories. Based on this, an overall conclusion on the extent and type of regulation in one of the categories within this jurisdiction is drawn.

The third approach, which appears to be related to the second approach, is functional. Legal rules serving a specific purpose are identified in each jurisdiction.[107] The main difference between the second and third approach is that the second approach does not take a functional starting point. This means that the taxonomy is necessarily based on the legal system of the jurisdiction being used as a starting point. The second approach thus essentially measures how similar other jurisdictions are to this first jurisdiction.[108] The functional approach takes into account that "the same functional role may be performed in different jurisdictions by rules with different formal classifications."[109]

The fourth approach uses empirical surveys on the empirical level. The investigator conducts interviews with a number of legal actors to survey legal practice.[110] The fifth approach measures a number of presumably key metrics, such as average duration of proceedings.[111] The sixth approach measures public perceptions about legal values.[112]

An overview of these measurements shows us that no single approach is the best. Furthermore, the different approaches gather qualitatively different data. For example, the fifth and sixth approach gather data that relates to the effect of law. The second and third approach gather data that relates to law itself.

## C. Law and Development

### *I. Law Matters*

As mentioned in the introduction of this chapter, the case for inclusion of a law-and-economics approach in this book is based on the premise that "law matters"; law influences the development of a society. Changes in law not only correlate with development, but there is also a causal relationship between the former and the latter. In this regard, an import specification needs to be made. "Development" for the purpose of this book means economic "development."

More specifically, law and development is concerned with a certain type of economic development: long-term sustainable economic growth, not transitory

---

[107] *Ibid* at 119–20.
[108] *Ibid* at 119.
[109] *Ibid* at 120.
[110] *Ibid* at 121–22.
[111] *Ibid* at 122–24.
[112] *Ibid* at 124.

economic growth. The first European countries to exhibit this type of growth were the Netherlands and Britain.[113] Transitory economic growth is growth based on conquest or exploitation of natural resources. Both sources of transitory growth are finite and unsustainable.[114]

The difference between sustainable and transitory economic growth can be illustrated by the fate of the former European colonies in America. A certain group of colonies, including for instance the Caribbean, experienced a period of rapid economic growth in the 15th to 18th century. These colonies were rich in natural resources. Another group of colonies, North America, and more specifically Canada and the United States, were relatively poor. Nowadays, the situation is reversed.[115] The explanation for the different outcomes is a matter of debate in economic literature. The "institutional theory" posits that the first group's reliance on exploiting natural resources meant that these colonies had no incentive to develop an efficient social and institutional framework, thus hindering sustainable economic growth.[116] The "legal origin theory" posits that it is the Civilian legal heritage of the former colonies in the first group was determinative.[117]

Both theories are foremost positive economic theories. They look at a real-life phenomenon – the different economic development of different countries – and try to develop a theoretical account that can explain the data. At the same time, the putatively positive description offered by the "legal origin theory" is easily combinable with a normative goal. If the description offered by the legal origin theory is correct – a lack of sustainable economic growth is a function of a Civilian legal heritage – and sustainable economic growth is the desirable

---

[113] Thomas S Ulen, "The Role of Law in Economic Growth and Development" in: Faure & Smits, eds, *Does Law Matter?, supra* note 103, 179 at 179.

[114] *Ibid* at 179.

[115] Kenneth W Dam, *The Law-Growth Nexus: The Rule of Law and Economic Development* (Washington, DC: Brookings Institution Press, 2006) at 58; Ulen, *supra* note 113 at 184–85. A descriptive account is offered by Daron Acemoglu, Simon Johnson & James A Robinson, "The Colonial Origins of Comparative Development: An Empirical Investigation" (2001) 91:5 Am Econ Rev 1369. See also Thorsten Beck, Asli Demirgüç-Kunt & Ross Levine, "Law, Endowments, and Finance" (2003) 70:2 J Financial Econ 137.

[116] Acemoglu, Johnson & Robinson, preceding note. Cf. Ulen, *supra* note 113 at 185.

[117] Simeon Djankov *et al,* "Courts" (2003) 118 Quart J Econ 453; Simeon Djankov, Caralee McLiesh & Andrei Shleifer, "Private Credit in 129 Countries" (2007) 84:2 J Financial Econ 299; Rafael La Porta *et al,* "Judicial Checks and Balances" (2004) 112 J Pol Econ 445; Rafael La Porta, Florencio Lopez-de-Silanes & Andrei Shleifer, "The Economic Consequences of Legal Origins" (2008) 46:2 J Econ Lit 285; Rafael La Porta *et al,* "Law and Finance" (1998) 106:6 J Pol Econ 1113 [La Porta et al., "Law and Finance"]; Rafael La Porta *et al,* "Legal Determinants of External Finance" (1997) 52:4 J Fin 1131. Particularly regarding secured transactions law, see Florencio Lopez-de-Silanes, "Turning the Key to Credit: Credit Access and Credit Institutions" in: Frederique Dahan & John Simpson, eds, *Secured Transactions Reform and Access to Credit* (Cheltenham: Edward Elgar, 2009) 3.

normative goal, it follows that legal reform should be undertaken that abandons Civilian heritage. This is the conclusion drawn by the reform proposals of the World Bank.[118]

Whether one can validly equate development and economic development is a matter of implicit debate in the law-and-development literature.[119] We can accept it for the purpose of this book, however, for two reasons. First, we are concerned not with law, or even private law, broadly understood, but only with movable property law and secured transactions law. There is a clear economic and commercial side to this area of the law. Second, this section is concerned with the legal origin theory. The legal origin theory claims a superiority of the Common Law based on the claim of alleged economic benefits associated with the Common Law legal system. While it is a legitimate counter-argument to say that economic growth is not everything– this would be an extrinsic argument –, this book is also concerned with the internal validity of this claim. In other words: If we accept the premise that secured transactions law and property law are concerned with economic growth and should only serve economic growth, does this really mean that Civilian property law needs to be replaced by a Common Law property law?

Law and development and institutional economics view law as instrumental in influencing the economic development of a country. Relating to the subject matter of this book, the agenda of this variety of law-and-development theory entails normative statements about property and secured transaction law. Property rights should be well-defined and alienable. Secured lending should enable creditors to take a wide variety of assets as collateral, to be informed about competing claims and interests in the collateral, and to seize and to sell the assets in the event of default. Bankruptcy regimes are to induce the exit of inefficient firms and redeployment of their assets to higher-valued uses.[120] A positive correlation between secure property rights and positive economic development has been found in a number of studies.[121] The success of England and the Netherlands in the second half of the second Millennium has been attributed to these countries' stable and secure property rights regime.[122]

---

[118] See e.g. World Bank (WB) & International Bank for Reconstruction and Development (IBRD), *World Development Report 2002: Building Institutions for Markets* (Oxford: Oxford University Press, 2002) and World Bank (WB) & International Bank for Reconstruction and Development (IBRD), *Doing Business in 2004* (Oxford: Oxford University Press, 2004).

[119] See Kevin E Davis & Michael J Trebilcock, "The Relationship between Law and Development: Optimists versus Skeptics" (2008) 56:4 Am J Comp L 895 at 898–99.

[120] *Ibid* at 903.

[121] Cf. Guangdong Xu, "The Role of Property Law in Economic Growth" in: Faure & Smits, eds, *Does Law Matter?, supra* note 103, 331 at 343.

[122] Cf. *ibid* at 341.

North underlines the importance of institutions in economic development.[123] He argues that there are two theories regarding the state's role in economics: the "contract theory" and the "predatory theory." The former theory views the state and its institutions as the framework within which private contracting takes place. The latter theory considers the state to be an instrument for the transfer of resources from one group to another. Both theories are obviously not mutually exclusive: the state can both provide a framework for contracting and play a role in resource allocation. Consequently, North's argument is that successful economic performance requires a successful combination of the two state roles.

### *II. Legal Origin*

#### *1. Common Law and Efficiency*

A very basic form of a positive economic account of law is the Common Law efficiency theory. A number of law-and-economics scholars have argued that the Common Law is inherently more efficient than the Civil Law.[124] One explanation offered argues that the common law process of law-making through judges leads to the evolution of ever more efficient rules. Inefficient rules, which greatly affect the common welfare, are more likely to be appealed than efficient rules.[125] In contrat to this, Trebilcock argues that a similar process would apply in cases of parliamentary law-making: inefficient rules are more likely to meet resistance from stakeholders, who would lobby against their enactment.[126]

Mahoney makes a final argument for the inherent efficiency of the Common Law. He argues that the

> "fundamental structural distinction between the common law and civil law lies in the judiciary's greater power to act as a check on executive and legislative action in a common-law

---

[123] This summary of Douglass C North, *Structure and Change in Economic History,* 1st edn (New York: Norton, 1981) is based on Daron Acemoglu & Simon Johnson, "Unbundling Institutions" (2005) 113:5 J Pol Econ 949 at 950.

[124] See e.g John C Goodman, "An Economic Theory of the Evolution of Common Law" (1978) 7:2 J Legal Stud 393; Posner, "Efficiency Norm", *supra* note 85; George L Priest, "The Common Law Process and the Selection of Efficient Rules" (1977) 6:1 J Legal Stud 65; Paul H Rubin, "Why Is the Common Law Efficient?" (1977) 6:1 J Legal Stud 51. See recently Paul G Mahoney, "The Common Law and Economic Growth: Hayek Might Be Right" (2001) 30:2 J Legal Stud 503. Cf. Trebilcock, *supra* note 64 at 129–32. See also Nuno Garoupa & Carlos Gómez Ligüerre, "Efficiency of the Common Law" in: Faure & Smits, eds, *Does Law Matter?, supra* note 103, 223.

[125] Goodman, preceding note; Priest, preceding note; Rubin, preceding note. See also Mahoney, preceding note at 506–7.

[126] Trebilcock, *supra* note 64 at 132.

system. Thus, although both the common and civil law provide strong protections for property and contract rights against other private actors, those rights may be more secure against the government itself in a common-law system."[127]

In the realm of contract law, the veracity of the Common Law efficiency theory is often based on the argument that parties would otherwise opt out of the application of Common Law rules.[128] This presumption of a rational choice by contract parties is not empirically verified. An actual analysis of choice-of-law clauses reveals that choice of law is more inspired by the interests of the legal profession than by the rational economic interest of the actual parties of a contract.[129]

### *2. The Legal Origin Theory*

Some authors – namely La Porta, Lopez-de-Silanes, Shleifer, and Vishny – suggest that, at least on average, Common Law jurisdictions will have stronger economic development than Civil Law jurisdictions.[130] They argue that

> "legal rules protecting investors vary systematically among legal traditions or origins, with the laws of common law countries [...] being more protective of outside investors than the laws of civil law [...] countries."[131]

They state that Civil Law is associated with a stronger governmental interference with property, implying that having a Civil Law system facilitates "greater corruption, larger unofficial economy, and higher unemployment."[132] Civil Law countries, they say, have overly formal judicial and enforcement procedures[133] and lack judicial independence.[134] These factors, in turn, weaken property rights.[135] The findings of the legal origins theory have been applied to secured transactions law as well.[136] Regarding two mechanisms of secured transactions law, Lopez-de-Silanes finds that Civil Law origin countries have significantly weaker control rights institutions in secured transactions law comparably strong level of information sharing institutions.[137]

---

[127] Mahoney, *supra* note 124 at 507.

[128] Trebilcock, *supra* note 64 at 132–33.

[129] Gilles Cuniberti, "The International Market for Contracts: The Most Attractive Contract Laws" (2014) 34:3 Nw J Int'l L & Bus 455.

[130] See La Porta, Lopez-de-Silanes & Shleifer, *supra* note 117.

[131] *Ibid* at 285–86.

[132] *Ibid* at 286.

[133] See Djankov *et al, supra* note 117; La Porta, Lopez-de-Silanes & Shleifer, *supra* note 117 at 286.

[134] La Porta *et al, supra* note 117; La Porta, Lopez-de-Silanes & Shleifer, *supra* note 117 at 286.

[135] La Porta, Lopez-de-Silanes & Shleifer, *supra* note 117 at 286.

[136] See Part III: § 11, "The Law and Economics of Secured Transactions".

[137] Lopez-de-Silanes, *supra* note 117 at 16–17.

As regards its economic method, legal origin theory is based on a benchmarking approach to law. One finding of the legal origin theory is that in poorer countries, enforcement is a more important variable than differences in substantive law.[138] Nevertheless, differences in creditor rights remains statistically significant in rich countries.[139] This leads to the conclusion that differences in creditor rights can still play a significant role in economic development once the foundations – that is to say, a functioning judiciary and enforcement mechanism – are put into place.

### *3. The Legal Origin Theory and Comparative Law Theory*

The legal origin theory is not possible without comparative law theory. In the legal origin theory, the object of study is legal families. The theory suggests that its findings must be related to the *defining* differences of legal families. However, it fails to demonstrate that the variance in variables such as "creditor rights" and "information sharing" are due to what makes a legal family a legal family: their *differentia specifica.*

When explaining their approach, the legal origin theorists refer to scholars such as Merryman,[140] Watson,[141] Reynolds and Flores,[142] and Zweigert and Kötz,[143] to explain what is meant by the terms "legal origin" or "legal family." The fact that the words seem to be used interchangeably implies that both mean the same thing. However, there is not one universally-accepted theory for what comparative law is and what its methodology should be. Thus, the terms themselves are not clearly defined in comparative law theory.

#### *a) Functionalism*

##### *aa) Functionalism as a Comparative Law Theory*

While legal origin scholarship often makes reference to Zweigert and Kötz,[144] it does not refer to their work on functionalism; rather, it cites their work on

---

[138] Djankov, McLiesh & Shleifer, *supra* note 117 at 316.

[139] *Ibid* at 316.

[140] John H Merryman, *The Civil Law Tradition: An Introduction to the Legal Systems of Western Europe and Latin America* (Stanford, Calif: Stanford University Press, 1969). See La Porta *et al,* "Law and Finance", *supra* note 117 at 1118.

[141] Alan Watson, *Legal Transplants: An Approach to Comparative Law* (Edinburgh: Scottish Academic Press, 1974). See La Porta *et al,* "Law and Finance", *supra* note 117 at 1115.

[142] See La Porta *et al,* "Law and Finance", *supra* note 117 at 1119.

[143] Konrad Zweigert & Hein Kötz, *Einführung in die Rechtsvergleichung auf dem Gebiete des Privatrechts,* 3rd edn (Tübingen: Mohr Siebeck, 1996). See e.g. La Porta *et al,* "Law and Finance", *supra* note 117 at 1118–19.

[144] Zweigert & Kötz, preceding note.

the classification of legal families.[145] Zweigert and Kötz stress the importance of functionalism for comparative law. For Zweigert and Kötz, functionalism enables one to determine if the subjects of the comparison are indeed comparable.[146] They start with the assumption that every legal system faces similar problems.[147] The goal of a functional approach is to examine how different legal systems tackle these similar problems.[148] Zweigert and Kötz point out that a legal system may even come up with a solution to a problem that could be considered to be "extralegal," such as, for instance, the legal rule of the *Grundbuch* (public register) of real estate in Germany and the system of title insurance companies in the United States.[149] Zweigert and Kötz add that there is a *praesumptio similitudinis* that, although the means may vary between legal systems, these systems tend to reach similar results.[150]

Zweigert and Kötz seem to be influenced by Jhering. In Zweigert's reading, Jhering stresses the importance of purpose for law.[151] At the same time, Jhering critiques law as being constructed from abstract legal concepts that have no bearing on social reality.[152] Zweigert and Kötz are also influenced by the way in which the problem of characterization is tackled in conflict of laws.[153] Rabel argued that the goal of conflict-of-laws rules is not to identify similar concepts in the invoked legal system, but rather to identify how a certain fact scenario is dealt with in that system.[154] Graziadei argues that the functional approach originated in Rabel's approach to characterization, which he sees as a a rejection of German 19th-century conceptualism and formalism.[155]

In summary, functionalism as a comparative law theory posits hat legal systems seem to be somewhat consistent in their function: they face similar problems and can be assumed to try to reach similar results. Therefore, they must agree on what the function of any legal or extralegal concept is in tackling these problems.

---

145 See Ralf Michaels, "The Functionalism of Legal Origins" in: Faure & Smits, eds, *Does Law Matter?, supra* note 103, 21 at 22.

146 Zweigert & Kötz, *supra* note 143 at 33.

147 *Ibid* at 33.

148 *Ibid* at 33.

149 *Ibid* at 37–38.

150 *Ibid* at 38.

151 Konrad Zweigert & Kurt Siehr, "Jhering's Influence on the Development of Comparative Legal Method" (1971) 19 Am J Comp L 215.

152 *Ibid* at 217.

153 Michele Graziadei, "The Functionalist Heritage" in: Pierre Legrand & Roderick Munday, eds, *Comparative Legal Studies: Traditions and Transitions* (Cambridge: Cambridge University Press, 2003) 100 at 104–6.

154 *Ibid* at 105–6.

155 *Ibid* at 104–5.

*bb) Functionalism and Legal Origin Theory*

There are several areas in which legal origin theory implicitly takes a functional approach. In its "origin story," legal origin scholarship assumes that the developments of the legal systems in France and England were faced with an alike problem: "protect law enforcers from being bullied with either physical force or bribes by powerful local interests."[156] From this starting point, legal origin theory assumes that there is a path dependency. The way in which the original problem was tackled by each of the different legal systems determines which new problems will result and which new functional approaches have to be taken to tackle these problems.[157] Last but not least, legal origin theory, when connected with a normative goal (*i.e.* welfare enhancement) shares with functionalism the idea that law is a tool for social engineering.[158]

*b) Legal Transplants*

In his work on the legal transplant approach to comparative law, Watson raises three arguments for the importance of the study of legal transplants as the subject of Comparative Law scholarship. Firstly, a study of a foreign legal system alone is not Comparative Law because it lacks a comparative component.[159] Secondly, Comparative Law cannot exhaust itself in being a description of legal families (*i.e.* of legal systems that share a strong commonality) because such exercise would "lack intellectual content."[160] Thirdly, Comparative Law should not consist of merely drawing comparisons between legal systems.[161] The reason for that is, according to Watson, that such comparison would rely on establishing comparability between legal systems. But any such comparability would need to be established on at least as many sociological reasons as legal reasons; therefore, such comparison would be as much sociology as it would be legal science.[162]

For these reasons, Watson proposes that Comparative Law should consist of studying the relationships between legal systems.[163] While Watson does not make it explicit, from his above-mentioned critique of Comparative Law as merely drawing comparisons, it follows that the study of such relationships should consist of a study of what is legal within these systems and not of a study of what would be a sociological background for these systems. He makes

---

[156] Edward L Glaeser & Andrei Shleifer, "Legal Origins" (2002) 117:4 Quart J Econ 1193 at 1195. Cf. Michaels, "The Functionalism of Legal Origins", *supra* note 145 at 23.

[157] Michaels, "The Functionalism of Legal Origins", *supra* note 145 at 24.

[158] *Ibid* at 24, referring to Zweigert & Kötz, *supra* note 143 at 45.

[159] Watson, *supra* note 141 at 4.

[160] *Ibid* at 4.

[161] *Ibid* at 4.

[162] *Ibid* at 5.

[163] *Ibid* at 7.

legal transplants the focus of his study. Legal transplants are "the moving of a rule or a system of law from one country to another, or from one people to another."[164]

Watson identifies three possible kinds of relationships. The first is the "historical relationship." This occurs when one legal system has evolved from an ancestor.[165] A second is an "inner relationship." Such a relation occurs when two legal systems are close in spirit to each other without any historical filiation.[166] He rightfully warns that such closeness must remain a hypothesis and cannot be proven.[167] The third, which Watson cautions against accepting, is an inherent relationship between legal systems that will all pass through similar evolutionary stages.[168]

Watson ends by contrasting the concept of legal transplants and Savigny's view that law is the expression of the *Volksgeist.*[169] While the latter view stresses the importance of a particular legal system as the expression of a nation's identity, the former admits that there is a history of borrowing of legal rules between societies.[170] But a legal transplant will not remain static in its new environment – it will evolve in its new host system.[171]

### *III. Legal Origin Appraised*

#### *1. Comparative Law Critique*

Michaels finds a number of points in legal origin scholarship which are problematic from a comparative law theory standpoint:[172] the focus of legal origin scholarship on formal law is overly narrow, its understanding of legal transplants is overly simplistic as is its understanding of the Civil Law/Common Law distinction.[173] I look at each of these points in turn.

First, the point that legal origin theory has an overly narrow focus on formal law. A critique of legal origin theory that could be made from a functionalist perspective is that simple benchmarking approach of legal origin theorists insufficiently accounts for functionally equivalent legal rules.[174] Essentially, certain supposedly functional characteristics of legal systems are measured by a

---

164 *Ibid* at 21.
165 *Ibid* at 7–8.
166 *Ibid* at 8.
167 *Ibid* at 8.
168 *Ibid* at 9.
169 *Ibid* at 21–22.
170 *Ibid* at 22.
171 *Ibid* at 27–29.
172 Michaels, "The Functionalism of Legal Origins", *supra* note 145 at 21.
173 On the last point see also Mathias M Siems, "Legal Origins: Reconciling Law and Finance and Comparative Law" (2007) 52:1 McGill LJ 55.
174 Michaels, "The Functionalism of Legal Origins", *supra* note 145 at 26.

quantification of similarity to the legal system of the United States. If a certain rule existing in the United States designed to achieve a certain purpose is lacking in the other system, this system will score lowly on the scale measuring this functional area, even though the legal system might have a very different rule designed to achieve the measured goal. Furthermore, the coding necessary for the benchmarking cannot sufficiently take into account the interdependency of legal rules.[175] Whether and to what degree a legal system contains a specific substantive rule of law is also a function of whether the same goal is not already partially achieved by other institutions, including non-legal ones. The critique is thus that legal origin scholarship is too focused on a micro-perspective where comparative law needs to include the macro-perspective.[176]

Second, the point that legal origin theory has a simplistic understanding of legal transplants. Pistor points out that legal origin scholarship takes a very straightforward approach to the relationship between legal systems and substantive rules. Legal rules in legal origin scholarship are a straightforward function of legal origins.[177] Legal transplants are thus ignored in legal origin scholarship.

Third, the claim that legal origin theory has a simplistic understanding of the Common Law/Civil Law divide. There are different approaches to comparative law and looking at the relationship between legal systems. A functionalist would make a distinction between legal systems by looking which countries use a similar rule to address the same problems. A legal transplant theorist may group legal systems by the origin of the legal rules and the extent of evolution of a transplanted rule. On the other hand, it is not clear that the legal origin scholars use any kind of "legal" criterion to establish what "legal origin" means; at least not a criterion that is related to private law. They write that

> "[they] adopt a broad conception of legal origin as a style of social control of economic life (and maybe of other aspects of life as well). In strong form (later to be supplemented by a variety of caveats), [they] argue that common law stands for the strategy of social control that seeks to support private market outcomes, whereas civil law seeks to replace such outcomes with state-desired allocations."[178]

This is an overly-broad definition that has more to do with constitutional theory or political philosophy than with private law. Yet the legal origin theorists pretend that their findings can be of guidance for private law legislation, such as secured transactions law.[179]

---

[175] *Ibid* at 27.

[176] *Ibid* at 27.

[177] See Katharina Pistor, "Rethinking the Law and Finance Paradigm" [2009] BYU L Rev 1647 at 1656–59, referring to La Porta *et al,* "Law and Finance", *supra* note 117.

[178] La Porta, Lopez-de-Silanes & Shleifer, *supra* note 117 at 286.

[179] See e.g. Lopez-de-Silanes, *supra* note 117.

Conveniently supporting their theory, the legal origin scholars group Québec, Scotland, and South Africa into the category of English legal origin.[180] By removing all major jurisdictions that would commonly be considered to be Civil Law jurisdictions but happened to be English or British possessions from their list of Civil Law jurisdictions, they thus make it unverifiable whether the economic development is really due to Common Law origin or to colonial history. A comparison between former British possessions, on the other hand, clearly shows that different economic development can be influenced to a large degree by the economic policy and political framework of the nation. I address this in the following sub-section.

### *2. The Colonial Approach*

The legal origin theory relies on analysing former colonies to arrive at conclusions about the ability of a legal system to influence economic development. The development history of colonies is thus an important area to look at.

It has already been shown that colonial history and colonizing powers are an important factor in shaping the kind and level of economic growth.[181] The colonial theory posits that it is not legal origin, but rather colonial history that played the decisive role in shaping the economic development of former colonies.[182] Colonial history does so by affecting "institutions." Institutions, in turn, influence economic development.

#### *a) History and Institutions*

Legal origin is often a function of colonial history.[183] But law is not the only area in which the colonial powers differed. Law is but one of many factors in colonial history that distinguished the European colonies from one another.[184] If analysed according to colonizing power rather than legal origin, "colonies which received French civil law not directly from the French but from another colonizing power, such as Spain or the Netherlands, were doing as well as British (ex-) colonies in 1960."[185] In the "origin countries" in which the legal systems developed, the legal system could just as well have been a function of the economic development as the other way around.[186]

---

[180] See e.g. La Porta, Lopez-de-Silanes & Shleifer, *supra* note 117 at 289.

[181] Graziella Bertocchi & Fabio Canova, "Did Colonization Matter for Growth?: An Empirical Exploration Into the Historical Causes of Africa's Underdevelopment" (2002) 46:10 Eur Econ Rev 1851.

[182] Daniel Klerman *et al,* "Legal Origin or Colonial History?" (2011) 3:2 J Leg An 379.

[183] *Ibid* at 380, 384.

[184] *Ibid* at 380.

[185] *Ibid* at 380.

[186] *Ibid* at 381.

In addition the legal systems of England and France developed as they did because of the conditions in those countries. Mahoney argues that the English Common Law was shaped by the aristocrats' and merchants' desire to have a law that offered a strong protection of property and contract rights and limited the Crown's ability to interfere in markets, while French law was seen as a means of altering property rights and ensuring less interference by judges.[187] The French legal system was plagued by cronyism and local fragmentation. Central control was a means of ensuring progress.[188] The idea of law being a function of other internal political factors also applies to those countries that voluntarily adopted a foreign legal system, such as Japan and Turkey; their choice of the legal system to be adopted can be seen as a function of their internal conditions.[189]

In conclusion, the colonial theory argues that "non-legal colonial explanations deserve to be taken seriously as explanations for the observed cross-country differences between 'common law' and 'civil law' countries."[190]

Acemoglu and Johnson add an important distinction to the legal origin analysis. First, they broaden the scope by shifting the analysis to "institutions" rather than "legal rules." Second, they distinguish areas of influence of legal origin. They claim that there is a strong relationship between legal origin and contract rights institutions on the one hand and colonial history on the other.[191] An important qualification to this result, however, is how the authors defined the respective institutions. They define "contracting institutions as the rules and regulations governing contracting between ordinary citizens, for example, between a creditor and a debtor" and "property rights institutions as the rules and regulations protecting citizens against the power of the government and elites."[192] In this definition, "property rights" are only tangentially concerned with private law relations. For the purpose of the following discussion, I thus refer to "private property law" when speaking about property law as private law rather than as a form of protection against state appropriation.

### *b) The Impact of Institutions on Economic Development*

If we take a Coasean view of private property law, private property law is nothing but a shorthand for private contracting.[193] Thus, for the purpose of Acemoglu and Johnson's study, private property law and secured transactions law would be better placed in the "contracting institutions" category rather than the

---

[187] Mahoney, *supra* note 124 at 504–5.
[188] *Ibid* at 509–11.
[189] Klerman *et al, supra* note 182 at 381.
[190] *Ibid* at 404.
[191] Acemoglu & Johnson, *supra* note 123.
[192] *Ibid* at 955.
[193] See Part II: § 8 C, "The Economic Analysis of Property Law".

confusingly named "property rights" category. Using this classification, it would follow – perhaps unsurprisingly – that there is a strong relationship between legal origin and private property law.

Placing private property rights in the contracting institutions category means that there would need to be a strong correlation between contracting institutions and economic development in order to maintain the validity of the legal origin theory in the area of private property law. If there were a strong correlation between contracting institutions and economic development, it would then also follow that legal origin does matter because legal origin does affect contracting institutions. However, once Acemoglu and Johnson "control for the effects of property rights institutions, contracting institutions seem to have no impact on income per capita, the investment to GDP ratio, and the private credit to GDP ratio."[194]

If we recall that in this terminology, "property rights" is essentially only protection against state infringement on private property and is mostly a function of colonial history, it follows that there is no demonstrable correlation between legal origin and economic development. More specifically, "the way in which countries were colonized, but not who colonized them, is a robust determinant of property rights institutions."[195]

Acemoglu and Johnson offer a theory on why contract institutions matter less than property rights institutions. They argue that individuals can structure contracts to reduce the adverse effects from contracting institutions.[196] Once again, this indicates a Coasean approach towards property rights analysis: a disadvantageous framework of private property rights can be circumvented by bargaining. The only costs incurred are bargaining costs. Thus, different contracting institutions, including significant differences in private property law, will only become a significant factor in economic development where transactions costs outweigh other costs. This conclusion is consistent with the finding by legal origin theorists who acknowledged that enforcement is a more important variable than differences in substantive law in poorer countries, while differences in creditor rights remain statistically significant in rich countries.

The colonial approach also offers an explanation as to why different colonies were colonized differently. Some colonies were set up as extractive colonies, showing a transitory economic growth. One possible explanation for this is that Europeans could not create the necessary institutions for long-term sustainable economic growth in places where they were confronted with a very high mortality rate (*e.g.* Congo or the Gold Coast).[197] In this context, it might be worthwhile to note that French and Spanish colonies tended to be in such

---

[194] Acemoglu & Johnson, *supra* note 123 at 953.

[195] *Ibid* at 971.

[196] *Ibid* at 988.

[197] Acemoglu, Johnson & Robinson, *supra* note 115 at 1395.

areas, thus skewing the results of the legal origin theory. The French colonial empire was never meant to create the institutions necessary for sustainable economic growth, and thus it follows that Civil Law will fare badly in a legal origin analysis which largely relies on former French colonies to quantify the Civil Law.

A policy approach – research that indicates that even where institutional factors are equivalent economic development will diverge because of a difference in policy[198] – presents an even stronger case for the denial of the importance of legal origins than the institutional approach. As Henry puts it,

> "the macroeconomic decisions of governments can exert just as much influence on the trajectory of the economy as the institutional framework within which those decisions take place. Countries have no control over their geographic location, colonial heritage, or legal origin, but they do have agency over the policies that they implement."[199]

However, it should be noted that even Henry does not deny that institutions – and thus the legal framework –can have an impact on economic development. Even in his view, law matters; it just matters a little less.

### *3. Bijuralism and Mixed Legal Systems in the Law-and-Economics Analysis*

Legal origin theory ignores mixed legal systems. One important contribution of the colonial approach consists in making a distinction between "pure" – or rather sufficiently pure – legal systems on the one hand and mixed legal systems on the other. I say "sufficiently pure" because there is a degree of reciprocal borrowing and legal transplantation between all legal systems. Mixed legal systems are important data points for the colonial approach because they are systems in which legal and colonial history do not coincide.[200]

In a legal origins-style analysis of mixed legal systems, Kim comes to the conclusion that mixed legal systems perform extremely well economically.[201] Her study was motivated by the realization that mixed legal systems are not treated separately in legal origins scholarship.[202] Positive accounts of the efficiency of Common Law tend to sweep the differences of mixed legal systems under the carpet as well. Mahoney recognized the problem posed by mixed legal systems but argued that for the purpose of his study, he could treat them

---

[198] See for an analysis on the impact of policies vs. legal institutions Peter B Henry & Conrad Miller, "Institutions versus Policies: A Tale of Two Islands" (2009) 99 Am Econ Rev 261.

[199] *Ibid* at 266.

[200] Klerman *et al, supra* note 182 at 390.

[201] Kensie Kim, "Mixed Systems in Legal Origins Analysis" (2010) 83:3 S Cal L Rev 693.

[202] *Ibid* at 701.

as Common Law jurisdictions because he was foremost concerned with Common Law as a constitutional arrangement.[203]

Kim contributes a distinct mixed system analysis to the legal origin debate. In order to identify them, she defines "mixed legal systems" as

> "political entities that have a presence of substantial common and civil law elements in their legal system — in other words, those countries in which we expect to find, 'in addition certainly to other mixed elements, that common law and civil law constitute the basic building blocks of the legal edifice.' Thus, a country with a mix of common law, civil law, and customary law (for example, South Africa) is included in this narrower definition of hybrid, but a country with a mix of civil law and customary law (for example, Japan) is not."[204]

Importantly for the subject of this book, this restrictive approach also means that Canada was not included as a mixed legal system because its "mixity"[205] is a function of regional differences; the same applies to the United Kingdom and the United States.[206] Presumably, Kim did not include Québec, Scotland, or Louisiana as individual political entities because there was not sufficient data on the subnational level to conduct the necessary analysis. Methodologically, she conducted her study by identifying a number of areas of law that have a proven relationship with economic performance: (private) property law, contract law, corporate and securities law, and procedural law.[207] Then, these areas of law were coded with either "0" (Common Law) or "1" (Civil Law).

One conclusion of this coding exercise is that not a single mixed system received a Common Law property rights coding. Property law was found to be "least susceptible to common law influence."[208] One account offered for this is the supposed resilience of property law and the difficulty of changing it retroactively.[209] However, the example of the abolition of the seigneurial system in Québec shows that property law can change quickly at a fundamental level.

The country coding data was then compared with the GDP growth rate for each country and the world average growth rate. The study showed that out of 14 mixed jurisdiction countries, three were underperforming in economic growth, six were over-performing and five were performing at an average or slightly above- or below-average rate.[210] Two of the three underperforming

---

[203] Mahoney, *supra* note 124 at 514.

[204] Kim, *supra* note 201 at 705 [references ommited].

[205] A term borrowed from Jane M Glenn, "Mixed Jurisdictions in the Commonwealth Caribbean: Mixing, Unmixing, Remixing" in: Esin Örücü, ed, *Mixed Legal Systems at New Frontiers* (London: Wildy, Simmonds & Hill, 2010) 78.

[206] Kim, *supra* note 201 at 705–6.

[207] *Ibid* at 710–11, 714.

[208] *Ibid* at 721.

[209] *Ibid* at 721.

[210] *Ibid* at 714.

countries had long periods of civil war in their recent history, which could account for their bad economic performance.[211]

## D. Conclusion

One problem with the legal origin theory is weak theoretical underpinning. The positive account for the efficiency of the Common Law places great reliance on the independence of judges in law-making.[212] However, the area of law analysed by the legal origin scholarship tends to be heavily influenced by statutory law in Common Law jurisdictions as well. Roe points out that an "inquiry into why secured credit and securitization are so strong in the United States" would lead to *Article 9 UCC,* "a code so richly drafted that it leaves little interpretive discretion for the judge."[213]

The legal origin theory is unable to provide any explanation or guidance for determining efficiency when analysing secured transactions and insolvency law. A better approach consists of a system-by-system individual analysis of a legal rule. This analysis should evaluate how each legal rule relates to theories of efficient (property or secured transaction law) and to what degree this legal rule is a function of its "legal system."

---

[211] *Ibid* at 718.

[212] See Part I: § 3 C.II.1, "Common Law and Efficiency".

[213] Mark J Roe, "Legal Origins, Politics, and Modern Stock Markets" (2006) 120:2 Harv L Rev 460 at 478.

Part II

# Property

## § 4 Property in Civil Law

This part of the book begins with a doctrinal exposition on property law. I first describe the black-letter law of property before offering theoretical insights into property law. The reason for this is, foremost, that I consider the difference between Civil Law and Common Law to be a difference of substance. If the legal origin theory posits that Civil Law is inherently less efficient than Common Law and consequently, the conclusion is drawn that it would be better to replace Civil Law rules with Common Law rules,[1] then we need clarity on what we mean when we speak of "Common Law" or "Civil Law" property. The approach often adopted in legal origins theory of taking a broad view of the meaning of the terms Common Law and Civil Law is of no great help in this respect.

If we recall the definitions of Common Law and Civil Law in legal origins theory ("common law stands for the strategy of social control that seeks to support private market outcomes, whereas civil law seeks to replace such outcomes with state-desired allocations"[2]) and its emphasis on judicial protection against the state as the defining characteristic of Common Law,[3] we quickly realize that this can be of no guidance in identifying differences in substantive law. Rather, we have to look at the black-letter law on property law and secured transactions law to validate the hypothesis that there is such a thing as *Common Law* property law and *Civil Law* property law.

This is particularly true if one rejects style of reasoning[4] and the role of precedent[5] as sufficient *differentia specifica* between the different legal systems. Even if one considers style of reasoning to be a defining difference, style

---

[1] See Part I: § 3 C.I, "Law Matters".

[2] Rafael La Porta, Florencio Lopez-de-Silanes & Andrei Shleifer, "The Economic Consequences of Legal Origins" (2008) 46:2 J Econ Lit 285 at 286.

[3] See Part I: § 3 C.III.2.a), "History and Institutions".

[4] See Colm P McGrath & Helmut Koziol, "Is Style of Reasoning a Fundamental Difference Between the Common Law and the Civil Law?" (2014) 78:4 RabelsZ 709.

[5] See e.g. Ernst J Cohn, "Precedents in Continental Law" (1935) 5:3 CLJ 366; Wolfgang Friedmann, "Stare Decisis at Common Law and Under the Civil Code of Quebec" (1953) 31

of reasoning could have an impact on substantive rules.[6] Beginning with an exposition on the black-letter legal doctrines of property law is thus warranted. This will show us that the substantive differences between property law in Common Law and Civil Law are significant.[7]

## A. Patrimony and Property

### *I. Patrimony*

The notion of patrimony is a *differentia specifica* between Québec Civil Law and the Common Law. The concept of patrimony is the starting point for an examination the modern Civil Law of property.[8] It arrived in Québec law by way of reception from other Civil Law systems. It is a doctrinal innovation. In the text of the *Code civil du Bas-Canada,* the notion of patrimony was barely found.[9] The same applies for the *Code civil des Francais,* where patrimony is not found as a term of art.[10] The modern notion of patrimony in Québec law is based on French law, which, in turn, was based on 19th-century German doctrinal writing by Zachariä and his third edition of a textbook on French law (which was the law of the land in parts of Germany).[11]

---

Can Bar Rev 723; Kurt Lipstein, "The Doctrine of Precedent in Continental Law with Special Reference to French and German Law" (1946) 28 J Comp Leg Int'l L 34; Max Radin, "Case Law and Stare Decisis: Concerning Präjudizienrecht in Amerika" (1933) 33:2 Col L Rev 199; Roland Wagner Döbler, "Präjudizien in deutschen, englischen und US-amerikanischen Gerichtsentscheidungen: Ein quantitativer Vergleich" (1995) 59 RabelsZ 113; Konrad Zweigert & Hans-Jürgen Puttfarken, "Statutory Interpretation: Civilian Style" (1969–1970) 44 Tul L Rev 704.

[6] See Jacques Auger, "Le style civiliste et le droit des sûretés réelles" in: Nicholas Kasirer, ed, *Le droit civil: avant tout un style?* (Montréal: Éditions Thémis, 2003) 48 at 48.

[7] Cf. Rudolf B Schlesinger, "The Past and Future of Comparative Law" (1995) 43:3 Am J Comp L 477.

[8] France Allard, "Entre le droit civil et la common law: La propriété en quête de sens" in: Jean C Gémar & Nicholas Kasirer, eds, *Jurilinguistique: Entre langues et droits* (Montréal: Éditions Thémis, 2005) 193 at 199.

[9] Pierre-Claude Lafond, *Précis de droit des biens,* 2d edn (Montréal: Éditions Thémis, 2007) at para 372.

[10] Christopher B Gray, "Patrimony" (1981) 22 C de D 81 at 95.

[11] Karl S Zachariä, *Handbuch des französischen Civilrechts,* 3rd edn (Tübingen: Mohr, 1827). See Rainer Becker, *Die Fiducie von Québec und der Trust: Ein Vergleich mit verschiedenen Modellen fiduziarischer Rechtsfiguren im Civil Law* (Tübingen: Mohr Siebeck, 2007) at 176–77; Gray, preceding note at 108. On the impact of French property law on Québec property law see Madeleine Cantin Cumyn, "Le droit privé des biens: À l'enseigne de la continuité" in: H P Glenn, ed, *Droit québécois et droit français: Communauté, autonomie, concordance* (Cowansville, Québec: Éditions Yvon Blais, 1993) 375 at 378.

The notion of patrimony is linked with the idea of the common pledge.[12] The term 'common pledge' *(gage commun)* is used to convey the notion that all assets owned by the debtor are available to satisfy any outstanding obligations.[13] In other words, a person's patrimony is the sum of that which that person offers in pledge to all her creditors to secure any of her obligations.

### *1. Patrimony in Roman Law*

While it is a doctrinal creation of the 19th century, the modern notion of patrimony has precursors. Gray has written an extensive analysis of the historical development of the notion of patrimony.[14] He begins his analysis with a look at patrimony in the *corpus iuris civilis* and concludes that patrimony was not an explicitly defined concept in the *corpus iuris civilis.*[15]

Notwithstanding the lack of a clearly defined notion of patrimony in Roman law, some shape can be given to the notion by looking at a related concept: the *peculium*. The *peculium* was a separate mass of monies dedicated by the *pater familias* to a son or a slave, but it was seen as a sub-division of the patrimony, showing the same characteristics. It was thus a "universality," not a discrete right. Liability incurred during the course of transactions out of the *peculium* was limited to the *peculium* itself.[16] Because of this, some writers have concluded that the idea of a person's patrimony as the sum – or "universality" – of assets and liabilities was not unknown to Roman law.[17]

Patrimony, in whatever limited sense it had in Roman law, was a class. As such, it consisted of members. Before Cicero, these members were things, not rights. With Cicero and the reception of Greek stoicism, the focus shifted. The right of ownership, not just the thing itself, became to be recognized as being a permissible member of the class. A change of ownership was no longer seen as the replacement of the "person" component in the thing-owner relationship, but as a transfer of a *right* of ownership.[18]

### *2. The Personal Theory of Patrimony*

The reception of patrimony concept in French doctrine took place through the writings of Aubry and Rau, who saw themselves in the tradition of the German

[12] Gray, *supra* note 10 at 97; Lafond, *supra* note 9 at paras 383–84; Roderick A Macdonald, "Reconceiving the Symbols of Property: Universalities, Interests and Other Heresies" (1994) 39 McGill LJ 761 at 770 [Macdonald, "Symbols"]; Claude Witz in: *JurisClasseur: Civil Code* (Paris: LexisNexis) Art 2284 et 2285 C. civ.

[13] *Code civil du Québec,* SQ 1991, c 64 [*CcQ*], art 2264.

[14] Gray, *supra* note 10.

[15] *Ibid* at 85–86.

[16] *Ibid* at 87.

[17] Cf. *ibid* at 87–88.

[18] *Ibid* at 88.

writer Zachariä.[19] Aubry and Rau posited that the notion of patrimony was linked to the notion of personality; patrimony is everything which could be subjected to and was expression of the person's will.[20] They also held that corporeal things are not in themselves part of the patrimony but only by virtue of the legal concept of "property" *(biens)*.[21] This echoes the development in Roman law. The classical notion of patrimony based on Aubry's and Rau's writing has three characteristics: first, everybody has a patrimony, even if it is empty;[22] second, everybody has but one patrimony;[23] third, every patrimony belongs to somebody.[24]

In Québec doctrine, a theory of property that requires all three conditions to be present as sufficient conditions for there to be patrimony is referred to as the 'personal theory of patrimony'.[25]

The will foundation for the notion of patrimony is important in several aspects. The third characteristic is the very outflow of the will foundation.[26] The will theory of patrimony serves as a reason for the inclusion of incorporeal property rights in the patrimony class (in other words: the recognition of incorporeal property). Because the patrimony is the sum of every legal relation subject to the agent's will, it should include both relations determined by things as well as relations determined without the notion of corporeality.[27] This explains why the Civil Law of Québec is more amenable to the recognition of incorporeal property than other Civil Law systems, such as modern German law, which does not have a doctrine of patrimony.[28] A further implication of the will theory is that a debtor's creditors cannot strip her of her patrimonial rights. They can only use the patrimonial rights to satisfy their debt.[29]

The personal theory of patrimony cannot account for all legal phenomena related to the patrimony. For instance, the patrimony of a deceased person passes to her successor, but can be held separate from the latter's patrimony

---

[19] Charles Aubry & Charles F Rau, *Cours de droit civil français: D'après la méthode de Zachariæ*, 4th edn (Paris: Marchal & Billard, 1873).

[20] *Ibid* at 229; Gray, *supra* note 10 at 106.

[21] Aubry & Rau, *supra* note 19 at 230.

[22] Becker, *supra* note 11 at 177; Lafond, *supra* note 9 at para 383; Macdonald, "Symbols", *supra* note 12 at 767.

[23] Becker, *supra* note 11 at 178; Lafond, *supra* note 9 at para 383; Macdonald, "Symbols", *supra* note 12 at 767.

[24] Becker, *supra* note 11 at 178; Lafond, *supra* note 9 at para 383; Macdonald, "Symbols", *supra* note 12 at 767.

[25] Lafond, *supra* note 9 at paras 383–84.

[26] Cf. Gray, *supra* note 10 at 106.

[27] *Ibid* at 147.

[28] *Ibid* at 147. On the limited role of patrimony in German law see Becker, *supra* note 11 at 174–75.

[29] Gray, *supra* note 10 at 107.

until all debts are settled.[30] One person may hold several universalities of patrimonial rights – a noteworthy example is unincorporated businesses.[31]

### *3. Patrimony by Appropriation*

In the *Code civil du Québec,* there is a different expression of patrimony. The theory of patrimony by appropriation considers the patrimony to be comprised of a class of property. Membership in this class is determined by an act of will carried out by a person; this process is called "appropriation."[32] Patrimony by appropriation has become very important as the foundation for Québec trust law. Thus, we look at this particular type of patrimony in more detail below.[33]

## *II. From Patrimonial Rights to Property*

Due to the acceptance of patrimony by appropriation, the third characteristic of classical patrimony (*i.e.* every patrimony belongs to somebody) is no longer a necessary condition for the existence of a patrimony in modern Québec law. Rather, in modern Québec law, patrimony is defined as a collection of rights *potentially* held by a person.[34] Regularly, the patrimony consists of all property appropriated by the holder of the patrimony.[35] In its generally accepted definition, the patrimony consists of an active side (that which is owned) and a passive side (that which is owed).[36]

On the active side, the elements of the patrimony are items of property. The word "property" *(bien)* has two meanings. It can mean either "a thing subject to appropriation" or a "patrimonial right."[37] The first meaning is sometimes thought not to be doctrinally precise,[38] but it is commonly – and, as I argue

---

[30] Macdonald, "Symbols", *supra* note 12 at 767.

[31] *Ibid* at 767.

[32] Lafond, *supra* note 9 at para 396.

[33] Part II: § 7 C.I, "Patrimony by Appropriation".

[34] Alain Sériaux, "La notion juridique de patrimoine: Brèves notations civilistes sur le verbe avoir" in: Ernest Caparros, ed, *Mélanges Germain Brière* (Montréal: Wilson & Lafleur, 1993) 312 at 313.

[35] Canada, Department of Justice, Bijuralism & Drafting Support Services Group Legislative Service Branch, "Proposals for Harmonizing the Bankruptcy and Insolvency Act with Quebec Civil Law" (2003) 37:1 RJT 19 at 38–39.

[36] Lafond, *supra* note 9 at para 375. However Sériaux, *supra* note 34 argues that the patrimony only consists of activa.

[37] Madeleine Cantin Cumyn & Michelle Cumyn, "La notion des biens" in: Sylvio Normand, ed, *Mélanges offerts au Professeur François Frenette* (Québec: Les Presses de l'Université Laval, 2006) 127 at 128.

[38] Cf. *ibid* at 128. However, the double meaning of property is a function of ambiguity in the Roman law sources, see below "Part II: § 4 D, Right and Object of Right."

below, correctly – used that way.[39] The definition of patrimony is similar in Québec Civil Law and French law.[40] Personality rights are an unchangeable function of personality; they cannot be appropriated. They are neither thought of as patrimonial rights,[41] nor are they property.[42] Some authors go further and imply that only things and rights that can be traded and consequently have a monetary value form part of the patrimony.[43] This, however, would mean that inalienable ownership would be a contradiction in itself, yet it is an accepted category of ownership.[44] Thus, a better criterion to determine the patrimonial or extra-patrimonial character of a right is to ask whether it depends on the existence of the person (such as a personality right) or can exist without the person (such as ownership of a *res extra commercium*).[45]

Property becomes part of a patrimony by appropriation – be it original acquisition or derivative acquisition. This means that possession is not a patrimonial right. Possession is not property. A right to possess is.[46]

### *III. Types of Property*

The taxonomy of property in Québec Civil Law follows two vectors. Article 899 *CcQ* provides as follows:

| | |
|---|---|
| "Property, whether corporeal or incorporeal, is divided into immovables and movables." | "Les biens, tant corporels qu'incorporels, se divisent en immeubles et en meubles." |

There is thus a distinction between movable and immovable property and a distinction between corporeal and incorporeal property.

#### *1. Corporeal and Incorporeal Property*

Lafond calls the distinction between corporeal and incorporeal property "la première grande division."[47] Based on the notion of property being anything subject to appropriation, he defines "corporeal property" as (1) any physical

---

[39] See Canada, Department of Justice, Bijuralism & Drafting Support Services Group Legislative Service Branch, *supra* note 35 at 38; Lafond, *supra* note 9 at paras 3–5.

[40] See Jean Carbonnier, *Droit civil* (Quadrige Manuels, Paris: Presses universitaires de France, 1964) at 45. On the continuing influence of French property law in Québec see Cantin Cumyn, "Le droit privé des biens", *supra* note 11 at 378.

[41] Macdonald, "Symbols", *supra* note 12 at 767.

[42] Canada, Department of Justice, Bijuralism & Drafting Support Services Group Legislative Service Branch, *supra* note 35 at 38–39; Lafond, *supra* note 9 at paras 376–80.

[43] Sériaux, *supra* note 34 at 315–16.

[44] Sylvio Normand, "La notion de modalité de la propriété" in: Normand, ed, *Mélanges offerts au Professeur François Frenette, supra* note 37, 255 at 262 [Normand, "Modalité"].

[45] Cf. Sériaux, *supra* note 34 at 317.

[46] *Ibid* at 320.

[47] Lafond, *supra* note 9 at 59.

good that is (2) subject to appropriation and that (3) has an economic value.[48] "Incorporeal property," on the other hand, is any right that has an economic value.[49] The latter criterion would exclude any rights that are a function of someone's personhood. Since these personality rights are not subject to appropriation, the second element of Lafond's definition of corporeal property does not differ from the third element; it is superfluous.

*2. Movable and Immovable Property*

Civil Law distinguishes between movable and immovable property. As mentioned in the introduction, this book is primarily concerned with movable property law. In Roman law, the distinction between movable and immovable property was of lesser importance and was straightforward: movable property was anything that could be moved and that was not attached to an immovable.[50] The distinction became more important in French law under the *Ançien régime.* Feudal law provided for different treatment of movables and immovables; immovables participated in the feudal scheme of land-holding. This also meant that the classification of a thing as movable or immovable was less a function of its natural properties and more a function of its importance for feudal societies. No longer were lands and their buildings immovable property. Rather, the term "immovable property" began to entail items such as seals, relicts, and rolls. Incorporeal property that could bear fruits was considered to be immovable, simple obligations which could not carry interest (for religious reasons) were movable.[51]

Modern Québec law has returned to the Roman principle of using the natural characteristics of a thing as the starting point for classification. At the same time, it has maintained a different framework for movable property on the one hand and immovable property on the other, just like feudal law.[52]

## B. Property Rights as Real Rights

In Québec Civil Law, there are two classes of rights: "personal rights" and "real rights." Personal rights confer a share in the common pledge of creditors to the creditor,[53] whereas real rights confer a right in the property itself, which ranks above the common pledge. Under the *CcBC,* real rights had two characteristics: they could be claimed only upon things (corporeal property), and they

[48] *Ibid* at para 65.
[49] *Ibid* at para 72.
[50] *Ibid* at paras 85–86.
[51] *Ibid* at paras 90–91.
[52] *Ibid* at paras 93–95.
[53] Macdonald, "Symbols", *supra* note 12 at 787.

were directly opposable to third parties.[54] Thus, we find two notions defining a property right: it has third-party effect and it relates to a thing, not a person.

We find similar formulations in case law:

"Pour sa part, *le droit réel est un lien de droit entre une personne et une chose;* il confère a son titulaire un pouvoir juridique direct et immédiat sur la chose, pouvoir qui s'exerce sans aucun intermédiaire. S il est principal (droit de propriété et ses démembrements), il porte sur la matérialité même de la chose; accessoire (p. ex. hypothèque, nantissement et privilège), il vise la valeur pécuniaire de la chose comme garantie de l'exécution d'une obligation principale. Le droit réel comporte comme attributs le droit de suite et le droit de préférence, ainsi que la possession et la faculté d'abandon."[55]

"Contrairement au *droit réel,* qui est *opposable aux tiers* sous réserve des règles de la publicité, le droit personnel est dit « relatif » puisqu'il ne lie que le créancier et le débiteur. [...] À l'inverse, le droit réel confère à son titulaire un pouvoir qui peut être exercé *directement sur un bien.* Il n'existe pas d'intermédiaire entre le titulaire du droit et le bien."[56]

Lafond maintains the same characteristics apply under the *CcQ,* but adds the right to unilaterally disavow the right to the definition of real rights.[57] Therefore, the term "real right" refers to the same concept that I refer to when using the term "property right" and the two terms will be used interchangeably when referring to Québec Law.

Outside the personal-real rights dichotomy are two further factual situations recognized by the law: detention and possession. Detention is the mere holding of property. Possession is detention combined with "an intention to exercise rights in the object as owner or other titulary of a real (by contrast with a personal) right."[58]

---

[54] Roderick A Macdonald, "Enforcing Rights in Corporeal Moveables: Revendication and Its Surrogates (Part 1)" (1986) 31:4 McGill LJ 573 at 584 [Macdonald, "Enforcing Rights I"]. Regarding the latter see also Yaëll Emerich, "La nature juridique des sûretés réelles en droit civil et en Common Law: Une question de tradition juridique?" (2010) 44:1 RJT 95 at 106.

[55] *Sacchetti v Lockheimer,* [1988] 1 SCR 1049 at 1056, Lamer J [references ommitted], ref'd to by *Anglo Pacific Group PLC c Ernst & Young inc*, 2013 QCCA 1323 at 61 [*Anglo Pacific*], Thibault JCA.

[56] *Anglo Pacific,* preceding note at 39–40, Thibault JCA [references ommitted, emphasis added].

[57] Lafond, *supra* note 9 at paras 442–53.

[58] Macdonald, "Enforcing Rights I", *supra* note 54 at 591.

## C. Ownership and Lesser Property Rights

### *I. Ownership*

An analysis of property rights in Québec Civil Law begins with ownership because other property rights are defined by their relation to ownership.[59] As defined above, "property" is everything that is subject to appropriation. "Appropriation" is the act of taking "ownership" *(propriété)* of property.[60] Civil Law has traditionally operated with a sharp distinction between ownership and possession. In Roman law, possession was actual enjoyment of property; ownership, on the other hand, was something very different.[61] The current notion of ownership in Québec law is defined in art 947 *CcQ:*

"Article 947 *CcQ*

| | |
|---|---|
| (1) Ownership is the right to use, enjoy and dispose of property fully and freely, subject to the limits and conditions for doing so determined by law. | (1) La propriété est le droit d'user, de jouir et de disposer librement et complètement d'un bien, sous réserve des limites et des conditions d'exercice fixées par la loi. |
| (2) Ownership may be in various modes and dismemberments. | (2) Elle est susceptible de modalités et de démembrements." |

Ownership is described as "absolute, exclusive and perpetual,"[62] it is "classiquement analysée comme un droit absolu, unitaire et indivisible."[63] The understanding of exclusivity entails unity and indivisibility.[64] The *CcQ* has broken with this traditional definition of ownership. It has replaced the notion of *absoluteness of ownership* with the notion of the right of ownership being "libre et complet."[65] I take a look at both notions in turn.

#### *1. The Genesis of the Traditional Notion of Absolute Ownership*

The idea of absolute ownership is a result of the abolition of the seigneurial system and feudal law.[66] This does not apply only to the Civil Law of Québec,

[59] See Part II: § 4 C.II, "Lesser Property Rights".

[60] Cf. Cantin Cumyn & Cumyn, *supra* note 37 at 143: "Dans une troisème acceptation, le mot bien désigne l'objet du droit de propriéte ou d'un des démembrements".

[61] Joshua C Tate, "Ownership and Possession in the Early Common Law" (2006) 48 Am J Legal Hist 280 at 281–82.

[62] Macdonald, "Enforcing Rights I", *supra* note 54 at 587.

[63] Yaëll Emerich, "Regard civiliste sur le droit des biens de la Common Law: Pour une conception transsystemique du droit de la propriété" (2008) 38:2 RGD 339 at 343.

[64] Macdonald, "Enforcing Rights I", *supra* note 54 at 587.

[65] See Lafond, *supra* note 9 at paras 654–56; Denis Vincelette, "Définition et notion de la propriété: Plaidoyer pour la vraisemblance" (2001) 31:4 RGD 677 at 681.

[66] Lafond, *supra* note 9 at para 651.

but to the Civil Law in general.[67] We have already looked at the seigneurial system as applied in Québec above.[68] At this point, I want to elaborate how the notion of ownership changed between feudal law and post-feudal Civil Law.

The ownership structure created by seigneurial law was a common feature of European feudal law. It was known as *duplex dominium.*[69] "Duplex dominium" meant that a lord and a vassal were both considered to be owners of immovable property (a fiefdom). They both held different rights in it, the *dominium directum* and the *dominium utile.* A precise definition of these rights was not a necessary condition of *duplex dominium. Duplex dominium* could thus encompass a variety of diverse legal relationships. Heirbaut calls it an "empty box."[70]

A duplex *dominium* could turn into a *multiplex dominium*: a vassal could, in his turn, enfeoff another vassal with the whole or part of what he had received from his lord. Thus, the vassal became a vassal and a lord, and a second vassal was created, resulting in three owners: the overlord and his vassal, the lord, having *dominium directum,* and the vassal at the bottom having *dominium utile.*[71]

Heirbaut claims that the reason for the abolition of the notion of *duplex dominium* was its ill-defined boundary. Because it lacked any further detail other than the fact that it allowed subinfeudation of property, it became associated with negative aspects of feudalism such as noble privileges and serfdom.[72] A further factor, Heirbaut claims, was its incompatibility with a principled approach to property law, furthered by the Enlightenment, which defined ownership as the foremost property right, the top of a pyramid of property rights.[73]

The abolition of the seigneurial system made it possible to create the notion of ownership *(dominium)* as an absolute right in property.[74] In the context of

---

[67] Kenneth GC Reid, "Property Law: Sources and Doctrine" in: Kenneth G Reid & Reinhard Zimmermann, eds, *A History of Private Law in Scotland* (Oxford: Oxford University Press, 2000) 185 at 190 makes this point for Scots law.

[68] See Part I: § 1 D, "The Abolition of the Seigneurial System".

[69] See Dirk Heirbaut, "Feudal Law: The Real Ius Commune of Property in Europe, or: Should We Reintroduce Duplex Dominium?" (2003) 11:3 Eur Rev Priv L 301. On the implication of duplex dominium for absolute ownership see Daniel Visser, "The Absoluteness of Ownership: The South African Common Law in Perspective" (1985) 1 Acta Juridica 39.

[70] Heirbaut, preceding note at 313.

[71] *Ibid* at 313.

[72] *Ibid* at 314.

[73] *Ibid* at 315.

[74] John EC Brierley, "Regards sur le droit des biens dans le nouveau Code civil du Québec" (1995) 47:1 Rev Int Dr Comp 33 at 35 [Brierley, "Regards"]; Cantin Cumyn, "Le droit privé des biens", *supra* note 11 at 376–77; Normand, "Modalité", *supra* note 44 at 255–56. Cf. Visser, *supra* note 69.

Scots law, Reid argues that abolition of feudalism must come before a codification of property law,[75] presumably because feudal structures of ownership are in the way of a coherent property law. Ownership in modern Civil Law is thus singular:

"Envisagé comme le droit le plus complet, celui qui accorde actuellement ou éventuellement la plénitude des prérogatives ou des avantages susceptibles d'être dérivés de son objet, le droit de propriété ne laisse aucune place pour un deuxième droit de même nature."[76]

### *2. The Notion of Ownership as a Complete Right*

The complete character of ownership means that all rights pertaining to the property originally belong to the owner.[77] These derivative rights of ownership can be classified. There are four classes of rights: the right to use, the right to the fruits, the power to dispose, and the right to accession.[78] The first three are also known by their Latin name: *usus (jus utendi), fructus (jus fruendi),* and *abusus (jus abutendi).*[79] The last right – the right to accession – is often omitted from the list. It refers to the owner's right to own anything which becomes one with the property and thus resembles the right to the fruits.[80] Frenette argues that there is a further right: the residual right he calls *vis attractiva.*[81] His argument is based on the observation that there is ownership even where the four preceding rights have been alienated separately. *Vis attractiva* then is the residual right to regain full ownership once a dismemberment comes to an end.

## *II. Lesser Property Rights*

Apart from ownership, there are other property rights in the *CcQ*. They are occasionally referred to as *jus in re aliena.*[82] These rights can be divided into two classes: the first class comprises non-accessory property rights, or "dismemberments of the right of ownership";[83] the second class of *jus in re aliena* is made up of accessory property rights.

---

[75] Reid, "Property Law", *supra* note 67 at 190.

[76] Madeleine Cantin Cumyn, "De l'existence et du régime juridique des droits réels de jouissance innommés: Essai sur l'énumération limitative des droits réels" (1986) 46 R du B 3 at 6 [Cantin Cumyn, "Droits réels innommés"].

[77] Normand, "Modalité", *supra* note 44 at 256: "[Le] propriétaire est, en principe, détenteur de la totalité des prérogatives inhérentes à la proriété." See also Lafond, *supra* note 9 at paras 664–65; Vincelette, *supra* note 65 at 682–83.

[78] Normand, "Modalité", *supra* note 44 at 256.

[79] See e.g. Lafond, *supra* note 9 at para 431.

[80] *Ibid* at para 667.

[81] François Frenette, "Du droit de propriété: Certaines de ses dimensions méconnues" (1979) 20:3 C de D 439 at 446–47.

[82] Macdonald, "Symbols", *supra* note 12 at 768.

[83] See the heading before *CcQ, supra* note 13, art 1119.

### *1. Principal Property Rights*

Dismemberments of ownership are also called principal property rights.[84] They are usufruct *(usufruit),*[85] use *(usage),*[86] servitude *(servitude),*[87] and emphyteusis *(emphythéose).*[88] The holder of a non-accessory property right is considered to possess the right and can thus avail herself of conservatory actions protecting her property.[89] The four dismemberments of property pertain to the four classes of rights of ownership mentioned above in different ways.[90]

The taxonomy of principal rights in the *CcQ* differs from the one in the *CcBC.* Section 405 *CcBC* provided that property rights were either the right of ownership, a grant of a derivative right of ownership, or a real servitude. The "real servitude" *(servitude réel)* denoted servitudes that were created in a servient land to the benefit of a dominant land; entitlement from the real servitude followed entitlement to the dominant land. For example, a right of passage would avail to the owner of a certain plot of land.

When derivative rights of ownership were transferred to a person and were capable of being held independently of other property, they were called "personal servitudes" *(servitudes personelles).* Despite being called "personal" servitudes, they were nevertheless property rights.[91] The *CcBC* contained a number of personal servitudes, just like the *CcQ* contains a number of dismemberments of ownership. In the *CcBC,* these were usufruct, use, habitation, and emphyteusis.[92]

There is an undeniable logic in no longer using the distinction between real and personal servitudes as a primary distinction of principal property rights. The two classes essentially differ only in how the acquisition of right takes place. Ownership of the governing property is a necessary condition to benefit from a real servitude. A personal servitude is transferred individually. But in regard to what is being carved out of the right of ownership in the serving property, both are the same.

#### *a) Usufruct, Use, and Servitude*

A "usufruct" gives the right-holder the right to use the item of property and to appropriate its fruit. A "use," on the other hand, only allows the right-holder to use the property, but not to draw its fruits. A "servitude" is right attached to

---

[84] *Sacchetti v Lockheimer, supra* note 55 at 1056, Lamer J .
[85] *CcQ, supra* note 13, art 1120.
[86] *Ibid,* art 1172.
[87] *Ibid,* art 1177.
[88] *Ibid,* art 1195.
[89] Lafond, *supra* note 9 at para 611.
[90] See Part II: § 4 C.I.2, "The Notion of Ownership as a Complete Right".
[91] Cantin Cumyn, "Droits réels innommés", *supra* note 76 at 9.
[92] *Ibid* at 9.

immovable property. It is what the *CcBC* referred to as real servitudes. By virtue of the servitude, certain limited rights of usage exist in the immovable property. The rights exist for the benefit of anyone holding a right in another – specific – immovable property.[93]

### *b) Emphyteusis*

An "emphyteusis" is a right in an immovable. By virtue of the emphyteusis, the right-holder has all rights enjoyed by the owner of the property, subject to three exceptions: she cannot alienate the property, she cannot destroy the property, and the right is limited in time.[94] An emphyteusis has been described as a temporary ownership.[95]

Heirbaut claims that emphyteusis is a resurrection of the notion of *duplex dominium.* Grouping it together with a right to superficies he writes:

> "Both give their holder real rights that are so extensive that *they violate the principle of unity of ownership.* In fact, when there is an emphyteusis or superficies, there are two owners: the landowner and the holder of the emphyteusis or superficies. The latter are inheritable and alienable, their only limitation being their duration, as they can no longer be perpetual [...]."[96]

Becker points out that the Civil Law concept of emphyteusis leads to a split of ownership interests in Civil Law that is similar to the Common Law position in regard to legal and equitable ownership.[97]

### *2. Accessory Property Rights*

Accessory property rights are "accessory" because their existence is contingent upon the existence of a personal right. Accessory rights guarantee an obligation and are thus neither directed at the property itself, nor at the derivative rights; rather, they are concerned with the pecuniary value of the property.[98] They are dealt with in their own chapter on security interests in Québec Civil Law in the part of this book which deals with secured transactions law.[99] A part of doctrine considers the hypothec to be a dismemberment of property as well, since the hypothec changes the allocation of the right to the value of the thing.[100]

---

[93] See Lafond, *supra* note 9 at para 435.

[94] *Ibid* at para 435.

[95] Cf. Cantin Cumyn, "Droits réels innommés", *supra* note 76 at 9.

[96] Heirbaut, *supra* note 69 at 317 [emphasis added].

[97] Becker, *supra* note 11 at 28, note 51. See also Jose R Cortina, "The Jus Emphyteuticarium and Trust: A Byzantine Solution for an Acadian Problem" (1981) 8:1 SUL Rev 95.

[98] Lafond, *supra* note 9 at para 440.

[99] See Part III: § 12, "Security Interests in Common Law".

[100] François Frenette, "De l'hyopthèque: Réalité du droit et métamorphose de l'objet" (1998) 39:4 C de D 803.

### *III. Ownership as a Property Right*

As Macdonald points out, there is ambiguity regarding the classification of ownership itself in the *CcQ*. He submits that is unclear whether it is a real right (or, in my terminology, a property right), a personal right, or a right *sui generis*.[101] The possible uncertainty arises because the *CcQ* specifies in art 1119 *CcQ* that usufruct, use, servitude and emphyteusis are real rights, and in art 2660 *CcQ* the same characterization is made for the hypothec. However, art 947 *CcQ* does not explicitly characterize ownership as a real right. As Macdonald says, characterizing ownership as a real right is the "more likely hypothesis."[102]

Macdonald's potential objection to a classification of ownership within the class of property rights is that this might result in a blurred distinction between personal rights and property rights; he bases this conclusion on the premise that if ownership were a real right, then a real right would be possible not only in things, but in personal rights as well, whereas in the traditional notion of a real right, such a right was only allowed in things.[103] However, this is an incorrect premise. As we will see in the next section, the premise that ownership is only possible in corporeal property – if it were ever correct– cannot be maintained under the *CcQ*. Thus, there is no objection to the classification of ownership among the class of property rights. It certainly conforms to the definition given above.[104]

## D. Right and Object of Right

### *I. Problem*

There is ambiguity and, subsequently, scholarly disagreement regarding the implications the new *CcQ* has on the notions of ownership and property – more specifically the object of ownership.[105] Because property, properly understood, is anything that is potentially subject to ownership, the question whether incorporeal property can exist under the new *CcQ* is simply a different wording of the question whether ownership is restricted to corporeal things or whether it can be extended to something incorporeal. The difficulty begins with the term "incorporeal." As a working definition, "something incorporeal" is meant to mean anything which is not a physical thing. Incorporeal property is thus anything which is not a thing, but in which an absolute right can be had.

---

101 Macdonald, "Symbols", *supra* note 12 at 797.
102 *Ibid* at 797.
103 *Ibid* at 787–88.
104 See Part II: § 4 B, "Property Rights as Real Rights".
105 Cf. Allard, "Entre le droit civil et la common law", *supra* note 8 at 211.

The answer to the question whether incorporeal property exists under the *CcQ* might seem straightforward, given that art 899 *CcQ* states that "property, whether corporeal or incorporeal, is divided into immovables and movables." However, the admission of incorporeal property requires the potential ownership of something incorporeal, which is seen as an innovation in Québec law from the state of law when the *CcBC* was still in force.[106]

The exclusion of incorporeal property and ownership of such property is not a necessary function of a Roman law heritage. Gaius distinguished between corporeal and incorporeal *res*. One example of corporeal *res* was land. Examples of incorporeal *res* were uses, usufructs, or obligations.[107] The term *res* could thus mean neither only "physical thing" nor only "right." Physical things were corporeals, incorporeals were rights, and thus *res* could not mean only either.[108]

Initially, ownership was not part of the Gaian scheme because there was no need to conceptualize the difference between having a *res* and having ownership of the *res*. To accommodate ownership, two competing theories were developed. According to the first theory, there is absolute entitlement to a *res*. Where the *res* is corporeal, one speaks of ownership; where it is incorporeal, there is no proper term for it.[109] According to the second theory, ownership conveys the idea that a *res* can be the subject of one's patrimony. The owner who says "I own this thing" thus expresses that this thing is in her patrimony.

In modern Québec law, we arguably find both theories operating at the same time. Not only does the right of ownership merge with the thing, but any patrimonial right can be owned.[110] Gretton has written the following about Reid's[111] conception of Civil Law ownership:

> "Ownership has a double role – or perhaps one should even speak of two sorts of ownership. First, ownership is a real right, the principal real right. Here one can speak of the ownership of land and bicycles. But secondly, ownership is also the relationship of a person to a right. This duality implies that, since rights can be owned, the right of ownership can be owned."[112]

For the reasons set out in the following paragraphs, I submit that the same applies to modern Québec law.

---

[106] Cf. *ibid* at 195: "La propriété est d'abord envisagée comme une institution juridique articulée en termes assez précis, ancrée traditionnellement dans une certaine corporalité."

[107] Inst 2.2.

[108] George L Gretton, "Ownership and Its Objects" (2007) 71:4 RabelsZ 802 at 805.

[109] *Ibid* at 807.

[110] *Ibid* at 825.

[111] Kenneth GC Reid, "Obligations and Property: Exploring the Border" [1997] AJ 225.

[112] Gretton, "Ownership and Its Objects", *supra* note 108 at 827.

*1. The Classical Notion of Property in the Code civil du Bas-Canada*

Under the *CcBC,* one could only own things *(choses),*[113] whereas now one owns property *(biens).*[114] In the earlier notion of property, developed under the *CcBC,* one was not an owner of incorporeal property; rather one merely held title to an incorporeal right. This distinction was drawn even though the Romans had already accepted that a patrimony was not composed of things, but rights in things.[115] Macdonald claims that the exclusion of incorporeal property was a function of the "distinction between persons and property."[116] Implicit in this notion is the idea that rights are not property because they relate to persons, not things.

The exclusion of incorporeal property from the class of accepted property was the general consensus under the *CcBC,* regardless of the Privy Council's decision in *Matamajaw Salmon Club v Duchaine,*[117] in which the Privy Council held that a fishing right can be property and thus owned.[118]

As Macdonald points out, there were other statutory rules amounting to exceptions proving the rule against incorporeal property, but "within the limits imposed by nineteenth-century exegesis of the Civil Code, a basic division of persons and property on phenomenal rather than noumenal grounds could be sustained."[119]

Gray argues that the exclusion of incorporeal property under the *CcBC* was only possible due to a form of conceptual trick. In order to maintain the idea that incorporeal property is not possible, doctrine had to uphold a semi-fictional distinction, Gray says: Mignault claimed that a property right in a corporeal thing is itself a corporeal item of property, while a right in a right is incorporeal.[120] A similar conclusion was drawn by Macdonald, who points out that

[113] See e.g. Macdonald, "Symbols", *supra* note 12 at 787–88.

[114] Brierley, "Regards", *supra* note 74 at 35–36; Cantin Cumyn & Cumyn, *supra* note 37 passim.

[115] See Part II: § 4 A.I.1, "Patrimony in Roman Law".

[116] Macdonald, "Enforcing Rights I", *supra* note 54 at 575. Cf. Yaëll Emerich, "Faut-il condamner la proprieté des biens incorporels?: Reflexions autour de la proprieté des créances" (2005) 46:4 C de D 905 at 907 [Emerich, "Proprieté des biens incorporels"].

[117] [1921] 2 AC 426 (Can PC) [*Matamajaw*].

[118] See critically Sylvio Normand, "Une relecture de l'arrêt Matamajaw Salmon Club" (1988) 29 C de D 807 [Normand, "Relecture"].

[119] Macdonald, "Enforcing Rights I", *supra* note 54 at 576.

[120] Cf. Gray, *supra* note 10 at 125. We find that a similar distinction was made in the earlier common law, cf. *Saskatchewan Minerals v Keyes* (1971), [1972] SCR 703, 23 DLR (3d) 573, Laskin J [dissenting]: "The language of 'corporeal' and 'incorporeal' does not point up the distinction between the legal interest and its subject-matter. On this distinction, all legal interests are 'incorporeal', and it is only the unconfronted force of a long history that makes it necessary in this case to examine certain institutions of property in the common

"[b]ecause traditional theory collapses the distinction between the right of ownership and the thing owned it follows that only tangible things (corporeals) may be owned, and that ownership is the only corporeal right. Intangibles (rights of action, debts and claims) must be understood merely as various species of rights vesting in their titulary. Again, all lesser rights in (*jus in re aliena*), or in respect of (*jus ad rem*), tangible objects are held to be incorporeal and cannot be owned."[121]

However, this is neither a conceptual trick nor a collapsing of categories, it is a function of the definition of "property." "Property" can be understood to mean not the right itself, but the object of the right.[122] It was and is conceptually possible to distinguish between the absolute right in a thing and the absolute right in that right. The former is "ownership" of the thing, while the latter can be called "title to ownership" or "ownership of ownership." The former is a right in corporeal property, the latter is a right in incorporeal property. However, where ownership is absolute, and only one right of ownership in a thing can exist at any one time, title to ownership is indistinguishable from ownership of the thing itself.

This is different when it comes to lesser real rights. A pledge of corporeal property still has corporeal property as its object. But an absolute right in the pledge is different from the pledge itself. The pledge is valid against the world (which is why the creditor-pledgee's right is "absolute"), but it does not make the pledged property part of the creditor's patrimony. The right the creditor-pledgee enjoys in the pledged thing, on the other hand, does form part of her patrimony. This right is available to the creditor's creditors. Thus, the pledge itself – the right – can be thought of as an item of property; but this was not done under the *CcBC*.

### *2. Property in the Code civil du Québec*

The question of admission of incorporeal property under the *CcQ* is complicated because notwithstanding the broad statement in art 899 *CcQ*, there appear to be provisions in the *CcQ* that follow the classical corporeal approach to ownership. For instance, art 953 *CcQ* gives the owner of property a right to revendicate the property against the possessor. Possession, in turn, is defined as the "exercise in fact" or "having detention."[123] Based on the ambiguous use of the words "property" and "things," Brierley consequently doubts whether the new *CcQ* indeed makes ownership of rights possible.[124]

---

law provinces through an antiquated system of classification and an antiquated terminology."

[121] Macdonald, "Enforcing Rights I", *supra* note 54 at 581.

[122] See Part II: § 4 A.II, "From Patrimonial Rights to Property".

[123] *CcQ*, *supra* note 13, art 921. See Macdonald, "Symbols", *supra* note 12 at 796–97.

[124] Brierley, "Regards", *supra* note 74 at 36.

Brierley's view is supported by an *obiter* remark made by the Court of Appeal of Québec in *Sani Sport inc c Hydro-Québec.*[125] This case revolved around the question whether a real right, a servitude[126] held by Hydro-Québec, reverted to the owner of the property. Hydro-Québec argued that according to art 916(2) *CcQ,* property of the state cannot be appropriated by prescription. The Court of first instance had held that a servitude is immovable property and that the exception of art 916(2) *CcQ* applied.[127]

This decision was based on an analysis that views the process of the extinction of a servitude as one of an acquisition of the servitude by the owner. As a result of the acquisition of the servitude by the owner of the property in which the servitude exists, the servitude – a dismemberment of the right of ownership – is reunited with the right of ownership because they are now held by the same person. In this analysis, a classification of the right of servitude as being itself an item of property is the necessary condition for the possibility of a re-acquisition of said item of property through the process of acquisitive prescription (*i.e.* the acquisition of property by passing of time). This classification, however, would have meant that acquisition should have been barred in the case at hand by the rule against acquisitive prescription of state property in art 916(2) *CcQ.*

The Court of Appeal held that the extinction of a servitude on land is best not described as a (re-)acquisition of the servitude by the owner, but rather as an extinction of a right. Since art 916(2) *CcQ* did not apply, the Court did not need to decide whether a right is property that can be appropriated and thus owned or whether it remains a right that is held. However, Morin JCA wrote that "Il convient donc d'affirmer que l'alinéa 2 de l'article art 916 *CcQ* ne soustrait pas au régime de droit commun de la prescription extinctive les biens de l'État et les droits réels qu'il détient sur ces biens."[128]

Thus, despite the wording of art 899 *CcQ,* the Court drew a distinction between property and real rights in the property which are themselves not property. An alternative view would have been to accept that a lesser real right in property is itself an item of property. Because lesser real rights would then already fall under the wording of art 916(2) *CcQ* (the rule applies to any "property"), this would have made it superfluous to broaden the scope of application of art 916(2) *CcQ* in order to include "property" and "real rights."

### *II. Analysis*

I submit that incorporeal property is not incompatible with the Civil Law notion of patrimony. Ever since the membership of patrimony was opened to

---

[125] *Sani Sport inc c Hydro-Québec*, 2008 QCCA 2498, [2009] RJQ 26.

[126] *CcQ, supra* note 13, art 1177.

[127] *Sani Sport inc c Hydro-Québec, supra* note 125 at para 30.

[128] *Ibid* at para 72, Morin JCA [emphasis added].

ownership rights rather than simply to corporeal things,[129] there has been no principled objection against recognition of ownership in incorporeal movables. The corporeality of the property is not a necessary condition for membership of the property in the class referred to as "patrimony."

The concept of ownership of incorporeal rights conflicts with the absolute nature of ownership envisioned by the first sentence of art 947 *CcQ*. A right is often restricted in transferability and other regards. This speaks for Brierley's view and against the possibility of ownership of rights. However, the second sentence of art 947 *CcQ* allows ownership in different modes,[130] and thus restricts the absolute nature of ownership. One important mode of ownership is inalienable ownership or ownership limited in alienability.[131] Thus, the *CcQ* itself already admits that ownership is not necessarily absolute. Consequently, one can safely assume that the ownership of rights is possible in the *CcQ*.[132]

Ownership of incorporeal property aligns with the general position of the *CcQ* if one considers ownership to be the fundamental real right. The *CcQ* specifically allows for other real rights pertaining to incorporeal property, specifically a hypothec in obligations.[133] Admitting a stronger real right, such as ownership, when the hypothec is already accepted as a real right in incorporeal property is thus not nothing fundamentally new, only something gradually stronger.[134]

The comparison with the hypothec helps to explain the apparent corporeal conception of ownership in the rules on vindication.[135] The case *Caisse populaire Desjardins de Val-Brillant c Blouin*[136] stands for the proposition that in the event of a hypothec in an obligation, *possession utile* is not something that needs to be in the physical realm; rather, it something that can be achieved by enabling a creditor to enforce a claim against a debtor.[137] Thus, possession is not necessarily something in the physical realm. This is acknowledged by Macdonald as well.[138] Thus, ownership of incorporeals can be vindicated as well.

---

[129] See Part II: § 4 A.I, "Patrimony".

[130] Normand, "Modalité", *supra* note 44 passim.

[131] *Ibid* at 262. See also Part II: § 4 G, "Restrictions on Alienability".

[132] Cf. *ibid* at 264–65.

[133] See Part III: § 14 B.IV, "The Object of the Hypothec".

[134] Consistent with his argument, Brierley considers the classification of a hypothec among real rights as problematic precisely because it is possible to hypothecate incorporeal property, see Brierley, "Regards", *supra* note 74 at 41.

[135] See Part II: § 4 H, "Vindication of Property Rights".

[136] *Caisse populaire Desjardins de Val-Brillant c Blouin,* 2003 SCC 31, [2003] 1 SCR 666, 225 DLR (4th) 577, 43 CBR (4th) 36.

[137] See Part III: § 14 B.V.2.b)aa), "The Val-Brillant Decision".

[138] Macdonald, "Symbols", *supra* note 12 at 799: "Article 1592 provides that the detention may be of property, and not just of a thing as under the Civil Code of Lower Canada, with the consequence, once again, that a personal right can generate a real right."

Finally, the acceptance of ownership in incorporeal property as a real right is supported by Québec case law. In *Greenberg c Gruber,*[139] shareholders initiated an action against other shareholders under s 241 *Canada Business Corporations Act.*[140] The *Canada Business Corporations Act* itself does not contain any rules on prescription, so the Court referred to the rules on prescription in the *CcQ* as the *droit commun.*[141] The Court then held that shares give the shareholders ownership in the company,[142] and ownership itself is not subject to prescription, but is instead perpetual.[143]

### *III. Conclusion*

In conclusion, the *CcQ* has led to a new notion of property: property can be either corporeal or incorporeal. Brierley highlights an important consequence of this wide notion of property: understood this way, property and real rights are less concerned with a thing-person relationship and are more seen as a means of protecting economic value.[144] This is noteworthy because, as we will see later, the corrective justice account of unjust enrichment posits that unjust enrichment is the means by which the (Common) Law protects value entitlements.[145] If property rights in Civil Law are concerned with value entitlements as well, there is a coherence between the normative goals of vindication of property rights in Civil Law[146] on the one hand and unjust enrichment in Common Law on the other.

## E. *Numerus Clausus* in Civil Law

Most Civil Law jurisdictions recognize that the class of property rights is a closed class. This is known as the *numerus clausus* of property rights. The *numerus clausus* is also codified in some legal systems.[147] The *numerus*

---

139 (2004), 2004 CanLII 14882 (Queb CA).

140 RSC 1985, c C-44.

141 *Greenberg c Gruber, supra* note 139 at para 25.

142 *Ibid* at paras 35–40.

143 *Ibid* at para 41. For an analysis of the case see also Cantin Cumyn & Cumyn, *supra* note 37 at 145–47.

144 Brierley, "Regards", *supra* note 74 at 48. Cf. Alain A Levasseur, "The Boundaries of Property Rights: La Notion de Biens" (2006) 54 Am J Comp L 145 at 147: "The justification or foundation for this 'legal wrapping' can be found in *one common denominator* which *binds together 'things' and 'ownership';* this common attribute lies in *the monetary or economic value of things and of the right of ownership.*" [Emphasis added].

145 See Part II: § 9 E.I, "Formalist Theory of Unjust Enrichment".

146 See Part II: § 4 H, "Vindication of Property Rights".

147 See e.g. *Code civil des Francais,* art 543 which provides "On peut avoir sur les biens, ou un droit de propriété, ou un simple droit de jouissance, ou seulement *des services fonciers*

*clausus* principle is important because it means that parties are not at total liberty to create property rights at will. This, in turn, means that any attempt by parties to modify the distribution of the debtor's property – her common pledge – in insolvency has to take place within a certain framework. The *numerus clausus* also provides the framework within which non-consensual changes of the distribution of the common pledge take place.

While the old *CcBC* contained a rule similar to art 543 *Code civil des Francais,*[148] the recognition of a *numerus clausus* principle was significantly challenged by the Privy Council's decision in *Matamajaw.*[149] In the decision, the Privy Council seemed to reject the notion of a *numerus clausus* of property rights.[150] The decision challenged both the *numerus clausus* and the Civil Law notion of unitary and indivisible ownership. The case revolved around the question whether a fishing right can be owned separately from the ownership of the river or whether such a right is a mere usufruct. This was important because by virtue of s 479 *CcBC,* a regular usufruct could only be granted for the lifetime of the usufructuary.[151] A real servitude could be granted in perpetuity, but would need to be granted in favour of a dominant. The Privy Council found that the fishing right was not a mere usufruct, but rather a discrete item of property that could be owned separately from the land in perpetuity. In doing so, the Privy Council admitted something that amounted to allowing a split ownership in land.[152] However, the Privy Council did not bother to precisely

---

*à prétendre.*" [Emphasis added] However, doctrine in France does not unequivocally recognize the existence of a numerus clausus; on this and for an overview of the numerus clausus principle in Civil Law see John H Merryman, "Policy, Autonomy, and the Numerus Clausus in Italian and American Property Law" (1963) 12:2 Am J Comp L 224; Bernard Rudden, "Economic Theory v Property Law: The Numerus Clausus Problem" in: John Eekelaar & John Bell, eds, *Oxford Essays in Jurisprudence: Third Series* (Oxford: Clarendon Press, 1987) 239 at 243. For an exposition of the numerus clausus principle in Scotland see e.g. Roderick RM Paisley, "Real Rights: Practical Problems and Dogmatic Rigidity" (2004) 9 Edin L Rev 267.

[148] *Code civil du Bas-Canada,* 29 Vict, c 41, s 405 was slightly different in wording than the French provision: "On peut avoir, sur les biens, ou un droit de propriété, ou un simple droit de jouissance, ou seulement des servitudes à prétendre." [Emphasis added].

[149] *Supra* note 117.

[150] Gray, *supra* note 10 at 143.

[151] A usufruct can still not be granted in perpetuity, see *CcQ, supra* note 13, art 1120.

[152] *Matamajaw, supra* note 117 at 434–35: "In considering which of these diverging sets of opinions is right, their Lordships are impressed with the necessity of bearing in mind that the principles on which the jurisprudence of Quebec with regard to rights in land rests are very different from those which obtain in the common law of England. In the latter country there has always been permitted great latitude in splitting up the title to the fee simple, with important results as regards the right of possession. But in other countries, such as those where the Roman law prevails, and in countries such as Scotland, which has its own system, the fee simple cannot be so freely disintegrated."

explain what this new right was: a split ownership, a perpetual usufruct, or a *sui generis* property right.[153]

It is not self-evident whether the *numerus clausus* principle applies in modern Québec law.[154] The *CcQ* no longer contains an equivalent to s 405 *CcBC*. Instead, art 1119 *CcQ* provides as follows:

"Article 1119 *CcQ*

| | |
|---|---|
| Usufruct, use, servitude and emphyteusis are dismemberments of the right of ownership and are real rights. | L'usufruit, l'usage, la servitude et l'emphytéose sont des démembrements du droit de propriété et constituent des droits réels." |

In the following paragraphs, I analyse doctrinal and judicial voices that argue that the *numerus clausus* opinion is at least not an insurmountable obstacle that prevents the recognition of property rights not codified in the *CcQ* or other specific laws.

### *I. Innominate Principal Property Rights*

In regard to the *CcBC,* Cantin Cumyn argued that the *numerus clausus* principle did not prevent the creation of innominate principal property rights.[155] Parties were not at total liberty to create property rights at will; rather, she argued, s 405 *CcBC* set up a framework for the transfer of innominate property rights.

In this scheme, innominate property rights had to fall into one of two categories: personal servitude or real servitude.[156] There was thus not a closed list of property rights, but rather a closed number of property right categories.[157] Cantin Cumyn argued that because innominate property rights were only possible as dismemberments of property and not as accessory property rights, they would have no impact on third parties. As dismemberments of property, they were transferred in the same way that any property transfer takes place, and thus third parties were sufficiently protected.[158] In regard to movable property, possession would protect the *bona fide* third party purchaser, while the communal-pledge creditor could avail herself of an avoidance action.[159]

Cantin Cumyn showed that there were a number of property rights apart from the numbered list. Their existence was either implicitly assumed in the

---

[153] See Normand, "Relecture", *supra* note 118.

[154] Some authors claim it does. Macdonald, "Symbols", *supra* note 12 at 787 writes "[R]eal rights, in principle, are limited in number." See also Denys-Claude Lamontagne, *Biens et propriété,* 6th edn (Cowansville, Québec: Éditions Yvon Blais, 2009) at 114.

[155] Cantin Cumyn, "Droits réels innommés", *supra* note 76. On principal property rights see Part II: § 4 C.II.1, "Principal Property Rights".

[156] *Ibid* at 39. On the taxonomy of servitudes see see Part II: § 4 C.II.1, "Principal Property Rights".

[157] *Ibid* at 7.

[158] *Ibid* at 29–30.

[159] *Ibid* at 30.

*CcBC,* or they were provided for by other laws, or they were recognized by the courts. Cantin Cumyn recognized that these rights were often re-characterized in order to fit within the scheme of numbered personal servitudes. But she argued that the *numerus clausus* principle had thus become devoid of any normative power; therefore one might do away with it as well.[160]

Brierley argues that in the case of the new *CcQ,* the lack of the definite article in art 1119 *CcQ* means that the *CcQ* has done away with the *numerus clausus* of property rights.[161] Frenette, who claims that the hypothec itself is a dismemberment of ownership, argues that the *CcQ* breaks any *numerus clausus* by providing for the hypothec, which is a dismemberment not listed in art 1119 *CcQ*.[162] On the other hand, the *CcQ* at one point was to contain an express provision allowing further dismemberments of property, but this did not become law.[163]

*II. Restrictive Approach to Innominate Property Rights*

The *numerus clausus* principle was extensively discussed in *Anglo Pacific Group PLC c Ernst & Young inc,*[164] a decision by the Court of Appeal of Québec. In its unanimous decision written by the Chief Justice of Québec, Thibault JCA, the Court accepted that parties can create property rights not listed in the *CcQ* under certain circumstances. In reaching its decision, the Court relied on the framework developed by Cantin Cumyn. However, the Court took a restrictive approach to the admission of innominate property rights.

The case revolved around the question whether a mining company, which later went insolvent, could grant one of its creditors a licence in its mining claim that would amount to a property right in the mined minerals themselves. This is an important distinction to keep in mind: the decision was not concerned with whether the debtor could validly transfer its own claim; rather it was concerned with whether the claim allowed the debtor to grant rights in the object of the claim.

The Court held that an innominate property right is created by a transfer of one of the derivative rights of ownership from transferor to purchaser.[165] The

---

[160] *Ibid* at 27: "Or, il ne parait pas logique de soutenir, d'une part, que les droits réels sont limités à ceux que la loi règlemente et de procéder, d'autre part, à la transformation de la règlementation légale pour accommoder des situations qui n'ont pas été prévues."

[161] *CcQ, supra* note 13, art 1119 provides as follows: "L'usufruit, l'usage, la servitude et l'emphytéose sont des démembrements du droit de propriété et constituent des droits réels." Brierley, "Regards", *supra* note 74 at 37. A similar argument is made by Frenette, "De l'hyopthèque", *supra* note 100 at 807, note 12.

[162] Frenette, "De l'hyopthèque", *supra* note 100 at 807. See Part II: § 4 C.II.2, "Accessory Property Rights".

[163] Cf. Lafond, *supra* note 9 at para 438.

[164] *Supra* note 55.

[165] *Ibid* at paras 57–58, 84.

granting of such an innominate principal property right means that the transfer transfers part of the derivative rights of ownerships.[166] The transferor herself needs to hold a right in the property.[167] This right needs to be a property right and the transferor needs to hold the *jus abutendi* of the property.[168]

The Court's decision in *Anglo Pacific* contained a very important restriction. The Court held that the transferor of a property right herself needs to hold the *jus abutendi* in relation to the property. From a conceptual standpoint, it is interesting to highlight the examples provided by Thibault JCA:

"Le démembrement du droit de la propriété relève de l'exercice de l'abusus qui est lié, comme je l'ai déjà expliqué, au droit de disposer de son bien. Par conséquent, il faut être, en principe, titulaire d'une partie de l'abusus pour consentir à un tiers un droit réel sur un bien. Par exemple, l'emphytéote a le pouvoir de créer une servitude sur le bien faisant l'objet de l'emphytéose. Le titulaire d'un bail minier, qui possède les droits et obligations d'un propriétaire, peut démembrer son droit en faveur d'un tiers pour la durée du bail (puisqu'on ne peut céder plus de droits que ce qu'on a acquis) et lui consentir un droit réel dans les substances minérales que son bail lui permet d'exploiter."[169]

She gave two examples of recognized principal property rights that entailed not only a transfer of the *jus utendi* and *jus fruendi,* but also granted their proprietor a *jus abutendi* not only in the right itself, but also in the object of the right. These rights were the emphyteusis and the leaseholder of a mine.

Madam Chief Justice Thibault then proceeded to determine whether the case of the mining claim is analogous.

"Qu'en est-il du claim? Dans le contexte de la Loi sur les mines, le propriétaire du droit aux substances minérales est l'État. C'est l'État qui démembre son droit de propriété en faveur d'une personne en lui attribuant un claim. Le titulaire de ce claim, qui est un droit réel immobilier distinct, peut-il, à son tour, démembrer sa propriété? [...] Le claim minier confère à son titulaire le droit de se servir du bien et celui de faire de l'exploration pour trouver des gisements. Ces droits sont susceptibles d'être démembrés. En revanche, le titulaire du claim minier n'a pas, à ce stade, un droit sur les substances minérales comme le détenteur du bail minier. Dans ce contexte, les débitrices avaient-elles la capacité de conférer à l'appelante un droit réel sur les substances minérales susceptibles d'être extraites advenant la découverte d'un gisement et l'octroi d'un bail minier?"[170]

That the owner of a mining claim could hold a *jus abutendi* in relation to the mined minerals was not already a function of being the proprietor of the claim. This conclusion was arrived at through analogous reasoning. Madam Chief

---

[166] *Ibid* at para 81, Thibault JCA: "La constitution d'un démembrement de la propriété nécessite un partage des attributs de la propriété, soit l'usus, le fructus ou l'abusus.

[167] *Ibid* at para 60, Thibault JCA.

[168] *Ibid* at para 69, Thibault JCA.

[169] *Ibid* at para 69, Thibault JCA.

[170] *Ibid* at para 70, Thibault JCA.

Justice Thibault argued that the case of a transfer of right in relation to a mining claim is comparable to a hypothec on future property.[171]

"À mon avis, c'est le cas. Même si la loi est muette sur ce sujet précis, j'estime que les principes applicables à l'hypothèque consentie par un non-propriétaire doivent être adaptés à la situation du titulaire du claim qui confère un droit réel sur des substances minérales extraites dont il deviendra propriétaire après l'octroi d'un bail minier. Il faut se rappeler que sous l'emprise du Code civil du Bas-Canada, le droit frappait de nullité l'hypothèque du bien d'autrui sous réserve d'une bonification du titre insuffisant ([s 2043 *CcBC*]). Le Code civil du Québec permet l'hypothèque sur le bien d'autrui ou sur le bien futur, mais il précise que cette sûreté prend effet lorsque le constituant devient propriétaire du bien hypothéqué ([art 2670 *CcQ*])."[172]

The analogy being made between the case of a hypothec on future property and the transfer of the claim is interesting for two reasons. First, it validates Frenette's argument that a hypothec is comparable to other principal property rights. Notionally, the debtor had granted its creditor a right in the mined minerals. Functionally, however, this amounted to a security interest in the mined minerals; because the mined minerals were not yet owned by the debtor, who held a mere expectancy by virtue of its claim, the grant should have only been allowed if a security interest would have been possible as well. This shows that while the list of property rights in the *CcQ* might not be exhaustive, it has a normative force. The Court would not admit an innominate property right which is essentially different from a recognized property right.

Second, the decision also poses a challenge to Cantin Cumyn's argument that the admission of innominate principal property rights only impacts purchasers and has no bearing on creditors. In fact, the decision showed how the transfer of an innominate property right can be used as a security interest. Because the innominate property right impacts third-party creditors, the Court was right in relying on the provisions of the *CcQ* regarding the hypothec in determining whether the parties could create such a security interest.

### *III. The Addressee of the Numerus Clausus Principle*

The difficulty with the argument against the *numerus clausus* put forward by Frenette and Cantin Cumyn is that they are based on a narrow understanding of *numerus clausus*. Frenette argues that any *numerus clausus* contained in art 1119 *CcQ* cannot be upheld because the *CcQ* itself adds the hypothec to this list. This resembles an alleged truism sometimes heard from Common Law scholars that a Civil Law system in general and its *numerus clausus* in particular are distinguished by the notion that neither parties nor courts may create a new type of property because this would contradict the code's status as the

---

[171] See Part III: § 14 B.IV, "The Object of the Hypothec".

[172] *Anglo Pacific, supra* note 55 at para 71, Thibault JCA.

exclusive source of legal obligation.[173] Cantin Cumyn makes her argument based on the implicit admission of property rights in statutes and by courts. However, it is possible to conceptualize the *numerus clausus* differently: the *numerus clausus* restricts the class of property rights and defines the members of this class by reference to certain characteristics,[174] but the *numerus clausus* only protects against the addition of members to the class by individual parties. Thus, it is not a breach of the *numerus clausus* principle if members are added to the class by the law or the courts.[175]

In conclusion, it can be said that the Civil Law of Québec recognizes a *numerus clausus* principle, but it does not do so strictly. A property transaction is not void simply because it does not conform strictly to the set of rules on property rights contained in the *CcQ*. Rather, parties can engage in property transactions and create innominate property rights as long as they conform to certain characteristics and principles regarding property rights provided for in the *CcQ* or in another statute.

## F. Acquisition of Ownership in Civil Law

Acquisition of ownership takes place through either derivative acquisition or original acquisition. "Derivative acquisition" means that the new owner acquires ownership by means of a transfer from a previous owner. "Original acquisition," on the other hand, means that ownership is created anew.[176] Derivative acquisition can also occur by way of inheritance where the acquirer is heir to the deceased. I will describe derivative acquisition of ownership between two living parties because it is here that we find challenges to the traditional Civil Law notion of ownership.

The *inter vivos* transfer of property in Québec law follows the principle of "consensualism." In this regard, Québec law differs from Roman law and follows an innovation introduced by French law. Nevertheless, the principle of consensualism resurrects a notion that existed under classical Roman law but was abolished during Justinian's reign: relativity of ownership.

---

[173] See e.g. Thomas W Merrill & Henry E Smith, "Optimal Standardization in the Law of Property: The Numerus Clausus Principle" (2000) 110:1 Yale LJ 1 at 9–10.

[174] See Jens T Füller, *Eigenständiges Sachenrecht?* (Jus Privatum, Tübingen: Mohr Siebeck, 2006) at 371–73.

[175] See Jan Jakob Bornheim, "Die Wirkung relativer dinglicher Rechte nach deutschem internationalen Sachenrecht" (2015) 79:1 RabelsZ 36 at 64–65 [Bornheim, "Relative dingliche Rechte"].

[176] Philippe Malaurie & Laurent Aynès, *Les biens,* 4th edn (Paris: Defrénois, 2010) at 551.

*I. Inter Vivos Transfer of Property in Roman Law*

The *inter vivos* transfer of ownership in Québec law differs from the traditional Roman law approach. In classical Roman Law, transfer of property was formalized. Depending on the property in question, ownership was transferred either by *mancipatio* or by *in iure cessio. In iure cessio* was done in the presence of a Roman praetor.[177] *Mancipatio* was done in the presence of five witnesses and a balance holder (*i.e.* a sixth person). The purchaser declared that he received ownership of the property and offered a symbolic bronze coin to the vendor in return. Only Romans could mancipate property.[178] Purchase by way of *mancipatio* was only possible in regard to certain property, which was called *res mancipi.*[179]

Aside from these two forms of transfer, transfer was possible by way of *traditio. Traditio* effected transfer of ownership by delivery of the property. Both mancipable and immancipable goods could be transferred through *traditio.* However, where mancipable goods were transferred by way of *traditio,* the vendor retained "Quiritian" title. The notion of Quiritan title refers to the fact that two systems of law operated concurrently in classical Roman law: Quiritian law – the law peculiar to the Romans – and Praetorian law – the supplementing general law. When mancipable property was transferred, the Quiritian title stayed with the vendor until a period of acquisitive prescription expired.[180] During that time, the vendor could vindicate the property against everybody with the exception of the purchaser; the purchaser was protected against an action by the vendor by an exception.[181] In a way, the purchaser's title could be classified as a form of "relative ownership."[182] As long as the vendor retained Quiritian title, the purchaser's right of ownership was not absolute. Only after the period of acquisitive prescription (*usucapio*) lapsed were Quiritian and Praetorian title reunited. However, the acquisition of full title was a function of the Quiritian *usucapio,* not of the Praetorian *traditio.*[183] The purchaser thus acquired a genuine original right; this was not a case of derivative

[177] G 1.24.

[178] *Ibid* 2.119.

[179] Henri Brun, "Les origines du consensualisme en matière de transfert de proprieté et des mitigations apportées au principe par le droit civil québecois" (1967–1968) 9:2 C de D 273 at 275.

[180] Eltjo JH Schrage, "Notes on the Transfer of Property: Modus et Titulus Dominii Transferendi" (1992) 1 *Fundamina* 91 at 102–5.

[181] *Ibid* at 105.

[182] Cf. Armand-Edmond Bouvier-Bangillon, *De la tradition considérée comme mode translatif de propriété en droit romain et dans l'ancien droit français* (Paris: F Pichon, 1877) at 208. See also Peter Birks, "The Roman Law Concept of Dominium and the Idea of Absolute Ownership" (1985) 1 AJ 1 at 29–31.

[183] See August Bechmann, "Zur Lehre von der usucapio pro emtore" (1889) 75:2 AcP 281; David LC Miller, "Derivative Acquisition of Movables" in: Robin Evans-Jones, ed, *The*

acquisition.[184] De Visscher argued that it was the main purpose of *usucapio* to enable the acquisition of full ownership in mancipable goods by way of *traditio.*[185]

In Roman law, a contract of sale created the obligation to deliver the property free of any claims that would require the purchaser to part with possession again.[186] The contract itself did not result in a transfer of ownership, nor was that one of the obligations created by a sales contract.[187] Rather, transfer of ownership was achieved by one of the above-mentioned mechanisms, most often as a result of delivery. Nevertheless, acquisition of ownership being a function of *usucapio,* not of delivery itself, delivery was only seen as a means of gaining a relative title, not as a means of gaining absolute ownership.[188]

During Justinian's reign, any reference in the *Corpus Iuris Civilis* to *mancipatio* was replaced by *traditio.*[189] This led to the adoption of the rule *traditionibus et usucapionibus, non nudis pactis dominia rerum transferuntur* ("property is transferred by tradition or prescription, not by mere contract"). This necessarily resulted in an abolition of the relative title of Praetorian law. This was part of a wider trend: at the same time, Justinian abolished the fiction that land outside of Italy was subject of the empire's *dominium,* resulting in the absolute ownership of these lands for the first time.[190]

Pre-revolutionary France followed the traditional approach to the transfer of property.[191] The same applies to Québec before the adoption of the *CcBC,*[192] to Louisiana before its adoption of a number of rules from the *Code civil des*

---

*Civil Law Tradition in Scotland* (Edinburgh: Stair Society, 1995) 128 at 138; Reuven Yaron, "Reflections on usucapio" (1967) 35:2 *Tijdschrift voor Rechtsgeschiedenis* 191 at 192.

184 Brun, *supra* note 179 at 275.

185 See Fernand de Visscher, "Auctoritas et Mancipio" (1956) 22 SDHI 87 at 98 and Fernand de Visscher, "Dualismo ed evoluzione della proprietà nella Roma repubblicana" (1957) 23 SDHI 26 at 28. But see Yaron, *supra* note 183 passim.

186 Robert L Theriot, "An Examination of the Role of Delivery in the Transfer of Ownership and Risk in Sales under Louisiana Law" (1985–1986) 60:5 Tul L Rev 1035 at 1043.

187 See Jan D Harke, *Besonderes Schuldrecht* (Berlin: Springer, 2011) at 10.

188 *Ibid* at 11.

189 Jan Hallebeek, "Transfer of Ownership: Traditionalism or Consensualism?" (2004) 45:1 *Codicillus* 6 at 8.

190 Birks, "The Roman Law Concept of Dominium and the Idea of Absolute Ownership", *supra* note 182 at 8–9.

191 Brun, *supra* note 179 at 273.

192 *Ibid* at 273.

*Francais,*[193] and to Scotland.[194] In Scotland, the traditional approach was partially replaced by the adoption of the Britain-wide *Sale of Goods Act, 1893,*[195] which follows a consensual approach.[196]

### *II. The Shift to Consensualism in French Law*

In pre-revolutionary France, sales contracts on immovables often contained a clause that deemed *traditio* to have taken place; this resulted in a de facto transfer of property through contract alone.[197] With the introduction of the *Code civil des Francais,* the mode of transfer of ownership changed. The transfer of property through transfer rather than delivery was no longer a mere practice; rather, it became the legal standard. This is known as "consensualism." In the *Code civil des Francais,* consensualism in sales of movables finds is defined in art 1583 *Code civil des Francais.*

"Article 1583 *Code civil des Francais*

[La vente] est parfaite entre les parties, et la propriété est acquise de droit à l'acheteur à l'égard du vendeur, dès qu'on est convenu de la chose et du prix, quoique la chose n'ait pas encore été livrée ni le prix payé."

Notwithstanding the fact that ownership passes from vendor to purchases, a third party can still acquire ownership if the property is delivered to her first.[198] The acquisition of ownership by the third party is not a passing of title from vendor to third party, but an original acquisition of ownership by the third party by means of immediate acquisitive prescription.[199]

---

[193] Theriot, *supra* note 186 at 1044.

[194] Miller, "Derivative Acquisition of Movables", *supra* note 183 at 130; Gordon Pugh, "Traditio in the Civil Law" (1962) 22:2 La L Rev 418 at 427–28.

[195] 56 & 57 Vict. See Pugh, preceding note at 428.

[196] See Part II: § 5 E.I, "Inter Vivos Transfer of Property in Common Law".

[197] See Eltjo JH Schrage, "Traditionibus et usucapionibus, non nudis pactis dominia rerum transferuntur: Die Wahl zwischen dem Konsens- und dem Traditionsprinzip in der Geschichte" in: Mario Ascheri, ed, *Ins Wasser geworfen und Ozeane durchquert: Festschrift für Knut Wolfgang Nörr* (Cologne: Böhlau, 2003) 913 at 913–14; Theriot, *supra* note 186 at 1043.

[198] *Code civil des Francais, supra* note 147, art 1141.

[199] See Sylvan J Steinberg (1955–1956) 30:1 Tul L Rev 153 at 154. Cf. Michael Scott, "Conversion and Revendication" (1961) 5:1 Mal L Rev 40 at 47. Stagl takes a similar position regarding German law on bona fide acquisition of ownership, see Jakob F Stagl, "Gutgläubiger Fahrniserwerb als „sofortige Ersitzung": Eine Neubestimmung der §§ 932 ff. BGB" (2011) 211:3–4 AcP 530.

### *III. Consensualism in Québec Law*

Modern Québec has the consensualism principle in common with French law.[200] Delivery is not a mode of transfer of property. The modes of acquisition of ownership are listed in art 916(1) *CcQ*.

"Article 916 *CcQ*

| | |
|---|---|
| (1) Property is acquired by contract, succession, occupation, prescription, accession or any other mode provided by law. | (1) Les biens s'acquièrent par contrat, par succession, par occupation, par prescription, par accession ou par tout autre mode prévu par la loi. |
| (2) [1]No one may appropriate property of the State for himself by occupation, prescription or accession except property the State has acquired by succession, vacancy or confiscation, so long as it has not been mingled with its other property. [2]Nor may anyone acquire for himself property of legal persons established in the public interest that is appropriated to public utility. | (2) [1]Cependant, nul ne peut s'approprier par occupation, prescription ou accession les biens de l'État, sauf ceux que ce dernier a acquis par succession, vacance ou confiscation, tant qu'ils n'ont pas été confondus avec ses autres biens. [2]Nul ne peut non plus s'approprier les biens des personnes morales de droit public qui sont affectés à l'utilité publique." |

In the area of sales contracts, art 1453 *CcQ* provides that contract transfers ownership. Unlike in French law, the second buyer is protected not by instantaneous prescription, but by a special rule. art 1454 *CcQ* protects the *bona fide* second purchaser who gains possession first, but this is not a case of the general *possession vaut titre* rule present in French law.[201]

The consensual transfer of property challenges the absolute notion of ownership. Gawkerere writes that "un véritable droit de propriété, au sens classique de la notion, n'est possible qu'après l'exécution complète des obligations des parties."[202]

## G. Restrictions on Alienability

Not all property is freely transferable. Sometimes, the law allows certain property to be inalienable. The general rule is found in art 1212 *CcQ:*

---

[200] See Jean P Gawkerere, "Que reste-t-il du transfert consensuel de la propriété des biens meubles en droit canadien?: Considérations sur la codification d'un principe dans un système bijuridique" (2005) 46:3 C de D 671 at 674.

[201] *Ibid* at 699.

[202] *Ibid* at 712.

"Article 1212 *CcQ*

(1) A restriction on the exercise of the right to dispose of property may only be stipulated by gift or will.

(2) A stipulation of inalienability is made in writing at the time of transfer of ownership of the property or a dismemberment of the right of ownership in it to a person or to a trust.

(3) [1]The stipulation of inalienability is valid only if it is temporary and justified by a serious and legitimate interest. [2]Nevertheless, it may be valid for the duration of a substitution or trust.

(1) La restriction à l'exercice du droit de disposer d'un bien ne peut être stipulée que par donation ou testament.

(2) La stipulation d'inaliénabilité est faite par écrit à l'occasion du transfert, à une personne ou à une fiducie, de la propriété d'un bien ou d'un démembrement du droit de propriété sur un bien.

(3) [1]Cette stipulation n'est valide que si elle est temporaire et justifiée par un intérêt sérieux et légitime. [2]Néanmoins, dans le cas d'une substitution ou d'une fiducie, elle peut valoir pour leur durée."

The provision appears to exclude all stipulations of inalienability made outside of the context of gifts or wills.[203] In the *CcBC,* s 970 *CcBC* prohibited any stipulation of inalienability in a property transfer for value. Article 1212 *CcQ,* on the other hand, entails not just stipulations of inalienability but also any "restriction on the exercise of the right" in any transfer that is neither a gift nor made by will.[204]

### *I. History*

In Roman law, a stipulation of inalienability was thought to be invalid, while in France during the *Ançien régime,* such stipulations were frequently employed by noble families and deemed valid.[205] After the enactment of the *Code civil des Francais* in France, there was no consensus on whether the new code outlawed stipulations of inalienability or not.[206] While courts were initially reluctant to uphold such stipulations, they soon began to uphold them in certain

---

[203] Michelle Cumyn, "Les restrictions à la liberté d'aliéner dans le Code civil du Québec" (1994) 39:4 McGill LJ 877 at 878–79.

[204] *Ibid* at 879.

[205] *Ibid* at 883–87. In fact, the desire to minimize the existence of private property held in semi-feudal tenure (fideicommissum) is one of the ratios behind the prohibition against restrictions on alienability in Germany, see Bornheim, "Relative dingliche Rechte", *supra* note 175 at 61; Jürgen Kohler in: Julius von Staudinger, *Kommentar zum Bürgerlichen Gesetzbuch mit Einführungsgesetz und Nebengesetzen, Buch 1. Allgemeiner Teil, §§ 134–138, Anh zu § 138: ProstG,* ed by Norbert Habermann (Berlin: Sellier-de Gruyter, 2011) § 137 BGB at para 7; Wolfram Timm, "Außenwirkungen vertraglicher Verfügungsverbote?" (1989) 44:1 JZ 13 at 17.

[206] *Code civil des Francais, supra* note 147, art 1598 provides: "Tout ce qui est dans le commerce, peut être vendu lorsque des lois particulières n'en ont pas prohibé l'aliénation." Cf. Cumyn, *supra* note 203 at 884.

instances. Notionally, this was supposed to be the exception, but the ratio allowing one to identify a clear pattern for when such an exception was warranted was not made explicit in the case law. This lead to doctrinal criticism. While some authors argued that the stipulations should be void as a matter of principle, Demolombe submitted they should be upheld if they are finite, in relation to a certain person, and justified by a serious reason.[207] He also identified two different ways in which a clause could operate: it either restricts a person's capacity to transfer the property, or it affects the property itself.[208] Bartin drew a different distinction: stipulations affecting the property itself and stipulations binding the parties only. The former were invalid, the latter were allowed.[209]

In Québec, the courts interpreted s 970 *CcBC* rather narrowly and allowed stipulations of inalienability outside of transfers of ownership for value. On the other hand, they upheld them in other transfers of property rights, even where the transfer was for value. One example is hypothecs.[210]

### *II. Purpose*

A stipulation of inalienability automatically removes the property from the common pledge; the property is thus no longer available to satisfy creditors trying to enforce a judgment.[211] This is seen as a necessary consequence of inalienability. Cumyn argues that if inalienable property could be seised in execution, it would not, in fact, be inalienable. If inalienable property were seisable, it would lose its third-party effect (so her argument goes) and since pure personal obligations to not transfer a property without third-party effect are generally valid,[212] there would thus be no reason to maintain a rule against restrictions on alienability.[213]

However, if we look at other Civil Law jurisdictions, we find that a rule against inalienability can be explained by reasons other than the protection of the common pledge. One of these reasons is the protection of the *numerus*

---

[207] Jean CF Demolombe, *Traité des donations entre-vifs et des testaments,* 1st edn (Cours de Code Napoléon, Paris: A Durand & L Hachette, 1861) at 294.

[208] *Ibid* at 291.

[209] Cf. Cumyn, *supra* note 203 at 884–85. This is in fact the solution adopted in Germany by *Bürgerliches Gesetzbuch,* s 137.

[210] Cumyn, *supra* note 203 at 888.

[211] *Ibid* at 879. The nexus of alienability and communal pledge exists in other Civil Law jursidictions as well, see Eberhard Wagner, "Rechtsgeschäftliche Unübertragbarkeit und § 137 S. 1 BGB" (1994) 194 AcP 451 at 472 and Rüdiger Liebs, "Die unbeschränkbare Verfügungsbefugnis" (1975) 175 AcP 1 (Germany).

[212] Cumyn, *supra* note 203 at 899.

[213] *Ibid* at 890.

*clausus.*[214] Furthermore, even if inalienable property were seisable, it would still not be transferable. A stipulation of inalienability removes the property from general commerce; it becomes *res extra commercium.*[215] Nevertheless, art 1215 *CcQ* clearly expresses that inalienable property does not form part of the common pledge.

### *III. Requirements*

Article 1212 *CcQ* contains three requirements: the stipulation needs to be made in writing, it needs to be temporary, and it needs to be "justified by a serious and legitimate interest." The first two elements are self-explanatory. In regard to what constitutes a sufficient interest, Cumyn submits there are three classes of reasons. In the first class, somebody could have an interest in a specific item of property, and it is this interest that needs to be protected. Examples include the interest of the last heir in the event of a hereditary substitution, or the interest of the beneficiary of a usufruct. The second class concerns the protection of the recipient of the property, who is to be protected against her inexperience. The third class is composed of reasons relating to the transferor's moral interest in not seeing the property that is being re-transferred right away.

### *IV. Consequence*

Aside from removing the property from the common pledge, a transfer violating a valid restriction on alienability is also relatively void. This means that the person bound by it can demand that the transfer be reversed.[216] At the same time, the voidness can also be invoked by the original transferor of the property who stipulated the restriction or a third party benefitting from it (for example, the holder of the right of the usufruct that is being protected).[217]

## H. Vindication of Property Rights

### *I. Principle*

In Civil Law property law, being the owner of a thing gives a person the right to demand specific restitution of the property if it is in the possession of another

---

[214] See BGH, 5 December 1996, V ZB 27/96, BGHZ 134, 182, NJW 1997, 861; Bornheim, "Relative dingliche Rechte", *supra* note 175 at 61–62; Kohler in: von Staudinger, *supra* note 205, § 137 BGB at para 7; Timm, *supra* note 205 at 16.

[215] Cumyn, *supra* note 203 at 881.

[216] *CcQ, supra* note 13, art 14201 1422.

[217] *Ibid,* art 1217.

who has no right to possession; this is known as the action to vindicate.[218] The reverse is true as well. Not only does a property right entitle to the protection of possession, but also is this protection of possession generally concerned with the protection of property rights.[219] This is a function of the exclusive nature of ownership, the fundamental property right.[220]

The right to revendicate was absent in early French law. The owner of property could demand recovery in criminal action. The right to revendicate was introduced in French law with the reception of Roman law.[221] In the *CcQ*, the right to vindicate immovable and movable property is a special form of the general right to have one's ownership right recognized and affirmed by the courts.[222] The right to vindicate is found in art 953 *CcQ*. The burden of proof when establishing an action to vindicate against a possessor rests on the owner. If the owner cannot establish her ownership, the possessor will prevail by virtue of being in possession.[223]

*II. Vindication of Incorporeal Property*

An important function of the notion of property and the notion of possession in the *CcQ* is that it is possible to revendicate incorporeal property such as accounts and other debts. This has been pointed out by Emerich.[224] She arrived at that conclusion without reference to the decision in *Caisse populaire Desjardins de Val-Brillant c Blouin*[225] by the Supreme Court of Canada. I would add, however, that the broadened notion of possession and control introduced by the Supreme Court in that case emphasizes that incorporeal property can be detained by third parties, making them liable in a vindication action.[226] It is important to note that in cases of accounts or other monies owed, the vindication will often include a case of subrogation; the debtor of the vindication action will often be unable to transfer the debt in specie or she will have changed the nature of the debt (for instance because monies have been mixed in her bank account). In that case, she owes an equivalent sum.[227]

---

[218] See for an analysis of the development of the right to vindication in Québec before the new Code civil Macdonald, "Enforcing Rights I", *supra* note 54 and Roderick A Macdonald, "Enforcing Rights in Corporeal Moveables: Revendication and Its Surrogates (Part 2)" (1986) 32:1 McGill LJ 1.

[219] Macdonald, "Enforcing Rights I", *supra* note 54 at 585.

[220] *Ibid* at 590.

[221] Scott, *supra* note 199 at 41–42.

[222] The latter is found in *CcQ, supra* note 13, art 912. See Lafond, *supra* note 9 at para 1195.

[223] Lafond, *supra* note 9 at para 609.

[224] Emerich, "Proprieté des biens incorporels", *supra* note 116 at 933–38.

[225] *Supra* note 136.

[226] See Part III: § 14 B.V.2.b)aa), "The Val-Brillant Decision".

[227] Emerich, "Proprieté des biens incorporels", *supra* note 116 at 934.

*III. Vindication of Property Held by Bankrupt Parties*

The right of vindication is a strong right for the owner. In *Transport international pool inc c St-Georges, Hébert Inc,*[228] Transport International Pool (TIP) loaned three trailers, registered in Ontario, to the defendant, St-Georges, Hébert Inc. on a long-term lease without registering the lease in accordance with art 1852 *CcQ*. According to art 1852 *CcQ,* long-term leases need to be registered in order to be effective against third parties. Subsequently, St-Georges went bankrupt. The trustee denied TIP's claim to the trailers because the long-term lease was not registered. The Court held that this did not exclude TIP's right to vindication because this right is an outflow of the Civil Law concept of ownership: "Or, c'est ce droit de propriété qui permet au locateur de reprendre son bien à la fin du bail, conformément à l'article 953 du Code civil du Québec. Ce droit de reprise, qui est un accessoire du droit de propriété, n'est pas non plus assujetti à la publicité."[229]

*IV. Assignability of the Right to Vindicate*

The question whether the action to revendicate can be assigned remains. Historically, the action to revendicate was assignable in a Civil Law system that was based on actions, not substantive rights.[230] In *Sauvé c Guildhall Insurance Co,*[231] the Court of Queen's Bench for Québec held that the subrogatee can revendicate as the successor to the original owner. The Superior Court later used this case as support for the ability of the assignee to revendicate in lieu of the owner.[232] This result was accepted in doctrine for the *CcBC.*[233]

But the reasoning of the Court in *Wawanesa Mutual Ins Co c Plante* is open to challenge. Subrogatee and assignee differ in that the former is the successor of all rights of the original owner, including ownership, while the latter only

---

[228] *Transport international pool inc c St-Georges, Hébert Inc*, 2005 QCCA 28, [2005] RJQ 374, 17 CBR (5th) 197.

[229] *Transport international pool inc c St-Georges, Hébert Inc,* preceding note at paras 31, 40, Morin JCA.

[230] Karl H Neumayer, "Die sogenannte Vindikationszession (§ 931 BGB) im dogmatischen Spannungsfeld zwischen Übereignung und procuratio in rem" in: Kurt Kuchinke, ed, *Rechtsbewahrung und Rechtsentwicklung: Festschrift für Heinrich Lange zum 70. Geburtstag, 25. März 1970* (Munich: CH Beck, 1970) 305 at 317; Jürgen Oechsler in: *Münchener Kommentar zum Bürgerlichen Gesetzbuch, vol 6, §§ 854–1296 BGB, WEG, ErbbauRG,* ed by Kurt Rebmann; Franz-Jürgen Säcker; and Roland Rixecker, 6th ed (Munich: CH Beck, 2013) § 929–936, Anh, BGB at para 11; Wolfgang Wiegand in: Julius von Staudinger, *Kommentar zum Bürgerlichen Gesetzbuch mit Einführungsgesetz und Nebengesetzen, Buch 3. Sachenrecht, §§ 925–984; Anh zu §§ 929 ff (Eigentum 2),* ed by Karl-Heinz Gursky (Berlin: Sellier-de Gruyter, 2011) § 931 BGB at para 15.

[231] [1961] BR 733.

[232] See *Wawanesa Mutual Ins Co c Plante,* [1967] CS 540.

[233] See Macdonald, "Enforcing Rights I", *supra* note 54 at 625, note 211.

receives certain rights. *Sauvé c Guildhall Insurance Co* could thus not be relied upon as authority for the case of assignment.

Furthermore, it should be noted that the *CcBC* did not include an equivalent to art 953 *CcQ.*[234] Article 953 *CcQ,* in turn, specifies that the right to revendicate is the *owner's* right. Thus, the right-holder must fulfill the personal condition of being the owner. In conclusion, because of the wording of the new art 953 *CcQ,* the right to vindicate should not be considered to be assignable.

Furthermore, it should be noted that even though the right to vindicate was assignable in traditional Civil Law, it was never sufficient to constitute delivery for the purpose of a transfer of possession.[235] Improvements

The good faith possessor of property can defend herself against a vindication claim by demanding that she be reimbursed for expenses that have led to an improvement of the property.[236] This right of the *bona fide* possessor was already recognized in Roman law.[237] It is conceptually similar to credit securities: it secures the possessor's right to reimbursement for improvements by giving her a right in property.[238]

## I. Possession in Civil Law

### *I. The Notion of Possession*

In Civil Law, possession is a question of fact, not a question of law.[239] Possession is defined by two elements: *corpus* and *animus.* Corpus is the actual control of the thing. It is often defined as physical control of a corporeal,[240] but this seems hardly sustainable in the wake of the Supreme Court's decision in *Val-Brillant.*[241] In *Val-Brillant,* the Court held that incorporeals can be delivered and that delivery means being put in possession.[242] *Animus* is the state of mind of the possessor. The possessor has animus if she exercises control by

---

[234] *Ibid* at 611.

[235] Miller, "Derivative Acquisition of Movables", *supra* note 183 at 150. Cf. Fabian Klinck, *Erwerb durch Übergabe an Dritte nach klassischem römischen Recht* (Berlin: Duncker & Humblot, 2004) passim, in particular at 356–358. Cf. Oechsler in: *MüKo-BGB, supra* note 230, § 929–936, Anh., BGB at para 11; Wiegand in: von Staudinger, *supra* note 230, § 931 BGB at para 15.

[236] *CcQ, supra* note 13, art 963 (immovables) and art 974 (movables).

[237] Andrew JM Steven, "Rights in Security over Moveables" in: Reid & Zimmermann, eds, *A History of Private Law in Scotland, supra* note 67, 333 at 350.

[238] *Ibid* treats the right of retention in the context of security interests.

[239] Lafond, *supra* note 9 at para 507.

[240] *Ibid* at para 514.

[241] *Supra* note 136.

[242] See Part III: § 14 B.V.2.b)aa), "The Val-Brillant Decision".

virtue of deeming herself either the owner of the thing or of a lesser real right in relation to that thing.[243]

The inclusion of the animus element of possession can be traced back to Savigny's work on possession, which influenced the Québec legislature.[244] Savigny claimed that protection of possession required an element of exercising one's will.[245] On the other side of the debate, Jhering argued that mere detention is enough to constitute possession.[246]

In Civil Law a possessor enjoys a number of rights. Among them are a presumption of ownership, the right to undertake conservatory acts (*i.e.* the possessor can prevent others from interfering with the property),[247] the right to reimbursement of certain expenses from the true owner,[248] and, in some cases, the right to enjoy fruits and revenues.[249]

### *II. Acquisitive Prescription Through Possession*

In certain circumstances, possession can become full ownership by way of "acquisitive prescription."[250] This makes it important to distinguish between possession and detention.[251]

---

[243] Lafond, *supra* note 9 at para 521.

[244] Yaëll Emerich, "Why Protect Possession?" in: Eric Descheemaeker, ed, *The Consequences of Possession* (Edinburgh: Edinburgh University Press, 2014) 30 at 38–39 [Emerich, "Possession"].

[245] Friedrich C von Savigny, *Das Recht des Besitzes,* ed by Adolf Friedrich Rudorff, 7th edn (Wien: Carl Gerold's Sohn, 1865).

[246] Rudolf von Jhering, *Der Besitzwille* (Jena: Gustav Fischer, 1889).

[247] See Part II: § 4 I.III, "The Possessory Action".

[248] See David Lametti & Audrey E Boctor, "Rewarding Ownership, Valuing Possessors: Making Sense of Articles 957–962 of the C.C.Q" in: Normand, ed, *Mélanges Offerts Au Professeur François Frenette, supra* note 37, 151.

[249] Lafond, *supra* note 9 at para 596; Michael H Lubetsky, "Adding Epicycles: The Inconsistent Use Test in Adverse Possession Law" (2009) 47 OHLJ 497 at 502.

[250] On acquisitive prescription see Lafond, *supra* note 9 at paras 2481–660; Lubetsky, preceding note.

[251] Macdonald, "Enforcing Rights I", *supra* note 54 at 592.

*III. The Possessory Action*

The action of vindication by the owner is different from the Civil Law action of *spuilzie* or the *actio spolii.*[252] This is an action by a person who is dispossessed against her will,[253] and requires no title.[254] The *actio spolii* is found in art 929 *CcQ,* according to which a possessor who has had possession in good faith[255] for more than a year "has a right of action against any person who disturbs his possession or dispossesses him in order to put an end to the disturbance or be put back into possession."

The wording of art 929 *CcQ* does not limit the action to immovable property. Case law indicates that the action should be restricted to immovable property,[256] but there is no convincing reason why that should be the case.[257] Emerich argues that in French law, the lack of possessory claims in regard to movable property are a function of the rule *la possession vaut titre* which benefits the dispossessor, but the same rule does not exist in Québec law.[258] If the possessory action is not limited to immovables, it would follow that it can be brought to recover debts as well.[259]

There are two competing accounts for the protection of possession in Civil Law, which were already implied by Savigny. The first is that possessory actions either protect society and the state's monopoly on violence or they protect the possessor.[260] The second account concedes that possession in itself is not a

[252] See for a historic account of the development of the possessory action in French law James Gordley & Ugo Mattei, "Protecting Possession" (1996) 44 Am J Comp L 293 at 312–18. See on the relationship between the two names Caterina Raffaele, "Concepts and Remedies in the Law of Possession" (2004) 8 Edin L Rev 267 at 270.

[253] Reid, "Property Law", *supra* note 67 at 210–16.

[254] *Ibid* at 213.

[255] *CcQ, supra* note 13, art 922 and art 927.

[256] Emerich, "Possession", *supra* note 244 at 49, referring to *Québec (Sous-Ministre du revenu) c Propriété Métro Industriel Inc,* [1999] JQ No 920 (Sup Ct).

[257] Lafond, *supra* note 9 at para 613.

[258] Emerich, "Possession", *supra* note 244 at 49–51.

[259] Cf. Emerich, "Proprieté des biens incorporels", *supra* note 116 at 933, note 119. See Part II: § 4 H.II, "Vindication of Incorporeal Property".

[260] Von Savigny, *Das Recht des Besitzes, supra* note 245 at 56: "In der Mitte zwischen diesen äussersten Fällen liegt der Fall da die der Person zugefügte Gewalt zugleich einen Besitz stört oder entzieht. Ein selbstständiges Recht ist in diesem Fall nicht neben der Person verletzt, aber in dem Zustand der Person ist doch etwas verändert zu ihrem Nachtheil, und soll das Unrecht, welches in der Gewalt gegen die Person liegt, in seinen Folgen gänzlich ausgetilgt werden, so kann dieses nur geschehen durch die Herstellung oder Beschützung jenes factischen Zustandes, worauf sich die Gewalt erstreckt hat." See Gordley & Mattei, *supra* note 252 at 296: "[This] suggests two rather different explanations for the protection of possession, each of which had its champions among the German jurists. According to the

right worthy of protection, but deems it an expression of the possessor's will. Protection of possession is thus a protection of a person's autonomy.[261] The accounts implicit in Savigny's writing are still identified as the basis for possessory protection in Québec law today.[262] Importantly, Savigny also strongly argued that possessory actions could not be explained as preliminary vindications;[263] in other words, the *raison d'être* for the possessory action can not be found in the presumption of ownership associated with possession.

The latter point might explain why Québec civil law used to contain an explicit rule against raising both the possessory action (*spuilzie*) and the petitory action (vindication) in s 772 *Code de procedure civile.*[264] The statutory rule itself was abolished, leading to a debate whether possessory and petitory action can now be combined in one proceeding.[265]

---

first, the law protects the peace and order of society against unlawfulness and force. According to the second, the law protects the victim himself." Emerich, "Possession", *supra* note 244 at 31 adopts both.

[261] Gordley & Mattei, *supra* note 252 at 296–97.

[262] Lafond, *supra* note 9 at paras 588–89.

[263] Von Savigny, *Das Recht des Besitzes, supra* note 245 at 54–57.

[264] RSQ, c C-25.

[265] Cf. Emerich, "Possession", *supra* note 244 at 53–54. Pro Lafond, *supra* note 9 at para 1203.

# § 5 Property at Common Law

The reader might be curious as to why the title of this chapter uses a different preposition than the title of the preceding chapter.[1] The reason is the Common Law's dual nature. This chapter is foremost concerned with property rights at law. The modification of common law property principles by equity will be looked at in more detail in the next chapter.[2]

The notion of patrimony is unknown to the Common Law.[3] Thus, this chapter follows a very different structure than the preceding one. The notion of property and also the notion of personal property in Common Law is very much a function of the development of a set of rules relating to personal property. These rules have developed over centuries after the Norman invasion of England. It is impossible to understand the diffuse notion of personal property in modern Common Law before first looking at the genesis of these common law rules. The reader will notice that this chapter makes more use of the past tense than the preceding chapter on Civil Law property.

## A. Personal Property

Above, I have mentioned the distinction between movable and immovable property in Civil Law.[4] Furthermore, I have limited the *scope* of this book to an examination of movable property law. Therefore, I have to make a similar distinction for Common Law as I made for Civil Law property law. As we shall see in the following paragraphs, the distinction is more complex in Common Law. Unlike in Civil Law, rights in relation to personal property are rather different from rights relating to real property.

---

[1] See Part II: § 4, "Property in Civil Law".

[2] See Part II: § 6, "Equitable Property Rights".

[3] Christopher B Gray, "Patrimony" (1981) 22 C de D 81 at 144.

[4] See Part II: § 4 A.III.2, "Movable and Immovable Property".

### *I. Real and Personal Actions*

The classification of property in English law into real and personal property is thought to be a function of the classification of actions into being either real or personal actions.[5]

The distinction between real and personal property is traced back to the works of Henry de Bracton, a lawyer living in England during the 12th century. In his work on the laws of England Bracton distinguished between actions regarding personal property and actions regarding real property; this was based on a division of his work into three parts: persons, things, and actions.[6] This classification was itself based on the classification of actions.

The English terminology derives from Roman law, which knew *actiones in rem* and *actiones in personam.* The *actio in personam* "was an action against a particular person to enforce the plaintiff's right to an act or forbearance on the part of the defendant."[7] The *actio in rem,* on the other hand, had a double meaning: it could be an action in relation to a thing or an impersonal action.[8] In an action relating to a thing, the claimant would claim either ownership of the thing or one of ownership's dismemberments.[9] One can merge both aspects by defining an impersonal action as

> "an action wherein the plaintiff does not allege the existence of an obligation between himself and the defendant, and the consequent personal liability of the defendant to do or forbear something for his satisfaction, but puts in issue the question whether he himself is invested with a right availing directly against some thing without the intervention of any other person's action, and correlative to a duty of forbearance imposed on all the world."[10]

In Common Law, on the other hand, classification is made by reference to the remedy obtained. A real action is one in which execution is made in a thing itself. In a personal action, satisfaction is achieved by making the defendant liable.[11]

In an action for the recovery of real property, the actions were *in rem* as they were

---

[5] TC Williams, "The Terms Real and Personal in English Law" (1888) 4 LQR 394 at 394 [Williams, "Real and Personal"].

[6] See David J Brennan, "Replevin and the Paradox of English Chattel Property" (2007) 36:4 Comm L World Rev 337 at 339. See also Williams, "Real and Personal", preceding note.

[7] Williams, "Real and Personal", *supra* note 5 at 395.

[8] Friedrich C von Savigny, *System des heutigen römischen Rechts* (Berlin: Veit & Comp, 1841), vol 5 at 23–28; Williams, "Real and Personal", *supra* note 5 at 395; Bernhard Windscheid, *Die Actio des römischen Civilrechts* (Düsseldorf: Julius Budeus, 1856) at 8–9.

[9] Part II: § 4 C.II, "Lesser Property Rights".

[10] Williams, "Real and Personal", *supra* note 5 at 396.

[11] *Ibid* at 398.

"given against a possessor, because he has or possesses the thing and can restore it or name its owner, as where one claims a specific thing [...] from another and asserts that he is its owner, and seeks the thing itself, not its price or its value or an equivalent of the same kind[.]"[12]

Regarding personal property, on the other hand, it was not the specific thing that was being restored. The action was not *in rem.*

"It seems at first sight that the action or plea ought to be both *in rem* and *in personam,* since a specific thing is being claimed and the possessor is bound to restore that thing. But in truth it will only be *in personam,* because he from whom the thing is sought is not bound to return the thing absolutely but disjunctively, to restore it or its value. By simply paying its value he is discharged, whether the thing itself is in existence or not."[13]

I take a look at the remedies available at law in more detail below.[14]

## *II. Real and Personal Property*

So far I have established that in Common Law, real property and personal property are different as regardws the type of actions that somebody claiming a right in relation to the property can bring. This does not tell us what we would find if we were to look into each class. It does not tell us whether something is real or personal property. In order to answer these questions, we first need to establish what is "property" and what is the *differentia specifica* of each group.

### *1. Property*

In Common Law, the term "property has a flexible meaning that needs to be constructed depending on context."[15] Just as in Roman law the word *res* could not just mean either "right" or "object of right" exclusively,[16] "property" in Common Law is sometimes used to mean either a right or the object of that right.[17] It is the second meaning with which I am concerned in this section. I

---

[12] Henry de Bracton, *On the Laws and Customs of England,* ed by George E. Woodbine (Cambridge, Mass: Harvard University Press, 1968) at 292.

[13] *Ibid* at 292 [emphasis added]. See also Robert Stevens, "When and Why Does Unjustified Enrichment Justify the Recognition of Proprietary Rights?" (2012) 92:3 Boston UL Rev 919 at 920.

[14] See Part II: § 5 F.I, "Common Law Torts for Wrongful Interference".

[15] Cf. *London Guarantee & Accident Co v George* (1906), 3 WLR 236 at 238 (Man KB); Canada, Department of Justice, Bijuralism & Drafting Support Services Group Legislative Service Branch, "Proposals for Harmonizing the Bankruptcy and Insolvency Act with Quebec Civil Law" (2003) 37:1 RJT 19 at 40.

[16] See Part II: § 4 D, "Right and Object of Right".

[17] See e.g. Yaëll Emerich, "Regard civiliste sur le droit des biens de la Common Law: Pour une conception transsystemique du droit de la propriété" (2008) 38:2 RGD 339 [Emerich, "Regard civiliste"], who uses the term "property" as the equivalent of the French "propriété".

prefer the term "property right" to describe the first meaning, and I will look at this term later.[18] However, the way in which "property" is used in the first sense can tell us something about what the second sense is.

In the first sense "property" means having a right over something to "some" degree of exclusion of others.[19] A licence for fishing, for instance, is property provided that and because it gives the holder an exclusive right to fishery if the holder conforms to the conditions of the license as well as a right to the fruits of the fishing, *i.e.* the fish.[20] Furthermore, the right must be "definable, identifiable by third parties, capable in its nature of assumption by third parties, and have some degree of permanence or stability."[21] If property in the second sense of the word is anything which is the object of property in the first sense, than "property" in the second sense – the meaning with which I will use it – is anything that can be the object of such a right of exclusion.

The property concept in Anglo-Canadian Common Law was recently re-examined in *Tucowscom Co v Lojas Renner SA.*[22] In this case, plaintiff and defendant had a dispute regarding a domain name. The legal question of interest was whether an Ontario court had jurisdiction over an out-of-province defendant based on the fact that personal property was located in Ontario. The potential personal property in question was the plaintiff's domain name. The Superior Court had held that there was no basis for jurisdiction in Ontario.[23] The Court of Appeal noted that American courts had already accepted domain names as property,[24] and that the same was true for England and Wales,[25] and Australia.[26] In *Tucowscom Co v Lojas Renner SA,* the Court of Appeal for Ontario applied the definition of property given above and concluded that the right to a domain name, *i.e.* a contract with the domain registrar, is property as well.

---

[18] Part II: § 5 B, "Property Rights in Personal Property".

[19] See *Manrell v Canada*, 2003 FCA 128 at 25, Sharlow JA: "It is implicit in this notion of 'property' that 'property' must have or entail some exclusive right to make a claim against someone else. A general right to do something that anyone can do, or a right that belongs to everyone, is not the 'property' of anyone."

[20] *Saulnier v Royal Bank of Canada,* 2008 SCC 58.

[21] *National Provincial Bank Ltd v Ainsworth,* [1965] AC 1175 at 1247–48 (HL), Wilberforce LJ, agreed with in *Tucowscom Co v Lojas Renner SA,* 2011 ONCA 548.

[22] Preceding note.

[23] *Tucowscom Co v Lojas Renner SA*, 2010 ONSC 5851 at paras 36–37.

[24] See *Kremen v Cohen,* 325 F3$^{d}$ 1035 (9$^{th}$ Cir 2003).

[25] *OBG Ltd v Allan,* [2007] UKHL 21.

[26] *Hoath v Connect Internet Services,* [2006] NSWSC 158.

*2. Real Property or Personal Property*

Real property is essentially land, while personal property is every property that is not real property.[27]

*3. Choses in Action*

A "chose in action" is essentially a right that will only be of benefit to the proprietor if and when she brings an action in court to realize this right.[28] A chose in action may exist either in relation to tangible property or independently of it.[29] In principle, a tort claim is a chose in action.[30] A chose in action is an item of property itself.[31]

## B. Property Rights in Personal Property

The purpose of this section is to analyse the notion of "property rights" or rights *in rem* in Common Law. The notion of property rights conveys the idea that somebody can hold a right in relation to an item of property that at least to a certain degree is severed from immediate control of the property. Immediate control of and right in the property are not the same. In this section, I first look at the idea that right and control are conceptually separate. I then look at what exactly characterizes the right in relation to the property in contrast to the class of rights called "personal rights."

*I. Rights in Personal Property*

Initially, in the first 150 years after the Norman conquest, English law – particularly in the works of Bracton – was described in terms borrowed from Roman law.[32] Based on Roman law, Bracton distinguished between "personal actions" (actions arising *ex contractu, ex maleficio,* or *ex delicto*) and "real actions" as well as between actions based on possession and actions based on a property right.[33] Seipp claims that the latter two types of actions constituted

[27] Alain A Levasseur, "The Boundaries of Property Rights: La Notion de Biens" (2006) 54 Am J Comp L 145 at 149–50.

[28] See Howard W Elphinstone, "What Is a Chose in Action" (1893) 9 LQR 311 at 311; TC Williams, "Is a Right of Action in Tort a Chose in Action?" (1894) 10 LQR 143 at 143 [Williams, "Right of Action"].

[29] Elphinstone, preceding note at 312.

[30] Williams, "Right of Action", *supra* note 28.

[31] Elphinstone, *supra* note 28 at 312.

[32] David J Seipp, "The Concept of Property in the Early Common Law" (1994) 12 Law & Hist R 29 at 35.

[33] *Ibid* at 36.

the class of real actions,[34] but as we have seen above,[35] Bracton rejected this classification for personal property. In other words, the distinction between personal and real actions does not correspond to the distinction between a property right and a personal right, unless one rejects the notion of property rights in personal property altogether.

Property and "ownership" could refer to any class of property, be it movable, immovable, or incorporeal.[36] However, there was a contradiction between the use of Roman terminology and the substantive law. In fact, even as far as chattel was concerned, English lacked "any right in movables that approached to the Roman *dominium.*"[37] Speaking of "ownership" of chattel is thus unhelpful. Rather, I will prefer the term "title" to chattel.[38]

The distinction drawn in the earliest accounts of Anglo-Norman law between actions based on possession and those based on a property right disappeared over time. The common law terminology between the end of the 12th century and the beginning of the 15th century lacked words to describe the notions of possession and ownership.[39] This has lead to the conclusion that the early common law did not draw any distinction between property rights and possession.[40]

At the same time, different terminology came to be applied regarding land chattels in the Year Books (the earliest reports of cases before English courts).[41] Property rights in chattels distinct from immediate possession were recognized before property rights in land were. Seipp suggest three possible explanations for this.

The "good feudal lawyer thesis" explains the different treatment by the fact that all land was held from the king by way of infeudation and sub-infeudation; the same did not apply to chattel.[42]

The "devisability thesis" is based on the difference in succession. While chattels could be devised to heirs by will, the succession to land was not possible by will until 1540. The problem with this account, so Seipp claims, is that these differences became less important over time with the increased use of "uses" (precursors to trusts) to devise land. If devisability were the driving

---

[34] *Ibid* at 36.

[35] See Part II: § 5 A.I, "Real and Personal Actions".

[36] Seipp, *supra* note 32 at 37.

[37] Frederic W Maitland, "Notes" in: Frederic W Maitland, ed, *Select Passages from the Works of Bracton and Azo* (London: Bernard Quaritch, 1895) 172 at 173.

[38] See Part II: § 5 C.I, "Title, Interest, and Estate".

[39] Seipp, *supra* note 32 at 31.

[40] Joshua C Tate, "Ownership and Possession in the Early Common Law" (2006) 48 Am J Legal Hist 280 at 313. See also Max Radin, "Disseisin of Chattels: The Title of a Thief" (1922) 11:4 Cal L Rev 259 at 259.

[41] Seipp, *supra* note 32 at 39–40.

[42] *Ibid* at 40.

force behind the distinction between property in chattels and the right in land, there should have been a chronological coincidence between the resurgence of a concept of "property in land" on the one hand and either the surge of practical evasion of indevisability of land or the point in time that lands became devisable at law in 1540 on the other. In actual fact, however, the notion of property in land developed somewhere in between, towards the end of the 15th century.[43] A temporal coincidence not noted by Seipp is the one between the acceptance of third-party effects of the use and the recognition of property rights in land.[44] The 15th century was the time period during which the Court of Chancery began to recognize that a "use" binds not just the parties to the use, but also creates effects on successors as well. Devising land through a use thus was no longer binding on the parties of the use but third parties as well. This may also explain why the idea of a property right in land became recognized.

A third account offered by Seipp is the "interference thesis." With chattel, the property could stray from its rightful possessor. A disconnect between land and the rightful possessor of land was far less likely. This made a distinction between possession and right to possession more necessary where chattel was concerned.[45] The problem with this hypothesis is the ease with which property was ascribed to a thief of or trespasser to personal property.[46]

### *II. Personal Rights and Property Rights*

Waters argues that the distinction between rights *in rem* and rights *in personam* does not have any meaning in the Common Law. His proposition is based on the fact that any right is relative in the Common Law, and thus a real *in rem* right cannot exist in a Common Law system.[47] I look at the notion of relativity of title below.[48] Waters' argument boils down to saying that the term *jus ad rem* is misleading because it negates the multitude of relationships between different people that is inherent in Common Law property. There is no one single right in any one item of property.

An alternative definition is to say that property rights are rights that affect third parties.[49] It is not necessary that they be good against the entire world. Rather, it is sufficient to speak of a property right in Common Law if the right

---

[43] *Ibid* at 44.

[44] See Part II: § 6 B.III, "Circumvention of the Feudal Land Law".

[45] Seipp, *supra* note 32 at 44–46.

[46] This ease is recognized by *ibid* at 48.

[47] Donovan WM Waters, "The Nature of the Trust Beneficiary's Interest" (1967) 45:2 Can Bar Rev 219 at 223–26.

[48] See Part II: § 5 C, "Title, Interest, and Ownership".

[49] Richard Calnan, *Proprietary Rights and Insolvency* (Oxford: Oxford University Press, 2010) at para 2.13; Iwan Davies, "Transferability and Sale of Goods" (1987) 7:1 LS 1 at 6–7.

is good against people with whom the claimant has no contract nor any other specific obligation, such as one arising from tort.[50]

For the purpose of this book, Waters' argument means that it might be unhelpful to think of property rights on the one hand and personal rights, on the other hand, in Common Law based on a terminology taken from Civil Law. Nevertheless, I want to maintain a parallel terminology between Common Law and Civil Law. In the context of this book, this means that I want to examine rights that are privileged in insolvency due to some nexus with a specific item of property. Insolvency law does make that distinction; it recognizes that certain rights are preferential *vis-à-vis* mere obligations because they have some relation to property. How this is so is the subject of a later part of this book.[51] As a working definition, it suffices to say that a property right in Common Law can be thought of as a right in relation to an item of property that is binding against an innominate class of people and which, because it does this, confers preferential treatment in insolvency.[52] It might very well be that the diffuse "relation" between right and item of property turns out to be stronger in Civil Law than in Common Law, but as I will show, both legal systems recognize that a right in relation to property is different than a right that only involves people.

## C. Title, Interest, and Ownership

When talking about Common Law property, we need to understand a number of terms and a related doctrine. These terms are "interest," "title," and "estate." The doctrine is that of "relativity of title." These three combined are important in order for one to understand what the term "ownership" might mean in relation to chattel. Gordley and Mattei argue that the doctrine of relativity of title does not exist in Common Law. I address their criticism later.[53] For now, I will merely define the terms as they are commonly understood and will wait to examine the veracity of the definition below.

---

[50] See Bernard Rudden, "Economic Theory v Property Law: The Numerus Clausus Problem" in: John Eekelaar & John Bell, eds, *Oxford Essays in Jurisprudence: Third Series* (Oxford: Clarendon Press, 1987) 239 at 239 [Rudden, "Numerus Clausus"].

[51] See Part IV: § 15, "Federal and Provincial Notions of Property and Security".

[52] Calnan, *supra* note 49 2:15.

[53] See Part II: § 5 G.I.1, "The Shortcomings of Possessory Protection".

### I. Title, Interest, and Estate

#### 1. Interest

An "interest" is a certain right in an item of property; examples are absolute interests, life interests (a right expiring at the end of life of the right-holder), a lease, or encumbrances of the property.[54]

#### 2. Estate

The "estate" is a group of rights held by a person. In Common Law, a simple way to describe estate is to see it as a bundle of rights and interests in a thing which are held by one person.[55] Historically, the term "estate" was only applied in regard to real property, but in the sense of "universality of interests held by one person," it can equally be applied to personalty.[56] Since historically, there was no ownership of land besides the ownership by the Crown,[57] Common Law did not require the possibility of ownership of the property in order for the property to be included within the estate. If the Common Law concept of "estate" would have taken ownership as its starting point, it would have excluded a large part of what is property, especially real property that could historically only be owned by the Crown. Common Law therefore always allowed for a variety of different legal and equitable rights and interests to be part of the estate.[58] This distinguishes the Common Law estate from the Civil Law patrimony.[59]

#### 3. Title

The interest is the object of title. "Title" is not entitlement to a thing, but to a type of right or interest in a thing.[60] In other words, to say "I have title to that

---

[54] Graham Battersby & AD Preston, "The Concepts of Property, Title and Owner Used in the Sale of Goods Act 1893" (1972) 35:3 Modern L Rev 268 at 268.

[55] John H Merryman, "Ownership and Estate: Variations on a Theme by Lawson" (1974) 48 Tul L Rev 916 at 927; Bruce H Ziff, *Principles of Property Law,* 5th edn (Toronto: Carswell, 2010) at 2.

[56] Levasseur, *supra* note 27 at 154.

[57] Merryman, "Ownership and Estate", *supra* note 55 at 927. See also Michael H Lubetsky, "Adding Epicycles: The Inconsistent Use Test in Adverse Possession Law" (2009) 47 OHLJ 497 at 503. But there was occasional reference to the "owner" of land in early common law, see Seipp, *supra* note 32 at 66.

[58] Gray, *supra* note 3 at 145; Merryman, "Ownership and Estate", *supra* note 55 at 928.

[59] See Part II: § 4 A, "Patrimony and Property".

[60] France Allard, "Entre le droit civil et la common law: La propriété en quête de sens" in: Jean C Gémar & Nicholas Kasirer, eds, *Jurilinguistique: Entre langues et droits* (Montréal: Éditions Thémis, 2005) 193 at 203 : "Contrairement au caractère allodial de la propriété en droit civil québécois, la common law fonde le rapport au bien-fonds sel un système de tenure. En vertu du mode allodial, la propriété porte directement sur le fonds, alors qu'en

interest" means that I am considered to be the right-holder in relation to that interest. In Common Law, several people can hold title in relation to the same thing at the same time, but regarding different interests.[61] However, the notion of title goes further. Several people can hold title not only in relation to the same thing, but also – so common wisdom goes – in relation to the same interest.[62]

The distinction between interest and title is a function of the possibility to allow a number of titles to the same interest. If the Common Law were to recognize only one title to any one interest, there would be no use in distinguishing the two.[63]

### *II. Ownership at Law*

#### *1. Ownership and Title*

There is a certain degree of confusion about the notion of ownership in Common Law. The term is occasionally used, but it lacks the precise definition that can be ascribed to it in Civil Law.[64] As we have seen in Civil Law, ownership means a right to control of a thing that is valid against the entire world; there is only one ownership at a time and all other property rights are defined as being carved out of the right of ownership.

In Common Law, on the other hand, there is an interest in property. The interest might be mere possession, it might be a right to possession, or it might be a combination of the two. Where two people claim the same property, the one with the better interest prevails. Thus, it might be enticing to ascribe ownership to the person with the best interest.[65] But at the same time, different

vertu du mode en tenure, le droit porte sur un intérêt. La notion de propriété est alors détachée du bien-fonds, elle est une pure abstraction, même si la notion d'intérêt foncier se rattache en principe a un héritage corporel qui est chose matérielle." Also Battersby & Preston, *supra* note 54 at 269.

[61] Allard, "Entre le droit civil et la common law", preceding note at 204; Battersby & Preston, *supra* note 54 at 269.

[62] Andreas Rahmatian, "A Comparison of German Moveable Property Law and English Personal Property Law" (2008) 3:1 J Comp L 197 at 203: "This relativity is expressed in the notion of 'title': the title measures the strength of a person's interest in relation to others. That interest in an object of property denotes the sum of rights over it which the person enjoys against others, but not always against all others."

[63] Battersby & Preston, *supra* note 54 at 270.

[64] See Donovan WM Waters, "The Institution of the Trust in Civil and Common Law" in: Académie du droit international, ed, *Recueil des cours* (Leiden: Sijthoff, 1995) 113 at 138: "The civil law can therefore speak of 'ownership' with a clarity of meaning that is not possible under the common law where 'ownership' is not a term of art."

[65] Cf. Rahmatian, *supra* note 62 at 203: "[An] owner of a chattel could be described as the person with the best possessory interest in it."

people can hold title to the same interest. So the owner is probably better described as the one holding the best title to the best interest. At the same time, it is not necessary to define ownership outside of litigation. The framework of title and interest can operate without having to rely on "ownership." Consequently, it is often argued that the Common Law lacks an absolute notion of ownership.[66]

*2. Ownership and Interest*

A different perspective of "ownership" is offered by Curwen. He points out that "ownership" is a term that has only been used fairly recently in Common Law, while the early common law operated with notions of "general property" and "special property."[67] "Property" in this context is not the object of the right, but the right itself.[68] In my terminology, I would thus speak of a general property right and a special property right. Curwen argues that "ownership" is essentially the most comprehensive interest imaginable in the property. The special property (right) then can have two meanings.

First, special property is a title created to the interest known as ownership. It is "special" because it ranks lower than another title: general property.[69] This, Curwen argues, is the case where there is a clear hiearchy of titles to the same interest. Thus, in the cases where there are a number of titles to the same interest, there is a multiplicity of owners, and who the owner is is a question of perspective.[70] This is essentially the notion of ownership presented in the preceding subsection.[71]

Second, special property can denote a type of interest. One can imagine situations in which there are different interests in the same property. Curwen's example is the pledge: the two interests are immediate possession and the reversionary right after the pledge's expiry. In this case, the general property

[66] Battersby & Preston, *supra* note 54 at 269: "[T]he phrase 'owner of property' assumes significance only in relation to a particular issue with a particular person." Francis S Philbrick, "Seisin and Possession as the Basis of Legal Title" (1938–1939) 24 Iow L Rev 268 at 203: "With the exception of a few rare situations our law has never undertaken to determine in one proceeding that one person, among all persons in the world, is the sole or true owner of certain land or chattels. Our doctrine of title has been for seven centuries one purely of relativity. It merely determines which of the parties to an actual dispute and (subject today to the new practice of declaratory judgments) between whom litigation has begun, holds the relatively better right." Rahmatian, *supra* note 62 at 277–78: "[O]wnership is, compared to possession, a more comprehensive superior right over a thing in a given dispute, but not an absolute right."

[67] Nicholas Curwen, "General and Special Property in Goods" (2000) 20:2 LS 181 at 181.

[68] Battersby & Preston, *supra* note 54 at 271.

[69] Curwen, "General and Special Property in Goods", *supra* note 67 at 182.

[70] *Ibid* at 181, 197.

[71] See Part II: § 5 C.II.2, "Ownership and Interest".

right refers to the reversionary interest; the special property right is the interest conferring a limited right to immediate possession. But, Curwen argues, both interests represent fractions of the comprehensive interest known as "ownership." He also implies that in these cases as well there is a multiplicity of owners because he speaks of "fragmented ownership."[72] Ames came to a similar conclusion when examining the idea of ownership at common law: "A true property may, therefore, be shortly defined as possession coupled with the unlimited right of possession. If these two elements are vested in different persons there is a divided ownership."[73]

Both perspectives of ownership – the title-based perspective, as well as the interest-based perspective – admit the possibility of multiple owners. The remainder of this chapter can be seen as my argument supporting the hypothesis that absolute ownership in one person is a concept unknown at common law. Whether the same is true in equity is a different matter and I discuss it further below.[74]

### *3. Ownership as Used in Statutes*

A clear definition of "ownership" as a term of art is generally avoided in Common Law statutes. For example, the *Personal Property Security Act*[75] makes passing reference to the owner mostly in connection with the registered owner of a vehicle. The *Sale of Goods Act*[76] makes reference to the owner in the context of a sale by a person other than the owner,[77] but it does not conceptualize a sale as a transfer of ownership; rather, it conceptualizes it as a transfer of property.[78]

When the Law Reform Commission of British Columbia suggested a reform of personal property law, they defined "owner" to mean "a person with an interest," while interest was defined as "[including] a security interest in property and a present or future right of possession or ownership of property."[79] The definition thus managed to achieve the feat of being circular and contradictory at the same time. It was circular because it defined an owner as somebody who had ownership of property, and it was contradictory because its definition of

---

72 Curwen, "General and Special Property in Goods", *supra* note 67 at 197.

73 James B Ames, "The Disseisin of Chattels (II): The Nature of Ownership" (1889) 3:7 Harv L Rev 313 at 314 [Ames, "Chattel Disseissin II"].

74 See Part II: § 10, "Proprietary Restitution".

75 RSO 1990, c P.10.

76 *Sale of Goods Act,* RSO 1990, c S.1.

77 *Ibid,* s 22.

78 *Ibid,* s 18.

79 Law Reform Commission of British Columbia, *Working Paper on Wrongful Interference with Goods* (Victoria: Law Reform Commission of British Columbia, 1992) at 53.

"interest" suggested that ownership was an interest distinct from a right of possession, but at the same time its definition of "owner" accepted that a right of possession was an interest that would be sufficient to constitute ownership.

### *4. Honoré's Notion of Ownership*

Notwithstanding what I have said in the previous paragraph, we can find the word "ownership" sometimes being used in reference to rights at law, but it has a very different meaning than the same word has in Civil Law. Based on the relativity of ownership, a different approach to ownership was taken by Honoré. He defined "ownership" as follows:

> "If ownership is provisionally defined as the greatest possible interest in a thing which a mature system of law recognizes, then it follows that, since all mature systems admit the existence of 'interests' in 'things,' all mature systems have, in a sense, a concept of ownership."[80]

As we can see, Honoré no longer ascribed any features to ownership, but simply defined "ownership" as a synonym for whatever best interest is admitted in property. In Civil Law, the claim to be the owner of property includes a statement about exactly what right I have in the property. Honoré's owner does not claim any right in the property. Rather, it is the outside world who ascribes ownership to her as the person who can currently claim to have the best interest. Honoré's definition also ignores both the difference between title and interest and the admission of concurrent title to the same interest. In other words, Honoré's definition of ownership does not include the idea that ownership is unique.

## D. Possession and Property

Above, I have argued that the notion of a property right is based on the idea that control of property and right to the property are conceptually different.[81] At the same time the connection between "control" and "property" is stronger in Common Law than in Civil Law. Another term for "control" is "possession." We have already looked at the notion of possession in Civil Law.[82] But in Common Law possession has a larger role to play. Property rights themselves are "thought of in terms of degrees of possession," property rights and especially

---

[80] Anthony M Honoré, "Ownership" in: Anthony G Guest, ed, *Oxford Essays in Jurisprudence* (Oxford: Oxford University Press, 1961) 107 at 108.

[81] See Part II: § 5 B, "Property Rights in Personal Property".

[82] See Part II: § 4 I, "Possession in Civil Law".

ownership are not fundamentally different from possession.[83] Possession is referred to as the "root of title."[84] This raises two questions. The first question regards the definition of possession. The second question concerns the type of relationship between possession and property rights. Rose poses a different second question: Why does possession give title?[85] This is a question of legal theory rather than one of black-letter law. It will thus be dealt with latter.[86]

### *I. Possession*

Regarding the first question, it has been said that the English law has never developed an exhaustive notion of possession.[87] Historically, possession had to accommodate only relationships between people and things in the physical world. Green argues that this is a function of exigency, not of design. Before the advent of the modern world, only physical, tangible things were of value. Thus, only they needed to be recognised for the purposes of determining possession. This meant that possession itself was manifested in the physical realm. Thus possession was initially seen as something self-evident to an outside observer, not something that needed to be conceptualized in an abstract fashion.[88]

Nevertheless, Harris has shown that an analysis of cases in which the concept of possession was applied allows one to develop a phenomenological definition of possession.[89] The phenomena associated with possession relate to two concepts: control and intention.[90] Pollock had earlier similarly defined "possession" as follows:

> "When the fact of control is coupled with a legal claim and right to exercise it in one's own name against the world at large, we have possession in law as well as in fact. We say as against the world at large, not as against all men without exception. *For a perfectly exclusive right to the control of anything can belong only to the owner.*"[91]

---

[83] David LC Miller, "Transfer of Ownership" in: Kenneth G Reid & Reinhard Zimmermann, eds, *A History of Private Law in Scotland* (Oxford: Oxford University Press, 2000) 269 at 269.

[84] Richard A Epstein, "Possession as the Root of Title" (1978–1979) 13:4 Ga L Rev 1221; Carol M Rose, "Possession as the Origin of Property" (1985) 52:1 U Chicago L Rev 73. See also Curwen, "General and Special Property in Goods", *supra* note 67 at 184.

[85] Rose, "Possession as the Origin of Property", preceding note at 75.

[86] See Part II: § 8, "Theory of Property Rights".

[87] *United States et al v Dollfus Mieg et Cie SA,* [1952] AC 582 at 605 (HL), Earl Jowitt.

[88] Sarah Green, "To Have and Hold?: Conversion and Intangible Property" (2008) 71:1 Modern L Rev 114 at 115.

[89] DR Harris, "The Concept of Possession in English Law" in: Guest, ed, *Oxford Essays in Jurisprudence, supra* note 80, 69.

[90] *Ibid* at 74–76 [emphasis added].

[91] Frederick Pollock & Robert S Wright, *An Essay on Possession in the Common Law* (Oxford: Clarendon Press, 1888) at 16.

I have emphasized the last part of this definition because a perfectly exclusive right to control personal property does not exist at law, and it is thus doubtful whether one can speak of ownership at law at all.[92] The second aspect – the relationship between possession and property rights – is the topic of the remainder of this chapter.

As regards the element of control,

> "the plaintiff's degree of physical control should not be considered in isolation, but in relation to the greatest degree of physical control which it is possible for the particular plaintiff to exercise over the particular chattel."[93]

The notion of possession is thus wide enough to accommodate a broad notion of property. Control does not need to be physical if the property is intangible.[94]

### *II. Seisin*

#### *1. The Notion of Seisin*

As it is generally understood "seisin" means a legally recognized form of possession of tenure (*i.e.* legal title in land subject to the ownership of the Crown).[95] In the words of Lord Mansfield, CJ, "[s]eisin is a technical term to denote the completion of that investiture, by which the tenant was admitted into the tenure; and without which, no freehold could be constituted or pass."[96] Seisin denotes a possession which is lawful not because of some contractual right, but because the seisee claims some right good against everybody in the seised property. Thus, regarding land, only somebody having a "freehold" in land is seised of the land.[97] Regarding the freehold, it is important to keep in mind that at common law, there is no allodial ownership of land, as the land is being held from the Crown; freehold is the strongest right in land admitted.

#### *2. Seisin of Personal Property*

The concept of seisin has not been applied to personal property since the end of the fifteenth century, but it did exist before.[98] Maitland has shown that previous to the end of the fifteenth century, there had been examples of seisin of personal property.[99] The modern distinction that real property is seised and

---

[92] See Part II: § 5 C.II, "Ownership at Law".

[93] Harris, *supra* note 89 at 74.

[94] Green, *supra* note 88 at 116.

[95] Philbrick, *supra* note 66 at 271.

[96] *Atkyns v Horde* (1757), 1 Burr 60 at 107 (KB), Lord Mansfield LCJ.

[97] Pollock & Wright, *supra* note 91 at 47.

[98] Frederic W Maitland, "Mystery of Seisin" (1886) 2 LQR 481 at 481 [Maitland, "Mystery"]; Frederic W Maitland, "The Seisin of Chattels" (1885) 1 LQR 314 at 324–25.

[99] Maitland, "The Seisin of Chattels", preceding note.

chattel possessed is a result of the parallel development of the notion of possession and the development of a distinct and more fully fleshed notion of a law of personal property during the fourteenth and fifteenth century.[100] But we find that certain notions that applied to seisin continue to be reflected in personal property law.

### *3. Seisin and Property Right*

Maitland claims that the common law notion of seisin is similar to ownership.[101] The similarity and the relationship between the notions of seisin and ownership regarding land are explained by the fact that there is no actual ownership as an absolute right in Common Law; land is held from the king. "Ownership" in this sense is only shorthand for saying "the prevailing relative entitlement." This prevailing entitlement is dependent on seisin where real property is concerned.[102] Seisin gave "ownership" good against all save those who had a better (older) title.[103] Taken this idea further, Maitland claims that analytically, a transfer of property was not in fact a transfer of a right between conveyor and purchaser. Rather, it is the thing itself that is delivered from conveyor to purchaser. Any right the latter received was not a result of a transfer of right, but was derived from her investiture, her seisin of the property.[104]

### *4. Disseisin*

A change in seisin is called "disseisin." Regarding land, disseisin had two consequences, regardless of whether it was legal or not. First, the disseisee was deemed to have lost title to the land. Second, the disseisee could avail herself of the *in rem* action for novel disseisin, which allowed her to recover possession of the land.[105] Arguably, the first consequence arose in cases of chattel as well. In many ways, disseisin of chattel property means that the disseisor received "absolute property in the chattel taken."[106] This suggests that the common law position was the thief had not only possession, but a property right in the property as well.[107] The disseisee was unable to devise any rights in the

---

[100] Philbrick, *supra* note 66 at 273–74.

[101] Maitland, "Mystery", *supra* note 98 at 481.

[102] *Ibid* at 481–82.

[103] *Ibid* at 488.

[104] *Ibid* at 489–90.

[105] Brennan, *supra* note 6 at 341.

[106] James B Ames, "The Disseisin of Chattels (I)" (1889) 3:1 Harv L Rev 23 at 28 [Ames, "Chattel Disseisin I"].

[107] See Radin, "Disseisin of Chattels", *supra* note 40 at 259, who points out that this explainable because "in the Year Books the two terms 'possession' and 'property' had not yet been fully differentiated."

property by will.[108] At the same time, the remedies available to the disseisee who lost possession of chattel were much more limited than the ones available for a loss of land. The law relating to a loss of personal property is explored in more detail below.[109] The question as to what extent a disseisin – a loss of possession – of personal property amounted to and still amounts to a loss of the property itself can not be answered until we have looked at these questions.

### *III. Non-Possessory Property Interests as Choses in Action*

Ames was a strong proponent of the theory that a non-possessory interest in personal property is a mere chose in action,[110] but his view has not gone unchallenged.[111] The historic position might have been that a non-possessory interest in property was a mere chose in action, not a right in the thing itself.[112] Bordwell claims that if a non-possessory interest in property was ever conceptualized as a chose in action, it ceased to be thusly described by the fifteenth century.[113] Williams, too, submits that a non-possessory interest in personal property is no longer accurately described as a mere chose in action.[114] At the same time, Bordwell admits that there is some logic to describing the non-possessory interest as a chose in action if one distinguishes between choses in possession and choses in action.[115] The question becomes relevant when one tries to conceptualize how a property right in personal property is acquired. If the non-possessory interest in personal property is a mere chose in action, the transfer of the property right by the transferor is governed by the rules of assignments of choses in action, and is thus conceptually very different from a transfer of a property right by a transfer of possession.

---

[108] Ames, "Chattel Disseisin I", *supra* note 106 at 25–26.

[109] See Part II: § 5 F.I, "Common Law Torts for Wrongful Interference".

[110] James B Ames, "The Disseisin of Chattels (III): Inalienability of Choses in Action" (1889) 3:8 Harv L Rev 337 [Ames, "Chattel Disseisin III"].

[111] Percy Bordwell, "The Alienability of Non-Possessory Interests" (1940) 19:3 NCL Rev 279 at 280 [Bordwell, "Alienability"].

[112] Cf. Elphinstone, *supra* note 28 at 312–13.

[113] Bordwell, "Alienability", *supra* note 111 at 280.

[114] Williams, "Right of Action", *supra* note 28 at 152–53.

[115] Bordwell, "Alienability", *supra* note 111 at 283.

## E. Acquisition of Property in Common Law

### *I. Inter Vivos Transfer of Property in Common Law*

### *1. From Delivery to Consensual Transfer*

#### *a) The Transfer of Property in Common Law*

The rule that a contract for the sale of specific goods in a deliverable state is capable of passing, and — unless the parties otherwise intend — does pass, title to the goods in question as soon as it is concluded is often characterized as an "old common law rule."[116] This view does not go unchallenged.[117] Maitland claims that the early common law required delivery. There could be no *donatio* without *traditio,* he claims.[118] But we find that by the fifteenth century, the courts accepted the consensual transfer of property without delivery.[119]

The move from a traditional approach to the transfer of property towards a consensual approach can also be seen in the remedies available to the purchaser. Towards the end of the 15th century, actions against the vendor of chattel for non-delivery were recorded as detinue actions (that is, action for the wrongful detention of somebody else's property), rather than debt actions.[120]

#### *b) The Sale of Goods Acts*

Nowadays, the transfer of property in the context of a sale is governed by statute. The first such statute was the *Sale of Goods Act, 1893.*[121] The *Sale of Goods Act, 1893* was replaced by the *Sale of Goods Act 1979.*[122] Throughout the Commonwealth, other Common Law jurisdictions have enacted substantially similar provisions – for instance, in Ontario, the *Sale of Goods Act.*[123] Under the statutes, a sales contract will transfer the property at the point in time intended

[116] See Birke Häcker, "Causality and Abstraction in the Common Law" in: Elise Bant & Matthew Harding, eds, *Exploring Private Law* (Cambridge: Cambridge University Press, 2010) 200 at 209. Cf. Jean P Gawkerere, "Que reste-t-il du transfert consensuel de la propriété des biens meubles en droit canadien?: Considérations sur la codification d'un principe dans un système bijuridique" (2005) 46:3 C de D 671 at 689–90.

[117] Cf. Gawkerere, preceding note at 689–90.

[118] Maitland, "Mystery", *supra* note 98 at 495–96, note 1.

[119] Bordwell, "Alienability", *supra* note 111 at 291.

[120] Stroud FC Milsom, "Sale of Goods in the Fifteenth Century" (1961) 77 LQR 257 at 273–78.

[121] 56 & 57 Vict.

[122] 1979, c 54 [*SGA*].

[123] *Sale of Goods Act, supra* note 76.

by the parties.[124] An assumption operates to the effect that the parties intend property to pass at the moment the contract is concluded.[125]

An interesting feature of the statutes is that they avoid the word "ownership." This can be explained by the way the statutes work. Merret explains that a transfer of property can have two effects: an absolute effect or a relative effect. The absolute effect takes place where the buyer acquires "absolute title, good against the apparent and true owner of the goods," in other words: good against the entire world. This is not what takes place in a transfer of property under the statute. While a buyer could once acquire indefeasible title in market overt, this option has been abolished.[126] Instead, the *nemo dat quod non habet* rule operates. The seller cannot confer a better title or a title in a better interest than she herself has. A sale thus affects priorities only between the parties to that transaction; it does not affect the priority of somebody with better title.[127] This also means that the question about "true ownership" becomes immaterial to an acquisition of property.

### 2. *Transfer of Property and Relativity of Title*

Ames characterizes the transfer of title in a sales transaction as consisting not of a transfer of a right but as one of a vendor's waiver of the right to possession. This, in turn, means that the purchasers' right to possession becomes the best possible right in the world.[128] This short explanation alone cannot explain title-acquisition in a consensual transfer without delivery.

In cases of transfer with delivery, it could easily be argued that the purchaser's right to possession is a good right to possession because she establishes possession without causing any distress to third parties. Thus, her possession is not open to challenge by third parties, but she can avail herself herself of protection in case her possession is wrongfully interfered with.

The same analysis cannot apply in cases where delivery has not yet taken place. In these cases, the purchaser's right to possession cannot yet be established by the peaceful taking of possession. The purchaser has no possession yet. However, title-acquisition can easily be explained by reference to the vendor's right of possession. The vendor, still in possession of the property, has the best right to possession, either because she acquired the property herself by virtue of a sales contract and delivery, or because she acquired it through other means (*e.g.* first taking of ownerless property, adverse possession, inheritance,

[124] *SGA, supra* note 122, s 18(1); s 17.

[125] *Ibid,* s 19; s 18.

[126] *Ibid,* s 23; s 22.

[127] Louise Merrett, "The Importance of Delivery and Possession in the Passing of Title" (2008) 67:2 CLJ 376 at 378.

[128] Ames, "Chattel Disseissin II", *supra* note 73 at 315. A similar account is offered by Walter W Cook, "The Alienability of Choses in Action" (1916) 29:8 Harv L Rev 816 at 817.

etc.). By entering the sales contract, the vendor subordinates her right to possession to the purchaser's right to possession.

### *II. Assignment of Choses in Action*

Originally, choses in action could not be transferred.[129] The assignability of choses in action began by admitting the assignee of a debt to sue as the attorney of the assignor.[130] Maitland argues that the rule against the assignability of a chose in action was a function of the delivery requirement.[131]

### *III. Adverse Possession*

The doctrine of adverse possession is the Common Law equivalent of acquisitive prescription.[132] At common law, there was no adverse possession of chattel.[133]

Very much like the transfer of property in a sales contract, adverse possession is not so overly concerned with the creation of the right of the possessor. The possessor who came into possession with clean hands already has a protected right to possession, good against anybody but the dispossessed. Instead, adverse possession is concerned with the extinction of the right of the dispossessed.[134] This mirrors the way in which the consensual transfer of property can be explained as the subordination of the vendor's right to possession to the purchaser's right. The extinction of the original possessor's right means that her title to the property cannot be restored after the period of adverse possession has lapsed, even should the adverse possessor disclaims her right; this applies to land just as much as it does to chattel.[135] This point is somewhat obscured by Bordwell, who describes the doctrine of adverse possession as one of "inchoate title which may ripen into perfect title by the lapse of time."[136] There is nothing inchoate about the adverse possessor's title other than the fact that until the original possessor's title becomes time-barred, it is defeasible.

---

[129] Ames, "Chattel Disseisin III", *supra* note 110 at 337; Cook, "The Alienability of Choses in Action", preceding note at 816.

[130] Cook, "The Alienability of Choses in Action", *supra* note 128 at 823.

[131] Maitland, "Mystery", *supra* note 98 at 495.

[132] See Lubetsky, *supra* note 57.

[133] AKR Kiralfy, "The Problem of a Law of Property in Goods" (1949) 12 Modern L Rev 424 at 428.

[134] Ames, "Chattel Disseissin II", *supra* note 73 at 318.

[135] *Ibid* at 320–21.

[136] Percy Bordwell, "Property in Chattels (Part I): Property in the Trespasser" (1916) 29:4 Harv L Rev 374 at 378.

*IV. Fruits, Accession*

In the early common law, the allocation of fruits of property came to depend on whether the nature of the thing had been altered. In such cases the property was allocated to the person who undertook the labour. Thus, trees growing in a field belonged to the person whose land it was, but crops sown on the same land belonged to the person who had sown them, even if she was a wrongful occupier.[137] By the doctrine of accession, materials worked by one into the property of another become part of that property.[138]

## F. Wrongful Interference with Personal Property

Above, we have seen that in Civil Law, the owner of property can vindicate her property right. She can essentially demand that a specific item of property be given back to her. The protection afforded to a property owner is independent of the possession of the item of property. The same is not true in Common Law – at least not at law. In a study commissioned by the Law Commission of Ontario and published in 1989, Simmonds, Stewart and Paciocco found that "[neither] the common law courts nor courts of equitable jurisdiction developed a remedial structure which vindicated property in goods by even a *prima facie* right to recovery in specie."[139] Because I have not looked at equity and property, I shall address the second part of that statement (no vindication in equity) in a later chapter.[140] The remainder of this section is concerned with the veracity of this statement at common law.

*I. Common Law Torts for Wrongful Interference*

Historically, the common law lacked distinctly proprietary remedies for the recovery of goods.[141] Instead protection of personal property always fell within the realm of tort law. Kiralfy suggests that this could be explained by the fact the common law remedies for the protection of personal property developed before the notion of a full-fledged property right in personal property became recognized.[142] On the other hand, it could also be said that the absence of distinctively proprietary remedies for the recovery of personal property are what

[137] Seipp, *supra* note 32 at 62–64.

[138] *Appleby v Mayers* (1867), 2 LRCP 651 (Exch Ch). See Anthony G Guest, "Accession and Confusion in the Law of Hire-Purchase" (1964) 27 Modern L Rev 505.

[139] Ralph L Simmonds, George R Stewart & David P Paciocco, *Study Paper on Wrongful Interference with Goods* (Toronto: Ontario Law Reform Commission, 1989) at 39 [emphasis in original].

[140] See Part II: § 10, "Proprietary Restitution".

[141] Kiralfy, *supra* note 133 at 424.

[142] *Ibid* at 424.

prevented the recognition of a personal property law. This point is raised by Ames. He claims that the "process by which the right *in personam* has been transformed into a real right may be traced in the expansion of the writs of replevin and detinue."[143] Whether the common law really has a "real right" regarding personal property is thus very much a function of the degree of protection offered by the remedies for personal protection against wrongful interference with personal property.

At common law, there are three actions for wrongful interference with chattel: they were *trespass to the chattel* for wrongful taking, *detinue* for wrongful holding, and *trover* for wrongful conversion.[144] All three are actions for damages, not restoration of possession. Additionally, there is an action for *replevin,* which differs from the preceding three actions because it allows a specific recovery of property as a matter of law. Finally, *larceny* protects personal property in the context of criminal proceedings. The "principle of parsimony" in early common law meant that the actions were clearly delimited. With the exception of larceny, none of the other actions could be combined with one another. She who brought a claim in trespass could not sue for replevin at the same time.[145] Regarding the combination of replevin and other torts, this no longer seems to be the position in all Canadian provinces.[146]

The current law of personal property torts is still very much influenced by the origin of these torts in the early common law.

> "particular the law of trover and conversion is a region still darkened with the mists of legal formalism, through which no man will find his way by the light of nature or with any other guide save the old learning of writs and forms of action and the mysteries of pleading."[147]

### *1. Larceny*

The "appeal of larceny" could be brought in connection with criminal proceedings against a thief.[148] This action was common during the early period after the Norman conquest. During that time, the Crown did not prosecute theft and robbery; the victims did this. The thief who was caught in possession of the stolen property was summarily executed and the goods were forfeited to his accuser. By the middle of the thirteenth century, larceny had gone out of use.[149]

---

[143] Ames, "Chattel Disseisin I", *supra* note 106 at 30–31 [emphasis in original].

[144] John W Salmond, "Observations on Trover and Conversion" (1905) 21 LQR 43 at 44.

[145] Ames, "Chattel Disseisin I", *supra* note 106 at 29, note 2.

[146] See Part II: § 5 F.I.5.a)aa), "The Claimant's Possession".

[147] Salmond, *supra* note 144 at 43.

[148] See Kathleen F Brickey, "The Jurisprudence of Larceny: An Historical Inquiry and Interest Analysis" (1980) 33:5 Vand L Rev 1101 at 1117–22 on the appeal of larcency.

[149] James B Ames, "The History of Trover" (1897) 11:5 Harv L Rev 277 at 278–82 [Ames, "Trover"].

It stands to reason that the action's decline coincided with the increase in criminal prosecution through the Crown. In fact, the structure of larceny was paralleled in public proceedings against the criminal. The thieves' property then no longer fell to the accuser, but to the Crown.[150] Larceny was a means of getting specific recovery, but its exercise was not without risk to the claimant. The Normans introduced trial by battle as a procedure in larceny proceedings,[151] which decreased enthusiasm for the action significantly.[152]

### 2. *Detinue*

#### *a) Requirements*

"Detinue" was an action brought against unlawful detention of property.[153] Detinue took two forms that related to the manner in which the defendant had gained possession. In *detinue sur bailment,* the defendant had gained the property through bailment or other contract from the claimant. In *detinue sur trover,* the defendant had gained the property without the claimant's consent. Other than the mode in which the property ways obtained, there was no difference between the two actions.[154] *Detinue sour bailment* was the older of the two actions.[155]

From the claimant's perspective, detinue had procedural disadvantages that led to it becoming gradually replaced by trover or conversion over time.[156] In an action for detinue, the defendant could defend herself by a wager of law. A wager of law consisted of an allegation of facts; the veracity of the allegation was affirmed by twelve witnesses. If they believed the defendant, the court was bound by this affirmation of facts. Salmond calls this form of fact-determination a "licence to perjury" and credits it with the relative unpopularity of the action of detinue.[157]

#### *b) Remedy*

Detinue originally allowed specific recovery of goods, but the defendant was always given the option of paying damages in lieu of recovery. Recovery was

---

[150] See Seipp, *supra* note 32 at 54.

[151] Brickey, *supra* note 148 at 1118.

[152] Ames, "Chattel Disseisin I", *supra* note 106 at 28–29.

[153] Salmond, *supra* note 144 at 44.

[154] *Ibid* at 45.

[155] Cynthia Hawes, *Tortious Interference with Goods in New Zealand: The Law of Conversion, Detinue and Trespass* (Ph.D. Thesis, University of Canterbury, 2010) <http://ir.canterbury.ac.nz/handle/10092/3834> accessed 20 June 2016 at 5, 10.

[156] Kiralfy, *supra* note 133 at 425; AWB Simpson, "The Introduction of the Action on the Case for Conversion" (1959) 75 LQR 364.

[157] Salmond, *supra* note 144 at 45. See also Edward Jenks, "A Blind Spot in English Law" (1933) 49 LQR 215 at 217.

thus never granted as of law.[158] Any exceptions made were in the discretion of the court.[159] This meant that detinue was a tort for damages for the detention of goods, in which the value of the goods was simply the basis of damages. Not until the 19th century was an order for the restitution of specific chattel possible in detinue,[160] and even then it was not granted as a matter of law. In some Canadian jurisdictions, the rules of courts prevent the defendant from satisfying a court order for the restitution of property by merely paying damages rather than returning the property.[161] But of course, this only becomes relevant after the plaintiff has already obtained an order to that effect, which – as just mentioned – is not available as of law, but as a matter of judicial discretion. Detinue has been merged with conversion in England by s 2 *Torts (Interference with Goods) Act 1977*.[162]

### *3. Conversion*

#### *a) Development of the Action for Trover or Conversion*

The modern day tort of trover or conversion is the successor to the old common law action of trover, without the formalities of the "action" regime of the old common law.[163] Unless context indicates otherwise, I use both terms interchangeably, but the word "trover" alone never means *detinue sur trover.*

Trover was the appropriate remedy for wrongful conversion – *i.e.* disposure – of property.[164] Originally, these cases were encompassed by detinue because a wrongful disposure requires a period of wrongful detention.[165] The elements of trover as a discrete action were modelled on those of the tort of *detinue sur trover.*[166] There were five: possession of the property by the claimant, loss of possession, finding by the defendant, refusal of delivery, and finally conversion the defendant's own use.[167] With the exception of the last element, all other elements became fictitious; the claimant only needs to prove the last.[168]

---

[158] Kiralfy, *supra* note 133 at 425.

[159] See *Kettle v Bromsall* (1738), 125 ER 1087 (Com Pl).

[160] Jenks, *supra* note 157 at 217.

[161] See e.g. QBR2013 10–27. See Ronald CC Cuming, "Secured Creditors' Non-Statutory Remedies: Unfinished Business" (2012) 91:2 Can Bar Rev 243 at 248.

[162] 1977, c 32.

[163] *Kuwait Airways Corporation v Iraqi Airways Company et al (Nos 4 and 5),* [2002] UKHL 19 at para 63, Lord Nicholls; *Hiort et al v The London & North Western Railway Company* (1879), 4 LR Ex D 188 at 199 (Engl and W CA), Thesiger LJ.

[164] Salmond, *supra* note 144 at 44.

[165] *Ibid* at 44.

[166] *Ibid* at 46.

[167] Ames, "Trover", *supra* note 149 at 277.

[168] *Ibid* at 277.

Over time, trover encroached on the area of detinue. Conversion came to encompass not just disposure of the property, but also any continued detention by the defendant. The reason for the expansion of trover was that there was no wager of law in a trover action.[169] The need to replace detinue with trover also explains why a number of elements for trover have become mere legal fictions. The common law was a system based on actions, and the scope of application of two actions could not overlap. Thus, trover and detinue could not cover the same set of facts. The additional elements required for trover allowed for it to be distinguished from detinue, but by turning them into legal fictions, plaintiffs could now bring an action for trover where before, they were forced to bring an action in detinue which would have allowed a wager at law.[170] The defendant who did not return the property to the claimant was deemed to have disposed of it; whether she had actually done so became immaterial.[171] The act of conversion can thus be defined as "an intentional dealing with a chattel which is seriously inconsistent with the possession or right to immediate possession of another person."[172]

The only instance of an act of detinue that does not also constitute conversion is where the defendant is merely unable to return the property without any malfeasance on her part.[173] This is because trover requires an element of adversity.

At the same time, a wrongful taking usually results in a wrongful detention of the property. Thus, the scope of trover and trespass overlap as well.[174] However, a distinction between the two is made in *Fouldes v Willoughby*.[175] There, the Court held that a taking of property only amounts to a conversion if it is done with the intent to deny the claimant's title to the property. Only then does the defendant set up an "adverse" claim.

*b) Requirements*

*aa) Adverse Detention*

The detention needs to be adverse. This means that the detention is in defiance of the claimant's right.[176] This is important for questions of limitation. If the

---

[169] Simpson, *supra* note 156.

[170] *Ibid.*

[171] Salmond, *supra* note 144 at 47–48.

[172] Michael Scott, "Conversion and Revendication" (1961) 5:1 Mal L Rev 40 at 41. Liability in conversion is sometimes said to be strict, see *Hambly v Trott* (1776), 98 ER 1136 at 1136 (KB), Lord Mansfield CJ: "An action of trover is not now an action *ex maleficio,* though it is so in form; but it is founded in property." [Emphasis added].

[173] Hawes, *supra* note 155 at 10.

[174] Salmond, *supra* note 144 at 51–52.

[175] *Fouldes v Willoughby* (1841), 151 ER 1153 (Ct Exch).

[176] Salmond, *supra* note 144 at 48.

defendant holds the property for a period of time without knowledge of the claimant's title before the claimant makes any demand of recovery, the limitation period for any claim of trover will not have commenced before the claim of recovery is made.[177] The element of adversity is also important for the third-party recipient. As long as no claim for recovery is made, the *bona fide* third-party recipient of property is not herself liable in conversion.[178]

*bb) The Claimant's Interest*

Trover requires an interference with the claimant's immediate right to possession, not merely her title.[179] At the same time, a right to possess is not only a necessary, but also a sufficient condition. Trover does not depend on the claimant having the best title; the claimant in possession will be able to successfully bring a claim in trover as much as the claimant who has a better title.[180] This can be explained by the fact that conversion is essentially an interference with the right to possess. In principle, the defendant cannot raise a third party's better title in response to a claim in conversion.[181] The only possible exception is the case in which the claimant had no actual possession at the time of conversion but a mere right to possess.[182]

*cc) Property Subject to Conversion*

In English law, conversion is not available for intangible property,[183] whereas in American law it is.[184] Lord Hoffmann argued that it was always implicit in the notion of conversion that the property was tangible.[185] While he does not state an explicit reason for the implicit notion of tangibility, it stands to reason that this is because otherwise, the property could not be subject to the fiction of a loss and finding. As we have seen, this fiction is a legacy of the old forms

[177] *Miller v Dell* (1890), [1891] 1 QB 468 (CA); *Spackman v Foster* (1883), 11 QBD 99 (QB). See Salmond, *supra* note 144 at 49.

[178] Salmond, *supra* note 144 at 50.

[179] *Ibid* at 54.

[180] *Bird v Fort Frances,* [1949] 2 DLR 791 (Ont HCJ). See also Ames, "Trover", *supra* note 149 at 277; John Kruse, "Replevin: Repeal or Retain?" (2001) 23:1 Liv L Rev 95 at 103; Bruce MacDougall, "The Debtor's Interest in Personal Property Under the PPSA" (1994) 33:1 Alta L Rev 80 at 82.

[181] Cuming, "Secured Creditors' Non-Statutory Remedies", *supra* note 161 at 250–51.

[182] *Ibid* at 251.

[183] See *OBG Ltd v Allan, supra* note 25. On the decision see Green, *supra* note 88.

[184] *Kremen v Cohen, supra* note 24.

[185] *OBG Ltd v Allan, supra* note 25 at 95–104, Lord Hoffmann.

of action. Lord Hoffmann thus allowed a legal fiction to remain a filter mechanism for conversion claims, even though it no longer exists and only ever existed to secure the best process for its claimants.[186]

It should be noted that there is strong indication that the House of Lords' decision would not be followed nowadays in Canadian courts. In *Royal Bank of Canada v Got & Associates Electric Ltd,*[187] the Supreme Court held that where an illegally appointed receiver of a company interferes with the company's assets, the receiver may be liable in conversion for her interference with the intangible assets. Because the Supreme Court has thus already recognized one form of conversion of intangible assets, there is no reason to deny it generally merely because intangible property cannot be subject to the old fictions of the common law action of trover. For example, conversion is also available where a bank collects a forged cheque.[188] The collecting bank commits an act of conversion regarding the forged cheque, which is deemed to be the property of the holder of the account upon which the cheque is drawn. The damages sound not only in the value of the physical object, but also in the amount drawn.[189]

### c) Remedy

A claim in conversion will result in an award for damages. The defendant cannot evade the payment of damages by return of the property, at least if the offer had not been made promptly after the act of conversion.[190] Conversion thus operates to extinguish the claimant's title to the property.[191] Execution takes place not *in specie* but in all goods held by the defendant.[192] The extinction of title by conversion becomes even more apparent where the claimant has been deprived of the property only temporality and then accepts the defendant's offer to return the property. In that case, the claimant is treated as having bought the property back from the defendant. The deemed purchase-price is set off with the claimant's claim for damages for the act of conversion (*i.e.* it is equal to the value of the property at that time). As a result, the measure of damages is the depreciation in value of the property during the period of the conversion

---

186 Green, *supra* note 88 at 115.

187 [1999] 3 SCR 408.

188 See MH Ogilvie, "The Tort of Conversion and the Collecting Bank" (2014) 91:3 Can Bar Rev 731 [Ogilvie, "Conversion"] on *Teva Canada Ltd v Bank of Montreal,* 2012 ONCA 486.

189 The position of Canadian courts regarding this matter is not uncontroversial, see Ogilvie, "Conversion", preceding note.

190 Cuming, "Secured Creditors' Non-Statutory Remedies", *supra* note 161 at 258.

191 Ames, "Chattel Disseissin II", *supra* note 73 at 326; Law Reform Commission of British Columbia, *supra* note 79 at 13, note 39, referring to *Sadler v Scott* (1946), [1947] 1 DLR 712 (BC CA).

192 Scott, *supra* note 172 at 43.

and not the damages suffered as a result of not having possession during that period.[193]

Nicholls argues that there is a fundamental problem with conversion and its remedy. Conversion is supposed to remedy loss of property, but it is the remedy that causes the loss. Before bringing an action for conversion, a claimant has lost possession of the property. After she has obtained judgment, her property right is extinguished once the defendant has paid up.[194] Avoiding this problem, the Privy Council's decision in *BBMM Finance (Hong Kong) Ltd v Eda Holdings Ltd*[195] suggests that the act of conversion already extinguishes the claimant's title.

### *4. Trespass*

Trespass developed out of the action for *trespass de bonis asportatis,* an action for the carrying away of a chattel.[196]

#### *a) Requirements*

Trespass originally lay where the defendant disseised the claimant of the property. It now protects possessors against direct interference with their possession of the chattel.[197] The possession must be physical possession or a right to immediate possession.[198] The interference has to be a direct act, such as taking away the chattel. The act has to be wilful, not merely involuntary.[199]

#### *b) Remedy*

Trespass is an action for damages only.[200] Much like trover, it extinguishes the dispossessed claimant's property right.[201]

### *5. Replevin*

Apart from the torts for wrongful interference, a claimant can avail herself of the action of replevin. The action of replevin was discussed extensively in a

---

[193] *BBMM Finance (Hong Kong) Ltd v Eda Holdings Ltd,* [1990] 1 WLR 409 (Hong Kong PC). See Cuming, "Secured Creditors' Non-Statutory Remedies", *supra* note 161 at 250.

[194] Nicholas Curwen, "The Remedy in Conversion: Confusing Property and Obligation" (2006) 26:4 LS 570 at 575.

[195] *Supra* note 193.

[196] Scott, *supra* note 172 at 41.

[197] Rahmatian, *supra* note 62 at 215.

[198] *Ibid* at 215.

[199] *Ibid* at 215.

[200] Ames, "Trover", *supra* note 149 at 285.

[201] Ames, "Chattel Disseissin II", *supra* note 73 at 326.

Canadian context in *Manitoba Agricultural Credit Corp v Heaman.*[202] Replevin is a way to achieve the specific recovery of goods.[203] This is the main distinction to the above-mentioned torts of trespass, detinue and trover. Replevin lay where the defendant had obtained possession of the property by unlawful distress.[204] Its origin can be found in feudalism.[205] The landlord was allowed to take his tenant's property for any arrears. This way of taking was referred to as "distress."[206] Originally, replevin was based on the fiction that the distrained tenant kept possession of the property.[207] The tenant could offer something else in pledge for the chattel taken – he would *replegiare.*[208]

### a) Requirements

#### aa) The Claimant's Possession

Replevin could historically only be brought by someone who was in possession of the property.[209] In *Mennie v Blake,*[210] the plaintiff lent money to Facey, who extinguished the debt by purchasing a horse and a cart "which were to be the property of the plaintiff."[211] Facey then left the country. At the pier, he gave horse and cart to the defendant, to whom he owned money as well. The plaintiff did not succeed in his action in replevin because, even though he owned cart and horse, he never had possession. The requirement that the distressee have former possession has been received in Canada.[212] In some Canadian provinces, former possession is, however, no longer a prerequisite.[213] The Canadian position appears to be to treat replevin not as a separate action, but as an interlocutory proceeding in an action brought for wrongful interference. The restitution of goods is thus not seen as the only and final remedy.[214]

---

[202] (1990), 70 DLR (4th) 518 (Man CA) [*Heaman*].

[203] *Mennie v Blake* (1856), 6 El & Bl 842 at 846 (KB).

[204] Kiralfy, *supra* note 133 at 424.

[205] Kruse, *supra* note 180 at 96.

[206] Brennan, *supra* note 6 at 342.

[207] *Ibid* at 345.

[208] *Ibid* at 343–44. See *Mennie v Blake, supra* note 203 at 849: "Replegiare is compounded of re and plagiare, as much as to say, as to redeliver upon pledges or sureties."

[209] See *Mennie v Blake, supra* note 203 at 849.

[210] *Ibid.*

[211] *Ibid* at 843.

[212] See *Freeman v Harrington* (1863), 5 NSR 352 (NS SC).

[213] For example in Saskatchewan, see *Agricultural Development Corp of Sask v Vigro Seed & Supply Ltd* (1989), 64 DLR (4th) 385 (Sask CA), but it is still required in Manitoba, see *Heaman, supra* note 202.

[214] *McCoig v Griffith* (1909), 2 Alta LR 335 (SC (TD)); *McGregor v McGregor* (1899), 6 BCR 432 (SC); *Great Western Railway v McEwan* (1869), 28 UCQB 528.

### *bb) The Claimant's Title*

A successful determination of title is not necessary. Replevin does not vindicate any and all property rights. "[If] A be in possession of goods in which B claims property, this [...] is not the writ to try that right."[215] While replevin is restoration of property, as Fleming writes, "restoration of the property is, of course, only provisional, pending determination of title."[216]

The defendant who claims that the claimant is not the "owner" of the property will not succeed if the claimant can establish that her right is better than the defendants' right in the property.[217] Even in those Canadian jurisdictions where there is no requirement of former possession, ownership is not necessary to succeed in replevin. It is sufficient if the claimant can show a better right to possession than the defendant.[218] What is no longer sufficient in Canadian law is mere possession.[219]

### *cc) The Interference*

Replevin was originally distinguished from cases of trespass by the type of interference with the good. Trespass protected against disseisin, while replevin protected against "distress." Distress was defined as the taking of the property as a type of security. In other words, the defendant in a replevin action did not deny the claimant's right of property. This was a crucial difference to a trespass claim.[220]

It has been suggested that with the introduction of the writ of *de proprietate probanda* – which allowed the claimant to prove her title to the property – the distress element became superfluous.[221] Rather than describing the claimant as a distressee, the broader term disseisee is preferable. The courts confirmed this extension.

"The question now to be decided is, simply, whether goods taken under a pretended authority can be replevied. *Prima facie* there is no doubt that they can; for though in ordinary practice it is applied only to distress for rent, yet replevin is, at common law, a remedy applicable in all cases where goods are improperly taken. And I find no satisfactory authority to shew that it will not lie where goods are improperly taken under the warrant of justice."[222]

---

[215] *Freeman v Harrington, supra* note 212 at 355, Young CJ.

[216] John G Fleming, *The Law of Torts,* 4th edn (Sydney: Law Book, 1971) at 72, cited as in *Heaman, supra* note 202 at 521.

[217] Seipp, *supra* note 32 at 61.

[218] *Agricultural Development Corp of Sask v Vigro Seed & Supply Ltd, supra* note 213 at 393, Bayda CJS.

[219] *Freeman v Harrington, supra* note 212 at 358, Young CJ.

[220] Ames, "Chattel Disseisin I", *supra* note 106 at 31.

[221] Brennan, *supra* note 6 at 346.

[222] *George v Chambers, Rees, and Brown* (1843), 152 ER 752 at 757 (Ct Exch), Parke B [emphasis added]. See also *Mellor v Leather & Clough* (1853), 118 ER 569 (QB).

But in *Mennie v Blake,* the Court of Queen's Bench reasoned that an action in replevin would not lie for any non-consensual detention. Rather, the disturbance of the disseisee's possession must be extraordinary.

> "[As] a general rule it is just that *a party in the peaceable possession of land or goods should remain undisturbed,* either by the party claiming adversely or by the officers of the law, until the right be determined and the possession shewn to be unlawful. But, *where, either by distress or merely by a strong hand, the peaceable possession has been disturbed, an exceptional case arises;* and it may be just that, even before any determination of the right, the law should interpose to replace the parties in the condition in which they were before the act done, security being taken that the right shall be tried, and the goods be forthcoming to abide the decision. Whatever may be thought of Lord Coke's etymology, *what he says of replegiare, while it shews his understanding of the law, gives a true account of what replevin is, a redelivery to the former possessor on pledges found. But this is applicable clearly to exceptional cases only.* If, wherever a party asserts a right to goods in the peaceable possession of another, he has an election to take them from him by a replevin, it is obvious that the most crying injustice might not unfrequently result."[223]

Canadian courts as well found that replevin cannot be based on a mere property right, but require some form of wrongful interference.[224]

#### *dd) The Defendant's Title*

In the early Common Law, title was a possible defence against a claim in replevin.[225] If the defendant argued that the property right was now vested in her, replevin could not succeed and the claimant was relegated to an action for trespass. This was changed over time and the writ of *de proprietate probanda* was introduced. It allowed the claimant to prove her property and follow through in a replevin action even when the defendant claimed a property right of her own in defence.[226] The introduction of the writ *de proprietate probanda* is identified as an important step in the development of the common law of personal property. It meant that in those circumstances where replevin lay, the distressor "could not thereafter gain absolute property in by his tort."[227]

### *b) Remedy*

The remedy in a replevin action consists in an order ordering the defendant to give the property back to the claimant.[228] Because replevin can result in the restitution of specific property, it seems to follow that is a real action, not a personal action. However, it is different from the real actions that are available

---

[223] *Mennie v Blake, supra* note 203 at 850–51, Coleridge J [emphasis added].
[224] *McGregor v McGregor, supra* note 214.
[225] Seipp, *supra* note 32 at 59.
[226] Ames, "Chattel Disseisin I", *supra* note 106 at 31–32; Brennan, *supra* note 6 at 346.
[227] Ames, "Chattel Disseisin I", *supra* note 106 at 32.
[228] *Mennie v Blake, supra* note 203 at 846.

for land because it does not depend on title to the property.[229] Replevin remedies the unlawful taking of the property; it does not vindicate the property right held by the claimant. Title to the property only becomes important at the defense stage; it is a shield, not a sword.

### *6. Summary of the Current State of the Law*

We find that the common law protects personal property without regard to the type of interest held by the claimant.[230] The Law Reform Commission of British Columbia stated that this is because, in the interest of social order, the law must protect both possessory and proprietary rights; wrongful actions affecting the possessor cannot be excused on the ground that a third party has a (better) interest in the property.[231] It appears however, that the common law goes further than that. It does not merely protect possession and property through the same set of torts; rather, it considers possession and property right to be essentially the same. In *Re Winkfield,* Collins MR expressed it thusly:

> "The root principle of the whole discussion is that, as against a wrongdoer, possession is title. The chattel that has been converted or damaged is deemed to be the chattel of the possessor and of no other, and therefore its loss or deterioration is his loss, and to him, if he demands it, it must be recouped. [...] *As between bailee and stranger possession gives title—that is, not a limited interest, but absolute and complete ownership*[.]"[232]

A claimant having title to a high-ranking interests, such as interest for perpetual possession (colloquially: the owner), cannot bring a personal property tort if somebody else has the immediate right to possession.[233] The case where the claimant does not have the immediate right to possession needs to be distinguished from cases in which the claimant has a right to possession, but the defendant defends herself by claiming that a third party has an even better right to the property. This is not a valid defence against a personal property tort. Because the defendant in a personal property action cannot bring a third party's better title as a defence, she may be equally liable to a number of claimants.[234]

---

[229] Williams, "Real and Personal", *supra* note 5 at 404.

[230] *Sprung Instant Structures Ltd v Royal Bank of Canada*, 2008 ABQB 30 at paras 13–16 [*Sprung*], Horner J.

[231] Law Reform Commission of British Columbia, *supra* note 79 at 20, referring to *Webb v Fox* (1797), 101 ER 1037 (KB).

[232] *Re Winkfield* (1901), [1902] P 42 at 60 (CA), Collins MR [emphasis added].

[233] See *Sprung, supra* note 230 at para 18, Horner J.

[234] Law Reform Commission of British Columbia, *supra* note 79 at 20.

*II. The Case for Reform*

The law relating to the protection of personal property has been the object of two law reform projects in Canada. First, the Law Commission of Ontario commissioned a study on the matter,[235] then the Law Reform Commission of British Columbia followed suit.[236] Both proposed legislative reform, but neither proposal was adopted.[237]

In Ontario, Simmonds, Stewart and Paciocco found the common law and equitable principles relating to the protection of personal property to be in need of reform. They argued for a *prima facie* restitution *in specie*. In their view, it seemed unprincipled to require the plaintiff who has successfully alleged a property right to show that damages are not sufficient because the plaintiff is, after all, "seeking to vindicate a property right."[238] Nevertheless, they advocated against "swinging the pendulum to the opposite extreme and making recovery *in specie* the presumptive remedy."[239]

The Law Reform Commission of British Columbia proposed a reform along four principles: a unitary action rather than the variety of common law torts; making it available to anyone with any type of interest in the property, including mere possession and personal rights; limiting compensation to loss; and widening the scope of remedies. In their conception, the type of interest alleged by the claimant would become important at the remedial stage,[240] but there was no suggestion that *in specie* restitution of personal property would have been available as of right in the event that the alleged interest was a superior property right.[241] As regards the range of available remedies, the Commission did specifically mention the possibility of declaring the defendant to be a constructive trustee.[242]

---

[235] Simmonds, Stewart & Paciocco, *supra* note 139.

[236] Law Reform Commission of British Columbia, *supra* note 79.

[237] Cuming, "Secured Creditors' Non-Statutory Remedies", *supra* note 161 at 246.

[238] Simmonds, Stewart & Paciocco, *supra* note 139 at 52.

[239] *Ibid* at 51 [emphasis added].

[240] Law Reform Commission of British Columbia, *supra* note 79 at 45.

[241] Cf. *ibid* at 45.

[242] *Ibid* at 46. I address the question to what extent the constructive trust can be seen as a remedy for the interference with a pre-existing property right below, Part II: § 9, "Property Unjustly Gained".

## G. Possessory or Proprietary Basis of Personal Property Law

### *I. The Case for a Property-Based Account of Personal Property*

#### *1. The Shortcomings of Possessory Protection*

Gordley and Mattei forcefully claim that the possession-based account of property in Common Law – and with it the notion of relativity of title – is wrong.[243] They submit that the doctrine of relativity of title that a possession-based account of property law enables is not ancient, but the 19th-century reaction of Common Law jurists to the Civil Law discussion of possession.[244] Their first argument against the possessory account of Common Law property rights is that the mere possessor cannot rely on her possession alone after she has abandoned it.[245] In other words, they claim that possession does not confer *persistent title.* Their second argument against the possessory account is that the possessory protection offered by the Common Law is not unique to this legal system: it exists in Civil Law as well.[246]

Gordley and Mattey's second argument is evidently true. Both Common Law and Civil Law protect possession. Their first argument is more complex, and I submit that it is not entirely convincing. It begins by referencing a dispute between two real property law scholars about the requirements for ejectment. Ejectment is the common law action for the recovery of possession of or title to land. It is thus an action for the recovery of a specific good, and thus resembles a vindication action in Civil Law. Hargreaves claimed that the claimant in ejectment had to show that she was a lessee or that she once had seisin,[247] but Holdsworth maintained that the claimant needs to show a title good against the entire world.[248] Gordley and Mattei base their argument against the possessory account of on how well each of these two submissions holds up in an analysis of selected real property cases of the common law from the end of the 17th century to the middle of the nineteenth century.[249]

The first problem of this argument is its applicability to personal property. Even if the analysis showed that ejectment is based on a notion of absolute title (*i.e.* ownership), rather than possession-based relative title, this would not prove that the same applies to personal property. The second problem with Gordley and Mattei's argument is that it contains a logical fallacy: they assume

---

[243] James Gordley & Ugo Mattei, "Protecting Possession" (1996) 44 Am J Comp L 293.

[244] *Ibid* at 301.

[245] *Ibid* at 303: "If Pollock were right, a possessor would have a title which, like an owner's, would not be extinguished when he abandoned the property."

[246] *Ibid* at 304.

[247] Anthony D Hargreaves, "Terminology and Title in Ejectment" (1940) 56:3 LQR 376.

[248] William Searle Holdsworth, "Terminology and Title in Ejectment: A Reply" (1940) 56:4 LQR 479.

[249] See Gordley & Mattei, *supra* note 243 at 319–29.

that the notion of absolute ownership exists at law and thus interpret any reference to "title" in the case law as a reference to absolute ownership.

In *Stokes v Berry,*[250] Lord Hold held that if A has possession for twenty years and then B gains possession, A can successfully bring an ejectment claim because twenty years possession "shall be a good title in him, as if he still had been in possession."[251] In *Roe dem Haldane & Urry v Harvey,*[252] Lord Mansfield held that an action in ejectment requires that the plaintiff show title. Gordley and Mattei claim that in neither case did the court have to decide a case where "neither party had title."[253] The fallacy is already at work here. By viewing *Stokes v Berry* and *Roe dem Haldane & Urry v Harvey* as cases in which "neither party had title," they assume that title is something more than what the plaintiffs had; presumably, they mean absolute title in the sense of ownership because that is how they themselves seem to use the term "title." But *Stokes v Berry* stands for the proposition that possession already confers a *sufficient title.* It also shows that possession confers a *persistent title* that survives dispossession.

In *Denn dem Tarzwell v Barnard,*[254] the claimant could not show a previous possession of twenty years. Lord Mansfield held that twenty years' possession was required to bring an ejectment action, but allowed the jury to assume that the period had lapsed even when the plaintiff was unable to prove the prior possession. In *Doe dem Hughes v Dyeball,*[255] the claimant showed that he had been in possession for a year and was forcibly dispossessed by the defendant. The defendant raised lack of title as a defence. Chief Justice Lord Tenterden held that if the plaintiff has possession and is dispossessed by the defendant, it is the defendant who must show title. In *Doe dem Smith & Payne v Webber,*[256] the plaintiff had legitimate possession for an unknown period. The Court held that this was *prima facie* evidence for bringing. an ejectment action. Gordley and Mattei rightfully point out that in all these cases, the ejectment action required a wrongful dispossession.[257]

In *Doe dem Carter v Barnard,*[258] Carter Sr. took possession of land in 1815 after he purchased it. The land was conveyed to him in 1824. His son lived on the land from 1815 to 1834 (for a total of 18 years). Then, his widow lived on the land for another 13 years. The Court held that the wife could not tack her

---

[250] (1699), 91 ER 366 (KB).

[251] *Ibid.*

[252] *Roe dem Haldane & Urry v Harvey* (1769), 98 ER 302 (KB).

[253] Gordley & Mattei, *supra* note 243 at 321.

[254] (1777), 98 ER 1259 (KB).

[255] (1829), 173 ER 1184 (Ass).

[256] (1834), 110 ER 1152 (KB).

[257] Gordley & Mattei, *supra* note 243 at 325.

[258] (1849), 116 ER 1524 (QB).

period of possession unto her husband's possession to avail herself of a combined period of possession of 31 years. Gordley and Mattei claim that the widow lost merely because the 18 years' possession by Carter Sr. were prima facie evidence that she did not have title.[259] I submit that a close reading of the court's decision shows otherwise.

> "The lessor of the plaintiff must therefore rely on her own possession for thirteen years as sufficient against the defendant who has turned her out and shews no title himself. According to the case of [*Doe dem Hughes v Dyeball*] that possession for thirteen years would be sufficient; for in that case the lessor of the plaintiff shewed only one year's possession. [...] Here, however, the lessor of the plaintiff did more, for she proved the possession of her husband before her for eighteen years, which was prima facie evidence of his seisin in fee; and, as he died in possession and left children, it was prima facie evidence of the title of his heir, against which the lessor of the plaintiff's possession for thirteen years could not prevail; and, therefore, she has by her own shewing proved *the title to be in another, of which the defendant is entitled to take advantage.*"[260]

What the quote shows is that the Court merely held that both the wife's possession was not as good a title than her husband's and that the defendant could avail himself of that title. The reason that defendant was entitled to take advantage of Carter Sr.'s title was that he took a mortgage in the property from Carter Sr. Using the mortgage as a sword had failed in an earlier action.[261] This does not mean that it failed as a shield, and I argue that the words "the defendant is entitled to take advantage" of another person's title do not mean that any defendant in an ejectment claim is entitled to take advantage of the fact that the claimant has not shown the world's best title. It simply expresses the fact that in the case at hand, the defendant was entitled to rely on Carter Sr.'s better title because he was the mortgagee. The Court seems to use the words "the title" to mean "the relatively best title." This is evidenced by the fact that the Court did not hold that the husband had absolute ownership in the property. He merely had longer and prior possession than the claimant.

In *Asher v Whitlock,*[262] Williams took possession of the waste of a manor. The waste was the common pasture of a demesne (*i.e.* land held by a lord of the manor in a feudal land tenure system). Thus, Williams clearly did not have best title in the land. Upon his death, Williams devised his interest in the waste land to his widow with remainder to his daughter upon the remarriage of his widow. Widow and daughter stayed in possession. Upon the widow's remarriage, the remainder fell to the daughter who died. The daughter's heir – effectively William's heir – then sued widow and new husband for ejectment. The Court allowed the action, even though the defendant could show that the lord

[259] Gordley & Mattei, *supra* note 243 at 325.

[260] *Doe dem Carter v Barnard, supra* note 258 at 1527, Patteson J [emphasis added].

[261] *Doe dem Goody v Carter* (1847), 115 ER 1505 (QB).

[262] (1865), 1 LRQB 1 (QB).

of the manor would have better title than William. Nevertheless, the claimant succeeded by virtue of having a better right than the defendant, the current possessor.

"I take it as clearly established, that possession is good against all the world except the person who can shew a good title; and it would be mischievous to change this established doctrine. [...] Suppose the person who originally inclosed the land had been expelled by the defendant, or the defendant had obtained possession without force, by simply walking in at the open door in the absence of the then possessor, and were to say to him, 'You have no more title than I have, my possession is as good as yours,' surely ejectment could have been maintained by the original possessor against the defendant."[263]

Two points are worth noting. First, Cockburn CJ speaks of "a good title" and no longer of "title," as if there was only one title. In this context, "good" title could be interpreted to mean "title better than the current possession." Second, he confirms that prior possession is enough to bring an action in ejectment. This quote also confirms that possession gives persistent title.

Gordley and Mattei claim that the cases just discussed show that there is no relativity of title. This argument only works if one sees title and possession as being opposed to each other. It collapses as soon as one recognizes that possession is title, a reading that I have taken in the preceding paragraphs. In the end, all Gordley and Mattei achieve is to show that at law, recovery of specific property does not rely on absolute title, but on possession. As regards their argument that there is no precedent that possession gives persistent title,[264] *Asher v Whitlock* and *Stokes v Berry* show otherwise. Their article ends with the conclusion that

"Continental and Anglo-American jurists have encountered difficulties because they equate a right to possession with ownership. But one can imagine a legal system that recognizes private and exclusive rights of possession but does not recognize ownership in the Western sense."[265]

One might even argue that the Common Law is such a system; the authors assume that ownership in the Civil Law meaning of the word exists in Common Law without proving it.

### *2. Extra-Judicial Rights Available to the Dispossessed Owner*

Ames argued that in cases of personal property the disseisor received title in the property and the disseisee loses title.[266] This argument can be maintained regarding personal property because there is no right at law to demand specific recovery. None of the torts grant a right to specific recovery as a matter of law.

---

[263] *Ibid* at 5, Cockburn J.

[264] Gordley & Mattei, *supra* note 243 at 328.

[265] *Ibid* at 329.

[266] See Part II: § 5 D.II.4, "Disseisin".

But Ames' view does not go unchallenged.[267] And it is certainly true that a dispossessed owner of personal property had rights at common law that went beyond a personal claim for damages. For instance, the dispossessed owner of personal property had a right to pursue her property in certain circumstances.[268] She could retake dispossessed property when it was found.[269]

### *3. Replevin*

Apart from the extra-judicial rights available to the dispossessed owner, another argument raised against a possession-based account of personal property is the availability of replevin.[270]

### *4. Third-Party Effects of Non-Possessory Personal Property Interests*

Another argument against the theory that property rights in personal property are entirely based on possession is the fact that a non-possessory interest is binding against third parties. This becomes particularly important if the possessor becomes insolvent. In that case, the claimant of a non-possessory property right can still avail herself of the personal property torts against the insolvent's estate. However, her right in Common Law is still not as strong as the corresponding Civil Law right. I discuss these matters below in the chapter on the impact of insolvency on property rights.[271]

## *II. The Case for a Possession-Based Account of Personal Property*

The analysis of the law relating to wrongful interference with personal property has revealed two things. First, ownership of property on its own is not a legal event that is in itself sufficient to trigger a restitutionary reply. Second, in common law there is no general restitution of specific personal property as a matter of law.

### *1. Possession, Not Property as the Legal Event*

If we distinguish property law as an area of the law different from the law of obligations, we have to answer the question "What distinguishes property law from the law of obligations?" One suggestion has been to describe property law by reference to a number of typical phenomena associated with property: specific recovery of property, persistency of title, encumbrances enforceable specifically against the property, and restrictions on users that are similarly

---

[267] See Bordwell, "Property in Chattels (Part I)", *supra* note 136.
[268] Bordwell, "Alienability", *supra* note 111 at 282, note 25.
[269] Williams, "Right of Action", *supra* note 28 at 153.
[270] See Brennan, *supra* note 6.
[271] See Part IV: § 16 C, "The Claimant's Non-Security Title in Insolvency".

enforceable. Put another way, an attribute of property is a right to exclude the world from possession. Described this way, there is arguably no property law relating to personal property.

In *Ward v Macauley,*[272] Lord Kenyon stated *obiter* that a plaintiff without an immediate right to possession might be able to bring trover. This was rejected in *Gordon v Harper.*[273] The English Law Reform Committee suggested that Lord Kenyon's view should be restored, and that any proprietary interest in a chattel should give title to sue for wrongful interference, but this suggestion was never implemented.[274]

This is not to say that the common law only protects immediate possession. The right being protected is not possession, but a right to possession. Where possession is due to revert to the claimant, she can avail herself of tort actions.[275] This has been established by a series of cases where the claimant was not possessed of the property, but only held a right that possession revert to her.[276]

### 2. Damages, Not Restitution as the Reply

The examination of tort law relating to personal property has revealed a lacuna in the common law. Tort claims relating to personal property are not concerned with absolute title to the property, only with relative entitlement.[277] Furthermore, with the exception of larceny and replevin, the torts do not allow recovery of the property. Conceptualised this way, the common law of personal property has not been separated from the law of possession. As soon as possession stops, any property right in the property potentially ends as well. In the words of Ames, disseisin of chattel can rest "absolute property in the chattel taken"[278] were it not for replevin.

### 3. Ownership, the Elusive Concept

Ownership in Common Law is "an elusive concept."[279] Because several people can have title to the same interest, "ownership" in Common Law is arguably

---

[272] (1791), 100 ER 1135 (KB).

[273] (1796), 101 ER 828 (KB).

[274] Andrew Tettenborn, "Reversionary Damage to Chattels" (1994) 53:2 CLJ 326 at 329, note 21.

[275] See *ibid.*

[276] *Mears v L & SWR* (1862), 142 ER 1029 (Com Pl); *Dame Harriet Lucy Tancred v Allgood* (1859), 157 ER 910 (Ct Exch); *Dean v Whittaker* (1824), 171 ER 1225 (KB); *Hall v Pickard* (1812), 170 ER 1350 (Ass). See Tettenborn, *supra* note 274 at 328–29.

[277] Kiralfy, *supra* note 133 at 425–26.

[278] Ames, "Chattel Disseisin I", *supra* note 106 at 29.

[279] Davies, "Transferability and Sale of Goods", *supra* note 49 at 2.

nothing more than shorthand to express "the relative best entitlement to the best possible interest."[280]

"The phrase 'owner of property' assumes significance only in relation to a particular issue with a particular person. [...] The *concept of absolute ownership,* by which is meant an indefeasible title to the absolute interest in the particular property, *is* as *elusive* in the realm of chattels as in that of land."[281]

McFarlane goes further and suggests that ownership in a Common Law legal system can be held by different people independently of each other, and reduces the meaning of ownership to a right of non-interference against an open class of third parties.[282] Relativity of title in his conception has no bearing on ownership, but is only used to resolve priority conflicts between the different owners.[283] Katz, on the other hand, argues that ownership is an exclusive concept; while the Common Law protects the possession of a multitude of parties, owner is the one who can set the agenda in relation to the object of property.[284] Her argument is that while different title-holders – lesser than the owner – are protected against interference with possession, only the owner is protected in relation to their agenda-setting power.[285] The challenge then is to determine what these other remedies are with which the Common Law protects the owner, or in other words which remedy is exclusive to the owner.

## H. *Numerus Clausus* in Common Law

Just like Civil Law, the Common Law is said to contain a *numerus clausus* of property rights.[286] With regard to the question of the relevance of this topic to

---

[280] See Allard, "Entre le droit civil et la common law", *supra* note 60 at 205; Battersby & Preston, *supra* note 54 at 269; Birke Häcker, "Das Trennungs- und Abstraktionsprinzip im englischen Recht: Dargestellt anhand der Übereignung" [2011] ZEuP 335 at 336.

[281] Battersby & Preston, *supra* note 54 at 269 [emphasis added].

[282] Ben McFarlane, *The Structure of Property Law* (London: Bloomsbury Publishing, 2008) at 144–46. Cf. Larissa Katz, "The Concept of Ownership and the Relativity of Title" (2011) 2:1 *Jurisprudence* 191 at 191.

[283] McFarlane, preceding note at 146.

[284] Katz, "The Concept of Ownership and the Relativity of Title", *supra* note 282 at 192.

[285] *Ibid* at 201: "[I]f we acknowledge that in substance ownership is a position of exclusive authority and exclusion is just one of the law's techniques for protecting it, owners and possessors emerge as different categories of right-holders."

[286] See Henry Hansmann & Reinier Kraakman, "Property, Contract, and Verification: The Numerus Clausus Problem and the Divisibility of Rights" (2002) 31:S2 J Legal Stud 373; Thomas W Merrill & Henry E Smith, "Optimal Standardization in the Law of Property: The Numerus Clausus Principle" (2000) 110:1 Yale LJ 1; John H Merryman, "Policy, Autonomy, and the Numerus Clausus in Italian and American Property Law" (1963) 12:2 Am J Comp L 224; Meredith Render, "The Concept of Property" (2017) 78 *Pittsburgh Law Review* 437;

this book, I refer to my earlier introduction to the *numerus clausus* principle in Civil Law: the *numerus clausus* provides the framework for the modification the pro-rata scheme of the common pledge.[287] An early example of a *numerus clausus* principle at work is arguably *Twyne's Case.*[288] A farmer owed his first creditor, Twyne, £400, and his second creditor £200. The second creditor brought an action to recover his debt. That is when the farmer sold his sheep to Twyne, but remained in possession of the sheep and continued to use them and appropriate their fruits. At the other creditor's instance, the sheriff came to collect the sheep. Twyne argued that he was a *bona fide* purchaser. The Court held that the transfer of the sheep to Twyne was not a genuine sale as it only served to secure the debt, and that English law at that time did not recognize non-possessory security interests in movables.[289] This case can be seen as precedent for the rule that parties are not at liberty to create arbitrary property rights in chattel.

### *I. Numerus Clausus Principle in 19th Century Case Law*

#### *1. Pro Numerus Clausus*

The leading case for the proposition of a *numerus clausus* of property in the Common Law is *Keppell v Bailey,*[290] which was decided in the Court of Chancery. The Supreme Court of the United States, which remarked *obiter* that a *numerus clausus* existed in every country, cited the case with approval.[291] *Keppell v Bailey* involved an undertaking by the lessees of real property to the proprietors of a railroad and quarry, on their own behalf and that of their successors. The lessees undertook to buy all their limestone from the quarry, carry the limestone along the railroad and pay a toll for doing so. The proprietors sought to enforce this covenant against a purchaser of the ironworks who had

---

Rudden, "Numerus Clausus", *supra* note 50. See also Rahmatian, *supra* note 62 at 202: "English law effectively operates a numerus clausus of real rights, obviously without a statutory basis, but with endorsement in case law and doctrine that has never seriously been challenged."

[287] See Part II: § 4 E, "Numerus Clausus in Civil Law".

[288] (1601), 3 Co Rep 80b (Engl and W St Ch).

[289] Arguably, in Shakespeare's "The Merchant of Venice" the rule against non-possessory security interests in chattel should have been sufficient to defeat Shylock's security interest in Antonio's flesh, but unlike the "Merry Wives of Windsor," which was released one year after *Twyne's* case, "The Merchant of Venice" is rarely analysed in a fraudulent-conveyance context, see Charles S Ross, "Shakespeare's Merry Wives and the Law of Fraudulent Conveyance" (1994) 25 *Renaissance Drama* 145.

[290] (1834), 39 ER 1042 (Ch).

[291] See *McDonogh's Ex'rs v Murdoch,* 15 How 367 at 392 (1853), curiam: "The principle that parties are not at liberty to invest new tenures of property and to impress such tenures on their lands, is one not peculiar to Louisiana, but is a part of the public policy of every country." Referring to *Keppell v Bailey,* preceding note.

purchased it with notice of the covenant. The Court held it could not because doing so would turn the private covenant into a property right.

"There are certain known incidents to property and its enjoyment; among others, certain burthens wherewith it may be affected, or rights which may be created and enjoyed over it by parties other than the owner; all which incidents are recognised by the law. [...] [G]reat detriment would arise and much confusion of rights if parties were allowed to invent new modes of holding and enjoying real property, and to impress upon their lands and tenements a peculiar character, which should follow them into all hands, however remote. Every close, every messuage, might thus be held in a several fashion; and it would hardly be possible to know what rights the acquisition of any parcel conferred, or what obligations it imposed."[292]

In *Hill v Tupper,*[293] the Court of Exchequer affirmed the principle. Hill and Tupper ran competing boating companies. Hill had entered into an exclusive licencing agreement with the Basingstoke Canal Co to hire boats out on the Basingstoke canal. He then sued Tupper in trespass to the land for renting boats out on the canal as well. The Court held that the contractual licencing agreement did not create any property right in Hill of which he could avail himself in an action against Tupper.[294] In *Stockport Waterworks v Potter,*[295] the Court held that "new rights of property cannot be created."[296]

### *2. Less Restrictive Approach to New Property Rights*

Just like the Civil Law *numerus clausus,* the Common Law *numerus clausus* is foremost a principle addressed towards the parties, not the courts.[297] Cases from the 19th century also highlight the courts' willingness to recognize new property rights.

*Tulk v Moxhay*[298] is a decision by the Court of Chancery. It was not concerned with property rights at law, but with property rights in equity.[299] Tulk was the owner of several parcels of land in Leicester Square. He sold a plot to

[292] *Keppell v Bailey, supra* note 290 at 1049, Lord Brougham LC.

[293] (1863), 159 ER 51 (Ct Exch).

[294] *Ibid* at 53, Pollock CB.

[295] *Stockport Waterworks v Potter* (1864), 159 ER 545 (Ct Exch).

[296] *Ibid.*

[297] Brendan Edgeworth, "The Numerus Clausus Principle in Contemporary Australian Property Law" (2006) 32:2 Monash UL Rev 387 at 394: "To identify the caution in the approach of the common law to creating interests outside the numerus clausus should not be taken to imply that there is no scope to accommodate novelty in the creation of property rights. In a large body of case law, courts have repeatedly emphasised the dynamism of the common law in the area of property law [...]." [Emphasis added].

[298] (1848), 41 ER 1143 (Ch).

[299] See *ibid* at 1145, Lord Cottenham LC: "With respect to the observations of Lord Brougham in Keppell v Bailey, he never could have meant to lay down that this Court would not enforce an equity attached to land by the owner, unless under such circumstances as would maintain an action at law."

another party. Both parties entered a covenant to keep the Garden Square "uncovered with buildings." The land was sold a number of times, before the defendant was purchased. The defendant intended to build on the property, so Tulk obtained an injunction to stop him. If the covenant were only binding between the original parties, the injunction could not have been upheld. But the Court decided that the covenant constituted an "equity in the land." If the purchaser has notice of the equity, she will be bound by it. Lord Cottenham gave two reasons for this. First, highlighting equity's occupation with notions of conscience and good faith, he argued that nothing could be more inequitable than allowing the first purchaser to acquire land for a lesser sum because it was subject to the covenanted obligation, and then to sell it the next day for a greater price to a second purchaser.[300] The problem with that argument is that the first purchaser was not the defendant. The second argument holds more sway. Lord Cottenham pointed out that the covenant benefitted Tulk's interest in the land he retained.[301]

It is this second reasoning which allows us to consider *Tulk v Moxhay* not as an example of complete liberty in the creation of property rights. Because the covenant was entered into for the benefit of a certain property, it was not completely fanciful. In fact, *Hill v Tupper* drove that point home by pointing out that at law, an easement can be created in favour of other land, but not any other way.[302]

Consequently, *Tulk v Moxhay* was considered to be precedent not for the suggestion that parties are not bound by a *numerus clausus,* but for the suggestion that a covenant as a property right is restricted to negative obligations in situations where the obligations is intended to run with the land and where the covenant relates to land.[303]

*De Mattos v Gibson*[304] was decided by the Court of Queen's Bench. It extended the principle of *Tulk v Moxhay* to personal property. *De Mattos v Gibson* was overruled by *Barker v Stickney,*[305] but its principle was again applied in a

---

300 *Ibid* at 1144, Lord Cottenham LC.

301 *Ibid* at 1144, Lord Cottenham LC: "[It] is now contended, not that the vendee could violate that contract, but that he might sell the piece of land, and that the purchaser from him may violate it without this Court having any power to interfere. If that were so, it would be impossible for an owner of land to sell part of it without incurring the risk of rendering what he retains worthless."

302 *Hill v Tupper, supra* note 293 at 53, Pollock CB: "[It] is not competent to create rights unconnected with the use and enjoyment of land, and annex them to it so as to constitute a property in the grantee." Referring to *Ackroyd v Smith* (1850), 138 ER 68 (Com Pl).

303 Edgeworth, *supra* note 297 at 397.

304 (1859), 45 ER 108 (QB).

305 (1918), [1919] 1 KB 121 (CA).

decision by the Privy Council in *Dominion Coal Co v Lord Strathcona Steamship Co.*[306] In *Strathcona,* a ship was chartered for ten seasons on the St. Lawrence river. It was used thusly for one season and then requisitioned for war service for three years. Afterwards, it was sold multiple times before being purchased by the defendants. The sale was said to be expressly subject to the charterer's rights. The defendants then refused to uphold the charter-party. The charterer relied on their charter-party. The Privy Council held that they could, essentially recognizing the charter-party as a property right.

Because it was a decision of the Privy Council for Canada, Justice Diplock held that while the Council "was entitled to respect which in a common law lawyer borders upon awe,"[307] *Strathcona* was not binding in England and neither its principle nor the principle of *De Mattos v Gibson* should be deemed good law.

### *3. The Meaning of English Case Law*

Edgeworth argues that the *numerus clausus* is best described as operating in the same way as one of Ronald Dworkin's "principles."[308] It exerts a "gravitational force" on the development of the law through doctrine and cases, and influences, but does not necessarily determine, the interpretation of rules in specific cases.[309]

## *II. The Numerus Clausus Principle in Canadian Common Law*

In Canada, the Supreme Court's decision in *Bank of Montreal v Dynex Petroleum Ltd*[310] can be seen as embracing the notion of a *numerus clausus* in the Common Law. The decision also highlights that the recognition of a *numerus clausus* does not mean that the law cannot evolve.

The issue of the case was whether a property right can be created in an incorporeal interest in land. Similar to the traditional notion of property in Civil Law,[311] the common law once viewed interests in corporeal property as corporeal property, but interests in these interests were seen as incorporeal interests. More precisely, the titular of certain interests in land was deemed to hold the land, while other interests only meant that the titular held an incorporeal interest in the property. The former was described as "corporeal hereditament," the latter as an "incorporeal hereditament." The distinction is important because

---

[306] (1925), [1926] AC 108 (Can PC).

[307] *Port Line v Ben Line Steamers,* [1958] 2 QB 146 at 165 (QBD), Diplock J.

[308] See Ronald M Dworkin, *Taking Rights Seriously* (Cambridge, Mass: Harvard University Press, 1978).

[309] Edgeworth, *supra* note 297 at 398.

[310] 2002 SCC 7 [*Dynex*].

[311] See Part II: § 4 D, "Right and Object of Right".

the proprietor of a corporeal hereditament could create a property right in the hereditament, while the proprietor of an incorporeal hereditament could not.[312]

As I have stated above when discussing Civil Law, this distinction is not logically necessary. One essentially draws a distinction between corporeal and incorporeal interests based not on the property the interest relates to, but based merely on the name of the right. This might be defensible where ownership of property is something significantly different from any other property right, but it is hard to defend in a legal system such as the Common Law, where such a unique interest does not exist, and which rather operates with a continuous spectrum of property interests. This was already recognized by Laskin J (as he then was) in *Saskatchewan Minerals v Keyes:*[313]

> "The language of 'corporeal' and 'incorporeal' does not point up the distinction between the legal interest and its subject-matter. On this distinction, all legal interests are 'incorporeal,' and it is only the unconfronted force of a long history that makes it necessary in this case to examine certain institutions of property in the common law provinces through an antiquated system of classification and an antiquated terminology."[314]

In 1971, Justice Laskin was in the minority and the majority of the Supreme Court deemed it unnecessary to decide whether the common law rule against interests in incorporeal hereditaments should be abandoned. But in *Dynex,* the Supreme Court followed Laskin's approach.

What makes the case significant to the current discussion of the *numerus clausus* principle in Common Law is the Court's reasoning. It did not decide that parties are at liberty to create any property right they want; rather, it held that the common law needed to evolve and admit the creation of interests in incorporeal hereditaments.[315] The decision is also interesting for its reliance on realist reasoning. Justice Major referred to Holmes' *dictum* it be "revolting to have no better reason for a rule of law than that so it was laid down in the time of Henry IV,"[316] and "still more revolting if the grounds upon which it was laid down have vanished long since, and the rule persists from blind imitation of the past"[317] – which was already embraced by the Court of Appeal below – as "compelling."[318] The search for "convincing policy reasons for maintaining the common law prohibition on the creation of an interest in land from an incorporeal hereditament other than fidelity to common law principles"[319] also reads

[312] *Dynex, supra* note 310 at para 8, Major J.
[313] (1971), [1972] SCR 703.
[314] *Ibid* at 722, Laskin J, dissenting.
[315] *Dynex, supra* note 310 at paras 14–21, Major J.
[316] Oliver W Holmes, "The Path of the Law" (1897) 10:8 Harv L Rev 457 at 469.
[317] *Ibid* at 469.
[318] *Dynex, supra* note 310 at para 19, Major J.
[319] *Ibid* at para 18, Major J.

like a rejection of legal formalism and a preference for a realist or even Law and Economics approach to property law.

As regards the position of the *Strathcona* principle in Canadian Common Law, it should be noted that the Privy Council found the purchaser of the ship to be a constructive trustee for the charterer. Yet it made no argument why the constructive trust was imposed.[320] Arguably, the development of the law relating to constructive trusts in Canada[321] has superseded the *Strathcona* principle. In a decision during her time at the Court of Appeal of British Columbia, McLachlin J (as she then was) declined to confirm the validity of the *Strathcona* principle in Canadian law.[322]

## I. Comparing Common Law and Civil Law Property

When comparing Common Law and Civil Law property, we notice differences and similarities.

### *I. Objects of Property*

One similarity is that both Common Law and Civil Law are able to accommodate a wide variety of objects of property, both corporeal and incorporeal. Emerich argues that the classical notion of property in Civil Law presupposes that something material is property, whereas the Common Law conceptualizes property as a right.[323] The problem with her argument is that it rests on an ambiguity in Civil Law and Common Law terminology. She equals *propriété* and property, but ignores the fact that the former is more likely to mean a certain type of right in relation to an object of property rather than the object itself, whereas the latter can mean both the right and the object.

### *II. Absolute Right in Property*

Emerich submits that Honoré's addition of a "residual right" to the incidents of ownership is a difference between the Civilian notion of ownership and the Common Law general property right (in Honoré's terminology: ownership).[324] However, this attribute of ownership is recognized in Civil Law as well.[325] I submit that it is unnecessary to include the subsidiary right to the property in

[320] MH Ogilvie, "Privity of Contract and the Third Party Purchaser" (1987) 13:4 CBLJ 402 at 419–20.

[321] See Part II: § 10 , "Proprietary Restitution".

[322] *Montreal Trust Co v Montreal Trust Co of Canada* (1988), 48 DLR (4th) 385 (BC CA).

[323] Emerich, "Regard civiliste", *supra* note 17 at 346.

[324] *Ibid* at 348, referring to Honoré, "Ownership", *supra* note 80 at 127.

[325] See Part II: § 4 C.I, "Ownership".

the list of rights associated with ownership if one already conceptualizes that ownership is the absolute right in the property itself. It then logically follows that the owner holds any residual lesser right or dismemberment of property that is not alienated.

The Civil Law notion of property is based on the idea that at any time, there can be only one owner of property. This means that there is no doctrine of estates. It also means that the protection of property is concerned with the identification of the owner, rather than with relative entitlement.[326] But a valid criticism of the traditional notion of ownership – and, by extension, property rights in general – is the conclusion that Civil Law ownership is not as absolute as it is traditionally thought to be.[327] We find this less-than-absolute ownership already in cases of consensual transfer of property where the relative entitlement between parties can differ depending on whether they were parties of the transaction or not.

### *III. The Value of Possession and Vindication of Ownership*

Emerich argues that possession is protected in both legal systems because it is connected with ownership.[328] She also argues that personal property torts, namely conversion, fulfil a role in Common Law that possessory action takes in Civil Law.[329] But as we have seen, there are other explanations for possessory protection in Civil Law. At common law, on the other hand, the protection of property is completely grounded in possession. An action of vindication presupposes a right of ownership. The common law protection of property through possessory torts is a consequence of its possession-based system.[330] It is also incomplete, as it lacks an action for the specific recovery of goods that would succeed by virtue of title alone.

Tettenborn credits the lack of a generalised tort relating to acts prejudicing the rights of property owners to the fact the English law is not "a particularly logical system."[331] Cuming argues that conversion protects possession because the right to possession is the most important right in the "bundle of rights" that is ownership at common law. Because common law lacks a clearly-defined concept of ownership, protection of property is concerned with protection of possession rather than protection of an abstract "right of ownership."[332]

---

[326] Roderick A Macdonald, "Enforcing Rights in Corporeal Moveables: Revendication and Its Surrogates (Part 1)" (1986) 31:4 McGill LJ 573 at 583.

[327] Emerich, "Regard civiliste", *supra* note 17 at 350–51.

[328] Yaëll Emerich, "Why Protect Possession?" in: Eric Descheemaeker, ed, *The Consequences of Possession* (Edinburgh: Edinburgh University Press, 2014) 30 at 43–44.

[329] *Ibid* at 52.

[330] Rahmatian, *supra* note 62 at 204.

[331] Tettenborn, *supra* note 274 at 326.

[332] Cuming, "Secured Creditors' Non-Statutory Remedies", *supra* note 161 at 248–49.

In Common Law, tort claims are not available only to the "owner" of personal property. Furthermore, at common law, the finder has sufficient title to bring an action of conversion against anyone at all except the owner or one with a better title.[333] Furthermore, the defendant in a Common Law jurisdiction cannot successfully defend herself with the allegation that the claimant is not the owner. Relatively better title is sufficient.[334] This applies regardless of whether the relative entitlement was embodied by possession at the time of interference or not.[335]

[333] See *Armory v Delamirie* (1722), 93 ER 664 (KB). See also Scott, *supra* note 172 at 44.

[334] *Armory v Delamirie,* preceding note. See Scott, *supra* note 172 at 45.

[335] Tettenborn, *supra* note 274 at 328.

# § 6 Equitable Property Rights

In the previous chapter, I have discussed the common law relating to personal property. However, the Common Law as a legal system is not merely made up of the rules of law. A distinct set of rules supplements the rules of common law. This set of rules is referred to as "equity." In a separate chapter, I will discuss the legal or equitable nature of *PPSA* security interests.[1] This influences the priority relationship between equitable claims and the *PPSA* security interest.[2] The purpose of this chapter is to explain the difference between law and equity and the types of equitable property interests. The "trust" concept in a Common Law legal system has a particular importance in regard to personal property because common law only recognizes a very limited number of rights in personal property. Rather than changing the *numerus clausus* of common law property rights, equity supplements the common law rules and thus modifies the common law forms of property rights.[3]

There is a distinction between consensual equitable interests, most notably the interest of a trust beneficiary, and equitable interests that are potentially the outflow of a pre-existing property right. The foremost representative of the latter category is the interest derived from a "constructive trust."[4] Apart from trust interests, equitable liens also confer equitable property interests.[5] The reason I include these non-consensual equitable interests is their impact on the priority relationship of these rights with security interests.

In the first section, I give a brief introduction to the origins of the trust and equity.[6] The trust is a conventional device (*i.e.* constituted by consent) whereas the constructive trust is not conventional. In that regard, they are fundamentally different. However, the trust and the constructive trust do share certain features. Thus, it is worthwhile to look at the basic features of the trust.[7] I then discuss

---

[1] See Part III: § 13 A, "Nature of the PPSA Security Interest".

[2] See Part III: § 13 D, "PPSA Security Interest and Equitable Property Rights".

[3] With a focus on consensual rights see Thomas W Merrill & Henry E Smith, "Optimal Standardization in the Law of Property: The Numerus Clausus Principle" (2000) 110:1 Yale LJ 1 at 17–19.

[4] See Part II: § 6 D, "Constructive Trusts".

[5] See Part II: § 6 G, "Equitable Liens".

[6] See Part II: § 6 A, "Law and Equity".

[7] See Part II: § 6 B, "Development of the Conventional Trust".

the constructive trust. There is disparity between jurisdictions and scholars about the precise nature, requirements, and beginning of the constructive trust,[8] questions which I analyse in this section.[9] I then look at the second variety of non-consensual trusts: the resulting trust.[10]

## A. Law and Equity

The Common Law is split into two branches; common law – or in a shorter form, "law" – and equity. The distinction derives from history and the jurisdiction of the courts in England. Historically, a plaintiff seeking relief in an English law court had to file an action, using a form called the "writ." In the late 13th century at the latest, the writ system became formalized; the number and content of writs became fixed.[11] If a royal subject sought judicial relief that could not be obtained by using a writ, he would plead to the King himself, who was the source of the judicial power in the first place. This plea to the King was not subject to the strict rules that were in force in the law courts, nor was there a limit to the kind of relief that would be granted by the King. The King, in turn, delegated the task of handling the pleas to his Chancellor. This is how the Court of Chancery came into being. The decisions of the Court of Chancery did not affect the rights the plaintiff and defendant were deemed to have at law, but rather put an equitable limit on how legal rights could be exercised.[12]

The co-existence of two bodies of law – common law and equity – naturally lead to a conflict between the two. Nowadays, if there is a conflict between law and equity, equity prevails. This rule harks back to a conflict between the courts of law and the Court of Chancery which found its climax in the *Earl of Oxford's Case.*[13] In that case, Lord Chancellor Ellesmere ruled that

> "In Chancery upon a Recognizance, a *Capias* may be awarded, and the Precedents of that Court, shall close up the Mouths of the Judges of the Common Law, notwithstanding the Statute of Magna Charta[. …] The Chancellor sits in Chancery according to an absolute and

---

[8] See Malcolm Cope, *Constructive Trusts* (North Ryde, NSW: Law Book, 1992) at 3–24; Albert H Oosterhoff *et al, Oosterhoff on Trusts,* 7th edn (Toronto: Carswell, 2009) at 748–52; David M Paciocco, "The Remedial Constructive Trust: A Principled Basis for Priorities over Creditors" (1989) 68 Can Bar Rev 315 at 315–16.

[9] See Part II: § 6 C, "The Trust Beneficiary's Right".

[10] See Part II: § 6 E, "Resulting Trusts".

[11] See Oosterhoff *et al, supra* note 8 at 4–5.

[12] *Ibid* at 7; William S Stevens, "The Common Law Origins of the Infield Fly Rule" (1974–1975) 123 U Pa L Rev 1474 passim. Cf. for a law-and-economics analysis of the infield fly rule Howard M Wasserman, "The Economics of the Infield Fly Rule" [2013] Utah L Rev 479.

[13] (1615), 21 ER 485 (Ch). See Mark Fortier, "Equity and Ideas: Coke, Ellesmere, and James I" (1998) 51 *Renaissance Quarterly* 1255.

uncontrolable [sic!] Power, and is to judge according to that which is alledged [sic!] and proved; but the Judges of the Common Law are to judge according to a strict and ordinary (or limited) Power."[14]

The conflict between the law courts and the Court of Chancery that resulted from the Lord Chancellor's decision was resolved by the King, presumably upon advice of the Attorney-General, Sir Francis Bacon, in favour of equity's primacy.[15] Equity's primacy in England was later codified in the Judicature Acts of the 1870s. These acts also merged the courts of equity and the common law. In Ontario, for example, the superiority of equity is expressed in s 96(2) *Courts of Justice Act*[16]: "Where a rule of equity conflicts with a rule of the common law, the rule of equity prevails."

## B. Development of the Conventional Trust

### *I. Introduction*

One of the most important legal institutions developed in equity is the "trust." The idea behind trusts can probably trace its origin back to the time after the Norman conquest, at which point they were still referred to as "uses." A use allowed one person to separate legal ownership of property, recognized at law, from the enjoyment, or use, of the property. The precise origins of the institution of the use are unclear.[17] Some authors argue it was solely or mostly derived from Germanic law,[18] others trace it back to the Roman *fideicommissum*.[19] Still others suggest Islamic law influences.[20]

[14] *Earl of Oxford's Case,* preceding note at 488, Lord Ellesmere LC.

[15] Oosterhoff *et al, supra* note 8 at 8; Frederick Pollock, *The Expansion of the Common Law* (London: Stevens and Sons, 1904) at 69–74.

[16] RSO, c C43.

[17] See for the current state of discussion Avisheh Avini, "The Origins of the Modern English Trust Revisited" (1996) 70:4 Tul L Rev 1139; Brendan F Brown, "The Ecclesiastical Origin of the Use" (1935) 10:4 Notre Dame L Rev 353 at 357; William F Fratcher, "Uses of Uses" (1969) 34:1 Mo L Rev 39; Monica M Gaudiosi, "The Influence of the Islamic Law of Waqf on the Development of the Trust in England: The Case of Merton College" (1987–1988) 136:4 U Pa L Rev 1231 at 1240–47; Shael Herman, "Utilitas Ecclesiae: The Canonical Conception of the Trust" (1996) 70:6 Tul L Rev 2239 at 2250 ff.

[18] See Oliver W Holmes, "Law in Science and Science in Law" (1899) 12:7 Harv L Rev 443 at 445 ff; Frederic W Maitland, "The Origin of Uses" (1894) 8:3 Harv L Rev 127 at 130.

[19] Brown, *supra* note 17; Vincent Vasey, "Fideicommissa and Uses: The Clerical Connection Revisited" (1982) 41:1 Jurist 201 at 203.

[20] Gaudiosi, *supra* note 17.

*II. Feudal Land Law and Mortmain*

The reason for the employment of uses can be traced to the property rules in place in the early common law. In that period, legal title to land was for life and could not be devised by will,[21] only through *feoffment (i.e. inter vivos* transfer) or – until the enactment of the *Statute Quia Emptores, 1290*[22] – through subinfeudation.

In the feudal land system, in case of death of the holder of land, the land would revert to the feudal lord, ultimately the Crown, unless the receiver would pay feudal duty. Thus, the Crown had an interest not to have the title pass to the Church, which never died.[23] Land held by the Church was referred to as land in *mortmain,* dead hand because the Church perpetually held it, it would never revert back to the Crown and it would render the Crown no more service, nor would it yield feudal duty.

"Some have said that it is called mortmaine, *manus mortua, quia possessio eorum est immortalis, mantis pro possessione, et mortua pro immortali,* and the rather, for that by the laws and statutes of the realme, all ecclesiastical persons are restrained to alien. Others say it is called *manus mortua per antiphrasin,* because bodies politique and corporate never die. Others say that it is called mortmaine by resemblance to the holding of a man's hand that is ready to die, for what he then holdeth he letteth not goe till he be dead. These and such others are' framed out of wit and invention; but the true cause of the name, and the meaning thereof, was taken from the effects, as it is expressed in the statute itself, *per quod quæ servitia ex hujusmodi feodis debentur, et quæ ad defensionem regni ab initio provisa fuerunt, indebitè subtrahuntur, et capitales domini eschaetas suas amittunt,* so as the lands were said to come to dead hands as to the lords, for that by alienation in mortmaine they lost wholly their escheats, and in effect their knights-services for the defence of the realme, wards, marriages, reliefes, and the like; and therefore was called a dead hand, for that a dead hand yeeldeth no service."[24]

Consequently, Edward I. had first passed the *Statute of Mortmain,*[25] which outlawed transfer of land to the church or other religious body. He reaffirmed this prohibition eleven years later in s 3 *Statute Quia Emptores, 1290:*

---

[21] Theodore FT Plucknett, *A Concise History of the Common Law,* 5th edn (London: Butterworths, 1956) at 712–24.

[22] *A Statute of Our Lord the King, Concerning the Selling and Buying of Land, 1290,* 18 Edw I, c 1.

[23] Cf. re the economic interest of the crown in the feudal services attached to land Albert H Oosterhoff, "The Law of Mortmain: An Historical and Comparative Review" (1977) 27 UTLJ 257 at 266.

[24] Edward Coke, *The First Part of the Institutes of the Laws of England: A Commentary Upon Littleton,* 1st edn (Philadelphia: Johnson & Warner, 1812), vol 1 6 (1.1.1.2.b.) [emphasis in original]. On the discussion surrounding the origin of the term mortmain see Oosterhoff, preceding note at 258–59.

[25] *Statute of Mortmain,* 7 Edw I.

"And it is to be understood, that by the said Sales or Purchases of Lands or Tenements, or any Parcels of them, such Lands or Tenements shall in no wise come into Mortmain, either in Part or in Whole, neither by Policy ne Craft, contrary to the Form of the Statute made thereupon of late."

### *III. Circumvention of the Feudal Land Law*

The use was employed to allow transfer of the property in case of death, circumventing the feudal land system.[26] The application of the use avoided legal transfer of title to the final recipient. Thus, the use allowed the bequeathal of real property to an heir. The use worked as follows: A holder of real property (the feoffor) would transfer the property to another living person (the feoffee) on the condition that the feoffor and his heirs would enjoy the use of the property. Along the same vein, a use could be made for the benefit of a religious body. Anybody enjoying the enjoyment of the use was called *cestui que use,* which is the short form of the Law French expression *cestui a que use le feoffment fuit fait.* This clause translates to "he to whose use the transfer was made." The institution itself was consequently called the "use." The rights of *cestui que use* were recognized in equity, but not at law, because *cestui que use* did not have legal title.[27]

In the fifteenth century, it was recognized that the use was not merely an agreement giving rights to feoffor, feoffee and *cestui que use,* but it was also binding upon the successor in title of the feoffee if they had notice of the use.[28]

### *IV. The Statute of Uses*

Uses deprived the Crown of income otherwise due upon the death of the feoffor as a feudal fee. For this reason, the *Statute of Uses*[29] was enacted during the reign of Henry VIII.[30] The *Statute of Uses* appeared to make uses impossible. By virtue of the *Statute of Uses, cestui que use* would receive immediate and outright title to the property. This operation of giving legal title to the equitable *cestui que use* is referred to as "executing the use."[31] The execution of the use would often conflict with the interests of the feoffor, who might want to keep enjoyment of the property for the remainder of his own land, and who would have otherwise assigned the property to *cestui que use* directly. There were

[26] For an account of the employment of uses in devising land to the church see Stephen W DeVine, "Ecclesiastical Antecedents to Secular Jurisdiction over the Feoffment to the Uses to Be Declared in Testamentary Instructions" (1986) 30:4 Am J Legal Hist 295.

[27] Oosterhoff *et al, supra* note 8 at 9.

[28] *Ibid* at 10.

[29] *An Act concerning Uses and Wills,* 27 Hen VIII, c 10.

[30] Oosterhoff *et al, supra* note 8 at 12.

[31] *Ibid* at 12.

cases, however, in which the use would not be executed, the most important of which was the use upon a use.[32]

Common law courts initially held that in cases of a use upon a use, the second use was inconsistent with the first use and thus void. The Court of Chancery, however, affirmed that a use upon a use was possible.[33] Thus, the use upon a use became a way of circumventing the *Statute of Uses*. The *Statute of Uses* would execute the first use, but not the second. To avoid linguistic repetition, the second "to the use of" would be replaced by "in trust for"[34] and thus the use became known as the "trust."

Another case in which the *Statute of Uses* would not execute the use was if the feoffee was not seised of the property.[35] At the time of the SU1536, the notions of seisin of real property and possession of personal property had already become differentiated.[36] Because the *Statute of Uses* did not operate upon non-seised property, it did not operate on a trust in personal property.

In 1660, feudal tenures were abolished in England.[37] While this removed one of the major incentives for the application of trusts regarding real estate,[38] the trust had developed into a recognized legal concept. Parties as well as courts had recognized its utility for a variety of applications. It thus survived the *Abolition of Tenures Act, 1660.*

## C. The Trust Beneficiary's Right

The trust yields an obligation of one party, who in modern trust law is referred to as the trustee, *vis-à-vis* other parties, who are called the settlor and the beneficiary; the obligation exists in "relation to particular property."[39] Consequently, one conceptualization is to say that the trust splits property rights into legal title and beneficial interest. Conceptually, viewing the trust this way is no problem in Common Law because feudal land law influenced Common Law property law, and the splitting of absolute ownership was a key feature of this

---

[32] See for all constellations *ibid* at 13.

[33] *Sambach v Dalston* (1633), 21 ER 188 (Ch); Oosterhoff *et al, supra* note 8 at 14.

[34] Oosterhoff *et al, supra* note 8 at 14.

[35] *Ibid* at 13.

[36] See Part II: § 5 D.II.1, "The Notion of Seisin".

[37] *An Act Takeing Away the Court of Wards and Liveries and Tenures in Capite and by Knights Service and Purveyance, and for Setling a Revenue Upon His Majesty in Lieu Thereof, 1660,* 12 Car II, c 24.

[38] Rainer Becker, *Die Fiducie von Québec und der Trust: Ein Vergleich mit verschiedenen Modellen fiduziarischer Rechtsfiguren im Civil Law* (Tübingen: Mohr Siebeck, 2007) at 24.

[39] Oosterhoff *et al, supra* note 8 at 18.

system.[40] This view aligns with the common conceptualisation before the *Statute of Uses;* at that time, a distinction was drawn between seisin (possession) and the use (fruits, profits, enjoyment) of land.[41] But at this stage, it should be noted that the split-title view of the modern trust beneficiary's right is not universally shared. Maitland argued that equitable rights are never rights in the thing itself.[42] This view has seen some judicial endorsement, and is known as the "grafting theory," based on the idea that the effect of the trust in that view is that rights are grafted on to the trustee's legal rights.[43] We will discuss the split-title or grafting question later.[44] At this stage, while potentially conceptually vague, the split-title theory can serve as the language which we use to discuss sommme of the keyfeatures of the beneficiary's right.

The splitting of legal title and beneficial interest means that the equitable interest is effective against any purchaser of the legal title, unless the purchaser is a *bona fide* purchaser for value without notice.[45] It furthermore means that the legal owner of the property is not barred from transferring legal title to any purchaser.[46]

Under the rule in *Saunders v Vautier,*[47] if all of the beneficiaries in the trust are of adult age and under no disability, the beneficiaries may require the trus-

---

[40] Henry Hansmann & Ugo Mattei, "The Functions of Trust Law: A Comparative Legal and Economic Analysis" (1998) 73 NYUL Rev 434 at 440. Cf. Ben McFarlane & Robert Stevens, "The Nature of Equitable Property" (2010) 4:1 J Equ 1 at 8: "One possible reason for the view that an equitable property right involves the creation of a right to a thing is that the common law permits several people to hold rights in relation to a single thing at the same time."

[41] Tobias Barkley, "Trustees' Bare Legal Title: Concept or Misconception?" (2017) 26:1 Austral Prop LJ 44 at 48–49, referring to NG Jones, "Uses and 'Automatic' Resulting Trusts of Freehold" (2013) 72:1 CLJ 91 at 95.

[42] Frederic W Maitland, "Lectures on Equity" in: Frederic W Maitland, *Equity, Also the Forms of Action at Common Law: Two Courses of Lectures,* AH Chaytor & WJ Whittaker (Cambridge: Cambridge University Press, 1910) 1 at 111–12.

[43] Barkley, *supra* note 41 at 45–47, referring to *DKLR Holding Co (No 2) Pty Ltd v Commissioner of Stamp Duties* (1980), 10 ATR 942 at 948–49 (NSW Sup Ct), which in turn endorses a different passage from Maitland, "Lectures on Equity", preceding note at 17.

[44] See Part II: § 8 E, "Theory of Equitable Property Rights".

[45] Hansmann & Mattei, *supra* note 40 at 440.

[46] *Ibid* at 440.

[47] (1841), 4 Beav 115 (Ch).

tee to transfer the legal estate to them and thereby terminate the trust. In principle, this applies to constructive trusts as well.[48] The transfer of the trust property to the trustee amounts to an equitable vindication of the property right.[49]

## D. Constructive Trusts

The conventional trust arises because of an agreement between the settlor and the trustee. However, a trust can also arise because by operation of law. It is then sometimes called a "remedial trust."[50] Because these trusts arise by operation of law,[51] I refer to them as "legal trusts." The distinction between conventional and legal trusts has been long recognized in English law. In the 17th century, Lord Nottingham classified trusts as follows: "All trusts are either, first, express trusts, which are raised and created by act of the parties, or implied trusts, which are raised or created by act or construction of law."[52]

This book is mostly concerned with the kind of legal trust known as the "constructive trust," but reference will be made to "resulting trusts" as well.[53] The reason for this focus is the role the constructive trust plays in restitution, unjust enrichment, and the possibility of a vindication of property rights in Common Law systems. Before I address these questions at the end of this part of the book, I introduce the constructive trust.

The constructive trust is a peculiarity of the Common Law with no obvious Civil Law equivalent. A constructive trust potentially limits the assets available to the debtor's estate in insolvency. Thus, a beneficiary (creditor) of a constructive trust may get priority over unsecured creditors and rank at par or even above secured creditors. This conflicts with the distribution scheme of bankruptcy regimes guided by the equal distribution principle among creditors (excepting secured creditors).

Internally, within the legal system according to which a claim for the constructive trust is put forward, this requires careful examination as to when the constructive trust should be awarded, so as not to disturb the distribution scheme unfairly. Giving clear shape to the constructive trust also enables other

---

[48] See *Giumelli v Giumelli,* [1999] HCA 10 at para 3, curiam: "A constructive trust of this nature is a remedial response to the claim to equitable intervention made out by the plaintiff. It obliges the holder of the legal title to surrender the property in question, thereby bringing about a determination of the rights and titles of the parties."

[49] Peter Birks, "Property and Unjust Enrichment: Categorical Truths" [1997] NZL Rev 623 at 650.

[50] See e.g. Oosterhoff *et al, supra* note 8 at 585.

[51] *Ibid* at 587.

[52] *Cook v Fountain* (1672), 3 Swans 585 at 591 (Ch), Lord Nottingham.

[53] See Part II: § 6 E, "Resulting Trusts".

jurisdictions to properly characterize the constructive trust in their conflict-of-laws regime.

The hypothesis advanced in this book is that the constructive trust serves a purpose that is comparable to the Civil Law concept of vindication. It thus becomes important to identify the line in Common Law that parallels the one found in Civil Law: the line between "unjustified enrichment" in its limited Civil Law meaning on the one hand and vindication on the other hand. Put differently, we need to draw lines between when the creditor should have a personal claim, determined by a monetary value, and when the creditor should have a claim to certain property. Finally, a clear characterization of the constructive trust also enables one to properly determine how insolvency law should deal with the constructive trust.

### *I. Nature of the Constructive Trust*

#### *1. English Law*

An early case involving constructive trusts in England is *Keech v Sandford.*[54] The trustee was party to a lease for the benefit of a minor. After the lease expired, the trustee first tried to have the lease renewed for the benefit of the child. After that failed, he renewed the lease in his name and for his benefit only. The Court of Chancery held that the trustee now held the lease in constructive trust for the beneficiary.

> "I must consider this as a trust for the infant; for I very well see, if a trustee, on the refusal to renew, might have a lease to himself, few trust-estates would be renewed to cestui que use; though I do not say there is a fraud in this case, yet he should rather have let it run out, than to have had the lease to himself. This may seem hard, that the trustee is the only person of all mankind who might not have the lease: but it is very proper that rule should be strictly pursued, and not in the least relaxed; for it is very obvious what would be the consequence of letting trustees have the lease, on refusal to renew to cestui que use. So decreed, that the lease should be assigned to the infant, and that the trustee should be indemnified from any covenants comprised in the lease, and an account of the profits made since the renewal."[55]

Lord Denning, in *Hussey v Palmer,* held that the constructive trust is a trust instituted "whenever justice and good conscience require it."[56] The Court of Appeal for New Zealand embraced this broad principle.[57] The Court followed a passage in Goff and Jones.[58]

---

[54] (1726), 61 Sel Cas T King 61 (Ch).

[55] *Ibid* at 62, King LC.

[56] *Hussey v Palmer,* [1972] 1 WLR 1286 at 1289–90 (CA Civ), Lord Denning MR.

[57] *Elders Pastoral Ltd v Bank of New Zealand,* [1989] 2 NZLR 180 at 185 (CA), Cooke P.

[58] Robert Goff & Gareth H Jones, *The Law of Restitution,* 3rd edn (London: Sweet & Maxwell, 1986) at 77: "Equity's traditional rules suggest that it is necessary to discover a fiduciary relationship before a plaintiff can trace his property. Now that law and equity are

Regarding New York law, the Chancery Division held that the constructive trust is substantive, not merely remedial.[59] It also held that the law in England is similar, if not the same.[60]

*2. Canadian Law*

In a number of cases, the Supreme Court evolved the constructive trust into a remedy for what it described as unjust enrichment (mainly in matrimonial property disputes).[61] Canadian case law is said to distinguish between two kinds of constructive trusts: the "remedial" constructive trust for cases of unjust enrichment as established in *Pettkus v Becker*[62] and the "institutional" constructive trust. In *Soulos v Korkontzilas,*[63] this distinction was maintained.[64] The remedial constructive trust is usually viewed as a judicial remedy for "unjust enrichment," the institutional constructive trust is instituted for wrongful acts like fraud and breach of duty of loyalty.[65]

However, importantly the Supreme Court indicated that both types of constructive trusts derive from one unifying underlying institution.[66] I submit that a distinction is not necessary, or at least that both types of constructive trusts

---

fused this requirement makes little sense, and it has been recently accepted that 'the receiving of money which consistently with conscience cannot be retained is, in equity, sufficient to raise a trust in favour of the party for whom or in whose account it was received.'" Cited as in *Elders Pastoral Ltd v Bank of New Zealand,* preceding note at 193, Somers J. The newest edition of *Goff & Jones* is Charles CJ Mitchell, Paul Mitchell & Stephen Watterson, *Goff & Jones: The Law of Unjust Enrichment,* 9th edn (London: Sweet & Maxwell, 2016).

[59] *Chase Manhattan Bank NA v Israel-British Bank (London) Ltd* (1979), [1981] 1 Ch 105 at 122–27 (Ch D) [*Chase Manhattan*], Goulding J.

[60] *Ibid* at 128, Goulding J.

[61] *Peter v Beblow,* [1993] 1 SCR 980; *Pettkus v Becker,* [1980] 2 SCR 834; *Rathwell v Rathwell,* [1978] 2 SCR 436; *Murdoch v Murdoch* (1973), [1975] 1 SCR 423.

[62] Preceding note.

[63] [1997] 2 SCR 217 [*Soulos*].

[64] Cf. Robert Chambers, "Constructive Trusts in Canada" (1999) 37 Alta L Rev 173, but arguing that the distinction needs only be maintained when one takes a narrow view of what constitutes "enrichment" Peter D Maddaugh & John D McCamus, *The Law of Restitution,* loose-leaf (Aurora, Ontario: Canada Law Book, 2004) 5:200.60; Oosterhoff *et al, supra* note 8 at 719 ff; Paciocco, *supra* note 8 at 318–19.

[65] *Soulos, supra* note 63 at para 17, McLachlin J (as she then was).

[66] *Ibid* at para 25, McLachlin J (as she then was): "[T]he law of constructive trust in the common law provinces of Canada embraces the situations in which English courts of equity traditionally found a constructive trust as well as the situations of unjust enrichment recognized in recent Canadian jurisprudence."

can be seen to be an expression of an underlying principle.[67] This is important for insolvency law[68] and the conflict of laws.[69]

*3. American Law*

In the United States, the constructive trust has also developed into a remedy for unjust enrichment.[70] Justice Cardozo expressed that "[a] constructive trust is the formula through which the conscience of equity finds expression."[71] In Texas, it was held that a constructive trust is not actually a trust, but rather an equitable remedy imposed by law to prevent unjust enrichment resulting from an unconscionable act;[72] it is not a fiduciary relationship but an equitable duty.[73] In California, the Court of Appeal held that "there is no cause of action for unjust enrichment. Rather, unjust enrichment is a basis for obtaining restitution based on quasi-contract or imposition of a constructive trust."[74] Other courts maintain that the constructive trust is structurally similar to the express trust.[75]

In the United States, five different approaches towards the constructive trust can be distinguished. The first class are jurisdictions that require for the constructive trust to be imposed an unjust enrichment plus an un-equitable element on the part of the debtor. In *New York* case law, the following requirements were formulated for a constructive trust: (1) a confidential or fiduciary relation, (2) a promise, (3) a transfer in reliance thereon and (4) unjust enrichment.[76] Unjust enrichment means that a party holds "property under such circumstances that in equity and good conscience he ought not to retain it."[77] Thus, a

---

[67] See Part II: § 10 F, "Analysis of Proprietary Restitution".

[68] See Part IV: § 16 D, "Proprietary Restitution and Insolvency".

[69] See Part V: § 19 A, "Characterization of Proprietary Restitution".

[70] See Cope, *supra* note 8 at 24–35; Roscoe Pound, "The Progress of the Law: 1918–1919 Equity" (1919–1920) 33 Harv L Rev 420 at 420–23.

[71] *Beatty v Guggenheim Exploration Co,* 122 NE 378 at 380 (NY 1919), Cardozo J.

[72] *Re Behring Intern, Inc,* 61 BR 896 at 906 (ND Tex 1986), McGuire CJ; *Ellisor v Ellisor,* 630 SW2[d] 746 at 748 (Tex 1[st] Dist 1982), Doyle J; *Lowther v Lowther,* 578 SW2[d] 560 at 561 (Tex 10[th] Dist 1979), McDonald CJ.

[73] *Re Behring Intern, Inc,* preceding note at 906, McGuire CJ.

[74] *McKell v Washington Mut, Inc,* 142 Cal App 4[th] 1457 at 1490 (Cal 2[d] Dist 2006).

[75] *Re Markair, Inc,* 172 BR 638 at 641 (9[th] Cir 1994), Jones BJ: "Unlike a resulting trust, '[a] constructive trust is not grounded in the intention of the parties, inferred or presumed; it is a remedial device of equity-a trust in invitum-to prevent unjust enrichment.' The distinction between resulting and constructive trusts may blur because, as an equitable remedy, a constructive trust remediates inequitable circumstances by imposing what the parties in equity should have intended." [References ommitted].

[76] *Re First Central Financial Corp,* 377 F3[d] 209 at 212 (2[d] Cir 2004); *Sharp v Kosmalski,* 351 NE2[d] 721 at 723 (NY 1976).

[77] *Simonds v Simonds,* 380 NE2[d] 189 at 194 (NY 1978). This in turn is a variation of the formula used in *Beatty v Guggenheim Exploration Co, supra* note 71 at 380, Cardozo J.

*bona fide* purchaser for value takes title free of the constructive trust, and a gratuitous donee does not.[78] Later, the four requirements were held to be a general guideline, whereas equity permits some flexibility in particular cases.[79] The field of application of a constructive trust for unlimited enrichment "is limited only by the inventiveness of men who find new ways to enrich themselves unjustly by grasping what should not belong to them."[80] Whether a party is unjustly enriched is still a legal, not a factual, question.[81] The constructive trust is held to be not substantively different from remedies in quasi-contract situations.[82]

The constructive trust is "fraud-rectifying" rather than "intent-enforcing."[83] A constructive trust should not be awarded when a written contract exists.[84] The law in *Florida*[85] and *Delaware*[86] is similar.

In a second class of jurisdictions such as *New Jersey,*[87] *Oregon,*[88] and *Texas*[89] an unjust enrichment alone is element enough. Thus, for instance, in New Jersey, a creditor who perfected her security interest in the debtor's property in

---

[78] *Simonds v Simonds,* preceding note at 194.

[79] *Re Koreag, Controle et Revision SA,* 961 F2ᵈ 341 at 353 (2ᵈ Cir 1992); *Bankers Sec Life Ins Soc v Shakerdge,* 49 NY2ᵈ 939 at 940 (1980).

[80] *Re Koreag, Controle et Revision SA,* preceding note at 353; *Latham v Father Divine,* 299 NY 22 at 27 (1949).

[81] *Re First Central Financial Corp, supra* note 76 at 213.

[82] *Ibid* at 213–14.

[83] *Ibid* at 215.

[84] *Ibid* at 213–16.

[85] See *Wadlington v Edwards,* 92 So2ᵈ 629 at 631 (Fla 1957), Thornal J: Intent is lacking when a constructive trust is imposed. Instead, "[the] trust is 'constructed' by equity to prevent an unjust enrichment of one person at the expense of another as the result of fraud, undue influence, abuse of confidence or mistake in the transaction that originates the problem."

[86] *Adams v Jankouskas,* 452 A2ᵈ 148 at 152 (Del 1982), Moore J: "The constructive trust does not arise from intent of the parties, but from un-equitable ('fraudulent, unfair, or unconscionable') act by the defendant, if this act led to an unjust enrichment of the defendant in relation to somebody to whom he owed a duty."

[87] *D'Ippolito v Castoro,* 51 NJ 584 at 588 (1968), Haneman J.

[88] *Derenco, Inc v Benj Franklin Federal Sav & Loan Ass'n,* 577 P2ᵈ 477 at para 15 (Ore 1978), Holman J: "Quasi-contracts and constructive trusts are parallel means at law and equity, respectively, of accomplishing substantial justice by preventing unjust enrichment and forcing restitution to the plaintiff of something which in equity and good conscience did not belong to the defendant. It is only proper touse a constructive trust when there is some specific property identified as belonging to the plaintiff. When the possession of no specific identifiable propertyissought and only a money judgment is requested, quasi-contract is the remedy."

[89] *Meadows v Bierschwale,* 516 SW2ᵈ 125 at 131 (Tex Sup Ct 1974), Johnson J: "Constructive trusts, being remedial in character, have the very broad function of redressing wrong or unjust enrichment in keeping with basic principles of equity and justice."

New York is entitled to have a constructive trust in the property imposed in her favour when the debtor moves merchandise to New Jersey without informing the creditor, thereby preventing the creditor from perfecting her security interest in that state.[90]

In a third class of jurisdictions, such as *Connecticut*[91] and *Minnesota,*[92] a constructive trust is imposed when property is conveyed to the creditor without express intent to create a trust but with the implied benefit of another person so that the creditor cannot equitably retain the property.

In *California,* a constructive trust has the following requirements:

> "(1) the existence of a *res* (property or some interest in property); (2) the right of a complaining party to that *res;* and (3) some wrongful acquisition or detention of the *res* by another party who is not entitled to it."[93]

In *Louisiana,* finally, the constructive trust was deemed to be incompatible with s 476 *Civil Code of Louisana,* which limits possible property interests under Louisiana civil law to the ones mentioned in the statute (*numerus clausus* of property interests).[94]

### *II. Beginning of the Constructive Trust*

The time when the trust comes into existence impacts the relationship of the constructive trust with other property rights; this becomes particularly important in bankruptcy: if the constructive trust arises before the court recognizes it, it can be effective in bankruptcy. There are two possibilities when a constructive trust comes into existence: it could either start *ab initio,* existing from the moment the unjust enrichment occurs,[95] or when the court orders the remedy.[96] The latter view again splits in two. The declaration of the remedy either has *ex nunc* effect,[97] or it has retroactive effect so that the constructive trust comes into existence *ex tunc.*[98] The consequence that constructive trusts exist that are not enforceable until a court declares them is occasionally

---

[90] *Re Howard's Appliance Corp,* 874 F2[d] 88 (2[d] Cir 1989).

[91] *Gulack v Gulack,* 30 Conn App 305 at 310 (App Ct 1993), Dupont CJ.

[92] *Knox v Knox,* 222 Minn 477 at 481 (1946), Matson J.

[93] *Communist Party v 522 Valencia, Inc,* 41 Cal Rptr 2[d] 618 at 623–24 (Cal 1[st] Dist 1995).

[94] *Plaquemines Parish Com'n Council v Delta Development Co, Inc,* 486 So2[d] 129 at 135–37 (La 4[th] Cir Ct App 1986).

[95] Paciocco, *supra* note 8 at 316, 319, note 21.

[96] Emily L Sherwin, "Constructive Trusts in Bankruptcy" [1989] U Ill L Rev 297 at 301. Cf. John P Dawson, *Unjust Enrichment: A Comparative Analysis,* Reprint 1999 (Holmes Beach, Fla: Gaunt, 1999) at 32.

[97] Cf. Sherwin, preceding note at 313.

[98] George E Palmer, *The Law of Restitution* (Boston: Little, Brown & Co, 1978) at § 1.4.

acknowledged.[99] If the constructive trust arises only at the point of the judgment, it can only be effective if the court's order has effect it before the estate passed to the trustee.[100]

*1. Canadian Law*

In Canada, the Court of Queen's Bench of Saskatchewan held that the remedial constructive trust does not arise until the moment of the court order.[101] In *Re Croteau,*[102] the Ontario High Court held that a constructive trust under the category established by *Pettkus v Becker* does arise before the order of the court.[103] In *Rawluk v Rawluk,*[104] finally, the Supreme Court in its majority opinion held that a remedial constructive trust arises at the time the duty to make restitution arises.

"It is important in this respect to keep in mind that a property interest arising under a constructive trust can be recognized as having come into existence not when the trust is judicially declared but from the time when the unjust enrichment first arose. As Professors Oosterhoff and Gillese state, 'the date at which a constructive trust arises … is now generally accepted to be the date upon which a duty to make restitution occurs' (Oosterhoff and Gillese, *A.H. Oosterhoff: Text, Commentary and Cases on Trusts,* 3rd ed. (Toronto, Carswell: 1987) at 579). Professor Scott has stated in *Law of Trusts* 4$^{th}$ ed. (Boston: Little Brown & Company, 1987) at 323–24 that: 'The beneficial interest in the property is from the beginning in the person who has been wronged. The constructive trust arises from the situation in which he is entitled to the remedy of restitution, and it arises as soon as that situation is created … It would seem that there is no foundation whatever for the notion that a constructive trust does not arise until it is decreed by a court. It arises when the duty to make restitution arises, not when that duty is subsequently enforced.' I agree completely with the position taken on this issue by the authors of these helpful texts."[105]

On the other hand, McLachlin J (as she then was) – in a minority opinion – held that the constructive trust of the remedial kind arises at the time of the order unless the court declares otherwise.

"Although the constructive trust is remedial, that is not to say that the remedial concept of constructive trust does not give rise to property interests. When the court declares a constructive trust, *at that point* the beneficiary obtains an interest in the property subject to the trust. That property interest, it appears, may be taken as extending back to the date when the trust was 'earned' or perfected. In *Hussey v Palmer,* in a passage referred to by Dickson J.

---

[99] *Ibid* at § 1.4.

[100] Sherwin, *supra* note 96 at 325–26.

[101] *Bedard v Schell* (1987), 59 Sask R 71 at para 13 (QB), Gerein J.

[102] (1985), 50 OR (2$^{d}$) 629 (HCJ).

[103] *Ibid* at 635, Potts J: "I have raised with counsel the question and they have agreed that the declaration as to ownership has a retroactive effect and takes place certainly as of the date of bankruptcy."

[104] [1990] 1 SCR 70.

[105] *Ibid* at 91–92, Cory J.

in *Rathwell v Rathwell* and relied on by the Court of Appeal in this case, Lord Denning postulated that the interest may arise at the time of declaration or from the outset, as the case may require. Scott views the trust as being in force from the outset, with a discretion in the court as to whether it should be enforced: op. cit., para. 462.2. Another American scholar regards it as coming into existence only on an order being made, but having retrospective operation: Bogert, *The Law of Trusts and Trustees* 2d ed. (St. Paul, West Pub. Co: 1978), at para. 472."[106]

### 2. English Law

In *Chase Manhattan Bank NA v Israel-British Bank (London) Ltd,* the Chancery Division held, in a case of mistaken payment, that the constructive trust begins on the day the event happened.[107] In *Re Sharpe,*[108] the Court held that under English law, even what may be considered a remedial trust begins prior to the judicial decree.[109]

### 3. American Law

The *ab initio* view is sometimes accepted in the US.[110] Other courts, on the other hand, held that the constructive trust arises at the time of the order.[111] This latter view thus has problems recognizing a constructive trust for the first time in bankruptcy proceedings.[112]

---

[106] *Ibid* at 103, McLachlin J (as she then was) [emphasis added].

[107] *Chase Manhattan, supra* note 59 at 128, Goulding J.

[108] [1980] 1 WLR 219 (Ch D).

[109] *Ibid* at 225–26, Browne-Wilkinson J (as he then was).

[110] *Re DVI, Inc,* 306 BR 496 at 499–500 (D Del Bankr 2004), Walrath J (Illinois); *Stansbury v United States,* 543 FSupp 154 at 157 (ND Ill 1982), Roszkowski DJ (Illinois).

[111] *Re Omegas Group, Inc,* 16 F3d 1443 at 1451 (6th Cir 1994), Batchelder Cir J: "Because a constructive trust, unlike an express trust, is a remedy, it does not exist until a plaintiff obtains a judicial decision finding him to be entitled to judgment 'impressing' defendant's property or assets with a constructive trust." Ref'd to by *Re Mark Benskin & Co, Inc,* 1995 WL 381741 (6th Cir 1995) (unpublished opinion).

[112] *Re Omegas Group, Inc,* preceding note at 1449, Batchelder Cir J: "Unless a court has already impressed a constructive trust upon certain assets [...] the claimant cannot properly represent to the bankruptcy court that he was, at the time of the commencement of the case, a beneficiary of a constructive trust held by the debtor." Cf. *Re Morken,* 182 BR 1007 at 1022 (D Minn Bankr 1995), Kressel BJ and *Re Markair, Inc, supra* note 75 at 641, Jones BJ: "Because it is a remedy, a constructive trust cannot affect rights in the *res* until it is imposed. A constructive trust imposed by state law pre-petition would therefore exclude the *res* from the debtor estate. If the remedy remains inchoate post-petition, however, it is subordinate to the trustee's strong arm power." [Emphasis added].

*III. Vendor-Purchaser Constructive Trusts*

Vendor-purchaser constructive trusts are trusts which are created in response to a failed or inchoate transfer of property at law.[113] Austin described them as follows:

"By the provisions of that part of the English law which is called equity, a contract to sell at once vests *jus in rem* or ownership in the buyer, and the seller has only *jus in re aliena.* But according to the conflicting provisions of that part of the English system called peculiarly law, a sale and purchase without certain formalities merely gives *jus ad rem,* or a right to receive the ownership, not ownership itself."[114]

In Maitland's conceptualisation,[115] this explanation of the vendor-purchaser constructive trust cannot be sustained, as he argued that equitable rights are never rights in the thing itself.[116] However, at this point, I am not yet concerned with the precise characterization of the right. I shall look at this question again later.[117] For the present purpose, it suffices to note that equity will recognize transfers of property which do not meet certain requirements that would be needed at law. Equity recognizes the transfer by creating a constructive trust between vendor and purchaser. Regarding chattel, failed transfers have become rare because of the particular implementation of consensualism.[118] Where a sales contract passes property by virtue of the agreement of the parties without the need of any further formalities,[119] a failed transfer of property becomes rare. However, failed transfers can happen, particularly when the parties agree to postpone the transfer of property and there is a subsequent failure. Courts have recognized a constructive trust in these circumstances.[120] Gretton goes further and argues that the function of the consensual principle in the *Sale of Goods Acts*[121] is that the purchaser becomes the equitable owner of the property upon the conclusion of the contract, but ownership in law passes only on delivery.[122] In other words, any sale of movable property becomes a purchaser-

---

[113] See on vendor-purchaser constructive trusts Anthony J Duggan, "Constructive Trusts from a Law and Economics Perspective" (2005) 55 UTLJ 217.

[114] John Austin, *Lectures on Jurisprudence: The Philosophy of Positive Law,* ed by Robert Campbell, 4th edn (London: J Murray, 1873), vol 1 at 388 [emphasis in original].

[115] See Part II: § 6 C, "The Trust Beneficiary's Right".

[116] Maitland, "Lectures on Equity", *supra* note 42 at 111–12.

[117] See Part II: § 8 E, "Theory of Equitable Property Rights".

[118] See also Birke Häcker, "Das Trennungs- und Abstraktionsprinzip im englischen Recht: Dargestellt anhand der Übereignung" [2011] ZEuP 335 at 344.

[119] See Part II: § 5 E.I, "Inter Vivos Transfer of Property in Common Law".

[120] *Taypotat v Surgeson,* [1985] 3 WWR 18 (Sask CA); *Hewett v Court* (1983), 149 CLR 639.

[121] *Sale of Goods Act 1979,* 1979, c 54, ss 17; 18 respectively *Sale of Goods Act,* RSO 1990, c S.1, ss 18(1); 19. See Part II: § 5 E.I, "Inter Vivos Transfer of Property in Common Law".

[122] George L Gretton, "Constructive Trusts (Part I)" (1997) 1:3 Edin L Rev 281 at 284.

vendor constructive trust. Delivery executes the trust and unites legal and equitable title in the purchaser. Conceptually, this explains why the good faith third-party second purchaser for value without notice can acquire full legal and equitable title, as she would not be different from any other third-party *bona fide* purchaser for value without notice purchasing property from a legal owner.[123]

Swadling criticizes the term "constructive trust" because, he argues, the duty to convey is the reason for which the constructive trust arises, not the result.[124] His criticism is based on the fact that the duty to convey is most interesting in the case of vendor-purchaser constructive trusts.[125] However, there is no reason to restrict the application of the rule in *Saunders v Vautier* to these types of trust, nor does Swadling state that it should be restricted. Consequently, any constructive trust would allow the claimant to demand that specific property be conveyed to her.

"Where a third party receives trust property, the beneficiary of the trust can bring either a claim for damages or demand recovery of the specific property.[126] Due to their complexity, questions on the exact nature and mechanism by which the beneficiary ascertains a right to the property *vis-à-vis* a third party are the subject of a later chapter."[127]

## E. Resulting Trusts

The term "resulting trust," or more precisely the "resulting," derives from Latin *resultare,*[128] meaning "to spring back." The resulting trust is difficult to define precisely, but it can be explained by reference to the cases in which it arises.[129] Phenomenologically, the resulting trust arises in two situations. A resulting trust is created either if an express trust fails, in which case the trustee holds the property in resulting trust for the settlor,[130] or in cases where property passes from A to B but equity presumes that B was not meant to receive the beneficial interest.[131] These two classes can thus be called "failed transfer resulting trust" and "presumptive intention resulting trusts."

---

[123] See Part II: § 6 C, "The Trust Beneficiary's Right".

[124] William Swadling, "The Fiction of the Constructive Trust" (2011) 64:1 Curr Legal Probs 399 at 408.

[125] See Part II: § 6 D.III, "Vendor-Purchaser Constructive Trusts".

[126] Nicholas Curwen, "The Remedy in Conversion: Confusing Property and Obligation" (2006) 26:4 LS 570 at 576.

[127] See Part II: § 10 , "Proprietary Restitution".

[128] William Swadling, "Explaining Resulting Trusts" (2008) 124 LQR 72 at 72.

[129] Oosterhoff *et al, supra* note 8 at 595.

[130] *Ibid* at 590; Swadling, "Explaining Resulting Trusts", *supra* note 128 at 73.

[131] Oosterhoff *et al, supra* note 8 at 590; Swadling, "Explaining Resulting Trusts", *supra* note 128 at 72–73.

Regarding the presumptive intention class, Birks argued that rather than explaining this class by the notion of presumptive intention, it is better explained by viewing the resulting trust as a response to defective non-beneficial transfers of property. This way, he tried to integrate the resulting trust into his theory of proprietary restitution.[132] The courts soundly rejected his submission:

"Professor Birks has argued for a wider role for the resulting trust in the field of restitution, and specifically for its availability in cases of mistake and failure of consideration. His thesis is avowedly experimental, written to test the temperature of the water. I feel bound to respond that the temperature of the water must be regarded as decidedly cold."[133]

Canadian courts developed the common intention theory win order to handle the presumptive intention class of resulting trusts. The common intention theory began in *Murdoch v Murdoch.* Under the common-intention theory, a spouse who made gratuitous contributions – either by contributing money or by maintaining the household, raising the children, etc. – to the intimate relationship could acquire a beneficial interest in the land owned by the other party, unless it could be shown that the contributing spouse meant her contributions as a gift. This trust is called a "common-intention trust" because it was presumed that the parties shared the common-intention that the land would be theirs together.[134] According to Oosterhoff and others, the common-intention trust was based on a misreading of the following passage in *Gissing v Gissing*[135] by Canadian courts:[136]

"Any claim to a beneficial interest in land by a person, whether spouse or stranger, in whom the legal estate in the land is not vested must be based upon the proposition that the person in whom the legal estate is vested holds it as trustee upon trust to give effect to the beneficial interest of the claimant as cestui que trust. The legal principles applicable to the claim are those of the English law of trusts and in particular, in the kind of dispute between spouses that comes before the courts, the law relating to the creation and operation of '*resulting, implied or constructive trusts.*' Where the trust is expressly declared in the instrument by which the legal estate is transferred to the trustee or by a written declaration of trust by the trustee, the court must give effect to it. [...] If it is not in writing it can only take effect as a resulting, implied or constructive trust [...].

A resulting, implied or constructive trust - and it is unnecessary for present purposes to distinguish between these three classes of trust - is created by a transaction between the trustee and the *cestui que trust* in connection with the acquisition by the trustee of a legal

[132] See Peter Birks, "Restitution and Resulting Trusts: Papers Presented at the First International Conference on Equity, the Faculty of Law, the Hebrew University of Jerusalem, June 1990" in: Stephen R Goldstein, ed, *Equity and Contemporary Legal Developments* (Jerusalem: Harry & Michael Sacher Institute for Legislative Research & Comparative Law, Hebrew University of Jerusalem, 1992) 335.

[133] *Westdeutsche Landesbank Girozentrale v Islington London Borough Council,* [1996] 1 AC 669 at 689 (HL), Lord Goff.

[134] See Oosterhoff *et al, supra* note 8 at 641–42.

[135] (1970), [1971] 1 AC 886 (HL) [*Gissing*].

[136] Oosterhoff *et al, supra* note 8 at 642–43.

estate in land, whenever the trustee has so conducted himself that it would be inequitable to allow him to deny to the *cestui que trust* a beneficial interest in the land acquired. And he will be held so to have conducted himself if by his words or conduct he has induced the *cestui que trust* to act to his own detriment in the reasonable belief that by so acting he was acquiring a beneficial interest in the land.

[...]

Difficult as they are to solve, however, these problems as to the amount of the share of a spouse in the beneficial interest in a matrimonial home where the legal estate is vested solely in the other spouse, only arise in cases where the court is satisfied by the words or conduct of the parties that it was their common intention that the beneficial interest was not to belong solely to the spouse in whom the legal estate was vested but was to be shared between them in some proportion or other."[137]

Oosterhoff and others argue that the reference in *Gissing* to the resulting trust was merely meant to illustrate the existence of non-written trusts, but not to declare that a resulting trust arises in cases of shared contributions.[138]

In *Kerr v Baranow,*[139] the Supreme Court of Canada effectively ended the availability of resulting trusts in the common intention cases:

"In this Court, since Pettkus, the common intention resulting trust remains intact but unused. While traditional resulting trust principles may well have a role to play in the resolution of property disputes between unmarried domestic partners, the time has come to acknowledge that there is no continuing role for the common intention resulting trust."[140]

The Court explained this with the fact that unjust enrichment now provides a more "comprehensive and more principled basis to address the wide variety of circumstances that lead to claims arising out of domestic partnerships."[141]

## F. The Rule Against Perpetuities

A trust has the potential to remove property from commerce for the duration of the trust.[142] This can be problematic if the duration of the trust is indeterminate. If the trust never terminates, there is never one person who can freely dispose of the property. This had led to the creation of the rule against perpetuities. The rule derives from the *Duke of Norfolk's Case.*[143] Henry Frederick Howard, 22^d Earl of Arundel devised certain titles to different branches of his descendants, with the remainder to other branches. All in all, the titles were

---

[137] *Gissing, supra* note 135 at 904–5, 909, Lord Diplock [emphasis added].

[138] Oosterhoff *et al, supra* note 8 at 643.

[139] 2011 SCC 10.

[140] *Ibid* at para 15, Cromwell J.

[141] *Ibid* at para 28, Cromwell J.

[142] See John H Merryman, "Policy, Autonomy, and the Numerus Clausus in Italian and American Property Law" (1963) 12:2 Am J Comp L 224 at 226.

[143] (1682), 3 Ch Cas 1 (Ch).

tied up for at least 200 years. The Court of Chancery held that property cannot be tied up for such an excessive period of time. In *Cadell v Palmer,*[144] the term was fixed at 21 years after the death of everyone alive at the creation of the trust. The common law rule has been modified in a few Canadian jurisdictions and England and Wales, but it has only been abolished in Manitoba.[145] Just as all interests need to vest within a certain period, a trust cannot be created for perpetuity.[146]

## G. Equitable Liens

The equitable lien is recognized in English law as a right to the property that confers a charge on the creditor until payment is made.[147] It is recognized in New Zealand as well,[148] and the High Court of Australia has considered it established law.[149]

As several authors note, the proper distinction between the equitable charge, which arises due to an agreement between the parties, and the equitable lien, which arises out of the parties' behaviour, is seldomly made.[150] For example, in *Swiss Bank Corp v Lloyds Bank Ltd,*[151] the Court used the term "equitable charge" to refer to the equitable lien.[152]

The terminology is rather confusing because the equitable lien is more akin to the consensual charge than to the consensual or legal lien because it secures payment of a sum of money not by way of retention, but rather by using the

---

144 (1833), 1 Cl & F 372 (HL).

145 See Oosterhoff *et al, supra* note 8 at 313.

146 *Ibid* at 314.

147 See Fiona R Burns, "The Equitable Lien Rediscovered: A Remedy for the 21st Century" (2002) 25 UNSWLJ 1 at 3–4; Barbara E Cotton, "The Equitable Lien: New Life in an Old Remedy" (1994) 16 Advocates' Q 385 at 386; John McGhee, *Snell's Equity,* 30th edn (London: Sweet & Maxwell, 2000) at paras 21.7, 28.2. With a particular focus on commercial transactions Sarah Worthington, "Equitable Liens in Commercial Transactions" (1994) 53 CLJ 263 at 263.

148 *Waitamo Wools (NZ) Ltd v Nelson (Nz) Ltd,* [1974] 1 NZLR 484 (CA); *Re Whitehead,* [1948] NZLR 1066 (CA).

149 *Giumelli v Giumelli, supra* note 48 at para 31, curiam, referring to *Chalmers v Pardoe,* [1963] 1 WLR 677 (Fiji PC).

150 Burns, "The Equitable Lien Rediscovered", *supra* note 147 at 4; Cotton, *supra* note 147 at 386.

151 [1980] 3 WLR 457 (CA Civ).

152 For another example see Burns, "The Equitable Lien Rediscovered", *supra* note 147 at 4, note 24.

proceeds from the property.[153] It is a hypothecation of the property.[154] This explains why, in passing, the High Court of Australia refers to it as "a charge or lien."[155]

The High Court of Australia pointed out that the term "equitable lien" and "constructive trust" are often used interchangeably in American law, but should in fact be distinguished – the latter giving title to property, the former giving a right of satisfaction.[156] However, they are distinct concepts in American law as well.[157]

The most pronounced difference between the equitable lien and the constructive trust is that the lien does not entitle the creditor to demand that legal title be transferred to her.[158] It is on this basis that the equitable lien, albeit not consensual, has a greater claim to be included in the list of security interests.[159] Burns argues that the equitable lien is to be used as an alternative to the constructive trust when the latter giving the beneficiary a right to the estate is inappropriate.[160]

The constructive trust seems to be the most common remedy effecting proprietary restitution in Canadian unjust enrichment cases. However, some cases on the equitable lien can be found. In *Mogus v Broz Family Trust,*[161] which involved real rather than personal property, the applicants argued that the registration of an interest by the respondents was invalid because s 62 *Land Titles Act*[162] provides that trusts cannot be entered in the land register. Here, the respondents argued that their interest was indeed an equitable lien, and thus could be registered under s 71 *Land Titles Act,* which allows the filing of notice to protect "unregistered estates, rights, interests or equities in registered land." *Ahone v Holloway* – also on real property – confirmed the existence of an equitable vendor's lien.[163] *Transwest Helicopters v Int Aviation Services*[164] confirmed the existence of an equitable lien in chattel. If it follows from that the

---

[153] McGhee, *supra* note 147 at para 21.7.

[154] Burns, "The Equitable Lien Rediscovered", *supra* note 147 at 4.

[155] *Giumelli v Giumelli, supra* note 48 at para 31, curiam.

[156] *Ibid* at para 32, curiam. For a historical analysis of the confusion see Burns, "The Equitable Lien Rediscovered", *supra* note 147 at 7–8.

[157] See with reference to American precedents Henry Monaghan, "Constructive Trust and Equitable Lien: Status of the Conscious and the Innocent Wrongdoer in Equity" (1960–1961) 38 U Det LJ 10 at 12–13. Cotton, citing case-law, points out that the American equitable lien is a floating equity, Cotton, *supra* note 147 at 392–93.

[158] Burns, "The Equitable Lien Rediscovered", *supra* note 147 at 10–11.

[159] *Ibid* at 11–12.

[160] *Ibid* at 16–24.

[161] (2007), 61 RPR (4th) 101 (Ont Sup Ct J).

[162] *Land Titles Act,* RSO 1990, c L.5.

[163] *Ahone v Holloway* (1988), 30 BCLR (2d) 368 (CA), appr'd by *1279017 Alberta Ltd v 1257613 Alberta Ltd*, 2009 ABCA 364.

[164] 2002 BCSC 1244.

vendor's lien still exists in Canadian common law, a vendor would have two available security interests, the *PPSA* purchase-money security interest[165] and the equitable lien. In *Thibodeau v Thibodeau,*[166] the Ontario Court of Appeal partly relied on *Swiss Bank Corp v Lloyds Bank Ltd*[167] and thus confirmed that the case is good law in Ontario too.[168] In *Tracy v Instaloans Financial Solutions Centres,*[169] the Court mentioned the equitable lien as an "alternative remedy" to the constructive trust in the traceable proceeds of wrongfully-received money.[170]

165 *Personal Property Security Act,* RSO 1990, c P.10, s 33.
166 2011 ONCA 110 [*Thibodeau*].
167 (1981), [1982] AC 584 (HL).
168 *Thibodeau, supra* note 166 at paras 56–58, Blair JA.
169 2010 BCCA 357.
170 *Ibid* at para 43, Newbury JA.

# § 7 The Civil Law Trust

It has been suggested that Civil Law jurisdictions cannot adopt a Common Law trust law because of the *numerus clausus* principle.[1] Because it is presumably always open to the legislature to introduce new property rights, this argument boils down to saying that an adoption of trusts comparable to Common Law trusts requires a type of property right that is fundamentally different from the traditional lists of property rights in Civil Law.

The purpose of this chapter is to show whether this is true and examine how and to what extent a concept comparable to the Common Law trust can be found in Civil Law. The existence of comparable institutions in the two component legal systems of Canadian bijuralism becomes particular important at the conflict-of-laws stage where property moves between jurisdictions.[2] In the first section I define the object of comparison. In the second section I look at the beginning of the reception of trust law in the *Code civil du Bas-Canada.* In the third section I look at how Québec Civil Law has developed its own notion of a trust with the new *Code civil du Québec.*

## A. The Object of Comparison

A comparison between the Common Law – or rather, equitable – trust and a Civil Law equivalent requires one to identify what exactly the object of comparison is. If I want to inquire if there is a trust in Civil Law, I need to know what a "trust" is.

---

[1] John H Merryman, "Policy, Autonomy, and the Numerus Clausus in Italian and American Property Law" (1963) 12:2 Am J Comp L 224 [Merryman, "Numerus Clausus"]. Cf. Rainer Becker, *Die Fiducie von Québec und der Trust: Ein Vergleich mit verschiedenen Modellen fiduziarischer Rechtsfiguren im Civil Law* (Tübingen: Mohr Siebeck, 2007) at 328–29; Henry Hansmann & Reinier Kraakman, "Property, Contract, and Verification: The Numerus Clausus Problem and the Divisibility of Rights" (2002) 31:S2 J Legal Stud 373 at 375.

[2] See Part V: § 19 C, "Proprietary Restitution and Change of Situs".

In his comparative study on trusts,[3] Becker gives a functional definition of the trust. His definition, however, only includes consensual trusts. In his definition, "trusts" and equivalent fiduciary concepts serve to allow a person to give power of administration of certain property to another person for the benefit of a third party or purposes while at the same making sure that "the other" is placed under certain restrictions in his administration of the property.[4] For brevity's sake, I shall refer to this other as the "trustee," and to the first one as the "settlor."[5]

Becker criticizes Waters[6] for giving an Anglocentric definition of the trust. However, this criticism is misguided for two reasons. *First*, Waters actually uses a definition very similar to the one given by Becker. Water cites Maitland's definition of a trust:

> "When a person has rights which he is bound to exercise upon behalf of another or for the accomplishment of some particular purpose he is said to have those rights in trust for that other or for that purpose and he is called a trustee."[7]

This definition, while given from the point of view of the trustee rather than of the property, is essentially the same as Becker's own. However, it true that Waters strays from the starting point of Maitland's definition further into his work on trusts. This is understandable, however, if we direct our attention to the *second* reason. As we have already seen in the preceding chapter, the Common Law trust encompasses more than just consensual trusts.[8] Consequently, a definition of "trusts" that includes non-consensual trusts cannot base its definition on the notion of a settlor who creates the trust by an act of will. The definition needs to be wider. Brierley has noted this as well. While Brierley initially defines a trust as triangular relationship between settlor, trustee, and beneficiary based on intent, he immediately broadens the definition of trust in order to understand any arrangement by which management and enjoyment of property are separated.[9] The Common Law trust has to fill a role that in Civil

---

[3] Becker, *supra* note 1.

[4] *Ibid* at 15–16.

[5] This terminology is also applied in Civil Law, see *Code civil du Québec,* SQ 1991, c 64 [*CcQ*], art 1261.

[6] Donovan WM Waters, "The Institution of the Trust in Civil and Common Law" in: Académie du droit international, ed, *Recueil des cours* (Leiden: Sijthoff, 1995) 113 at 125 ff.

[7] Frederic W Maitland, *Equity,* ed by A. H. Clayton and W. J. Whittaker (Cambridge: Cambridge University Press, 1936) at 4, cited as in Waters, "The Institution of the Trust in Civil and Common Law", preceding note at 125.

[8] See Part II: § 6 , "Equitable Property Rights".

[9] John EC Brierley, "The New Quebec Law of Trusts: The Adaption of Common Law Thoughts to Civil Law Concepts" in: H P Glenn, ed, *Droit québécois et droit français: Communauté, autonomie, concordance* (Cowansville, Québec: Éditions Yvon Blais, 1993) 383 at 385: "[T]he trust proceeds upon the idea that, as a matter of fundamental principle, the beneficial enjoyment of property can be separated from its management."

Law has been filled by other legal concepts such as *negotiorum gestio* and unjustified enrichment.[10] While I have already mentioned this in the chapter on equitable property rights,[11] the application of trusts to unjustified enrichment situations in Common Law will also be the subject of its own chapter.[12] What is important for the present purpose is to accept that the trust is not merely definable by the aspect of triangularity and intent; instead, it can be defined more broadly. A wide understanding of "trust" enables us to better translate all aspects of the Common Law trust into Civil Law. This will become particularly important when looking at the recognition of restitutionary trusts in conflict of laws.[13]

## B. The Trust in the *Code civil du Bas-Canada*

In the trust-adjacent area, the *CcBC* differed from the revolutionary *Code civil des Francais*. Notably, the *CcBC* allowed substitutions,[14] including *inter vivos* substitutions.[15] But it was thought that the trust framework of the *CcBC* left a lacuna: it admitted charitable foundations and permitted fiduciary substitutions, but it contained no general framework for fiduciary donations.[16] Due to pressure by Anglo-Quebeckers, the *CcBC* was amended and the trust was introduced in Québec law.[17]

The Québec trust, however, was not the same as the Common Law trust: it did not create a split between legal and equitable title.[18] Common Law did not

---

[10] Becker, *supra* note 1 at 25. Max Rheinstein, "Traite Theorique Et Pratique Des Trusts by Pierre Lepaulle" (1934) 43:6 Yale LJ 1049 at 1053 points out that the unjust-enrichment constructive trust in American law serves a role taken over by the rei vindicatio in French law.

[11] See Part II: § 6 D, "Constructive Trusts".

[12] See Part II: § 10 , "Proprietary Restitution".

[13] See Part V: § 19 C, "Proprietary Restitution and Change of Situs".

[14] *Code civil du Bas-Canada,* 29 Vict, c 41, s 964.

[15] *Ibid,* s 925.

[16] John EC Brierley, "Regards sur le droit des biens dans le nouveau Code civil du Québec" (1995) 47:1 Rev Int Dr Comp 33 at 43 [Brierley, "Regards"].

[17] Madeleine Cantin Cumyn, "L'origine de la fiducie québécoise" in: McGill University, Faculty of Law, ed, *Mélanges Paul-André Crepeau* (Cowansville, Québec: Éditions Yvon Blais, 1997) 199 at 216 ff. Cf. Donovan WM Waters, "Unification or Harmonization?: Experiences with the Trust Concept" in: Walter A Stoffel, ed, *Conflits et harmonisation: Mélanges en l'honneur d'Alfred E. von Overbeck à l'occasion de son 65ème anniversaire* (Fribourg: Édition universitaire, 1990) 591 at 595.

[18] *Royal Trust Co v Tucker,* [1982] 1 SCR 250 [*Royal Trust*]*; Curran c Davis,* [1933] SCR 283; *GM O'Meara v Bennett,* [1922] 1 AC 80 (Can PC).

form the foremost authority in the application of the trust provisions of the *CcBC*.[19] The foremost provisions were ss 981a; 981b *CcBC*.

"Section 981a *CcBC*

All persons capable of disposing freely of their property may convey property, moveable or immoveable, to trustees by gift or by will, for the benefit of any persons in whose favor they can validly make gifts or legacies.

Section 981b *CcBC*

Trustees, for the purposes of their trust, are seized as depositaries and administrators for the benefit of the donees or legatees of the property, moveable or immoveable, conveyed to them in trust, and may claim possession of it, even against the donees or legatees for whose benefit the trust was created … . [T]he trustees may sue and be sued and take all judicial proceedings for the affairs of the trust."

The effect of these two provisions was that a trust could only be settled for no value. There was also a certain contradiction in the two provisions: s 981a *CcBC* envisioned that the property be conveyed to the trustee, implying they would receive ownership of it; however, s 981b *CcBC* did not speak of the trustee in terms of ownership, but rather stated that trustees were "seized as depositaries and administrators" of the property. This created doubt as to what was meant by the "conveyance of property."

Instead of splitting ownership, the trustee received a *sui generis* right of ownership.[20] However, the precise patrimonial consequence of trust property was the subject of a dispute in doctrine.[21] One school of thought held that the trustee owns the property.[22] A second held that the beneficiary has to be considered owner of the property.[23] A third considered the settler the owner.[24] A fourth considered the trust property to have legal personhood.[25] The idea of an ownerless patrimony under the administration of a trustee was not considered

---

[19] *Laverdure v Du Tremblay,* [1937] AC 666 (Can PC); *Curran c Davis,* preceding note at 301, Rinfret J; *Laliberté v Larue,* [1931] SCR 7. See also Yves Caron, "The Trust in Quebec" (1980) 25 McGill LJ 421 at 424.

[20] *Royal Trust, supra* note 18 at 272–73, Beetz J. See also Yves Rossier, "Etude comparée de certains aspects patrimoniaux de la fiducie" (1988) 34:4 McGill LJ 817 at 896–98.

[21] See Becker, *supra* note 1 at 146. Caron, *supra* note 19, at 426 ff provides a comprehensive overview of the theories.

[22] Caron, *supra* note 19 at 426–28.

[23] *Ibid* at 428.

[24] *Ibid* at 429–30.

[25] Madeleine Cantin Cumyn, "Les personnes morales dans le droit privé du Québec" (1990) 31:4 C de D 1021 at 1043–45; Caron, *supra* note 19 at 430–32.

in Québec at that time.[26] It was, however, argued that the trust forms a separate patrimony.[27]

The Supreme Court of Canada gave a certain shape to this *sui generis* ownership. It held that the trustee is the owner of the trust property,[28] that "ownership cannot remain in suspense,"[29] and that the beneficiary merely has an obligatory right against the trustee.[30]

## C. The Trust in the *Code civil du Québec*

### *I. Patrimony by Appropriation*

In the context of the trust in the law of Louisiana, McAuley asks the question whether a trust can only be called a trust if the trustee receives title to the trust property.[31] If so, the trust envisioned by the *CcQ* is not a trust. Rather than relying on a transfer of title to the trustee, the *CcQ* introduced the notion of a "patrimony by appropriation."

Patrimony by appropriation is a genuine innovation of Québec law. It stands in sharp contrast to the situation under the *CcBC*. Rather than relying on a *sui generis* ownership right, the legislature abolished the notion that ownership cannot remain in suspense. Patrimony by appropriation entails ownerless property. Any notion that the settlor retains ownership is clearly contradicted by art 1265 *CcQ:*

"Article 1265 *CcQ*

Acceptance of the trust divests the settlor of the property, charges the trustee with seeing to the appropriation of the property and the administration of the trust patrimony and is sufficient to establish the right of the beneficiary with certainty.

L'acceptation de la fiducie dessaisit le constituant des biens, charge le fiduciaire de veiller à leur affectation et à l'administration du patrimoine fiduciaire et suffit pour rendre certain le droit du bénéficiaire."

The *CcQ* makes it abundantly clear that neither settlor, nor trustee, nor beneficiary have a property right in the trust property:

---

[26] Becker, *supra* note 1 at 146–47.

[27] See Rossier, *supra* note 20 at 881 ff. Cf. Cantin Cumyn, "Les personnes morales dans le droit privé du Québec", *supra* note 25 at 1043.

[28] *Royal Trust, supra* note 18 at 272–73, Beetz J.

[29] *Ibid* at 272–73, Beetz J.

[30] *Ibid* at 272–73, Beetz J.

[31] Michael McAuley, "Truth and Reconciliation: Notions of Property in Louisiana's Civil and Trust Codes" in: Lionel D Smith, ed, *Re-imagining the Trust: Trusts in Civil Law* (Cambridge: Cambridge University Press, 2012) 119 at 125.

"Article 1261 *CcQ*

The trust patrimony, consisting of the property transferred in trust, constitutes a patrimony by appropriation, autonomous and distinct from that of the settlor, trustee or beneficiary and in which none of them has any real right.

Le patrimoine fiduciaire, formé des biens transférés en fiducie, constitue un patrimoine d'affectation autonome et distinct de celui du constituant, du fiduciaire ou du bénéficiaire, sur lequel aucun d'entre eux n'a de droit réel."

Rather, the trust property becomes part of an impersonal "patrimony by appropriation." The act of appropriation is not subject to any publicity requirements; only where the conveyance act regarding certain property itself is subject to special rules (*e.g.* the conveyance of immovables) would the same apply to the conveyance of this property to the trust patrimony.[32]

The notion of patrimony by appropriation allows the trust to be integrated within the Civil Law framework. It provides an alternative to the concept of split title in Common Law.[33] It relies on a fundamental cornerstone of Civil Law property law: patrimony.[34] Lepaulle first suggested the notion of a trust as a patrimony by appropriation.[35] He developed the notion based on the concept of a "purpose patrimony"[36] *(Zweckvermögen)* which had evolved in German law and then spread to French doctrine.

Brinz developed the precursor of the modern patrimony by appropriation.[37] Bekker further developed it.[38] Brinz developed the notion to explain the recognition of corporations without the fiction of legal personality. He explained that property could not only be appropriated by a person but also for a purpose. In the latter case, no owner was necessary. Bekker's contribution was to draw a

[32] Becker, *supra* note 1 at 290–91.

[33] Brierley, "The New Quebec Law of Trusts", *supra* note 9 at 383.

[34] Brierley, "Regards", *supra* note 16 at 45. On the utility of the notion of patrimony in integrating a trust into a Civil Law property framework from a Scots perspective see George L Gretton, "Trusts Without Equity" (2000) 49:3 ICLQ 599.

[35] Pierre Lepaulle, *Traité théorique et pratique des trusts en droit interne, en droit fiscal et en droit international* (Paris: Rousseau, 1932); Pierre Lepaulle, "Trusts and the Civil Law" (1933) 15:1 J Comp Leg Int'l L 18.

[36] I have adapted the English terminology from Rheinstein, *supra* note 10 at 1050, who calls it a "purpose fund."

[37] In the second edition of his work on the Roman law as received in Germany, Brinz dedicated an entire sub-volume to the notion of the "purpose patrimony." Alois Brinz, *Das Zweckvermögen,* 2[d] edn (Lehrbuch der Pandekten, 321, Erlangen: Andreas Deichert, 1879–1882).

[38] Ernst I Bekker, *System des heutigen Pandektenrechts* (Weimar: Hermann Böhlau, 1886), vol 1 at 206–7; Ernst I Bekker, "Zur Lehre vom Rechtssubjekt: Genuß und Verfügung; Zwecksatzungen, Zweckvermögen und juristische Personen" (1873) 12 Jb Dogm 1; Ernst I Bekker, "Zweckvermögen, insbesondere Peculium, Handelsvermögen und Actiengesellschaft" [1861] ZHR 499.

distinction between the ownerless patrimony by appropriation, a unitary patrimony, and the purpose patrimony in the middle.[39] A connection can be made between Jhering's works[40] and the theories advanced by Brinz and Bekker.[41] Jhering distinguished his theory of rights from the will theory. He argued that a right existed not by reference to a person's will but by virtue of a legitimate interest protected by law;[42] however, unlike Bekker and Brinz, Jhering did not believe that a right could exist without being held by a natural person.[43]

The notion of a partially separate patrimony has been applied in French doctrine to explain the separation of the main patrimony of a person and other funds such as matrimonial property.[44] The modern French trust is another example. A third example found in Québec law was the old *CcBC* trust, which could be understood as a separate patrimony.[45]

When the *CcQ* modernized and extended trust law, it merely did away with the notion that property in a separate fund such as this still had to be owned by somebody. This notion had already been held to be a fiction in parts of doctrine.[46]

### *II. Trustee, Beneficiary, and Trust Property*

#### *1. Management of the Trust by the Trustee*

In principle, the trustee's personal patrimony is not liable for any debt incurred in the management of the trust.[47] Trust liabilities are not part of the trustee's patrimony. At the same time, all rights relating to the patrimony are exercisable by the trustee.[48] The trustee has a power of agency with regard to the trust.[49]

---

[39] Bekker, "Zur Lehre vom Rechtssubjekt", preceding note at 69 ff.

[40] See Rudolf von Jhering, *Geist des römischen Rechtes,* 1st edn (Leipzig: Breitkopf & Härtel, 1865), vol 31 and Rudolf von Jhering, "Passive Wirkungen der Rechte: Ein Beitrag zur Theorie der Rechte" (1871) 10 Jher Jb 387.

[41] Becker, *supra* note 1 at 173.

[42] Von Jhering, *Geist des römischen Rechtes, supra* note 40 at 320 ff. See also Gerhard Wagner, "Rudolph von Jherings Theorie des subjektiven Rechts und der berechtigenden Reflexwirkungen" (1993) 193:4 AcP 319.

[43] Von Jhering, "Passive Wirkungen der Rechte", *supra* note 40 at 390.

[44] Becker, *supra* note 1 at 180.

[45] *Ibid* at 181.

[46] Pierre Charbonneau, "Les patrimoines d'affectation: Vers un nouveau paradigme en droit quebecois du patrimoine" (1983) 85 R du N 491.

[47] Brierley, "Regards", *supra* note 16 at 47.

[48] *CcQ, supra* note 5, art 1278.

[49] *Ibid,* art 1278(2). See Becker, *supra* note 1 at 207.

Where the trustee exceeds her power, she is personally liable[50] unless the beneficiary authorizes the transaction[51] or it is a beneficial transaction for the trust.[52]

Any property purchased with means coming from the trust patrimony will become part of the trust patrimony, not part of the trustee's patrimony. This is known as "real subrogation" *(subrogation réel).*[53] Its application to the administration of the trust patrimony by the trustee is not explicitly codified in the *CcQ,* but legislative intent and doctrinal voices both assume it applies.[54] Brierley views this as a function of the separate nature of the trust patrimony, separate from the trustee's patrimony.[55] Indeed, the notion of real subrogation has always been considered to be an integral part of Aubry and Rau's notion of patrimony.[56]

*2. The Beneficiary's Right in Relation to the Trust*

From a law-and-economics standpoint, the attractiveness of a trust law framework is largely determined by the attractiveness of the trust for the beneficiary.[57] In order for the Québec trust to be a successful way of structuring estate planning and reducing the outflow of capital to other provinces, the protection of the beneficiary and her rights are essential.

The beneficiary of the trust has no real right in the trust property.[58] But as a function of the admission of incorporeal property, the beneficiary's right in the trust itself is property. In other words, the beneficiary might have no property right in the trust property, but she does have a property right in relation to her

---

[50] *CcQ, supra* note 5, art 1320.

[51] *Ibid,* art 1320.

[52] *Ibid,* art 1321.

[53] On real subrogation in Civil Law see Henri Capitant, "Essai sur la subrogation réelle" (1919) 18 RTD 385.

[54] Becker, *supra* note 1 at 210; Brierley, "Regards", *supra* note 16 at 46; Brierley, "The New Quebec Law of Trusts", *supra* note 9 at 391; Gil Rémillard, ed, *Code civil du Québec: commentaires du Ministre de la justice* (Montréal: Publications Dacfo, 1993) at 370.

[55] Brierley, "Regards", *supra* note 16 at 46; Brierley, "The New Quebec Law of Trusts", *supra* note 9 at 391.

[56] Charles Aubry & Charles F Rau, *Cours de droit civil français: D'après la méthode de Zachariæ,* 4th edn (Paris: Marchal & Billard, 1873) at 236: "Il suit de cette régle que, lors de la délivvrance ou de la restitution d'une universalité juridique, celui auquel doit se faire cette délivrance ou cette restitution, est toujours en droit d'exiger la remise de l'objet qui est venu remplacer, dans cette universalité, celui qui en est sorti."

[57] See Ugo Mattei, "Efficiency in Legal Transplants: An Essay in Comparative Law and Economics" (1994) 14:1 Int'l Rev L & Econ 3 at 8–10.

[58] *CcQ, supra* note 5, art 1261. See Brierley, "Regards", *supra* note 16 at 47.

right against the trust. This means, for instance, that the beneficiary can charge her interest with a hypothec.[59]

### *a) Rights of Enjoyment and in Regards to Management*

The right of the beneficiary is described in art 1284 *CcQ:*

"Article 1284 *CcQ*

| | |
|---|---|
| While the trust is in effect, the beneficiary has the right to require, pursuant to the constituting act, either the provision of a benefit granted to him, or the payment of the fruits and revenues and of the capital or the payment of one or the other. | Pendant la durée de la fiducie, le bénéficiaire a le droit d'exiger, suivant l'acte constitutif, soit la prestation d'un avantage qui lui est accordé, soit le paiement des fruits et revenus et du capital ou de l'un d'eux seulement." |

Notwithstanding both the fact that the beneficiary does not hold a "real right" in the trust property[60] and the limited right described by art 1284 *CcQ,* the beneficiary of the trust does have a number of quasi-property rights. She can take legal action in the place of the trustee when the latter refuses or neglects to act or is prevented from acting. The beneficiary can also void acts of the trustee that are in fraud of her rights and obtain injunctive relief.[61]

### *b) Protection of the Trust Property*

In cases of wrongful disposal of trust property, the beneficiary should also be entitled to follow her property into third-party hands by applying the general provision of art 1699 *CcQ* on the restitution of wrongfully-received property by a third party to the trust.[62] The reason for the nullity of the transaction is that the trustee's power to administer does not include a power to wrongfully dispose of the property. An act with regard to the property that is committed by the trustee and that exceeds her power is void.[63] Because transfer of property is in principle based on a consensual principle, not the principle of separation of obligation and transfer,[64] the nullity encompasses the transfer of property.[65]

---

[59] Becker, *supra* note 1 at 233. See Part III: § 14 B.IV.2, "Hypothecs in Incorporeal Property".

[60] *CcQ, supra* note 5, art 1261.

[61] *Ibid,* arts 1290; 1291. See also Brierley, "The New Quebec Law of Trusts", *supra* note 9 at 395.

[62] Brierley, "The New Quebec Law of Trusts", *supra* note 9 at 395; Lionel D Smith, "Unauthorized Dispositions of Trust Property: Tracing in Quebec Law" (2013) 58:4 McGill LJ 795 at 799.

[63] Smith, "Unauthorized Dispositions of Trust Property", preceding note at 799. But cf. Becker, *supra* note 1 at 193.

[64] See Part II: § 4 F.III, "Consensualism in Québec Law".

[65] Becker, *supra* note 1 at 219.

Nullity is relative and thus can be invoked by the beneficiary.[66] Yet the beneficiary is under no duty to invoke the nullity.[67] This corresponds to her right to authorize wrongful disposals.[68]

If the conditions of a restriction on alienability are met, the same result can be reached not by reference to power, but by reference to the provisions on restrictions on alienability.[69] Becker even argues that art 1212(3)(2) *CcQ* allows restrictions on alienability even where the transfer is not gratuitous.[70] In this case, the beneficiary's power to follow the trust property into a third party's hand would always be a function of the provisions of art 1212 *CcQ ff,* provided its formal requirements are met. Inalienability creates effects similar to the principle of following in Common Law trusts.[71]

In cases where the trustee wrongfully disposes trust property but the property cannot be followed into a third party's hands, the beneficiary should be able to claim a right in the substitute received by the trustee. This is an application of the real subrogation principle to cases where the trustee explicitly breaches the trust. Smith argues that the principle of real subrogation should also apply in case of unauthorized dispositions of trust property by the trustee.[72]

### *c) The Nature of the Trust Beneficiary's Right*

Given the number of rights that protect the trust beneficiary, it seems doubtful to which extent the exclusion of property rights in the trust property by art 1261 *CcQ* – based on a strong dichotomy between personal and property rights – is warranted. Macdonald argues that the *CcQ* has abolished the traditional dichotomy between absolute property right and relative personal right.[73] As I have argued above, this is true insofar as absolute rights are only admitted in corporeals, and all other rights are considered to be incorporeal.[74] However, it is possible to understand the beneficiary's right as an absolute right, and thus uphold the property right-personal right dichotomy. The beneficiary's right is not an absolute right in the individual properties that constitute the trust patrimony; rather, it is a property right in the trust patrimony itself.

---

[66] *CcQ, supra* note 5, art 1420.

[67] Becker, *supra* note 1 at 220–21.

[68] See Part II: § 7 C.II.1, "Management of the Trust by the Trustee".

[69] See Part II: § 4 G, "Restrictions on Alienability".

[70] Thus limiting the scope of *CcQ, supra* note 5, art 1212(1). See Becker, *supra* note 1 at 194.

[71] Cf. Merryman, "Numerus Clausus", *supra* note 1 at 231.

[72] Smith, "Unauthorized Dispositions of Trust Property", *supra* note 62.

[73] Roderick A Macdonald, "Reconceiving the Symbols of Property: Universalities, Interests and Other Heresies" (1994) 39 McGill LJ 761. See also Becker, *supra* note 1 at 234–58.

[74] See Part II: § 4 D, "Right and Object of Right".

# § 8 Theory of Property Rights

The purpose of this chapter is to look at theories of property rights and try to find a general theory of property that describes both Civil Law and Common Law property. Now is the appropriate time to do so, as the understanding of the black-letter law of both Common Law and Civil Law relating to movable property allows us to understand the relation between the theory and the legal rules. At the same time, the theories are not merely descriptive. As I will demonstrate, they make normative predictions that influence the Common Law regarding proprietary restitution[1] and provide a framework for an economic theory of secured transaction law.[2] A theory of property rights has to address what the specific difference is that distinguishes property rights from personal rights. There are two common descriptions: either a property right is seen as a right in a (physical) thing, or a property right is a right good against the entire world.[3] In their absoluteness, both theories cannot explain common law property law, which recognizes neither an absolute best right (or at least does not conceptually require it), nor restricts property rights to rights in corporeals.

## A. Theory of Property: Why Property?

There are competing theories of why property exists. In itself, this book does not concern the theoretical justification for property rights. However, it is helpful to provide a brief overview of those theories that affect the justification of the *numerus clausus*.

### *I. The Natural Account of Property*

The natural account of property posits that property and property rights are an institution unto themselves. The recognition of property rights does not serve any extrinsic goal; rather, property is recognized as a value in itself. In a sense, property predates its legal recognition.

---

[1] See Part II: § 10 , "Proprietary Restitution".

[2] See Part III: § 11 , "The Law and Economics of Secured Transactions".

[3] Cf. Robert Stevens, "When and Why Does Unjustified Enrichment Justify the Recognition of Proprietary Rights?" (2012) 92:3 Boston UL Rev 919 at 920–21.

*1. Will Theory of Property*

Aubry and Rau adopted a natural approach to the origin of property. Their will-based theory of patrimony considered patrimony to be something pre-legal to which recognition is given by the law.[4] At the same time, the will theory of patrimony is also found in the writings of Savigny. In the Savignian conception of law, "law is a power of the individual. Within the limits of this power, the will of the individual is supreme."[5]

There is a theoretical link between the Saviginan approach to law and Kant legal philosophy. Kant posited that it is law's purpose to facilitate the co-existence of the will of one person with the will of another. Law's empire is the avoidance of conflict between competing wills.[6] The use of property is the realization of the owner's "free and purposive agency." The owner asserts a right that others also have with respect to their own property.[7] The recognition of property rights is the way in which each owner's will can co-exist with the others' will. Weinrib describes Kant's theory of property as being based on three conceptual steps.[8] The first step is the postulate that the single innate right of a human being is to be free; this freedom extends insofar as external exercise can co-exist with all other human beings' freedom.[9] The second step is the postulate that first step enables anybody to appropriate something to her will.[10] The third step is the postulate that it is the state who provides the framework within which the freedom of one person co-exists with the freedom of the others'.[11] Property rights are the way in which the state does so in regards to the freedom of the individual to appropriate things.[12]

For Hegel too, property is about the exercise of one's will. Property is the way in which individuals interact with the material world. Hegel argues that property supplies the tools through which individual will may be realized in

---

[4] See Christopher B Gray, "Patrimony" (1981) 22 C de D 81 at 112.

[5] *Ibid* at 114.

[6] See *ibid* at 119.

[7] Ernest J Weinrib, *The Idea of Private Law,* 2[d] edn (Oxford: Oxford University Press, 2012) at 200.

[8] Ernest J Weinrib, *Corrective Justice* (Oxford: Oxford University Press, 2012) at 270–77.

[9] Immanuel Kant, "Metaphysik der Sitten: Rechtslehre" in: Immanuel Kant, *Werke,* ed by Wilhelm Weischedel, 3rd ed (Darmstadt 1971), vol 4, 306 at 345 [Kant, "Rechtslehre"]. See also previously *ibid* at 339–40 and *ibid* at 337.

[10] *Ibid* at 355.

[11] *Ibid* at 430–31.

[12] Weinrib, *Corrective Justice, supra* note 8 at 276.

the world. Appropriation represents the imposition of a person's will on the world.[13]

### 2. Locke's Notion of Property

Locke argued that property rights ought to be recognized for two reasons.[14] First, the recognition of property rights creates an incentive for human beings to make use of the resources available to them.[15] Second, a person has the rights to the fruits of her labour.[16] Locke's conception of property is reflected in the notion that possession is the origin of property.[17] In this account, the state – and thus the law – serves to protect the innate right of man.[18]

### 3. The Natural Account of Property and Incorporeal Property

An important point about the natural account of property is that in itself, the account does not necessitate limiting property to corporeal property. In principle, any resource that can be used by somebody is subject to appropriation.[19] The exclusion of incorporeal property by Kant and Savigny requires recourse to some higher rule, which for them is the fundamental impossibility to speak of property rights in relation to human beings; doing so would negate human freedom.[20]

## II. Utilitarian Account of Property

Gordley and Mattei give an example of a utilitarian account of property. They argue that property is a solution to two problems. First, property allocates scarce resources among people who want them. Second, property rights solve

---

[13] Georg Wilhelm Friedrich Hegel, *Grundlinien der Philosophie des Rechts* (Berlin: Nicolaische Buchhandlung, 1821) at 47–61. See also Nestor M Davidson, "Standardization and Pluralism in Property Law" (2008) 61:6 Vand L Rev 1597 at 1620.

[14] See Sibyl Schwarzenbach, "Locke's Two Conceptions of Property" (1988) 14:2 Soc Th & Pract 141 at 150; Dan Wielsch, "Differenzierungen des Eigentums: Zur Entwicklung eines rechtlichen Grundbegriffs" in: Stefan Keller & Stefan Wiprächtiger, eds, *Recht zwischen Dogmatik und Theorie: Marc Amstutz zum 50. Geburtstag* (Zürich, St Gallen: Dike, 2012) 329 at 335.

[15] John Locke, *Two Treatises of Government,* ed by Thomas Hollis (London: A Millar et al, 1764) at 215–18.

[16] *Ibid* at 216–17.

[17] Cf. Carol M Rose, "Possession as the Origin of Property" (1985) 52:1 U Chicago L Rev 73.

[18] Davidson, *supra* note 13 at 1621.

[19] See Marietta Auer, *Der privatrechtliche Diskurs der Moderne* (Tübingen: Mohr Siebeck, 2014) at 103–4; Dieter Schwab, "Eigentum" in: Otto Brunner, Werner Conze & Reinhart Koselleck, eds, *Geschichtliche Grundbegriffe: Historisches Lexikon zur politisch-sozialen Sprache in Deutschland* (Stuttgart: Klett-Cotta, 1975), vol 2, 65 at 85–87.

[20] See Auer, preceding note at 103–8.

the problem of deciding how resources will be used. Property rights delegate this decision to the owner.[21] A utilitarian view of property does not recognize property as being independent of the state; rather, the state uses property to implement the goals of the polity.[22]

### *III. Realist Account of Property*

The realist approach to property views property as a means of shaping human interaction.[23] In this view, property rights exist to reflect social relationships. Different property rights exist to reflect the variety of social relationships that can exist.[24]

## B. Bundle of Rights or Institution: How Property?

A second question that needs to asked is how exactly a property right can be conceptualized. The two competing theories are that property is a right in a thing, or a right in relation to others. The two competing theories can be expressed differently: Is a property right a bundle of rights, or is it one unitary right (*i.e.* an institution)? While these two wordings sound like two accounts of two different theoretical contests, we will see that they can be understood to be two sides of the same coin. Furthermore, the bundle-of-rights picture also has a role to play in conceptualizing the *numerus clausus* of property rights. If property rights are understood as bundles of rights, any property right is a sub-bundle; the *numerus clausus* thus governs how the bundles can be arranged.

---

[21] James Gordley & Ugo Mattei, "Protecting Possession" (1996) 44 Am J Comp L 293 at 331.

[22] Cf. Davidson, *supra* note 13 at 1645.

[23] See Hanoch Dagan, "The Craft of Property" (2003) 91:6 Cal L Rev 1517 at 1558–65 [Dagan, "Craft"].

[24] See Part II: § 8 D.III, "Realist Theory of the Numerus Clausus".

### *I. The Bundle-of-Rights Picture*

The bundle-of-rights picture for property rights is associated with two legal theorists, Hohfeld[25] and Honoré.[26] Each has contributed to one aspect of the metaphor. Hohfeld described property rights as being composed of a set of inter-personal rights, while Honoré described ownership as being composed of a set of discrete rights in relation to a thing.

#### *1. The Hohfeldian Concept of Property*

##### *a) The Hohfeldian Scheme*

Hohfeld created a language to analyse rights. In his terminology, there were two sets of four pairs of atomic terms. The two sets were distinguished by how the pairs were grouped together. The first set grouped pairs by opposites. In this scheme, a right is the opposite of a no-right; a privilege is the opposite of a duty; a power is the opposite of a disability; and an immunity is the opposite of a liability. The second set grouped the pairs by correlation. A right in one person correlates with a duty in another; a privilege of one person correlates with a no-right in another; a power in one person correlates with a liability in another; and an immunity in person correlates with the disability of another person.[27]

Hohfeld continued to give meaning to the atomic terms. Another word for "right" is "claim."[28] A "right" or "claim" is essentially the capacity to require that somebody else do something. "Duty" is the obligation by the other person.[29] A "privilege" is the capacity to do something. The corresponding "no-right" means that the no-right holder cannot demand the capacity holder to not do the something.[30] A power is the capacity to change the right-duty tie between

[25] Wesley N Hohfeld, "Some Fundamental Legal Conceptions as Applied in Judicial Reasoning" (1913) 23:1 Yale LJ 16 [Hohfeld, "Fundamental Conceptions I"], republished as Wesley N Hohfeld, "Some Fundamental Legal Conceptions as Applied in Judicial Reasoning (I)" in: Wesley N Hohfeld, *Fundamental Legal Conceptions as Applied in Judicial Reasoning and Other Legal Essays,* ed by Walter W Cook (New Haven: Yale University Press, 1923) 23 and Wesley N Hohfeld, "Fundamental Legal Conceptions as Applied in Judicial Reasoning" (1917) 26:8 Yale LJ 710 [Hohfeld, "Fundamental Conceptions II"], republished as Wesley N Hohfeld, "Fundamental Legal Conceptions as Applied in Judicial Reasoning (II)" in: Hohfeld, *Essays,* this note, 65.

[26] Anthony M Honoré, "Ownership" in: Anthony G Guest, ed, *Oxford Essays in Jurisprudence* (Oxford: Oxford University Press, 1961) 107.

[27] Hohfeld, "Fundamental Conceptions I", *supra* note 25 at 30.

[28] *Ibid* at 32.

[29] *Ibid* at 32.

[30] *Ibid* at 32–44.

at least two persons, or a multitude of two-person relationship.[31] The corresponding liability is thus the description of a person being subject to another person's power.[32] "Immunity" is the opposite of liability. It means being free from somebody else's power in regards of certain rights.[33] Correspondingly, a "disability" means that the disability-holder lacks the power to affect certain rights in relation to a certain somebody.[34] Hohfeld saw this language as the toolkit with which all rights could be described.

*b) The Notion of Property Rights and Hohfeld*

Hohfeld applied his descriptive language to property rights in a later essay.[35] He started with the premise that property rights cannot not be understood as rights in the thing because rights are only ever rights between human beings; inter-human relations is all the law can affect.[36] According to Hohfeld, whether or not somebody has a property right is foremost a function of the quantity of rights a right-holder has in relation to other people. Whether the right-holder has rights in relation to all people or only in relation to specified individuals is not decisive. The right-holder is one who holds a bundle of fundamentally similar rights; she is owed a bundle of fundamentally similar duties.[37] Consequently, Hohfeld preferred the term "multital right" over "property right."[38] Notwithstanding Hohfeld's preference, I continue to use the terminology of this book and speak of property rights. In Hohfeld's analysis, property rights could be classified according to what type of duty they entailed in others.[39] However, Hohfeld's analysis is *per se* nothing more than a tool. It answers neither the question why a certain property right entails certain duties, nor the question why it creates duties in a certain class of people.[40]

*c) The Transfer of Property and Hohfeld*

Ames' theory of how a transfer of property takes place has much in common with the Hohfeldian concept of property.[41] It is also worth noting that Cook,

---

[31] *Ibid* at 44–53.

[32] *Ibid* at 53–54.

[33] *Ibid* at 55.

[34] *Ibid* at 55.

[35] Hohfeld, "Fundamental Conceptions II", *supra* note 25.

[36] *Ibid* at 721.

[37] *Ibid* at 723. See James E Penner, "The Bundle of Rights Picture of Property" (1996) 43 UCLA L Rev 711 at 726 [Penner, "Bundle of Rights"].

[38] See e.g. Hohfeld, "Fundamental Conceptions II", *supra* note 25 at 712.

[39] See e.g. *ibid* at 734. Cf. Penner, "Bundle of Rights", *supra* note 37 at 726–27.

[40] Penner, "Bundle of Rights", *supra* note 37 at 727.

[41] Percy Bordwell, "The Alienability of Non-Possessory Interests" (1940) 19:3 NCL Rev 279 at 286–87.

the legal realist, essentially gave a similar account of a transfer of property.[42] Cook credited Hohfeld with laying the foundation for his account.[43] A Hohfeldian influence in Cook's account of the rule against the assignability of rights is clearest when he states that it is a truism that "all legal rights are from their nature not, in the strictest sense, transferable."[44] In Cooke's analysis, the rule against the assignability of choses in actions can be explained with the Hohfeldian account of rights. Rights only exist between persons. If a chose in action is assignable, it means that both assignor and assignee are given the power to create a right-duty relationship between assignee and those third parties by which the original duty was owed. This would violate the fundamental idea that two parties cannot negatively impact third parties by bargaining.

### *2. Honore's Bundle of Rights*

Honoré's contribution to the modern bundle-of-rights picture consists in describing "ownership" – by which he means the "the greatest possible interest in a thing which a mature system of law recognizes"[45] – as not being one unitary right, but rather as being composed of a class of individual rights. Neither of these rights was a necessary condition for ownership, but in combination, they gave a phenomenological description of ownership.[46] At some point – so the assumption goes – a right-holder uniting a sufficient number of these individual rights in her hands would reach the tipping point and be described as the owner.

#### *a) Property Rights as Person-Thing Rights or Person-Person Rights*

While Honoré described ownership as something in relation to a thing,[47] it could also be understood to be a description of Hohfeld's right-duty set. While Honoré argues that ownership should be understood to be in a thing, he does so because he wants to highlight that the property right has a certain relation to the thing.[48] It is a right in relation to a thing. However, Honoré shares Hohfeld's position that properly understood, rights can only exist between people.[49]

---

[42] See Cook's account at Walter W Cook, "The Alienability of Choses in Action" (1916) 29:8 Harv L Rev 816 at 817.

[43] See *ibid* at 819, note 3, referring to Hohfeld, "Fundamental Conceptions I", *supra* note 25.

[44] Cook, "The Alienability of Choses in Action", *supra* note 42 at 818.

[45] Honoré, "Ownership", *supra* note 26 at 108.

[46] *Ibid* at 112.

[47] See Penner, "Bundle of Rights", *supra* note 37 at 732.

[48] Honoré, "Ownership", *supra* note 26 at 134.

[49] *Ibid* at 134.

*b) Necessary Incident of Ownership*

It is worthwhile to take a look at the first incident of ownership according to Honoré. In the introduction, he mentions that in any legal system the "owner" can use her property, stop others from using it, lend it, or transfer it.[50] This can be translated into Hohfeldian terminology. "Using" means the owner has a privilege against everyone, while everyone else has a no-right in relation to the owner. "Stopping use of others" means the owner has a right to demand that everyone stop using it, while everyone else is under a duty to stop using it.

It is at this point that we note a weakness in Honoré's premise that ownership exists in every Western legal system. The English common law does not prevent a third party from claiming personal property and converting it to her own use. So while it might be said that everybody is under a duty not to convert personal property (use it as their own) and this duty is enforced by monetary damages, there is in fact no corresponding right of the right-holder. So in fact, there is not even a duty not to convert personal property; rather, there is a duty not to convert without monetary compensation.

*c) Multititularity*

Honoré makes a second claim about ownership which raises an issue for the Common Law. This problem is due to the multititular nature of English property law. Multititularity describes a legal system where different persons can create title in to the same interest in property without one person deriving her title from another. The English system is one of multititularity. As seen above,[51] a possessor can create title to an item of property that does not depend on the title of the previous possessor.[52] Honoré claims that it is necessary that any multititular system resolves conflicts of title.[53] As I will show below, the Common Law does not resolve any conflict of title.[54]

*d) The Incidents of Ownership*

Honoré lists the following incidents as being typically associated with ownership: the right to possess, the right to use, the right to manage, the right to income, the right to the capital, the right to security, transmissibility, perpetuality, and residuarity.[55]

With regards to the right to possess, Honoré reiterates his claim that the right to possess "is the foundation on which the whole superstructure of ownership

---

[50] *Ibid* at 108.
[51] See Part II: § 5 D, "Possession and Property".
[52] See also Honoré, "Ownership", *supra* note 26 at 141.
[53] *Ibid* at 141.
[54] See Part III: § 13 D, "PPSA Security Interest and Equitable Property Rights".
[55] Honoré, "Ownership", *supra* note 26 at 113–21.

rests."[56] He defines "possession" as "to have exclusive physical control of a thing, or to have such control as the nature of the thing admits."[57] The latter arguably allows incorporeal things. The right to possession is composed of the right to be put in exclusive control of a thing and the right to remain in control of the thing (*i.e.* the claim that others should not interfere without permission).[58] Once again, we find this to be problematic with regard to Common Law. Does the right to be put in control of the thing include the right to regain control of the thing which one formerly had in her possession but then lost? In other words, is a right to revendicate a thing a necessary condition of ownership? We do not find it at common law. Furthermore, Honoré claims that not any one condition is a necessary condition; on the other hand, he lists the two rights relating to possession as the "foundation" upon which the entire concept of ownership rests. This sounds very much like a necessary condition. So if we have to answer the question just raised in the affirmative, it would follow that there is no concept of ownership of personal property at common law. This adds a further dimension to my conclusion above that Civil Law ownership is unknown at common law. Honoré seems to recognize this contradiction in his argument by saying that the right to possession is already sufficiently protected where there is some pressure on the defendant to hand the property over.[59] This would potentially allow one to conclude that the common law torts relating to wrongful interference are sufficient.

Cuming argues that the bundle of rights picture explains why the Common Law tort law requires possession for the protection of personal property.

> "From early times, the principal proprietary right protected by the law was possession or immediate right to possession. Conversion remains as a remedy that protects 'proprietary rights' to the extent that those rights arise out of possession or an immediate right to possession of personal property. The lack of a clear concept of ownership of personal property at common law resulted in the development of an action in tort that focuses on the 'wrong' of interference with the possessory rights of the claimant and not damage to the claimant's property interest."[60]

### *3. Discrete Property Rights in the Bundle-of-Rights Picture*

Combining Hohfeld and Honoré, an extreme version of the bundle-of-rights picture conceptualizes a property right as an infinite number of person-person relations (rather: a finite number equalling the population of the world); each of these relations can be broken down into infinitesimally small right-duty

---

[56] *Ibid* at 113.
[57] *Ibid* at 113.
[58] *Ibid* at 113.
[59] *Ibid* at 115.
[60] Ronald CC Cuming, "Secured Creditors' Non-Statutory Remedies: Unfinished Business" (2012) 91:2 Can Bar Rev 243 at 249.

sets.[61] Reversely, this would mean that it will never be possible to find the threshold that needs to be reached in order for a bundle to be classified as a property right. There is no hard line between personal rights and property rights. This extreme version of the bundle-of-rights picture can be contrasted with a more nuanced version that argues that property rights are not arbitrary bundles, but can be conceived of as pre-packaged bundles, or modules.[62] In this theory, property rights are the pre-packaged bundles recognized by the law.

Dagan argues that property rights are a combination of bundles and forms. In his analysis, the bundle-of-rights picture is true, but the list of recognized property rights creates forms that predetermine which sticks become parts of the bundle.[63] Thus, in his view, the form "ownership" would be a form that entails all possible sticks, while other forms take only a subset of available sticks and convey them to the property right holder.

Penner argues that property rights are best understood not according to an amorphous bundle of right picture but according to a criteria test. The criteria theory holds that it is not arbitrary whether a criterion applies or not, rather, there are rules which criteria apply in which circumstances. Property does have a predefined meaning. It differs depending on context, but it differs in a predictable fashion.[64] The foremost criterion Penner identifies is the one that "property rights" refers to rights that exist only between persons, but in respect of items of property.[65] This then requires one to define what can be an item of property.[66] He comes to the conclusion that something is an item of property if it can be held by anyone.[67] Property is what can be held impersonally.

### *II. Property Law as the Law of Things*

Smith has expanded on the modular approach that I described above. He denies that the bundle-of-rights picture is a theory of property at all because it fails to describe the notion of property rights as such by breaking down a property right into an infinite number of infinitesimal inter-personal rights; the content of any bundle becomes arbitrary.[68] Smith's contribution to this description of the shortcomings of the bundle-of-rights picture is to say that the modules are not arbitrary. Their shape is determined the fact that property rights are different

---

[61] Cf. Penner, "Bundle of Rights", *supra* note 37 at 734.

[62] For different varieties of this account see Dagan, "Craft", *supra* note 23; Thomas W Merrill, "Property as Modularity" (2012) 125:1 Harv L Rev 151; Penner, "Bundle of Rights", *supra* note 37. See also Henry E Smith, "Property as the Law of Things" (2011) 125:7 Harv L Rev 1691.

[63] Dagan, "Craft", *supra* note 23 at 1526–35.

[64] Penner, "Bundle of Rights", *supra* note 37 at 767–97.

[65] *Ibid* at 771.

[66] *Ibid* at 799.

[67] *Ibid* at 802.

[68] Smith, *supra* note 62 at 1694–700.

from other rights by exclusion of others in an object of property (in Smith's terminology: a thing). In Hohfeld's terminology, property rights create no-rights and duties in everybody but the right holder, and they create rights in the right holder. The *differentia specifica* of property rights is that they do so not by virtue of personal behaviour, but by taking an object as their starting point.[69] Exclusion of others – *i.e.* the imposition of no-rights, the removal of privileges, and the creation of duties – is the defining mechanism of property rights.[70] The extent of exclusion and the class of excluded of people is defined by the purpose of the property right.[71] This would explain, for example, why the "owner" of property is able to exclude more people from doing more things than the lease-holder. At the same time, the grant of a lesser property right such as a security interest by the owner can be conceptualized as a modification of the extent of exclusion due to ownership. What is important is that exclusion necessarily requires an object of exclusion. Smith is thus able to explain why property law is a law of property and not merely a law of specific interpersonal relationship.[72]

## C. The Economic Analysis of Property Law

The economic analysis of law arguably owes its theoretical underpinning to realism and utilitarianism; just like these two schools of legal theory, it is also concerned with how law can purposefully shape human interaction to achieve a certain purpose.[73] For the economic analysis of the law this purpose is welfare.[74] We thus find similarities between the economic analysis of property law on the one and, and realist and utilitarian theories of property law on the other. The purpose of this section is to detail some concepts applied in the economic analysis of property law.

Economic analysis of property law has to define its subject. From a purely economic perspective, property rights are a mechanism for the allocation of

[69] *Ibid* at 1703–8.

[70] *Ibid* at 1705. See also RC Nolan, "Equitable Property" (2006) 122 LQR 232 at 234–35 and Kevin J Gray, "Property in Thin Air" (1991) 50:2 CLJ 252 at 299.

[71] Smith, *supra* note 62 at 1705. On the function of exclusion for property see also Larissa Katz, "Exclusion and Exclusivity in Property Law" (2008) 58:3 UTLJ 275.

[72] The absence of the person-thing relationship in accounts of property law has been lamented by Thomas W Merrill & Henry E Smith, "What Happened to Property in Law and Economics?" (2001) 111:2 Yale LJ 357.

[73] Cf. Michael J Trebilcock & Paul-Erik Veel, "Property Rights and Development: The Contingent Case for Formalization" (2008) 30:2 U Pa J Int'l L 397 at 409.

[74] See Part I: § 3 , "Law and Economics".

authority regarding the access to and use of resources.[75] Supposedly, "property right" is a wider concept in economics than in legal scholarship.[76] The economic definition does not depend on a legal theory of what property means in substantive law. It thus easily includes not only procedural mechanisms, but also extra-legal mechanisms. Xu claims that the economic view of property rights stands in sharp contrast to legal scholarship which views property rights as "relations between people respecting things."[77] However, as we have seen in the preceding section, this is but one view of property rights. Furthermore, Xu uses the example of the thief to highlight the contrast between economic and legal rights. Thieves, he claims, lack legal rights over stolen property, but are able to consume it, exclude others from it, derive income from it, and alienate it; each of these capabilities is an attribute of ownership and hence thieves have economic rights in stolen property. However, his premise that thieves have no legal rights in stolen property is not entirely accurate as a matter of law with regard to the common law of personal property.[78]

Four types of property rights can be found in a law-and-economics discussion: private property rights, common property rights, state property rights, and open access.[79] Open access rights are characterized by a state in which everybody has a right of access to the resource and no-one has the right to exclude others from access to it.[80]

### *I. Efficiency of Private Property Rights*

In regards to property rights, the "Coase theorem" and the "Hobbes theorem" postulate that in a world of zero transactions costs, the allocation of property rights would not matter; however, because transactions costs are not zero, property rights should be created to assign rights to the party deriving the highest welfare from it, and they should resemble the result of bargaining.[81]

Private property rights are a prerequisite for the operation of market mechanisms.[82] Then again, the creation, distribution and enforcement of private property rights create costs. Furthermore, property rights are costly for those who want to enter into transactions that cannot be reproduced by one of the established discrete property rights; they will have to bargain around the misfit,

---

[75] Guangdong Xu, "The Role of Property Law in Economic Growth" in: Michael Faure & Jan M Smits, eds, *Does Law Matter?: On Law and Economic Growth* (Cambridge: Intersentia, 2011) 331 at 333.

[76] See e.g. Richard A Posner, *Economic Analysis of Law,* 7th edn (New York: Aspen Publishers, 2007) at 48.

[77] Xu, *supra* note 75 at 334.

[78] See Part II: § 5 D, "Possession and Property".

[79] Xu, *supra* note 75 at 335.

[80] *Ibid* at 335.

[81] See Part I: § 3 A.IV.2, "Coase's Contribution".

[82] Xu, *supra* note 75 at 337.

which will result in bargaining costs. Therefore, law should only recognize property rights where their benefit outweighs their costs.[83]

Economic theory recognizes a number of ways in which private property rights influence economic development. First, private property encourages individuals to put resources to effective use by internalizing costs.[84] Second, a stable property regime allows individuals to divert resources from self-defence towards productive investment.[85] Third, a stable property rights regime makes it possible to invest in high-return portable assets and long-term projects.[86] Presumably, the reason why an unstable property rights framework diverts investment towards low-yield immovable assets rather than high-yield portable assets is that immovables are easier to possess and thus easier to defend against expropriation by other individuals. Fourth, a well-tailored property rights framework minimises transactions costs.[87] Fifth, security of title allows secured lending, which is believed to increase credit reliability.[88]

These arguments all lead one to conclude that an economic property rights framework stresses security of title and predictability of content.[89] This would contradict the predictions of the legal origin theory. With regards to the blackletter law, common law property is less formal and less secure than Civil Law property.[90] Another important factor when considering whether Civil Law rules should be replaced by Common Law rules is that a disturbance of established rules might create a disturbance in commonly-used forms of transaction that outweigh the marginal benefit.[91]

### *II. Tragedy of the Commons*

The phrase "tragedy of the commons" describes the problem that open and unregulated access to a resource will lead to the overuse and demise of this resource. It can occur because each individual can maximize her own profit by increasing the exploitation of the resource. Any negative impact this behaviour has on the resource is borne not by the exploitative individual, but the community as a whole.[92] For open-access property, the users do not internalize the

[83] Trebilcock & Veel, *supra* note 73 at 453; Xu, *supra* note 75 at 337.

[84] Harold Demsetz, "Toward a Theory of Property Rights" (1967) 57:2 Am Econ Rev 347 at 349; Trebilcock & Veel, *supra* note 73 at 404; Xu, *supra* note 75 at 340.

[85] Trebilcock & Veel, *supra* note 73 at 408, 417.

[86] Xu, *supra* note 75 at 340.

[87] *Ibid* at 341.

[88] Trebilcock & Veel, *supra* note 73 at 408; Xu, *supra* note 75 at 341. On the efficiency of secured transactions regimes see Part III: § 11 , "The Law and Economics of Secured Transactions".

[89] Cf. Trebilcock & Veel, *supra* note 73 at 410.

[90] See Part II: § 5 I, "Comparing Common Law and Civil Law Property".

[91] Cf. Trebilcock & Veel, *supra* note 73 at 447.

[92] Garrettt Hardin, "The Tragedy of the Commons" (1968) 162:3859 Science 1243.

external costs of a decrease in the resource.[93] Private property rights remedy the tragedy of the commons by internalizing the costs and syncing costs and yields of resource access.

*III. Tragedy of the Anti-Commons*

The tragedy of the anti-commons is the reverse of the tragedy of the commons. In the "tragedy of the anti-commons," excessive private property rights allow individuals to use their private property to prevent a form of resource use that would increase the common welfare.[94] A tragedy of the anti-commons can occur wherever private property rights are admitted. Common property rights or can address both the shortcomings of excessive private property rights as well as problems created by an open access regime.[95]

## D. Theory of *Numerus Clausus*: Which Property?

Both Common Law[96] and Civil Law[97] recognize the doctrine of the *numerus clausus* of property rights. While the assertion that the *numerus clausus* is a part of the black-letter law is uncontroversial, the desirability of and reasons for this principle have become the subject of a number of contributions in recent years.[98] This stands in contrast to earlier doctrinal analysis, which was less concerned with a justification of the *numerus clausus* principle.[99] Theories of the *numerus clausus* have to explain two phenomena: why the *numerus clausus* exists and why the *numerus clausus* contains the types of property rights it

---

[93] Xu, *supra* note 75 at 336.

[94] Michael A Heller, "The Tragedy of the Anticommons: Property in the Transition from Marx to Markets" (1998) 111:3 Harv L Rev 621.

[95] Trebilcock & Veel, *supra* note 73 at 405; Xu, *supra* note 75 at 337.

[96] See Part II: § 5 H, "Numerus Clausus in Common Law".

[97] See Part II: § 4 E, "Numerus Clausus in Civil Law".

[98] See particularly Dagan, "Craft", *supra* note 23; Davidson, *supra* note 13; Henry Hansmann & Reinier Kraakman, "Property, Contract, and Verification: The Numerus Clausus Problem and the Divisibility of Rights" (2002) 31:S2 J Legal Stud 373; Michael A Heller, "The Boundaries of Private Property" (1999) 108:6 Yale LJ 1163; Thomas W Merrill & Henry E Smith, "Optimal Standardization in the Law of Property: The Numerus Clausus Principle" (2000) 110:1 Yale LJ 1; Bernard Rudden, "Economic Theory v Property Law: The Numerus Clausus Problem" in: John Eekelaar & John Bell, eds, *Oxford Essays in Jurisprudence: Third Series* (Oxford: Clarendon Press, 1987) 239 [Rudden, "Numerus Clausus"].

[99] See e.g. John H Merryman, "Policy, Autonomy, and the Numerus Clausus in Italian and American Property Law" (1963) 12:2 Am J Comp L 224 [Merryman, "Numerus Clausus"].

does. There is no inherent justification for the *numerus clausus* in Civil Law or Common Law.[100]

In his analysis of the *numerus clausus* principle, Rudden offers a variety of potential explanations, which he groups into classes as follows:[101] "legal reasons," "philosophical reasons," and "economic reasons." I adopt Rudden's framework, but make some changes to his terminology. I also add the realist account to the list. Adapting Rudden's terminology, I refer to rights that are not admitted as property rights as a result of the *numerus clausus* principle as "fancies."[102] It should be noted that Lord Brougham did not use "fancy" as the name of the right itself, but as an adjective. He rejected the proposition that "incidents of a novel kind can be devised and attached to property at the fancy or caprice of any owner." Thus, one might also refer to "fancies" as "fanciful incidents" or, adopting the terminology of this book, "fanciful property rights."[103] Rather than "legal reasons," I shall refer to "formalist" reasons because essentially these are reasons that are internal to the law.

### *I. Formalist Account of the Numerus Clausus*

The class of formalist reasons consist of "absence of notice," "absence of consent," "pyramiding,"[104] and "undue restraints on alienation."

#### *1. Absence of Notice*

The "absence of notice" argument explains the *numerus clausus* by pointing out that the purchaser might face uncertainty in determining whether any fancies are attached to the property.[105] But there are two problems with the absence-of-notice explanation. First, when there is a property register, the register can contain notice of the fancies.[106] This argument of course only refers to property subject to registration. Second, Rudden claims, in no legal system is notice is necessary or sufficient for the validity of all property rights.[107]

---

[100] Merrill & Smith, "Optimal Standardization in the Law of Property", *supra* note 98 at 10 argue that the numerus clausus in Civil Law is the outflow of the stright codal nature of Civil Law and thus a function of a Civil Law system beyond justification, but see Part II: § 4 E, "Numerus Clausus in Civil Law".

[101] Rudden, "Numerus Clausus", *supra* note 98.

[102] *Ibid* at 239, referring to *Keppell v Bailey* (1834), 2 My & K 517, 39 ER 1042 (Ch), Lord Brougham LC.

[103] *Keppell v Bailey,* preceding note at 1049, Lord Brougham LC.

[104] Rudden, "Numerus Clausus", *supra* note 98 at 245–49.

[105] *Ibid* at 246.

[106] *Ibid* at 246.

[107] *Ibid* at 246.

*2. Absence of Consent*

The "absence of consent" argument explains the *numerus clausus* by the law's general reluctance to impose obligations on parties when they did not agree.[108] Rudden argues that this argument alone cannot explain the *numerus clausus* because most legal systems recognize that certain duties exist regardless of consent, listing obligations of an owner of land *vis-à-vis* neighbouring properties as an example.[109] Another example that comes to mind is the neighbour principle in negligence.[110] I owe a duty of care to my neighbour whether I consented to it or not. The fundamental issue with this argument is that it alone cannot explain why property rights are recognized at all. If all duties required consent of the obligor, there could not be any third-party effect of property rights.

*3. Pyramiding*

The "pyramiding" objection to fancies posits that it is undesirable that an item of property can become "encrusted with layers of obligations."[111] Rudden rejects this argument. He claims that regarding land law, feudal law was abolished not because of the excess of subinfeudation – attaching layers of rights in land and binding the proprietor in possession – but because it led to a situation where land was not valued properly. Furthermore, where such excess exists, the legislature or courts could intervene.[112] But of course Rudden's argument here is entirely impractical once it is being generalised: the legislative intervention against the excesses of feudalism, be it the *Statute Quia Emptores, 1290*[113] in England or the abolition of the seigniorial system in Québec addressed one particular class of fancyful incidents; a complete abolition of the *numerus clausus* would potentially create a wide diversity of fanciful property rights, and it might be impractical to expect the legislature to address each and any undesirably fancy. Furthermore, if a court could easily invalidate any fancy, it would in fact not be a secure property right at all. Finally, neither the pyramiding argument nor Rudden's counter-argument decide the question whether fanciful property rights are desirable and why they are desirable.

---

[108] See also Merryman, "Numerus Clausus", *supra* note 99 at 226.

[109] Rudden, "Numerus Clausus", *supra* note 98 at 247.

[110] See *M'Alister or Donoghue v Stevenson* (1931), [1932] AC 562 (HL).

[111] Rudden, "Numerus Clausus", *supra* note 98 at 248.

[112] *Ibid* at 248.

[113] *A Statute of Our Lord the King, Concerning the Selling and Buying of Land, 1290,* 18 Edw I, c 1.

*4. Restraints Against Alienation*

The "restraints against alienation" argument posits that the *numerus clausus* operates to prevent parties from placing third parties under a restraint of alienation. The German Supreme Court in its decision on the German trust has explicitly rejected the argument that the *numerus clausus* protects the alienability of property in Germany by stating that freedom of alienation and *numerus clausus* are two different explanations for the rule against restrictions on alienation.[114]

*5. Conclusion*

In conclusion, the formalist arguments against the admission of fanciful property rights might show how the *numerus clausus* principle relates to other legal concepts such as consent in contract law and notice. But a formalist analysis does not itself offer any argument for or against the *numerus clausus.*

*II. Philosophical Reasons for the Numerus Clausus*

In his account of philosophical reasons, Rudden offered both a Kantian and a Hegelian explanation for the *numerus clausus,* and used Hohfeld's framework as a tool in a descriptive analysis of the *numerus clausus.*[115]

For Kant, only those acts that respected the freedom of the other were lawful.[116] Thus, an obligation that binds every subject of a legal system can be imposed only by that system itself and not by an individual.[117] An echo of Kant's legal philosophy can be found in Honoré's account of property rights: "[D]uties corresponding to claims *in personam* are created by particular titles [...] duties corresponding to claims *in rem* are created by a general title – the fact of being subject to a given legal system."[118]

For Hegel, property rights are linked with an individuals freedom of will. Free property is the means through which freedom of will expresses itself, and is that which allows free will to operate. The *numerus clausus* in this view is

---

[114] BGH, 5 December 1996, V ZB 27/96, BGHZ 134, 182, NJW 1997, 861, referring to Jürgen Kohler, "Vormerkbarkeit eines durch abredewidrige Veräußerung bedingten Rückerwerbsanspruchs" [1989] DNotZ 339. The rule against restrictions on alienation is found in *Bürgerliches Gesetzbuch,* s 137.

[115] Rudden, "Numerus Clausus", *supra* note 98 at 249–52.

[116] Kant, "Rechtslehre", *supra* note 9 at 337: "Eine jede Handlung ist recht, die oder nach deren Maxime die Freiheit der Willkür eines jeden mit jedermanns Freiheit nach einem allgemeinen Gesetze zusammen bestehen kann." See also Part II: § 8 A.I.1, "Will Theory of Property".

[117] Rudden, "Numerus Clausus", *supra* note 98 at 249.

[118] Anthony M Honoré, "Rights of Exclusion and Immunities Against Divesting" (1960) 34:3 Tul L Rev 453 at 456 [emphasis in original].

necessary to ensure the freedom of property. Restrictions on property are restrictions on people.[119]

Rudden applies the Hohfeldian bundle-of-rights picture to illustrate the effect fanciful property rights have on third parties. His example is one of a fanciful property right given by White to Black in an item of property. Before White transfers the fancy to Black, everybody in the world has the same fanciful right in relation to anybody else in the world except for White. After White has transferred the fancy to Black, everybody in the world still has the same right against each other except for White *and* Black. This shows that even beneficial fancies make third parties worse off.[120]

### *III. Realist Theory of the Numerus Clausus*

As mentioned above, legal realism views property as a means of shaping human interaction. Different property rights or "forms" of property can promote desired values.[121] Property law regulates the toolkit of forms because this is how competing social and political goals can be realized in private interactions.[122] However, a critical analysis of property rights in action can show that the existing rules relating to certain property rights might be an imperfect embodiment of and a less-than-ideal mix between the desired values. This would mean that the form of property needs to be changed to better conform to the underlying value.[123]

Because the list of forms is not static but subject of an evolution catalysed by forces such as courts, private parties, and legislators, the actual *numerus clausus* needs constant critical analysis.[124] This echoes Holmes' notion that it be "revolting to have no better reason for a rule of law than that so it was laid down in the time of Henry IV. It is still more revolting if the grounds upon which it was laid down have vanished long since, and the rule simply persists from blind imitation of the past."[125] Doctrinalism in itself is no justification for the actual *numerus clausus* in force.

---

[119] Rudden, "Numerus Clausus", *supra* note 98 at 250.

[120] *Ibid* at 251.

[121] Dagan, "Craft", *supra* note 23 at 1559–61.

[122] Davidson, *supra* note 13 at 1601. A similar view is expressed by Meredith Render, "The Concept of Property" (2017) 78 *Pittsburgh Law Review* 437 at 443–44: "*Numerus clausus* is first and foremost a coordinating tool." [Emphasis original]. Render's account of the *numerus clausus* differs in that she does not express any position as to what the toolkit is used for.

[123] Davidson, *supra* note 13 at 1601.

[124] *Ibid* at 1616. On the interaction of parties and courts in the evolution of consensual aspects of property rights see Carol M Rose, "Crystals and Mud in Property Law" (1988) 40:3 Stan L Rev 577.

[125] Oliver W Holmes, "The Path of the Law" (1897) 10:8 Harv L Rev 457 at 469.

In the realist account, an evaluation of property rights requires one to identify the promoted values and then see how the *numerus clausus* and the current list of admitted property rights affects these values and whether it does so in a desirable. The law-and-economics analysis of the *numerus clausus* does this with one particular value in mind: welfare. In a federal state, a certain competition between competing property rights frameworks is a function of the close union of competing legal systems.[126] The competition becomes more influential where the legal systems offer significantly different approaches: a competition between a Common Law and Civil Law legal system is more likely to result in more sweeping changes in one legal system than a competition between two broadly similar Common Law jurisdictions.

*IV. Economic Reason for the Numerus Clausus*

Economic analysis of property rights sometimes adopts a wider definition of the term "property right," distinguishing between "formal" and "informal" property rights. "Formal property rights" are property rights "defined and enforced by the state."[127] "Informal property rights" are the result of individual bargaining and areprivately enforced.[128] Implicit in this definition is that property rights are rights of access to an item of property. In the legal terminology adopted in this book, only the first class of property rights should be referred to as "property rights." The *numerus clausus* principle stands in contrast to the principle of freedom of contract, which is deemed to be desirable because it allows the efficient distribution of resources.[129] But a closed list of discrete property rights has advantages as well.[130]

*1. Information Costs*

The *numerus clausus* can operate to limit information costs in a variety of ways. First, it makes it easier to determine the class of available property rights in available properties.[131] Because there are only a limited number of property rights that can be purchased, a potential purchaser can more easily survey the market for which property rights are for sale in which properties. Second, the potential purchaser can easily see which third-party rights are attached to her

---

[126] Davidson, *supra* note 13 at 1617.

[127] Xu, *supra* note 75 at 351.

[128] *Ibid* at 351.

[129] Merrill & Smith, "Optimal Standardization in the Law of Property", *supra* note 98 at 5.

[130] Rudden, "Numerus Clausus", *supra* note 98 at 252–60.

[131] Merrill & Smith, "Optimal Standardization in the Law of Property", *supra* note 98 at 26; Rudden, "Numerus Clausus", *supra* note 98 at 254–55.

object of desire.[132] Third, tortfeasors can understand with which property rights they must not interfere.[133]

### 2. Transaction Costs

Well-defined property rights reduce transaction costs.[134] Rather than having to negotiate the precise content of each party's entitlement, the parties can rely on the discrete property right for the content of the acquired rights.

### 3. Market

Fanciful property rights can potentially remove property from the free flow of commerce.[135] Personal rights do not have the same effect.[136] The market argument is the economic variant of the formalist argument that fancies put an undue restraint on alienation.[137]

### 4. Fragmentation

Building on the "tragedy of the anti-commons," the *numerus clausus* can be seen as a device for minimizing the effects of durable property rights on those dealing with the property in the future; by closing the list of available property rights, the law avoids a fragmentation of access rights to the resource.[138] The problem with the anti-commons argument is that the law does not take a principled stance against fragmentation. Any item of property can have an unlimited number of co-owners.[139] Fragmentation of access to a resource is not *ex-ante* undesirable; rather, it is desirable because it allows efficient use of a resource. Fragmentation often only becomes a problem if the circumstances change and the titular of a property right is no longer able to draw income from the resource. Thus, an anti-commons approach accounts for why the law should provide for the possibility of the ex-post extinction of property rights creating

[132] Merrill & Smith, "Optimal Standardization in the Law of Property", *supra* note 98 at 26; Rudden, "Numerus Clausus", *supra* note 98 at 255.

[133] Merrill & Smith, "Optimal Standardization in the Law of Property", *supra* note 98 at 26.

[134] Rudden, "Numerus Clausus", *supra* note 98 at 253; Xu, *supra* note 75 at 351.

[135] Rudden, "Numerus Clausus", *supra* note 98 at 254.

[136] Honoré, "Rights of Exclusion and Immunities Against Divesting", *supra* note 118 at 468.

[137] Merrill & Smith, "Optimal Standardization in the Law of Property", *supra* note 98 at 24.

[138] See Heller, "The Boundaries of Private Property", *supra* note 98.

[139] Hansmann & Kraakman, *supra* note 98 at 417–19; Merrill & Smith, "Optimal Standardization in the Law of Property", *supra* note 98 at 51–52.

a fragmentation; it cannot explain an *ex ante* prohibition against the creation of a fancy.[140]

*5. Delimiting Use*

Haansmann and Kraaken argue that efficient use of the same resource by two parties requires that they each have a shared understanding of the other's right. Otherwise, they may over- or underuse the property. This is the problem of "co-ordination." Furthermore, they need to be able to protect themselves against infringement of their rights in the property. This is the problem of "enforcement." The solution to both problems is "verification." Formal property rights are better defined than informal property rights.[141] Through the process of verification, each party can verify the other party's understanding of the parties' respective rights. In enforcement, a third-party enforcer, such as a judge, verifies the parties' understanding of their respective rights. Pre-defining property rights is the way in which verification is achieved.[142] With regards to the enforcement aspect, discrete property rights are more easily enforced by the state, which has a monopoly on violence.[143]

The theory advanced by Haansmann and Kraaken allows one normative prediction about law. Possession is the easiest means of verification.[144] This can explain why possession is a title and is recognised as the root of ownership. It can also explain why common law is more concerned with the protection of possession than with the protection of a more abstract and difficult notion such as ownership. At the same time, the possession rule fails with regard to more sophisticated applications of property.[145] In other words, were the *numerus clausus* principle only concerned with keeping verification costs at a minimum, all property rights would depend on and revolve around possession. This is clearly not the case. The admission of non-possessory property rights must thus have a benefit that offsets the higher costs of verification.

*V. Creating the List of Discrete Property Rights*

Closing the list of admitted property rights does not only have benefits. Otherwise, there would be only one property right.[146] Since bargaining costs are not zero in the real world, admitting only one property right would create excessive costs associated with constant bargaining between the property right holder and

[140] Hansmann & Kraakman, *supra* note 98 at 418.
[141] Xu, *supra* note 75 at 351.
[142] Hansmann & Kraakman, *supra* note 98 at 382–84.
[143] Xu, *supra* note 75 at 351.
[144] Hansmann & Kraakman, *supra* note 98 at 384–85.
[145] *Ibid* at 385.
[146] Merrill & Smith, "Optimal Standardization in the Law of Property", *supra* note 98 at 35.

the class of access seekers. The *numerus clausus* can thus be explained as an equilibrium between maximum standardization – one property right – and no standardization at all.[147] The exact shape of the *numerus clausus* – the content of the list of admitted discrete property rights – should be the result of the interests of the parties and the bargaining costs. Where either bargaining costs are high, or the interest of the party is very common, it is efficient to create a property right that mirrors this interest.

The private parties' interests are decisive in shaping the content of property rights by defining the possible combinations of rights into recognized bundles and formulating the criteria test.[148]

## E. Theory of Equitable Property Rights

Above,[149] I have conceptualized property rights as rights – arguably: discrete bundles of rights – in relation to objects of property. The relation between property right and property object is one of exclusiveness: a person holds a property right if it can exclude others from the object of property. This theory of property rights differs from the working definition of property rights I have adopted in the chapters on the black-letter law of property, where I defined property rights as being enduring in insolvency. This distinction matters because the latter definition easily includes equitable property rights. The purpose of this section is to analyse whether equitable rights can really be thought of as property rights within the theory of property rights, or whether the insolvency-based working definition has lead to a wrong classification of equitable rights.[150] Legal interests are straightforward to understand in relation to their right/duty aspect. The legal right in the thing corresponds with the third-party duty not to interfere. The person-thing relationship that is at the heart of property at law is summarized by Penner's conceptual understanding of legal property where "the thing itself 'mediates' the normative relationship between the right holder and the duty bearer."[151]

---

[147] *Ibid* at 38–40.

[148] Anthony Scott, "Property Rights and Property Wrongs" (1983) 16:4 Can J Econ 555. Scott does not use the term "criteria test," I have changed his terminology to conform to the one used by Penner, "Bundle of Rights", *supra* note 37 at 767–97. See also Part II: § 8 B.I.2, "Honore's Bundle of Rights".

[149] See Part II: § 8 B, "Bundle of Rights or Institution: How Property?".

[150] This question is also examined in Elena C Zaccaria, "The Nature of the Beneficiary's Right Under a Trust: Proprietary Right, Purely Personal Right or Right Against a Right?" [2019] LQR 460.

[151] James E Penner, "The (True) Nature of a Beneficiary's Equitable Proprietary Interest under a Trust" (2014) 27:2 Can JL & Juris 473 at 475 [Penner, "True Nature"].

### *I. The Contractarian View*

Langbein argues that the law of trusts can be based on a contractarian foundation,[152] but this does negate the role trusts have to play in relation to property. In fact, Langbein has to exclude non-consensual trusts from his analysis to reach this conclusion.[153] His contractarian view is sustainable even in relation to constructive trusts, in the sense that a law-and-economics approach to property rights always proceeds from the premise that any property right should anticipate a bargaining result.[154] Understood this way, the contractarian view does not add anything to the personal-property right debate.

### *II. The Personal / Property Dichotomy*

As mentioned in the preceding chapter on equitable property rights, one view holds that equitable rights, exemplified by the trust beneficiary's right are not rights in relation to property, but rights in relation to the trustee.[155] Maitland provides us with a more detailed account of the personal right and property right positions. He described the two opposing positions thusly:

> "(1) *Cestui que trust* has rights enforceable against any person who has undertaken the trust, all who claim through or under him as volunteers (heirs, devisees, personal representatives, donees) against his creditors, and against those who acquire the thing with notice actual or constructive of the trust.
>
> Or
>
> (2) *Cestui que trust* has rights enforceable against all save a *bona fide* purchaser ('purchaser' in this context always includes mortgagee) who for value has obtained a legal right in the thing without notice of the trust express or constructive."[156]

Later, Scott and Stone argued similar positions.[157] Scott argued that because the beneficiary has a right against an indeterminate class of people, she has a property right in the trust property. Stone maintained that the beneficiary has a

---

[152] John H Langbein, "The Contractarian Basis of the Law of Trusts" (1995) 105 Yale LJ 625.

[153] *Ibid* at 631.

[154] Anthony J Duggan, "Constructive Trusts from a Law and Economics Perspective" (2005) 55 UTLJ 217 provides such an analysis for a subset of constructive trusts. See also Part II: § 8 C, "The Economic Analysis of Property Law".

[155] See Tobias Barkley, "Trustees' Bare Legal Title: Concept or Misconception?" (2017) 26:1 Austral Prop LJ 44 at 45–47, referring to NG Jones, "Uses and 'Automatic' Resulting Trusts of Freehold" (2013) 72:1 CLJ 91 at 95.

[156] Frederic W Maitland, *Equity, Also the Forms of Action at Common Law: Two Courses of Lectures,* ed by A. H. Chaytor and W. J. Whittaker (Cambridge: Cambridge University Press, 1910) at 120 [emphasis in original]. Maitland preferred the first definition.

[157] Austin W Scott, "The Nature of the Rights of the Cestui Que Trust" (1917) 17:4 Col L Rev 269; Harlan F Stone, "The Nature of the Rights of the 'Cestui Que Trust'" (1917) 17:6 Col L Rev 467. See also Donovan WM Waters, "The Nature of the Trust Beneficiary's Interest" (1967) 45:2 Can Bar Rev 219 at 221–22.

personal right against the trustee although he does admit that the right itself can be described as property.

The personal theory is supported by reference to the trust's historical predecessor, the use. At the time before the *Statute of Uses.*[158] property rights in relation to land were conceptually split into two: the seisin (rightful possession) and the right to use (fruits, profits, enjoyment). The creation of a use assigned these rights to different parties.[159] The function of the *Statute of Uses* was that an arrangement in which the person seised held for the use of another would be executed, meaning that the rightful possession would be transferred to the person who held the right to use.[160] As Barkley argues, the *Statute of Uses* thus lead to a recharacterization of uses, which became known as trusts.[161] In a trust, the trust beneficiary's right was no longer conceived as a right in the property but instead as a right against the trustee. This would prevent the execution of the second use.[162] Implicit in this argument is that the *Statute of Uses* would have excuted any proprietary right of the *cestui que trust* regardless of whether it was legal or equitable. Classifiying the right of the *cestui que trust* as non-proprietary was thus necessary to avoid execution of the trust.

In Maitland's concept of equitable rights there is no such thing as an equitable property right. All equity does is having two aspects to the recognition of the trustee's personal duties. First it recognizes the trustee's obligation to exercise their legal rights for the benefit of the beneficiary. Second it is willing "to shift this personal obligation to (or, if 'shift' is tendentious, to impose a like obligation on) third party recipients of the property from the trustee."[163] Similarly arguing against the view that equitable rights protects rights in things, Smith writes that

> "Equity simply understood the idea of an obligation differently from the common law and differently from the civil law tradition. Equity was, and is, much more willing to let obligations (if they relate to the benefit of particular property) have effects on third parties, at least those who were not good faith purchasers for value of the property in question."[164]

---

[158] *An Act concerning Uses and Wills,* 27 Hen VIII, c 10.

[159] Barkley, *supra* note 155 at 48–49.

[160] *Ibid* at 48–50; Jones, *supra* note 155 at 106; DEC Yale, "The Revival of Equitable Estates in the Seventeenth Century: An Explanation by Lord Nottingham" (1957) 15:1 CLJ 72 at 83.

[161] See Part II: § 6 B.IV, "The Statute of Uses".

[162] Barkley, *supra* note 155 at 49; Jones, *supra* note 155 at 106; Yale, *supra* note 160 at 83.

[163] Penner, "True Nature", *supra* note 151 at 476.

[164] Lionel D Smith, "Trust and Patrimony" (2009) 28 ETPJ 332 at 345.

### *III. Rights Against Rights*

Recently, a third view of the beneficiary's right has been proffered as well. The right-against-a-right view of the trust beneficiary's right posits that the trust beneficiary has no right in the trust asset itself, but only a right in the right held by the trustee.[165] McFarlane has recently re-opened the debate by offering a third class of rights other than property rights and personal rights. He argues for a definition of legal and equitable rights that defines the former as "property rights" (rights against things) and the latter as "persistent rights" (rights against rights against things).[166] The argument against understanding the beneficiary's right as a property right is that the rules of trust law amount to a rejection of a direct relationship between beneficiary and trust property.[167] McFarlane's argument is that equitable rights cannot be understood to mean rights in things because the equitable right holder – the beneficiary – depends on an intermediary: the trustee.[168] At the same time, the beneficiary's right against the trustee is persistent because it prevents third parties from interfering with the trustee's right to the beneficiary's disadvantage.[169]

### *IV. Analysis*

As the three preceding subsections show, there are different ways to conceptualize equitable rights. We have already seen that the pure contractarian view does not add much to our understanding of equitable property rights as understood in this chapter[170]. Let us now turn to the personal right conceptualization of the beneficiary's right. A number of reasons have been submitted to support the denial of a property right classification of equitable rights in regard to trust property. The first argument is that if a third party wrongfully causes damage to the trust property, there is no claim by a beneficiary against the third party.[171] This is not a convincing argument. It is like saying the title-holder of property has no property right because she cannot vindicate property. That is a reason why she might not be the "owner," or rather why there is no ownership at common law, but not an argument for denying any title, unless one considers the

---

[165] Cf. Penner, "True Nature", *supra* note 151 at 473, referring to Robert Chambers, *An Introduction to Property Law in Australia,* 1st edn (Sydney: Thomson Law Books, 2001) at 115; Ben McFarlane & Robert Stevens, "The Nature of Equitable Property" (2010) 4:1 J Equ 1; Smith, "Trust and Patrimony", preceding note.

[166] See Ben McFarlane, *The Structure of Property Law* (London: Bloomsbury Publishing, 2008) and McFarlane & Stevens, preceding note.

[167] Smith, "Trust and Patrimony", *supra* note 164 at 344.

[168] McFarlane & Stevens, *supra* note 165 at 2.

[169] *Ibid* at 2.

[170] See Part II: § 8 E.I, "The Contractarian View".

[171] McFarlane & Stevens, *supra* note 165 at 8; Smith, "Trust and Patrimony", *supra* note 164 at 343.

action for damages the defining element of a property right, in which case this is a very arbitrary *differentia specifica.* In fact, the beneficiary might very well have an unjust enrichment claim against the interferor and I will later argue that the unjust enrichment principle in Common Law does operate to complete the protection of property rights.[172]

The second argument says that the claims of the beneficiary against third parties are not based on interference with the property but on interference with the trustee's obligation in regard to the property.[173] But this is essentially the question whether property rights are rights in things or rights against others in relation to things. To consider the beneficiary as "beneficial owner" – that is, somebody having a property right in relation to the trust property – relates to a certain extent to the realist Hohfeldian conception of the law, which considers the law to be concerned with personal relations, rather than relations between persons and things that have no bearing on the social sphere. Further, the trust beneficiary can exclude others from access to the trust property.[174] Nolan argues that the beneficiary's right of enjoyment in the trust property is not a multital right because she can only enforce it against a limited class: the trustee.[175] However, this is not entirely true: the beneficiary can enforce her right in the item of property against the trustee only, but the class of people who are the trustee is open-ended because whoever wrongfully receives the trust property becomes the constructive trustee. What is true is that the trustee owes certain personal duties which she only ever owes by virtue of being appointed trustee. These do not relate to a certain property so they cannot be classified as property rights.[176]

Against Maitland's view that saw equitable rights as personal rights capable of shifting,[177] it can be argued that the shifting of obligation that equity recognizes in relation to the trustee's obligation *vis-à-vis* the beneficiary is not different from what is the specific difference of any property right in general in a Hohfeldian understanding of property: its ability to effect shifting or imposition of a duty without the consent or breach of a duty by those parties who are or become liable.[178] In summary, the personal rights theory of the trust beneficiary's equitable right is not reconcilable with the understanding of property rights developed in this chapter.

Let us then turn to right-against-rights view of equitable rights. In the right-against-rights view, the exclusion of equitable rights from the class of property

---

[172] See Part II: § 10 , "Proprietary Restitution".
[173] Smith, "Trust and Patrimony", *supra* note 164 at 343.
[174] Cf. Nolan, *supra* note 70 at 236.
[175] *Ibid* at 236.
[176] *Ibid* at 254.
[177] See Part II: § 8 E.II, "The Personal / Property Dichotomy".
[178] See Part II: § 8 B.I.1, "The Hohfeldian Concept of Property".

rights depends on a concept of a property right being an an immediate right to an asset. Further, in Penner's reading of the right-against-right view

> "the only facilitative power one has under the law of trusts is to undertake a personal obligation, with the result that the law of trusts really belongs within the law of obligations. It is the undertaking of the obligation by the trustee to hold specific property for another that is the relevant obligation, and it is equity's willingness to treat a 'right, to a right' as binding on third parties which creates the trust by operation of law."[179]

Understood this way, the right-against-a-right view is not convincing because that is akin to saying that no one has the power to transfer title at law, only to agree that title be transferred, and iti s the law that gives effect to this agreement. This view of trust law is also not necessary to safeguard a *numerus clausus* because the power to declare trusts is not a violation of the Common Law *numerus clausus* principle; a trust is not a fancy.[180]

Regardless of Penner's argument, I do not believe that a third category of rights adds anything to the personal/property dichotomy as far as property rights as understood in this book are concerned.[181] This then leaves the question whether the property right conceptualization of the beneficiary's right is sound, defensible, and useful. I would argue it is, provided one widens one's understanding of the person-thing relationship that characterizes property law. Equitable property rights are not concerned with physical agenda-setting in relation to the item of property.[182] Instead, they protect the specific value, use and enjoyment that the beneficial owner can have in the property.

Penner defends the position that a trust entails a split of legal title and beneficial ownership, or as he calls it a split of the rights and powers. Whereas the legal owner holds the powers to deal with the property, the beneficial owner is the one who has the right to benefit from the property.[183] I would argue that a better expression of this view is that upon creation of a trust, the entitlement is split: the legal title protects possession, the equitable title protects value, and the legal owner must use their power for the benefit of the latter, the value. If there is no split, the legal owner is also entitled to the value, *i.e.* value entitlement is generally an incident of ownership.

Rudden argues that the distinction between equity and legal rights is a function of understanding rights not as rights in objects of property but as rights in value.[184] If any non-personal right were defined in relation to an object, the distinction between legal entitlement and equitable title would collapse. This

---

[179] Penner, "True Nature", *supra* note 151 at 492.
[180] Nolan, *supra* note 70 at 261–62; Penner, "True Nature", *supra* note 151 at 492.
[181] See Part II: § 8 B, "Bundle of Rights or Institution: How Property?".
[182] See Part II: § 8 B.I.2.b), "Necessary Incident of Ownership".
[183] Penner, "True Nature", *supra* note 151 at 477.
[184] Bernard Rudden, "Things as Thing and Things as Wealth" (1994) 14:1 Oxford J Legal Stud 81.

might explain why the Civil Law does not operate with the notion of equitable property rights, but it is evident that the Common Law does not share this view of a person-thing relationship in property law. The distinction between equity and law is very much alive in case law at the moment. If anything, this book can be seen as a modest contribution in showing that equity does play a role in complementing the incomplete person-thing relationship provided for by the common law.

The import of a specific value embedded in a trust property can also explain why trusts are so important to modern economic reality. Most modern trusts are not based on the trustee's possession of a corporeal trust asset, as there either is no such asset (wealth management trust), or because the beneficiary has possession themselves (*e.g.* trusts for land, but also partnership property if subject to a trust). The beneficiary's protection is consequently not a function of the beneficiary getting the trustee to enforce the latter's possessory right. Either the beneficiary has possession themselves, in which case their possession is protected by legal remedies; or they are concerned with value protection, or more precisely, it is the interest in the asset's value that the Common Law protects.[185]

Penner argues that to describe equitable ownership in Common Law legal systems, one does not need to choose between a notion that pits equitable ownership against legal ownership, the "sausage meat" conception of equitable interests – that equitable ownership is the valuable sausage meat within the skin of legal title – or the Roman notion of ownership, but proposes a fourth option. Ownership, he argues, is about title, which "which comprises the powers to transfer, confer rights in, or otherwise dispose of (within the confines of the *numerus clausus*) the right to possess tangibles or the right (through legal action or equitable suit) to realise the value of intangibles."[186] It is then the purpose of the law/equity split to potentially assign these different aspects of ownership to different people. But the quitable right also gives the beneficiary the option to reunite these different aspects. Penner writes that

> "[i]t is not the beneficiary['s] right [in] the trustee's right to immediate, exclusive possession which benefits the beneficiary but his right that, the trustee exercise his power of legal title to put the beneficiary into possession, so that he acquires at common law the right to immediate, exclusive possession, which is good against the whole world, including the trustee[.]"[187]

This is an important point. This makes it clear that a beneficiary's legal right is a function of their equitable right; in other words, the equitable right is the gateway to getting a legal right that is directly enforcable against the entire world.

---

[185] Cf. Penner, "True Nature", *supra* note 151 at 481–82.
[186] *Ibid* at 486–88.
[187] *Ibid* at 482.

# § 9 Property Unjustly Gained

As we have seen above, common law lacks the strong protection of property offered by Civil Law.[1] At the same time, theories of property favour strong protection of property rights and a clear delimitation of entitlement.[2] In the following two chapters, I argue that the Common Law as a legal system provides for a Civilian level of protection of property through the area of law described as the "law of unjust enrichment" or the "law of restitution."

Lord Justice Mummery characterized a claim for unjust enrichment as "not a claim for compensation for loss, but for recovery of a benefit unjustly gained."[3] But the focus of my analysis is narrower than that; in the end, I am not concerned with *any* form of benefit a defendant might have gained unjustly; rather, I am only interested in *property* that is unjustly received. Other forms of benefit are, for instance, services.[4] The mere receipt of such a benefit is outside the scope of our analysis, unless the receipt of a non-proprietary benefit triggers a proprietary response.[5] Nevertheless, since cases tend to treat unjust receipt of another's property as falling into the same category as the unjust receipt of service, reference to cases not involving property is necessary.

Referring to the area of law I analyse in this chapter as either the law of "restitution" or "unjust enrichment" already gives an answer to the important question whether it is fundamentally described by its cause or its remedy.[6] In fact, for Birks unjust enrichment is but one of the reasons for restitution.[7] For

---

[1] See Part II: § 5 I, "Comparing Common Law and Civil Law Property".

[2] See Part II: § 8, "Theory of Property Rights".

[3] *Boake Allen Ltd v HMRC,* [2006] STC 606 at para 175 (CA Civ).

[4] See e.g. *Benedetti v Sawiris,* [2010] EWCA Civ 1427.

[5] See e.g. *Kerr v Baranow,* 2011 SCC 10, [2011] 1 SCR 269, 328 DLR (4th) 577; *Pettkus v Becker,* [1980] 2 SCR 834, 117 DLR (3d) 257 [cited to SCR].

[6] Dennis Klimchuk, "The Normative Foundations of Unjust Enrichment" in: Robert Chambers, Charles C Mitchell & James E Penner, eds, *Philosophical Foundations of the Law of Unjust Enrichment* (Oxford: Oxford University Press, 2009) 81 at 82.

[7] Peter Birks, "Property and Unjust Enrichment: Categorical Truths" [1997] NZL Rev 623 at 626; Peter Birks, *Unjust Enrichment,* 2d edn (Oxford: Oxford University Press, 2005) at 4–5.

Virgo as well, there are three principles which give rise to a claim for restitution: unjust enrichment, disgorgement, and vindication of property rights.[8] Because "unjust enrichment" has become the established term in Canadian law,[9] this is the term I have chosen for this chapter. Nevertheless, this does not anticipate a substantive statement whether restitution is always based on the same legal event, or whether certain classes of events are different from others. Notably, I am not yet making a statement whether restitution does or does not entail vindication of property rights, which is better classified separately from other unjust-enrichment events. This is essentially the topic of the next chapter.[10]

Before I turn my focus to the Common Law, I look at the law of unjustified enrichment in two Civil Law systems. The development in the two Common Law jurisdictions of England and Common Law Canada was influenced by their Civil Law neighbours, Québec and Scotland. Thus, I give a brief overview of the law of unjustified enrichment in these two jurisdictions. However, I should note at the outset that Civilian legal systems do not recognize property rights as the result of an unjust enrichment claim.[11] Thus, while the comparison with unjustified enrichment in Civil Law is worthwhile because of its structural similarities to unjust enrichment in Common Law, Civil Law's remedies have no bearing on the subject of this book. In other words: were it not for the structural similarities, Civil Law unjustified enrichment would not make an appearance in this book, whereas Common Law restitution law does because it can result in a property right.

In a system of law that is no longer defined by its writs or actions, the areas of the law should be organized by causes of action rather than remedies sought.[12] However, in the context of this book, I think it is permissible to approach the law through its defining remedy. A restitutionary remedy can be a proprietary right – for instance, a "remedial" trust or an equitable lien. The choice to set the primary focus on the remedy (restitution) is thus a function of the over-arching topic of this book: property rights, stemming from a Common Law or a Civil Law system, and their effect in insolvency. Consequently, I use

---

[8] Graham Virgo, *The Principles of the Law of Restitution,* 3rd edn (Oxford: Oxford University Press, 2016) at 8 [Virgo, *Restitution*].

[9] As well as in English law; compare the change in booktitles between Robert Goff & Gareth H Jones, *The Law of Restitution,* ed by Gareth H. Jones, 7th edn (London: Sweet & Maxwell, 2007) [*Goff & Jones*[7]] and Charles CJ Mitchell, Paul Mitchell & Stephen Watterson, *Goff & Jones: The Law of Unjust Enrichment,* 8th edn (London: Sweet & Maxwell, 2011).

[10] Part II: § 10, "Proprietary Restitution".

[11] See Birks, *Unjust Enrichment, supra* note 7 at 32.

[12] Mitchell McInnes, "The Canadian Principle of Unjust Enrichment: Comparative Insights Into the Law of Restitution" (1999) 37 Alta L Rev 1 at 3–4.

the law of restitution as my starting point for the analysis of the Common Law in section B.

In section DC I look at the recognition of the unjust enrichment principle as the foundation of restitution law in England and Canada. In section D, I discuss the question of what exactly constitutes the "unjust factor" in unjust enrichment law. In section E, I discuss theoretical accounts of unjust enrichment law.

## A. Unjustified Enrichment in Civil Law

### *I. Québec Law of Unjustified Enrichment*

Under the *Code civil du Bas-Canada,*[13] the general principle of unjust enrichment was not codified, but the Supreme Court of Canada acknowledged there exists a general principle against allowing a defendant to retain an unjust enrichment within the Civil Law:

> "Dans le champ d'opération des quasi-contrats nous rencontrons d'abord la gestion d'affaires et ensuite l'action *de in rem verso* qu'on aurait tort de confondre avec l'action que donne cette gestion.
>
> L'action *de in rem verso* n'est pas nommée dans notre code pas plus que dans le Code Napoléon; elle existe pour tant dans notre droit comme dans le droit français qui la tiennent tous deux du droit romain. Son fondement juridique est le grand principe d'équité que nul ne s'enrichir au détriment d'autrui.
>
> Autre chose est l'action *de in rem verso.* Elle suppose que le demandeur fait une dépense d'argent ou d'activité dont résulte l'enrichissement du défendeur."[14]

In Québec, the term was used to designate a wider variety of cases. It basically encompassed any case where there was "(1) an enrichment of the defendant, (2) an impoverishment of the plaintiff, (3) a correlation between the enrichment and impoverishment and (4) an absence of a civilly valid cause for this factual correlation."[15] The idea that the *actio de in rem verso* encompassed such a general principle was endorsed by the Supreme Court in *Cie immobilière Viger*

---

[13] *Code civil du Bas-Canada,* 29 Vict, c 41.

[14] *Regent Taxi & Transport Co v Congregation des Petits Frères de Marie,* [1929] SCR 650, [1930] 2 DLR 353, Mignault J [dissenting on the outcome, emphasis original]. See also *Price v Neault* (1886), 12 App Cas 110, 13 QLR 287 (PC). The term de in rem verso is already used in the Roman digests Ulpian, *Digests* 15.3.3.2: "et regulariter dicimus totiens *de in rem verso* esse actionem, quibus casibus procurator mandati vel qui negotia gessit negotiorum gestorum haberet actionem quotiensque aliquid consumpsit servus, ut aut meliorem rem dominus habuerit aut non deteriorem." [Emphasis added].

[15] JD Fine, "Cause in the Quebec Law of Enrichment without Cause" (1973) 19:4 McGill LJ 453 at 455.

*Ltée c Lauréat Giguère Inc.*[16] In its decision, the Court held that, while unjustified enrichment was not codified, the *CcBC* did not contain the entire *droit commun:*

"On peut également trouver un tel support dans un extrapolation des multiples dispositions du Code civil qui n'en sont que des applications particulières. Le Code civil ne contient pas tout le droit civil. Il est fondé sur des principes qui n'y sont pas tous exprimés et dont il appartient à la jurisprudence et à la doctrine d'assurer la fécondité."[17]

It thus accepted the existence of a general principle of unjustified enrichment.[18]

In the *Code civil du Québec,*[19] the principle was finally codified in art 1493 *CcQ.*

"Article 1493 *CcQ*

| | |
|---|---|
| A person who is enriched at the expense of another shall, to the extent of his enrichment, indemnify the other for his correlative impoverishment, if there is no justification for the enrichment or the impoverishment. | Celui qui s'enrichit aux dépens d'autrui doit, jusqu'à concurrence de son enrichissement, indemniser ce dernier de son appauvrissement corrélatif s'il n'existe aucune justification à l'enrichissement ou à l'appauvrissement." |

Unjustified enrichment in Québec law operates under a principle of weak subsidiarity. This means that where the claimant has a claim other than an unjust enrichment claim, she has to rely on that claim. Failure to do so prevents her from bringing an unjust enrichment claim.[20]

## *II. Scots Law of Unjustified Enrichment*

In Scots law, the principle is that "[a] person may be said to have received unjustified enrichment at another's expense when he has obtained a benefit from his actings or expenditure, without there being a legal ground which would justify him in retaining that benefit."[21]

---

[16] (1976), [1977] 2 SCR 67.

[17] *Ibid* at 76, Beetz J.

[18] See also, writing extrajudicially, Pierre-Basile Mignault, "L'enrichissement sans cause" (1934–1935) 13 R du D 157.

[19] *Code civil du Québec,* SQ 1991, c 64.

[20] *Ibid,* art 1494. See Lionel D Smith, "Property, Subsidiarity and Unjust Enrichment" in: David Johnston & Reinhard Zimmermann, eds, *Unjustified Enrichment: Key Issues in Comparative Perspective* (Cambridge: Cambridge University Press, 2002) 588 at 607–8. See also Alexis Posez, "La subsidiarité de l'enrichissement sans cause: Étude de droit Français à la lumière du droit comparé" (2014) 91:2 Rev dr int dr comp 185 at 224 on Québec in particular.

[21] *Dollar Land (Cumbernauld) Ltd v CIN Properties Ltd,* [1996] SC 331 at 348–49 (Ct Sess, In H), Lord Cullen. See also *Shilliday v Smith,* [1998] SLT 976, [1998] SC 725 (Ct Sess, In H).

### *1. The Condictiones*

Based on Roman law, Scots law distinguishes different categories of unjustified enrichment, called *condictiones.* They are: the *condictio indebiti;* the *condictio causa data, causa non secuta;* and the *condictio sine cause.*[22] These categories are substantive in the sense that if a fact pattern can be subsumed into one of these categories, the unjustified enrichment is to be reversed.[23] Even where a transfer of property is based on contract and the contract fails, the duty to reverse the enrichment is explicitly not based on contract law, instead forming part of the law of unjust enrichment.[24]

### *2. Unjustifed Enrichment in the Map of Scots Law*

#### *a) Unjustified Enrichment and the Law of Obligations*

Scots law has recognized unjustified enrichment as a separate area of law, distinct from tort and contract, since the 16th century.[25] Unlike English law, Scots law has always rejected the implied contract theory in unjustified enrichment cases.[26] Another difference between Scots law and English law is that unjustified enrichment is seen as a unitary institution and not one that is – or at least was – split between law and equity.[27]

Above I have described how the Scots law of unjustified enrichment consists of the several *condictiones.* In Stair's classification of the law, the *condictiones* are one of two categories of restitution. Restitution encompasses all cases where debtor and claimant are connected by a defective transfer of ownership. Unjust enrichment encompasses the cases where the transfer, while defective, is not invalid.[28] This classification – notably the difference between restitution in cases of an invalid transfer of ownership and restitution in cases of a defective, yet not invalid, transfer of ownership – was retained by later doctrine.[29]

---

[22] *Shilliday v Smith,* preceding note at 727, Rodger LP.

[23] *Ibid* at 728.

[24] *Ibid* at 730.

[25] Peter Birks, "Restitution: A View of Scots Law" (1985) 38 Curr Legal Probs 57 at 58–59.

[26] See *ibid* at 60–61, Birks points out that there were occasional exceptions in jurisprudence, referring to *Masters and Seamen of Dundee v Cockerill* (1869), 8 M 278 at 281 (Ct Sess, In H), Neaves LJ: "The action of *condictio indebiti* implies *indebiti solutio.* It is a peculiar action well known in our law. It depends not on contract, but on quasi contract. When a payment is made which is supposed to be due, but which is not due, the law makes a contract between the parties such as they would have made had the real truth been known." [Emphasis original].

[27] Birks, "Restitution", *supra* note 25 at 61.

[28] See Robin Evans-Jones & Phillip Hellwege, "Some Observations on the Taxonomy of Unjustified Enrichment in Scots Law" (1998) 2 Edin L Rev 180 at 181–83.

[29] *Ibid* at 183–86.

### *b) Unjustified Enrichment and Property Law*

As is common in a Civilian legal system,[30] in Scots law, there is a sharp distinction between property law and the law of unjustified enrichment. Generally, a claim in unjustified enrichment is not *in rem.*[31] An enrichment claim is one for personal restitution, while a property claim is one for vindication.[32] The two cases can be distinguished by the allocation of ownership: in cases of personal restitution, ownership lies with the defendant; however, in cases of vindication, the claimant still retainsher ownership. Furthermore, in cases of vindication, the claimant will rely only on her ownership. In enrichment cases, she must rely on the fact that the defendant is unjustly enriched.[33]

The sharp distinction between enrichment restitution and vindication is of particular importance in Scots law because the transfer of ownership can be separate and abstract from the underlying causal contract;[34] thus a void contract may still result in a transfer of title from claimant to defendant.

## B. Origins of Restitution

If we turn our attention from the Civil Law to the Common Law, we find that unjust enrichment was not initially recognized as a discrete area of the law. The Common Law developed from a number of cases at common law in which a right to restitution of a monetary sum was recognized. These categories of cases became known the "common counts." At the same time, a right to restitution was recognized in equity. How these common law common counts and the cases of equitable restitution were then found to be based on the underlying principle of "unjust enrichment" is the topic of the next section.[35]

### *I. The Common Counts*

Historically, the law of restitution arose from the common law action of *indebitatus assumpsit* or *assumpsit* (which effectively translates as "debt undertaken").[36] The action *assumpsit* literally concerned a promise to repay a debt.

---

[30] Kenneth GC Reid, "Unjustified Enrichment and Property Law" [1994] JRNS 167 at 167–68. Cf. Birks, *Unjust Enrichment, supra* note 7 at 32.

[31] Reid, "Unjustified Enrichment and Property Law", preceding note at 167–68.

[32] *Ibid* at 169.

[33] George L Gretton, "Proprietary Issues" in: Johnston & Zimmermann, eds, *Unjustified Enrichment, supra* note 20, 571 at 573; Reid, "Unjustified Enrichment and Property Law", *supra* note 30 at 169.

[34] See Part II: § 4 F.I, "Inter Vivos Transfer of Property in Roman Law".

[35] See Part II: § 9 C, "Development of the Unjust Enrichment Principle".

[36] *Goff & Jones*[7], *supra* note 9, at para 1.2; Virgo, *Restitution, supra* note 8 at 45.

The writ of *assumpsit* originated in the Common Law courts, specifically the Court of King's Bench.[37] The acceptance of the action for *assumpsit* can be traced back to a competition between the Court of King's Bench and the Court of Common Pleas. The action for *assumpsit* was more flexible and more efficient than its Common Plea counterpart, so claimants would have preferred to pursue their claim by virtue of the *assumpsit* action in the Court of King's Bench.[38] Furthermore, basing a claim on *assumpsit* allowed the claimant to initiate the case at the Court of King's Bench, whereas usually, he would have been required to file it at the Court of Common Pleas.[39] The undertaking of the debt by the defendant did not need to be explicit; rather, it could be implied from the circumstances. In *Slade's Case,*[40] the Exchequer Chamber condoned the practice of the Court of King's Bench to imply the undertaking of the debt.

*Assumpsit* evolved to encompass four counts: *money had and received, money paid* to the defendants' use, *quantum meruit,* and *quantum valebat.*[41] Since the terminology of *assumpsit* is still used in modern cases, it might be helpful to briefly explain what these four counts were. "Money had and received" refers to the case where the claimant paid money to the defendant by mistake or under duress, or if there was a failure of consideration.[42] "Money paid" encompasses cases where money was paid from the claimant to a third party, which subsequently led to a benefit for the defendant. Originally, the action for money paid would require that the defendant made the payment upon request, but law could imply this request.[43] The two *quantum* counts would be for reasonable hypothetical remuneration for services and goods rendered by the claimant.[44]

### *II. Moses v Macferlan*

The case considered to be the "source of the modern law of restitution"[45] is *Moses v Macferlan.*[46] The facts of the case were as follows: Moses had endorsed promissory notes to Macferlan. Macferlan had promised Moses that Moses would suffer no prejudice because of the endorsement. Nevertheless,

---

[37] *Goff & Jones*[7], *supra* note 9, at para 1.6.

[38] *Ibid* at para 1.6.

[39] See *Peel v Canada,* [1992] 3 SCR 762, 98 DLR (4th) 140 [*Peel,* cited to SCR], McLachlin J (as she then was).

[40] *Slade's Case* (1602), 4 Co Rep 92, 76 ER 1074 (KB).

[41] See *Peel, supra* note 39 at 153–54, McLachlin J (as she then was); *Goff & Jones*[7], *supra* note 9, at para 1.2.

[42] *Goff & Jones*[7], *supra* note 9, at para 1.2.

[43] *Ibid* at para 1.2.

[44] *Ibid* at para 1.2.

[45] The words used in a prior edition by Graham Virgo, *The Principles of the Law of Restitution,* 2d edn (Oxford: Oxford University Press, 2006) at 6 [Virgo, *Restitution*[2]].

[46] *Moses v Macferlan* (1760), 2 Burr 1005, 97 ER 676 (KB).

Macferlan pursued Moses in court for payment of the endorsed notes. He succeeded because the Court held that, in view of the formal nature of the promissory notes and the rules of procedure, it was barred from hearing any informal evidence on Macferlan's promise to Moses that he should suffer no prejudice. Moses had to make good on the promissory notes and pay. He then pursued Macferlan in the Court of King's Bench to recover the money had and received, based on the argument that Macferlan was not entitled to the money. Lord Mansfield wrote that

> "[t]his kind of equitable action, to recover back money, which ought not in justice to be kept, is very beneficial, and therefore much encouraged. It lies only for money which, *ex æquo et bono,* the defendant ought to refund [...] In one word, the gist of this kind of action is, that the defendant, upon the circumstances of the case, is obliged by the ties of natural justice and equity to refund the money."[47]

It should be noted that Lord Mansfield, being a justice at the Court of King's Bench, uses the word "equitable" in the sense of "natural justice," not in the sense of "falling under the equitable jurisdiction of the Court of Chancery."[48]

The importance of the decision lies in the fact that under the circumstances, it was obvious that Macferlan had never undertaken to repay the money to Moses.[49]

### *III. Equitable Restitution*

Restitution based on *assumpsit* originated in the common law courts. Apart from the common law cases, a second line of restitution cases arose in the courts of equity, beginning with *Keech v Sandford.*[50] In equitable restitution cases, the causes of action were based on equitable principles such as undue influence, breach of confidence, and breach of fiduciary duty.[51] In these cases, the constructive trust was awarded as a means of restitution.

---

[47] *Ibid* at 1012, Lord Mansfield LCJ.

[48] Smith, "Property, Subsidiarity and Unjust Enrichment", *supra* note 20 at 610.

[49] *Goff & Jones*[7]*, supra* note 9, at para 1.8. See also Peter Birks, "English and Roman Learning in Moses V Macferlan" (1984) 37 Curr Legal Probs 1 at 9–13.

[50] *Keech v Sandford* (1726), 61 Sel Cas T King 61, 25 ER 223 (Ch).

[51] McInnes, "The Canadian Principle of Unjust Enrichment", *supra* note 12 at 17–18.

## C. Development of the Unjust Enrichment Principle

This section deals with the relationship between unjust enrichment and restitution. The word "unjust enrichment" encompasses two notions. Unjust enrichment is both descriptive as well as a substantive legal notion.[52] In the descriptive sense, unjust enrichment means that the defendant has a gain that she cannot retain.[53] In the substantive sense, it is the unifying legal concept of unjust enrichment (rather than something as heterogeneous as the common counts based on *assumpsit*) that stipulates conditions which, if met, will give rise to a claim for restitution.

### *I. Rejection of the Implied Contract Theory*

#### *1. England*

*Assumpsit* was based on the idea that the defendant had undertaken to repay a sum of money to the claimant, but the existence of this promise became a fiction.[54] This process was promoted by *Moses v Macferlan,*[55] because as we have just seen, the facts in that case did not permit an implied promise on Macferlan's part to repay.

*Assumpsit* played an important role in the development of the law of restitution. It prevented the development of a third category of personal obligations different from contract and tort:[56]

"I think it excludes from the law of England any claim *in personam* based even on the circumstance that the defendant has been improperly enriched at the expense of the plaintiff by a transaction which is *ultra vires.* All analogies drawn from other systems, such as that of the Roman law, appear to me to be qualified in their application by two considerations. The first is that, broadly speaking, so far as proceedings *in personam* are concerned, the common law of England really recognizes (unlike the Roman law) only actions of two classes, those founded on contract and those founded on tort. When it speaks of actions arising *quasi ex*

---

[52] See Virgo, *Restitution, supra* note 8 at 8–10.

[53] Cf. Mitchell McInnes, "Resisting Temptations to Justice" in: Chambers, Mitchell & Penner, eds, *Philosophical Foundations of the Law of Unjust Enrichment, supra* note 6, 100 at 102 [McInnes, "Resisting Temptations"]; Mitchell McInnes, "Taxonomic Lessons for the Supreme Court of Canada" in: Ross Grantham & Charles Rickett, eds, *Structure and Justification in Private Law: Essays for Peter Birks* (Oxford: Hart, 2008) 77 at 96.

[54] Virgo, *Restitution, supra* note 8 at 39. The point was made in more detail in the previous edition, see Virgo, *Restitution*$^2$*, supra* note 45 at 19.

[55] *Goff & Jones*$^7$*, supra* note 9, 1.8–9.

[56] Andrew S Burrows, *The Law of Restitution,* 3rd edn (Oxford: Oxford University Press, 2010) at 28 [Burrows, *Restitution*]. For a positive account of the value of the implied contract theory see Steve Hedley, "Implied Contract and Restitution" (2004) 63:2 CLJ 435.

*contractu* it refers merely to a class of action in theory based on a contract which is imputed to the defendant by a fiction of law."[57]

Viscount Haldane's rejection of analogies to Roman law is puzzling if one keeps in mind that both *assumpsit* as well as Lord Mansfield's approach in *Moses v Macferlan* were based on Roman law origins.[58]

In modern times, courts recognized that the implied promise theory was a result of the formal constraints of the action-based civil procedure in England.

"The writ of *indebitatus assumpsit* involved at least two averments, the debt or obligation and the *assumpsit.* The former was the basis of the claim and was the real cause of action. The latter was merely fictitious and could not be traversed, but was necessary to enable the convenient and liberal form of action to be used in such cases."[59]

The abolition of the old forms of proceedings led to the rejection of the implied contract theory.[60] Instead, courts saw restitutionary claims as falling into the category of legal obligations. The claims were based on obligations created by law, not on the intention of the parties.

"In these quasi-contractual cases the court will look at the true facts and ascertain from them whether or not a promise to pay should be implied, irrespective of the actual views or intentions of the parties at the time when the work was done or the services rendered."[61]

Over time, the fiction of a contract was abandoned as a leftover of the old forms of action.

"These fantastic resemblances of contracts invented in order to meet requirements of the law as to forms of action which have now disappeared should not in these days be allowed to affect actual rights. When these ghosts of the past stand in the path of justice clanking their mediæval chains the proper course for the judge is to pass through them undeterred."[62]

In a passage in *Fibrosa Spolka Akcyjna v Fairbairn Lawson Combe Barbour Ltd*[63] relied on later by the Supreme Court of Canada in *Deglman v Guaranty Trust Co & Constantineau,*[64] Lord Wright made the following observation:

---

[57] *Sinclair v Brougham,* [1914] AC 398, [1914] All ER Rep 622 (HL), Viscount Haldane LC [emphasis added]. For a critical account see Peter Birks & Grant McLeod, "The Implied Contract Theory of Quasi-Contract: Civilian Opinion Current in the Century Before Blackstone" (1986) 6 Oxford J Legal Stud 46 at 52–53.

[58] See Birks, "English and Roman Learning in *Moses v Macferlan*", *supra* note 49; Birks & McLeod, preceding note.

[59] *Fibrosa Spolka Akcyjna v Fairbairn Lawson Combe Barbour Ltd,* [1943] AC 32 at 63 (HL), Lord Wright [emphasis added].

[60] *Goff & Jones*[7], *supra* note 9, at para 1.9.

[61] *William Lacey (Hounslow) Ltd v Davis,* [1957] 1 WLR 932 at 936 (QBD), Barry J.

[62] *United Australia, Ltd v Barclays Bank, Ltd,* [1941] AC 1 at 29 (HL), Lord Atkin. See furthermore for the development in English law *Goff & Jones*[7], *supra* note 9, at para 1.11.

[63] *Supra* note 59.

[64] *Deglman v Guaranty Trust Co & Constantineau,* [1954] SCR 725, [1954] 3 DLR 785.

"It is clear that any civilized system of law is bound to provide remedies for cases of what has been called unjust enrichment or unjust benefit, that is to prevent a man from retaining the money of or some benefit derived from another which it is against conscience that he should keep. Such remedies in English law are generically different from remedies in contract or in tort, and are now recognized to fall within a third category of the common law which has been called quasi-contract or restitution."[65]

Notwithstanding the recognition of "restitution" as a third category of liability distinct from contract and tort, English courts continued to occasionally use the language of "implied contracts" until the 1990s,[66] but in *Westdeutsche Landesbank Girozentrale v Islington London Borough Council,*[67] this language was rejected by Lord Browne-Wilkinson.[68]

*2. Canada*

The Supreme Court of Canada followed English authority in abandoning the implied contract theory. In the leading case *Deglman,* the claimant performed services for his aunt based on an oral understanding which was unenforceable as a contract; it would have violated the version of the *Statute of Frauds*[69] then in force. After the aunt died, he made a claim against the estate. The Supreme Court of Canada recognized that his claim for restitution on a *quantum meruit* basis was founded on unjust enrichment rather than on an implied contract because it would have been impossible to imply a contract while the actual contract was voided by the *Statute of Frauds.*[70]

*II. Recognition of the Unjust Enrichment Principle*

*1. Canadian Law*

The difference between Canadian and English law was that Canadian law not only abandoned the implied contract theory, but it was also quicker in basing restitution on the unjust enrichment principle. After the recognition of the unjust enrichment principle, the next stage was the widening of the unjust enrichment principle to encompass not just common law claims of the former *assumpsit* category but equitable claims as well. This was achieved through

---

[65] *Fibrosa Spolka Akcyjna v Fairbairn Lawson Combe Barbour Ltd, supra* note 59 at 61, Lord Wright.

[66] See William Swadling, "The Fiction of the Constructive Trust" (2011) 64:1 Curr Legal Probs 399 at 404.

[67] *Westdeutsche Landesbank Girozentrale v Islington London Borough Council,* [1996] 1 AC 669, [1996] 2 All ER 961 (HL) [*Westdeutsche Landesbank,* cited to AC].

[68] *Westdeutsche Landesbank Girozentrale v Islington London Borough Council,* [1996] 1 AC 669, [1996] 2 All ER 961 (HL), Lord Browne-Wilkinson.

[69] *Statute of Frauds,* RSO 1990, c S19.

[70] *Deglman, supra* note 64.

several steps in the case law of the Supreme Court. These cases involved matrimonial property disputes. Canadian law arrived at the unjust enrichment principle by combining matrimonial property disputes with unjust enrichment.

*a) Murdoch*

The matrimonial property disputes involved cases where spouses or common law partners separated without providing for a division of property acquired by one of the spouses (typically the husband) during the course of the relationship. These cases were initially seen as cases of resulting trusts. In *Murdoch v Murdoch*[71] the Court held that a spouse is only entitled to an equitable interest in the other spouses' property if a common-intention resulting trust claim can be made out. Writing for the majority, Justice Martland relied on English authorities and concluded that they stand for the proposition that matrimonial property can be divided if a resulting trust can be shown to exist.[72] But already in this case, Justice Laskin, in a minority opinion, suggested that a claim for a constructive trust can be made if the common-intention resulting trust claim fails.[73]

*b) Rathwell*

The decision in *Murdoch* was revisited in *Rathwell v Rathwell.*[74] In this case, the spouses owned a joint bank account in which all monies were deposited. Funds from this account were then used to purchase land. Titles to the land were registered in the husband's name. An equitable interest for the wife was never discussed. The land was used for farming. Mrs. Rathwell made considerable contributions to the farm: she did chores while her husband was busy on the farm, looked after the garden, canned produce, milked the cows, sold the cream, drove machinery, bailed hay, provided for third-party workers, and kept the books. After the breakdown of the marriage, the wife claimed an equitable proprietary interest in half of the real and personal property owned by her husband. The trial judge rejected her claim but the Court of Appeal allowed it in respect of certain lands. The husband appealed. The Supreme Court dismissed the appeal.

In an opinion delivered by Dickson J, with whom Laskin CJC and Spence J concurred, it was held that the wife's claim can succeed whether based on a resulting trust or a constructive trust. Based on the facts of the case, Dickson J

---

[71] *Murdoch v Murdoch* (1973), [1975] 1 SCR 423, 41 DLR (3[d]) 367.

[72] *Ibid* at 437, Mardland J, referring to *Gissing v Gissing* (1970), [1971] 1 AC 886, [1970] 3 WLR 255, [1970] 2 All ER 780 (HL); *Pettit v Pettit* (1969), [1970] AC 777, [1969] 2 WLR 966, [1969] 2 All ER 385 (HL).

[73] *Murdoch, supra* note 71 at 455, Laskin J (as he then was).

[74] *Rathwell v Rathwell,* [1978] 2 SCR 436, 83 DLR (3[d]) 289 [*Rathwell,* cited to DLR (3[d])].

did not accept the submission that property legally owned by the husband should be excluded from a matrimonial property distribution.[75]

After having examined the resulting trust claim, finding it should succeed, Dickson J turned to the question of the constructive trust. He based the constructive trust on the principle of prevention of unjust enrichment.

"Analysing the facts from the remedial perspective of constructive trust, it is clear that only through the efforts of Mrs. Rathwell was Mr. Rathwell able to acquire the lands in question. Assuming, *arguendo,* that Mrs. Rathwell had made no capital contribution to the acquisitions, it would be unjust, in all of the circumstances, to allow Mr. Rathwell to retain the benefits of his wife's labours. His acquisition of legal title was made possible only through 'joint effort' and 'team work' as he himself testified; he cannot now deny his wife's beneficial entitlement."[76]

Justices Martland, Judson, Beetz, and de Grandpré disagreed that the constructive trust can be applied in such cases. Justices Ritchie and Pigeon found it unnecessary to make any findings on the constructive trust issue.

*c) Pettkus v Becker*

The next step in the development towards the unjust enrichment principle was the Supreme Court's decision in *Pettkus v Becker.*[77] This decision was important in two regards. First, it accepted the constructive trust as a form of relief in matrimonial property disputes. Second, it established the principle that unjust enrichment is the basis for common law remedies, such as *quantum meruit,* and equitable remedies, including the constructive trust.

The facts of the case were the following. Mr. Pettkus and Ms. Becker were common law spouses. Initially Ms. Becker supported Mr. Pettkus for five years. Mr. Pettkus, who was also working, used the resulting savings to save for the purchase of a farm in Québec; it is a curious quirk in the development of the law of unjust enrichment in Common Law Canada that the facts of its leading case were probably properly partially governed by the civil law of Québec. Title to the farm was in Mr. Pettkus' name. Both then worked on a farm, and used the proceeds from the farming to buy two further properties in Ontario. Later, they moved to one of their Ontario properties.

At the beginning of his discussion of the resulting trust doctrine and its applicability in marital property disputes, Justice Dickson states his ambition to "clarify the equivocal state in which the law of matrimonial property was left"[78]. The common-intention approach had been criticised by Waters in a

[75] *Ibid* at 457, Dickson J.

[76] *Ibid* at 439, Dickson J.

[77] *Pettkus v Becker, supra* note 5.

[78] *Ibid* at 841–42, Dickson J.

1974 article.[79] McCamus suggests that Dickson J's reasoning was partly motivated by his wish to address the issues raised by Waters.[80] Indeed, Dickson J addresses Waters' criticism head-on. He approvingly cites two passages from Water's critical case comment.[81]

Based on the findings at trial, Dickson J found it impossible to discern any common intention. Justice Dickson thus turns to the constructive trust. He starts his analysis with the statement that "[t]he principle of unjust enrichment lies at the heart of the constructive trust."[82] He then identifies three requirements for unjust enrichment:

> "In *Rathwell* I ventured to suggest there are three requirements to be satisfied before an unjust enrichment can be said to exist: an enrichment, a corresponding deprivation and absence of any juristic reason for the enrichment. This approach, it seems to me, is supported by general principles of equity that have been fashioned by the courts for centuries […]."[83]

### 2. *English Law*

English courts were initially more reluctant to accept the unjust enrichment principle.

> "My Lords, the exact status of the law of unjust enrichment is not yet assured. It holds a predominant place in the law of Scotland and, I think, of the United States, but I am content for the purposes of this case to accept the view that it forms no part of the law of England and that a right to restitution so described would be too widely stated."[84]

Unjust enrichment as a cause of action was not fully recognized in England until *Lipkin Gorman v Karpnale Ltd.*[85] In *Lipkin Gorman v Karpnale Ltd,* the House of Lords accepted a claim as being based on unjust enrichment. The plaintiff was a firm. C was a partner at the firm and had authority to draw cheques from the firm's client's account. He obtained cheques from the cashier of the firm, payable to cash, that were drawn on the client's account. C signed the cheques and the cashier cashed them and handed the money over to C. C then exchanged the cash for gambling chips at the defendant's casino. In one instance, C presented a banker's draft for over £3 735 in favour of the firm, which the casino accepted. The plaintiff sued for money had and received for

---

[79] Donovan WM Waters, "Matrimonial Property Disputes - Resulting and Constructive Trusts - Restitution" (1975) 53:2 Can Bar Rev 366.

[80] John D McCamus, "Restitution on Dissolution of Marital and Other Intimate Relationships: Constructive Trust or Quantum Meruit" in: Jason W Neyers, Mitchell McInnes & Stephen G Pitel, eds, *Understanding Unjust Enrichment* (Oxford: Hart, 2004) 359 at 362.

[81] *Pettkus v Becker, supra* note 5 at 843, Dickson J.

[82] *Ibid* at 847, Dickson J.

[83] *Ibid* at 848, Dickson J.

[84] *Reading v Attorney General,* [1951] AC 507 at 513–14 (HL), Lord Porter.

[85] [1991] 2 AC 548, [1991] 3 WLR 10, [1992] 4 All ER 512 (HL) [cited to AC].

an invalid contract, for conversion regarding the £3 735 and as beneficiaries of a constructive trust regarding the property interest in the money.[86]

Their Lordships held that an innocent recipient of stolen money is liable to repay the money to the original owner when the recipient has not given full consideration for the money and therefore is unjustly enriched at the expense of the owner. Furthermore, the plaintiff was holder of the *chose in action* constituted by the indebtedness of the bank. It could therefore trace the money. Finally, the casino was liable for conversion of the draft.

### *III. Opposition to the Unjust Enrichment Principle*

Even though the case law indicates that unjust enrichment is the reason for restitution both in law and equity,[87] the validity of such a statement is not accepted throughout the Common Law world.[88] There are two strains of arguments against the unjust enrichment principle as the basis of restitution.

The first objection argues that basing restitution on unjust enrichment is akin to the tail wagging the dog because in Common Law, the outcome of a case is not based on principle; rather, legal principles develop by following the case law.

The second objection to the unjust enrichment view is that unjust enrichment can only be considered to be at the heart of restitution in the descriptive sense of the word, not the substantive sense of the word.[89] A variant of the second strain of criticism is to say that there may in fact be no underlying substantive institution that unifies all cases in which a restitutionary remedy is awarded.[90] In other words, these critics argue that there may be a "law of restitution," but not a "law of unjust enrichment."

---

[86] *Lipkin Gorman v Karpnale Ltd,* [1991] 2 AC 548, [1991] 3 WLR 10, [1992] 4 All ER 512 (HL).

[87] See *Pavey & Matthews Pty Ltd v Paul* (1987), 162 CLR 221; *Deglman, supra* note 64; *Re Cleadon Trust* (1938), [1939] Ch 286 at 307 (CA), Greene MR.

[88] See *Roxborough v Rothmans of Pall Mall Australia Ltd,* [2001] HCA 68 at paras 70–75, 208 CLR 516 [*Rothmanns*]. See with references on the differing position in Australia Gerald HL Fridman, "Unjust Enrichment (Dis)Contented" in: Neyers, McInnes & Pitel, eds, *Understanding Unjust Enrichment, supra* note 80, 35 at 44–45. See also Steve Hedley, "Unjust Enrichment as the Basis of Restitution: An Overworked Concept" (1985) 5 LS 56.

[89] See e.g. Peter Jaffey, "The Unjust Enrichment Fallacy and Private Law" (2013) 26 Can JL & Juris 115 [Jaffey, "Fallacy"]; Peter Jaffey, "Two Theories of Unjust Enrichment" in: Neyers, McInnes & Pitel, eds, *Understanding Unjust Enrichment, supra* note 80, 139 [Jaffey, "Two Theories"].

[90] Hedley, "Unjust Enrichment as the Basis of Restitution", *supra* note 88 at 58–60.

### *1. The Tail Wagging the Dog*

The proponents of the tail-wagging-the-dog argument caution against an overly rigid approach to legal rules:

> "To the lawyer whose mind has been moulded by civilian influences, the theory may come first, and the source of the theory may be the writing of jurists not the decisions of judges. However, that is not the way in which a system based on case law develops; over time, general principle is derived from judicial decisions upon particular instances, not the other way around.
>
> Unless, as this Court indicated in *David Securities Pty Ltd v Commonwealth Bank of Australia,* unjust enrichment is seen as a concept rather than a definitive legal principle, substance and dynamism may be restricted by dogma. In turn, the dogma will tend to generate new fictions in order to retain support for its thesis. It also may distort well settled principles in other fields, including those respecting equitable doctrines and remedies, so that they answer the newly mandated order of things. Then various theories will compete, each to deny the others."[91]

While this passage from *Roxborough v Rothmans of Pall Mall Australia Ltd* is very illuminating regarding the difference between a Common Law approach and a Civil Law one, it does not substantially argue against an unjust enrichment foundation. All it does is remind us that the question is not whether it is desirable to base restitution on unjust enrichment, but rather whether case law supports this hypothesis. As the two preceding subsections have shown, it does, at least in England and Canada.

### *2. Event and Response*

#### *a) Argument*

A more substantial criticism of the unjust enrichment principle is to say that the statement "restitution is based on unjust enrichment" is only true in a trivial way. In other words, it is argued there is only a relationship between unjust enrichment and restitution when using the term "unjust enrichment" in its descriptive meaning. Consequently, saying that a claim is one in unjust enrichment does nothing to determine the necessary conditions for successfully establishing such a claim.[92] Jaffey analyses the cases in which restitution has been awarded. He argues that in cases where there is a pre-existing property right, restitution is a result of this pre-existing property right. This, Jaffey says, means that the restitution it cannot simultanously be based on unjust enrichment.[93] In cases where there is a contractual relationship between the parties

---

[91] *Roxborough v Rothmans of Pall Mall Australia Ltd,* [2001] HCA 68, 208 CLR 516 at para 70–75, Gummow J, referring to *David Securities Pty Ltd v Commonwealth Bank of Australia* (1992), 175 CLR 353.

[92] Jaffey, "Two Theories", *supra* note 89 at 142–43. See also Jaffey, "Fallacy", *supra* note 89.

[93] Jaffey, "Two Theories", *supra* note 89 at 146–51.

and restitution was based on the failure to meet an implied condition (a Civilian would refer to these cases as a *condictio ob rem*), the claim is a contractual one.[94] *Quantum meruit* cases are either straightforward contract cases (where only the amount itself is in dispute)[95] or cases of "imputed contracts."[96] Furthermore, there is a category of restitution for wrongs which is essentially tort law.[97]

*b) Counter-Argument*

A reply to the second argument against the unjust enrichment principle requires us to take a look at terminology and taxonomy. Birks divided private law into two categories: "events" and "responses."[98] All rights and duties are consequences of the events.[99] There are, in Birks' view, four categories of events: "consent," "wrong," "unjust enrichment," and "miscellaneous".[100] A response is the right-duty relationship that arises because of the event.[101] "Remedies," on the other hand, are the orders of a court to relieve the plaintiff of his grievance.[102]

In this taxonomy, unjust enrichment is an event, restitution is a response.[103] This is a helpful distinction to keep in mind when addressing Jaffey's criticism. It allows us to phrase the criticism in other words: Jaffey argues that because unjust enrichment is not the only event that causes restitution, the former cannot be the reason for the latter.

This statement, however, is true only to a certain extent. It simply means that unjust enrichment cannot be the *only* reason for restitution. Nevertheless,

---

[94] *Ibid* at 152–54.

[95] *Ibid* at 155–56.

[96] *Ibid* at 158.

[97] *Ibid* at 159–63.

[98] See principally Peter Birks, "Definition and Division: A Meditation on Institutes 3.13" in: Peter Birks, ed, *The Classification of Obligations* (Oxford: Clarendon Press, 1997) 1; Peter Birks, "Equity in the Modern Law: An Excercise in Legal Taxonomy" (1996) 26 UWAL Rev 1; Peter Birks, "Rights, Wrongs, and Remedies" (2000) 20 Oxford J Legal Stud 1; Ross Grantham & Charles Rickett, "Property Rights as a Legally Significant Event" (2003) 62:3 CLJ 717 at 718 [Grantham & Rickett, "Property as Event"].

[99] Birks, "Rights, Wrongs, and Remedies", preceding note at 5; Grantham & Rickett, "Property as Event", preceding note at 718–19.

[100] Birks, "Definition and Division", *supra* note 99 at 19–20; Birks, "Rights, Wrongs, and Remedies", *supra* note 99 at 21, 37; Grantham & Rickett, "Property as Event", *supra* note 99 at 719.

[101] Birks, "Rights, Wrongs, and Remedies", *supra* note 99 at 5.

[102] Grantham & Rickett, "Property as Event", *supra* note 99 at 719; Michael Tilbury, "Remedy as Right" in: Grantham & Rickett, eds, *Structure and Justification, supra* note 53, 421 at 421, note 3.

[103] Birks, "Definition and Division", *supra* note 99 at 20; William Swadling, "A Claim in Restitution?" [1996] LMCLQ 63 at 63, note 1.

Smith and others argue that the use of the word "restitution" for responses to cases that are not unjust enrichment is inappropriate.[104] As mentioned in the introduction, Birks[105] and Virgo[106] use the term "restitution" to refer to any response that aims at transferring value back to the claimant. Thus, for Virgo there are three principles that lead to restitution: unjust enrichment, disgorgement and vindication of property rights.[107] Smith and others would only call the first response "restitution," and the response in the second case is referred to as "disgorgement." The third principle does not exist in Smith and others's approach, but could be called vindication. In effect, there are thus two ways of addressing Jaffey's criticism. The first one is to say that restitution is not necessarily mono-causal. The second reply is to limit the meaning of restitution and use it only when the event to which it responds is unjust enrichment.

When evaluating case law to see whether it supports the hypothesis that unjust enrichment in its substantive sense is a reason for restitution, one needs to keep in mind that originally, law and equity differed in their approach to restitution. Law courts, on the one hand, based restitution on *assumpsit.* Equity courts, on the other hand, clearly used an approach that merely looked at a defective transfer of value without a charge of wrongdoing,[108] in effect unjust enrichment, in cases based on the principle enunciated in *Keech v Sandford.*[109] Jaffey's approach is not able to account for the existence of these cases.

In conclusion, basing restitution on unjust enrichment allows one to distinguish it both from contract and tort. It differs from the former because it is not based on the intention of the parties[110] and from the latter because there is not necessarily a charge of wrongdoing against the defendant.[111]

On a final note, it should be kept in mind that this definition does not make a statement regarding whether "unjust enrichment" excludes cases where there is a charge of wrongdoing against the debtor. There is certainly a strong case that can be made for including these cases under the "unjust enrichment" heading.[112] However, for the purpose of this book, it is already sufficient to show

---

[104] See Lionel D Smith *et al, The Law of Restitution in Canada* (Toronto: E. Montgomery Publications, 2004) at 41.

[105] Birks, *Unjust Enrichment, supra* note 7 at 4–5.

[106] Virgo, *Restitution, supra* note 8 at 7–8, subject to the disclaimer that one needs to be careful not to be "too simplicistic" in drawning any conclusions from that formulation.

[107] *Ibid* at 7–8.

[108] Calling this the phenomenon of "liability without fault" in unjust enrichment Lionel D Smith, "Restitution: The Heart of Corrective Justice" (2001) 79:7 Tex L Rev 2115 at 2115.

[109] Fridman, *supra* note 88 at 38–39.

[110] *Ibid* at 36–37.

[111] *Ibid* at 39.

[112] See Kit Barker, "The Nature of Responsibility for Gain: Gain, Harm, and Keeping the Lid on Pandora's Box" in: Chambers, Mitchell & Penner, eds, *Philosophical Foundations of the Law of Unjust Enrichment, supra* note 6, 146; Kit Barker, "Understanding the Unjust Enrichment Principle in Private Law: A Study of the Concept and its Reasons" in: Neyers,

that it is necessary to have unjust enrichment as a legal event that gives rise to a legal response. This has succeeded because there are cases where restitution cannot be explained by a charge of wrongdoing – something that would allow one to view restitution as a tort-based response. Smith points out that in cases of restitution for wrongdoing, the claimant need not show that the debtor is enjoying an enrichment corresponding to her own deprivation. Therefore, he argues, disgorgement for wrongdoing is fundamentally different from restitution for unjust enrichment.[113] It does not necessarily follow, though, that a claimant cannot make *both* claims: a claim for disgorgement if the defendant has wrongfully deprived her, and a claim for unjust enrichment if the defendant has deprived her (regardless of the charge of wrongdoing) *and* there is a corresponding enrichment.

### *IV. Requirements of the Action for Unjust Enrichment*

In Canadian law, a claim in unjust enrichment involves that three elements are shown: there must be an enrichment of the defendant, a corresponding deprivation of the claimant, and, finally, an unjust element.[114] As regards the question of enrichment and deprivation, the Supreme Court of Canada "has consistently taken a straightforward economic approach to the first two elements of the test for unjust enrichment."[115] However, the element of deprivation may be lacking if the reason for the giving of the plaintiff is the friendship between the parties.[116] The last element will be discussed in the next section.

---

McInnes & Pitel, eds, *Understanding Unjust Enrichment, supra* note 80, 79. On restitution for "wrongful enrichment" see also Peter Birks, "At the Expense of the Claimant: Direct and Indirect Enrichment in the English Law" in: Johnston & Zimmermann, eds, *Unjustified Enrichment, supra* note 20, 493; Peter Birks, "Unjust Enrichment and Wrongful Enrichment" (2001) 79 Tex L Rev 1767; Ross Grantham & Charles Rickett, "Disgorgement for Unjust Enrichment?" (2003) 62:1 CLJ 159; Mitchell McInnes, "Interceptive Subtraction, Unjust Enrichment and Wrongs: A Reply to Professor Birks" (2003) 62:3 CLJ 697.

[113] Smith, "Restitution", *supra* note 109 at 2116.

[114] *Garland v Consumers' Gas Co*, 2004 SCC 25, [2004] 1 SCR 629, 237 DLR (4th) 385, 9 ETR (3d) 163, Iacobucci J; *Peel, supra* note 39 at 151, 164, McLachlin J (as she then was); *Pettkus v Becker, supra* note 5 at 848, Dickson J. For English Law see *Banque Financière de la Cité v Parc (Battersea) et al* (1998), [1999] 1 AC 221, [1998] 2 WLR 475, [1998] 1 All ER 737 (HL), Lord Steyn, and *ibid* at 234, Lord Hoffmann.

[115] *Peter v Beblow*, [1993] 1 SCR 980, 101 DLR (4th) 621, McLachlin J (as she then was). For an extensive discussion of the concepts of deprivation and enrichment see James J Edelman, "The Meaning of Loss and Enrichment" in: Chambers, Mitchell & Penner, eds, *Philosophical Foundations of the Law of Unjust Enrichment, supra* note 6, 211 passim and, dealing specifically with what constitutes enrichment, Robert Chambers, "Two Kinds of Enrichment" in: Chambers, Mitchell & Penner, eds, *Philosophical Foundations of the Law of Unjust Enrichment, supra* note 6, 242 passim.

[116] *Brennan v Gardy Estate*, 2011 BCSC 1337 at para 27.

## D. No Basis or Unjust Factors

In the preceding section, I argued that unjust enrichment is a *reason for* restitution, and have concluded that this aptly summarizes the position of English and Canadian courts. But there is a further question that needs to be resolved, namely the "unjust question": Can the "unjustness" of the enrichment be inferred from *one* single underlying cause, or is an enrichment only then unjust if one out of a number of various unjust factors is present?[117]

The proponents of the first theory follow a Civilian-influenced "no-basis approach," while the proponents of the second theory follow the "unjust factors approach." Broadly speaking, the two approaches to unjust enrichment are as follows: either one says that enrichment is unjust if there is no juristic reason for the *enrichment,* or one says that the enrichment is unjust if the claimant can establish that the *retention* of the enrichment is unjust.

"There are two distinct doctrinal approaches to restitution at common law. The first is the traditional 'category' approach. It involves looking to see if the case fits into any of the categories of cases in which previous recovery has been allowed, and then applying the criteria applicable to a given category to see whether the claim is established. The second approach, which might be called the 'principled' approach, developed only in recent years."[118]

---

[117] See Birks, *Unjust Enrichment, supra* note 7 at 40–45, 101–28; Andrew S Burrows, "Absence of Basis: The New Birksian Scheme" in: Andrew S Burrows & Alan Rodger, eds, *Mapping the Law: Essays in Memory of Peter Birks* (Oxford: Oxford University Press, 2006) 33; Burrows, *Restitution, supra* note 56 at 95–116; Thomas Krebs, "In Defence of Unjust Factors" in: Johnston & Zimmermann, eds, *Unjustified Enrichment, supra* note 20, 76; Mitchell McInnes, "Garland's Unitary Test of Unjust Enrichment: A Response to Professor McCamus" (2011) 38:2 Advocates' Q 165 [McInnes, "Garland's Unitary Test"]; Mitchell McInnes, "Making Sense of Unjust Enrichment: Unjust Enrichment after Garland v Consumers' Gas" (2004–2005) 42 Alta L Rev 399; Mitchell McInnes, "The Reason to Reverse: Unjust Factors and Juristic Reason" (2012) 92 Boston UL Rev 1049 [McInnes, "Reason"]; Sonja Meier, *Irrtum und Zweckverfehlung: Die Rolle der Unjust-Gründe bei rechtsgrundlosen Leistungen im englischen Recht* (Studien zum ausländischen und internationalen Privatrecht, Tübingen: Mohr Siebeck, 1999); Sonja Meier, "No Basis: A Comparative View" in: Burrows & Rodger, eds, *Mapping the Law,* this note, 343; Charles CJ Mitchell, Paul Mitchell & Stephen Watterson, *Goff & Jones: The Law of Unjust Enrichment,* 9th edn (London: Sweet & Maxwell, 2016) at paras 1.21–1.25; Lionel D Smith, "Demystifying Juristic Reasons" [2007] CBLJ 281 [Smith, "Demystifying"]; Lionel D Smith, "The Mystery of Juristic Reason" (2000) 12 Sup Ct L Rev 211 [Smith, "Mystery"].

[118] *Peel, supra* note 39 at 151, McLachlin J (as she then was). See also the synopsis in McInnes, "The Canadian Principle of Unjust Enrichment", *supra* note 12 at 8. See also Brice Dickson, "Unjust Enrichment Claims: A Comparative Overview" (1995) 54:1 CLJ 100 at 115.

The former no-basis approach is also the approach in Civil Law systems, while the latter unjust factors approach is the traditional Common Law approach.[119]

Several authors argue that the no-basis theory is more befitting of a Civilian system that uses an inductive top-to-bottom approach for arriving at a rule governing the facts at hand, whereas the unjust factors theory is grounded in the Common Law's deductive approach of finding rules in each individual case which together are to form a coherent whole.[120] McInnes goes as far as to suggest that the Civil Law embraced a broad no-basis-approach because it is "more inclined to become involved in day-to-day life."[121]

### *I. Unjust Factors*

The traditional approach in English law is to require the existence of unjust factors. Whether enrichment is unjust is determined by seeing whether any of the factors is met.[122]

An early description of the unjust factors was given by Lord Mansfield in *Moses v Macferlan:*

> "It lies for money paid by mistake; or upon a consideration which happens to fail; or for money got through imposition (express, or implied;) or extortion; or oppression; or an undue advantage taken of the plaintiff's situation, contrary to laws made for the protection of persons under those circumstances. In one word, the gist of this kind of action is, that the defendant, upon the circumstances of the case, is obliged by the ties of natural justice and equity to refund the money."[123]

The unjust factors developed in later case law are grouped in three categories: claimant-based factors, defendant-based factors, and policy-based factors.[124]

### *II. No-Basis Approach*

The other approach to unjust enrichment is the no-basis approach. In this approach, an enrichment is unjust if there is no reason for the retention of the enrichment by the defendant.

---

[119] Chris DL Hunt, "Decline of Juristic Reasons: Unjust Enrichment and the Supreme Court of Canada" (2010) 43:1 UBCL Rev 173 at 173–74.

[120] *Ibid* at 176; Krebs, *supra* note 118 at 99; McInnes, "Making Sense of Unjust Enrichment", *supra* note 118 at 402.

[121] McInnes, "Reason", *supra* note 118 at 1054.

[122] Stephen A Smith, "Unjust Enrichment: Nearer to Tort Than Contract" in: Chambers, Mitchell & Penner, eds, *Philosophical Foundations of the Law of Unjust Enrichment, supra* note 6, 181 at 202–3.

[123] *Moses v Macferlan, supra* note 46 at 1012.

[124] See Virgo, *Restitution, supra* note 8 at 121. See also Hunt, *supra* note 120 at 175.

*1. The English Position: The Swap Cases and Their Aftermath*

The law of unjust enrichment was the subject of many lawsuits in England because of the swap cases. An interest swap is an agreement by virtue of which two parties agree to pay each other interest rates on a notional sum. One party will pay a fixed interest rate, the other a floating rate, using a reference rate such as the "London Interbank Offered Rate." The party agreeing to pay a floating rate will thus make a gain if the reference rate falls because the payment she receives is fixed. In England, local authorities entered such agreements to finance their loans. However, in *Hazell v Hammersmith & Fulham London Borough Council,*[125] their Lordships decided that a swap entered by a municipal body was *ultra vires* and that the contract was void. Consequently, the local authority had a right to restitution for the monies paid pursuant to the swap agreement.

Meier argues that in the ensuing restitution cases,[126] restitution can be more aptly described as being based on a no-basis approach rather than on an unjust factor because these cases do not fit the traditional unjust factors approach.[127] Birks agreed:

> "The disagreement between the majority and the minority turns on whether one can be retrospectively mistaken in any sense relevant to restitutionary relief. The majority holds that one can, and in so holding it appears to have approved a notion of operative mistake of law which is not only broader than operative mistake of fact but broader than the rationale underlying relief for mistake. Without saying so expressly, it has moved English law towards a civilian *condictio indebiti.* [*Condictio indebiti*] means 'Claim in respect of something not due.'"[128]

Birks consequently argued that the English law of unjust enrichment is based on a no-basis approach rather than an unjust-factor approach.[129]

*Deutsche Morgan Grenfell Group plc v Inland Revenue Commissioners & another*[130] is cited as proof that English law has not (yet) embraced a no-basis

[125] *Hazell v Hammersmith & Fulham London Borough Council,* [1992] 2 AC 1, [1991] 2 WLR 372, [1991] 1 All ER 545 (HL).

[126] *Kleinwort Benson v Lincoln City* (1998), [1999] 2 AC 349, [1998] 3 WLR 1095, [1998] 4 All ER 513 (HL); *Westdeutsche Landesbank, supra* note 67.

[127] Sonja Meier, "Unjust Factors and Legal Grounds" in: Johnston & Zimmermann, eds, *Unjustified Enrichment, supra* note 20, 37 at 67–69.

[128] Peter Birks, "Private Law" in: Peter Birks & Francis Rose, eds, *Restitution and Equity* (London: Mansfield Press, 2000), vol 1, 1 at 14, cited as in *Deutsche Morgan Grenfell Group plc v Inland Revenue Commissioners & another,* [2006] UKHL 49 at para 153, [2007] 1 AC 558 [*Morgan Grenfell*] [emphasis added].

[129] Birks, *Unjust Enrichment, supra* note 7. See also Meier, "No Basis", *supra* note 118.

[130] *Deutsche Morgan Grenfell Group plc v Inland Revenue Commissioners & another,* [2006] UKHL 49, [2007] 1 AC 558.

approach.[131] The case arose because the claimant had paid taxes. If the company had been a British company, it would have had the option to defer the payment. Because it was a foreign company, it had no such option. After the courts struck down the distinction, the claimant claimed restitution of the benefit enjoyed by the state (*i.e.* the interest that accrued due to the early payment). If English law had taken a no-basis approach, so the argument goes, the claim could not have succeeded because the tax liability existed.

Using *Morgan Grenfell* as an argument against the no-basis approach thus hinges on denying that premature payment is enrichment. It is not logically necessary to take the position that premature payment is not enrichment, and the fact that capital creates interest speaks for the classification of premature payment as enrichment because premature payment accrues interest against the defendant that would not have otherwise accrued. In fact, German law contains a provision that specifies that premature payment is in principle not to be treated as an unjustified enrichment, which implies that it would otherwise be one.[132] Premature payment is considered to be an unjust enrichment in German law where the recipient was in breach of a statutory duty in accepting the payment prematurely.[133]

The reasoning of the House of Lords also implies that the premature payment of a debt is a payment of a debt not due and thus without basis. Lord Hoffmann implies that the claimant's case would have been more straightforward had it been argued on a no-basis approach, and the only reason why the no-basis question was not determinative was that the claim succeeded on the unjust factor approach, using the unjust factor of mistake, as well.[134] Lord Walker explicitly embraced the Birksian scheme, albeit *obiter.*[135]

### 2. Canadian Position on the Unjust Question

Compared to the English position, the no-basis or absence of juristic reason approach has been more firmly embraced by the Supreme Court of Canada in the Anglo-Canadian Common Law.[136]

---

[131] McInnes, "Garland's Unitary Test", *supra* note 118 at 173–74; McInnes, "Reason", *supra* note 118 at 1061–62.

[132] *Bürgerliches Gesetzbuch,* s 813(2); Stefan Lorenz in: Julius von Staudinger, *Kommentar zum Bürgerlichen Gesetzbuch mit Einführungsgesetz und Nebengesetzen, Buch 2. Recht der Schuldverhältnisse, §§ 812 - 822 (Ungerechtfertigte Bereicherung),* ed by Norbert Horn (Berlin: Sellier-de Gruyter, 2007) § 813 BGB at paras 16–9.

[133] BGH, 22 March 2007, VIII ZR 268/05, BGHZ 171, 364, NJW 2007, 1947.

[134] *Morgan Grenfell, supra* note 129 at para 28, Lord Hoffmann.

[135] *Ibid* at para 158, Lord Walker.

[136] Smith, "Demystifying", *supra* note 118.

Traditionally, Anglo-Canadian law followed the unjust factors approach in order to tackle the unjust question.[137] The Supreme Court first hinted at a changing approach in *Rathwell,* where Dickson, J wrote:

"As a matter of principle, the court will not allow any man unjustly to appropriate to himself the value earned by the labours of another. That principle is not defeated by the existence of a matrimonial relationship between the parties; but, for the principle to succeed, the facts must display an enrichment, a corresponding deprivation and the absence of any juristic reason — such as a contract or disposition of law — for the enrichment."[138]

Justice Dickson reiterated that approach in *Pettkus v Becker,* when he wrote:

"[T]here are three requirements to be satisfied before an unjust enrichment can be said to exist: an enrichment, a corresponding deprivation and absence of any juristic reason for the enrichment. This approach, it seems to me, is supported by general principles of equity that have been fashioned by the Courts for centuries [...]."[139]

However, Dickson, J then added "It must, in addition, be evident that the retention of the benefit would be 'unjust' in the circumstances of the case."[140] As a result, it was not clear if that addition meant that the unjust factors still played a role in Canadian unjust enrichment law.[141] This was strongly criticized in legal scholarship. The argument against the adoption of a Civilian no-basis approach was that the Common Law has no basis from which a list of accepted juristic reasons could be derived; thus, it would be a more predictable development of the law to search for a reason to reverse rather than to compel the defendant to provide a reason for the retention of the benefit.[142]

In *Garland v Consumers' Gas Co,*[143] the Supreme Court unequivocally introduced a Civilian-inspired test for lack of juristic reason:

"The test for unjust enrichment has three elements: (1) an enrichment of the defendant; (2) a corresponding deprivation of the plaintiff; and (3) an absence of juristic reason for the enrichment. The proper approach to the juristic reason analysis is in two parts. The plaintiff must show that no juristic reason from an established category exists to deny recovery. The established categories include a contract, a disposition of law, a donative intent, and other valid common law, equitable or statutory obligations. If there is no juristic reason from an established category, then the plaintiff has made out a prima facie case. The *prima facie* case is rebuttable, however, where the defendant can show that there is another reason to deny recovery. Courts should have regard at this point to two factors: the reasonable expectations of the parties and public policy considerations.

In my view, this approach to the juristic reason analysis is consistent with the general approach to unjust enrichment endorsed by McLachlin J in *Peel v Canada* where she stated

---

[137] Hunt, *supra* note 120 at 178.

[138] *Rathwell, supra* note 74 at 455, Dickson J.

[139] *Pettkus v Becker, supra* note 5 at 848, Dickson J.

[140] *Ibid* at 848, Dickson J.

[141] On the resulting confusion see Hunt, *supra* note 120 at 178–79.

[142] Smith, "Mystery", *supra* note 118.

[143] *Supra* note 115.

that courts must effect a balance between the traditional 'category' approach according to which a claim for restitution will succeed only if it falls within an established head of recovery, and the modern 'principled' approach according to which relief is determined with reference to broad principles. It is also, as discussed by Professor Smith, generally consistent with the approach to unjust enrichment found in the civil law of Quebec (see, for example, [art 1493 *CcQ* and art 1494 *CcQ*]."[144]

Unfortunately, in a number of cases following *Garland* – namely *Pacific National Investments Ltd v Victoria (City),*[145] *Kingstreet Investments Ltd v New Brunswick (Department of Finance),*[146] and *BMP Global Distribution Inc v Bank of Nova Scotia*[147] – the Supreme Court of Canada did not apply the no-basis approach consistently.[148] The Supreme Court used unjust factors such as mistake in one case involving an *ultra vires* contract with a municipal government,[149] and compulsion in another case involving *ultra vires* taxation.[150] In both these cases it made notional reference to *Garland.* In *BMP Global* it made no reference to *Garland* at all and relied on a "straightforward" application of an unjust factors analysis.[151] This led McCamus to conclude that the "no-basis" approach only applies where the case does not fall into an established "unjust factor" category.[152] However, the Supreme Court cases after *Garland* can be explained by the fact that the Court deemed that unjust enrichment analysis should not apply in constitutional cases,[153] as a function of the parties pleading,[154] or because unjust factors were used to show why there is in fact no juristic reason.[155]

---

[144] *Ibid* at paras 44–47, Iacobucci J [references omitted], referring to Smith, "Mystery", *supra* note 118.

[145] *Pacific National Investments Ltd v Victoria (City),* 2004 SCC 75, [2004] 3 SCR 575, 245 DLR (4th) 211.

[146] *Kingstreet Investments Ltd v New Brunswick (Department of Finance),* 2007 SCC 1, [2007] 1 SCR 3, 276 DLR (4th) 342.

[147] *BMP Global Distribution Inc v Bank of Nova Scotia,* 2009 SCC 15, [2009] 1 SCR 504, 304 DLR (4th) 292, 58 BLR (4th) 1.

[148] See for an extensive criticism of this confusion Hunt, *supra* note 120.

[149] *Pacific National, supra* note 146 at para 31, Binnie J.

[150] *Kingstreet, supra* note 147 at para 58, Bastarache J.

[151] *BMP Global, supra* note 148 22, Deschamps J. See the case comments by John D McCamus, "Mistake, Forged Cheques and Unjust Enrichment: Three Cheers for B.M.P. Global" (2009) 48:2 CBLJ 76 [McCamus, "Three Cheers"] and Mitchell McInnes, "The Unitary Action in Unjust Enrichment" (2009) 48 CBLJ 102 [McInnes, "Unitary Action"].

[152] See McCamus, "Three Cheers", preceding note.

[153] *Kingstreet, supra* note 147.

[154] *BMP Global, supra* note 148. See McInnes, "Garland's Unitary Test", *supra* note 118 at 188.

[155] *Pacific National, supra* note 146 at paras 27–52, Bastarache J.

### *III. The Relationship Between Unjust Factors and No-Basis Approach*

Choosing between an unjust factors approach or a no-basis approach is an either/or decision. Both approaches are fundamentally diametrical. In one approach, the defendant must find a juristic reason for which she is entitled to retain the enrichment. In the other approach, the claimant must find a reason, an unjust factor, for which she should be granted restitution.[156]

Because both approaches are diametrically opposed, the unjust question must be answered by reference to one approach; both cannot apply at the same time.[157] This is because absence of juristic reason is not simply an unjust factor. It is wider.[158] In the no-basis approach, on the other hand, the basis has to be positively established. Evidently, unjust factors cannot be used to establish juristic reason because even absence of an unjust factor would not necessarily establish juristic reason.[159]

The no-basis approach is straightforward when there is no juristic reason apparent for which the defendant should be able to claim the retention of the enrichment. However, there are also cases where there is a potential basis that fails to establish such a foundation. One example would be a contract that turns out to be void. In these cases, to say that the absence of a juristic reason alone is enough to explain the claim in unjust enrichment is not satisfactory because it does not explain why the potential basis is not a sufficient juristic reason.[160] In these cases, recurse can be had to the unjust factors.[161] This is admitted by Birks himself in his pyramid model of unjust enrichment:

> "A pyramid can be constructed in which, at the base, the particular unjust factors such as mistake, pressure, and undue influence become reasons why, higher up, there is no basis or the defendant's acquisition, which is then the master reason why, higher up still, the enrichment is unjust and must be surrendered."[162]

The Birksian pyramid has already been applied by the Supreme Court of Canada. The Court used unjust factors to demonstrate why there is no juristic reason for an enrichment.[163]

The specific contribution of unjust factors in an unjust enrichment analysis is their nature as expressions of unjust-enrichment-specific negative reasons

---

[156] Cf. Hunt, *supra* note 120 at 177 and McInnes, "Unitary Action", *supra* note 152 at 123.

[157] Birks, *Unjust Enrichment, supra* note 7 at 44; Burrows, "Absence of Basis", *supra* note 118 at 33; Hunt, *supra* note 120 at 176; McInnes, "Unitary Action", *supra* note 152 at 123.

[158] Birks, *Unjust Enrichment, supra* note 7 at 114–16; Hunt, *supra* note 120 at 177.

[159] Hunt, *supra* note 120 at 177; McInnes, "Unitary Action", *supra* note 152 at 123.

[160] Cf. Hunt, *supra* note 120 at 181.

[161] See *ibid* at 181–82.

[162] Birks, *Unjust Enrichment, supra* note 7 at 116.

[163] See *Pacific National, supra* note 146 at paras 27–52, Bastarache J.

for retention. The unjust enrichment reasons for retention are not the same as reasons that would compel the unjust enrichment claimant to confer the prestation in the first place. For example, donative intent is not an established category of liability, but it is a reason to retain a benefit. Unjust factors can rebut a presumption of donative intent.[164]

## E. Explaining Unjust Enrichment

Even though unjust enrichment is a valid category in the system of law, we do not yet know whether unjust enrichment is the expression of an underlying legal principle or merely a theory that is able to explain individual cases in which the court held that a transfer of value is defective and needs to be reversed. Newton's theory of gravity explains the real-world phenomenon of gravity on a fairly satisfactory basis for most practical purposes, but it does not offer any reason why gravity exists in the first place. But whereas physics is not concerned with why the world is the way it is,[165] a legal theory could explain why we recognize unjust enrichment.

### *I. Formalist Theory of Unjust Enrichment*

One potential approach is the corrective justice approach to justifying unjust enrichment.[166] As Weinrib notes, the corrective nature of corrective justice is intuitively obvious.[167] He demonstrates this using a quote from *Kingstreet:*

> "Restitution is a tool of corrective justice. When a transfer of value between two parties is normatively defective, restitution functions to correct that transfer by restoring parties to their pre-transfer positions."[168]

The judgment itself also cites the following passage from *Peel:* "The concept of 'injustice' in the context of the law of restitution harkens back to the Aris-

---

[164] Smith, "Demystifying", *supra* note 118 at 290–91.

[165] Physics deals with the Goldilocks dilemma of why the world is the way it is by pointing out that theories of the universe are constrained by the necessity to allow an observer capable of postulating the theory, see *Oxford English Dictionary,* 3rd edn sv anthropic principle.

[166] On the theory of corrective justice see generally Ernest J Weinrib, *Corrective Justice* (Oxford: Oxford University Press, 2012).

[167] Ernest J Weinrib, "Correctively Unjust Enrichment" in: Chambers, Mitchell & Penner, eds, *Philosophical Foundations of the Law of Unjust Enrichment, supra* note 6, 31 at 31 [Weinrib, "Correctively"].

[168] *Kingstreet, supra* note 147 at para 32, Bastarache J. Cf. McInnes, "Resisting Temptations", *supra* note 53 at 107; Weinrib, "Correctively", preceding note at 31.

totelian notion of correcting a balance or equilibrium that had been disrupted."[169] What then does it mean to view the law of unjust enrichment as part of corrective justice?

According to Aristotle, there are two kinds of justice: distributive justice and corrective justice. Aristotle writes, "[t]he one remaining form of what is just is the rectifying kind, which we find in transactions both voluntary and involuntary."[170]

In Aristotle's word, any transfer is correlative.[171] In a claim for unjust enrichment, the defendant's gain is therefore the plaintiff's loss. Unjust in a context of corrective justice means that one has made a gain and the other a loss; before this event occurred, there was equality.[172] Yet Aristotle offers no explanation as to how the initial equilibrium can be determined.[173]

In a corrective justice account of unjust enrichment, the correlative nature of unjust enrichment is stressed.[174] The transfer of value from plaintiff to defendant essentially creates the correlativity between plaintiff and defendant.[175] The purpose of a claim in unjust enrichment is thus to right the wrong and repair the imbalance, thus restoring corrective justice.[176] Weinrib stresses the value of property rather than the item of property itself, and expresses value entitlement as the foremost incident of property.[177]

### *II. Legal Realism and Unjust Enrichment*

The starting point of the realist approach to unjust enrichment and restitution is the emphasis on the coercive nature of law. Private law is enforced through the state because the state has the monopoly on coercive power.[178] Realism tries to deconstruct and reveal the reasoning and policy behind legal rules.[179]

---

[169] *Peel, supra* note 39 at 165, McLachlin J (as she then was).

[170] Aristotle, *Nicomachean Ethics* (Indianapolis: Bobbs-Merrill, 1962) 1131b 1.

[171] *Ibid* at 1132a 1–6.

[172] *Ibid* at 1132a 1–6. Cf. McInnes, "Resisting Temptations", *supra* note 53 at 108–9.

[173] McInnes, "Resisting Temptations", *supra* note 53 at 110.

[174] Klimchuk, *supra* note 6 at 86–87; Weinrib, "Correctively", *supra* note 168 at 31.

[175] This nexus is established by the Supreme Court itself in the aforemention quote: "Restitution is a tool of corrective justice. When a transfer of value between two parties is normatively defective, restitution functions to correct that transfer by restoring parties to their pre-transfer positions." *Kingstreet, supra* note 147 32, Bastarache J. See Weinrib, "Correctively", *supra* note 168 at 33.

[176] See Virgo, *Restitution, supra* note 8 at 4–5; Ernest J Weinrib, "Corrective Justice in a Nutshell" (2002) 52 UTLJ 349. See also *Peel, supra* note 39 at 165.

[177] Weinrib, "Correctively", *supra* note 168 at 33–34, referring to Georg Wilhelm Friedrich Hegel, *Grundlinien der Philosophie des Rechts* (Berlin: Nicolaische Buchhandlung, 1821) at 77, 98.

[178] Hanoch Dagan, "Restitution's Realism" in: Chambers, Mitchell & Penner, eds, *Philosophical Foundations of the Law of Unjust Enrichment, supra* note 6, 54 at 56–57.

[179] *Ibid* at 57.

Consequently, legal realism views restitution as a function of the underlying social values that determine the plaintiff's and defendant's rights, not necessarily making reference to the correlativity between the two.[180] This approach is open to attack from the corrective justice standpoint at two points. First, the realist approach does not sufficiently explain why the two parties in unjust enrichment cases are linked together or why the plaintiff should have exactly these rights *vis-à-vis* the defendant.[181] At best, it can be said that the justification from a realist standpoint is to say that the reason can be seen in the underlying values from which private law derives. However, the realist approach gives no response to the question what these values should be,[182] thus rendering the content of the law arbitrary.

A realist's response to this criticism is to say that it may well be true that without specifying the underlying value, the content of law is arbitrary; yet a formalist approach to law, such as the corrective justice approach, does not fare better at predicting the content of the law.[183] Dagan further argues that the more important defence of realism is to say that realism is not void of a core set of values. Dagan lists these values: "autonomy, utility, and community."[184]

### *III. Conclusion*

Dagan's second defence seems paradoxical. The revolutionary approach of legal realism is to see law as a means to an end. If the defence of this approach is to say that realism is not completely arbitrary because the content of the law can be partly constructed and determined by unchangeable core values, this yields nothing but another formal approach to law. If we want to look at the core values that underlie the law, we have to look elsewhere.

However, it is not the purpose of this book to develop a general theory of unjust enrichment law. Rather, the ambition is more modest. In the next chapter, I want to analyse how the small subset of unjust enrichment law that yields proprietary restitution can be accounted for. Having said that, I can already make one anticipated prediction: the corrective justice approach to unjust enrichment does not fully account for proprietary restitution because it emphasizes value rather than the item of property itself.

[180] *Ibid* at 65–66.

[181] Ernest J Weinrib, "Book Review: Restoring Restitution" (2005) 91 Va L Rev 861 at 869 [Weinrib, "Restoring"].

[182] James J Edelman, "Review: The Law and Ethics of Restitution" (2006) 69 Modern L Rev 131 at 134; Weinrib, "Restoring", preceding note at 868.

[183] Dagan, "Restitution's Realism", *supra* note 179 at 70.

[184] *Ibid* at 71.

# § 10 Proprietary Restitution

Restitution in most cases is personal. It refers to an economic benefit received by the defendant, and it does not confer a higher rank in insolvency.[1] However, restitution can be proprietary. It is important to note that by calling it "proprietary restitution," I do not mean to anticipate the result that the claim itself is an outflow of a pre-existing property right. Rather, the word "proprietary" is used to describe the fact that the claim is one in regard to certain property – conferring a higher rank in insolvency – rather than a personal claim.[2]

Canadian courts regularly award proprietary remedies such as the constructive trust in what they call unjust enrichment cases. Other Common Law jurisdictions – such as England – recognize proprietary restitution as well. This raises the question what the basis for the award of proprietary restitution is. Birks was a strong proponent of the unjust enrichment account of proprietary restitution.[3] However, there are other possibilities. The answer to this question also depends on whether we consider the constructive trust to be a completely discretionary remedy, a "semi-remedial" trust[4] (which means that there are certain guidelines for when it is an appropriate remedy), or completely institutional (meaning that in certain events a constructive trust necessarily arises).

Canadian courts commonly call the constructive trust a "remedial" device. They thus imply that the trust is discretionary and not bound by rules. I argue that such an unprincipled understanding of the constructive trusts is not desirable. Whether proprietary restitution is restitution for unjust enrichment or replies to another legal event, its recognition should be the result of an identifiable principle. When I use the word "remedy," I do not mean to imply that the court is free in its discretion to select the remedy. Furthermore, this terminology does not make a statement regarding the possible remedies. It allows one

---

[1] Andrew S Burrows, "The English Law of Restitution: A Ten Year Review" in: Jason W Neyers, Mitchell McInnes & Stephen G Pitel, eds, *Understanding Unjust Enrichment* (Oxford: Hart, 2004) 11 at 23–24.

[2] See Peter Jaffey, "Two Theories of Unjust Enrichment" in: Neyers, McInnes & Pitel, eds, *Understanding Unjust Enrichment,* preceding note, 139 at 147.

[3] Peter Birks, *Unjust Enrichment,* 2[d] edn (Oxford: Oxford University Press, 2005) at 32.

[4] David M Paciocco, "The Remedial Constructive Trust: A Principled Basis for Priorities over Creditors" (1989) 68 Can Bar Rev 315 at 318–21 draws a similar distinction.

to talk of personal remedies (such as the order to pay money), as well as proprietary remedies (such as the institution of a constructive trust).

It is theoretically possible to admit only rights *in personam* as a response to unjust enrichment,[5] as this is the choice of Civilian systems.[6] In Common Law, it is less clear whether property rights can respond to unjust enrichment. Thus, the question is not whether it is possible that proprietary restitution *can* arise as a response to unjust enrichment. Rather, the questions are whether it *does and should* and – provided the answer to the first two questions are affirmative – *when*.

## A. Proprietary Restitution

### *I. Canadian Law*

Canadian courts have awarded constructive trusts in a variety of cases. Three broad categories can be identified: breakdown of intimate relationships, defective transfers, and breaches of fiduciary duties.

#### *1. Intimate Relationships*

#### *a) Principle*

We have already encountered an important class of proprietary restitution cases in the preceding chapter. Canadian courts regularly recognize a constructive trust as a restitution for unjust enrichment in the context of marital or other intimate, non-formalized (common law), relationships.[7] In *Pettkus v Becker,*

---

[5] Birks, *Unjust Enrichment, supra* note 3 at 32.

[6] See *ibid* at 32; Robert Stevens, "When and Why Does Unjustified Enrichment Justify the Recognition of Proprietary Rights?" (2012) 92:3 Boston UL Rev 919 at 919.

[7] Leading cases are *Peter v Beblow,* [1993] 1 SCR 980; *Sorochan v Sorochan,* [1986] 2 SCR 38 [*Sorochan*]; *Pettkus v Becker,* [1980] 2 SCR 834 and *Kerr v Baranow,* 2011 SCC 10 [*Kerr*]. On the Anglo-Canadian law of proprietary restitution in the context of marital and common law partnerships see Robert Leckey, "Unjust Enrichment and De Facto Spouses" (2012) 114 R du N 475; John D McCamus, "Restitution on Dissolution of Marital and Other Intimate Relationships: Constructive Trust or Quantum Meruit" in: Neyers, McInnes & Pitel, eds, *Understanding Unjust Enrichment, supra* note 1, 359; Anne Sanders, "Cohabitants in Private Law: Trust, Frustration and Unjust Enrichment in England, Germany and Canada" (2013) 62:3 ICLQ 629 and Donovan WM Waters, "Resulting Trusts and the Canadian Remedial Constructive Trust: Reconciling the Two" (2013) 19:9 T & T 1 [Waters, "Reconciling"]. See also Simone Wong, "Constructive Trusts over the Family Home: Lessons to Be Learned from Other Commonwealth Jurisdictions?" (1998) 18:3 LS 369, comparing the Canadian law with the situation in England and John Mee, "Property Rights and Personal Relationships: Reflections on Reform" (2004) 24:3 LS 414 on the possibility of a reception of

the Supreme Court held that a constructive trust can arise as a remedy for the unjust enrichment of one spouse due to services rendered by the other. However, the Supreme Court did not address the question what other forms of relief are available and whether relief is always proprietary. This may have been due to the fact that *Pettkus v Becker* involved a fact pattern situation in which the former common-intention resulting trust barely failed. Thus, the Court was not concerned with a general theory of remedies available for unjust enrichment, but only with a remedy similar in effect to the established resulting trust.[8] In *Sorochan v Sorochan,* the Court pointed out that a constructive trust is not the only available remedy for unjust enrichment.[9] In *Peter v Beblow,* the majority of the Court found that presumption operates in favour of non-proprietary relief. Justice McLachlin (as she then was) held that a personal remedy might be inappropriate where it is insufficient and the claimant's efforts have given her a special link to the property.[10]

*b) The Test for Proprietary Restitution*

*Kerr v Baranow* stands for two proposition: first, proprietary relief can take another form than the constructive trust; second, proprietary relief requires some form of a link between the claimant and the property.

*aa) Alternative Remedies*

While the cases just presented all involve the recognition of a constructive trust, this is not the only proprietary remedy for cases of unjust enrichment. Another option is recognizing that the claimant has a security interest in the property[11] – in other words an equitable lien.[12] From the claimant's point view, both remedies have the advantage of securing the claimant's position and rank in insolvency.[13]

---

Canadian law in England, but see also Charles CJ Mitchell, "Restitutionary Claims for Services: Identifying and Quantifying the Benefit" [2011] LMCLQ 504 at 515, arguing that the Canadian approach is unlikely to be adopted in England.

[8] McCamus, "Restitution on Dissolution of Marital and Other Intimate Relationships", preceding note at 369.

[9] *Sorochan, supra* note 7 at 47, Dickson CJ.

[10] *Peter v Beblow, supra* note 7 at 997, McLachlin J (as she then was).

[11] See Graham Virgo, *The Principles of the Law of Restitution,* 3rd edn (Oxford: Oxford University Press, 2016) at 4 [Virgo, *Restitution*].

[12] For examples, see e.g. *Biehl v Strang*, 2011 BCSC 1373 at paras 398–99 and *Tracy v Instaloans Financial Solutions Centres,* 2010 BCCA 357 at para 43, Newbury J (outside the intimate-relationship context).

[13] Virgo, *Restitution, supra* note 11 at 4.

*bb) The Link*

The problem with the broad regarding the requirement of a link between the claimant's contribution and the defendant's gain is that some form of link already exists because of the nature of the unjust enrichment claim: any enrichment is a function of a deprivation of the claimant.[14] *Kerr* specified the link requirement in more detail:

"As to the nature of the link required between the contribution and the property, the Court has consistently held that the plaintiff must demonstrate a 'sufficiently substantial and direct' link, a 'causal connection' or a 'nexus' between the plaintiff's contributions and the property which is the subject matter of the trust [...]. As Dickson C.J. put it in *Sorochan*, the primary focus is on whether the contributions have a 'clear proprietary relationship' [...] Indirect contributions of money and direct contributions of labour may suffice, provided that a connection is established between the plaintiff's deprivation and the acquisition, preservation, maintenance, or improvement of the property [...]. The plaintiff must also establish that a monetary award would be insufficient in the circumstances [...]. In this regard, the court may take into account the probability of recovery, as well as whether there is a reason to grant the plaintiff the additional rights that flow from recognition of property rights."[15]

*2. Defective Transfers*

A second category of constructive trusts involves cases of defective transfers of property. One important class of these constructive trusts are cases where the parties intended a transfer of property, but the transfer fails for some reason. In these cases, the constructive trust of the vendor-purchaser constructive trust class arises.[16] The reverse cases are resulting trusts, in which the transfer from transferor to purchaser was not meant to convey the equitable interest.[17] In a third class, the constructive trustee has received the property through a transfer that suffers from some vitiating defect.

The case of *Bank of Montreal v iTrade Finance Inc* can be seen as an example of the third class. A, based on fraud, induced the plaintiff, iTrade, to transfer certain monies to it. Later, the plaintiff obtained a tracing order to determine "whether any of the funds that originated with iTrade remain in the hands of, or can be traced into assets in the hands of, persons other than *bona fide* purchasers for value without notice."[18] In the meantime, A had used proceeds from the money transfer to open an investment account with the defendant, BMO. As traceable proceeds of the original funds transferred by iTrade, the investment account was covered in principled by the tracing order.

---

[14] McCamus, "Restitution on Dissolution of Marital and Other Intimate Relationships", *supra* note 7 at 378.

[15] *Kerr, supra* note 7 at paras 51–52, Cromwell J [references omitted, emphasis original].

[16] See Part II: § 6 D.III, "Vendor-Purchaser Constructive Trusts".

[17] See Part II: § 6 E, "Resulting Trusts".

[18] *Bank of Montreal v iTrade Finance Inc*, 2009 ONCA 615 at paras 5–6 [*iTrade (ONCA)*].

A also held a credit card account with an unpaid balance. The defendant and A agreed that the investment account would be pledged to secure the credit card debt. The agreement was partly documented, but no formal security agreement was executed or registered.[19] The plaintiff requested a motion to the effect that it was entitled to the monies in the investment account.

The motion court held that A acquired no interest in property that is traceable proceeds of fraudulently acquired monies. The Court of Appeal disagreed, reaffirming that the fraudulent person obtains a voidable interest in the transferee for purposes of creating a security interest.[20] Furthermore, once the property is transferred to a *bona fide* purchaser for value, the interest of the fraudulent person is no longer voidable.[21] The stated rationale is that "the great object of the law is to afford certainty and repose to titles honestly acquired."[22] The Court held that a person who parts with property is less deserving of protection than a person who departs only with possession.[23] Consequently, the Court held that BMO was a *bona fide* purchaser for value and therefore broke the tracing link.[24]

The Court of Appeal then turned to the question of unjust enrichment. It reiterated the conditions of unjust enrichment in Anglo-Canadian law as "(a) a benefit to or enrichment of one party, (b) a corresponding detriment to or deprivation suffered by the other party, and (c) the absence of any juristic reason for the benefit or enrichment."[25] The Court of Appeal did not find it necessary to decide whether BMO was enriched at all by taking security in exchange for extending credit to A.[26] It instead found that BMO had juristic reason for any enrichment, not least of all because it was a *bona fide* purchaser for notice and

---

[19] *Ibid* at paras 6–11.

[20] *Ibid* at para 20. See also *Gray v Royal Bank of Canada* (1997), 143 DLR (4th) 179 (BC SC) and *R v Canadian Imperial Bank of Commerce*, [2000] OJ No 4149 (CA).

[21] *iTrade (ONCA), supra* note 18 at para 20.

[22] Orlando Bump & James McIlvaine Gray, *A Treatise Upon Conveyances Made by Debtors to Defraud Creditors*, 4th edn (Washington, DC: WH Lowdermilk & Co, 1896) at 489–90, cited as in *iTrade (ONCA), supra* note 18 at para 21. The passage by Bump & Gray had already been approved by *Bank of Nova Scotia v Simpson* (1984), 1984 CarswellNS 22 at para 25 (SC).

[23] *iTrade (ONCA), supra* note 18 at paras 22–23. Cf. *Central Newbury Car Auctions Ltd v Unity Finance Ltd* (1956), [1957] 1 QB 371 at 381–82 (CA), Denning LJ dissent. See already *R v Canadian Imperial Bank of Commerce, supra* note 20 at para 7, curiam.

[24] *iTrade (ONCA), supra* note 18 at para 29.

[25] *Ibid* at para 32. Cf. *Canada (Attorney General) v Confederation Life Insurance Co* (1995), 24 OR (3d) 717 (Gen Div); *Peter v Beblow, supra* note 7; *Pettkus v Becker, supra* note 7; *Rathwell v Rathwell*, [1978] 2 SCR 436, affirmed by *Canada (Attorney General) v Confederation Life Insurance Co* (1997), 32 OR (3d) 102 (CA) (this point not dealt with).

[26] *iTrade (ONCA), supra* note 18 at para 36.

"equity has long protected the interests of someone in such a position."[27] Thus, the plaintiff lost the case.

The Court of Appeals judgment was confirmed by the Supreme Court in *iTrade Finance Inc v Bank of Montreal.*[28] The Supreme Court affirmed that the plaintiff's interest was an equitable interest – either an equitable lien or a constructive trust.[29] Since the Court also affirmed that BMO was a *bona fide* purchaser of the investment account, the decision of the Court of Appeals was affirmed. Because the defendant BMO was a purchaser by virtue of being the purchaser of a pledge, rather than by acquiring legal title, it was in fact a secured creditor. The judgment thus also clarifies the priority relationship between an equitable property right and a security interest. On that point, the judgment will be discussed later in this book.[30]

### 3. Breach of Fiduciary Duties

#### a) Lac Minerals

In *Lac Minerals Ltd v International Corona Resources Ltd,*[31] the Supreme Court of Canada dealt with possible limits on the availability of a constructive trust. Plaintiff and defendant were both mining corporations. The plaintiff carried out exploration of its property that led to the conclusion that minerals could be found on its property and on an adjacent property. The defendant learned about the exploration and contacted the plaintiff. Consequently, the plaintiff informed the defendant about the results in more detail. At that meeting, confidentiality of the information was not discussed. Later, the possibility of a joint venture regarding the exploitation of the plaintiff's property as well as the adjacent property was discussed. Subsequently, the plaintiff tried to acquire the adjacent property. However, the defendant also submitted a competing and ultimately successful offer for the adjacent property. The plaintiff sued the defendant for liability regarding the adjacent property.[32]

Writing for the majority of the Supreme Court of Canada, LaForest J held that a constructive trust is an available remedy for unjust enrichment.[33] He further indicated that he considers claims for unjust enrichment and restitution to be the same.[34] In unjust enrichment, proprietary remedies and personal remedies are available and the court has to choose the appropriate remedy.[35] The

---

[27] *Ibid* at para 41.
[28] 2011 SCC 26.
[29] *Ibid* at paras 31–32, Deschamps J.
[30] See Part III: § 13 D.II.1, "Priority of the Equitable Property Right".
[31] [1989] 2 SCR 574 [*Lac Minerals*].
[32] *Ibid* at 575–76.
[33] *Ibid* at 673–74, LaForest J.
[34] *Ibid* at 674, LaForest J.
[35] *Ibid* at 674–75, LaForest J.

remedy of constructive trust should not be limited to cases where a pre-existing right to property is recognized,[36] nor should a special relationship between the parties be a condition. For the latter conclusion, the Court relied on *Chase Manhattan Bank NA v Israel-British Bank (London) Ltd*[37] as authority for the proposal that a constructive trust can be the remedy where no special relationship exists.[38]

In his dissent, Sopinka J expressed his view that a constructive trust is inappropriate in actions based on breach of confidence because these cases are concerned with plaintiff's loss rather than the defendant's gain.[39]

*b) Soulos v Korkontzilas*

In *Soulos v Korkontzilas,*[40] the defendant was an estate agent. The plaintiff was his client. The plaintiff instructed the defendant to arrange the purchase of a house. The vendor of the property agreed to a price, but the defendant did not relay this to the plaintiff; rather, he informed his wife, who bought the property and then transferred it to the defendant and herself as joint tenants. When the plaintiff learned that the defendant had purchased the property for himself, he sued, alleging that the defendant held the property in constructive trust for him. The property held special value for the plaintiff because its tenant was his banker and being one's banker's landlord was a source of prestige in the Greek community to which the plaintiff belonged. The trial judge found that the defendant K had breached a duty of loyalty owed to the plaintiff, but held that a constructive trust was not an appropriate remedy because the plaintiff had not been "enriched." The Court of Appeal, in a majority decision, reversed the judgment and ordered that the property be conveyed to the plaintiff subject to appropriate adjustments.

The Supreme Court of Canada affirmed the Court of Appeal's decision. It agreed that the conditions of an unjust enrichment were not met because the property had deprecated in value, but it found that the purpose of the constructive trust is

> "not only to remedy unjust enrichment, but to hold persons in different situations to high standards of trust and probity and prevent them from retaining property which in 'good conscience' they should not be permitted to retain."[41]

---

[36] *Ibid* at 676, LaForest J: "[It] is not the case that a constructive trust should be reserved for situations where a right of property is recognized. That would limit the constructive trust to its institutional function, and deny to it the the status of a remedy, its more important role."

[37] (1979), [1981] 1 Ch 105, [1979] 3 All ER 1025 (Ch D) [*Chase Manhattan,* cited to All ER].

[38] *Lac Minerals, supra* note 31 at 675–76.

[39] *Ibid* at 618, Sopinka J.

[40] *Soulos v Korkontzilas,* [1997] 2 SCR 217 [*Soulos*].

[41] *Ibid* at para 17, McLachlin J (as she then was).

Justice McLachlin's (as she then was) statement appears to contradict Justice Dickson's statement that "[t]he principle of unjust enrichment lies at the heart of the constructive trust."[42]

It also seems to contradict the Supreme Court's decision in *Lac Minerals,* where the Court integrated trusts based on a breach of a fiduciary duty with the unjust enrichment principle. Certainly, the difference between *Lac Minerals* and *Soulos* is that in the latter case, the property deprecated in value. But it seems overly complex to thus conclude that both cases were fundamentally different types of constructive trusts. The Supreme Court indicated that both types of constructive trusts derive from one unifying underlying institution, and – without embracing that theory – that they can be understood to both be based on unjust enrichment if one interprets "'enrichment' [...] very broadly to extend beyond pecuniary claims."[43]

### *II. English Law*

#### *1. Defective Transfers*

##### *a) Chase Manhattan*

This case stands for the proposition that restitution can be based on a subsisting property right. The plaintiff, a New York bank, was instructed to pay money to the benefit of defendant's account held by M, another New York bank. It mistakenly paid twice. The defendant then turned insolvent. In the first instance, the legal effects of the mistaken payment were to be determined by New York law as *lex causae,* whereas the legal remedies were to be determined under the *lex fori.* The plaintiff claimed that the defendant held the money in trust for the plaintiff and that it was entitled to trace and recover the money. The defendant argued first that this was not part of the substantive law of New York; rather it was a remedy and that remedies were to be characterized as procedural. If that were true, they would be governed by the *lex fori.* Second, under applicable English law, the remedy of tracing and recovery required an initial fiduciary relationship between the parties, which was lacking. Third, all property of the defendant was held in statutory trust by the trustee in bankruptcy. Therefore, to recover, the plaintiff needed to be a creditor in the insolvency proceedings.[44]

The Court held that under English and New York law, the plaintiff continued to hold equitable property in the money. Therefore, the plaintiff had a right to trace and recover the money. Justice Goulding held that it was common ground that the law of New York as the *lex causae* must determine the effects of the

[42] *Pettkus v Becker, supra* note 7 at 847, Dickson J.

[43] *Soulos, supra* note 40 at paras 25–26, McLachlin J (as she then was).

[44] *Chase Manhattan, supra* note 37 at 1028.

mistaken payment.[45] On the substantive question, he referred to the case *Re Berry.*[46] In that case, Justice Coxe held that money paid by mistake never becomes property of the receiver.[47] Justice Coxe accepted authority that money paid by mistake is held in trust.[48] Justice Goulding held that this is a rule of equity in England as well.[49] He further held that the necessary fiduciary relationship to enable tracing can arise from mistaken payment.[50] Important for the holding that the plaintiff continued to have a property right in the money was the fact that the plaintiff continued to hold an equitable interest in the property.[51]

*b) Macmillan*

*Macmillan Inc v Bishopsgate Investment Trust Plc (No 3)*[52] recognized that certain restitutionary claims must be characterized as being part of the law of property, at least as far as conflict of laws is concerned. The plaintiff was a Delaware corporation. It had a majority holding in B, a New York corporation and the registry for B's shares. It transferred the shares to the first defendant to hold as nominee for the plaintiff under an agreement governed by the laws of New York. The first defendant transferred the shares to the second, third, and fifth defendants in breach of the trust agreement and without the plaintiff's knowledge in order to secure a loan. After the default of the first defendant, the plaintiff brought an action against the banks, alleging that the shares were transferred in breach of trust, that the plaintiff's interest was superior to the banks' interest and that the banks held the shares in constructive trust for the plaintiff. The banks argued that they held the shares with no defect in title because they acquired them in good faith.

In the High Court,[53] Justice Millet held that the issue whether the banks were *bona fide* purchasers had to be determined according to the law of New York; this was the *lex loci actus.* The appeal concerned the question whether the question of title was to be determined by English or New York law.[54]

The Court of Appeal held that the applicable law of the cause of action does not govern all issues in the suit. For each issue, the applicable law must be determined separately. As regards the question of title, this was a question of

---

[45] *Ibid* at 1029.

[46] 147 F 208 (2^d Cir 1906).

[47] *Ibid* at 210.

[48] *Ibid* at 211.

[49] *Chase Manhattan, supra* note 37 at 1031.

[50] *Ibid* at 1032.

[51] *Ibid* at 1033.

[52] (1995), [1996] 1 All ER 585 (CA Civ) [*Macmillan*].

[53] *Macmillan Inc v Bishopsgate Investment Trust Plc (No 3)* (1993), [1995] 1 WLR 978 (Ch D).

[54] *Macmillan, supra* note 52 at 591–94, 602–3, 611–12.

property law and therefore was to be determined by the *lex situs* and not the *lex loci actus,* although the two were the same laws in the present case.

Lord Justice Staughton identified three stages in determining the applicable law. First, the nature of the issue must be determined. This is called characterization. Second, the conflict rule containing the connecting factor must be identified. Third, through application of the connecting factors, the applicable law is to be identified.[55] Lord Justice Staughton embraced the approach of characterizing according to the content and purpose of the conflict-of-laws rule of the *lex fori,*[56] as did Auld LJ.[57] Although they did not mention it specifically, the characterization implies that the conflict-of-laws system has divided the bundle of laws that exist in a jurisdiciton into sub-bundles such as property law, matrimonial law, etc.[58] However, Auld LJ emphasized that the characterization should not be constricted by the categories of the domestic substantive law alone.[59] He identified the issue at hand as being either one of a "receipt-based restitutionary claim or about property" and acknowledged that the former category may be alien to other legal systems.[60]

Macmillan argued before the Court that because its claim is restitutionary, the issue should be characterized as obligational.[61] Lord Justice Staughton distinguished this case on the basis that there was a proprietary claim to trace the money as well as a claim at law for money had and received.[62] He further remarked that the plaintiff's claim is "to some extent proprietary."[63] He continued that he was willing to accept that the plaintiff's claim is restitutionary in nature;

---

[55] *Ibid* at 589.

[56] *Ibid* at 589–90.

[57] *Ibid* at 604.

[58] On the characterization of proprietary restitution in the conflicts of law see Part V: § 19 A, "Characterization of Proprietary Restitution". See also Stephen GA Pitel, "Characterisation of Unjust Enrichment in the Conflict of Laws" in: Neyers, McInnes & Pitel, eds, *Understanding Unjust Enrichment, supra* note 1, 331 and Pattarapas Tudsri, "Characterization of Proprietary Restitution in the Conflict of Laws" (2013) 44:2 Ottawa L Rev 261. For an introduction to the problem of characterization in private international law see "Characterisation and the Incidental Question" in: Lawrence Collins & Jonathan Harris, eds, *Dicey, Morris and Collins on the Conflict of Laws,* 15th ed (London: Sweet & Maxwell, 2012), vol 1, 38; Kurt Lipstein, *Private International Law: Characterization,* ed by Konrad Zweigert, Ulrich Drobnig, and Kurt Lipstein (International Encyclopedia of Comparative Law, III-5, Tübingen: Mohr Siebeck, 1999); Stephen GA Pitel & Nicholas S Rafferty, *Conflict of Laws* (Toronto: Irwin Law, 2010) at 211–17 and Ernst Rabel, "Das Problem der Qualifikation" (1931) 5 RabelsZ 241.

[59] *Macmillan, supra* note 52 at 604.

[60] *Ibid* at 604.

[61] *Ibid* at 594.

[62] *Ibid* at 594.

[63] *Ibid* at 595.

thus the former rule 230 in Dicey, Morris and Collins[64] should apply.[65] Lord Auld pointed out that the plaintiff's submission that his claim is "restitutionary rather than proprietary" relies on a certain interpretation of *Chase Manhattan Bank NA v Israel-British Bank (London) Ltd* regarding the law applicable on unjust enrichment, while in fact that case actually made no express decision on the issue.[66] The Court agreed that the issue now at hand is not about the claim, but whether the defendant can raise the defence that they acquired their title without fault because they were in good faith.[67] From this case, some scholars deduce that actions for restitution should be considered to be proprietary if based on a property right, and personal if based on money had and received, at least as far as the conflict of laws is concerned.[68]

*c) Westdeutsche Landesbank*

In *Westdeutsche Landesbank Girozentrale v Islington London Borough Council,*[69] the House of Lords considered a restitutionary claim after a failed transfer to be personal in nature. The plaintiff entered into an interest rate swap agreement with the defendant, a local authority. Under the agreement, the plaintiff paid £2.435m to the defendant. The defendant was obliged to pay interest on a notional sum of £25m. In an unrelated case, entering into a swap agreement was held to be *ultra vires* for a local authority and void *ab initio*. The plaintiff sued the defendant for repayment of the initial sum minus payments made in the meantime by the defendant, plus interest from the commencement date of the agreement.

The appeal concerned the award of compound interest. Both the trial court as well as the appeals court held that the plaintiff had a right either under money had and received or because they were entitled to trace the money in equity. However, the substantive right upon which recovery was based was not subject of the appeal before the Lords. The plaintiff argued that while its legal title was extinguished, it continued to be the beneficial owner of the assets. Furthermore,

---

[64] Lawrence Collins, ed, *Dicey, Morris and Collins on the Conflict of Laws,* 14th edn (London: Sweet & Maxwell, 2006) at para 34.1. Rule 230 has been substantially modified due to the entry into force of the *Regulation (EC) No 864/2007 of the European Parliament and of the Council of 11 July 2007 on the Law Applicable to Non-Contractual Obligations* [2007] OJ L177/40, see "Unjust Enrichment, Equitable Claims and Negotiorum Gestio" in: Lawrence Collins & Jonathan Harris, eds, *Dicey, Morris and Collins on the Conflict of Laws,* 15th ed (London: Sweet & Maxwell, 2012), vol 2, 2289 at para 36.8.

[65] *Macmillan, supra* note 52 at 596.

[66] *Ibid* at 604.

[67] *Ibid* at 596–605, 614.

[68] Joanna Bird, "Choice of Laws Rule for Priority Disputes in Relation to Shares" [1996] LMCLQ 57 at 61; Adrian Briggs, "Restitution Meets the Conflict of Laws" (1995) 3 RLR 94 at 99.

[69] [1996] 1 AC 669 (HL) [*Westdeutsche Landesbank*].

it submitted that the separation of legal and beneficial title automatically resulted in a trust.[70] Had that argument succeeded, the plaintiff would have been awarded compound interest because prior to this decision, courts would award compound interests in equity when and only when the holder of the money was trustee.

Their Lordships held that because the plaintiff's claim was personal and not proprietary, the Court had no jurisdiction to award compound interest. Lord Goff and Lord Woolf dissented. It is important to note that they agreed in principle that an action for money had and received is a personal action based on total failure of consideration, not an action based on implied contract or an equitable property right. Their dissent was based on the view that equity should allow compound interest to extend to personal claims.

Lord Goff's dissent was based on his opinion that equity jurisdiction should be extended to allow compound interest on personal claims.[71] He concurred with the majority that the action was personal, not proprietary, but recognized that restitution can be achieved by means of a proprietary claim, relying on *Sinclair v Brougham*[72] as authority for the proposition that restitution can take place by means of an equitable property right.[73]

Their Lordships raised the question why a plaintiff should have the additional benefits of a proprietary claim, namely protection from insolvency of the defendant.[74] Lord Goff pointed out that in cases such as the present where the plaintiff has entered into a transaction with the defendant, it has already assumed the insolvency risk of the other party.[75] Lord Wilkinson-Browne warned against the bad results that would come from awarding the claimant in restitution cases priority over all other creditors.[76]

Lord Goff identified a conflict between restitution lawyers and equity lawyers. The former wanted to embrace the trust as a remedy in restitution law because in their view, restitution law is based upon the principle of unjust enrichment, and the constructive and resulting trust are meant to reverse unjust enrichment. Equity lawyers, on the other hand, were concerned that the princi-

---

[70] *Ibid* at 672–73, Lord Goff.

[71] *Ibid* at 692–98, Lord Goff.

[72] [1914] AC 398 (HL).

[73] *Westdeutsche Landesbank, supra* note 69 at 687, Lord Goff.

[74] The insolvency consideration is also highlighted by Gareth Jones, "Ultra Vires Swaps: The Common Law and Equitable Fall-Out" (1996) 55:3 CLJ 432 at 434: "The consequences [of treating the bank as a trustee] would be startling. *Ultra vires* creditors would be in a more favourable position than *intra vires* creditors; a party to a commercial transaction might receive priority over general creditors on the other party's insolvency; and offbalance-sheet liabilities would exist of which businessmen would be unaware."

[75] *Westdeutsche Landesbank, supra* note 69 at 690, Lord Goff.

[76] *Ibid* at 712, Lord Browne-Wilkinson.

ples of equity are distorted if the concept would be annexed to the law of restitution.[77] Lord Wilkinson-Browne identified four principles of trust law with which the extension of the trust to the current case would be incompatible. First, equity operates on the legal title holder's conscience. Conscience requires her to either carry out the purpose for which he received title or do what the law imposes upon her in reply to unconscionable conduct. Second, a trust cannot be imposed until the title-holder becomes unconscionable. Third, there must be identifiable trust property. The exception is where the title holder receives the assets in breach of a fiduciary duty. Fourth, the beneficiary of a trust has an interest in the trust assets from the date of establishment.[78]

Lord Goff distinguished the case from *Sinclair v Brougham.*[79] In his view, the former case concerned an action for money had and received when a borrowing contract was void. The House of Lords then held that an action for money had and received was not permissible in such a case. If an action for money hand and receive would lie, it would become immaterial whether or not contract was valid. However, not providing for any remedy would enrich the recipient of the money. Therefore, the Court recognized a resulting trust to allow the depositors of the money to trace and recover their money in equity.[80] Lord Goff then addressed other reasons for recognizing the trust as a response to unjust enrichment – namely an article by Birks[81] – calling for wider availability of proprietary remedies in restitution; Lord Goff squarely rejected that call.

> "Professor Birks has argued for a wider role for the resulting trust in the field of restitution, and specifically for its availability in cases of mistake and failure of consideration. His thesis is avowedly experimental, written to test the temperature of the water. I feel bound to respond that the temperature of the water must be regarded as decidedly cold."[82]

His reasons were twofold. First, at the time the money is still identifiable, the recipient has no knowledge of the failure of consideration. Once he has this knowledge, the assets to which the trust is to be attached is no longer identifiable.[83] Second, he stated that there is no general rule that the property and beneficial interest in money does not pass to the recipient in the event of frustration

---

[77] *Ibid* at 685, Lord Goff.

[78] *Ibid* at 705, Lord Browne-Wilkinson.

[79] *Sinclair v Brougham, supra* note 72.

[80] *Westdeutsche Landesbank, supra* note 69 at 687–88, Lord Goff.

[81] Peter Birks, "Restitution and Resulting Trusts: Papers Presented at the First International Conference on Equity, the Faculty of Law, the Hebrew University of Jerusalem, June 1990" in: Stephen R Goldstein, ed, *Equity and Contemporary Legal Developments* (Jerusalem: Harry & Michael Sacher Institute for Legislative Research & Comparative Law, Hebrew University of Jerusalem, 1992) 335.

[82] *Westdeutsche Landesbank, supra* note 69 at 689, Lord Goff.

[83] *Ibid* at 689, Lord Goff.

or breach of contract; there is no compelling reason why it should be otherwise in cases of mistake or initial failure.[84]

*2. Wrongful Taking*

The cases of proprietary restitution for cases of wrongful taking could easily be subsumed under the defective transfer class. The main difference is that in cases of wrongful taking, the transfer is defective not because of some defect in the will of the transferor, but becaue the transfer is not a result of an exercise of the transferor's will at all.

*a) Lipkin v Gorman*

In *Lipkin Gorman v Karpnale Ltd,*[85] the House of Lords recognized unjust enrichment as a discrete area of English law. However, that case was not concerned with a claim based on an equitable property right because the plaintiff did not advance such a claim.[86] Lord Goff held that the plaintiff was able to trace his property in the *chose in action* to the money drawn by C, and the defendants then conceded that the property remained vested in the plaintiff.[87] Lord Goff remarked that, even though the action of money had and received required that legal title in the money was vested in the plaintiff at one point, the claim was still a personal claim, not a proprietary claim.[88] This means that the restitutionary claim was personal, not *in specie.*[89]

*b) Foskett v McKeown*

In *Foskett v McKeown,*[90] the House of Lords clearly characterized a claim in restitution as being both *proprietary* and *not based on unjust enrichment.* The plaintiffs entrusted money to M for land development. M, in breach of trust, misappropriated some £20 440 of the money to pay two premiums of a life insurance policy. The policy provided for a payment of either £1m or the aggregate value of units notionally assigned to the policy, whichever sum was greater. M assigned the beneficial interest in the policy to the third to fifth defendant. Upon M's suicide, £1m was paid to the trustees of the policy, the first and second defendants. The plaintiffs claimed part of the payout as their contribution to the value of the policy. The plaintiffs obtained a declaration

[84] *Ibid* at 689–90, Lord Goff.
[85] [1991] 2 AC 548 (HL).
[86] *Ibid* at 572.
[87] *Ibid* at 572, 574.
[88] *Ibid* at 572.
[89] David Fox, "Legal Title as a Ground of Restitutionary Liability" [2000] RLR 465 at 466.
[90] (2000), [2001] 1 AC 102 (HL).

that the land and the shares in the land development company were held in trust for them. They furthermore obtained £600 000 as a compromise with the bank where their funds were originally held. The Court of Appeals held that the plaintiffs did not hold an equitable interest in the benefits, nor did they have a claim to the benefit proportionate to the share of the misappropriated sum to the premiums paid overall. It held the plaintiffs were limited to a charge over the benefits to the extent their money could be traced into the premiums with interest.[91]

The House of Lords held that the plaintiffs were entitled to a proprietary remedy. Consequently, their earlier compensation could not diminish their proprietary interest in the benefit. Their proprietary interest in the benefits was proportionate to the share of the misappropriated sum to the premiums paid overall. Where a trustee misappropriates trust money, the beneficiaries can claim either a proportionate share of the proceeds or enforce a lien upon them to secure his personal claim.

The defendants asserted that the plaintiffs, by virtue of their earlier compensation, did not retain any interest in the deposit monies. Furthermore, they asserted that the plaintiffs' claim is one of vindication of property rights, not a case of unjust enrichment. Therefore, they argued that the defendants were only entitled to the amount originally misappropriated.[92]

Lord Browne-Wilkinson characterized the key question of the case as "who enjoys the ownership of the property in which the loss or the unexpected benefit is reflected"?[93] He stated that the plaintiffs' claim is not one based on unjust enrichment but one "based on the assertion by the purchasers of their equitable proprietary interest in identified property," and "it is a case of hard-nosed property rights."[94]

Lord Millett stated that

> "[t]he transmission of a claimant's property rights from one asset to its traceable proceeds is part of our law of property, not of the law of unjust enrichment. There is no 'unjust factor' to justify restitution (unless 'want of title' be one, which makes the point). The claimant succeeds if at all by virtue of his own title, not to reverse unjust enrichment."[95]

According to Lord Millett, the plaintiffs sought to *vindicate* their property rights.[96]

Because the original item of property – the monies – was gone, the case dealt with tracing the plaintiffs' original right into the proceeds.[97] But tracing

---

[91] *Ibid* at 107–8, 111–12.
[92] *Ibid* at 105.
[93] *Ibid* at 106.
[94] *Ibid* at 108–9.
[95] *Ibid* at 127.
[96] *Ibid* at 129.
[97] *Ibid* at 109, 127.

was not the claim or cause of action itself, only the means to pursue the claim.[98] Because the plaintiffs were able to trace their property rights into the proceeds, they were entitled to a proportionate proprietary interest in the benefits of policy. This is not a reversal of unjust enrichment, but the consequence of property rights.[99]

### *3. Breach of Fiduciary Duty*

In a number of cases, English courts have recognized that a defendant can become a constructive trustee when she has breached a fiduciary duty. In *Reading v Attorney General,*[100] a member of the army had accepted bribes during the course of his duty. After he was found out, the army confiscated the bribes. His action for recovery failed because he was considered to hold the bribes in trust for the army. The House of Lords held that it was not in a position to base the trust on the principle of unjust enrichment; rather the trust arose because the soldier could only make the money by virtue of being in service.[101] In *Attorney General for Hong Kong v Reid,*[102] the Privy Council held that a Crown prosecutor who accepted bribes in order to obstruct the prosecution, and then used those bribes to buy land, held the land in trust for the Crown. In *Sinclair Investments (UK) Ltd v Versailles Trade Finance Ltd,*[103] Lord Neuberger MR (as he then was) for the Court of Appeal, considering himself to be bound by precedent, clarified that in English law, the equitable entitlement of the claimant is personal, not proprietary, where the property in question was acquired with

> "funds which, although they could not have been obtained if he had not enjoyed his fiduciary status, were not beneficially owned by the claimant or derived from opportunities beneficially owned by the claimant."[104]

However, in *FHR European Ventures LLP v Cedar Capital Partners LLC*[105] the Supreme Court of the United Kingdom, in a unanimous decision of all seven sitting justices and written by Lord Neuberger himself, overruled *Sinclair Investments (UK) Ltd v Versailles Trade Finance Ltd,* and held that a constructive trust arises when the defendant has accepted bribes. Consequently, the claimant has an equitable property right. The case made no reference to unjust enrichment principles.

---

[98] *Ibid* at 128.

[99] *Ibid* at 110.

[100] [1951] AC 507 (HL).

[101] *Ibid* at 514–15, Lord Porter.

[102] (1993), [1994] 1 AC 324 (Hong Kong PC).

[103] [2011] EWCA Civ 347.

[104] *Ibid,* Lord Neuberger MR (as he then was). See also Robert Pearce & Jennifer Shearman, "The Pursuit of Proprietary Remedies for Breach of Fiduciary Duty" (2012) 24 Denn LJ 191.

[105] [2014] UKSC 45 [*FHR*].

## B. Explaining Proprietary Restitution

### *I. Preliminary Remarks*

In this section, I look at how legal scholarship accounts for the existence of proprietary restitution. When trying to explain the existence of proprietary restitution, there are two factors that need to be distinguished: first, whether proprietary restitution forms part of the framework of unjust enrichment law, or stands outside of it; second, whether there are policy reasons to consider because proprietary restitution has profound impacts in insolvency. The second aspect is dealt with in the chapter on the constructive trust and insolvency.

### *1. Equity's Preference for Personal Remedies*

Equity generally favours personal over proprietary remedies.[106] There are several explanations for that. First, there is no substantive reason for this, but rather stems from the fact that equity courts did not want to interfere with the jurisdiction of law courts.[107] Second, proprietary remedies are potentially disadvantageous for third parties.[108] Third, proprietary remedies are more intrusive for the defendant.[109] Whatever the reason, Canadian jurisprudence indicates that proprietary remedies should only be awarded as a last resort.[110]

The constructive trust is a heavy burden on the defendant. A less intrusive proprietary remedy would be an equitable lien. That would allow the defendant to dispose the lien without the consent of the plaintiff, whereas the plaintiff who has a constructive trust has a hold on the defendant.[111] The lien would give the plaintiff equal protection against the insolvency of the defendant. Whereas a true proprietary remedy requires the plaintiff to be either able to identify the property or trace it, this standard is not required in restitutionary cases.[112]

### *2. Requirements of a General Theory of Proprietary Restitution*

The explanatory models for proprietary restitution are not all comprehensive. Some of the models focus on certain classes of proprietary restitution only. But if one only looks at one class, it becomes difficult to elaborate a general theory of proprietary restitution. The categories of proprietary restitution that need to

---

[106] MM Litman, "The Emergence of Unjust Enrichment as a Cause of Action and the Remedy of Constructive Trust" (1987–1988) 26 Alta L Rev 407 at 454.

[107] *Ibid* at 454.

[108] *Ibid* at 454.

[109] *Ibid* at 454.

[110] *Ibid* at 454.

[111] *Ibid* at 456.

[112] *Ibid* at 456–57.

be accounted for are defective transfer of title, wrongful taking, and the intimate relationship cases. I also have to address the question whether proprietary restitution can take place in straightforward unjust enrichment cases that are neither characterized by a certain property transfer (*e.g.* defective transfer or wrongful taking) nor by the intimate relationship pattern.

### *II. The Unjust Enrichment Model*

#### *1. Event and Response*

The unjust enrichment model gives an explanation as to why proprietary responses follow from unjust enrichment and what form this response can take. For Birks, the question whether English law recognizes proprietary restitution for unjust enrichment was decidedly settled. He wrote "The rationality of 'women and children first' may require re-examination, but shipwreck is not the time to attempt a re-assessment."[113]Smith holds an equally strong opinion

> "One way to approach this question would be to ask whether the law *should* grant proprietary remedies for unjust enrichment, as if we were working with a blank sheet of paper and designing a new system from scratch. On that approach, a number of criteria could be applied to answer the question. If one took an instrumentalist approach to private law, it could be applied here. Such an approach, however, does not accord any respect to the institutional practices of the law. Such practices, built up over the years in the form of legal traditions, cannot be treated as dispensable without imperilling the fundamental requirement of justice that like cases be treated alike."[114]

Birks and Smith have come to the conclusion that there have already been cases in English law where property rights where used as a response to unjust enrichment. Birks sharply criticizes attempts to abolish this established possibility. He states that due the implication of a property right on insolvency, the question whether to disallow property rights in unjust enrichment cases is a question better left to Parliament than to be decided when the case arises.[115]

Birks says it is not self-evident that the law of unjust enrichment should not know the response of a property right.[116] He argues that the claim that unjust enrichment cannot give rise to a property right may be based on the confusion of unjust enrichment as the event in response to which the right arises and the response itself.[117] He argues that property rights are responses and not

---

[113] Birks, *Unjust Enrichment, supra* note 3 at 181.

[114] Lionel D Smith, "Philosophical Foundations of Proprietary Remedies" in: Robert Chambers, Charles C Mitchell & James E Penner, eds, *Philosophical Foundations of the Law of Unjust Enrichment* (Oxford: Oxford University Press, 2009) 281 at 281 [emphasis in original].

[115] Birks, *Unjust Enrichment, supra* note 3 at 181.

[116] *Ibid* at 181.

[117] *Ibid* at 37.

events,[118] and denies that property rights can ever be events that trigger responses. For instance, he argues that the fact that a fixture built on land becomes the property of the proprietor of the land[119] is not a function of a property right.[120]

Therefore, proprietary restitution responds to an event other than a pre-existing property right and unjust enrichment can be one of these events. This conception is based on two premises. First, according to Birks, all events are occurrences in the natural world.[121] Second, something cannot be response and event at the same time.[122] Therefore, for Birks, the right to reclaim one's property from the possessor does not rest on the property right itself, but upon a different event. At law, that event is either the unjust enrichment or the wrong.[123] In equity, where a direct vindication is permitted, the event is the receipt of property that is not the possessor's own.[124]

For Birks, even the case of *Foskett v McKeown* can be explained as a case of proprietary restitution of unjust enrichment. That is the explanation Birks gives, even though he acknowledges that the House of Lords chose to give a different explanation. He states that the House of Lords' view can only be explained by the fiction of persistence, which Birks views as the Common Law equivalent of real subrogation in Civil Law.[125] However, a legal fiction is only necessary when no other explanation can be given. According to him, explaining the outcome of the case as a response to unjust enrichment would be the missing explanation.[126] Birks contrasts his view with the Virgo approach,[127] which he says influenced the House of Lords.[128]

According to Birks, the fact that unjust enrichment cases can all be consolidated under the "no basis" approach is an argument for a unitary response.[129] According to Birks, one should sharply distinguish between event and response. The decision to allow a property right as a response is a second step,

---

[118] Peter Birks, "Property, Unjust Enrichment, and Tracing" (2001) 54:1 Curr Legal Probs 231 at 238. Cf. Ross Grantham & Charles Rickett, "Disgorgement for Unjust Enrichment?" (2003) 62:1 CLJ 159 at 719.

[119] See Part II: § 5 E.IV, "Fruits, Accession".

[120] Birks, "Property, Unjust Enrichment, and Tracing", *supra* note 118.

[121] Grantham & Rickett, "Disgorgement for Unjust Enrichment?", *supra* note 118 at 720.

[122] *Ibid* at 720.

[123] *Ibid* at 720.

[124] *Ibid* at 721.

[125] Cf. Rainer Becker, *Die Fiducie von Québec und der Trust: Ein Vergleich mit verschiedenen Modellen fiduziarischer Rechtsfiguren im Civil Law* (Tübingen: Mohr Siebeck, 2007) at 357, pointing out that the Civil Law takes a narrow approach to real subrogation. See also Henri Capitant, "Essai sur la subrogation réelle" (1919) 18 RTD 385.

[126] Birks, *Unjust Enrichment, supra* note 3 at 35–36.

[127] See Part II: § 10 B.III, "The Property Rights Model".

[128] Birks, *Unjust Enrichment, supra* note 3 at 36–37.

[129] *Ibid* at 185.

which is distinct from the first step (identifying the event).[130] The response may take the shape of a property right or a personal obligation of the defendant.[131] Birks identifies three property rights as responses to unjust enrichment in English law: an immediately vested beneficial right *in rem* (*i.e.* a trust), powers *in rem,* and security interests (*i.e.* equitable liens).[132] Birks says that even with this underlying common explanation for unjust enrichment, two lines can be drawn to distinguish cases of unjust enrichment. First, there is a difference between cases of initial and cases of subsequent failure. Second, there is a difference between cases where the plaintiff asserts an interest in the thing originally received and those where he asserts an interest in the traceable proceeds of the thing originally received.[133] Therefore, Birks distinction is based on two criteria. The one looks at the cause of unjust enrichment, the other one looks at the claim of the plaintiff.

Smith recognizes that the Supreme Court of Canada in *Pettkus v Becker* did not clearly distinguish between unjust enrichment as the cause of action and the constructive trust as the remedy. However, he argues that this was later clarified in *Sorochan.*[134] Smith also uses *Peter v Beblow* to support his position. He says that the Supreme Court in *Peter v Beblow* proposed that another proprietary response to unjust enrichment is an equitable lien.[135] He argues that in the case of *Re Estate Gareau*[136] the ordering of "constructive trusts as way of security" must mean an "equitable lien because of unjust enrichment."[137] Smith proposes that "equitable proprietary interests" can be used as a "remedy" to solve cases where no enrichment currently exists but where it is likely to arise in the future.[138]

*2. The Proprietary Restitution Test in the Unjust Enrichment Approach*

If proprietary restitution can be the response to unjust enrichment, this leads to the question when proprietary restitution should be available in an unjust enrichment claim. After all, not every unjust enrichment triggers a proprietary response.

---

[130] *Ibid* at 33.

[131] *Ibid* at 33.

[132] *Ibid* at 183–84.

[133] *Ibid* at 183–85.

[134] Referring to Litman, *supra* note 106. See Lionel D Smith *et al, The Law of Restitution in Canada* (Toronto: E Montgomery Publications, 2004) at 334–35.

[135] Smith *et al,* preceding note at 355.

[136] [1995] OJ No 2117 (Gen Div).

[137] Smith *et al, supra* note 134 at 356.

[138] *Ibid* at 356–57. Smith refers to *Republic Resources Ltd v Ballem* (1981), 33 AR 385 (QB) as an example of such a case.

### a) The Birksian Model

#### aa) Two Necessary Conditions

The Birksian unjust enrichment model requires that two conditions be met to trigger the proprietary response. First, the enrichment of the defendant must consist of property that is either a direct subtract from the claimant's estate or its traceable proceeds.[139] Second, if there was ever a point in time during which the defendant was not liable in unjust enrichment (first fact pattern), the response should be personal, but where the defendant's right to the property was always subject to the claim (second fact pattern), the response can be proprietary.[140] From this description, we can already gather that the Birksian scheme is primarily concerned with defective transfer cases.

#### bb) The Temporal Element

When looking at the second condition, the first class of fact patterns concerns cases of subsequent failure of basis, the second concerns cases of an initial absence of basis.[141] For his analysis, Birks relied particularly on *Chase Manhattan,* along with cases of failed trusts.[142] Birks acknowledges that this analysis is contradicted by the outcome of *Westdeutsche Landesbank.*[143] There, their Lordships only awarded a personal remedy, even though the basis for the transfer of the monies had always been absent. In Birks' view, their Lordships neglected to properly analyse whether *Westdeutsche Landesbank* was a case of initial failure or one of subsequent failure because they were not aware of the temporal element in deciding between personal and proprietary response.[144]

Birks distinguishes one pattern in which subsequent failure does not prevent a proprietary response. These cases are cases of "ring-fenced funds" – that is, funds that were transferred from the claimant to the defendant not at the latter's free disposal, but earmarked for a specific purpose.[145] These cases are known as "Quistclose trusts."[146]

From a policy standpoint, the second condition is justified by the fact that if there was a point in time in which the defendant was entitled to the property,

---

[139] Burrows, "The English Law of Restitution", *supra* note 1 at 26–27. On the concept of tracing see Lionel D Smith, *The Law of Tracing* (Oxford: Clarendon Press, 1997).

[140] Birks, *Unjust Enrichment, supra* note 3 at 181–82. See also Burrows, "The English Law of Restitution", *supra* note 1 at 27.

[141] Birks, *Unjust Enrichment, supra* note 3 at 181–82.

[142] *Ibid* at 186–87.

[143] *Supra* note 69.

[144] Birks, *Unjust Enrichment, supra* note 3 at 190–91.

[145] *Ibid* at 195–98.

[146] Named after the House of Lord's decision in *Barclays Bank Ltd v Quistclose Investment Ltd* (1968), [1970] AC 567 (HL) [*Quistclose Investment*].

and there was a subsequent failure of consideration, the claimant assumed the risk of the defendant's insolvency.[147]

The Birksian scheme alone cannot explain the family law cases decided by the Supreme Court of Canada, nor can they account for breach of fiduciary duty. Birks would argue that these are cases not of unjust enrichment, but of restitution for wrongdoing.[148]

*cc) Choosing the Appropriate Proprietary Response*

In Birks' view, the proprietary response to unjust enrichment is both an equitable lien and beneficial ownership if the property held by the defendant is a traceable proceed of the original property.[149] He acknowledges that there may be no clear guideline for cases in which cases the equitable lien is the *only* response.[150]

*b) Stevens' Model*

Stevens' model of proprietary restitution also concerns defective transfers. He argues that a constructive trust arises where both the transfer of right and the transfer of value are conditional and both of these conditions fail. In cases where only the transfer of value fails, the property right still passes and the claim is personal.[151] This seems like an introduction of a principle of separation and abstraction: the proprietary entitlement becomes separated from the causal obligation, and its effects are abstract from the effect of the causal obligation.

Stevens submits that his theory for constructive trusts is different but similar to the explanation for vendor-purchaser constructive trusts.[152] The conceptual similarity is not explicitly spelled out, but his implicit argument is that in cases of vendor-purchaser constructive trusts, the agreement to transfer an item of property already constitutes an equitable property right in the purchaser. Thus, the value of the property is transferred by the agreement and payment of the price: the purchaser is now entitled to the property's value and has a property right in it. Thus, the vendor becomes a constructive trustee. A similar explanation can even be applied in cases of theft or other rogue acquisitions of property. Where the rogue obtains property, she is not entitled to its value. At the

---

[147] Burrows, "The English Law of Restitution", *supra* note 1 at 27.

[148] Birks, *Unjust Enrichment, supra* note 3 at 11–13.

[149] *Ibid* at 201–2.

[150] *Ibid* at 202.

[151] Stevens, "When and Why Does Unjustified Enrichment Justify the Recognition of Proprietary Rights?", *supra* note 6 at 925–27.

[152] See *ibid* at 923–25. Stevens concludes his section on vendor-purchaser constructive trusts with the remark that "[w]e find precisely the same pattern within the law of unjustified enrichment."

same time, the claimant retains a property right in the property and even arguably has an equitable right in it. Thus, she can make a proprietary restitution claim. In conclusion, if Stevens' model is described not in terms property transfer, but in terms of separation of value and equitable right on the one hand and immediate possession of the property on the other hand, it can account for a variety of proprietary restitution cases.

### c) *Moore v Sweet*

A recent case involving the test for the recognition of a proprietary right is *Moore v Sweet.*[153] In *Moore,* the claimant and a third party, the claimant's former spouse, had entered into a contractual arrangement by virtue of which the claimant would pay all premiums of a life insurance on the third party's life; in return, the third party had undertaken to nominate the claimant as sole beneficiary. In fact, he had nominated his new partner, the defendant, as the irrevocable beneficiary.[154] The issue was whether – after the third party had deceased – the proceeds of the life insurance policy were impressed with a constructive trust in the claimant's favour.The Court of Appeal had found they were not,[155] but the majority of the Supreme Court found they were, with Gascon and Rowe JJ, in a joint opinion, dissenting.

There was another basis of the claimant's claim, who argued that she was the assignee of the life insurance policy proceeds. However, the Court noted that the designated beneficiary of a life insurance policy enjoys a strong protection under the *Insurance Act*:[156] while the benefit is a chose in action, assignment is only valid if the beneficiary notifies their consent, so the Court said.[157] This appears inconsistent. If the beneficiary is the beneficiary then of course they have to consent to an assignment, because they are the the creditor of the claim being assigned; they are the owners of the chose in action; they are the effective assignor. But the Court treated this as if the insured party were the owner of the chose in action and thus the assignor. This seems inconsistent.

Rejecting the assignment of the claim, the question is whether the claimant can make a claim based on unjust enrichment remedied by proprietary restitution. The first-instance court found that the defendant had been unjustly enriched at the claimant's expense and that the proceeds of the policy were subject to a constructive trust. There was no juristic reason for the entitlement *vis-à-vis* the claimant; the designation as beneficiary did not constitute such a juristic reason in relation to the claimant; the oral agreement between the claimant and the third party amounted to an equitable assignment of the proceeds to

---

[153] 2018 SCC 52 [*Moore*].
[154] *Ibid* at para 2.
[155] *Moore v Sweet,* 2017 ONCA 182.
[156] RSO 1990, c I 8.
[157] *Moore, supra* note 153 at paras 16–17, Côté J.

the claimant.[158] The majority of the Court of Appeal overturned the first-level decision. They found that *Garland* mandated a two-stage approach, and that in applying this approach, the designation of the defendant as beneficiary constituted a valid juristic reason for their enrichment. They found that the question whether there is a category of constructive trusts outside the unjust enrichment category exists does not need deciding because there are no indications that such a good-conscience constructive trust would arise in the present context.[159]

The majority of the Supreme Court reversed the Court of Appeal's decision on the basis that it did find that there was an unjust enrichment situation that needed being remedied by a constructive trust. It based its decision on what it called the principled unjust enrichment principle, *i.e.* the principle that any unjust enrichment is based on an absence of basis for the enrichment. The majority of the Supreme Court described the "principled" unjust enrichment approach as a theory explaining the unjust categories; they are different expressions of the same principle.[160]

The majority of the Supreme Court identified two main issues: first, was there a deprivation suffered by the claimant that correspondend to the defendant's enrichment; second, whether the *Insurance Act* provided a juristic reason.[161]

In relation to the first question, the majority found that to establish that the defendant was enriched and the claimant correspondingly deprived, it must be shown that a "tangible benefit" passed from the latter to the former.[162] From the outcome of the decision, we can gather that this tangible benefit is not necessarily a specific item of property, but it might be enough to argue it gives rise to a property right in an item of property. After all, the money paid by the third party was not identical to the proceeds of the insurance. The majority also points out that the deprivation and the gain do not need to be the exact same thing and support this by reference to the Québec law of unjustified enrichment.[163]

Turning to the question whether there was a juristic reason for the defendant's enrichment, the majority reasoned that the *Insurance Act* does not destroy "prior rights" and thus the claimant can still claim the proceeds.[164] This mention of prior rights is interesting as it confirms that there is an underlying pre-

---

[158] As summarized by the Supreme Court in *ibid* at paras 19–20.

[159] As summarized by the Supreme Court in *ibid* at paras 22–24.

[160] *Ibid* at paras 36–37, Côté J.

[161] *Ibid* at para 40.

[162] *Ibid* at para 41, referring to *Kerr, supra* note 7 at para 38; *Pacific National Investments Ltd v Victoria (City),* 2004 SCC 75 at para 15; *Peel v Canada,* [1992] 3 SCR 762 at 790.

[163] *Moore, supra* note 153 at para 45, Côté J, referring to *Cie immobilière Viger Ltée c Lauréat Giguère Inc* (1976), [1977] 2 SCR 67 at 79 and *Lacroix v Valois,* [1990] 2 SCR 1259 at 1278–79.

[164] *Moore, supra* note 153 at 62–73.

existing entitlement that is merely vindicated by the declaration of the constructive trust.

The majority describes the underlying difference between them and the minority as follows: The minority characterizes the claim the claimant has in the insurance proceeds as a contractual claim against the third party (or rather their estate because it is the very nature of the life insurance that the proceeds arise upon death of the insured third party) and this contractual right is extinguished by the provision of the *Insurance Act.*[165] Again, implicit in this argument is to say that the claimant's right was always more than a personal claim. It was, I would argue, always an inchoate equitable property right in the proceeds, which are in essence the future time value of the claimant's deprivation.

Turning to the appropriate remedy, the majority found that "courts will impress the disputed property with a constructive trust only if the plaintiff can establish two things: first, that a personal remedy would be inadequate; and second, that the plaintiff's contribution that founds the action is linked or causally connected to the property over which a constructive trust is claimed."[166] The second requirement is akin to saying that the claimed assets must be a fruit of the defendant's original deprivation. This approach is a little more difficult to sustain in the cohabitation cases, but there, it might be argued that the claimant's contribution to the common undertaking is a reason for an original acquisition of a property right.

### *III. The Property Rights Model*

The property rights model is the most distinct of all approaches; it denies that a proprietary response, such as the constructive trust, can ever arise as a response to unjust enrichment. Virgo states that "there is simply no empirical evidence to support the assertion that property rights can derive from the defendant's unjust enrichment."[167] Only insofar as unjust enrichment is used in its descriptive sense can one talk of unjust enrichment because in a trivial sense, the holder of property that rightfully belongs to another person is unjustly enriched.[168]

For Virgo only personal but no proprietary responses are available in substantive unjust enrichment cases.[169] Like Birks, Virgo sharply distinguishes between restitution as a response and the legal cause to which the restitution responds. Virgo cites a number of cases where the courts characterized a response as being restitutionary and proprietary but not, in his interpretation, as based

---

[165] *Ibid* at para 80, Côté J.
[166] *Ibid* at para 91, Côté J.
[167] Virgo, *Restitution, supra* note 11 at 16, 563.
[168] *Ibid* at 12.
[169] *Ibid* at 16.

on unjust enrichment.[170] He includes *Lipkin Gorman v Karpnale Ltd* in this list of cases involving the vindication of property rights, not unjust enrichment, because the remaining property interest of the plaintiff until the moment the defendant acquired the money was key.[171]

The property rights model is based on the premise that Birks' taxonomy of legal events was not exhaustive. It is possible for further categories to emerge from the miscellaneous other categories.[172] Consequently, Grantham and Rickett disagree with Birks' conclusion that property rights cannot be a legally significant event.[173] First, they say that Birks' first premise is not correct. Events are not merely something occurring in the natural world; rather, they are always something constructed in the mind by legal thought and interpretation of the natural world.[174] They disagree with Birks' second premise as well. While they concur that something cannot be its *own* cause, they say it is not impossible that a category of rights sometimes is a response, sometimes an event.[175] Therefore *in rem* rights can be a legally significant event.[176] As a legal event, it logically follows that they can give rights to legal responses.

However, in Grantham and Rickett's view, the response itself can only be an *in personam* right.[177] In their words, the declaration of the *in rem* situation by the court is "inert."[178] This is similar to Birks' view that the law itself may respond to an event by the creation of legal relationships without the need for a court to order remedies.[179] The initial legal response may be the creation of an *in rem* right such as the trust, which the court then recognizes. This conforms to Birks' view that the trust is a response.[180] However, an additional legal response in the form of an *in personam* right against the defendant is necessary to vindicate the plaintiff.[181] Furthermore, the order cannot be the event that gives right to the *in personam* right because a court order is declaratory of

---

[170] *Foskett v McKeown, supra* note 90; *Macmillan, supra* note 52; *Lipkin Gorman v Karpnale Ltd, supra* note 85. See Virgo, *Restitution, supra* note 11 at 559–65.

[171] Virgo, *Restitution, supra* note 11 at 560–61.

[172] Mitchell McInnes, "Taxonomic Lessons for the Supreme Court of Canada" in: Ross Grantham & Charles Rickett, eds, *Structure and Justification in Private Law: Essays for Peter Birks* (Oxford: Hart, 2008) 77 at 81.

[173] Ross Grantham & Charles Rickett, "Property and Unjust Enrichment: Categorical Truths or Unnecessary Complexity?" [1997] NZL Rev 668 at 671.

[174] Grantham & Rickett, "Disgorgement for Unjust Enrichment?", *supra* note 118 at 723–26.

[175] *Ibid* at 727.

[176] *Ibid* at 728.

[177] *Ibid* at 730–31.

[178] *Ibid* at 731.

[179] See Peter Birks, "Rights, Wrongs, and Remedies" (2000) 20 Oxford J Legal Stud 1.

[180] Peter Birks, "Definition and Division: A Meditation on Institutes 3.13" in: Peter Birks, ed, *The Classification of Obligations* (Oxford: Clarendon Press, 1997) 1 at 32–33.

[181] Grantham & Rickett, "Disgorgement for Unjust Enrichment?", *supra* note 118 at 731.

rights.[182] There must be a pre-existing event which gives rise to the legal response. This is the *in rem* right recognized by the court and from which a personal obligation of the defendant in possession of the plaintiff's property to conform to the *in rem* right stems.[183] Therefore, the plaintiff's property right in this view emerges independently from and prior to the court order.

Consequently, wherever there is a traceable subsisting proprietary right, the case is not one of unjust enrichment.[184] Grantham and Rickett see *Foskett v McKeown* as proof of their view.[185] The advantage of viewing certain cases as being a vindication of property rights instead of viewing them as based on unjust enrichment is, in Grantham and Rickett's view, the fact that that way, a subsisting property right can be vindicated without the defences of unjust enrichment being available.[186] Finally, the remedy of imposing a lien is not a response to the original property right, but a proprietary remedy for the breach of the trust to secure the personal obligation.[187] Similarly, Watts proposes that proprietary responses should be reserved for cases where there was no consent regarding transfer of title.[188] In Virgo's analysis, there are three events to which restitutions responds: unjust enrichment, wrongdoing, and the vindication of property rights.[189]

### *IV. The Power Model*

Häcker suggests that proprietary restitution follows what she calls a "generalized power model."[190] She argues that restitution after impaired consent transfers should always take the form of a power that has to be exercised before any property right revests. The power can exist in combination with a personal claim for restitution based on unjust enrichment. Exercise of the power revests a property right in the claimant and extinguishes the unjust enrichment claim

---

[182] *Ibid* at 731–32.

[183] *Ibid* at 732.

[184] *Ibid* at 744–45.

[185] Ross Grantham & Charles Rickett, "Unjust Enrichment: Reason, Place and Content" in: Grantham & Rickett, eds, *Structure and Justification, supra* note 172, 5.

[186] Grantham & Rickett, "Disgorgement for Unjust Enrichment?", *supra* note 118 at 734.

[187] *Ibid* at 748.

[188] Peter Watts, "Birks and Proprietary Claims, with Special Reference to Misrepresentation and to Ultra Vires Contracts" in: Grantham & Rickett, eds, *Structure and Justification, supra* note 172, 361 at 365.

[189] Virgo, *Restitution, supra* note 11 at 7.

[190] Birke Häcker, "Proprietary Restitution After Impaired Consent Transfers: A Generalised Power Model" (2009) 68:2 CLJ 324. See also Birke Häcker, *Consequences of Impaired Consent Transfers: A Structural Comparison of English and German Law* (Studien zum ausländischen und internationalen Privatrecht, Tübingen: Mohr Siebeck, 2009).

because the defendant can then no longer be said to be unjustly enriched.[191] Häcker's theory is not a generalized theory of proprietary restitution; rather, it is only meant to explain failed transfer cases.

### *V. The Principled Approach*

The "principled approach," elaborated by Oosterhoff and others, is a formalist-doctrinal approach to proprietary restitution. It distinguishes between the two types of constructive trusts: first, there are cases where there is a direct link between the claimant's loss and the defendants gain; this is "subtractive unjust enrichment." The second category encompasses cases where the direct link is lacking, and the constructive trust is a disgorgement of the defendant's gain that she acquired through her wrongdoing.[192] They note that in the latter case it may be more appropriate to speak of restitution not as a response to unjust enrichment but as a response to wrongdoing. If restitution does not respond to subtractive unjust enrichment, it may be more appropriate to speak of disgorgement only and to banish the term "restitution" for those cases.[193]

In explaining when a constructive trust arises, the principled approach starts with the premise that a constructive trust is only possible when the defendant holds an asset to which the trust can attach.[194] This must be logically true. In the next step, for the recognition of a constructive trust this approach requires that the asset constitute the unjust enrichment the defendant received.[195] Thus, a constructive trust cannot be recognized for a service, unless the service creates the asset.[196] This approach limits the constructive trust to cases where the right to restitution arose before the defendant received full beneficial ownership of the asset.[197] Supposedly, this means full beneficial ownership aside from any equitable interest *by the claimant.*[198] If the unjust enrichment is based upon a conveyance of an asset which is not void *ab initio,* but which becomes

---

[191] Häcker, "Proprietary Restitution After Impaired Consent Transfers", preceding note at 346–47.

[192] Albert H Oosterhoff *et al, Oosterhoff on Trusts,* 7th edn (Toronto: Carswell, 2009) at 728.

[193] Cf. Mitchell McInnes, "The Measure of Restitution" (2002) 52 UTLJ 163; Oosterhoff *et al,* preceding note at 729–30; Lionel D Smith, "The Province of the Law of Restitution" (1992) 71 Can Bar Rev 672. For an example in a judicial decision where the term "disgorgement" is used in that sense see *Heward v Eli Lilly & Company* (2008), 295 DLR (4th) 175 (Ont Sup Ct J).

[194] Oosterhoff *et al, supra* note 192 at 796.

[195] Robert Chambers, "Constructive Trusts in Canada" (1999) 37 Alta L Rev 173 at 199; Oosterhoff *et al, supra* note 192 at 796–97.

[196] Oosterhoff *et al, supra* note 192 at 797.

[197] Chambers, "Constructive Trusts in Canada", *supra* note 195 at 219; Oosterhoff *et al, supra* note 192 at 797.

[198] This derives from Oosterhoff *et al, supra* note 192 at 797 last paragraph.

void for failure to meet a condition subsequent,[199] then the imposition of a constructive trust should depend on whether or not the claimant intended to transfer full title to the defendant, or whether she intended to retain beneficial ownership. Only in the latter case should a constructive trust be imposed on the asset and its traceable proceeds.[200]

### *VI. The Specific Performance Approach*

The specific performance approach holds that a constructive trust should only be imposed when common law remedies do not grant equal relief.[201] There is support for this view in the Restatement, First, Restitution, claiming that equitable jurisdiction should not be given when the remedies at law are sufficient to grant relief.[202] Canadian law seems to indicate otherwise, but *Sorochan* – the decision cited by Paciocco to support his claim that the constructive trust is available in addition to legal remedies[203] – spoke of the availability of different remedies in general; it was not required that all available remedies were available to the case at hand. In fact, the decision specifically addresses the need to have a test to determine when a constructive trust is inapplicable *in concreto.*[204] Paciocco rejects the specific performance approach because it begs the relevant question:

> "In my view, the adequacy doctrine should be rejected in both family and commercial cases alike. It produces curious and unsatisfactory results. In particular, it begs the very question that needs to be answered: when is it just and appropriate to confer on a plaintiff the priority over the general creditors of the defendant? The answer according to the inadequacy doctrine appears to be 'when that priority is required.'"[205]

### *VII. Inability to Perform Personal Obligation*

This approach imposes a constructive trust when the defendant is unable or obviously unwilling to perform the personal obligation. This approach has been

---

[199] Cf. *Twinsectra Ltd v Yardley,* [2002] UKHL 12 and *Quistclose Investment, supra* note 146.

[200] Oosterhoff *et al, supra* note 192 at 797–98.

[201] See Malcolm Cope, *Constructive Trusts* (North Ryde, NSW: Law Book, 1992) at 487.

[202] American Law Institute, *Restatement of the Law, Third, Restitution, Draft No. 6* (Philadelphia: American Law Institute, 2008) at § 166, comment c.

[203] Paciocco, *supra* note 4 at 417.

[204] *Sorochan, supra* note 7 at 47, Dickson CJC: "Other remedies, such as monetary damages, may also be available to rectify situations of unjust enrichment. We must, therefore, ask when and under what circumstances it is appropriate for a court to impose a constructive trust."

[205] Paciocco, *supra* note 4 at 339 [references ommitted].

applied in Canadian case law in cases such as *Peter v Beblow* and *Zaidan Group Ltd v London (City).*[206]

*VIII. Summary*

In summary, there are a variety of explanations for the constructive trust. Some explanations are not principled in the sense that they make proprietary restitution dependent on the specifics of the claimant-defendant relationship without taking into account why the claimant should be given a better right in the property than the defendant's other creditors. This is the shortcoming of the last two theories. Other theories can account for specific instances of proprietary restitution, but without further generalization cannot account for all instances; admittedly, this is not their ambition. Such theories include the unjust enrichment model, the proprietary restitution model, and the generalized power model. The principled approach finally acknowledges that it itself is not one general theory of proprietary restitution; rather it gives two accounts for but two types of proprietary restitution. Before I submit my own theory of proprietary restitution, there are a number of phenomena that I want to look at first. The first concerns the persistence of property rights surviving a change in claimant, defendant, or property. This will be the topic of the next two sections, which follow a structure similar to the first two sections of this chapter: first, the black-letter law is described in the next section, and then theories are given in the section after the next section. The second phenomenon is the admission of proprietary restitution in cases of retention of title – or more plainly: the question whether a thief is liable in proprietary restitution. This is the topic of section E.

## C. Persistence of Rights

There are three ways in which a property right survives change: subrogation, following, and tracing. Each one responds to a different type of change. "Subrogation" covers cases of a change of claimant, "following" a change of defendant, "tracing" a change of property.

---

[206] (1987), 36 DLR (4th) 443 (Ont HCJ).

*I. Subrogation*

In its general sense "subrogation" means that the claimant is assigned the rights of another party.[207] Apart from contractual subrogation, there is also the remedy of subrogation for unjust enrichment.[208] The claimant can be assigned proprietary rights as well as personal rights.[209] In *Banque Financière de la Cité v Parc (Battersea) et al*[210], the plaintiff advanced an unsecured loan to Parc. Parc used the loan to pay off a first-ranking secured loan. The defendant was a secured party of the second rank. When Parc became insolvent, the plaintiff claimed to be subrogated to the rights of the first lender. Their Lordships held that the claimants were indeed subrogated to the right of the first chargee, thus giving them priority against the defendant. This was justified because otherwise the defendant would have been unjustly enriched at the expense of the claimants. If the plaintiff had been subrogated *vis-à-vis* the entire world, this would have given them the benefit of a first charge, which would have placed them in a better position than they had bargained for; they never thought that they had a charge against Parc which would give them security against all Parc's creditors.[211] Thus, the subrogation was relative only, only taking effect between plaintiff and defendant, not against other secured or unsecured creditors.[212]

*Banque Financière de la Cité v Parc (Battersea) et al* stands for the proposition subrogation occurs where it is appropriate to reverse the creditor's unjust enrichment. Watterson argues that subrogation can be explained by what he calls the "liability model," as opposed to the "orthodox model". In the orthodox model, the claimant immediately acquires rights.[213] In the liability model, the claimant

"does not immediately acquire rights which are equitable replicas of X creditor's extinguished rights, as subrogation-justifying facts occur. Instead, those legally significant facts merely trigger a liability on D and relevant others to be subjected by subsequent court order to legal relations equivalent to those which previously existed, if this is needed to reverse

[207] Virgo, *Restitution, supra* note 11 at 20; Stephen Watterson, "Modelling Subrogation as an 'Equitable Remedy'" (2016) 2:2 CJCCL 609 at 611–12.

[208] *Banque Financière de la Cité v Parc (Battersea) et al* (1998), [1999] 1 AC 221 at 231–32 (HL), Lord Hoffmann. See also *Eileen Joan Rosina Filby v Mortgage Express (No 2) Ltd,* [2004] EWCA Civ 759.

[209] Andrew S Burrows, *The Law of Restitution,* 3rd edn (Oxford: Oxford University Press, 2010) at 147 [Burrows, *Restitution*].

[210] *Supra* note 208.

[211] Burrows, *Restitution, supra* note 209 at 154.

[212] *Banque Financière de la Cité v Parc (Battersea) et al, supra* note 208 at 237, Lord Hoffmann.

[213] Watterson, *supra* note 207 at 634.

their unjust enrichment (and a concomitant entitlement in C to bring proceedings to obtain such relief)."[214]

### *II. Following*

Following property is the process by which the claimant asserts that she continues to hold a property right in the same item of property that is now being held by a different party. Following is thus important when the claimant wants to assert a legal right in property. But because legal property rights only give rise to personal claims, the claimant might want to follow an equitable right. According to the rule in *Barnes v Addy,*[215] a third-party recipient of trust property becomes herself a constructive trustee.[216] The judgment offered three cases in which somebody becomes a constructive trustee:[217]

(1) A trustee de son tort
(2) Knowing assistance to the breach of trust
(3) Knowing receipt of trust property

Where the defendant is a *bona fide* purchaser for value without notice, this extinguishes the beneficiaries claim.[218] Constructive notice is sufficient.[219] Knowing receipt will trigger two different responses: personal liability or the imposition of a constructive trust.[220] For the purpose of this work, we can focus on the proprietary claim.

Following equitable property rights can be explained in two ways. Either, the claimant has a persistent right in the property good against everybody, or there is a chain of equitable rights, each one arising anew every time property and legal title to it passes from one person to the next.[221] The latter was Maitland's view.[222] The causative event giving rise to the new equitable property right can be described as one of unjust enrichment.[223]

---

[214] *Ibid* at 635.

[215] (1874), 9 LR Ch App 244.

[216] On the application of this case in Canadian courts see Michael Bryan, "The Receipt-Based Constructive Trust: A Case Study of Personal and Proprietary Restitution in the Supreme Court" (1999) 37 Alta L Rev 73.

[217] *Barnes v Addy, supra* note 215 at 251–52, Selborne, LC.

[218] See *Lennox Industries (Canada) Ltd v The Queen* (1987), 34 DLR (4th) 297 (Fed TD).

[219] *Twinsectra Ltd v Yardley, supra* note 199 at para 105, Lord Millet.

[220] See also *Westdeutsche Landesbank, supra* note 69 at 707–8, Lord Browne-Wilkinson; Bryan, *supra* note 216 at 89; David Salmons, "Claims Against Third-Party Recipients of Trust Property" (2017) 76:2 CLJ 399 at 401. For a discussion on the knowing receipt framework in England, Australia, and Canada compared see Mark Leeming, "The Comparative Distinctiveness of Equity" (2016) 2:2 CJCCL 403 at 412–15.

[221] Becker, *supra* note 125 at 39.

[222] John H Langbein, "The Contractarian Basis of the Law of Trusts" (1995) 105 Yale LJ 625 at 647–48. See Part II: § 8 E, "Theory of Equitable Property Rights".

[223] Lionel D Smith, "Unravelling Proprietary Restitution" (2004) 40:3 CBLJ 317 at 326.

While mostly focussing on the personal claim, Chambers draws parallels between the constructive trustee in a knowing receipt situation and the position of the possessor *vis-à-vis* the holder of the legal title. He argues that the knowing recipient is a trustee because anyone other than a *bona fide* purchaser who holds assets transferred to them in breach of trust is subject to a duty to "preserve those assets and restore them to the proper persons."[224] Knowing receipt in this sense is thus the vindication of the equitable interest enjoyed by the beneficiary, just like the legal remedies for wrongful interference vindicate the interference with the possessory legal title. With reference to cases on bailment, Chambers argues that the knowing recipient is akin to the deemed bailee of chattel. Just like a bailee owes duty to the owner of the property, so does the knowing recipient owe duties to the constructive trustee.[225] A similar argument was made by Smith, who wrote that "[i]t appears that the best view of knowing receipt is that it is equity's analogue to the common law's claim in conversion".[226] This again underscores that equity performs a function akin to legal rights, with the difference that it is concerned with value, not possession. Equitable ownership is about value, legal ownership about control or possession. But that also means that equity, while originally developed in relation to tangibles, is much better equipped to handle ownership of incorporeal property.

Salmons argues that the claim against the knowing recipient is not a continuation of the right against the original trustee but rather, it is a new right created by the recipient's wrongdoing; further, keeping the right against the original trustee and the knowing recipient conceptually separate, he argues, is an expression of a principle of equitable property rights, which require that the beneficiary primarily assert a right against the trustee, who in turn can pursue third parties, not against third parties directly.[227] In relation to this argument, two things can be said. First, rather than saying that the wrongdoing provides a reason for the creation of a new property right,[228] one could argue that is the reason why the original property right has not been extinguished. Second, Salmons' argument based on an equitable principle of pursuing the trustee primarily[229] begs the real question. If the claimant has a proprietary claim against the recipient of trust property, that recipient has become the trustee. The real enquiry should be if there is a normative justification for making the third party a constructive trustee. Salmons somehow suggests that the proprietary claim against the recipient is a *sui generis* equitable claim. But it is not, it is a claim

---

[224] Robert Chambers, "The End of Knowing Receipt" (2016) 2:1 CJCCL 1 at 7–8.

[225] *Ibid* at 8–9.

[226] Lionel D Smith, "W(h)ither Knowing Receipt" (1998) 114:3 LQR 394, in a note discussing the judgment in *Citadel General Assurance Co v Lloyds Bank Canada,* [1997] 3 SCR 805.

[227] Salmons, *supra* note 220 at 407–9.

[228] *Ibid* at 407.

[229] *Ibid* at 409.

brought by the beneficiary of a constructive trust against the constructive trustee. At the end of the day the only equitable property right is is the trust.

## *III. Tracing*

### *1. The Basic Rules*

Tracing is the procedure by which it is determined whether property is legally the substitute for other property.[230] Tracing in itself does not establish a claim. In other words, the exercise of tracing is only used to establish that one item of property has replaced another; it does not establish the claimant's claim in either the traced property or the substitute.[231] It is important to note that it is the property's value that is being traced.[232]

Traditionally, tracing requires a clean substitution. If the claimant alleges a right in certain coins or bills and a rogue uses these coins or bills to purchase something, the claimant can trace her right into the purchased item. But her claim would fail when the defendant mixed the hard money with other monies.[233] While the Court of King's Bench in *Taylor v Plumer* was concerned with tracing an equitable property right,[234] the case now stands for the proposition that tracing at common law is concerned with clean substitution only; where money or other property becomes part of a mixed fund, tracing a legal title will not succeed.[235] While tracing through clean substitutions sounds like it is limited in scope, one example of a clean substitution is money drawn from a bank account. The money is a traceable proceed of a chose in action: the account holder holds title to the indebtedness of the bank, which is a chose in action.[236]

### *2. Tracing Through Mixed Funds*

A distinction is often made between tracing in equity and tracing at law. Unlike common law tracing, equitable tracing allows tracing property into and through

---

[230] Burrows, "The English Law of Restitution", *supra* note 1 at 30–31; Burrows, *Restitution, supra* note 209 at 117.

[231] Smith, *The Law of Tracing, supra* note 139 at 11–14.

[232] Robert Chambers, "Tracing and Unjust Enrichment" in: Neyers, McInnes & Pitel, eds, *Understanding Unjust Enrichment, supra* note 1, 263 at 263.

[233] *Taylor v Plumer* (1815), 105 ER 721 (KB); Burrows, *Restitution, supra* note 209 at 123–24.

[234] See *Jones & Sons (Trustee) v Jones* (1996), [1997] Ch 159 at 169 (CA Civ), Millet LJ, referring to Lionel D Smith, "Tracing in Taylor v Plumer: Equity in the Court of King's Bench" [1995] LMCLQ 240. See also Smith, *The Law of Tracing, supra* note 139 at 168–69.

[235] Burrows, *Restitution, supra* note 209 at 124.

[236] *Lipkin Gorman v Karpnale Ltd, supra* note 85; Burrows, *Restitution, supra* note 209 at 129–30.

mixed funds.[237] Where the rogue obtains $100 and mixes it with her own funds, tracing into the mixed fund allows the claimant to follow her right into the mixed fund. When the rogue then uses the mixed fund to buy a horse, the tracing allows the claimant to follow her right into the horse, potentially establishing a *pro rata* property right in the horse. The distinction between tracing at law and in equity requires that the claimant must have had an equitable right in the traced property in order for equitable tracing to take place.[238]

I should note that Smith makes a strong argument that the rules of tracing at law and in equity are not different, but the same; the difference only manifests itself at the level of the claims available to remedy an equitable right or a legal right. The gist of the argument is the simple observation that tracing is an exercise determining facts, not rights and remedies.[239] There is undeniable force in this argument; however, for the purpose of this chapter, the debate is not relevant. I have come to the conclusion that the range of remedies available to the holder of a property right *at law* is deficient. Thus, I concern myself with the remedies available to the holder of an equitable right. Because the argument is that the more generous rules of tracing available in equity should apply at law, and not vice versa, whether or not there is a unitary law of tracing has no bearing on claims based on equitable rights.

Burrows argues that the inability to trace a legal property right through mixed funds presents a particular challenge where the the defendant has acquired the property from the claimant by way of theft. He argues that a thief acquires no legal title to stolen property, thus equitable tracing should not be possible, which he considers to be absurd and contrary to *obiter* authority.[240] I will look at this argument in more detail in the next section.[241] At the moment, I suffices to say that the argument that the thief has no title at all is at best

---

[237] *Agip (Africa) v Jackson* (1990), [1991] Ch 547 at 566 (CA Civ), Fox LJ; *Re Diplock,* [1948] Ch 465 at 520 (CA), Lord Greene MR. On the rules of equitable tracing into mixed funds see also Burrows, *Restitution, supra* note 209 at 133–1436 and Smith, *The Law of Tracing, supra* note 139 at 169–242.

[238] *Re Diplock,* preceding note at 540, Lord Greene MR, referring to *Sinclair v Brougham, supra* note 72.

[239] Smith, *The Law of Tracing, supra* note 139 passim.

[240] Burrows, *Restitution, supra* note 209 at 132, note 70, referring to *Westdeutsche Landesbank, supra* note 69 at 716, Lord Browne-Wilkinson: "I agree that the stolen moneys are traceable in equity. But the proprietary interest which equity is enforcing in such circumstances arises under a constructive, not a resulting, trust. Although it is difficult to find clear authority for the proposition, when property is obtained by fraud equity imposes a constructive trust on the fraudulent recipient: the property is recoverable and traceable in equity. Thus, an infant who has obtained property by fraud is bound in equity to restore it." [References ommitted].

[241] See Part II: § 10 E, "The Problem of Title".

misleading. As we have seen in the analysis of common law property, the thief does acquire a property right.[242]

### *3. The Multiplication of Property Rights*

One argument against the proprietary view of tracing is the "multiplication" argument. If the claimant's right in the traced property is a function of her property right in the original property right, the claimant who can both follow and trace her property now has two property rights: one in the original property, one in the traced property. In many cases, such as where the property is money and the purchaser of the property is a *bona fide* purchaser for value without notice, the property right in the original property becomes extinguished.[243]

But there are cases where the property right in the original property does not become extinct. If the property is not money, the *nemo dat quod non habet* rule operates and the *bona fide* purchaser of a legal right cannot acquire better title than the claimant. The claimant would then have a property right in the original property and in the substitute found by tracing. The proposed solution is the power of election.[244] The claimant can either assert her interest in the original property, or exercise her power to trace the property, in which case she will lose her right in the original property but turn her inchoate property right in the traced property into a full property right.[245] This resembles the election in conversion, where the payment of damages extinguishes the claimant's property right in the converted goods.[246]

## D. Explaining Tracing

### *I. Tracing in the Unjust Enrichment Model and Property Rights Model*

A number of authors draw a sharp distinction between following and tracing to the effect that while following is concerned with the assertion of a property right, tracing has nothing to do with the pre-existing property right.[247] Birks

---

[242] See Part II: § 5 G.II, "The Case for a Possession-Based Account of Personal Property".

[243] Chambers, "Tracing and Unjust Enrichment", *supra* note 232 at 263.

[244] Lionel D Smith, "Tracing" in: Andrew S Burrows & Alan Rodger, eds, *Mapping the Law: Essays in Memory of Peter Birks* (Oxford: Oxford University Press, 2006) 119 at 121.

[245] Burrows, *Restitution, supra* note 209 at 131. See also Peter Birks, "Mixing and Tracing: Property and Restitution" (1992) 45 Curr Legal Probs 69 at 95.

[246] Burrows, *Restitution, supra* note 209 at 131.

[247] *Ibid* at 121–22, 170; Chambers, "Tracing and Unjust Enrichment", *supra* note 232 at 266.

soundly rejected what he called the "fiction of persistence."[248] His argument goes that it is fictional to say that a claimant is given a right in the item of property that is found by the tracing exercise because she had a property right in the original property; rather, the claimant may be given a new right in the traced property to reverse the defendant's unjust enrichment at the claimant's expense.[249] In this respect tracing differs significantly from entitlement to the fruits of property.[250] This part of legal scholarship argues that unjust enrichment is the principle that explains why the claimant can assert a right in substitute property.[251] The alternative view of persistence argues that either a feature of all property rights is a right to the proceeds of sale of those rights, or that a right to the proceeds of sale of property rights is one of the ways in which those rights are enforced.[252]

*1. The Argument Against Persistence*

The argument against persistence is that a property right cannot be separated from its object and its enforceability against everybody.[253] But expressed this broadly, it is difficult to coherently conceptualize property rights in Common Law. After all, it is accepted that property rights at law are inherently relative.

*2. The Argument Against Property Including a Right to Proceeds*

The argument against viewing the right to the traced property as an incident of the right in the traced property is essentially that it is not a necessary incident.[254] That is akin to saying, "Just because I have ownership of a thing does

[248] Birks, *Unjust Enrichment, supra* note 3 at 36, referring to Andrew S Burrows, "Proprietary Restitution: Unmasking Unjust Enrichment" (2001) 117 LQR 412 [Burrows, "Unmasking"]. See also Birks, "Property, Unjust Enrichment, and Tracing", *supra* note 118 at 244, calling the property righs justification for the right in the substitute property a "leech theory of the behaviour of proprietary rights in and through substitutions. There is one right which, detached from the original *res,* will wait to sink its head in any passing substitute. The right in the [substitute property] is then the same right as the right in the [original property ...]." [Emphasis added].

[249] Burrows, "Unmasking", preceding note at 417–18; Burrows, *Restitution, supra* note 209 at 121–22.

[250] Burrows, "Unmasking", *supra* note 248 at 430: "[T]here is a fundamental difference between, on the one hand, asserting that a person's ownership of a pig carries with it ownership of her piglets; and, on the other hand, asserting that a person's ownership of a pig carries with it ownership of the horse which a defendant has traceably substituted for the pig."

[251] Chambers, "Tracing and Unjust Enrichment", *supra* note 232 at 266.

[252] Cf. *ibid* at 266.

[253] *Ibid* at 273.

[254] *Ibid* at 277. Cf. Lionel D Smith, "Unjust Enrichment, Property and the Structure of Trusts" (2000) 116 LQR 420 at 424–25.

not explain why no-one can take it away from me." Of course it does not. The reason why no-one can take it away is the law's understanding of what a property right should entail. But the argument that "unjust enrichment" is a sufficient reason does nothing to justify the proprietary remedy either.

### *3. The Argument Against Tracing Being a Means of Enforcement*

A third proprietary explanation of the right in traced property is to view the right to the substitute property as a means of enforcing the original property right.[255] This is conceptually similar to viewing it as an incident of the property right.[256] The argument against this view is that the claimant can trace property rights as well as personal rights. But this again confuses object of property and title to property. This argument is based on a narrow understanding of property rights, not allowing the recognition of a property right in choses in action. But choses in action are permissible objects of property even though they themselves are only personal rights. Thus, the right at the start of the tracing exercise is not the personal right; it is the proprietary entitlement to that personal right.

## *II. Challenging Foskett v McKeown*

The unjust enrichment model argues that the property right in substitute property is founded on the unjust enrichment principle. Property is a kind of right, while unjust enrichment is a source of rights.[257] On this basis, the House of Lord's classification of the *Foskett v McKeown* claim as proprietary has been attacked.[258] But this presupposes a rejection of the property rights model that posits that property can be both an event and a reply. From this perspective, Lord Millet was not talking about "property rights" in the sense of a legal response when classifying the claim in *Foskett v McKeown.* The property rights model would argue that he was merely classifying the cause of action as one pertaining to property law. While it might be argued that there is no reason not to consider property law claims that are structurally similar to unjust enrichment claims to be part of the unjust enrichment law, this creates the danger that one starts to broaden these claims and neglects a principled basis for when a property right could be created as a response to an unjust enrichment event.

Another argument against the House of Lord's decision in *Foskett v McKeown* under the unjust enrichment model is that tracing is not restricted to the law of property. Value can be traced into and through personal rights, such as

---

[255] See Grantham & Rickett, "Property and Unjust Enrichment", *supra* note 173 at 680 referring to it as an "indirect enforcement" of a property right [emphasis in original]; Ross Grantham & Charles Rickett, "Tracing and Property Rights: The Categorical Truth" (2000) 63:6 Modern L Rev 905.

[256] Cf. Chambers, "Tracing and Unjust Enrichment", *supra* note 232 at 278.

[257] *Ibid* at 265.

[258] *Ibid* at 265.

a bank account.[259] This is an interesting example. The right I have against the bank is not a property right, but my entitlement to it is a property right because the right is a chose in action. Classified this way, it is hard to envision cases where tracing does not operate on property rights. But the unjust enrichment criticism against *Foskett v McKeown* in this regard can be countered on a more fundamental level. Lord Millet's statement can be understood to mean not that "tracing is part of our law of property," but rather that the right resulting in the tracing exercise that uses a property right as a starting point is part of property law.

*III. Conclusion*

In conclusion, the unjust enrichment model is not the only logically necessary explanation of the claimant's right in the substitute property. Viewing the claimant's right in the substitute property as an incident of the right in the original property is an equally possible rationalization of existing law.

## E. The Problem of Title

In short, the "problem of title" refers to the question whether and how a claimant can make an a restitutionary claim even where she retains title to the property. The straightforward example involves the thief. A significant share of legal doctrine does not view these cases as cases of unjust enrichment because the rogue is not enriched if she does not get title.[260] On the other hand, Lord Browne-Wilkinson stated *obiter* that the thief is a constructive trustee, albeit without basing this in unjust enrichment.[261] My submission in this section is that the unjust enrichment view is correct.

The existence of proprietary restitution has often been listed as the Common Law equivalent of Civil Law vindication.[262]

"However, in the great majority of cases where Anglo-American law creates constructive trusts, the creditor is favored in actual French law in quite a similar manner. If A has transferred an object to B and the transfer is made in pursuance of an invalid legal act (the typical

---

[259] *Ibid* at 265.

[260] See e.g. Robert Chambers, "Trust and Theft" in: Elise Bant & Matthew Harding, eds, *Exploring Private Law* (Cambridge: Cambridge University Press, 2010) 223 at 227. Cf. Fox, *supra* note 89 at 485; William Swadling, "A Claim in Restitution?" [1996] LMCLQ 63; William Swadling, "Ignorance and Unjust Enrichment: The Problem of Title" (2008) 28:4 Oxford J Legal Stud 627. Cf. Robert Stevens, "Three Enrichment Issues" in: Burrows & Rodger, eds, *Mapping the Law, supra* note 244, 49 at 62–64.

[261] *Westdeutsche Landesbank, supra* note 69 at 716, Lord Browne-Wilkinson.

[262] See e.g. Ross Grantham & Charles Rickett, "Property Rights as a Legally Significant Event" (2003) 62:3 CLJ 717 at 736–39 [Grantham & Rickett, "Property as Event"].

situation in Anglo-American constructive trust cases), the French doctrine of causa deprives B of any rights in the object. The legal ownership remains with A; he is entitled as against B – to use the Romanistic term – not only to an obligatory claim of *condictio* but to a real action of *rei vincidatio*. In effect, A has a *droit de suite* and a right of reclamation against B's other creditors, he is in almost the same privileged position as a constructive trustee. Hence, the need of the constructive trust does not exist for French law; it possesses it already, although under another technical name, it is true, and with certain differences in detail."[263]

Curwen argues there is no convincing reason as to why there is no specific recovery remedy at common law but there is in equity.[264] Implicit in his argument is the functional equivalency between the constructive trust as a remedy and the vindication of property. The functional equivalency would not exist if thieves were not liable in a proprietary restitution claim. This in itself is of course not an argument for the existence of proprietary restitution against a rogue. Differences between Civil Law and Common Law are not an argument, but rather descriptive statements. Rather, the question should be whether the persistence of title pre-empts a restitutionary response or not and what is the relationship between this response and the law of unjust enrichment.

The often-made case against an unjust enrichment claim in cases where the claimant retains a legal title (*e.g.* cases of theft) is that the claimant retains title, and this title is better than the title acquired by the rogue.[265] This broad argument actually entails a number of narrower arguments that are a function of the notion of property in Common Law. The first argument is that the retention of better title allows the claimant to avail herself of the common law remedies for wrongful interference with property. The second argument is that the retention of title means that the claimant retains the equitable property right, and thus any restitutionary response does not require any further justification. The third argument is to deny the correlativity between the rogue's enrichment and a deprivation on the claimant's side. In addition to these arguments, Grantham and Ricket put forward an argument against unjust enrichment liability in cases of retention of title based on their structural understanding of unjust enrichment. I look at each argument in turn and defend my submission that the thief can be considered to be a constructive trustee.

---

263 Max Rheinstein, "Traite Theorique Et Pratique Des Trusts by Pierre Lepaulle" (1934) 43:6 Yale LJ 1049 at 1053.

264 Nicholas Curwen, "The Remedy in Conversion: Confusing Property and Obligation" (2006) 26:4 LS 570 at 578.

265 See e.g. Chambers, "Trust and Theft", *supra* note 260 at 227. Cf. Fox, *supra* note 89 at 485; Swadling, "A Claim in Restitution?", *supra* note 260; Swadling, "Ignorance and Unjust Enrichment", *supra* note 260. Cf. Stevens, "Three Enrichment Issues", *supra* note 260 at 62–64.

### I. Common Law Remedies for the Recovery of Personal Property

The first argument mentioned above is that a claimant who retains title to the property acquired by a rogue can avail herself of the arsenal of claims available at law.[266] The obvious problem with this argument is that in that case, the claimant who did not lose legal title would be worse off than the claimant who lost it. This is a function of the shortcoming of the remedies available at law. There are two main potential common law remedies. The common law claim in conversion is not necessarily *in specie* restitution. A non-proprietary restitution claim for money had and received will also only give a claim for damages, not a proprietary claim for the thing.

#### 1. Conversion

If the rogue has received a $100 bill, the claimant can sue for conversion. But it is possible that a claim for proprietary restitution or unjust enrichment is more advantageous for the claimant when compared with a claim in conversion.[267] On one level, this might depend on the availability of defences. Where a defendant can defeat a tort claim but not an unjust enrichment claim, it might be better to bring the unjust enrichment claim. But more importantly, there is no action at law whereby the claimant will regain the property as a matter of right. Such an action will be for damages. In other words, the title retained by the claimant is defeasible, or at least it would be unless we recognized that she has a right for proprietary restitution. This would obviously be more important where the property is not money because presupposing a solvent debtor, a claim for a $100 bill or a claim for damages amounting to $100 is of equal value to the claimant.[268]

The common law regarding the vindication of personal property is deficient in three regards. First, as seen above, the common law does not contain an action for the specific recovery of chattel. Furthermore, while specific performance of a legal obligation is a remedy available in equity, it is rarely applied

---

[266] See e.g. Chambers, "Tracing and Unjust Enrichment", *supra* note 232 at 291. On the protection of property through common law torts see Part II: § 5 F.I, "Common Law Torts for Wrongful Interference".

[267] Stevens, "Three Enrichment Issues", *supra* note 260 at 63.

[268] William M Cheyne, *Is the Thief a Trustee?: Principled Approaches to Proprietary Restitutionary Remedies* (University of Otago) <http://www.otago.ac.nz/law/research/journals/otago043955.pdf> accessed 6 November 2017 at 31 argues that outside insolvency, proprietary restitution of specific property is not necessary because the claimant can demand specific recovery at law, but of course this is a matter of discretion. The point is that there is no right at law.

in cases of chattel recovery.[269] Second, protection of property is based on interference with possession, not with an abstract interest.[270] Third, personal property torts are not available regarding all types of personal property.[271]

*2. Money Had and Received*

Apart from bringing an action based on a common law tort, the claimant can also bring a personal unjust enrichment claim for money had and received. *Lipkin Gorman v Karpnale Ltd* was one such case.[272] Another potential such case of this nature was *Jones & Sons (Trustee) v Jones*[273]. In this case, Mr. Jones transferred £11 000 from the account of the plaintiff to the defendant, Mrs. Jones. She speculated with that money and multiplied it, then deposited her gains in a bank account opened for the purpose. When the plaintiff went bankrupt, its trustee demanded that the bank pay out the proceeds to him. But this case can be analysed as not being about unjust enrichment, but as being a dispute about entitlement to a chose in action.[274] Because the bank was solvent, the question whether the claim was proprietary or personal did not arise.

The option of pursuing a restitutionary claim rather than a common law tort has been long established.[275] In *Clarke v Shee and Johnson,*[276] Lord Mansfield CJ found that a third party who receives money to which the plaintiff has a legal title is liable in an action for money had and received. Briefly summarized, the facts of *Clarke v Shee and Johnson* involve Clarke, his employee Wood, and Shee. Wood misappropriated monies collected for Clarke and entered into a betting contract with Shee on the outcome of a state lottery. The statute establishing the lottery voided betting contracts outside the lottery scheme. Shee was thus not a purchaser for value. In such cases, the claimant's retention of title can be seen as the reason for the unjustness of the enrichment, thus triggering the personal restitutionary response.[277]

In the earlier law, the advantage of the money had and received claim over conversion was that the claimant did not have to allege an act of conversion.[278] Furthermore, the claimant did not have to rely on a right in specific coins or

---

[269] Edward Jenks, "A Blind Spot in English Law" (1933) 49 LQR 215 at 217, note 4.

[270] See Part II: § 5 G.II, "The Case for a Possession-Based Account of Personal Property".

[271] See Part II: § 5 F.I.3.b)cc), "Property Subject to Conversion".

[272] See Part II: § 10 A.II.2.a), "Lipkin v Gorman".

[273] *Supra* note 234.

[274] See Peter Millett, "Jones V Jones: Property or Unjust Enrichment" in: Burrows & Rodger, eds, *Mapping the Law, supra* note 244, 265.

[275] Other cases include *Holiday v Sigil* (1826), 172 ER 81 (KB).

[276] (1774), 1 Cowp 197, 98 ER 1041 (KB).

[277] Fox, *supra* note 89 at 484.

[278] *Ibid* at 469–70.

bills, but could allege an entitlement in a fund.[279] The latter factor is less important if one considers choses in action to be capable of being converted, but it was important where the property that was being protected was physical.

Fox comes to the conclusion that *Lipkin Gorman v Karpnale Ltd* can be seen as a case of property rights vindication.[280] Grantham and Rickett argue that money had and received claims must be categorized as pure vindication actions, wholly separate from the unjust enrichment principle.[281] But the objection to this is that if they were, there would be no reason why the remedy should be purely personal. Grantham and Rickett come to that conclusion because they deny that unjust enrichment ever succeeds where the claimant can still assert her property right,[282] but there is no compelling reason why a claimant cannot have both a claim for vindication and a claim for unjust enrichment and for there thus to be a concurrent liability. In essence, they argue that the property right can be vindicated without any reference to unjust enrichment at all, and that English law operates on a principle of subsidiarity whereby unjust enrichment is limited as a subsidiary cause of action if everything else fails.[283]

### *II. Retention of Equitable Title*

The second argument against viewing the thief as a constructive trustee on the basis of their unjust enrichment is to say that the claimant always retains an equitable right and thus there is no deprivation.[284] This argument runs into the obstacle that the equitable right does not exist unless somebody else has legal title. In other words, the claimant has no equitable right she can retain. This point is expressed clearly by Lord Browne-Wilkinson in *Westdeutsche Landesbank.*

> "A person solely entitled to the full beneficial ownership of money of property, both at law and in equity, does not enjoy an equitable interest in that property. The legal title carries with it all rights. Unless and until there is a separation of the legal and equitable estates, there is no separate equitable title. Therefore to talk about the bank 'retaining' its equitable interest is meaningless. The only question is whether the circumstances under which the money was paid were such as, in equity, to impose a trust on the local authority. If so, an equitable interest arose for the first time under that trust."[285]

But this does not mean that no equitable right can arise – rather than be retained – for the benefit of the claimant where somebody else establishes a possessory

---

[279] *Ibid* at 470.

[280] See *ibid* at 491.

[281] Grantham & Rickett, "Property and Unjust Enrichment", *supra* note 173 at 678.

[282] *Ibid* at 682.

[283] Grantham & Rickett, "Property as Event", *supra* note 262 at 741–44.

[284] See e.g. Peter Birks, "Property and Unjust Enrichment: Categorical Truths" [1997] NZL Rev 623 at 629.

[285] *Westdeutsche Landesbank, supra* note 69 at 706, Lord Browne-Wilkinson.

title to the property. Lord Browne-Wilkinson was evidently talking about cases where there is only one legal title to property. In those cases, no equitable right can exist.

The case is different where a rogue has obtained property. Notwithstanding the legal title still held by the claimaint, the rogue does receive a title to the property, albeit one inferior to the legal right held by the claimant. Thus, the retention of title by the claimant would only prevent the trusteeship of the defendant if the defendant's right could not be held in trust.[286] But in fact this right that can be held in trust.[287] Furthermore, it is important to note that the thief of movable property arguably has a better right to possession than the claimant because the claimant has no means of being restored in possession as a matter of common law.

### *III. No Correspondence Between Enrichment and Deprivation*

The third argument is to say that the defendant's enrichment consists of a title that is inferior to the title held by the claimant.[288] Thus it cannot be said that the defendant has gained something *at the expense of* the claimant.[289] We sometimes even encounter the claim that this is the position of Civilian systems: where the claimant retains title, the conditions of an unjust enrichment claim are not present.[290] This is not true. In German law, the dispossessed owner can bring a personal unjust enrichment claim or a proprietary vindication claim.[291] It is true that in German law, the owner's claims for use and fruits against the possessor without a right to possession are subject to a special regime, which

---

[286] This argument is made by Susan Barkehall Thomas, "Thieves, Owners and the Problem of Title (I): Chattel" (2011) 5 J Equ 46 and Susan Barkehall Thomas, "Thieves, Owners and the Problem of Title (II): Money" (2012) 6 J Equ 33.

[287] John Tarrant, "Thieves as Trustees: In Defence of the Theft Principle" (2009) 3 J Equ 170. See also Chambers, "Trust and Theft", *supra* note 260 at 228–30.

[288] Chambers, "Trust and Theft", *supra* note 260 at 232.

[289] Swadling, "Ignorance and Unjust Enrichment", *supra* note 260 at 650–51.

[290] Cf. Smith, "Tracing", *supra* note 244 at 132: "If the defendant is in possession of something that belongs to the claimant, this in itself does not generate a claim in unjust enrichment; enrichment is legally prevented."

[291] See Karl-Heinz Gursky in: Julius von Staudinger, *Kommentar zum Bürgerlichen Gesetzbuch mit Einführungsgesetz und Nebengesetzen, Buch 3. Sachenrecht, §§ 985–1011,* ed by Karl-Heinz Gursky (Berlin: Sellier-de Gruyter, 2012) Vorbemerkungen zu §§ 985–1007 BGB at para 8 and Stefan Lorenz in: Julius von Staudinger, *Kommentar zum Bürgerlichen Gesetzbuch mit Einführungsgesetz und Nebengesetzen, Buch 2. Recht der Schuldverhältnisse, §§ 812 - 822 (Ungerechtfertigte Bereicherung),* ed by Norbert Horn (Berlin: Sellier-de Gruyter, 2007) § 812 BGB at para 73.

displaces the general unjust enrichment law and is found alongside to the vindicatory action.[292] But importantly, these are still personal claims[293] and they are easily understood as particular unjust enrichment claims protecting a certain class of possessors based on their degree of good faith.[294] What is important to take away from this is that the general statement that Civilian systems deny that the factual conditions for an unjust enrichment claim are met when the claimant retains ownership is not true. Whether or not the unjust enrichment claim with regard to the property is subsidiary to a vindication claim is another question.[295]

Taking the retention of title argument in Common Law further is the argument that denies that the possession gained by the defendant constitutes an enrichment because her right to possession is inferior to the claimant.[296] This argument recognizes that the defendant has gained something, but deny its value. But this argument is circular. The rogue's interest to possession can hardly be said to be inferior in all but name unless the claimant has a right to *in specie* restitution of the property, which can only be provided as of law by proprietary restitution for the unjust enrichment of the rogue. The mere fact that the defendant's inferior right allows the claimant to avail herself of certain personal actions is not an argument against a proprietary claim.[297]

In a third variety, the title-based claim is said to differ because the enrichment of the defendant is not causally linked to the claimant's deprivation. Instead, title replaces the causality link. Tracing is said to show not a causal link, rather but a title link between claimant and defendant.[298] However, tracing shows that the value lost by the claimant is the one received by the defendant. Granted, tracing is no intent-based causality, but it does demonstrate a link between value lost and value received. Thus, the argument is based on the

[292] Karl-Heinz Gursky in: von Staudinger, preceding note, Vorbemerkungen zu §§ 987–993 BGB at paras 43–63.

[293] *Ibid* at para 36.

[294] Lionel D Smith, "Property, Subsidiarity and Unjust Enrichment" in: David Johnston & Reinhard Zimmermann, eds, *Unjustified Enrichment: Key Issues in Comparative Perspective* (Cambridge: Cambridge University Press, 2002) 588 at 594 hints at a similar analysis of German law.

[295] See Part II: § 9 A.I, "Québec Law of Unjustified Enrichment".

[296] Chambers, "Trust and Theft", *supra* note 260 at 234–35.

[297] A similar point is made by Fox, *supra* note 89 at 488: "It is alien to the security of property interests that the conduct of a person who receives the plaintiff's asset should affect the plaintiff's right to enforce his property in it. It is in the nature of a proprietary interest that it should remain enforceable against persons generally, provided the conditions for its continuing survival are fulfilled."

[298] Smith, "Unjust Enrichment, Property and the Structure of Trusts", *supra* note 254 at 417–21. It should be noted that Smith does eventually concede that title-based claims are based in unjust enrichment.

premise that the link between deprivation and enrichment is one of intent at every stage. This is not self-evident.

*IV. Grantham and Rickett's Argument*

Grantham and Rickett's argument against an unjust enrichment claim where the claimant has retained title is that retention of title will rarely constitute an unjust factor.[299] Of course, this requires one to reject the no-basis approach to unjust enrichment law. The validity of this argument has thus become doubtful in England; it can be rejected for Canadian law.

*V. Conclusion*

In conclusion, the better view is to the thieve's role as constructive trustee as being a response to their unjust enrichment. Doing so illuminates an important point of the relationship between unjust enrichment and property law. Unjust enrichment and the persistence of a property right do not have to be mutually exclusive. Birks argued that unjust enrichment and property law relate to each other by way of an event-response relationship.[300] But Birks' model still had problems explaining the proprietary remedy in cases where the title continued. Birks argued that in cases where the claimant retains title, but the defendant is in possession of the property, the claimant who elects to bring a claim in unjust enrichment elects to extinguish her legal right, thus allowing an equitable right to exist.[301] But this is an unnecessary fiction if one accepts that unjust enrichment can operate on more than just the best title. In fact it can operate on any property right, including possession-based rights such as the ones enjoyed by the rogue.

## F. Analysis of Proprietary Restitution

In the preceding sections, I have looked at proprietary restitutions. The first two sections were concerned with proprietary restitution and an internal account for it. Before submitting my own theory of proprietary restitution, I have looked at particular questions related to proprietary restitution: rights in relation to traced property and the problem of title. The claim made in this section is that proprietary restitution cannot be explained by unjust enrichment alone; rather, there is link between property rights and proprietary restitution as the respone. This holds true despite the fact that some situtations of proprietary

---

[299] Grantham & Rickett, "Property and Unjust Enrichment", *supra* note 173 at 682.

[300] See Birks, *Unjust Enrichment, supra* note 3 at 37–38; Smith, "Tracing", *supra* note 244 at 120. See also Part II: § 10 B.II.1, "Event and Response".

[301] Birks, *Unjust Enrichment, supra* note 3 at 66–69.

restitution, such as the restitution due from the thief to the original owner, were described as unjust enrichment in the preceding section.

### *I. Formalist Accounts of Unjust Enrichment and Proprietary Restitution*

Linking proprietary restitution to a pre-existing property right helps to overcome a problem in the formalist account of unjust enrichment. Weinrib's corrective justice account of unjust enrichment appears to exclude proprietary restitution or at least place it squarely outside unjust enrichment. For him, unjust enrichment is about value entitlement, and value entitlement is necessarily personal.

> "Ownership of the thing of value involves a relationship between the transferee and the rest of the world; the claim to the value independently of the thing of value involves a relationship between the transferee and the transferor. The bilaterality of the transfer endows the value with a juridical significance that is separate from the one it has as an incident of a thing of value."[302]

Property law, on the other hand, is based on the view of property law as the law in objects of property. Vindication is an elemental building block of a law in things because it keeps the relationship between proprietor and property intact. But as we have seen when discusing whether equitable rights are property rights, it is possible to recognize equitable rights as property rights in a two-track approach: legal rights relate to possession, equitable rights relate to value, and this value can sometimes be value that relates to a specific item, such was when the value is the value represented by the the item of a specific corporeal item of property.[303] Once one recognizes this, one can add that economic theory of property stresses the need for certainty and persistence of this relationship.

### *II. Doctrinal Reasons for a Principled Approach*

There is a doctrinal reason for grounding proprietary restitution in something more than unjust enrichment alone. First, proprietary restutiton completes the common law property law. Because of the common law's conservatism regarding changes in the form of property rights, it is the proprietary restitution that to vindicate personal property. The vendor-purchaser constructive trust can serve as an example of this. In common law, transfer of property is transfer of title. Title passes by consent alone. However, the transfer of title does not give an absolute remedy for the vindication of the transferred property. Tort actions do not give a remedy for specific restitution of the item as a matter of course. They would also not avail against a second buyer (subject to the conditions of

---

[302] Ernest J Weinrib, "Correctively Unjust Enrichment" in: Chambers, Mitchell & Penner, eds, *Philosophical Foundations of the Law of Unjust Enrichment, supra* note 114, 31 at 38.

[303] See Part II: § 8 E, "Theory of Equitable Property Rights".

s 25 *Sale of Goods Act 1979*[304] or its equivalents). The vendor-purchaser constructive trust fills this gap. It gives meaning to the "transfer of property" in giving the buyer a true ownership-like right to vindicate the purchased property. Unlike specific performance, it is robust in insolvency.

On the other hand, linking proprietary restitution to a vindication of property rights helps addressing the uncertainty brought into Canadian personal property law by *Dominion Coal Co v Lord Strathcona Steamship Co.*[305] A *numerus clausus* principle is desirable and continuing down the *Strathcona* road (*i.e.* every purchaser with notice of a fanciful covenant is a constructive trustee) is not desirable.

A principled approach minimizes the risk of the constructive trust becomeing purely discretionary with no predictability. Waters warns that before

> "unjust enrichment may ultimately become an apex principle in Canada for a restitution structure that employs discretionary remedy for all apparent unjust enrichment situations, [...] there is reason to consider when such a step should be taken."[306]

### *III. Shortcomings of the Unjust Enrichment Account*

The unjust enrichment principle justifies restitution. If one accepts the premise that one should not be enriched at the expense of the other without there being a reason for it (or with the presence of an unjust factor), restitution follows in certain circumstances. However, unjust enrichment does not give a reason for *in species* or proprietary restitution. Neither unjust enrichment nor property can explain proprietary restitution on its own. I will explain this more in the following sub-section.

### *IV. Compatibility of Proprietary Restitution with Unjust Enrichment Law*

#### *1. Subsidiarity*

I submit that proprietary restitution in English and Canadian law can be understood as a form of "unjust enrichment plus."[307] They are not mutually exclusive because they are two distinct areas of legal events. This is also Virgo's view. Nor are they mutually exclusive because one is only ever an event, the other is only ever a response. Rather, both are events which, when combined, trigger proprietary restitution. Proprietary restitution is a reply to an unjust enrichment with a little extra. This little extra is the fact that the defendant has something to which the claimant is entitled. Unjust enrichment and property are thus not mutually exclusive.

---

[304] 1979, c 54.

[305] (1925), [1926] AC 108 (Can PC).

[306] Waters, "Reconciling", *supra* note 7 at 9.

[307] This appears to be approach adopted by Craig Rotherham, "Tracing Misconceptions in Foskett v McKeown" [2003] RLR 57 at 62.

Smith points out that the subsidiarity of unjust enrichment claims to a vindication action in German law can be explained by the fact that the vindication action itself can be understood as being aimed at preventing unjust enrichment. He only makes that argument with regard to certain accessory aspects of the vindication action; the claim for fruits and use value.[308] But *fructus* and *usus* are as much incidents of ownership as the right of exclusion associated with ownership, which is protected by a vindication. I thus submit that the vindication action itself is based on the unjust enrichment principle. If it were not for the *actio vindicatio,* a claim in unjustified enrichment would lie.[309] The reason the *actio vindicatio* displaces the "unjustified enrichment proper" claim is the underlying property right enjoyed by the claimant. The argument for the admission of unjust enrichment claims where title has not passed is that there is no common law action to vindicate property.[310]

The problem with my submission is that in it itself, it does not yet explain why proprietary restitution takes place. The proprietary element is easily identifiable in cases where the defendant has simply taken the property. It is even possible to find a principle in cases of defective transfers. These cases would simply require elaboration to identify where the defect is so severe to at least create an equitable interest for the benefit of the claimant. But services rendered is a problematic case for my theory of proprietary restitution. This can be seen in the Canadian family law cases where unjust enrichment was said to be the reason for proprietary restitution of services rendered. I submit that just like the language of "implied contract" cast a shadow preventing the recognition of unjust enrichment as a cause of action, so does the current language of "unjust enrichment" cast a shadow that makes it difficult to recognize that while property claims are structurally similar to plain unjust enrichment claims, the difference is that they are not value-based: the unjust enrichment is not the retention of some value; rather it is the retention of an item of property. This necessitates a different type of response, and this property-related feature is a *differentia specifica* that sets property-based unjust enrichment – or vindication, if you will – apart from value-based unjust enrichment, which only generates a personal claim. If this *differentia specifica* is present, proprietary restitution will ensue. The "institutional" constructive trust cases can be explained by some "unfair" retention of property to the detriment of the claimant as well. In the Canadian family law cases, the *differentia specifica* is present because of the "link" requirement elaborated in *Kerr.*

Recognizing unjust enrichment as a discrete area of law does not mean that an unjust enrichment claim can always be decided without reference to other

---

[308] Smith, "Property, Subsidiarity and Unjust Enrichment", *supra* note 294 at 594.

[309] An actio possessionis, see *ibid* at 594.

[310] *Ibid* at 619–21; Lionel D Smith, "The Mystery of Juristic Reason" (2000) 12 Sup Ct L Rev 211 at 222.

areas of law. The question whether an enrichment is unjust because an apparent contract fails at least touches on questions of contract law.[311] It is not merely an unjust enrichment law question. Just as "absence of contract" is characterized as forming part of the realm of contract law, one might argue that the "creation of an equitable property interest in communal property" – *i.e.* the constructive trust – should be characterized as forming part of property law.

*2. Stevens' Unjust Enrichment Model*

Stevens' unjust enrichment model of proprietary restitution[312] has a shortcoming: it alone cannot explain constructive trusts of the intimate-relationship category, nor of the breach of fiduciary obligation category. In many of the family law cases, there was only a service, no right. So either Stevens' model is wrong, or he is implicitly saying that there must be a different underlying reason for recognizing a property right of the claimant in these cases.

One way of integrating the intimate-relationship category is to say there was one event through which Ms. Becker received a right in the farming enterprise. While the relationship was intact, she agreed to not assert her right, which would be comparable to a conditional transfer of the right to Mr. Pettkus. She also agreed to render the services for free during the duration of the relationship. But after the failure of the relationship, her assertion of the right by way of a constructive trust is a second separate event.

This account has the advantage of being equally applicable to the constructive trusts of the fiduciary duty category. The difference between *Lac Minerals* and *Soulos* can be explained by admitting that in both cases, the property right did not arise in response to an unjust enrichment, but was a property right in response to a fiduciary duty. In both cases, the unjust enrichment then consisted in the retention of property that was held despite the property right of another.

I argue that this theory is compatible with the Canadian approach to constructive trusts. Justice McLachlin (as she then was) suggested that "institutionary" and "remedial" constructive trusts can be united under the "unjust enrichment" term if one establishes that unjust enrichment entails more than pecuniary entitlement. Webb has shown that such a wider-than-value principle exists in the Common Law. He points out that "many restitutionary claims are founded on the receipt of a benefit deriving from the claimant and without the latter's consent, something more is needed if such a claim is to be recognized. [...]"[313] This additional element is not only found in a pecuniary loss by the

[311] Cf. Mitchell McInnes, "The Reason to Reverse: Unjust Factors and Juristic Reason" (2012) 92 Boston UL Rev 1049 at 1058–59 [McInnes, "Reason"].

[312] See Part II: § 10 B.II.2.b), "Stevens' Model".

[313] Charlie Webb, "Property, Unjust Enrichment, and Defective Transfers" in: Chambers, Mitchell & Penner, eds, *Philosophical Foundations of the Law of Unjust Enrichment, supra* note 114, 335 at 350.

defendant. Rather, "[t]he extra element in such claims is better expressed by saying that the benefit received by the defendant must be one to which the claimant was exclusively entitled, one which the law had reserved for him."[314] Consequently, a restitutionary claim fails if the claimant cannot show exclusive entitlement to the item of property with which the defendant interfered.[315]

Expressing this argument in more property-related terminology, Smith similarly argues that a deprivation can be shown to exist whenever the defendant has interfered with a "bundle of rights" held by the claimant.[316] Applied to property claims, claims for proprietary restitution should succeed where the claimant can establish that she has an exclusive right to the property which is being interfered with. For example, in *Edwards v Lee's Administrator,*[317] the defendant charged the public for access to caves that were partly under the claimant's land. The plaintiff succeeded in claiming the profits thus gained. As Smith argues, the case could be viewed as a case of restitution for wrong, but "it can also be viewed as a claim to traceable proceeds. It is a disposal by the defendant of part of the bundle of rights that make up the claimant's assets. The profits are a traceable product."[318]

### *V. Explaining Proprietary Restitution Upon the Dissolution of Intimate Relationships*

The creation of a property right for a spouse can be explained by the economic account of *numerus clausus.* As I have argued above, it is efficient to recognize a property right when either the transactions costs are high, or the type of access is commonly sought.[319] While the monetary costs of bargaining between spouses about their relative entitlement to the yields of their marriage might be relatively low, the idealistic costs associated with it are high. Furthermore, common-enterprise relationships are very common. It is thus efficient for the law to recognize the need for each spouse's spouses property right – not just the spouse who acquires title at law – in the yields of the enterprise. We find a similar approach in *Gauthier v Gauthier,*[320] where Lee J characterized the proprietary entitlement in common law relationships – as opposed to less stable intimate relationships – as a form of anticipated result of bargaining.

---

[314] *Ibid* at 351, referring to *Bradford Corp v Pickles,* [1895] AC 587 (HL) and *Victoria Park Racing and Recreation Grounds Company Ltd v Taylor* (1937), 58 CLR 479.

[315] Webb, "Property, Unjust Enrichment, and Defective Transfers", *supra* note 313 at 351–52.

[316] Smith, "Tracing", *supra* note 244 at 130–31.

[317] 96 SW2d 1028 (Ky Ct App 1936).

[318] Smith, "Tracing", *supra* note 244 at 130.

[319] See Part II: § 8 D.V, "Creating the List of Discrete Property Rights".

[320] 2013 ABQB 566.

"Manderscheid J in Behiels at para 16, referred to the legal principle outlined by our Court of Appeal in *Panara* v *Di Ascenzo*, 2005 ABCA 47 at para 22, 361 AR 382 where Russell JA said: 'In a common law relationship there is no presumed entitlement to property sharing. However, remedies are available to unmarried partners who are unfairly disadvantaged upon breakdown of the relationship … [emphasis added]' He concluded that unlike persons divorcing after a marriage, any claim based on common-law relationship by parties who are unmarried partners, must therefore have a basis in equity.

The analytical significance of my conclusion that the pre-marriage relationship between Michel and Donnalee was not a common-law relationship is that there is no legally presumed entitlement to property sharing between them."[321]

With regards to the realist theory of property, the recognition of a property right in matrimonial contexts can be seen as an expression of a certain social value – that is, the equal valuation of each spouse's contribution.[322]

The view of seeing the proprietary restitution constructive trust as the making good of an inchoate property interest has a parallel in Watterson's conception of the unjust enrichment approach to subrogation.[323] Watterson's claim that a subrogation situtation always lead to an inchoate subrogation and that all the court does is ending the inchoate state if doing so is necessary to prevent unjust enrichment is an interesting parallel structure to saying "certain legal relationships, e.g. familial relationships, always trigger an inchoate property right and the court merely recognized this if necessary to reverse unjust enrichment".

### *VI. Certainty and Discretion in the Law of Proprietary Restitution*

One issue relating to the law of proprietary restitution concerns the difference between remedial trusts and institutional trusts. If proprietary restitution is to be seen as an effective remedy for an interference with a proprietary interest then its availability should be certain. Calling the constructive trust a remedial trust implies that it is discretionary for the court to choose the appropriate remedy, and this is a view that is implicitly taken by those who characterize the trust as such.[324] On the other hand, an equitable claim is only discretionary when it is available in addition to other legal remedies.[325] In many cases where a constructive trust is imposed, there is no other remedy available.[326] Further,

---

[321] *Ibid* at paras 35–36, Lee J.

[322] See Part II: § 8 D.III, "Realist Theory of the Numerus Clausus". On values expressed through the forms of property see Hanoch Dagan, "The Craft of Property" (2003) 91:6 Cal L Rev 1517. Recognizing the impact of values in matrimonial contexts cf. Nestor M Davidson, "Standardization and Pluralism in Property Law" (2008) 61:6 Vand L Rev 1597 at 1632.

[323] See Part II: § 10 C.I, "Subrogation".

[324] Oosterhoff *et al, supra* note 192 at 739–40.

[325] *Ibid* at 739.

[326] *Ibid* at 739–40.

courts occasionally treat the constructive trust as if it were a right in some cases, most notably in cases of mistaken payment.[327] This thus requires to assess what is meant by institutional and remedial, and whether these are accurate labels.

There are two ways of understanding the term "remedial trust." First, the remedial constructive trust describes a form of implied trust which does not mirror express trusts in referring to the settlor's intention as a constituent requirement. Second, the term remedial trust describes trusts which do not arise automatically by operation of law but because the court orders it into existence. The date of it coming into existence then is a function of the court's order. It is that latter sense in which Lord Browne-Wilkinson used the term remedial constructive trust in *Westdeutsche Landesbank.*[328] The orthodox view is that English law only recognises the non-remedial trust when categorizing trusts according to Lord Browne-Wilkinson's terminology.[329]

The idea of remedial trusts arising not by operation of law but as a function of court's exercise of discretion is elaborated by Liew. Using Austin's distinction between primary and secondary rights, where primary rights are rights that exist *per se,* whereas a secondary right only exists after a breach of duty by the defendant,[330] Liew argues that constructive trusts are best understood as remedies to secondary rights.[331] Primary rights have "a limited range of potential remedies,"[332] whereas there is a range of discretion in relation to the selection of a specific remedy out from a (non-discretionary) range of possible remedies where the right in question is a secondary right.[333] Analytically, in the context of common-intention constructive trusts, Liew identifies a primary duty to deal with the property consistent with the mutal assumptions.[334] The breach of this duty gives rise to a right to compensation. This, Liew argues, is the secondary right.[335]

---

[327] *Ibid* at 740 with further references.

[328] Charlie Webb, "The Myth of the Remedial Constructive Trust" (2016) 69:1 Curr Legal Probs 353 at 353–56 [Webb, "Myth"], referring to *Westdeutsche Landesbank, supra* note 69 at 714–15, Lord Browne-Wilkinson.

[329] Webb, "Myth", preceding note at 353–56, referring to *Bailey v Angove's Pty Ltd,* [2016] UKSC 47 at para 27, Lord Sumption.

[330] John Austin, *Lectures on Jurisprudence: The Philosophy of Positive Law,* ed by Robert Campbell, 4th edn (London: J Murray, 1873), vol 2 at 821.

[331] Ying K Liew, "The Secondary-Rights Approach to the 'Common Intention Constructive Trust'" [2015] Conveyancer 210 at 210.

[332] *Ibid* at 210.

[333] *Ibid* at 211.

[334] *Ibid* at 219.

[335] *Ibid* at 220.

The problem with Liew's approach is that one could just as well argue that the recognition of a constructive trust should never be the response to secondary right. Rather it should be the result of certain defined events, just like the acquisition of legal title to property is the result of certain events, but any secondary rights should be a question of whether or not to enforce the trust, or whether the enforcement of the trust is estopped for certain reasons (*e.g.* the beneficiary's unjust enrichment *vis-à-vis* third-party creditors, or because damages are sufficient). Connecting this point more broadly to the constructive trust as a response to unjust enrichment one could argue that the equitable property right could be said to always exist, all that the unjust enrichment question answers is whether it should be enforced at the moment. This is akin to the enforcement of a legal property right, particularly if we look at Civil Law as an example. The owner is always the owner, but they can only assert their ownership if the defendant interferes with their ownership, and this inquiry also includes an inquiry into whether the claimant/potential owner (1) ever acquired ownership, and (2) did not lose ownership at some point.

Instead of viewing the constructive trust as the result of a vaguely defined exercise of discretion, one could argue that constructive trusts responding to unjust enrichment are in fact defined with certainty. Any rule on the recognition of a property right is not just a rule for the sake of having a rule. It is a rule that expresses some notion of what is considered fair in this legal system. These notions of fairness require a distribution and sometimes a redistribution of property entitlements in a way that is not always predictable to the parties.[336] Using a Dworkian understanding of rules, Webb argues that the difference between institutional and remedial trusts is not that the latter are a form of palm-tree justice, but rather that institutional trusts are trusts whose coming into existence is fully determined by rules whereas remedial trusts are trusts where rules circumscribe the judicial discretion, but do not bind the court completely (yet).[337] In other words, remedial trusts cover situations in which the very nature of deductive rule-making in Common Law has not yet led to the development of a fully set rule.

Virgo goes even further. He argues that the recognition of the remedial constructive trust requires the recognition of a cause of action for which the trust is a remedy. He argues that in Canada, unjust enrichment – and unjust enrichment alone – is the cause of action and the trust is an apparently discretionary remedy.[338] In English law, something more is needed.[339]

---

336 Webb, "Myth", *supra* note 328 at 357–60.

337 *Ibid* at 361–63, referring to Ronald M Dworkin, *Taking Rights Seriously* (Cambridge, Mass: Harvard University Press, 1978) at 24–28.

338 Graham Virgo, "The Genetically Modified Constructive Trust" (2016) 2:2 CJCCL 579 at 588 [Virgo, "Genetically Modified"], referring to *Kerr, supra* note 7; *Soulos, supra* note 40; *Pettkus v Becker, supra* note 7.

339 Virgo, "Genetically Modified", preceding note at 588.

Despite the apparent distinction between remedial and institutional trusts, Virgo argues that the distinction between institutional and remedial constructive trust are nothing but "lazy characterisation" and that it should be abandoned.[340] Virgo takes issue with the implication of the language of institutional and remedial constructive trusts that implies that remedial constructive trusts are somehow less predictable and subject to more unfettered judicial arbitrariness. In fact, Virgo argues, the remedial constructive trust is restrained by rules and only takes place within parameters making it predictable.[341] The same parameters that define judicial discretion in relation to the remedial constructive in Canada and Australia are partially recognized in England, where the remedial constructive trust ostensibly does not exist.[342] Trusts such as the one recognized in *FHR*,[343] where assets acquired by a fiduciary from as bribes or secret commissions in breach of their fiduciary duty were subject to a constructive trust, are rule-determined and thus institutional.

While Virgo's model of proprietary restitution begins with the subsistence of the property right as its starting point,[344] Virgo recognizes that there are cases where the property right right is created or persists because of a breach of duty.[345] At least in English law, the institutional constructive trust, the only form of constructive trust in English law, arises because of the breach of a duty.[346] However, Virgo goes further and argues that a stringent analysis of cases in which Canadian courts have awarded a constructive trust as a remedy allows one to clearly identify a set of cases where "the trust arises by operation of law," and that this set of cases in fact encompasses all cases of constructive trusts.[347] In other words, Virgo argues that the distinction between institutional and remedial constructive trusts[348] is not helpful for Canadian law either.

While the Court as the law-maker had discretion when making the rule as to whether trusts should be recognized in circumstances such as the one in *FHR* the discretion was spent once the rule had been formulated. Now, like cases will be treated alike and a trust arises in comparable circumstances.[349] However the incomplete nature of rules means that a rule will never decide all cases for

---

340 *Ibid* at 589.

341 *Ibid* at 590.

342 *Ibid* at 591–93.

343 *Supra* note 105.

344 Virgo, *Restitution, supra* note 11 at 569–70.

345 *Ibid* at 570. See also Ross Grantham, "Doctrinal Bases for the Recognition of Proprietary Rights" (1996) 16 Oxford J Legal Stud 561.

346 Virgo, *Restitution, supra* note 11 at 595.

347 See Virgo, "Genetically Modified", *supra* note 338. The quoted passage is from *ibid* at 606.

348 See Part II: § 6 D.I.2, "Canadian Law".

349 Webb, "Myth", *supra* note 328 at 363–65.

all future.[350] This, I would add, is a function of Gödel's incompleteness theorem as applied to law.[351]

*Pennington v Waine*[352] is an example that sometimes the necessity for courts to complete existing rules by adding to existing rules is due to the fact that the court in the earlier case refused to promulgate a general rule and instead contented itself with promulgating a narrow rule.[353] Another case in which a court might want to "complete" an existing rule applies where the pre-existing rule is general, but the court wants to now carve out an exception to the existing rule. While rules can be formulated more precisely than the Court did in *Pennington,* and the scope for a rule-completing exercise of discretion thus minimized, the logical and linguistics restrictions make it impossible to exclude all rule-making discretion *a priori.*[354]

There are two supporting arguments to underline the rule-boundness of the constructive trust. First, equity is by necessity rule-bound.[355] Second, at the level of the domestic law, there might be a dichotomy between "institutional" rights, and "remedial" rights, but if we accept that remedies are not arbitrary, but the function of an exercise of judicial "discretion" strictly bound by rules, then arguably at least on the level of vertical and horizontal interactions within a system of bijuralism, these rules should be recognized as the legal basis for the recognition of rights.

This raises the question as to how the rule set applying to constructive trusts can be summarized. Virgo argues that the cause of action for constructive trusts is a two-step process. First, a constructive trust should be *prima facie* recognized when the defendant has obtained property in breach of a subjective fiduciary duty. Second, the recognition of the constructive trust should be subject to a modification. This modification should be made by reference to the three key implications: (1) priority over unsecured creditors; (2) the increase in value of the trust property; and (3) the ability to follow the trust property into third-party hands.[356]

In relation to the first step, it might be argued that it seems unfair to make the recognition of a constructive trust a function of subjective standard because apart from giving the beneficiary a *Saunders v Vautier*[357] claim to recieve the specific trust property, one of the main consequences of the trust is that third parties lose out. It seems unfair then to say that the defendant's behaviour on

---

350 *Ibid* at 366–67.

351 See Part I: § 3 A.III.2.b), "The Incompleteness Theorem".

352 [2002] EWCA Civ 227.

353 Webb, "Myth", *supra* note 328 at 367–68.

354 *Ibid* at 368–69.

355 See e.g. David Neuberger, "Equity: The Soul and Spirit of All Law or a Roguish Thing?" (Paper presented to the University of New South Wales, Sydney, 4 August 2014).

356 Virgo, "Genetically Modified", *supra* note 338 at 593–95.

357 (1841), 4 Beav 115 (Ch).

its own should have an impact on third-party status. But this would be tempered by the modification step of the recognition of the constructive trust.

With reference to Australian and English case law,[358] Virgo tests his analytical framework in relation to the thief-as-constructive-trustee problem, arguing that there is no reason to restrict the constructive trust by reference to unsecured creditors (who stand to make a bargain from including the property in the thief's estate), that there is no reason why the thief should retain the profits of the stolen property, and third that the third-party beneficiary is sufficiently protected by the *bona fide* purchaser rule.

In relation to mistaken payment, Virgo claims that the cause for the imposition of the constructive trust is the subjective knowledge of the recipient.[359] Again, he argues there is no reason why the unsecured creditors should enjoy a windfall, or why the recipient of the payment should retain the profit. Virgo points out that the claimant can follow their proprietary right into third-party hands if the third party did not provide value, which Virgo rejects.[360] But the reason for this would simply be that the third party has not provided value and we thus have a priority contest between a person who made a mistake, and a person who received something for nothing. It is not unfair to let the former person win.

In relation to the receipt of property from third parties in breach of a fiduciary duty,[361] Virgo argues that the reason for the imposition of the constructive trust is the agency of the defendant for the claimant. There is no reason why the claimant – to whom the fiduciary duty was owed – should outrank unsecured creditors, that the defendant should not retain the benefit, and that a third party *de lege ferenda* but not *de lege lata* should not be liable as constructive trustee if they received the trust property in ignorance of the original breach.[362] The discretion in this case could be guided by the extent to which the fiduciary duty resembles an agency relationship.

### *VII. Conclusion*

I am now in a position to formulate my theory of proprietary restitution: Proprietary restitution is an appropriate response to unjust enrichment wherever the retention of property by the defendant amounts to a negation of the property right retained or received by the claimant without a juristic reason. The property right here is the right to the value, use, and enjoyment of the item of property. This is the type of property right with which equity is concerned., whereas

[358] *Black v Freedman* (1910), 12 CLR 105 *Westdeutsche Landesbank, supra* note 69.

[359] *Westdeutsche Landesbank, supra* note 69 at 709, Lord Browne-Wilkinson.

[360] Virgo, "Genetically Modified", *supra* note 338 at 595–99.

[361] Rejected in *Lister & Co v Stubbs* (1890), 45 Ch D 1 (CA) but recognized in *FHR, supra* note 105.

[362] Virgo, "Genetically Modified", *supra* note 338 at 599–605.

property at law is possession and control for the time being without reference to who in substance is entitled to the benefit of the asset.[363]

Anchoring proprietary restitution within unjust enrichment explains why the no-basis approach is necessary. A use of unjust factors alone would not vindicate these property rights as they would not effectively protect the value entitlement. Property should be absolute and the ability to protect and regain property should not hinge on the existence of an unjust factor. Using a comprehensive conceptual basis is not "Civilian meddling,"[364] but rather a consequence of attempting to find a coherent basis of the existing law and how it assigns entitlement. Where the claimant's property right protects the claimant's interest in a specific item of property, that is the value arising from or use of a specific asset, proprietary restitution should take the form of a constructive trust. Where the property right protects the claimant's pure monetary value entitlement, restitution should take the form of an equitable lien. Proprietary restitution is the way in which the Common Law vindicates a person's property right by preventing the defendant from negating the claimant's title; if it were not for proprietary restitution, this would be possible because of the absence of a right of specific recovery at law. The exercise of this right to vindicate might be subject to Virgo's exceptions as discussed in the preceding subsection.

In cases of defective transfers or wrongful taking, the claimant's property right is a function of the incomplete property transfer. This encompasses any initial absence of basis for the transfer as well as resulting trusts whereby the transferor/claimant intended to create an equitable right for herself. Conversely, where the transferor/defendant intended to transfer the property right to the purchaser/claimant, a vendor-purchaser constructive trust situation arises.

---

363 Cf. Tobias Barkley, "Trustees' Bare Legal Title: Concept or Misconception?" (2017) 26:1 Austral Prop LJ 44 at 50.

364 See McInnes, "Reason", *supra* note 311 at 1054.

Part III

# Secured Transactions

## § 11 The Law and Economics of Secured Transactions

The legal origin theory posits that Common Law is inherently more efficient than Civil Law. Before I look at secured transactions in Common Law and Civil Law in the next four chapters, I consider the economic theory of secured transactions law in this chapter. After all, a comprehensive theory of legal origins as applied to substantive secured transaction law would require one to identify what exactly makes secured transaction law efficient and how these mechanisms are more easily implemented in Common Law than in Civil Law.

### A. Introduction

#### *I. The Economic Nature of Secured Transactions*

Secured transactions law is to a large extent determined by economic considerations. The reason itself behind having a secured transactions law is described as a desire to increase the availability of credit, to make credit less expensive, and to minimize the risk of credit for the creditor.[1] A firm's ability to use its assets as collateral in order to secure credit expands the firm's access to credit.[2] Secured transactions law is thus facilitative in nature.[3] Because of its essential commercial nature, secured lending is very amenable to an economic analysis of law.[4]

---

[1] Roderick A Macdonald, "Change of Terminology? Change of Law?" (1992) 23 RGD 357 at 359.

[2] See Mehnaz S Safavian, "Firm-Level Evidence on Collateral and Access to Finance" in: Frederique Dahan & John Simpson, eds, *Secured Transactions Reform and Access to Credit* (Cheltenham: Edward Elgar, 2009) 110.

[3] See Frederique Dahan & John Simpson, "Legal Efficiency of Secured Transactions Reform: Bridging the Gap Between Economic Analysis and Legal Reasoning" in: Dahan & Simpson, eds, *Secured Transactions Reform and Access to Credit,* preceding note, 122 at 132.

[4] Moritz Brinkmann, *Kreditsicherheiten an beweglichen Sachen und Forderungen: Eine materiell-, insolvenz- und kollisionsrechtliche Studie des Rechts der Mobiliarsicherheiten*

In this book, I have chosen to restrict analysis to the area of movable property. In a modern developed economy, about half of business property is movable, the other half is immovable.[5] For small to medium-sized businesses, movable property may take up to 100 percent of assets.[6] Thus, it follows that for the development of new businesses, an efficient secured transactions law in movable property is of greater concern than one in immovable property.[7] This focus on movable credit distinguishes commercial lending from consumer credit. A large share of consumer debt is based on using the consumer's house as collateral.[8]

Just as consumer credit uses mostly another type collateral (*i.e.* immovable property) the intended benefit behind consumer secured transactions law may be different. For example, secured transactions in immovable property might be governed by access-to-housing concerns.[9] Since the consumer credit market uses primarily immovable property as collateral and the influence of movable property is stronger in commercial credit, it follows that the analysis and measure of efficiency may be different between secured transactions law in movables and secured transactions law in immovables.

With regard to the economic analysis of secured transactions law, we again find the two approaches that characterize the economic analysis of law: a positive one and a normative one.[10] The positive approach analyses different rules in different jurisdictions, measures different economic data points in these jurisdictions, and postulates theories that explain differences in data. The normative analysis postulates *ex ante* theories of what an efficient secured transactions law should be like.

The problem with which the economic analysis of secured transactions law is faced is that there are not many recorded data sets that can be the starting point for a positive analysis.[11] We thus only find a limited positive account of secured transaction law. Importantly, empirical data supports the conclusion that firms that cannot use their property for collateral have trouble accessing

---

*vor dem Hintergrund internationaler und europäischer Entwicklungen* (Jus Privatum, Tübingen: Mohr Siebeck, 2011) at 68.

[5] Heywood Fleisig, "The Economics of Collateral and of Collateral Reform" in: Dahan & Simpson, eds, *Secured Transactions Reform and Access to Credit, supra* note 2, 81 at 88

[6] *Ibid* at 89.

[7] See also Safavian, *supra* note 2 at 119–21.

[8] Cf. John Simpson & Frederique Dahan, "Mortgages in Transition Economies" in: Dahan & Simpson, eds, *Secured transactions reform and access to credit, supra* note 2, 172.

[9] Cf. Dahan & Simpson, "Legal Efficiency of Secured Transactions Reform", *supra* note 3 at 132, referring to "social functions" of the mortgage market. See also Simpson & Dahan, preceding note at 176.

[10] See Part I: § 3 B.I, "Positive and Normative Economic Analysis of Law".

[11] Brinkmann, *supra* note 4 at 68.

the credit market.[12] Lopez-de-Silanes comes to the conclusion that legal origins affect secured transactions law. He argues that "creditor rights and collateral rules are statistically significantly weaker in French and socialist legal origins than in common law nations and even in German legal origin countries."[13] However, his argument heavily relies on differences in procedural aspects of enforcement. It should thus not be taken as a statement about the content of the substantive rules.

Because of the limited number of empirical studies with limited scope, the economic theory of secured transaction combines normative and positive approaches. Theories of secured transactions explain why secured transactions exist and how they can be beneficial, but at the same time, each explanatory theory may contain a normative element, in essence stating that secured transactions are only beneficial if certain conditions are met. A critical analysis of the legal origins predictions thus requires us to distill the normative predictions and to analyse to what extent a Civil Law origin and property law background are in fact an obstacle to the realization of the normative calls to secured transaction law.

### *II. The Efficiency of Secured Transactions*

An economic theory of secured transactions requires one to explain why secured transactions are efficient. A security interests allows the debtor to use her asset for two purposes simultaneously. The debtor can enjoy the uses of the property and use it as means of securing her obligations at the same time.[14] This explains the necessity of non-possessory security interests. Requiring a creditor to take possession of the collateral increases the cost of granting security, and impedes the debtor's ability to conduct her business.[15]

Other inefficiencies may arise at all levels. They may be due to the exclusion of certain property as possible collateral or cumbersome laws relating to creation, priority, publicity, and enforcement.[16] Exclusion of certain types of property from the pool of potential collateral makes it difficult for a business to access credit.[17] The share of these dead assets is typically especially large

---

[12] Safavian, *supra* note 2.

[13] Florencio Lopez-de-Silanes, "Turning the Key to Credit: Credit Access and Credit Institutions" in: Dahan & Simpson, eds, *Secured Transactions Reform and Access to Credit, supra* note 2, 3 at 3.

[14] Henry Hansmann & Reinier Kraakman, "Property, Contract, and Verification: The Numerus Clausus Problem and the Divisibility of Rights" (2002) 31:S2 J Legal Stud 373 at 404.

[15] John Armour, "The Law and Economics Debate About Secured Lending: Lessons for European Lawmaking?" in: Horst Eidenmüller & Eva-Maria Kieninger, eds, *The Future of Secured Credit in Europe* (Berlin: Walter de Gruyter, 2008) 3 at 14.

[16] Fleisig, "The Economics of Collateral and of Collateral Reform", *supra* note 5 at 90.

[17] Safavian, *supra* note 2 at 118–19.

among movable property.[18] Thus, some territories put emphasis on enlarging the pool of potential assets; one example is Slovakia,[19] whose secured transactions law is hailed as business-friendly.[20]

Above, I have mentioned that property law is essentially distributive. Resources are limited and property law allocates these resources among persons. Because of this, it is difficult to envision cases in which a secured transaction law can be said to be fully Pareto efficient. This would require at least one person benefited from a rule while no-one else suffered a disadvantage. This is hard to imagine in a case of distribution of limited resources. Efficiency is thus usually measured using the Kaldor-Hicks criterion: one assesses whether the benefits accruing to at least one party outweigh the costs accruing to all parties.[21]

Schwartz argues that secured transactions regimes can be Pareto efficient if one assumes that unsecured creditors – *i.e.,* the class of creditors worse off by admitting secured transactions – will fully compensate by taking higher interest and at the same time and that the decrease in interest rate charged by the secured creditor will more than offset the increase by the secured creditor. Schwartz does concede, however, that in reality, not all unsecured creditors will be sophisticated enough to do so.[22] If one were to assume that all unsecured creditors are perfectly rational market participants and thus fully compensatet the increase in risk to them that results from the granting of secured credit, a Pareto efficient secured transactions regime would depend on providing sufficient information to unsecured creditors to allow them to set off their risk. The secured transactions regime would need to be structured in a way that allows unsecured creditors to gain the information cheaply enough so that they would not have to increase their interest rate to a degree that exceeds the reduction in interest rate by the secured creditor. At the same time, the information system must be so cheap that the costs incurred by debtor and secured creditor do not exceed the reduction either.

What, then, does efficiency mean in the context of secured transactions law? Dahan and Simpson define efficiency as the "extent to which a law and the way it is used provide the benefits that it was intended to achieve."[23]

---

[18] *Ibid* at 119.

[19] See Katarina Mathernová, "The Slovak Secured Transactions Reform: Ingredients of a Successful Reform and Reflection on Its Achievements" in: Dahan & Simpson, eds, *Secured Transactions Reform and Access to Credit, supra* note 2, 207 at 216–17.

[20] See "Slovak Solution: Why Slovakia Has the World's Best Rules on Collateral" *The Economist* (25 January 2003) 70–1.

[21] See Part I: § 3 B.II.2, "Measures of Efficiency".

[22] Alan Schwartz, "Security Interests and Bankruptcy Priorities: A Review of Current Theories" (1981) 10:1 J Legal Stud 1 at 2, note 7.

[23] Dahan & Simpson, "Legal Efficiency of Secured Transactions Reform", *supra* note 3 at 133.

This is essentially an application of the general welfare analysis inherent in the economic analysis of law.[24] It hinges on the definition of "benefit." The intended benefit of secured transactions law primarily consists in facilitating access to credit.

Dahan and Simpson analyse what criterion can be used to establish whether a law provides the benefits it was intended to achieve. They reject the approach that simply measures whether the volume of secured transactions has increased after a reform.[25] Instead, the law should be "simple, fast and inexpensive, there should be certainty as to what the law is and how it is applied, and it should function in a manner which fits to the local context."[26] Regarding the last measure, they elaborate that the law must respond to certain economic needs, fit the context of the financial system, fit existing market practices, achieve acceptance, and be tailored towards a specific purpose.[27] They offer the functionalist approach of *Article 9 UCC* as an example of a law that may be unfit for certain local contexts. This may be because, unlike the pre-*Article 9 UCC* situation in the United States, potential reform countries may face a lack of types of security interests rather than an abundance of them, or because the functional *Article 9 UCC* approach would "touch on fundamental elements of its legal system such as freedom of contract and ownership rights."[28]

## B. The External Argument Against the Secured Creditor's Priority

A common argument against the permissibility of secured transactions is an external argument. It is external not only in the sense of not being a formalist legal argument, but because it refers to reasons beyond the lending transactions. The external argument against the secured creditor's priority posits that the secured creditor should not have priority over each subset of the class of

---

[24] See Part I: § 3 B.II.1, "Welfare and Efficiency".

[25] Dahan & Simpson, "Legal Efficiency of Secured Transactions Reform", *supra* note 3 at 132. Interestingly enough, this seems to be the approach of Lopez-de-Silanes, who simply measures the credit-to-GDP-ratio, see Lopez-de-Silanes, *supra* note 13 at 25, or Fleisig, who notes that reform increased the collateralized-property-to-GDP ratio in Romania, see Fleisig, "The Economics of Collateral and of Collateral Reform", *supra* note 5 at 90–91.

[26] Dahan & Simpson, "Legal Efficiency of Secured Transactions Reform", *supra* note 3 at 134.

[27] *Ibid* at 136.

[28] *Ibid* at 137 explanatory footnotes ommited.

unsecured creditors because there are policy arguments against such a priority.[29] For example, the argument is often made that tort creditors do not assume the risk of the debtor's insolvency, and that the subordination of tort claims to secured credit is undesirable from a policy standpoint.

More generally, secured credit upsets the *pro rata* distribution in bankruptcy; Common Law courts have traditionally placed such attempts in the vicinity of fraud, particular where the security interest was a non-possessory security interest.[30]

As regards the empirical side of the distribution argument, in an analysis of three classes of firms subject to massive tort claims – *i.e.* tobacco, asbestos, and pharmaceutical companies – Listokin found that these debtors on average carry less debt than other firms and that there is no empirical evidence that secured credit is used to shift capital from tort claimants to lenders.[31] Listokin concedes that this does not argue against granting tort claimants priority over secured creditors, but that the laws do not need to be changed to address an "empirically insignificant problem."[32] Nevertheless, one cannot help but to notice that the three fields of enterprises examined include companies that are typically large and profitable. It is thus not surprising that one finds a low level of secured debt there.

The external argument against secured transactions could be countered by providing mechanisms that protect the party to whose detriment the pro-rate scheme is disturbed. The recognition of inchoate property interests for certain classes of creditors, which are then remedied by the constructive trust,[33] could be seen as such a safeguard. In this sense, the co-existence of secured transactions law and proprietary restitution within one provincial legal system in Canada can be seen as an expression of choice by that province on how to balance certain competing policy goals. Whether this choice needs to respected in federal insolvency law is a second-level question to be examined later.[34]

---

[29] Lucian A Bebchuk & Jesse M Fried, "The Uneasy Case for the Priority of Secured Claims in Bankruptcy" (1996) 105:4 Yale LJ 857; Lucian A Bebchuk & Jesse M Fried, "Uneasy Case for the Priority of Secured Claims in Bankruptcy: Further Thoughts and a Reply to Critics" (1996) 82:6 Cornell L Rev 1279; John Hudson, "The Case Against Secured Lending" (1995) 15:1 Int'l Rev L & Econ 47; Lynn M LoPucki, "The Unsecured Creditor's Bargain" (1994) 80:8 Va L Rev 1887; Elizabeth Warren, "Making Policy with Imperfect Information: The Article 9 Full Priority Debates" (1997) 82:6 Cornell L Rev 1373.

[30] See e.g. *Twyne's Case* (1601), 76 ER 809 (St Ch). In *Zartman v First Nat Bank,* 82 NE 127 at 128 (NY 1907), Vann J the court refused to give effect to a security interest in after-acquired property because "the result would deprive the general creditors with superior equities so far as after-acquired property is concerned, of their only chance to collect debts".

[31] Yair Listokin, "Is Secured Debt Used to Redistribute Value from Tort Claimants in Bankruptcy?: An Empirical Analysis" (2008) 57 Duke LJ 1037.

[32] *Ibid* at 1078–79.

[33] See Part II: § 10 F, "Analysis of Proprietary Restitution".

[34] See Part IV: § 16 D, "Proprietary Restitution and Insolvency".

## C. The Traditional Case for Secured Transactions

One argument for permitting parties to enter into a security agreement is an internal argument for secured transactions. This argument is not based on an economic analysis, but views the right to use one's property in secured transactions as an outflow of the property right itself.[35] It thus follows a formal approach to law.[36]

The traditional economic argument in favour of allowing a debtor to use her property to secure credit claims that the debtor who offers collateral minimizes the creditor's risk that is associated with the debtor's default. Thus, the creditor will charge a lower interest rate. Interest is thus at least partly an insurance against default.[37]

## D. Shortcomings of the Argument for Secured Transactions

The traditional case for secured transactions is not fully borne out by empirical studies. At least in the UK, Germany, and France, secured loans are not associated with significantly lower interest rates than unsecured loans.[38] The relationship becomes stronger in less-developed economies with smaller loans.[39]

Secured transactions carry with them higher transaction costs compared to unsecured lending. Thus, security only makes sense for bigger loans, not for smaller loans or loans where the debtor has a stable credit history.[40]

### *I. The Modigliani-Miller Hypothesis*

The Modigliani-Miller hypothesis postulates that in a perfect world, every gain achieved by a change in one part of a firm's capital structure will result in an

---

[35] Steven L Harris & Mooney, Jr, Charles W, "A Property-Based Theory of Security Interests: Taking Debtors' Choices Seriously" (1994) 80:8 Va L Rev 2021. Harris & Mooney's formalist approach has been criticized by Alan Schwartz, "Taking the Analysis of Security Seriously" (1994) 80:8 Va L Rev 2073.

[36] See Part I: § 3 A.I, "Formalism".

[37] Brinkmann, *supra* note 4 at 72; Thomas H Jackson & Anthony T Kronman, "Secured Financing and Priorities Among Creditors" (1979) 88 Yale LJ 1143 at 1151–52.

[38] Armour, *supra* note 15 at 10; Sergei A Davydenko & Julian R Franks, "Do Bankruptcy Codes Matter?: A Study of Defaults in France, Germany, and the UK" (2008) 63:2 J Fin 565 at 599.

[39] Heywood Fleisig, Mehnaz S Safavian & Nuria de La Peña, *Reforming Collateral Laws to Expand Access to Finance* (Washington, DC: World Bank Publications, 2006) at 6.

[40] Fleisig, "The Economics of Collateral and of Collateral Reform", *supra* note 5 at 99.

offsetting of costs to other parts of the capital structure.[41] The Modigliani-Miller hypothesis contains a significant challenge to any theory of secured transaction law. Applied to secured transaction law, it predicts that changes in ratio of secured and unsecured credit will not affect the overall cost of credit to the firm. Any reduction in the cost of credit – *i.e.* any a lower interest – because the credit is secured is offset by the higher interest demanded by unsecured creditors whose lending has become more risky as a result of their being subordinated to secured creditors.[42] Furthermore, secured transactions are not cost-neutral. Because the creation of a credit security involves costs, the effect of secured credit should in fact be negative for the debtor.[43] This argument assumes that the increase in interest for the non-secured loan plus the cost of security always exceeds the decrease in interest for the loan. This however, requires perfect information on the side of the non-secured debtors. Where such a perfect information does not exist, secured transactions allow cost-shifting from secured creditors to unsecured creditors; the debtor can participate in this debt shifting. Thus, this argument explains why the debtor grants secured credit, but it does not answer the question whether secured transactions are efficient if the costs and gains of all parties are taken into account.

### *II. Kaldor-Hicks Efficiency*

As described above, secured transactions can be Kaldor-Hicks efficient if they can be shown to accrue a benefit to at least one party that outweighs all the losses accrued by other parties. Applying this criterion, there is no straightforward case for the efficiency of secured transactions.

#### *1. The Third-Party Creditor's Loss*

If we assume that the secured creditor has a gain from secured credit, there is still no apparent reason for a macroeconomic gain. The unsecured creditor's loss offsets any secured creditor's gain,[44] particularly since there are creditors who do not know about the security interest or who are for some other reason

---

[41] Franco Modigliani & Merton H Miller, "The Cost of Capital, Corporation Finance and the Theory of Investment" (1958) 48:3 Am Econ Rev 261.

[42] Michael G Bridge, "The Quistclose Trust in a World of Secured Transactions" (1992) 12:3 Oxford J Legal Stud 333 at 337–38; Jackson & Kronman, *supra* note 37 at 1154; Steven L Schwarcz, "The Easy Case for the Priority of Secured Claims in Bankruptcy" (1997) 47:3 Duke LJ 425 at 429; Alan Schwartz, "The Continuing Puzzle of Secured Debt" (1984) 37:5 Vand L Rev 1051 at 1052–55; Robert E Scott, "A Relational Theory of Secured Financing" (1986) 86:5 Col L Rev 901 at 905–6.

[43] Schwartz, "Security Interests and Bankruptcy Priorities", *supra* note 22 at 7–8; Scott, "A Relational Theory of Secured Financing", preceding note at 905–6.

[44] Homer Kripke, "Law and Economics: Measuring the Economic Efficiency of Commercial Law in a Vacuum of Fact" (1985) 133:5 U Pa L Rev 929 at 948–49.

unable to respond to secured creditors.[45] This latter group stands to make an even greater loss.

### 2. Minimizing the Impact on Third-Party Creditors

An efficient secured transaction regime should minimize the disadvantages associated with unsecured creditors. Armour lists three ways in which this can be done.[46] The first mechanism is the use of registries. The second mechanism is the *numerus clausus* principle. Because the *numerus clausus* only allows a limited number of rights in property, creditors can find out about third-party rights by asking a closed list of questions. Armour claims that this is a Civilian approach,[47] but as we have seen, the *numerus clausus* operates in Common Law as well.[48] The third mechanism is selective enforcement. The enforcement of non-possessory rights against third parties can be limited to cases where the third party's costs to discover the right's existence would be lower than the costs the holder of the right would incur to publicise the right's existence. Armour claims that the third mechanism is more efficient than the second because it allows "greater innovation in financial contracts."[49] Combined with his earlier statement that the *numerus clausus* principle is Civilian, this would readily imply that the Common Law is superior in this regard. But above,[50] I discussed the decision in *Anglo Pacific Group PLC c Ernst & Young inc.*[51] This decision shows that Civilian legal systems can also take a liberal approach to the *numerus clausus* and operate it in a way which results in selective enforcement.

### III. Moral Hazard

Another argument against secured transactions is that they allow the creditor to be fully protected. Lenders no longer make a selection between viable and unviable projects.[52] The main beneficiaries from secured transactions thus seem to be firms engaged in unprofitable enterprises.

---

[45] Bebchuk & Fried, "The Uneasy Case for the Priority of Secured Claims in Bankruptcy", *supra* note 29 at 882–91; Bebchuk & Fried, "Uneasy Case for the Priority of Secured Claims in Bankruptcy", *supra* note 29 at 1293–314.

[46] Armour, *supra* note 15 at 25–26.

[47] *Ibid* at 25.

[48] See Part II: § 5 H, "Numerus Clausus in Common Law".

[49] Armour, *supra* note 15 at 26–27.

[50] See Part II: § 4 E.II, "Restrictive Approach to Innominate Property Rights".

[51] *Anglo Pacific Group PLC c Ernst & Young inc*, 2013 QCCA 1323.

[52] Bebchuk & Fried, "The Uneasy Case for the Priority of Secured Claims in Bankruptcy", *supra* note 29 at 898–900.

## E. Economic Arguments for the Efficiency of Secured Transactions

There are a number of theories that complement the traditional case for secured transactions which explain why the benefits associated with secured transactions outweigh the disadvantages.

### *I. Signalling*

One theory of why credit security exists is the "signalling theory." It posits that debtors offer collateral to signal their creditworthiness. It is thus not a theory that explains why secured credit is efficient, merely why it exists. It has not been shown that the benefit from such signalling exceeds its costs. Furthermore, signalling might be insufficiently clear.[53] It is a theory that does not withstand empirical reality: in reality, there is a reverse proportional relationship between the use of credit security and creditworthiness.[54]

### *II. The Unsecured Creditor's Benefit*

There are also cases imaginable in which the unsecured creditor will benefit from secured credit. A debtor in distress will find it difficult to receive capital to make the necessary investments that would help her to overcome difficulties. By allowing the debtor to use her property as collateral, the debtor might still receive some credit, which could prevent her insolvency. This benefit accrues to all creditors, including unsecured creditors whose claim would have been reduced the most in insolvency.[55]

### *III. Information and Control Rights*

The "information" view postulates that the more access to credit is facilitated, the more access to information the creditor has.[56] The "control rights" view argues that the more assured the creditor is that her control in the collateral will be maintained, the easier access to credit is for the debtor.[57] Both views are not mutually exclusive; rather they may be complimentary.[58] The two views connect with secured transactions law in different ways. Proceeding from the information view, collateral is seen as a means of alleviating the information gap between borrower and lender.[59] An analysis of credit access from the control

---

[53] Schwartz, "Security Interests and Bankruptcy Priorities", *supra* note 22 at 14–21.

[54] Armour, *supra* note 15 at 6.

[55] Schwarcz, *supra* note 42 at 441–45.

[56] See Lopez-de-Silanes, *supra* note 13 at 3.

[57] See *ibid* at 4.

[58] *Ibid* at 3.

[59] *Ibid.*

rights perspective has its focus in particular on collateral rules and creditor rights and contract enforcement.[60] A lender will be more likely to lend money for better terms, the more protected her rights are in case of default.[61]

### *1. Information Asymmetry*

Secured transactions law facilitates credit because it help to avoid economic processes that minimize access to credit. These processes relate to information asymmetry.[62] Giving security for a loan addresses the problem of information asymmetry in several ways.

#### *a) Adverse Selection*

*First,* creditors can use collateral to counteract "adverse selection."[63] Adverse selection describes a process where there is an asymmetry of information between one party (the creditor) to a transaction and the pool of potential contracting parties (the potential debtors). This, in turn, leads the creditor to make a decision that actually minimizes the number of desirable potential partners in the pool. Applied to credit, this means the following. Consider there are two types potential of debtors: people who expect to make repay the credit and those who either already intend to default (the fraudsters) or do not understand a credit transaction at all (the fools). If credit could not be secured, creditors would charge higher interest to insure themselves against the risk of default. By charging higher interest, the number of desirable partners diminishes because there are less people who expect enough return from the credit to be able to repay. The number of fools and fraudsters, on the other hand, would remain about the same. Thus, the pool is less desirable for the creditor.[64]

#### *b) Moral Hazard*

*Second,* collateral deals with moral hazard. The higher the unsecured loan is, the bigger the incentive for the debtor to default on the loan. Creditors could insure themselves against that by slowly increasing the size of each individual

---

[60] *Ibid.*

[61] Philippe Aghion & Patrick Bolton, "An Incomplete Contracts Approach to Financial Contracting" (1992) 59:3 Rev Econ St 473; Oliver Hart *et al,* "A New Bankruptcy Procedure That Uses Multiple Auctions" (1997) 41 Eur Econ Rev 461; Oliver Hart & John Moore, "A Theory of Debt Based on the Inalienability of Human Capital" (1994) 109 Quart J Econ 841; Oliver Hart & John Moore, "Default and Renegotiation: A Dynamic Model of Debt" (1998) 113 Quart J Econ 1; Lopez-de-Silanes, *supra* note 13 at 7; Robert M Townsend, "Optimal Contracts and Competitive Markets with Costly State Verification" (1979) 21 J Econ Th 265.

[62] George J Stigler, "The Economics of Information" (1961) 69 J Pol Econ 213.

[63] George A Akerlof, "The Market for Lemons: Quality Uncertainty and the Market Mechanism" (1970) 84:3 Quart J Econ 488.

[64] Fleisig, "The Economics of Collateral and of Collateral Reform", *supra* note 5 at 85.

loan given out to a particular creditor. However, this may be adverse for the economic development at large as it may prevent a matching of debtors who undertake high-yield projects with a loan appropriate for such big projects, which are untypical for the debtor's prior credit history. Securing the loan through collateral allows for a sudden increase of loan size while minimizing the incentive of default.[65]

*c) Monitoring*

The information rights associated with secured credit also benefit unsecured creditors. The unsecured creditors benefit from the monitoring undertaken by the secured creditor.[66] There is some empirical evidence to the effect that monitoring can explain why secured transactions take place. Smaller, younger, and riskier firms are more likely to have to enter a security agreement to secure credit. This is exactly the group of companies that most likely needs to be monitored.[67]

For these types of firms, access to other finance such as selling shares in the company is typically limited or undesirable because it would entail a loss of control. By entering a secured credit transaction, these companies can essentially sell an investment opportunity to the creditor. In return, the creditor receives limited control and monitoring rights.[68]

*d) Normative Results*

Legal institutions provided for by some secured transactions laws such as property registries are seen as a means of narrowing the information gap.[69] Property registries perform two tasks: registering the security interests against the property and tracking title.[70] Thus, in order for it to be efficient, the registration system must make it easy to both file as well as retrieve title and collateralization information.[71]

The secured creditor will have a stronger incentive to monitor the debtor where the security interest is not in one specific item of property, but is a floating interest in all present and after-acquired property. Only then is there a nexus between the debtor's performance and the effectiveness of the security interest. Thus, to maximize the benefits associated with monitoring, the secured transactions law should allow global interests in present and after-acquired property.

---

[65] *Ibid* at 85–87.
[66] Brinkmann, *supra* note 4 at 81.
[67] Armour, *supra* note 15 at 9, 11.
[68] Scott, "A Relational Theory of Secured Financing", *supra* note 42.
[69] Lopez-de-Silanes, *supra* note 13 at 7.
[70] *Ibid* at 7–8.
[71] *Ibid* at 8.

*2. Control Rights*

An analysis of collateral control rights can proceed in three stages. *First,* businesses may face a shortcoming of property that can be effectively collateralized. Thus, an efficient legal framework should allow for the use of a wide array of property as collateral.[72] *Second,* the wider the scope of the rights in the collateral, the less collateral relative to the value of the loan is required. Thus, the framework granting more rights in the collateral becomes more efficient in its need for collateral.[73] *Third,* collateral rights must be easily enforceable.[74] The efficiency of such enforcement procedures can also be measured.[75]

*IV. Purchase-Money Security Interests in Economic Theory*

Secured transactions law will often allow a creditor to obtain a priority even though there are other pre-existing secured creditors. This can be explained as well. A distinction can be drawn between the types of transaction that are being financed. Where the credit is given so that the debtor purchases new property and the security interest is granted in the new property, the transaction is neutral from the point of view of the other creditors. The transaction has neither increased nor decreased the class of assets available to other creditors. There is thus no disadvantage in these cases of purchase-money security interests (PMSI).[76]Alternatively, PMSI allow the debtor to develop projects on its own that a general creditor would veto.[77] PMSI financers are also often specialized financers – for example, lending institutions in the car market – so they can provide a specialized form of monitoring not available to other creditors.[78] Normatively, this explains why the PMSI lender should have priority over other creditors.

*V. Priority Relationship*

In accounting for secured transactions, one also needs to explain the priority system of secured transaction. This can be done by conceptualizing the priority framework of secured transactions as an attempt to anticipate bargaining. In this sense, the admission of interests in present and after-acquired property as

[72] *Ibid* at 10.

[73] *Ibid* at 10.

[74] *Ibid* at 11.

[75] See Simeon Djankov *et al,* "Courts" (2003) 118 Quart J Econ 453.

[76] Brinkmann, *supra* note 4 at 76.

[77] Jackson & Kronman, *supra* note 37 at 1167–74; Scott, "A Relational Theory of Secured Financing", *supra* note 42 at 962–63; Robert E Scott, "The Politics of Article 9" (1994) 80:8 Va L Rev 1783 at 1798.

[78] Scott, "A Relational Theory of Secured Financing", *supra* note 42 at 962–63; Scott, "The Politics of Article 9", preceding note at 1798. Cf. Barry E Adler, "Limits on Politics in Competitive Credit Markets" (1994) 80:8 Va L Rev 1879 at 1881.

well as the priority granted to PMSI reflect the average interest of debtor and creditors. The first creditor will usually demand to receive priority in relation to every usable collateral, but has no objection to super-priorities in property that could not be purchased otherwise.[79]

## F. Conclusion

The analysis of the law-and-economics debate about secured transactions has shown that there is some empirical evidence regarding the impact of secured transactions law on economic performance and availability of credit. Nevertheless, a comprehensive economic account of secured transactions has not emerged. The economic arguments in favour of a secured transactions regime favour publicity of secured transactions, the admission of non-possessory security interests, and the permission of security interests in present and after-acquired property. They also argue in favour of priority of purchase-money security interests. Creditors need sufficient control rights that correlate to their security interest. These factors have to be balanced with competing policy goals, as well as the general property law principle stressing security of title.

---

[79] Alan Schwartz, "A Theory of Loan Priorities" (1989) 18 J Legal Stud 209.

# § 12 Security Interests in Common Law

In the preceding chapter, I have looked at the economic theory of secured transaction law. The purpose of the next four chapters, including this one, is to look at the relationship between economic theory and the substantive secured transaction law. The legal origin theory would require that the normative demands in a secured transaction law are more easily realized in Common Law than in Civil Law. Whether or not this is so depends on the relationship between Common Law and Civil Law secured transactions law and the respective property law frameworks to which secured transaction law belongs. Thus, I also look at this relationship.

## A. Common Law Security Interests

### *I. Overview of Common Law Security Devices*

Secured transactions in personal property in all Common Law jurisdictions are governed by *Personal Property Security Acts (PPSAs).*[1] Historically, before the enactment of *PPSAs,* Anglo-Canadian secured transaction law followed English law, which is still largely unchanged from the common law position. It is worth looking at the English common law security devices for two reasons: first, this enables one to better understand the innovations introduced by the *PPSAs;* second, as I show, priority between *PPSA* security interests and other equitable interests continues to be governed by common law principles. Take note that I use the words "common law" to make a distinction from the statutory *PPSA* framework; no statement about the legal or equitable nature of the interest is intended.[2] It should also be noted that there may be statutes relating to common law security devices. But a feature of these devices is that their origin is not statutory; rather, the device came first, and then a regulating statute was enacted.

---

[1] For instance the *Personal Property Security Act,* RSO 1990, c P.10 [*PPSA* (*Ont*)].

[2] See Part III: § 13 A, "Nature of the PPSA Security Interest".

It is said that in Common Law jurisdictions, contractual freedom means there is no limit to the kinds of security interests that can be created.[3] However, it is possible to come up with a taxonomy that encompasses all possible kinds of security interests that can be created.[4] Goode suggests four kinds of security interests: the pledge, the contractual lien, the mortgage, and the charge.[5] Bridge and others omit the lien.[6]

### *1. Pledge*

The original security interest in chattel is the "pledge" or "pawn." A pledge involves the transfer of possession from the debtor to the creditor with the understanding that the latter may sell the property if the debtor defaults on her obligation.[7] If the debtor pays, she is entitled to regain possession. In the mortgage context, this is known as the "equity of redemption,"[8] a term which can be applied universally to describe the debtor's persistent interest in the property. Since the creditor is not the legal owner of the property, she cannot foreclose the debtor's equity of redemption.[9]

### *2. Legal Lien*

At law, the lien is a right to retain possession of the property – without the right to sell the property – until a payment is made.[10] The legal lien can be classified along two vectors. First, a legal lien can arise by operation of law or from contract. Second, legal liens can be distinguished by scope: a particular lien is associated with a particular debt; a general lien secures all outstanding debts

---

[3] Michael G Bridge *et al,* "Formalism, Functionalism, and Understanding the Law of Secured Transactions" (1999) 44 McGill LJ 567 at 636; Iwan Davies, "The Reform of English Personal Property Security Law: Functionalism and Article 9 of the Uniform Commercial Code" (2004) 24 LS 295 at 314; Royston M Goode, *Goode on Legal Problems of Credit and Security,* ed by Louise Gullifer, 5th edn (London: Sweet & Maxwell, 2013) at para 1.06 [*Goode on Security*], note 207.

[4] Bridge *et al,* preceding note at 636; *Goode on Security,* preceding note, at para 1.46, note 207.

[5] *Goode on Security, supra* note 3, at para 1.46.

[6] Bridge *et al, supra* note 3 at 636. For further pinpoints to cases dealing with a possible re-characterization of the lien see *Goode on Security, supra* note 3, at para 1.53.

[7] For an extensive discussion of the pledge see *Donald v Suckling* (1866), 1 LRQB 585 (QB).

[8] See Part III: § 12 A.I.3, "Chattel Mortgage".

[9] *Donald v Suckling, supra* note 7.

[10] See *Hammond v Barclay* (1802), 102 ER 356 (KB). See also, with exceptions to the rule, John McGhee, *Snell's Equity,* 30th edn (London: Sweet & Maxwell, 2000) at para 28.1. For Australian law see Fiona R Burns, "The Equitable Lien Rediscovered: A Remedy for the 21st Century" (2002) 25 UNSWLJ 1 at 2–3.

of the creditor/possessor.[11] The lien differs from the other security interests in that it does not confer a *permanent title* to the collateral (like the mortgage after foreclosure), or a *permanent right to the proceeds* of the collateral. The right conferred by the legal lien in the property is necessarily temporary. For this reason, legal liens are outside of the scope of my analysis. Liens arising by operation of law can be found in a number of statutes in Canadian Common Law jurisdictions. They operate in favour of suppliers of certain goods or services, and are found in particular statutes dealing with certain types of contracts such as those of innkeepers, repairmen, or storage providers.[12]

I have already mentioned the equitable lien.[13] This type of lien is in fact very different from the type of lien just defined because it does not confer a right of retention. The common characteristic of the legal lien and the equitable lien is that the creditor has a "nexus on a particular thing," which is why – based on "the natural meaning of 'lien' in French as a bond or tie" – both institutions came to be grouped under the same heading.[14]

### *3. Chattel Mortgage*

Originally, when the pledge was the only recognized security interest in chattel, there was a presumption of fraud if the debtor granted the creditor a security without a transfer of possession.[15] However, the absence of non-possessory credit securities turned out to be an impediment for commerce. Therefore, once the law developed and no longer associated fraud with such a transaction, non-possessory securities developed.

The first non-possessory security is the chattel mortgage. In cases of a legal mortgage the mortgage consists of the transfer of legal title to the collateral from the debtor to the creditor. Possession remains with the debtor. Furthermore, the debtor has a right to receive title back once she fulfills her obligation. This is called the "equity of redemption." This right is recognized in equity.

"[T]he equity of redemption of a mortgage is the right of a mortgagor upon payment of a mortgage debt to a re-conveyance of the legal estate that was vested in the mortgagee by

---

[11] See with references to case law Burns, "The Equitable Lien Rediscovered", preceding note at 3.

[12] See Anthony J Duggan & Jacob S Ziegel, *Secured Transactions in Personal Property: Cases, Text and Materials,* 5th edn (Toronto: Emond Montgomery Publications, 2009) at 373–98; Roderick J Wood & Michael I Wylie, "Non-Consensual Security Interests in Personal Property" (1992) 30:4 Alta L Rev 1055.

[13] See Part II: § 6 G, "Equitable Liens".

[14] Andrew JM Steven, "Rights in Security over Moveables" in: Kenneth G Reid & Reinhard Zimmermann, eds, *A History of Private Law in Scotland* (Oxford: Oxford University Press, 2000) 333 at 352. For a comparison of the two see Adrian Wong, "An Introduction to Liens in Commercial Transactions" (1999) 20 Sing L Rev 134.

[15] *Twyne's Case* (1601), 76 ER 809 (St Ch). See also William C Hillman, "What's in a Name: The U.C.C. Filing System in the Courts" (1991) 44 Okla L Rev 151 at 151.

reason of the mortgage [...] Justice Dickson (later C.J.C.) summarised a number of cases defining the legal nature of the equity of redemption. He concluded that it is a 'right of property' and an interest in land."[16]

A similar definition applies *mutatis mutandis* for personal property.[17] There is doctrinal disagreement whether the equity of redemption is a property right or a personal one,[18] but the Supreme Court of Canada has held that an equity of redemption is a property right and it is treated as such in bankruptcy proceedings.[19] If the debtor defaults, the creditor can either apply to the court for a foreclosure order to extinguish the debtor's equity of redemption and take the collateral in satisfaction of the obligation, or she can sell the collateral and apply the proceeds to the debt.

If the creditor does not receive legal title, but rather an equitable interest in the property, the mortgage is an equitable mortgage.[20] Thus, any failed legal mortgage that transfers an equitable right to the creditor is an equitable mortgage. Furthermore, the security trust is a form of equitable mortgage.[21]

### 4. Equitable Charge

The second non-possessory security is the equitable charge. It does not involve transfer of an existing title, but rather consists in a hypothecation[22] of the property. This means that title (and possession) remains with the debtor, but the creditor grants the hypothetical right to realize the proceeds from the collateral in the event of the debtor's default. An equitable mortgage entails an equitable charge as well because apart from the beneficial title to the property, the creditor also receives the right to realize on the collateral.[23]

---

[16] *Scotia Mortgage Corporation v Davidson Estate,* [2009] OJ No 1781 at para 25 (Sup Ct J), Quigley J [references ommitted].

[17] Bridge *et al, supra* note 3 at 689, note 72; Edward I Sykes, *The Law of Securities: An Account of the Law Pertaining to Securities over Real and Personal Property under the Laws of Australian Jurisdictions,* 5th edn (North Ryde, NSW: Law Book, 1993) at 610.

[18] See Bridge *et al, supra* note 3 at 589, note 72; Sykes, preceding note at 145–47. Cf. *Alberta (Treasury Branches) v MNR,* [1996] 1 SCR 963 at paras 90–96, Major J dissenting.

[19] *Alberta (Treasury Branches) v MNR,* preceding note at para 34, Cory J, referring to *Federal Business Development Bank v Québec,* [1988] 1 SCR 1061. See also *Bank of Montreal v Hester Creek Estate Winery Ltd et al*, 2004 BCSC 724 at para 23, Tysoe J.

[20] *Goode on Security, supra* note 3, at para 1.56.

[21] *Ibid* at para 1.57.

[22] *Ibid* at para 1.55.

[23] See *ibid* at para 1.56.

### 5. Floating Charge

Finally, the last kind of security interest is the floating charge. For the purpose of having a four-fold taxonomy, the floating charge is not substantially different from the fixed equitable charge. The difference consists in the fact that, unlike a fixed charge, the floating charge does not attach to any specific collateral until it crystallizes. This characteristic was explicitly recognized for the first time in *Re Panama, New Zealand & Australian Royal Mail Company.*[24] The charge is a floating, rather than a fixed, charge:

> "(1.) if it is a charge on a class of assets of a company present and future; (2.) if that class is one which, in the ordinary course of the business of the company, would be changing from time to time; and (3.) if you find that by the charge it is contemplated that, until some future step is taken by or on behalf of those interested in the charge, the company may carry on its business in the ordinary way as far as concerns the particular class of assets I am dealing with."[25]

The floating charge thus allows the debtor to dispose of the collateral in the ordinary course of business free of the security. The creditor, on the other hand, may potentially hold the entire property of the debtor as collateral. The floating charge is therefore beneficial for both parties. The floating charge is a right *in rem.*[26] It is not attached to specific property until it crystallizes, but exists before crystallization.[27]

### II. Legal or Equitable Nature of Common Law Security Devices

Of the types of security interest mentioned in this subsection, two confer a legal right to the creditor: the pledge and the legal mortgage. The equitable mortgage and the equitable charge confer an equitable interest to the creditor. The lien confers a right of retention.

To be recognized at law, the creditor's security interest must be conferred by virtue of a transfer of present property to which the debtor has legal title, to the creditor personally, in accordance with any statutory requirements.[28]

From that, it follows that any interest in future property is equitable, a rule established by *Holroyd v Marshall.*[29] The security interest in after-acquired

---

[24] (1870), 5 LR Ch App 318.

[25] *Re Yorkshire Woolcombers Association,* [1903] 2 Ch 284 at 295 (CA), Romer LJ.

[26] See *Goode on Security, supra* note 3, at para 4.1.

[27] *Evans v Rival Granite Quarries, Ltd,* [1910] 2 KB 979 at 999 (CA), Buckley LJ.

[28] *Goode on Security, supra* note 3, at para 1.10.

[29] (1862), 10 HL Cas 191.

property exists before the property becomes the debtor's property as an inchoate security interest.[30] Since it is an equitable consensual security interest, it follows that it is an equitable charge.

As for the question of whether such an interest can be fixed or whether it is always a floating charge, precedent is that such a charge may be fixed.[31] However, the recent English decision in *National Westminster Bank plc v Spectrum Plus Limited*[32] has cast some doubt on the characterization of these charges as fixed; one lord went so far as to say that his refusal to change the law was only because it would affect the rights of the parties in the insolvency proceedings.[33]

### *III. Quasi-Security Devices in Common Law*

Apart from these security devices, "quasi-security"[34] transactions also existed. These were based on the allocation of title. They were the conditional sales agreement, the hire-purchase and the finance lease. In all these cases, the creditor reserved title to the collateral. The difference between the hire-purchase and the finance lease is that the latter does not necessarily include the sale of the property, but the debtor may buy the property at the end of the lease period based on its residual value. In cases of a hire-purchase, the debtor may not be obliged to buy the property, but she is encouraged to realize upon the buying option by a penalty she has to pay if she chooses not to buy.[35] Provincial *Con-*

---

[30] *Tailby v Official Receiver,* this note, at 533, Lord Watson; *Holroyd v Marshall,* preceding note at 220, Lord Chelmsford. See also *Royal Bank of Canada v Radius Credit Union Ltd,* 2010 SCC 48 at para 20, Charron J.

[31] *Agnew & Kevin James Bearsley v The Commissioner of Inland Revenue (Re Birtwhistle),* [2001] UKPC 28 (NZ); *Siebe Gorman & Co Ltd v Barclays Bank Ltd* (1978), [1979] 2 Lloyd's Rep 142 at 159 (Ch D), Slade J. The same is true for pre-PPSA Canadian law, see *Evans Coleman & Evans Ltd v RA Nelson Construction Ltd* (1958), 16 DLR (2[d]) 123 (BC CA).

[32] [2005] UKHL 41.

[33] *Ibid* at para 74, Lord Hope.

[34] As they are referred to in the modern English context, see Law Commission, *Company Security Interests: A Consultative Report* (LAW COM, vol 176, London: Her Majesty's Stationery Office, 2004) xvii.

[35] Jacob S Ziegel, "Should Canada Adopt an Article 2A Type Law on Personal Property Leasing?" (1989–1990) 16 CBLJ 369 at 370–71.

*ditional Sales Acts* governed conditional sales and hire-purchases, but not finance leases, nor simple leases without a sales component.[36] Accounts receivable were assignable in a security assignment.[37] In cases of a security assignment to several creditors, priority was determined according to which creditor was the first one to notify the account-debtor.[38]

The leading case for the use of retention of title for security purposes in England is *Aluminium Industrie Vaassen BV v Romalpa Aluminium Ltd.*[39] Aluminium Industrie Vaasen (AIV) sold aluminium foil to Romalpa Aluminium. The sales contract stipulated that ownership of the foil would only be transferred to Romalpa when the purchase price had been paid in full. Romalpa was to have the power to sell the manufactured articles in the course of business as a deemed agent of AIV. Romalpa became insolvent. Its receiver wanted the aluminium to be subject to a floating charge held by the creditor bank. AIV argued that it retained title to the goods. The courts agreed with AIV's position.[40]

### *IV. Personal Property Security Law Reform in England*

There have been several attempts to reform personal property security law in England.[41] The most recent complete set of proposals was presented by the Law Commission in 2004.[42] However, this proposal did not deal with security interests consented to by individuals, even though the need for reform is equally present there.[43] These would have been continued to be governed by the *Bills of Sale Acts 1878–1882,* which may receive modest reforms on the area of consumer protection,[44] but no complete overhaul, let alone comprehensive *PPSA* regime, is currently planned.

---

[36] Duggan & Ziegel, *Secured Transactions in Personal Property, supra* note 12 at 7–9. For a historical perspective on the *Conditional Sales Acts* see GVV Nicholls, "The Law Governing Conditional Sales in Canada" (1939) 21:1 JCompLeg 1.

[37] Duggan & Ziegel, *Secured Transactions in Personal Property, supra* note 12 at 9–10.

[38] See *Dearle v Hall* (1823), 38 ER 475 (Ch).

[39] [1976] 1 WLR 676 (CA Civ).

[40] *Ibid.*

[41] See Noel McGrath, "Book Review: The Reform of UK Personal Property Security Law: Comparative Perspectives" (2011) 31 LS 159 at 159.

[42] Law Commission, *supra* note 34.

[43] See McGrath, *supra* note 41 at 160.

[44] See Department of Business Innovation & Skills, *A Better Deal for Consumers: Consultation on the Proposal to Ban the use of Bills of Sale for Consumer Lending* (London: Her Majesty's Stationery Office, 2009).

## B. The *PPSA* Approach to Security Interests in Personal Property

### *I. Enactment of PPSAs*

The situation in the Canadian Common Law provinces is different from English law. In Common Law Canada, *PPSAs* were passed. The reform process began in Ontario, where the precursor to the modern *Personal Property Security Act* was passed by the provincial legislative assembly in 1967. The Canadian Bar Association established a committee that prepared a Uniform Personal Property Security Act. Acts based on this uniform act were enacted, some with significant innovations, in Manitoba (1973),[45] Saskatchewan (1979, modernized in 1993),[46] Prince Edward Island (1990),[47] New Brunswick (1993),[48] the Northwest Territories (1994, also in force in Nunavut),[49] Nova Scotia (1995–96),[50] Yukon (1981),[51] Alberta (1988),[52] British Columbia (1989),[53] and Newfoundland and Labrador (1998).[54] The fact that each common law jurisdiction has its own *PPSA* should be kept in mind, but to make the text simpler to read, I use the singular generic *PPSA* unless I make reference to a particular case. When making reference to specific statutory provisions outside the context of an actual case, I use the *PPSA (Ont)* as an example.

The Canadian legislation has much in common with the American *Article 9 UCC*. But unlike in the United States, the process of *PPSA* legislation did not become necessary because of a shortage of credit securities. The common law list of secured transactions – particularly the recognition of the floating charge – meant that creditors had a variety of effective ways of securing credit. But it was felt that the common law approach was unsystematic and did not result in a coherent priority scheme.[55]

---

[45] *Personal Property Security Act,* CCSM, c P35.

[46] *Personal Property Security Act,* SS 1993, c P-6.2.

[47] *Personal Property Security Act,* RSPEI 1998, c P-3.1.

[48] *Personal Property Security Act,* SNB, 1993, c P-3.1.

[49] *Personal Property Security Act,* SNWT 1994, c 8.

[50] *Personal Property Security Act,* SNS 1995–1996, c 13.

[51] *Personal Property Security Act,* RSY, 2002, c 169.

[52] *Personal Property Security Act,* RSA 2000, c P-7.

[53] *Personal Property Security Act,* RSBC 1996, c 359.

[54] *Personal Property Security Act,* SNL 1998, c P-7.1.

[55] See Ronald CC Cuming, "Article 9 North of 49°: The Canadian PPS Acts and the Quebec Civil Code" (1995) 29 Loy L Rev 971 at 972–73; Ronald CC Cuming, "The Internationalization of Secured Financing Law: The Spreading Influence of the Concepts UCC, Article 9 and Its Progeny" in: Ross Cranston, ed, *Making Commercial Law: Essays in Honour of Roy Goode* (Oxford: Clarendon Press, 1997) 499 at 508.

## *II. The Functionalist Approach to Security Interests*

### *1. Concept*

The *PPSA* introduced the unitary concept of a "security interest." This concept entails both common law security devices (*i.e.* mortgage, pledge, charge) as well as quasi-security devices based on the allocation of title and applies the same rule to them, regardless of their formal appearance. However, the *PPSA* does not touch the underlying legal concepts used to establish the security interest but instead govern the exercise of those rights used for the security purpose that derive from the security interests. Thus, allocation of title may for instance still be of interest for tax purposes, but the rights and obligations of creditor and debtor as far as the security purpose is concerned do not change based on allocation of title, and the *PPSA* is based on the rejection of deriving any consequences from property law concepts.[56] The claim that the *PPSA* negates the title of the transferor in a retention-of-title sales contract thus goes too far.[57]

Furthermore, the *PPSA* applies to certain transactions regardless of whether or not they are used for a security purpose or not. These are called "deemed security interests." They are transfers of accounts and chattel paper[58] and all long-term leases for a period of over a year,[59] as well as consignments that secure a debt.[60] If deemed security interests do not secure a debt, the part in the *PPSA* on rights and remedies is inapplicable.[61] However, the priority regime is still in place.

### *2. Criticism*

The *PPSA* concept of a unitary security interest has not been met with universal acclaim.[62] Bridge and others raise three points against the apparent break of the *PPSA* with property concepts.

First, the *PPSA* includes transactions (*e.g.* long-term leases, assignment of accounts or chattel paper) that are not meant to secure credit within their scope

---

[56] Bridge *et al, supra* note 3 at 573.

[57] Cf. Michael G Bridge, "The Scope and Limits of Security Interests" in: Horst Eidenmüller & Eva-Maria Kieninger, eds, *The Future of Secured Credit in Europe* (Berlin: Walter de Gruyter, 2008) 180 at 195; Cuming, "The Internationalization of Secured Financing Law", *supra* note 55 at 523.

[58] *PPSA (Ont), supra* note 1, s 2(b).

[59] *Ibid,* s 2(c). However, long-term licenses do not fall under the scope of a *PPSA,* see *Stoke Resources & Consulting Inc v Auto Body Services Red Deer Ltd*, 2011 ABCA 370.

[60] *PPSA (Ont), supra* note 1, s 2(a)(ii). For an overview see Duggan & Ziegel, *Secured Transactions in Personal Property, supra* note 12 at 55–60.

[61] *PPSA (Ont), supra* note 1, s 57.1.

[62] See Bridge *et al, supra* note 3. In the English context see Davies, "The Reform of English Personal Property Security Law", *supra* note 3.

because certain elements of these transaction approach credit securities. This may be contrary to the expectations of the parties when they contract, who thus do not expect to have secured transaction law to apply.[63]

Second, there is a logical breach within the *PPSA* when it includes certain ownership interests within its scope. The fact that the *PPSA* had to resort to the technique of a legal fiction to include certain ownership interests within its scope shows that even under the *PPSA,* ownership and security interest are different concepts.[64] Bridge and others criticize this approach because the *PPSA* purports to promote function over form. However, if interests serving a clearly proprietary purpose (such as certain long-term leases) are included in the scope of the *PPSA* for formal reasons, this puts form over function again.[65] Against this criticism, it can be argued that the *PPSA* may use a formal criterion such as the length of the lease to include a transaction within its scope. However, this formalism is not an end in itself. Rather, it lowers transaction costs by establishing a clear criterion that is foreseeable for the parties. The object of criticism in the second point of criticism is thus nothing but an answer to the first point of criticism.

The third point of criticism is that the *PPSA* relies on the very concept of property because a security interest is an interest in property. Thus, property itself still needs to be defined.[66] However, this point is addressed in the *PPSA* itself,[67] which provides that common law and equity continue to apply for questions not governed by the *PPSA*. Thus, the *PPSA* still makes reference to the common law to provide a definition of "property." The gap within the *PPSA* is intentional.

## C. The *PPSA* Framework

After having looked at how the functionalist approach of the *PPSA* security interest differs from the common law approach to security interests in the preceding sections, the purpose of this section is to give a brief overview of the concrete working mechanism of a *PPSA* security interest. First, the creation (in *PPSA* terminology: "attachment") and perfection of the interest is explained, then I take a look at the rights deriving from the security interest and how a conflict of competing interests is resolved within the *PPSA*.

---

[63] Bridge *et al, supra* note 3 at 575.
[64] *Ibid* at 575.
[65] *Ibid* at 575.
[66] *Ibid* at 575–76.
[67] See e.g. *PPSA (Ont), supra* note 1, s 72.

### *I. Creation of the Security Interest: Attachment*

When entering a security agreement, the parties conclude two distinct legal acts: the security agreement as a contract, and the creation of the security interest itself as a proprietary right. It is the latter that in *PPSA* terminology is referred to as "attachment."[68]

Attachment requires that three conditions be met: value must be given by the secured party, the debtor must have a right in the collateral, and the agreement must be evidenced either in writing or by the creditor's possession of the collateral. The last of these conditions is also called the "evidentiary element".[69]

#### *1. Value*

The *PPSA* concept of value does not differ from its common law definition. "Value [...] means any consideration sufficient to support a simple contract."[70]

#### *2. Rights in the Collateral*

The condition that the debtor has a property right in the property is an important bridge between the *PPSA* framework and general property law. The right in the property which is being used as collateral need not be an ownership right. Yet because of the *nemo dat quod non habet* rule, the creditor will only be a purchaser of the pre-existing debtor's property right.[71] If the property right is only a possesory right, then the *nemo dat quod non habet* rule means that the purchaser of the security interest will not prevail against a person having title to a better interest.[72]

From this rule it follows that equities attached to the property prior to the attachment remain impressed on the property.[73] Cuming, Walsh and Wood argue that this is not true for a creditor who takes property subject to a trust even if the debtor conveys in breach of trust under the condition that the creditor does not know about the trust. However, as is discussed in more detail later in this book,[74] this is only a function of the rules of equity, not a particular characteristic of the *PPSA* security interest.

---

[68] See Ronald CC Cuming, Catherine E Walsh & Roderick J Wood, *Personal Property Security Law,* 2[d] edn (Toronto: Irwin Law, 2012) at 240–46.

[69] *PPSA (Ont), supra* note 1, s 11(2). See Cuming, Walsh & Wood, *Personal Property Security Law,* preceding note at 241.

[70] *PPSA (Ont), supra* note 1, s 1(1).

[71] *Gray v Royal Bank of Canada* (1997), 143 DLR (4[th]) 179 at 25 (BC SC).

[72] *Ibid,* referring to *Armory v Delamirie* (1722), 93 ER 664 (KB). The latter was affirmed by *Bird v Fort Frances,* [1949] 2 DLR 791 (Ont HCJ).

[73] *Agar v 762250 Ontario Ltd* (1994), 6 PPSAC (2[d]) 292 (Ont Gen Div).

[74] See Part III: § 13 D, "PPSA Security Interest and Equitable Property Rights".

A true exception to the *nemo dat* rule appears to take place if the debtor holds the property by virtue of a conditional sales contract or security-lease. In this case, the second creditor does not receive a security interest subject to the pre-existing legal rights of the first creditor. Rather, priority between the two is determined by the *PPSA* scheme. This is a result of the fact that, due to the functional *PPSA* approach, the first creditor's initial right becomes subject to the *PPSA* framework. Cuming, Walsh and Wood argue that these cases do not form an exception to the *nemo dat, but rather* that they should be explained by treating the debtor as the owner of the property for the purpose of the *PPSA* framework[75] This problem is further discussed in the section looking at the particular problems of the interaction of the *PPSA* with general property law.[76]

The *PPSA* allows the debtor to grant a security interest in property not currently held by her. This security interest in "after-acquired property" attaches to the property as soon as the debtor receives a property right in the property provided the other conditions are met.[77]

### *3. The Evidentiary Element*

Regarding the evidentiary element, in all jurisdictions but Ontario, it is only required for attachment to be considered to have taken place with regard to third parties, but not between creditor and debtor. In other words, if s 11(2) *PPSA (Ont)* is read literally, in Ontario the evidentiary element is a requirement for the security interest itself to have effect between the parties of the security agreement. However, even if the evidentiary element is not yet met, effect to the agreement is usually given effect in the relationship between the parties in Ontario as well.[78]

## *II. Perfection of the Security Interest*

In the *PPSA* context, "perfection" means that a security interest is eligible to participate in the *PPSA* priority scheme.[79] The effects of perfection are restricted to secured transactions law. For example, the fact that a security interest was duly registered is not a defence against a claim by a purchaser without notice of the interest for breach of the implied warranty that the property be unencumbered.[80] In order for the security interest to be eligible for perfection,

[75] Cuming, Walsh & Wood, *Personal Property Security Law, supra* note 68 at 256.

[76] See Part III: § 13 B, "The Debtor's Right in the Collateral and the Object of Attachment".

[77] Cuming, Walsh & Wood, *Personal Property Security Law, supra* note 68 at 262; *PPSA (Ont), supra* note 1, s 12(1).

[78] Cuming, Walsh & Wood, *Personal Property Security Law, supra* note 68 at 241–42.

[79] *Ibid* at 296–97.

[80] *Zuker v Paul* (1982), 37 OR ($2^d$) 161 (HCJ). See also Jacob S Ziegel, "Interaction of Sales Law and the OPPSA, and Related Questions" (1982) 7 CBLJ 338.

the interest must have already attached to the property.[81] The two principal means of perfection are registration[82] and possession.[83]

If the debtor transfers the property without the knowledge of the creditor, the security interest remains perfected until the end of a grace period of thirty days after the creditor learns either about the transaction or the sale, whichever is later.[84] If the creditor also holds a security interest against the purchaser, a discharge of the second security interest does not un-perfect the security interest in the transferred property, even if the pre-existing security interest in the creditor-purchaser relationship is a security interest in all present and after-acquired property.[85]

### *III. Creditor Rights Deriving from a Security Interest*

As a consequence of the unitary concept of a security interest, the *PPSA* provides for a unitary set of rights resulting from the security. The creditor may take the collateral in satisfaction of the obligation,[86] but only insofar as debtor and other interested third parties do not object. If the latter object, the creditor may apply to the court to render the objection ineffective.[87] If the creditor does not take the collateral, she must sell and account for the collateral according to s 63 *PPSA (Ont).* The statute thus deems sale of the collateral the default way of realizing the credit security. This is an outflow of the primary "hypothecary character"[88] of the *PPSA* security interest: the creditor's foremost non-possessory right in somebody else's property to satisfy an outstanding obligation.[89] They seem to refer to the difference between the old Common Law chattel mortgage – which was based on transfer of ownership to the creditor and where foreclosure of the debtor's equity would have been the default realization option – and the *PPSA* security interest, where the default option is the power to dispose of somebody else's property.

---

[81] Cuming, Walsh & Wood, *Personal Property Security Law, supra* note 68 at 242.
[82] *PPSA (Ont), supra* note 1, s 23.
[83] *Ibid,* s 22.
[84] See *ibid,* s 48(2).
[85] See *Lisec America, Inc v Barber Suffolk Ltd,* 2012 ONCA 37.
[86] *PPSA (Ont), supra* note 1, s 65(2).
[87] *Ibid,* s 65(5).
[88] Cuming, Walsh & Wood, *Personal Property Security Law, supra* note 68 at 8.
[89] *Ibid* at 7–8. See also Yaëll Emerich, "La nature juridique des sûretés réelles en droit civil et en Common Law: Une question de tradition juridique?" (2010) 44:1 RJT 95 at 117.

## *IV. Priority*

### *1. General Rule*

As a general rule, priority between competing *PPSA* security interests is determined by order of perfection.[90] If the conflict is between two security interests that are perfected by registration, then priority is decided by order of registration rather than order of perfection.[91] There are three types of security interests that are subject to special priority rules, which can be divided into two classes. The first class contains the narrowly focused production money security interest in animals and crops,[92] which mostly relates to farming ventures, and the broad purchase-money security interest. I focus on the latter. The second class contains security interests in securities.

### *2. Purchase-Money Security Interests in the PPSA*

Unlike other security interests, purchase-money security interests (PMSI) are subject to a special priority rule. A PMSI is either a security interest which secures payment of the price or the repayment of o loan that was advanced for the purpose of buying the property, or a long-term lease.[93] Where both seller and lender obtain a PMSI, the seller will prevail.[94] A PMSI creditor must perfect her interest within a certain time frame to gain priority over all other security interests in the same property.[95]

In *MacPhee Chevrolet Buick GMC Cadillac Ltd v SWS Fuels Ltd,*[96] the Court of Appeal for Nova Scotia held that the PMSI creditor only receives priority if the security interest is perfected within the defined period after the debtor has obtained "possession *as a debtor*" (in case of s 33(2) *PPSA (Ont):* 15 days), and more specifically that the meaning of the phrase "*as a debtor*" does not mean that the debtor must have obtained possession as the debtor of the creditor.[97] As a result, if the debtor has obtained possession of property as the debtor of one first secured creditor and then continues to possess the property while title to the property is transferred to the second creditor, the second

---

[90] *PPSA (Ont), supra* note 1, s 30.

[91] *Ibid,* s 30(1)(1).

[92] See e.g. *ibid,* s 32. Unlike other *PPSAs,* the Yukon and Ontario statutes do not cover animals, see Cuming, Walsh & Wood, *Personal Property Security Law, supra* note 68 at 469.

[93] *PPSA (Ont), supra* note 1, s 1(1). See for more details Cuming, Walsh & Wood, *Personal Property Security Law, supra* note 68 at 435–39.

[94] *PPSA (Ont), supra* note 1, s 33(3). Se also Cuming, Walsh & Wood, *Personal Property Security Law, supra* note 68 at 465–67.

[95] *PPSA (Ont), supra* note 1, s 33(2).

[96] 2011 NSCA 35 [*MacPhee*].

[97] *Ibid* at para 41.

creditor can no longer avail herself of a PMSI. The Court also held that the debtor does not have constructive possession for the new PMSI creditor.[98]

As a matter of policy, this is right. It would be unclear as to when the constructive possession is supposed to have taken place. Possible moments are the purchase of title by the new PMSI creditor from the old creditor or the time of the new agreement by the new PMSI creditor and the debtor. The first moment is not appropriate because the debtor does not necessarily know about the transfer of title. The second moment is not suitable because by virtue of the PMSI agreement, the debtor receives a right to possession. It would be contradictory to construct constructive possession by the debtor for the creditor when the agreement intends to give the debtor a right to possession against the creditor.

The resulting weak position of the purchaser of collateralized property is a result of the policy embodied by the *PPSA:*

> "The Legislature has not conditioned the PMSI's super-priority on the date the debtor 'first possesses collateral as a debtor to each new creditor, despite that the debtor earlier had obtained his possession of this collateral as a debtor with another creditor.' Whether [s 35 *PPSA (Ont)*] should embody that language is a policy choice for the Legislature."[99]

On the other hand, it is possible to obtain a PMSI in collateral which the debtor already possessed or even had some property right in. As long as the debtor does not have the best title to the best interest, the creditor can always advance money that allows the debtor to get a better interest in the property. If this happens, the creditor has advanced money for the purchase of the property and can avail herself of PMSI super-priority.[100]

The current *PPSA* PMSI scheme is not without problems. First, there is an issue relating to PMSIs if the debtor buys and sells large quantities of inventory. Technically, a PMSI relates to one specifically purchased item, which creates high transaction costs when purchasing lots of inventory. The PMSI priority status is lost where the debtor takes out a new credit and uses the money to discharge the PMSI credit in a refinancing transaction.[101] The financer would be required to constantly keep track whether or not the PMSI property has been sold. They might also lose out against a global financing bank with a regular security interest. There have been decisions to the effect that that PMSI priority

---

[98] *Ibid* at para 44.

[99] *Ibid* at para 41.

[100] *Greyvest Leasing Inc v CIBC* (1991), 1 PPSAC (2d) 264 (Ont Gen Div), referring to *North Platte State Bank v Production Credit Ass'n of North Platte,* 189 Neb 44 (1972).

[101] Canadian Conference on Personal Property Security Law, Working Group (CCPPSL Working Group), *Report to the Canadian Conference on Personal Property Security Law on Proposals for Changes to the Personal Property Security Acts,* (2017) at 25–26, referring to *MacPhee, supra* note 96; *Unisource Canada Inc v Laurentian Bank of Canada* (2000), 47 OR (3d) 616 (CA) [*Unisource*]*; Battlefords Credit Union Limited v Ilnicki* (1991), 82 DLR (4th) 69 (Sask CA) [*Ilnicki*].

should extend to the new debt,[102] but the statutory wording is not clear in that regard. To avoid these issues, the CCPPSL Working Group suggests extending the PMSI priority to "related transactions."[103]

Second, the *PPSAs* do not account the fact that a debtor may owe several debts to their creditor, only one of which qualifies as a PMSI. In that case, there needs to be a repayment ranking scheme.[104] The CCPPSL Working Group proposes that by default, absent a different intention, payments are credited towards unsecured, then secured non-PMSI debts, and finally to PMSI debts.[105] In Saskatchewan, both suggestions will be implemented,[106] but in relation to the first point, it will merely codify the case law in that jurisdiction.[107]

### *3. Securities*

Securities are essentially certificated rights in the assets of an enterprise.[108] Security interests in securities can be perfected by control or by the regular means,[109] but perfection by control will give the creditor super-priority.[110] Whether or not a creditor has control is determined by the *Securities Transfer Act,* not the *PPSA (Ont).*[111] Primary means of getting control are delivery of the security, or a control agreement between the creditor and the security issuer or intermediary. The *PPSAs* do not provide for a means of control being used to perfect a security interest in a bank account, unlike the *Code civil du Québec.* As an example of vertical co-ordination in a bijural system, this will be addressed below.[112]

### *4. Electronic Chattel Paper*

A chattel paper is a paper that represents a monetary obligation and a security interest in specific tangible personal property.[113] Under the *PPSA* framework,

---

[102] *Unisource,* preceding note; *Ilnicki,* preceding note.

[103] CCPPSL Working Group, *supra* note 101 at 18–19, 26–27.

[104] *Ibid* at 28.

[105] *Ibid* at 30.

[106] *Personal Property Security Amendment Act,* SS 2019, c 15.

[107] See David G Gerecke & Fraiba Jalal, "Amendments to PMSI Rules in Saskatchewan" (*Miller Thomson,* 12 February 2019) <https://www.millerthomson.com/en/publications/communiques-and-updates/financial-services-insolvency-communique/february-12–2019-fsi/amendments-to-pmsi-rules-in-saskatchewan/> accessed 13 May 2019.

[108] *Securities Transfer Act,* SO 2006, c 8 [*STA*], s 1.

[109] *PPSA (Ont), supra* note 1, s 30.1(8).

[110] *Ibid,* s 30.1(2).

[111] *Ibid,* s 1(2); *STA, supra* note 108, s 25; s 24; s 23.

[112] See Part IV: § 15 B, "Crown Privileges".

[113] CCPPSL Working Group, *supra* note 101 at 4.

a (possessory) pledge of the chattel paper gives the pledgee priority over secured creditors with a merely registered security interest in the chattel paper.[114] This approach is ostensibly problematic where the chattel paper is an electronic document because it would be unclear who would be first to take possession of the electronic document.[115] As a result, the CCPPSL Working group has recommended that the concept of control should be used to allow possession of electronic chattel paper.[116] This change has been accepted in Saskatchewan.[117] However, it is difficult to share the enthusiasm for electronic chattel paper from a third-party perspective. Given that the CCPPSL Working Group defines "control" in a way that it essentially creates a private security register,[118] it is unclear what the advantage over the general *PPSA* register is.

## D. Conclusion

The advantage of the *PPSA* approach to secured transaction is that it does away with traditional concepts of property law. Instead of relying on traditional notions of title and interest, *Article 9 UCC* – and in its wake the *PPSA* – instituted the new concept of a "security interest." Arguably, it is this very abandonment of traditional property law concepts that make the *PPSA* approach to secured transactions exportable.

However, two examples, to be looked at in the following chapters, show that the relationship between secured transactions law and general property law cannot be left unresolved. First, there is the example of the relationship between *PPSA* security interests and equitable property interests.[119] Second, there is the relationship between a *PPSA* security interest and a *Bank Act* security interest, a property right created at the federal level and thus at the vertical plane of bijuralism.[120] These two examples show that it is necessary to put secured transaction law on a more robust property law foundation.

[114] *Ibid* at 5.
[115] CCPPSL Working Group, *supra* note 101 at 6–7.
[116] *Ibid* at 9.
[117] *Personal Property Security Amendment Act, supra* note 106.
[118] CCPPSL Working Group, *supra* note 101 at 12–13.
[119] See Part III: § 13 D, "PPSA Security Interest and Equitable Property Rights".
[120] See Part IV: § 15 A.V.1, "Common Law: Nemo Dat".

# § 13 *PPSA* Security Interests and Property Law

## A. Nature of the *PPSA* Security Interest

One question whose answer is not immediately apparent is whether the *PPSA* creates a legal or an equitable right. There is some support for a legal characterization in legal scholarship. As regards interests in after-acquired property, Cuming, Walsh and Wood argue that the reason they were not recognized at law under the common law framework was that a legal right combined with the *nemo dat* rule would have given the creditor too strong a hold on the property. As long as these interests were equitable, this situation was remedied by the equitable *bona fide* purchaser exception. Within the *PPSA* framework, the *bona fide* purchaser protection is now made possible by the security interest publicity requirement. Consequently the security interest could be recognized as a legal right.[1] Cuming, Walsh and Wood suggest a uniform legal characterization of all *PPSA* security interests, but stress that a characterization is no longer needed *within* the *PPSA* framework.[2] Other doctrinal writers also advocate a legal characterization of the *PPSA* interest.[3]

One straightforward argument for characterizing the security interest as legal would be to say that all property interests created by statute are legal. There are, however, instances of statutory equitable property interests. Equitable interests and estates in land under s 1(3) *Law of Property Act, 1925*[4] are but one example.

While it had already hinted at a re-characterization of all security interests as legal,[5] recently, the Supreme Court of Canada held that the interest is indeed

---

[1] See Ronald CC Cuming, Catherine E Walsh & Roderick J Wood, *Personal Property Security Law,* 2[d] edn (Toronto: Irwin Law, 2012) at 262.

[2] *Ibid* at 262.

[3] See Anthony J Duggan & Jacob S Ziegel, *Secured Transactions in Personal Property: Cases, Text and Materials,* 5[th] edn (Toronto: Emond Montgomery Publications, 2009) at 116; Marc-Alexandre Poirier, "Analysis of the Interaction Between Security Under Section 427 of the Bank Act and Provincial Law: A Bijural Perspective" (2003) 63 R du B 287 at 360; John GH Stumbles, "The PPSA: The Extended Reach of the Definition of the PPSA Security Interest" (2011) 34:2 UNSWLJ 448 at 454.

[4] 15 & 16 Geo V, c 20.

[5] See *Royal Bank of Canada v Sparrow Electric Corp,* [1997] 1 SCR 411 at 44–53 [*Sparrow*], Gonthier J.

legal in nature; the Court also suggested that the legal nature of the *PPSA* security interest is not a function of the wording of the security agreement.

"[I]t is clear that *PPSA* security interest, just as the Bank Act security interest, is a statutorily created interest and, as such, an interest recognized at law. While some of the historical forms of security created equitable rather than legal interests, the effect of the *PPSA*'s functional approach, which covers all of these antecedent security interests, is to treat them all equally as 'security interest' under the *PPSA*. This conclusion is also the consensus found in the academic commentary, and I see no reason to depart from it."[6]

This result is qestioned in *Re Production Enhancement Group Inc,*[7] where the Court of Queen's Bench of Alberta held that the *Personal Property Security Act*[8] does not prevent the parties from creating an "equitable charge." However, that case revolved around the question whether language that under common law would have created an equitable charge is a security agreement resulting in a *PPSA* security interest. It was not concerned with the legal or equitable nature of the resulting interest. In conclusion, the *PPSA* security interest can be classified as a legal property right.

## B. The Debtor's Right in the Collateral and the Object of Attachment

The *PPSAs* permit the creation of a security interest in the debtor's property. This reference to the common law concept of property raises a number of issues. The first relates to the very notion of property. I have already made reference to the Supreme Court's decision in *Saulnier v Royal Bank of Canada* above.[9] *Saulnier* relied on a characterization of a fishing licence as akin to *profit à prendre,* a common law right transferring the right to the fruits to the transferee. Justice Binnie identified policy reasons for including a fishing licence in the property category for the purpose of creating a *PPSA* security interest as well as doctrinal formal reasons (the formal proximity of the fishing licence to a *profit à prendre*).[10] The problem is that these two reasons work together in case of a fishing licence, but not necessarily in case of other licences that cannot be compared to a *profit à prendre.* In those cases, the two lines of

---

[6] *Bank of Montreal v Innovation Credit Union,* 2010 SCC 47 at para 42, Charron J. See also Stumbles, *supra* note 3 at 453–56.

[7] 2011 ABQB 350.

[8] RSA 2000, c P-7.

[9] See Part I: § 2 B.II.3.b), "The Notion of Property in Federal Law".

[10] *Saulnier v Royal Bank of Canada,* 2008 SCC 58 at paras 25–50, Binnie J.

reasoning are actively opposed to each other.[11] For example, the analogy is much harder to make in relation to other licences such as taxi concessions.[12] The *profit à prendre* analogy in *Saulnier* cannot work for intellectual property licences and other contractual licences either.[13] Other licences thus bring a tension between a formal and policy-based/realistic approach to the law at the forefront. This is a problem that the Civilian monolithic approach to property, which views contractual rights as regular patrimonial objects, does not have.[14]

The second problem relating to the debtor's right in the collateral regards the proper conceptualization of the conditional-sales agreement and of other cases in which the creditor retains a better title to the property.[15] The *PPSA* does not explain to what the security interest of the vendor attaches. If title never passes to the debtor, the security interest cannot attach to the property right transferred to the debtor. There must be some other form of property to which the security interest may attach.

It cannot attach to any form of equity of redemption vested in the debtor because if she has not made any payment whatsoever towards the property, she has not received such equity. However, the *PPSA* allows for the security interest to attach before the assumed creation of such equity.[16] Section 23 *Personal Property Security Act*[17] is the general rule on perfection through registration and it does not mention that payment of the first rate as a condition for perfection, meaning the existence of an equity is not required. If perfection is possible, the security interest must have attached already because attachment is a condition for perfection according to s 20(1) *PPSA (Ont)*.

One way to avoid the problem is to accept that the treatment of a legal event by the *PPSA* is somewhat inconsistent with the characterization of the same event outside the law of secured transaction.[18] Alternatively, Ziegel and Denomme suggest that the *PPSA* transfers beneficial ownership of the collateral to the debtor:

"It is intrinsic to the creation of security under the Canadian legislation that the beneficial title in property subject to a security interest is, or remains, in the debtor and that once the

---

[11] Anthony J Duggan, "Current Issues in Secured Transactions Law in Canada: An Ontario Perspective" in: Louise Gullifer & Orkun Akseli, eds, *Secured Transactions Law Reform: Principles, Policies and Practice* (Oxford, Portland: Hart, 2016) 95 at 99.

[12] Canadian Conference on Personal Property Security Law, Working Group (CCPPSL Working Group), *Report to the Canadian Conference on Personal Property Security Law on Proposals for Changes to the Personal Property Security Acts,* (2017) at 33.

[13] *Ibid* at 34.

[14] See Part II: § 4 D, "Right and Object of Right".

[15] Cuming, Walsh & Wood, *Personal Property Security Law, supra* note 1 at 124.

[16] See *ibid* at 124.

[17] RSO 1990, c P.10.

[18] See Cuming, Walsh & Wood, *Personal Property Security Law, supra* note 1 at 124.

secured obligation has been discharged the debtor becomes the unencumbered owner of the collateral."[19]

The use of the phrase "beneficial title" implies that the *PPSA* convey a kind of equitable title to the property to the owner even in case of a conditional-sale agreement. This, however, would go against the equitable principle that there is no property alienation without consent.[20] Another, less dogmatic analysis is to say that the *PPSA* treats any substantial security agreement as a security agreement, and therefore, for the purpose of the *PPSA*, a conditional-sale agreement is a security agreement, not a retention of title by the seller. Therefore, under a *PPSA* analysis, the debtor/buyer acquires title. However, under this analysis, the *PPSA* goes even further in that it transfers not only an equitable interest, but also full legal title without consent.

An alternative approach consists of saying that the debtor always has a possession and possession is a right. This right is sufficient for attachment.[21] MacDougall also directs us to the cases of *Jordan v Butler*[22] and *Re Samuels & Co, Inc.*[23] In both cases, the court held that the fact that the debtor held a voidable title was sufficient for the security interest to attach because she who has voidable title can confer good title to a *bona fide* purchaser.[24] But of course these cases could also be explained on a mere possessory basis.

A final issue arising in relation to the object of collateralization arises where a bank takes security in its own debt towards its customers. Because this problem exemplifies the vertical vector if interaction in a bijural system, we will look at it below in the relevant chapter.[25]

## C. *PPSA* and the Wrongful Interference with Personal Property

The *PPSA* contains rules about creation, priority, and enforcement of statutorily recognized security interests in personal property. The question as to which other rights the secured creditor has in relation to the property is left to the

---

[19] Jacob S Ziegel & David L Denomme, *The Ontario Personal Property Security Act: Commentary and Analysis* (Aurora, Ont: Canada Law Book, 1994) at 63.

[20] Michael G Bridge *et al*, "Formalism, Functionalism, and Understanding the Law of Secured Transactions" (1999) 44 McGill LJ 567 at 589–90.

[21] Bruce MacDougall, "The Debtor's Interest in Personal Property Under the PPSA" (1994) 33:1 Alta L Rev 80, referring to *Kinetics Technology Intern Corp v Fourth Nat Bank of Tulsa*, 705 F2$^{d}$ 396 (10$^{th}$ Cir 1983).

[22] 156 NW2$^{d}$ 778 (Neb 1968).

[23] 526 F2$^{d}$ 1238 (5$^{th}$ Cir 1975).

[24] MacDougall, *supra* note 21 at 96–98.

[25] See Part IV: § 15 B, "Crown Privileges".

general law.[26] Due to the possessory basis of the common law torts relating to wrongful interference with personal property, common law torts leave a gap in respect of a range of important issues that may arise in relation to a wrongful interference with personal property.[27] This is particularly problematic where the property right is non-possessory.

A *PPSA* security interest is conceptually independent of a right to possession. The *PPSA* right is not a right to possession, but a hypothecary right to use somebody else's property to satisfy an outstanding debt.[28] First, while the *PPSA* creditor has a right to seize the collateral,[29] this is a function of default. The right to possess is not the same as her security interest, and its condition precedent is default.[30] Second, the right to possession enjoyed by the *PPSA* creditor is conceptually different from the right to possession envisioned by common law torts. While the *PPSA* creditor might take permanent possession in lieu of satisfaction of the debt, this possibility is not absolute, but rather subject to objections by the debtor and other creditors.[31] If they object, the creditor can only seize the collateral as a first step in her attempt to monetize the collateral. This right is different from having a right to possession allowing use and enjoyment of property. Arguably, it is the latter which is protected by the common law torts.[32] At the same time, where the *PPSA* creditor can successfully bring a conversion claim, she could obtain higher damages than what is protected by her security interest.[33]

Because a purchaser of property subject to a perfected security interest comes under the scope of the *nemo dat* rule, the *PPSA* creditor can seize property in the hands of the third party.[34]

Cuming thus argues that the *PPSA* should contain a statutory remedy that allows the compensation of any prejudice suffered because the collateral is no longer able to serve its function as collateral.[35]

---

[26] See Ronald CC Cuming, "Secured Creditors' Non-Statutory Remedies: Unfinished Business" (2012) 91:2 Can Bar Rev 243; Cynthia Hawes, *Tortious Interference with Goods in New Zealand: The Law of Conversion, Detinue and Trespass* (Ph.D. Thesis, University of Canterbury, 2010) <http://ir.canterbury.ac.nz/handle/10092/3834> accessed 20 June 2016 at 148–55.

[27] Cuming, "Secured Creditors' Non-Statutory Remedies", preceding note at 245.

[28] See Part III: § 12 C.III, "Creditor Rights Deriving from a Security Interest".

[29] See Part III: § 12 C.III, "Creditor Rights Deriving from a Security Interest".

[30] Cuming, "Secured Creditors' Non-Statutory Remedies", *supra* note 26 at 257.

[31] See Part III: § 12 C.III, "Creditor Rights Deriving from a Security Interest".

[32] Cuming, "Secured Creditors' Non-Statutory Remedies", *supra* note 26 at 257.

[33] *Ibid* at 258–59.

[34] *Ibid* at 258.

[35] *Ibid* at 262–74.

## D. *PPSA* Security Interest and Equitable Property Rights

### *I. Common Law Priority Rules*

In this subsection, I look at the priority framework for competing legal and equitable interests at common law and equity; because both areas of law are non-statutory, they can be described as common law rules in the wider sense of the word "common law." The common law framework continues to shape the *PPSA* analysis, which I will discuss in the next subsection.

#### *1. Priority of Fixed Security Interests*

##### *a) Competing Legal and Equitable Interests*

Provided that the only consensual security interest involved is a fixed one, the priority of this security interest and the competing interest is governed by law and equity.[36] In case of a floating charge, rules similar to agency come into play as well.[37]

First, it should be said that the rules of law and equity are subject to modification by statutory registration requirements. However, where two consensual security interests are both equally perfected or unperfected, in most cases, the common law rules apply again.[38] According to common law, priority is defined by two rules.

First, the *nemo dat quod non habet* rule applies; thus, once the property is partly alienated, the same interest cannot be given again. This rule is modified by cases of ostensible authority and apparent ownership. For the successive assignment of accounts, the rule in *Dearle v Hall*[39] provides that the assignee who first gives notice to the account debtor has priority.

Second, a *bona fide* purchaser for value of a legal title without notice of any equitable interest ranks above the holder of the equitable interest.[40] A "purchaser" is anyone who acquires the interest by virtue of consent rather than by operation of law (for instance, the heir takes by operation of law); "for value" means that the transfer was not gratuitous.[41] The existence of notice is decisive

---

[36] Royston M Goode, *Goode on Legal Problems of Credit and Security,* ed by Louise Gullifer, 5th edn (London: Sweet & Maxwell, 2013) at para 5.2 [*Goode on Security*].

[37] *Ibid* at para 5.2.

[38] See for a more detailed analysis *ibid* at paras 5.24–5.35.

[39] (1823), 38 ER 475 (Ch).

[40] See *Goode on Security, supra* note 36, at para 5.09; John McGhee, *Snell's Equity,* 30th edn (London: Sweet & Maxwell, 2000) 4.8–32; Lionel D Smith, *The Law of Tracing* (Oxford: Clarendon Press, 1997) at 386–87.

[41] Smith, *The Law of Tracing,* preceding note at 386, note 35.

at the time the purchaser makes the advance.[42] The *bona fide* rule also applies to equitable liens.[43]

The rule enables the holder of low-ranking equitable interest to jump ahead of a higher-ranking holder of an equitable interest by making an advance for the purchase of legal title if she has no notice of the higher-ranking equity at the time of the advance. The higher priority of the legal purchase then tacks to the lower-ranking priority as well.[44] When a consensual security interest competes with a non-consensual interest, the general rules just described apply.[45]

### *b) Competing Equities*

Finally, when all concerned interests are equitable, the rules of equity apply. The general rule is that the first-in-time equity will prevail over later equities.[46] The reason is that every conveyance of an equitable interest is also based on the good conscience of the conveyee.[47] This rule only applies between equal equities. Where one conveyee has demonstrated partly inequitable behaviour, her interest will be subdued to the "better" equitable interest.[48]

## *2. Priority of Floating Charges*

The most important modification to the priority framework in cases of floating charges is that the debtor is authorised to deal with the property in the ordinary course of his business, which includes using the property for security.[49] The rule in *Dearle v Hall* does not apply and the creditor of a floating charge cannot gain priority over another secured creditor by giving notice to the account

---

[42] See *Goode on Security, supra* note 36, at para 5.09.

[43] McGhee, *supra* note 40 at para 28.2.

[44] *Dodds v Hills* (1865), 2 H & M 424 (KB), affirmed by *Macmillan Inc v Bishopsgate Investment Trust Plc (No 3)* (1993), [1995] 1 WLR 978 at 1001, 1003–4 (Ch D), Millet J, affirmed by *Macmillan Inc v Bishopsgate Investment Trust Plc (No 3)* (1995), [1996] WLR 387 (CA Civ) (dealing with conflict of laws issues). The rule in *Dodds* was also affirmed in real-estate cases, see *Taylor v Russell,* [1892] AC 244 (HL) and *Bailey v Barnes,* [1894] 1 Ch 25 (CA). See also *Goode on Security, supra* note 36, at para 5.9.

[45] *Goode on Security, supra* note 36, at para 5.37.

[46] See McGhee, *supra* note 40 at para 4.6.

[47] *Phillips v Phillips* (1861), 4 De GF & J 208 at 215 (QB), Lord Westbury LC: "I take it to be a clear proposition that every conveyance of an equitable interest is an innocent conveyance, that is to say, the grant of a person entitled merely in equity passes only that which he is justly entitled to and no more."

[48] For details, see McGhee, *supra* note 40 at paras 4.38–4.41.

[49] *Cox Moore v Peruvian Corporation, Ltd,* [1908] 1 Ch 604 (Ch D); *Re Hamilton's Windsor Ironworks Co* (1879), 12 Ch D 707 (Ch D). See also *Goode on Security, supra* note 36, at para 5.40.

debtor.[50] If the terms of the floating charge include a provision that prohibits the secured transaction, the floating charge retains its priority because any use of the property for security is a breach of the fiduciary duty, thus making the charge an encumbering equity, and the priority of the charge is then determined by the fact that it has been an inchoate security right.[51] It follows that it can be defeated by a *bona fide* purchaser for value without notice.[52] The same is not necessarily true for a purchase outside of the ordinary course of business.[53]

### *II. Priority in Relation to PPSA Security Interests*

In this subsection, I look at the priority between the *PPSA* security interests and equitable property rights. As in English law, the laws of *PPSA* jurisdictions no longer solely rely on the common law to determine priority. Rather, the *PPSA* contain its own priority framework, which is one of its advantages.[54]

However, this framework only determines the interaction of interests otherwise governed by the *PPSA*. The relationship between non-consensual equitable interests and consensual *PPSA* security interests is not governed by the *PPSA,* but by common law principles.[55] Thus, this subsection is mostly an application of the principles enumerated above.

#### *1. Priority of the Equitable Property Right*

There are two possible approaches for the holder of an equitable property right – for example, the beneficiary of a constructive trust or the creditor of an equitable lien – to assert priority over the *PPSA* security interest.

##### *a) General Priority Rules*

The first option available to the beneficiary or equitable creditor consists in the application of the general priority rules. Because the *PPSA* security interest is legal in nature, the equitable creditor could claim that the *PPSA* creditor is not a *bona fide* purchaser for value without notice.

On the other hand, if the *PPSA* creditor can show that she is a *bona fide* purchaser, her interest will outrank the interest of the beneficiary. Since the

---

[50] *Re Ind, Coope & Co Ltd,* [1911] 2 Ch 223 (Ch D); *Ward v Royal Exchange Shipping Company* (1887), 58 LT 174 (Ch D). See also *Goode on Security, supra* note 36, at para 5.40.

[51] *Wilson v Kelland,* [1910] 2 Ch 306 (Ch D); *English & Scottish Mercantile Investment Co Ltd v Brunton,* [1892] 2 QB 700 (CA). See also *Goode on Security, supra* note 36, at para 5.41.

[52] *English & Scottish Mercantile Investment Co Ltd v Brunton,* preceding note.

[53] See *Goode on Security, supra* note 36, at para 5.42.

[54] *Ibid* at para 5.2.

[55] Cuming, Walsh & Wood, *Personal Property Security Law, supra* note 1 at 514.

priority relationship between beneficiary and secured creditor is not one between two *PPSA* creditors, the *PPSA* priority scheme is inapplicable. Thus, the secured creditor will outrank the beneficiary even though her interest only conforms to the legal or equitable rules and remains unperfected under the *PPSA* rules.[56]

*b) The Rule in Barnes v Addy*

The second way in which the original beneficiary may preserve her priority is provided by the rule from *Barnes v Addy.*[57] Because the potentially liable *PPSA* creditor receives an interest in the trust property, she is appropriately put in the third category, as a knowing recipient. The next question is whether the constructive trust binds beneficiary and trustee in such a way that the claim for knowing receipt against the *PPSA* creditor can be made. Since the constructive trustee does not necessarily know about the constructive trust, the constructive trustee must act against the conscience.[58]

Lastly, the question whether not only the beneficiary of a constructive trust, but also the creditor of an equitable lien can make a "knowing receipt" claim remains. First, a claim for knowing receipt does not require a trust, but can be made for any breach of fiduciary relationship.[59] In Canadian law, this is true for the claim for knowing assistance,[60] and the requirements here are the same for knowing receipt.[61] Furthermore, it is suggested that the claim can be made based on any equitable relationship.[62] Then it would follow that the equitable lien is sufficient for a claim for knowing receipt as well. However, this leads to one particular result. If the *PPSA* creditor becomes constructive trustee by virtue of knowing receipt of property subject to an equitable lien, the creditor of the equitable lien suddenly becomes beneficiary of a trust, whereas before, she was only creditor of an equitable lien. That means her interest in the property is stronger than before. It would thus seem necessary not to make her a beneficiary, but rather to let the *PPSA* creditor become a debtor of an equitable lien.

---

[56] *iTrade Finance Inc v Bank of Montreal,* 2011 SCC 26 at para 58 [*iTrade*], Deschamps J.

[57] (1874), 9 LR Ch App 244. See Part II: § 10 C.II, "Following".

[58] Albert H Oosterhoff *et al, Oosterhoff on Trusts,* 7th edn (Toronto: Carswell, 2009) at 963. See also *Twinsectra Ltd v Yardley,* [2002] UKHL 12, in particular at para 76, Lord Millet.

[59] McGhee, *supra* note 40 9.42–43.

[60] Oosterhoff *et al, supra* note 58 at 963–64.

[61] Cf. for English law McGhee, *supra* note 40 at para 9.43.

[62] See Oosterhoff *et al, supra* note 58 at 963–64 with further references.

*2. Priority of the PPSA Security Interest Over Equitable Property Rights*

Because the *PPSA* security interest is considered to be a legal right, it defeats a prior equitable property right if the creditor is a *bona fide* purchaser for value without notice.[63] This rule was applied in *iTrade Finance Inc v Bank of Montreal.*[64] An exception such as the one in s 136 *LPA, 1925* is not part of the *PPSA* framework. Furthermore, if the holding of the Supreme Court of Canada in *Bank of Montreal v Innovation Credit Union* can be considered to be good law for all varieties of *PPSA* security interests,[65] the *PPSA* would re-characterize all former equitable security interests. Thus, the *PPSA* creditor enjoys a much better protection from any equitable interests than her non-statutory counterparts. Regarding the notice requirement, it could be argued that a *PPSA* creditor will always have constructive notice of the equitable property right because it is the result of a court order. But the constructive trust attaches even before the court makes its order. The decision in *iTrade* was unclear whether "purchaser" means "purchaser" as meant in common law and equity or as defined in the *PPSA.*[66] In that particular case, the defendant met both definitions. While both definitions are essentially the same, it seems to me that the right definition is the one pre-dating the *PPSA*. In effect, the application of the *bona fide* rule is operating outside of the *PPSA* framework and thus no recourse should be had to *PPSA* concepts.

The same is not true if the *PPSA* security interest comes first in time. The priority seems straightforward in a first fact pattern: where the debtor already has title to the property, the *PPSA* security interest is created, and the equitable property right is then created later. In this pattern the *nemo dat* rule should apply and the equitable property right can only attach to whatever right the debtor has.[67] It should be noted, however, that *Board of Industrial Relations v Avco Financial Services Realty Ltd et al*[68] involved a chattel mortgage, not a charge. The application of the *Board of Industrial Relations v Avco Financial Services Realty Ltd et al* principle in *Royal Bank of Canada v Sparrow Electric Corp* is thus not self-evident. In other words, *Board of Industrial Relations v Avco Financial Services Realty Ltd et al* can only stand for the proposition that

[63] Jamie Glister, "The Role of Trusts in the PPSA" (2011) 34:2 UNSWLJ 628 at 632, note 22 draws the same conclusion.

[64] *Supra* note 56 at paras 58–62, Deschamps J.

[65] See Part III: § 13 A, "Nature of the PPSA Security Interest".

[66] *iTrade, supra* note 56 at 62–66, Deschamps J.

[67] With regards to statutory deemed trusts see *Sparrow, supra* note 5 at 46, Gonthier J dissenting on the outcome referring to *Board of Industrial Relations v Avco Financial Services Realty Ltd et al,* [1979] 2 SCR 699 at 706, Martland J and *Dauphin Plains Credit Union Ltd v Xyloid Industries Ltd,* [1980] 1 SCR 1182 at 1199, Pigeon J.

[68] Preceding note.

the *nemo dat* rule applies where the mortgagor has transferred title to the mortgagee. Its application to cases of charges – where no transfer of title takes places from chargor to chargee – might be explained by a functionalist reasoning. But it is not self-evident from general property law principles that a chargor cannot create an equitable interest in the charged property to which she retains title.

The second fact pattern entails cases in which the constructive trust – or the inchoate property right in my analysis[69] – arises before the property is acquired. In these cases, the order of creation of *PPSA* security interest and trust would not change the fact that the debtor only acquires the property subject to the equitable property right. The *PPSA* creditor is arguably not a *bona fide* purchaser if she has already made the entire secured loan. Cuming, Wood and Walsh argue that a creditor with a security interest in after-acquired property could avail herself of the *bona fide* purchaser rule as well, at least if she makes subsequent advantages without notice.[70]

### 3. Avoiding the Equitable Interest

#### a) Canadian Law

In bankruptcy cases which I will discuss in the chapter dealing with property rights in insolvency[71] Canadian courts previously held that when the debtor is insolvent, a constructive trust can only be obtained when other unsecured creditors would otherwise benefit from the immoral behaviour of their debtor and be thus unjustly enriched because "an otherwise unsecured creditor is seeking, in effect, to 'jump the queue over other unsecured creditors in the bankruptcy.'"[72]

While the cases discussed later are concerned with the protection of the unsecured creditors in bankruptcy, not the secured creditor, their analysis should be equally valid when the imposition of the constructive trust remedies an unjust enrichment otherwise accruing to a secured *PPSA* creditor. There is no reason why the unjust enrichment of the secured creditor is to be treated differently than the one of unsecured creditors. The same goes for the deprivation of secured creditors by the beneficiary who tries to "jump the queue."

---

[69] See Part II: § 10 F, "Analysis of Proprietary Restitution".

[70] Cuming, Walsh & Wood, *Personal Property Security Law, supra* note 1 at 515. See also *Hopkinson v Rolt* (1861), 11 ER 829 (HL).

[71] See Part IV: § 16 D, "Proprietary Restitution and Insolvency".

[72] *Baltman v Coopers & Lybrand Ltd (in re Melnitzer)* (1996), 43 CBR ($3^{d}$) 33 (Ont Gen Div), Killeen J.

*b) Australian Law*

The Australian High Court case *Giumelli v Giumelli*[73] gives certain guidance when a constructive trust may be inappropriate. It requires a court that recognizes a constructive trust to look at the interests of third parties affected by the trust. It also held that a constructive trust is inappropriate where the expectation of the presumptive trustee is equally met by giving a lien over the property.[74]

*c) Statement*

At first glance, it appears that the approach adopted in these cases requires for the imposition of a constructuve trust require that the constructive trust be a remedy, rather than an institutional constructive trust that *has* to be recognized whenever certain conditions are met and that it would not be consistent with a view of the constructive trust as a vindication of pre-existing property rights.[75] However, it is equally possible to view these cases as a form of priority contest between two competing property right: the right held by the *PPSA* creditor and the right of the beneficiary of the constructive trust. Instead of "recognizing the constructive trust," what courts really do is deciding the priority competition between these rights in favour of the constructive trust beneficiary.

*4. Priority in the Event of Two PPSA Security Interests*

At common law, it would not have been possible to confer two legal security interests in the same property. Once the legal title is alienated, the debtor can only charge her property in equity. Thus, a second security interest would have needed to be an equitable security interest. It would have competed with an equitable property interest under the rules of equity (*i.e.* the first in time rule). The second security interest would have lost a priority competition with the competing constructive trust.

Under the *PPSA,* it is perfectly possible to collateralize the same property more than once, and priority between the different security interests is determined by the *PPSA* framework (*i.e.* largely by order of perfection). This means that the second security interest will rank lower than the first security interest. Now consider property that is subject to a *PPSA* security interest and impressed with an equitable property right, either because the equitable property interest attached after the *PPSA* security interest in spite of the considerations mentioned above,[76] or because the first *PPSA* creditor had notice of the equitable

[73] [1999] HCA 10.

[74] *Ibid* at para 51, curiam. See also Fiona R Burns, "Giumelli v Giumelli Revisited: Equitable Estoppel, the Constructive Trust and Discretionary Remedialism" (2001) 22 Adel L Rev 123 particularly at 134.

[75] This issue is discussed in detail in Part II: § 9 , "Property Unjustly Gained".

[76] See Part III: § 13 D.II.1, "Priority of the Equitable Property Right".

interest. Then imagine a second *PPSA* security interest that ranks below the first *PPSA* security interest, but that – because it attached after the equitable property right and the second *PPSA* creditor is a *bona fide* purchaser for value without notice – enjoys priority over the equitable property right. This leads to a priority circle. The second *PPSA* security interest is subdued to the first *PPSA* security interest. The first *PPSA* security interest is subdued to the equitable property right. The equitable property right in turn is subdued to the second *PPSA* security interest.[77] This situation is specific to the *PPSA* framework because in common law, it would not be possible to have two competing legal rights. Either the rights would consist of titles in relation to different interests, or the relativity of title would unambiguously decide the priority competition.

## E. *Bona Fide* Purchase of Negotiable Property

A specific type of priority contest involves a secured creditor and the purchaser of negotiable instruments. The *PPSAs* include rules to provide for the negotiability of money and other defined instruments. However, the level of protection varies. In all jurisdictions other than Ontario, a creditor who receives an instrument as payment of a debt takes priority over somebody having a security interest in it. But only Saskatchewan and Manitoba address the transfer of electronic funds. This rule was developed for electronic instruments in Saskatchewan by *Flexi-coil Ltd v Kindersley District Credit Union Ltd.*[78] But it was not accepted universally. In *CFI Trust v Royal Bank of Canada*[79], the Supreme Court of British Columbia rejected an extension of the rule to electronic transfers.[80]

The CCPPSL Working Group notes the absence of a rule that gives priority to a purchaser of an instrument – or in the case of Saskatchewan[81] and Manitoba, the purchaser of an instrument or recipient of a cheque – who is not a creditor, unless they are *bona fide* purchasers.[82] The Working Group argues that as a matter of policy, the purchaser/recipient of an instrument or transfer should be treated the same as a recipient of money. It also recommends that the rules for perfected and unperfected security provisions be harmonized and integrated into one rule to avoid results where a recipient takes free of a perfected, but not

[77] On priority circles in general and other specific circular situations in secured transaction law see Roderick J Wood, "Circular Priorities in Secured Transactions Law" (2010) 47:4 Alta L Rev 823.

[78] (1993), 107 DLR (4th) 129 (Sask CA).

[79] 2013 BCSC 1715.

[80] See CCPPSL Working Group, *supra* note 12 at 53–55.

[81] *Personal Property Security Act,* SS 1993, c P-6.2, ss 20; 31.

[82] CCPPSL Working Group, *supra* note 12 at 55–56.

of an unperfected security interest.[83] The CCPPSL Working Group proposals have been implemented in Saskatchewan.[84]

The CCPPSL Working Group proposals do not take into account that the receipt of money, instruments, or transfers could be unjust enrichment by a third party triggering a proprietary response. The recipient could be unjustly enriched at the expense of the secured creditor whose security interest is ostensibly destroyed by the receipt. In that case, the secured creditor might make a proprietary unjust enrichment claim. However, the Working Group's proposals mitigate the unjust enrichment effect by requiring that a person who receives money as a gift takes free of a security interest only if they have no knowledge of the security interest and a transferee who gives value will always take precedence. The same applies to transfers of funds or instruments.[85] This raises the question what happens if the third party has knowledge of a higher ranking security interest (which thus survives) but takes free of a lower ranking security interest. In that case, the lower ranking party might bring an unjust enrichment claim, provided the requirements for such a claim are met. This would then result in a priority contest between the formerly lower-ranking party and the secured creditor whose interest survived the transfer.

---

[83] *Ibid* at 55–56.

[84] *Personal Property Security Amendment Act,* SS 2019, c 15.

[85] CCPPSL Working Group, *supra* note 12 at 62.

# § 14 Security Interests in Civil Law

## A. Secured Transactions Law Framework in the *Code civil du Québec*

### *I. Classification of Credit Security*

In Québec Civil Law, a credit security is by definition a device that secures payment of an obligation; it cannot exist without a causal obligation, the execution of which it guarantees.[1] This is referred to as the "accessory nature" of a credit security. The types of security can be classified according to the means by which security is given. Thus, a security for credit can be either real or personal. A real security right attaches to property *(biens).* A personal credit security, on the other hand, attaches to the patrimony of the person giving the personal security.[2] In this chapter, I will discuss real security rights.

There are several real legal mechanisms in Québec civil law that can serve to secure a debt. The first kind is a credit security that gives a right of preferential satisfaction, and in certain cases following, on property. This sub-group contains the hypothec and prior claims, as well as credit security deriving from federal law.[3] The second group of debt-securing mechanisms work through the allocation of title. They include the retention of title and fiduciary ownership for security purposes (*i.e.* a security trust), a sale under a resolutory clause, the instalment sale, the sale with the option of re-buying the property, and hire-purchase. However, the primary purpose of the mechanisms in the second group is not to secure credit.[4] Therefore, the main focus of this chapter will lie on security rights in the first group, namely prior claims and hypothecs. A hypothec is subject to the prior claims enumerated in art 2651 *Code civil du Québec*[5]. Creditors of a prior claim are satisfied in preference to creditors of a hypothec and ordinary creditors.[6]

---

[1] Marc Boudreault, *Les sûretés,* 3rd edn (Montréal: Wilson & Lafleur, 2008) at para 1.

[2] *Ibid* at paras 3–4.

[3] *Ibid* at para 4.

[4] See *Ouellet (Syndic de),* 2004 SCC 64 at paras 9, 13.

[5] *Code civil du Québec,* SQ 1991, c 64 [*CcQ*].

[6] See Boudreault, *Les sûretés, supra* note 1 at para 470.

If classified by how a real credit security right comes into existence, one can distinguish contractual security rights and legal security rights from each other. The former includes the hypothec and security rights under the *Bank Act*. The latter includes priorities, legal hypothecs, and, at least one author argues, the title retention.[7]

In the next two sections, I will discuss the two primary real security rights in Québec law, the hypothec and the prior claim. I will then look at quasi-security devices in Québec law, *i.e.* transactions that work with the allocation of title. However, before turning our attention to the specific security devices, the *remaining* two subsections *in this section* will discuss the conceptual framework of real security in the *CcQ*.

### *II. Common Pledge of Creditors*

A credit security is understood to be a device by which the creditor may avoid the *pari passu* rule regarding the distribution of the proceeds of a judicial sale in execution.[8] The object of a regular personal action – that is, an action to extinguish a personal obligation – is the entire patrimony of the debtor. Patrimony is the sum of the debtor's assets (*i.e.* objects of ownership) and liabilities that can be assigned a pecuniary value.[9] This patrimony of the debtor is referred to as the "common pledge" of the creditors.[10] Any property right, whether it is ownership, a fractional dismemberment of ownership (*i.e.* personal servitudes), charges on land (*i.e.* real servitudes), or collateral rights securing an obligation (*i.e.* real security), on the other hand, is enforced by an action in the thing itself.[11] Thus, a credit security enables the creditor to take the property out of the common pledge and use it solely to satisfy her own claim.[12]

Bridge and others write that "much more than the [C]ommon [L]aw, the [C]ivil [L]aw distinguishes between owing and owning."[13] This quote summarizes the relationship between the debtor's patrimony (*i.e.* all property owned by her) and the assets generally available to the debtor's creditor. This becomes important with regard to the treatment of title-based transactions. These are transactions in which the creditor retains ownership of an asset. At first, one

---

[7] *Ibid* at para 7.

[8] Michael G Bridge *et al,* "Formalism, Functionalism, and Understanding the Law of Secured Transactions" (1999) 44 McGill LJ 567 at 651.

[9] *Ibid* at 651.

[10] *CcQ, supra* note 5, art 2644. See Bridge *et al, supra* note 8 at 651.

[11] Bridge *et al, supra* note 8 at 651.

[12] Roderick A Macdonald, "Reconceiving the Symbols of Property: Universalities, Interests and Other Heresies" (1994) 39 McGill LJ 761 at 780.

[13] Bridge *et al, supra* note 8 at 651.

might think that as a consequence of the common pledge, any preferential treatment can only arise from the security rights provided for in the *CcQ*. These are prior claims and hypothecs.

"En effet, l'article 1801 C.c.Q. rend nulle toute stipulation suivant laquelle, pour garantir l'exécution de l'obligation, le créancier se réserve le droit de devenir propriétaire irrévocable du bien ou d'en disposer. Le Code réaffirme le principe que les biens, tous les biens du débiteur, sauf stipulation particulière (art. 2645 C.c.Q.), sont le gage de ses créanciers (art. 2644 C.c.Q.). Si tous les créanciers ont, règle générale, des droits égaux sur les actifs de leur débiteur, le Code prévoit que la distribution du prix de leur vente puisse avantager ceux qui bénéficient 'des causes légitimes de préférence' (art. 2646 C.c.Q.). Or, stipule l'article 2647 C.c.Q. : 'les causes légitimes de préférence sont les priorités et les hypothèques'. Les premières sont établies par la loi alors que les secondes sont conventionnelles ou légales, mobilières avec ou sans dépossession ou immobilières. Les sûretés sont habituellement sujettes à l'obligation de publicité."[14]

However, this alone does not rule out any form of security working with title modification.[15] This type of security confers preferential treatment on the creditor because it removes the property out of the debtor's patrimony entirely and thus removes it from the common pledge.

*III. No Presumption of Hypothec*

While the common pledge of all creditors and the regime of the *CcQ* do not rule out any additional forms of secured credit, the *Loi sur l'application de la réforme du Code civil* prohibits certain types of quasi-security devices based on title allocation (namely the security transfer of title).[16] However, the *CcQ* does not prohibit the use of other types of concepts that can have the effect of a credit security, such as the instalment sale.[17] This is a difference between Civil Law and Common Law. The latter, as discussed above, is based on a functional approach to the *PPSA* security interest.

The fact that the *CcQ* maintains a distinction between its primary security interest, the hypothec, and title-allocation devices based on their formal differences has been criticized.[18] Bridge and others identify four approaches through

---

[14] *Boisclair (Syndic de) c Banque de Montréal,* [2001] RJQ 2815 at para 17 (CA), Gendreau JA.

[15] *Ibid* at para 18, Gendreau JA: "On aurait pu, sans doute, arguer que la cession de créance à titre de garantie collatérale pourrait trouver sa place dans ce système, n'eut été la Loi sur l'application de la réforme du Code civil qui scelle l'intention du législateur."

[16] See *ibid* at para 18.

[17] See *CcQ, supra* note 5, art 1745. See also Part III: § 14 D, "Quasi-Security Devices in Civil Law".

[18] See Roderick A Macdonald, "Change of Terminology? Change of Law?" (1992) 23 RGD 357 [Macdonald, "Change"]; Louis Payette, *Les sûretés réelles dans le Code civil du Québec,* 5th edn (Cowansville, Québec: Éditions Yvon Blais, 2015) at paras 156–58.

which a legislature can react to the fact that title-allocation may be used to create an additional security right:

"A *first* means for controlling title security would be its outright prohibition. No right in property securing performance of an obligation other than a hypothec could be taken. A *second* approach would be the enactment of a general deeming provision that would not prohibit title transactions, but would simply recharacter, them as hypothecs. An example is the 'presumption of hypothec' suggested by the Civil Code Revision Office. Instalment sales and financial leases, for example, would automatically become ordinary sales with a hypothec back in favour of the seller, regardless of the intention of the parties to them. *Third,* the legislature could adopt a 'substance of the transaction' principle. The transaction would remain as the parties intended, but the registration and enforcement regime would be the same as that applicable to ordinary hypothecs. In fact, this was the approach taken by the legislature in 1964. *Fourth,* the legislature could simply leave all forms of title transaction unregulated as security devices. Each of these four approaches purportedly regulate all transactions on the basis of their intent, their object, or their consequence."[19]

Bridge and others then identify the main question one has to ask when choosing between the four alternatives. They state that

"[t]he question is whether non-security concepts are seen as parasitic upon the concept of security, or whether the concept of security is parasitic upon the other basic concepts of private law, notably those relating to property and obligation."[20]

Under a rule following the second approach, any transaction that is substantially comparable to a hypothec would have been subject to the same requirements. Macdonald argued for the second approach,[21] which in his view would have been more coherent with the Civil Law.[22] Common Law lawyers as well have argued that the single unified security interest found in *Article 9 UCC* and the *PPSA* is based on the Civilian concept of the hypothec and thus harmonizes very well with a Civil Law legal system.[23] This was also the approach suggested by the *Office de révision du Code Civil.*[24]

Eventually, however, the second approach was rejected by the legislature in favour of a variant of the third approach whereby certain effects of title-based

[19] Bridge *et al, supra* note 8 at 657 [emphasis added].

[20] *Ibid* at 657–58.

[21] See fundamentally Roderick A Macdonald, "Faut-il s'assurer qu'on appelle un chat un chat?: Observations sur la méthodologie législative à travers l'énumération limitative des sûretés, «la présomption d'hypothèque» et le principe de «l'essence de l'opération»" in: Ernest Caparros, ed, *Mélanges Germain Brière* (Montréal: Wilson & Lafleur, 1993) 527.

[22] Macdonald, "Change", *supra* note 18 at 367.

[23] See Harry R Sachse, "Report to the Louisiana Law Institute on Article Nine of the Uniform Commercial Code: Part I" (1967) 41:3 Tul L Rev 505 at 535.

[24] Paul-André Crépeau, ed, *Rapport sur le code civil du Québec* (Québec: Éditeur officiel, 1978), vol 2 t. 1, 431.

transactions would be subject to rules similar to the ones for the hypothec.[25] The same goes for trusts. A trust constituted to secure a debt is subject to the same publicity requirements as a hypothec.[26]

In favour of his approach, Macdonald argued that the *CcQ* already partly restricts the effects of title allocation by requiring registration of title in certain cases, and a broader generalization of the rule would thus not introduce an incompatibility with the *CcQ*.[27] Macdonald argued that jurisprudence should adopt a substance-of-the-transaction rule even though such a rule is absent in the *CcQ* because it creates coherence between the abstract policy goals and the specific rules of the *CcQ*.[28]

The Supreme Court of Canada rejected Macdonald's suggestion.

"The coming into force of the [*CcQ*] marked an important step in the evolution of the Quebec law of real security [...]. The legislature reorganized this field of civil law, structuring it primarily around a single type of security, the hypothec, which applies to both movable and immovable property, although it also recognized, in [art 2647 *CcQ*], another type of right, the prior claim, which protects certain kinds of claims. [...] This solution was adopted in preference to the presumption of hypothec recommended by the Civil Code Revision Office, which would have grouped all forms of security, including 'ownership securities' (*sûretés-propriétés*), under a single concept: the hypothec [...]. That proposal had attracted strong objections from many critics. [...] Thus, instead of agreeing to organize the law of real security around the concept of presumption of hypothec, the Quebec legislature set up a simplified, unified security system that nevertheless maintained the fundamental distinction between the legal concepts of security and ownership in relation to the creation and exercise of real securities."[29]

The Court made a clear distinction between title retention and a security interest: the former depends on the creditor's ownership, the latter depends on hypothecation, which in turn depends on the debtor's ownership of the hypothecated property.[30] By using language that stresses the fundamental difference between the two concepts, the Court has implicitly refused to introduce a presumption of hypothec.

The Court's decision has been criticised by Grenon. In Grenon's view, the difference between title retention and hypothec in Québec Civil Law conflicts with insolvency law policy. Bringing the law regarding quasi-security devices using title-retention more in line with the law on hypothecs would have been a

---

[25] Gil Rémillard, "Présentation du projet de Code civil du Québec" (1991) 22 RGD 5 at 55. On the treatment of title-based transactions in the *CcQ, supra* note 5, see also Part III: § 14 D, "Quasi-Security Devices in Civil Law".

[26] *CcQ, supra* note 5, art 1288.

[27] Macdonald, "Change", *supra* note 18 at 368–69.

[28] *Ibid* at 372.

[29] *Lefebvre (Syndic de); Tremblay (Syndic de),* 2004 SCC 63 at para 20, LeBel J [references ommitted].

[30] *Ibid* at para 21; *Ouellet (Syndic de), supra* note 4 at paras 9, 13.

way to resolve this conflict.[31] Because Grenon's argument is one of insolvency law, I address it later in the section on the interaction between insolvency law and provincial law.[32]

Doctrine has also made arguments against the adoption of the presumption of hypothec. The presumption of hypothec in its strictest form would change the contractual title arrangement and thus contradict contractual freedom.[33] Furthermore, it would create uncertainty about the attribution of ownership.[34] To understand this argument, one should recall that ownership in Civil Law is absolute, and there is no continuous spectrum of property rights. Thus an analysis such as the one in *Re Giffen*[35] stating that the debtor's possessory interest can be part of her estate in the event of bankruptcy cannot be applied to the Civil Law patrimony.[36] Additionally, the *CcQ* created a unitary credit security for movable and immovable property. The law governing immovables in particular requires a clear allocation of title with which the presumption of hypothec would conflict.[37]

## B. Hypothec

The hypothec is the consensual security device established by the *CcQ*. According to Cuming, Walsh and Wood it is on fundamental level similar to the security interest governed by the *PPSA* in that one underlying concept governs security rights in all kinds of movable property, be it present or after-acquired, and can secure any kind of obligation, be it past, current or future, be it determinate or indeterminate.[38]

---

[31] See Aline Grenon, "La problématique entourant les « sûretés-proprietés » au Québec: Lefebvre (Syndic de); Tremblay (Syndic de) et Oulllet (Syndic de)" (2005) 35 RGD 285 passim.

[32] See Part IV: § 16 B.III.2, "Civil Law Quasi-Security Devices in Insolvency".

[33] Payette, *supra* note 18 at para 160.

[34] *Ibid* at para 160.

[35] [1998] 1 SCR 91.

[36] *Ibid* at para 34.

[37] Payette, *supra* note 18 at para 160.

[38] Ronald CC Cuming, Catherine E Walsh & Roderick J Wood, *Personal Property Security Law,* 1st edn (Toronto: Irwin Law, 2005) at 47. The relevant sub-section has changed in Ronald CC Cuming, Catherine E Walsh & Roderick J Wood, *Personal Property Security Law,* 2d edn (Toronto: Irwin Law, 2012) at 89. In particular, the commonality between *PPSA*s and *Code civil du Québec* is no longer described as a "philosophic commonality," which was the wording in the first edition.

### *I. Roman Law Origins of the Hypothec in Movable Property*

The modern hypothec in Québec law derives from Roman law.[39] In fact, the *CcQ* has brought the hypothec closer to its origins because it once again allows the hypothecation of movables. In Roman law, there were four security rights in movables. They were the *fiducia cum creditore* where the creditor takes title and asset. Second, there were those security rights where title is with the creditor, but the debtor had possession (know as *pace commissoire*). Third, there was the *pignus,* where the creditor took possession and the debtor retained title.[40] Finally there was the *hypotheca,* where the creditor had neither title nor possession, but only a conditional "right to seize and sell the secured asset, either by judicial process or privately."[41]

The *hypotheca* developed from the Praetorian edicts. The first cases of hypothecs were agreements between the lessor and the lessee of immovables. The lessee would grant the lessor a security on all movables that the lessee would bring onto the land of the lessor. Unlike with the *fiducia cum creditore*[42] (security trust) and the *pignus*[43] (pledge), the creditor thus did not take possession of the collateral. The possessory link was substituted by the fact that the debtor brought the collateral onto the creditor's land.[44] Later, the praetor no longer required that the collateral be on the creditor's land and thus allowed hypothecation in any other debtor-creditor relationship.[45] The hypothec had *in rem* effect and included a right to follow the property.[46]

### *II. The Hypothec as a Property Right*

#### *1. Hypothec and Patrimony*

Both the *Code civil du Bas-Canada* and the *CcQ* define the hypothec as a real right. In the terminology of this book it is thus a property right. Occasionally,

[39] On the Roman law of secured transactions see generally Willem J Zwalve, "A Labyrinth of Creditors: A Short Introduction to the History of Security Interests in Goods" in: Eva-Maria Kieninger, ed, *Security Rights in Movable Property in European Private Law* (Cambridge: Cambridge University Press, 2004) 38.

[40] Bridge *et al, supra* note 8 at 653–54.

[41] *Ibid* at 654.

[42] See Paul van Warmelo, *An Introduction to the Principles of Roman Civil Law* (Cape Town: Juta, 1976) at 113–14.

[43] See *ibid* at 115–16.

[44] Paul Jörs *et al, Römisches Recht,* $4^{th}$ edn (Enzyklopädie der Rechts- und Staatswissenschaft Abteilung Rechtswissenschaft, Berlin: Springer, 1987) at 203–4.

[45] See van Warmelo, *supra* note 42 at 116–19.

[46] Jörs *et al, supra* note 44 at 205.

the hypothec has been characterized as a partial alienation of the right of ownership.[47] However, the Québec Court of Appeal held that the accessory nature of the hypothec contradicts any characterization of it as a (partial) alienation of the property because the real right the creditor receives depends on the existence of the underlying obligation, whereas principal property rights are absolute and unconditional.

"C'est ce caractère accessoire de l'hypothèque qui la distingue d'un véritable démembrement de propriété. Essentiellement elle confère un droit réel accessoire servant à garantir l'exécution d'une obligation en donnant au créancier le droit d'être préféré sur le produit de la vente[48]."

The debtor retains the right to *usus, fructus,* and *abusus* of the collateral.[49] If the fruits and revenues are collected by the creditor of a pledge, she must hand over the fruits to the debtor and apply the revenues to expenses, interest, and the main debt related to the pledge.[50]

Macdonald identifies a shortcoming of the hypothec under the *CcQ*. According to him, a lesser property right such as the hypothec (an accessory property right), can only exist in something which can be subject to the absolute and foremost property right: ownership.[51] He claims that in classical Civil Law doctrine, only corporeals can be object of ownership.[52] It would thus follow that a right in property that cannot be owned cannot be a property right. Thus, it is contradictory to consider the hypothec a property right if it can attach to all types of things. However, the Civil Law of Québec, according to Macdonald, requires that something is a property right in order for it to be recognized as having priority in insolvency.[53] The monolithic concept of one hypothec for all kinds of property thus creates a concept of property and ownership in one section of the *CcQ* that is incompatible with the concepts as they are used in the rest of the *CcQ*.[54]

The gist of Macdonald's argument is that the admission of a property right in incorporeal property introduces an inconsistency within the Civil Law. This criticism can be rejected. As discussed above,[55] the *CcQ* redefined the concept of property rights, permitting ownership not only in things but also in other

---

[47] *Loewen c MacCabees Mutual Life Insurance Co,* [1973] CA 1094 at 1095; *Caisse populaire de Lévis c Maranda,* [1950] BR 249 at 254.

[48] *Banque Canadienne Impériale de Commerce c Marcano,* [1990] RJQ 28 at 31 (CA), Nichols JA.

[49] *CcQ, supra* note 5, art 2733.

[50] *Ibid,* art 2737.

[51] Macdonald, "Change", *supra* note 18 at 370.

[52] *Ibid* at 370.

[53] *Ibid* at 369, note 17, with references.

[54] *Ibid* at 370.

[55] See Part II: § 4 D, "Right and Object of Right".

rights as well. Admitting the same for the hypothec is only consistent. Admittedly, it seems circular that I have used the possibility of a hypothec in incorporeal right to argue why ownership in incorporeal property is possible while considering ownership as a real right, whereas now I use the possibility of ownership to argue why a hypothec in incorporeal property does not contradict the hypothec's characterization as a property right. Yet in this circumstance, the circular logic is permissible because its only purpose is to show that such a characterization is in fact consistent. Having admitted property rights in incorporeal property, one can even go one step further and conceptualize the hypothec as a property right not in the final object of property, but as a right the debtor's right in property.[56] Conceptualized this way, there is no fundamental difference between hypothecs secured by corporeal collateral and those secured by incorporeal collateral.

### 2. *Right to Follow*

The hypothec gives the creditor the right to follow the property "into whosever [sic!] hands it may be."[57] This means that the hypothec remains attached to the property even if the ownership passes to a third party,[58] subject to the rules on opposability of the hypothec.[59] The right to follow is restricted to alienations outside the debtor's ordinary course of business.[60]

### 3. *Real Subrogation*

In general, the hypothec does not include an element of real subrogation, that is, if the debtor alienates the property (which she may) the hypothec remains attached to the original property, but the creditor does not receive a right to the property the debtor has received as proceeds of the alienation. In certain cases, a new hypothec in the proceeds may arise for the benefit of the creditor. Where the hypothec was in individual property alienated during the ordinary course of business the creditor has to file notice.[61] A hypothec on a universality of goods always contains an element of real subrogation if the debtor has a business and the original property is alienated in the ordinary course of business.[62]

---

[56] François Frenette, "De l'hyopthèque: Réalité du droit et métamorphose de l'objet" (1998) 39:4 C de D 803 at 808–9. See also Part II: § 4 D, "Right and Object of Right".

[57] *CcQ, supra* note 5, art 2660.

[58] See Payette, *supra* note 18 at paras 322–26.

[59] See Part III: § 14 B.VI, "Opposability of the Hypothec".

[60] *CcQ, supra* note 5, art 2700.

[61] *Ibid,* art 2674:2.

[62] *Ibid,* art 2674(1).

The subrogation replaces the right to follow mentioned in the preceding paragraph.[63]

Ordinary course of business in that context means that the property must have been dedicated for alienation. It is not alienation in the ordinary course of business if the debtor who runs a construction business sells a truck to replace it with a new one.[64] This is, however, not a continuation of the old right.[65]

#### *4. Accessory Nature of the Hypothec*

The establishment of a contractual security requires that the underlying obligation be recognized.[66] In Québec law, the recognition of a debt can be qualified as a unilateral contract whose purpose it is to serve as written proof of the existence of the underlying debt.[67]

The obligation can be monetary or otherwise. The hypothec can also guarantee future obligations. In the last case, simple performance of the debt never extinguishes the hypothec because it remains in existence in case a future obligation arises.[68]

### *III. Taxonomy of Hypothecs*

Hypothecs can be classified by collateral (*e.g.* hypothec on movables or immovables, on particular property or on all property, on obligations, or on property represented by an instrument), whether they occur with delivery (a "pledge"[69]) or without it, or by their effect (*hypothèque ordinaire ou ouvert*).

### *IV. The Object of the Hypothec*

Apart from certain restrictions for hypothecs on movables, the collateral can be any property. Property that cannot be the object of the execution of a judgement according to the rules of execution contained in the *Code de procedure civile,*[70] and property that forms part of the debtor's residence or that is material to her daily life cannot be hypothecated. Whether the first exception includes

---

[63] Yaëll Emerich, "La nature juridique des sûretés réelles en droit civil et en Common Law: Une question de tradition juridique?" (2010) 44:1 RJT 95 at 108 [Emerich, "Sûretés réelles"].

[64] *Banque de développement du Canada c Constructions Boyer & Truchon Inc (syndic),* [1997] JQ No 1274 at para 28 (Sup Ct).

[65] See Payette, *supra* note 18 at para 320.

[66] Boudreault, *Les sûretés, supra* note 1 at para 54.

[67] *Caisse populaire de Rivière-du-Moulin c Lavoie,* [1973] RL 385 (Queb Prov Ct); Boudreault, *Les sûretés, supra* note 1 at para 55.

[68] Boudreault, *Les sûretés, supra* note 1 at para 171.

[69] *CcQ, supra* note 5, art 2665(2) defines "pledge" as a synonym for hypothec with delivery.

[70] *Code de procedure civile,* RSQ, c C-25.

inalienable property is unclear. Inalienable property in this case refers whose right of ownership cannot be transferred to another person. The argument for the hypothecation is that hypothecation not only allows for a remedy that would necessitate the transfer of title, but also – as the case may be – the right to enjoy the fruits and use of the property.[71] The hypothec can be granted in respect of future property not yet owned by the debtor but by somebody else. In such cases case, it becomes valid as soon as the debtor acquires the property.[72]

### *1. Hypothecs in Corporeal Property*

There is no fundamental difference between a hypothec in movables and in immovables. Rather, both are different expressions of the same legal institution, and unless otherwise provided, the provisions governing a hypothec are applicable to both. In this regard, the Québec approach is comparable to the one used in Slovakia.[73]

According to art 2695 *CcQ,* a hypothec on rents is considered to be a hypothec on immovables as well. This raises the question whether art 2710 *CcQ* and art 2713 *CcQ* – the rules on hypothecs on obligations – are applicable to such a hypothec because they are found in the section on hypothecs on movables.[74]

If a hypothec is in movable property that then in turn – by virtue of art 903 *CcQ* – becomes immovable property, the hypothec remains a hypothec on movables. If the property is used for business purposes, it remains movable property.[75] A natural person cannot enter into a hypothec agreement regarding most of her movable property unless she undertakes a business.[76]

### *2. Hypothecs in Incorporeal Property*

An obligation (*e.g.* an account) can be hypothecated as well. Before the *CcQ,* if an obligation was to be used as collateral, the security assignment was used for security purposes. The debtor would assign the account to the creditor. Except by a convention for sale and re-sale and in a security trust, the security assignment of an obligation is no longer permissible because it would allow

---

[71] Boudreault, *Les sûretés, supra* note 1 at para 179; Payette, *supra* note 18 at paras 441–45.

[72] *CcQ, supra* note 5, art 2670.

[73] Katarina Mathernová, "The Slovak Secured Transactions Reform: Ingredients of a Successful Reform and Reflection on Its Achievements" in: Frederique Dahan & John Simpson, eds, *Secured Transactions Reform and Access to Credit* (Cheltenham: Edward Elgar, 2009) 207 at 217.

[74] Boudreault, *Les sûretés, supra* note 1 at para 125.1.

[75] *Loi sur l'application de la réforme du Code civil,* SQ 1992, c 57, s 48.

[76] See Boudreault, *Les sûretés, supra* note 1 at para 142.

the creditor to circumvent publicity requirements.[77] Rights in relation to a trust can be hypothecated as well.[78]

### *3. Floating Hypothec*

A hypothec can be granted on all property forming a universality.[79] Only natural persons, or, arguably, a corporation undertaking a business can grant a hypothec on all goods.[80] Similarly, only these debtors can grant a floating hypothec.[81]

### *4. Hypothecs in Securities*

The *Assemblée nationale* excluded most possible ways of constituting a possessory hypothec through delivery unless the hypothecated obligation was represented by a negotiable instrument in the wake of *Caisse populaire Desjardins de Val-Brillant c Blouin.*[82] However, the legislature also included a specific new category of possessory hypothecs – namely hypothecs in securities – which allow delivery of obligations not represented by a negotiable instrument. The necessity of this particular regime arises in the context of the delivery, which plays a role in creation and opposability of the hypothec. I will address the particularities relating to the hypothec in securities below.[83]

## *V. Creation of the Hypothec*

### *1. General Rule*

The pledge in Roman law and under the *CcBC* required delivery as a constitutive element of the pledge.[84] The *CcQ* now distinguishes between creation of a hypothec with or without delivery. In both cases, as we will see, the hypothec is created by agreement. In cases of a hypothec without delivery, the hypothec

---

[77] *Boisclair (Syndic de) c Banque de Montréal, supra* note 14 at paras 16–17; Boudreault, *Les sûretés, supra* note 1 at para 134.1.

[78] See Part II: § 7 C.II.2, "The Beneficiary's Right in Relation to the Trust".

[79] *CcQ, supra* note 5, art 2666.

[80] See for the discussion of the ability of a corporation Boudreault, *Les sûretés, supra* note 1 at para 142.1.

[81] *Ibid* at para 201.

[82] 2003 SCC 31 [*Val-Brillant*].

[83] See Part III: § 14 B.IV.4, "Hypothecs in Securities".

[84] Aurore Bernadiba, "La Loi sur le transfert des valeurs mobilieres et l'obtention des titres intermédiés: Ou les excès d'un régime d'exception en matière de sûretés mobilières" (2012) 53:2 C de D 303 at 308–9.

is created by a legal act evidenced in writing.[85] The act only needs to be notarized where the hypothec secures payment of an issued bond.[86] A written contract establishing the obligation of a party to create a hypothec is not sufficient.[87] In this respect, Québec law operates with a principle of separation. A hypothec with delivery (or pledge) is constituted by delivery.[88] Delivery must be accompanied by the intention of the parties to create the security interest.[89]

The wording of art 2696 *CcQ* and art 2702 *CcQ* reveals an easily overlooked difference.

"Article 2696 *CcQ*

| | |
|---|---|
| A movable hypothec without delivery shall, on pain of absolute nullity, be granted in writing. | L'hypothèque mobilière sans dépossession doit, à peine de nullité absolue, être constituée par écrit." |

"Article 2702 *CcQ*

| | |
|---|---|
| A movable hypothec with delivery is granted by physical delivery of the property or title to the creditor or, if the property is already in his hands, by his continuing to physically hold it, with the grantor's consent, to secure his claim. | L'hypothèque mobilière avec dépossession est constituée par la remise matérielle du bien ou du titre au créancier ou, si le bien est déjà entre ses mains, par le maintien de la détention matérielle, du consentement du constituant, afin de garantir sa créance." |

The hypothec without delivery must be created in writing on pain of nullity, whereas the movable hypothec is "granted by delivery." The reason for the different wording is easily explained. The different wording reveals that the parties can agree to a hypothec in writing first and then later decide to convert it into a hypothec with delivery. In such cases, the hypothec was initially created by the written agreement; the additional effect of delivery is the opposability of the hypothec.

Bernadiba claims that a pledge can only be created by delivery.[90] However, I submit that the recognition of the hypothec without delivery and the decision to view the hypothec with or without delivery as but two varieties of the same underlying institution mean that it is undesirable to say that delivery is an essential condition for constituting a pledge. I submit that delivery is sufficient to constitute a hypothec. The intention of the parties must only relate to the creation of one security interest: the hypothec. The difference between Bernadiba's position and mine results from the fact that I consider there to be only

[85] *CcQ, supra* note 5, art 2696.
[86] *Ibid,* art 2692.
[87] Payette, *supra* note 18 at para 773.
[88] *CcQ, supra* note 5, art 2702.
[89] Payette, *supra* note 18 at para 845.
[90] Bernadiba, *supra* note 84 at 310.

one framework for all hypothecs, whereas Bernadiba maintains a sharp distinction between hypothecs without delivery and pledges. The difference could be one of mere terminology, but it could also lead one to conclude that parties who agreed to constitute a hypothec without delivery would no longer be at liberty to simply switch to a pledge by mere delivery. If one were to classify hypothecs without deliveries and pledges as substantially different concepts, one would require the delivery to be accompanied by evidence that the parties intended to create a new security interest. Parties would need to agree to create a pledge rather than a hypothec without delivery. A dichotomy between pledges and hypothecs without delivery thus increases the burden of proof on the creditor.

*2. Delivery*

The defining condition of a pledge is that the creditor gains control and exclusive authority over the collateral.[91] In cases of pledges, the possession of the collateral by the creditor is the condition of opposability of the hypothec against third parties. Possession of the collateral also has a "publicity effect," for it replaces the register publicity.[92]

*a) Delivery to a Third Party*

If third party has possession for the creditor, the publicity effect of the possession does not take place until the third party receives written proof of the hypothec.[93] Until then, the hypothec is not opposable against anybody outside the creditor-debtor relationship.

*b) Delivery of an Obligation*

If incorporeal property represented by a negotiable instrument is hypothecated, delivery takes place by delivery of the instrument.[94] Initially, it was unclear whether it would be possible to "deliver" obligations not represented by negotiable instruments. The Supreme Court answered that question in the affirmative in *Val-Brillant.*[95]

*aa) The Val-Brillant Decision*

This decision essentially dealt with the meaning of the legal term "delivery" in Québec Civil Law. Above, I explained that a real hypothec requires effective

---

[91] Cf. *Grobstein c A Hollander & Son Ltd,* [1963] BR 440 at 442; Payette, *supra* note 18 at para 862.

[92] See Part III: § 14 B.VI, "Opposability of the Hypothec".

[93] *CcQ, supra* note 5, art 2705. Cf. Boudreault, *Les sûretés, supra* note 1 at para 204.

[94] See also Bernadiba, *supra* note 84 at 309–10.

[95] *Supra* note 82.

control of the collateral by the creditor. However, it was unclear how effective control of a debt not represented by a negotiable instrument could be achieved.

One stream of doctrine argued that in order to achieve effective control of an obligation not represented by a negotiable instrument, the conditions for opposability of the assignment *vis-à-vis* the debtor need to be met.[96] These conditions of opposability are enumerated in art 1641 *CcQ*. Furthermore, according to this provision, if these conditions are met, the assignment of an account is opposable against the debtor of the account. In other words, art 1641 *CcQ* contains the sufficient conditions that allow the assignee to oppose the hypothec in a debt not represented by a negotiable instrument *vis-à-vis* the debtor.

Payette argued against the possibility of pledging of an account through the fulfillment of the conditions of opposability. His argument goes as follows: the *CcBC* had specified that the creditor gained *possession utile* sufficient for the pledge if the conditions of the opposability of the assignment were met;[97] however, the *CcQ* lacked such a provision, and therefore, the meeting of these conditions should no longer constitute *possession utile.*[98] This argument seems to implicitly rely on a definition of "possession" as something that is in the physical realm. Thus, absent a statutory provision re-defining the word, "possession" only entails events in the physical realm, but not abstract legal events such as notice to the debtor of the assigned or pledged obligation.

The majority of the Supreme Court, however, adopted the first view.[99] The Court justified its decision by reference to the Common Law. It stated:

> "[T]he approach adopted above also has the advantage of being compatible with the most recent developments in the North American law of real security. Legislation in relation to personal property security that has been enacted in the common law provinces of Canada allows individuals to grant security interests in claims that are not represented by negotiable instruments, which are considered to be intangibles."[100]

It is important to note that the Court still conceptualized the delivery as one whereby the creditor is put in possession.[101] Thus, *Val-Brillant* also stands for the proposition that possession is not something that needs to be manifested in the physical realm or something that is only possible regarding corporeal property.

---

[96] Boudreault, *Les sûretés, supra* note 1 at para 196.

[97] See *Fiduciaires de la Cité et du District de Montréal Ltée c Brosseau,* [1970] CA 419 at 422; *Re Civano Construction Inc* (1961), [1962] CS 45.

[98] Payette, *supra* note 18 at para 837, there text accompanying n 1658.

[99] *Val-Brillant, supra* note 82 at para 14, Gonthier J.

[100] *Ibid* at para 22, Gonthier J.

[101] See *ibid* at para 20, Gonthier J: "[Art.] 2076 of the French Civil Code ('C.C.'), which has never been amended and which applies to all pledges, requires, as do arts. 2702 and 2703 C.C.Q., that the creditor be put in possession."

*bb) Reactions to Val-Brillant in Doctrine*

The decision of the Supreme Court has been met with criticism from doctrine. First, the Court gave a too liberal meaning to the word "possession." Second, by extending the applicability of the pledge to obligations not represented by negotiable instruments, the Court undermined the publicity function of possession.[102]

This criticism hails back to earlier criticism made against the security assignment that was permissible under the *CcBC*. Macdonald argued that the security assignment allows a security mechanism that is outside a registration or publicity regime.[103] The pledging of obligations creates the same problem because there as well, the pledging may be public for creditor and debtor (first debtor) of the secured obligation, and the debtor of the pledged obligation. It is undetectable, however, for other creditors of the first debtor.

Boudreault has defended the decision as bringing certainty.[104] Furthermore, he had already argued for a similar legislative approach while the Supreme Court had not yet rendered its decision.[105]

*cc) Subsequent Amendments to the Code civil*

In 2008, with the adoption of the *Loi sur le transfert de valeurs mobilières et l'obtention de titres intermédiés,*[106] the *Assemblée nationale* added the word "physical" to art 2702 *CcQ,* specifically to overturn the decision of the court.[107] The word "physical" does so in two ways. First, it clarifies that delivery cannot mean the mere fulfillment of the conditions of opposability,[108] because they contain no "physical" element. Second, physical delivery seems to imply that the collateral must somehow be manifest in the physical world and not just be

---

[102] See Pierre Ciotola & Antoine Leduc, "Arrêt Val-Brillant: Évolution ou régression de l'hypothèque mobilière avec dépossession, en droit civil quebecois" (2006) 40 RJT 5 passim.

[103] Macdonald, "Change", *supra* note 18 at 368.

[104] See Boudreault, *Les sûretés, supra* note 1 at para 199.

[105] See Marc Boudreault, "Développements en droit des sûretés" in: Jacques Beaulne, Roxanne Guérard & Michèle Lafontaine, eds, *Mélanges Ernest Caparros* (Montréal: Wilson & Lafleur, 2002) 175.

[106] *Loi sur le transfert de valeurs mobilières et l'obtention de titres intermédiés,* SQ 2008, c 20 [*LTVM*].

[107] See Québec, Assemblée nationale, Commission des finances publiques, *Journal des débats,* vol 40, no 47 (June 12, 2008, Pierre Charbonneau) <http://www.assnat.qc.ca/fr/travaux-parlementaires/commissions/cfp-38–1/journal-debats/CFP-080612.html> accessed 18 September 2019: "[L]'article 134 a pour effet de mettre un terme aux incertitudes qui découlent de la décision de la Cour suprême." On the problems of intertemporal law see Payette, *supra* note 18 at para 135.

[108] *CcQ, supra* note 5, art 1641.

an abstract legal right.[109] An exception – allowing the continued hypothecation of insurance policies to the benefit of the person paying the premiums – is contained in art 2479.1 *CcQ*. Furthermore, pledges in securities are still possible without delivery.[110]

### *VI. Opposability of the Hypothec*

#### *1. General Rule*

A hypothec is opposable against third parties either when it is published,[111] or – for the pledge – upon delivery.[112]

#### *2. Publication*

The hypothec on immovables is registered in the register of immovables. A hypothec on movables is registered in the "Register of personal and movable real rights."[113] This latter register consists of two files. One file contains the name and date of birth (for natural persons) or postal code (for legal persons and trusts) of the debtor. The second file contains the description of the collateral if the collateral has a vehicle identification number (VIN).[114]

For cases in which a hypothec is granted in an obligation that is itself secured by a hypothec, registration of the second hypothec is a necessary element. However, Boudreault argues this is not a condition for valid publication of the second hypothec. Given that the debtor of the original hypothec must be given notice of the registration of the second hypothec, it is rather a condition of opposability of the second hypothec *vis-à-vis* the debtor of the first hypothec so that she knows who to pay.[115]

If the first hypothec is a hypothec in immovables, the Court of Appeal for Québec has decided that the second hypothec need only be registered in the register of personal and movable real rights.[116] This decision can be criticized because a hypothecation of a claim secured by a hypothec transfers the rights resulting from the first hypothec to the creditor of the second hypothec; the register on immovables then no longer discloses to whom the rights resulting

---

[109] Michel Deschamps, "Le nouveau régime québécois des sûretés sur les valeurs mobilières" (2009) 68 R du B 545 at 556, note 30. See also *Caisse populaire Desjardins de l'Est de Drummond v Canada,* 2009 SCC 29 at para 129, Marie Deschamps J dissenting on the outcome. Cf. the "real" (*i.e.*) physical, nature of the pledge in Civil Law Payette, *supra* note 18 at para 821.

[110] See Part III: § 14 B.IV.4, "Hypothecs in Securities".

[111] *CcQ, supra* note 5, art 2663.

[112] *Ibid,* art 2703.

[113] *Ibid,* art 2980.

[114] Boudreault, *Les sûretés, supra* note 1 at paras 232–35.

[115] See *ibid* at paras 238, 284.

[116] *Caisse populaire Desjardins de La Ouareau c Dandurand,* [2003] RJQ 412 (CA).

from the hypothec belong.[117] Doctrine before the Court of Appeal decision widely held that publication of the second hypothec in the register on immovables is necessary.[118] When Boudreault agrees with position, he contradicts his earlier position that the registration of the second hypothec is done solely for the benefit of the debtor of the first.

### *VII. Hypothec in Securities*

#### *1. The Notion of Securities*

Securities (*valeurs mobilières*) in Québec are governed by the *Loi sur les valeurs mobilières,*[119] while trade in securities are governed by the *LTVM.* Both acts contain similar, yet not comprehensive,[120] definitions of "security." Broadly speaking, a security symbolizes the obligation of the issuer to pay an obligation, a share in a legal entity, or a right to the patrimony of a legal entity.[121] A security can be represented by a physical certificate or be uncertificated, in which case it is tracked in a register.[122]

Furthermore, securities can be held directly or indirectly. In the first case, the investor holds the security directly from the issuer. In the second case, an intermediary, who, in turn, registers the rights of the investors, holds the security. Most securities are held in a pyramidal structure, where a central depositor holds the actual security for the benefit of an intermediary. The intermediary, in turn, holds her right in the security for the benefit of another intermediary or the final customer.[123]

#### *2. Hypothecation of Securities*

The hypothec published in a register did not conform to the business practices of the financial service industry.[124] Therefore, there was considerable interest in establishing a framework for a "possessory" hypothec in securities.

Prior to the enactment of the *LTVM,* there was uncertainty whether the majority opinion of the Supreme Court would allow hypothecation with delivery

[117] Boudreault, *Les sûretés, supra* note 1 at para 239.

[118] See *ibid* at para 239, note 439.

[119] *Loi sur les valeurs mobilières,* RSQ, c V-1.1 [*LVM*].

[120] See Suzie Lanthier, *Les sûretés sur les valeurs mobilières: Le mouvement d'uniformisation d'origine américaine est-il transposable universellement?: Vers une approche québécoise à la question* (LL.M. Thesis, Université de Montréal, 2009) <http://hdl.handle.net/1866/3770> accessed 19 October 2017 at 12.

[121] Cf. *ibid* at 12–13.

[122] See *ibid* at 14.

[123] Bernadiba, *supra* note 84 at 315–16.

[124] Ciotola & Leduc, *supra* note 102 at 30–32; Michel Deschamps, "Les sûretés sur des titres détenus auprès d'un intermédiaire en droit canadien" (2005) 10 Unif L Rev 189 at 203; Lanthier, *supra* note 120 at 4–5.

of securities.[125] One problem stems from the fact that the decision in *Val-Brillant* only established a framework for delivery of obligations, whereas the concept of a security is wider.[126] In case of indirectly held securities, it was argued that the analysis of the Supreme Court could have been applied as well because the security holder has a claim against the intermediary.[127] However, this analogy was neither widely accepted nor applied by courts.[128]

It is this situation that the *LTVM* responded to. The law introduced a particular regime for hypothecs on securities with delivery found in the newly-introduced art 2714.1 *CcQ*-art 2714.7 *CcQ.*[129] Now securities regulated by the *LTVM* can be delivered either by delivery of the title – regardless of whether the title is a negotiable or non-negotiable instrument[130] – or by the creditor gaining control of the securities according to the *LTVM.* Control can be achieved in three ways. Either the creditor can be become the titular holder of the security, the creditor can enter a control agreement over the security agreement with the holder, or a third party can become the fiduciary holder of the security.[131]

### *VIII. Rights Deriving From a Hypothec*

#### *1. Indivisibility of the Hypothec*

The hypothec is indivisible.[132] This means that each piece of property guarantees the entire debt, and each part of the entire debt is guaranteed by all collateralized property.[133] The creditor can thus choose which collateralized property she wants to use to satisfy her claim.

---

[125] Lanthier, *supra* note 120 at 4–5.

[126] *Ibid* at 114.

[127] Deschamps, "Les sûretés sur des titres détenus auprès d'un intermédiaire en droit canadien", *supra* note 124 at 203–4.

[128] Lanthier, *supra* note 120 at 114–15.

[129] On the particularities of the framework for hypothec in securities see Deschamps, "Le nouveau régime québécois des sûretés sur les valeurs mobilières", *supra* note 109.

[130] *CcQ, supra* note 5, art 2714.7 provides as follows: "La dépossession opérée par la remise et la détention matérielles de certificats de valeurs mobilières ne requiert pas que ces certificats soient négociables lorsqu'ils représentent des valeurs mobilières visées par la Loi sur le transfert de valeurs mobilières et l'obtention de titres intermédiés; la dépossession s'effectue par la livraison des certificats conformément à cette loi."

[131] *LTVM, supra* note 106, s 113. See also Lanthier, *supra* note 120 at 139–40.

[132] *CcQ, supra* note 5, art 2662.

[133] Boudreault, *Les sûretés, supra* note 1 at para 450.

### 2. Judicial Sale of Collateral

The hypothec gives the creditor right of preferential payment from the proceeds of the collateral.[134] In *Anjou (Ville d') c CAC Realty Ltd et autres,*[135] the Supreme Court had held that property can be sold in a judicial sale subject to hypothecs because s 670 *Code de procedure civile* allows a judicial sales notice to include the mention of pre-existing "charges." The decision not only was subject to a doctrinal controversy,[136] but also contained a harsh dissent by Beetz and de Grandpré, JJ, who argued that the words "charge" and "real rights" in the *Code de procedure civile* only

> "refer to rights carved out of ownership such as usufruct, use and habitation, which cannot be given effect without the support of the immovable to which they are attached. The old law put in the same category as these rights land charges – several of which were payable in kind – which were owed by the estate rather than by its owner. It would not be fair to the holder of these rights if the sheriff's sale were necessarily to discharge them. The same does not apply to hypothecs and privileges: the claim they guarantee can be satisfied by money, without the immovable, specifically by the proceeds of a judicial sale of the immovable which is subject to them, with their beneficiary – this is his only right – being paid directly from the proceeds in accordance with the priority of his security."[137]

Unlike the *CcBC,* the *CcQ* addresses this problem. According to art 2792 *CcQ,* a creditor of a hypothec can no longer demand that the collateral be sold subject to a hypothec in the event of a sale by judicial authority. The new provision is applicable for hypothecs on both movables – where the same result already derives from s 611.1 *Code de procedure civile* – and immovables[138] The legislature has thus overturned the decision of the Supreme Court.

### 3. No Right of Foreclosure

Under the *CcQ,* the creditor has nothing that amounts to a right to foreclosure whereby she becomes full owner of the collateral in satisfaction of the outstanding debt. Any such clause in the security agreement is void.[139]

### 4. Floating and Universal Hypothecs

A floating hypothec requires crystallization before the creditor can pursue her rights from the hypothec. "Crystallization" refers to a notice by the creditor

---

[134] *CcQ, supra* note 5, art 2647; art 2660. See Boudreault, *Les sûretés, supra* note 1 at paras 464–67.

[135] (1977), [1978] 1 SCR 819.

[136] Boudreault, *Les sûretés, supra* note 1 at para 467.

[137] *Anjou (Ville d') c CAC Realty Ltd et autres, supra* note 135 at 834, Beetz J.

[138] See *Caisse populaire Ste-Famille de Sherbrooke c Belzile* (1994), [1995] RDJ 137 (Queb Sup Ct); Boudreault, *Les sûretés, supra* note 1 at para 467, note 814.

[139] *CcQ, supra* note 5, art 1801. See Boudreault, *Les sûretés, supra* note 1 at para 538.

after which she can have all rights *vis-á-vis* third parties of a regular hypothecary creditor in regards to the property charged with the floating hypothec.[140] The floating hypothec nevertheless produces effects even before the crystallization because according to art 2720 *CcQ,* the sale of an enterprise affected by a floating hypothec is void relative to the creditor of the floating hypothec.

## C. Prior Claims

### *I. Nature of Prior Claims*

Prior claims are legal securities. They can be defined as a right of preferential satisfaction from the proceeds of the sale of a good, accorded by law to a creditor by virtue of the creditor having a claim deriving from a certain, named kind of obligation.[141] The obligations which make a creditor a creditor with a prior claim are listed in art 2651 *CcQ*. I look at the several categories listed there and their respective particularities in the next subsection. Prior claims enjoy priority even over hypothecs.[142] According to art 2655 *CcQ,* prior claims take priority even though they are not published. If several priorities attach to the same property, law determines their rank. If several hold the same rank, they share in the proceeds concurrently.[143]

Prior claims differ from hypothecs in two respects. First, they do not give the creditor a real right to action, meaning she cannot enforce her right directly into the particular property, but rather must follow the ordinary execution procedures against the debtor. Second, they generally do not contain a right to follow the property, meaning that the prior claim only attaches to the property as long as it is the debtor's property.[144] That means that the creditor cannot take possession of the property in lieu of payment, and she can only force the sale of the property if she pursues a personal action against the debtor.[145] For these reasons, as regards the *Bankruptcy and Insolvency Act,* a creditor with a prior claim is not considered to be a secured creditor.[146]

---

[140] *CcQ, supra* note 5, art 2718; art 2719.

[141] Payette, *supra* note 18 at paras 188, 310.

[142] *Ibid* at para 188.

[143] *CcQ, supra* note 5, art 2651; art 2657.

[144] See Boudreault, *Les sûretés, supra* note 1 at para 29; see Payette, *supra* note 18 at paras 196–202, highlighting the existence of this right in a few particular instances only.

[145] Payette, *supra* note 18 at para 201.

[146] *Ibid* at para 147.

Because prior claims derive from law, the parties are not at liberty to modify, nor create prior claims through a contractual agreement.[147] Unlike a hypothecary creditor, a creditor of a prior claim cannot cede his rank.[148]

### *II. Certain Particular Prior Claims*

#### *1. Prior Claim of a Supplier and the Right to Resolve the Contract*

Under s 1998 *CcBC* and s 1999 *CcBC,* the vendor of merchandise had a privilege, a right of re-vindication to the sold merchandise, and a right to resolve the contract. According to art 2651 *CcQ,* on the other hand, the vendor has a regular prior claim with no attached real right. She still maintains her right to resolve the contract, however, and if she does so, she can revendicate her property.[149] The right to revendicate is a function of the consensual nature of the transfer of property. Where the sales contract has been rescinded, property has not passed and the vendor becomes owner again.[150]

The right to revendicate creates one possible conflict with federal law. According to art 1741 *CcQ,* the right to resolve requires that the property has not been surrendered to a hypothecary creditor. It is unclear whether the term "hypothecary" is used here because the hypothec is the only hypothecary credit security under the *CcQ* or because it should specifically exclude federal credit securities such as the one under s 427 *Bank Act.* Under the old law, the supplier could take the property back regardless of a security under the *Bank Act.*[151] Payette argues this case law should still be authority because the security under s 427 *Bank Act* is a right of ownership rather than a hypothecary right.[152]

#### *2. Right of Retention*

Article 2651(3) *CcQ* accords a prior claim to all creditors who have a right of retention. Article 2741 *CcQ,* in turn, stipulates that the debtor may not demand restitution of property owned by her but held by a hypothecary creditor (in a pledge) until she has performed the secured debt. If one were to qualify the resulting right of the creditor as a right of retention within the meaning of art 2651(3) *CcQ,* the creditor of a pledge would always also enjoy priority over all other secured creditors by virtue of her prior claim. This would undermine the priority scheme set out by the registration and perfection scheme of the

---

[147] Cf. *Kouri c Ferguson & Canada Maple Exchange Ltd* (1922), 33 BR 208; Boudreault, *Les sûretés, supra* note 1 at para 28.

[148] *Municipalité de Baie-Trinité c Caisse populaire Desjardins de Baie-Comeau,* (2003), [2003] RDI 460 (Queb CA); Boudreault, *Les sûretés, supra* note 1 at para 28, note 58.

[149] *CcQ, supra* note 5, art 1741.

[150] See Part II: § 4 F.III, "Consensualism in Québec Law".

[151] *Banque nationale du Canada c William Neilson Ltd,* [1991] RJQ 712 (CA).

[152] Payette, *supra* note 18 at para 244.

*CcQ*. Therefore, doctrine states that the right deriving from the pledge is not a right of retention in the sense of art 2651(3) *CcQ*.[153] This result can also be explained by an insolvency argument. If the creditor of a pledge enjoys a prior claim as well, other secured creditors have an incentive to put the debtor in bankrupty. The pledgee would – by virtue of her prior claim – enjoy priority over other secured creditors. Insolvency would extinguish the prior claim. Thus, any secured creditor who had priority over the pledgee were it not for the prior claim would benefit from putting the debtor into bankruptcy.

As regards certain federal laws that give a creditor a right to retain property,[154] the Supreme Court has held that federal law already comprehensively determines all further rights deriving from such a right of retention.[155] Therefore, a right of retention that derives from federal law cannot be the basis for a prior claim.

### 3. Prior Claims for State Claims

The *CcQ* does not specify whether prior claims for the state include prior claims in favour of the federal government. For this interpretation speaks the fact that the *CcQ* occasionally uses the term "Québec" to refer to Québec specifically and that the term "État" in the French version is given a wide meaning in art 3077 *CcQ*.[156] However, it is widely assumed that the *CcQ* only intends to create prior claims for claims of the Crown in the right of Québec.[157] Payette list several arguments for this. First, in art 3017 *CcQ* and art 3068 *CcQ*, state refers to Québec.[158] Second, Payette list several arguments that relate to the relationship between the federal government and Québec. art 2654 *CcQ* requires the state in its role as creditor of a prior claim to disclose its claims to a creditor who prepares to execute her claim. If the state claims were to include federal state claims, the provincial legislature would thus have imposed a duty on the federal government, which according to Payette, would be *ultra vires*.[159]

### 4. Municipal Property Taxes

The *CcQ* underwent one significant change regarding prior claims for municipalities. While these prior claims relate to immovable property and are thus generally outside the scope of this book, the difference between municipal

---

[153] Boudreault, *Les sûretés, supra* note 1 at para 534; Payette, *supra* note 18 at paras 868–70.

[154] See Payette, *supra* note 18 at para 276.

[155] *Canada 3000 Inc, Re; Inter-Canadian (1991) Inc (Trustee of)*, 2006 SCC 24 at paras 78–82.

[156] Payette, *supra* note 18 at para 283.

[157] See Boudreault, *Les sûretés, supra* note 1 at para 37 with further references.

[158] Payette, *supra* note 18 at para 283.

[159] *Ibid* at para 283.

property tax prior claims and other prior claims highlights an important difference in insolvency,[160] which is why I include them here. Initially, these prior claims were the same as all other prior claims. While a purchaser of an immovable would still be held liable for unpaid taxes on that immovable, she would not have been liable for the original obligation. Rather, after the purchase, a new obligation with a new prior claim would arise.[161]

Article 2654.1 *CcQ* now specifically provides that prior claims of municipalities and school boards for property taxes on immovables constitute a real right and give the creditors a right to follow the property. Thus, the prior claim remains attached to the property if it changes hands to a new owner., however, the law does not envision any special real right of action for these creditors. Consequently, no prior claim entails any kind of real right of action. The reference in art 2656 *CcQ* to a real right of action thus is either without meaning or simply a reference to the execution of the personal judgment.[162] The latter is "real" only in the sense that it is a realization of the common pledge of the creditors, but if the term were interpreted that way, all rights against a private law subject would be real rights because the common pledge is always the means of realizing a private law right.

## D. Quasi-Security Devices in Civil Law

As mentioned above, the *CcQ* does not prohibit or re-characterize title-based transactions that serve to secure credit. The following title-based transactions that can secure credit are recognized:[163] a sale with a retention of title,[164] a sale with a faculty of redemption,[165] a purchase lease (a lease agreement where the lessor buys the property and confers a right to possess the property to the lessee),[166] and the security trust.[167] In all these cases, the creditor – respectively the trustee in the last case – can only rely on her rights if the transaction is published according to the rules on hypothecs. In addition, certain long-term leases need registration regardless of whether they secure credit or not.[168] This is akin to deemed security interests in Common Law.[169]

---

[160] See Part IV: § 16 B.II, "Characterization of Prior Claims as a Credit Security".
[161] Payette, *supra* note 18 at para 303.
[162] *Ibid* at paras 201–2.
[163] Emerich, "Sûretés réelles", *supra* note 63 at 124–27.
[164] *CcQ, supra* note 5, art 1749.
[165] *Ibid,* art 1750; art 1756.
[166] *Ibid,* art 1842; art 1847.
[167] *Ibid,* art 1263.
[168] *Ibid,* art 1852.
[169] See Part III: § 12 B.II, "The Functionalist Approach to Security Interests".

For a Civil Law legal system, it is conceptually difficult to integrate title-retention schemes into a general secured transactions framework. As we have seen in the analysis of Civil Law and Common Law property, possession is a property right in the Common Law, but not in the Civil Law. Civil Law thus faces a problem when trying to explain how the debtor can create a competing security interest in collateral if the debtor has only a possessory interest, be it because the unpaid seller of goods has reserved full ownership in the goods, or because the lessor has retained full ownership in the property.[170]

## E. Appraisal of Québec Secured Transactions Law Reform

I submit that, notwithstanding its shortcomings, Québec secured transactions law can be seen as an example of a secured transaction law that is as efficient as its Common Law counterparts, while at the same time retaining a coherency with Civilian principles and general property law. The coherency with property law is even an advantage Québec secured transaction law has over the *PPSA* approach in its current form.

The reform of secured transactions law in the *CcQ* had two goals. The first goal was the preservation of the Civilian heritage.[171] The second goal was the adoption of a uniform approach to credit securities based on a functionalist approach comparable to the *PPSA* and *Article 9 UCC*. A functionalist reform requires consideration of the policy goals behind secured credit. If the main goal is to facilitate credit by making it less expensive, it follows that secured credit legislation should minimize the transactions costs of secured lending.[172] I take a look at both notions in turn. In the first sub-section, I look at the compatibility of secured transactions law with Civilian property law. In the second subsection, I compare the efficiency of the Québec secured transaction law framework and that of its Common Law counterpart.

### *I. Civilian Property Law and Secured Transactions in the Code civil*

#### *1. Title-Based Devices*

It is argued that the difference between Common Law and Civil Law secured transactions is that the Civil Law operates with a formal approach, while the

[170] Michael G Bridge, "The Scope and Limits of Security Interests" in: Horst Eidenmüller & Eva-Maria Kieninger, eds, *The Future of Secured Credit in Europe* (Berlin: Walter de Gruyter, 2008) 180 at 193. Cf. Aline Grenon, "Major Differences between PPSA Legislation and Security over Movables in Quebec under the New Civil Code" (1996) 26 CBLJ 391 at 397 [Grenon, "Differences"].

[171] Macdonald, "Change", *supra* note 18 at 358–59.

[172] *Ibid* at 360.

Common Law takes a functional approach.[173] The Civil Law method is to deduce a number of rules from the legal characterization of a fact pattern. A fact pattern that can be qualified as a hypothec evokes the legal rules on hypothecs, which, in turn, evokes the legal rules on accessory real rights, and so forth.[174]

In a way, the Civil Law is inherently functional. Uniting similar concepts under one general rule and adding specific rules for certain particular patterns is an essential Civil Law technique.[175] A notable characteristic of the new *CcQ* framework is the unification of all credit securities under the heading "hypothec."[176] This is at least very similar to a functional approach to secured transactions.[177] Functionally similar concepts are united in one meta-concept.

The limit of the Civilian functionalism is reached where title-based transactions are concerned. Here a conflict arises. On the one hand, prohibiting title-based credit securities and creating a presumption of hypothec is Civilian because it recognizes that one function – securing credit – should be governed by one institution – the hypothec.[178] On the other hand, there is nothing to which the hypothec could attach if ownership does not rest with the debtor. Therefore, a presumption of hypothec would require one to re-allocate ownership. Because of the fundamental importance of ownership in Civil Law, this would create a legal result that differs completely from the parties' intention. This is not Civilian style.[179] The *CcQ* resolved this conflict in favour of the parties' intention and left the chosen allocation of ownership intact while subsuming title-based devices under a regime comparable to the hypothecary regime.[180]

### *2. Possession in Civil Law Secured Transaction Law*

The old law distinguished mainly between securities with or without delivery.[181] Security in movable property right without delivery was not admitted, but this was mainly a function of the technical difficulties in creating an efficient registry for movable property, not an essential function of Civil Law.[182] The admission of non-possessory hypothecs in movable property is thus not a break with Civilian tradition.

---

[173] Cf. Emerich, "Sûretés réelles", *supra* note 63 at 102.

[174] *Ibid* at 103–4.

[175] Jacques Auger, "Le style civiliste et le droit des sûretés réelles" in: Nicholas Kasirer, ed, *Le droit civil: avant tout un style?* (Montréal: Éditions Thémis, 2003) 48 at 66–72.

[176] *Ibid* at 62.

[177] Emerich, "Sûretés réelles", *supra* note 63 at 120–21.

[178] Auger, *supra* note 175 at 74–75.

[179] *Ibid* at 76–77.

[180] See also Part III: § 14 D, "Quasi-Security Devices in Civil Law".

[181] Auger, *supra* note 175 at 62–63.

[182] *Ibid* at 63–64.

### 3. Securities Law and Civil Law Property

#### a) The Property Concept in the Code civil and in Securities Law

It is interesting to note that the legislature decided to split the regulation of securities in general[183] – and of transactions on securities in particular[184] – off of the *CcQ*, but decided to include the framework for hypothecs in securities in the *CcQ*. The decision to split the securities framework from the *CcQ* can be explained by viewing this framework as a law *sui generis* for the participants in the financial market,[185] and is not unique to Québec in the French Civil Law family.[186]

Lanthier identifies a possible conflict between the Civil Law property concept and securities. According to her, there are three interrelated uncertainties. First, it is not clear whether securities are corporeal or incorporeal.[187] Certain authors maintain that one can only be the owner of corporeal goods.[188] Second, the beneficiary could be owner or holder of the security.[189] While this may raise less problems in cases where the debtor is the holder of a certificated security, it is more complex when the debtor uses indirectly-held securities as collateral. Neither the *LTVM* nor the *LVM* contain an explicit re-characterization of the property concept, nor an explanation how the property concept in securities law relates to the general notion of property in the *CcQ*. Lanthier submits that this was partly due to the fact that the legislature was in a hurry to regulate securities law and did not take the time ground the new framework dogmatically within the *droit commun*.[190] There is clear indication in the legislative history that the securities concept was indeed legislated without regard to the Civilian notion of ownership.

"[N]ous avons une préoccupation au niveau de la notion de propriété. Globalement, on peut poser la question suivante: Qui est le propriétaire des titres intermédiés? Est-ce le courtier? Est-ce l'investisseur? Est-ce le créancier du courtier? La définition fondamentale, en droit civil, de 'propriété' ne nous semble pas claire, et c'est inquiétant. Nous parlons ici de l'épargne de milliers de Québécois investisseurs qui se retrouve sur un terrain législatif glis-

---

[183] *LVM, supra* note 119.

[184] *LTVM, supra* note 106.

[185] Lanthier, *supra* note 120 at 157.

[186] *Ibid* at 156, note 757, citing France, Belgium, Switzerland and Louisiana.

[187] *Ibid* at 161.

[188] Cf. Pierre-Claude Lafond, *Précis de droit des biens*, 2[d] edn (Montréal: Éditions Thémis, 2007) at 433; Lanthier, *supra* note 120 at 161.

[189] Lanthier, *supra* note 120 at 161.

[190] Lanthier, *supra* note 120 at 163.

sant. La ministre des Finances, qui dit vouloir protéger sans réserve les épargnants du Québec, ferait mieux d'être très prudente avec les modifications qu'elle entend apporter au droit des valeurs mobilières.[191]

[J]e dois vous dire au départ que la question de propriété, vous ne la retrouverez pas dans le projet de loi. Il n'y a personne qui est propriétaire des titres. L'intermédiaire, c'est indiqué expressément, je pense, à l'article 104, il n'est pas propriétaire des titres, de l'actif. Et par ailleurs, la question de la nature juridique des droits de ceux qui acquièrent des titres, le projet ne se prononce pas là-dessus. Est-ce que ce sont des droits réels ou des droits de créance? L'important, c'est que ce sont des droits qu'il peut exercer à l'encontre de l'intermédiaire. Ça fait que la question du droit de propriété ne se pose pas dans ce projet-là, et c'est volontaire. Ça a été volontaire aussi dans les autres provinces. On n'avait pas à se prononcer sur la nature juridique du titre en question."[192]

In France, the concept of what constitutes a good was extended to allow the subsumption of the interest of a securities holder under the concept of ownership.[193] As Mercier puts it: "[a]bstraction faite des droits qu'elles confèrent à leur propriétaire à l'encontre de la société émettrice, l'associé dispose d'un droit réel de propriété sur la valeur du titre dématérialise."[194]

I submit that it would have been possible to integrate the concept of securities into the Civil Law notion of ownership. Two problematic points raised by Lanthier were the ownership of incorporeal goods and the position of the intermediary. With regard to both points, it would have been possible to integrate securities into Civil Law property law. I have submitted that ownership of incorporeals is possible;[195] thus even uncertificated securities can be owned. With regard to the position of the intermediary of the security, it is possible to characterize the securities held by the intermediary to be a separate patrimony by appropriation. The holder of the securities can be characterized as the owner of the rights in that patrimony akin to the position of the beneficiary of a trust, who is not owner of the property constituting the trust patrimony, but owner of rights in the patrimony.[196] As an owner of an (incorporeal) good, she could hypothecate her rights in the items of that patrimony. Neither ownership nor hypothecation of securities thus poses a conceptual challenge to Quebec Civil Law.

---

[191] Québec, Assemblée nationale, Commission des finances publiques, *Journal des débats,* vol 40, no 47 (June 12, 2008, Christian Lévesque).

[192] Charbonneau, "", *supra* note 107.

[193] Lanthier, *supra* note 120 at 163.

[194] Virginie Mercier, *L'apport du droit des valeurs mobilières à la théorie générale du droit des biens* (Presses Universitaires D'Aix Marseilles: Aix-en-Provence, 2005) at 454, cited as in Lanthier, *supra* note 120 at 163.

[195] See Part II: § 4 D, "Right and Object of Right".

[196] See Part II: § 7 C.II, "Trustee, Beneficiary, and Trust Property".

### *b) The Hypothecation of Securities in the Code civil*

One point of criticism against the hypothecation of securities is that the hypothec in securities requires one to admit an ownership in incorporeals which contradicts the traditional corporeal notion of ownership.[197] I have addressed this point in the preceding paragraph.

A further problematic issue surrounding the hypothecation of securities is the relationship between the concepts of delivery and control. As Lanthier also points out,[198] delivery is a concept utilized by the *CcQ* to prevent "the debtor from being able to use the collateral to receive further credit."[199] The control concept, however, is "a new functional concept that has to be analysed on its own terms, without resort to analogy and legal fiction."[200] Lanthier consequently criticizes the fact that the legislature tried to square this new concept with the *CcQ* concept of delivery rather than treating it as a new concept.[201] Bernadiba argues that the *LTVM* breaks with the traditional notion of the pledge and the rules on its creation and opposability.[202] First, the *LTVM* supposedly changes the publicity meaning of possession. Bernadiba argues that the traditional role of delivery in a pledge is to inform third parties of the existence of a pledging contract,[203] but a security can be pledged by delivering a non-negotiable title.[204] Where the hypothec is constituted without delivery of the instrument, but through a control agreement or by entering it in a the issuer's register, the issuer of the security is not bound to disclose the existence of the pledge to third parties.[205] Second, the control agreement gives the creditor a *jus abutendi*. Her possession thus amounts to something akin to ownership.[206] This reveals a Common Law notion of possession as title. Bernadiba relates this proprietary nature of possession to Jhering's theory of possession.[207] However, the reduced publicity effect of possession is a function of the admission of incorporeal property. A similar reduced publicity occurred with regard to other incorporeal

---

[197] Bernadiba, *supra* note 84 at 326–27.

[198] Lanthier, *supra* note 120 at 160.

[199] Payette, *supra* note 18 at para 829 [translated by the author].

[200] Robert M Scavone, "Stronger than Fictions: Canada Rethinks the Law of Securities Transfers in the Indirect Holding System" (2007) 45 CBLJ 67 at 86.

[201] Lanthier, *supra* note 120 at 160.

[202] Bernadiba, *supra* note 84, passim in particular at at 306–7.

[203] *Ibid* at 307.

[204] *Ibid* at 319. See also Part III: § 14 B.IV.4, "Hypothecs in Securities".

[205] *Ibid* at 320–21.

[206] *Ibid* at 325.

[207] *Ibid* at 322–23.

property in the wake of *Val-Brillant*.[208] A *jus abutendi* by non-owning possessors is also not unheard of; one example is the *bona fide* rule which allows a second purchaser to acquire ownership from a non-owner in possession.[209]

A final point of criticism is that the hypothec in securities does not have the same priority scheme as other hypothecs.[210] A hypothec in securities constituted by control trumps all other means of perfection.[211] This mirrors the Common Law rule.[212] However, there is nothing inherently Civilian or Uncivilian about the choice of priority. It might turn out that the super-priority of the creditor in control turns out to have detrimental economic effect and the rule needs to be changed, but this is a question that is separate from whether or not the hypothec in securities is faithful to Civil Law concepts. As it stands right now, the uniformity of priority of security interests in securities in Common Law and Civil Law is desirable because it facilitates uniform expectations of the market throughout the Dominion.

### *II. Efficiency of the Code civil*

#### *1. General Framework*

For Macdonald, the goal of secured lending is to reduce transaction costs. From this, he derives several conclusions about the substantive content of secured transactions law. First, the rank of the security should be made clear as early as possible, preferably when the transaction is entered into. Second, once established, the security should be as firm as possible and should not be defeasible by later rights. Third, these rules should apply regardless of the form of the security.[213]

There are several reasons why secured transactions law in the *CcBC* did not meet these objectives. First, the *CcBC* viewed secured transactions mostly as a means of consumer property acquisition and not as a tool of business.[214] Second, the fine-tuning to very specific purpose of credit securities created a variety of securities, distinguished on a set of overly formal criteria.[215] In this way, the variety of tailor-made credit securities with a narrow scope of application prevented parties from adopting credit securities for their specific needs and limited contractual freedom.

In Macdonald's view, the reform fails to make coherent choices. He acknowledges that the *CcQ* minimizes the occurrence of secret *ex post facto*

---

[208] See Part III: § 14 B.V.2.b)aa), "The Val-Brillant Decision".

[209] See Part II: § 4 F.III, "Consensualism in Québec Law".

[210] Bernadiba, *supra* note 84 at 340–43.

[211] *Ibid* at 341.

[212] See Part III: § 12 C.IV.3, "Securities".

[213] Macdonald, "Change", *supra* note 18 at 359–60.

[214] *Ibid* at 360.

[215] *Ibid* at 360.

securities such as legal hypothecs or priorities, which make the rank of a security unclear. But he also maintains several points of criticism. First, title-based transactions are still permitted and treated differently from hypothecs.[216] Second, the relationship between securities and patrimony is unclear if the patrimony is modified by, for example a matrimonial regime, other forms of communal property, or statutory deemed trusts.[217] Third, unregistered preferred claims continue to exist.[218] Fourth, the uniform treatment of movables and immovables and corporeals and incorporeals is perilous. This is because immovables are usually not as tradable as movables. Furthermore, territories and buildings are relatively stable, whereas movables are transformed and mixed. By treating hypothecs on immovables and on movables as uniform, the *CcQ* imposes rules for immovables on movables more often than is necessary and thus makes movables less likely to be able to function as collateral.[219]

With regard to the maintained distinction between hypothecs and title-based transactions, I refer to my earlier submissions.[220] Apart from the *CcQ,* which addresses the effects of a distinction between hypothecs and title-based transactions at the level of property law, an efficient use of property also requires that insolvency law addresses these effects. Parliament has taken up this task and amended the *BIA* accordingly; I address this below in the chapter on property in insolvency.[221] The relationship between security interests and patrimony modifications through matrimonial property regimes is outside the scope of this book, but in the next chapter I do analyse the relationship between statutory deemed trusts under federal law and security interests and come to the conclusion that Civil Law fares better in this analysis than Common Law.[222] Furthermore, it appears to me that the issue of the compatibility of deemed trusts with secured transactions law should be addressed by federal Parliament intervening in the general provincial property law, not the provincial legislature. With regard to the continued admission of unregistered prior claims, these benefit either suppliers or the state. Giving preference to suppliers does not necessarily disadvantage other creditors because suppliers add property to the debtor's patrimony, which benefits other unsecured creditors.[223] Admittedly, giving preference to the state, on the other hand, is not uncommon and the *CcQ* prior claims benefitting the state are functionally similar to Crown privileges benefitting the Crown in right of Canada.[224] Uniting hypothecs on movables and immovables

---

[216] *Ibid* at 361–62.
[217] *Ibid* at 362.
[218] *Ibid* at 362.
[219] *Ibid* at 362–63, 370–71.
[220] See Part III: § 14 E.I.1, "Title-Based Devices".
[221] See Part IV: § 16 B.III, "Title-Based Security Devices in Bankruptcy".
[222] See Part IV: § 15 B, "Crown Privileges".
[223] See Part III: § 14 E.II.2, "Purchase Money Security Interests in the Code civil".
[224] See Part IV: § 15 B, "Crown Privileges".

under one heading does not mean that each type of hypothec is subjected to the exact same rule set. Rather, the *CcQ* follows an approach in which things are united under one heading but distinguished insofar as distinctions are necessary. This is evidenced by the fact that the chapter on hypothecs contains general provisions, a section on movable hypothecs, and a section on immovable hypothecs.

### 2. *Purchase Money Security Interests in the Code civil*

Economic theory suggests that it is beneficial to grant purchase financers a super-priority over other secured creditors.[225] The *PPSA* implements this by providing for the super-priority of the PMSI.[226] The advantage of the Common Law PMSI is that it allows general *PPSA* security interests to attach to the same collateral as the PMSI. If, for example, the debtor has entered a general security interest in after-acquired property and then purchases new collateral pursuant to a PMSI, the collateral is subject to a first-ranking PMSI and a second-ranking *PPSA* security interest in after-acquired property. The *CcQ* does not contain a PMSI, only limited priorities.[227] A vendor's hypothec will have priority over prior hypothecs provided it is created in the contract of sale and published within 15 days after the sale,[228] but third party financers cannot avail themselves of this priority.

However, third party financers can make use of the hire-purchase framework to create a PMSI-like priority. In this scenario, the vendor sells the collateral to the titular/creditor who then enters a hire-purchase agreement with the purchaser/debtor. The titular in a hire-purchase who has duly registered her interest will prevail over other unsecured creditors inside and outside insolvency.

A potential downside is that the use of title to allow this type of security would seem to make it impossible for the debtor to use the same collateral twice. If the debtor does not own the property, she cannot grant a hypothec in it. A pre-existing universal hypothec from a general financing agreement would not attach to the purchased collateral. But because the *CcQ* allows the hypothecation of obligations, the debtor who is the purchaser in a hire-purchase agreement should be able to hypothecate her claim that she receive ownership at the end of the hire-purchase. While the object of the hire-purchase – the purchased collateral – and the object of the hypothec – the incorporeal claim – are notionally distinct, this would economically to a double use of the collateral.

---

[225] See Part III: § 11 E.IV, "Purchase-Money Security Interests in Economic Theory".

[226] See Part III: § 12 C.IV.2, "Purchase-Money Security Interests in the PPSA".

[227] Grenon, "Differences", *supra* note 170 at 401.

[228] *CcQ, supra* note 5, art 2954.

### *3. Control Rights*

Just as in Common Law, the hypothecary creditor can only bring a possessory action if she has been in possession of the property.[229] However, the position of the Civil Law creditor is still better than that of her Common Law counterpart.[230] As a titulary of a property right, the hypothecary creditor is also able to avail herself of the action to vindicate her property.[231]

[229] Lafond, *supra* note 188 at 611.

[230] See Part III: § 13 C, "PPSA and the Wrongful Interference with Personal Property".

[231] Cf. Roderick A Macdonald, "Enforcing Rights in Corporeal Moveables: Revendication and Its Surrogates (Part 1)" (1986) 31:4 McGill LJ 573 at 640–53.

Part IV

# Vertical Co-ordination

## § 15 Federal and Provincial Notions of Property and Security

The preceding two parts of this book dealt with property rights. First, in part two, I looked at general property rights and the most comprehensive property right that exists in each legal system: ownership in Civil Law and the best title to the best interest in Common Law. An important focus of the second part of this book was how the Common Law protects property rights by ways of proprietary restitution. Part three of this book dealt with accessory property rights; security interests are property rights that secure certain obligations. The purpose of this current part and the next part is to analyse how these property rights interact. The interaction takes place on two levels. The first level – the topic of this part – is the interaction between property rights and federal law. This is an interaction along the second vector of bijuralism.[1] The next part will deal with the treatment of property rights on the second level: the conflict of laws. As we will see, this is an interaction along the first vector of bijuralism.[2]

This current part discusses two ways in which federal law interacts with provincial law along the vertical vector of bijuralism. First, in this chapter, we look at how federal law influences and is influenced by provincial notions of property and security where federal law itself regulates secured transactions. In the next chapter, we will discuss how federal law interplays with provincial notions of property and security where the federal law itself does not govern secured transactions or property rights, but relies on their creation in provincial law.

While the general secured transactions law framework falls within the realm of provincial jurisdiction, federal Parliament has enacted a number of laws that create security interests. These federal security interests are created in connec-

[1] See Part I: § 2 B.II, "The Second Vector: Federal Law and Provincial Law".
[2] See Part I: § 2 B.I, "The First Vector of Interaction: Common Law and Civil Law".

tion with laws whose general subject matter falls under the jurisdiction of federal Parliament. According to s 91(15) *Constitution Act, 1867,*[3] federal Parliament can legislate in the area of banking law. As a result Parliament enacted the *Bank Act,*[4] which also contains a dedicated secured transactions law framework.[5] Federally-regulated financial institutions can avail themselves of this *Bank Act* security interest. In an even more specialized subject area, federal Parliament has enacted legislation dealing with secured transactions in intellectual property.[6] Furthermore, federal Parliament has created a number of deemed trusts that secure the Crown's claims against a debtor's obligation ("Crown privileges").[7] The interaction of these federal security interests with provincial property law and secured transactions law raises its own particular problems of bijuralism along the vertical vector of bijuralism.[8] I have decided to look at the *Bank Act* security interest as it is the most comprehensive federal security interest.[9] I also look at Crown privileges. Both rights raise issue of priority co-ordination between federal and provincial law.

## A. *Bank Act* Security Interest

### *I. The Bank Act Framework*

The *Bank Act* security interest is only open to banks or authorized foreign banks listed in Schedules I, II, or III of the *Bank Act.* The *Bank Act* security interest contained a number of innovations.[10] For example, it was the first secured transaction law framework to operate with notice filing as a publicity element.[11]

---

[3] 30 & 31 Vict, c 3 [*Constitution Act*].

[4] SC 1991, c 46.

[5] On the constitutionality of a federal secured transactions framework as an annex for banking law jurisdiction see *Bank of Montreal v Hall,* [1990] 1 SCR 121 [*Hall*]; *Tennant v Union Bank of Canada,* [1894] AC 31 (Can PC); Marc-Alexandre Poirier, "Analysis of the Interaction Between Security Under Section 427 of the Bank Act and Provincial Law: A Bijural Perspective" (2003) 63 R du B 287 at 297.

[6] *Constitution Act, supra* note 3, s 91(22); s 91(23). See Anthony J Duggan & Jacob S Ziegel, *Secured Transactions in Personal Property: Cases, Text and Materials,* 5th edn (Toronto: Emond Montgomery Publications, 2009) at 553.

[7] See e.g. *Income Tax Act,* RSC 1985, c 1 (5th Supp.) [*ITA*], s 227.

[8] See Part I: § 2 B.II, "The Second Vector: Federal Law and Provincial Law".

[9] See Roderick J Wood, "The Nature and Definition of Federal Security Interests" (2000) 34:1 CBLJ 65 at 71.

[10] *Ibid* at 71–73.

[11] *Ibid* at 72.

The basic rules for the *Bank Act* security interest are found in s 427 *Bank Act.* The security interest requires that the parties agree in writing that a security interest is to be created. The delivery of this document must coincide with the making of the loan. Finally, the debtor must be "owner" of the collateral. The meaning of "ownership" is not defined by the act. The notice-filing renders the interest effective against third parties.[12] The notice does not describe the loan or the collateral; its function is to trigger further inquiry by other creditors.[13]

*II. The Debtor's Original Interest*

The *Bank Act* security interest requires that the debtor has a property right in the property. This left it uncertain whether the security interest in after-acquired property only attaches once the debtor receives title to the property,[14] or whether the *Bank Act* security interest attaches retroactively as soon as the debtor obtains title. The Supreme Court initially left the question open,[15] but embraced the latter approach in *Royal Bank of Canada v Radius Credit Union Ltd.*[16] At the same time, the Court stressed that the property right does not arise until the debtor acquires the property.

The Court found that the notion that the property right can only come into existence when the debtor acquires it is a conclusion that "finds support in the majority of the Canadian jurisprudence and virtually all academic commentary."[17] The Court added that the attached property right is not the only interest conferred to the *Bank Act* creditor. A *Bank Act* creditor receives an additional interest. This is an interest in whatever right the debtor already has in the property and be it a mere expectancy.[18] The Supreme Court explains this additional interest by referring to the development of security interests in after-acquired property. Whereas at common law, one could not grant security unless one already had title to the property, equity allowed the granting of security in after-acquired property.[19] This equitable security interest would only attach to the

---

[12] Poirier, *supra* note 5 at 316.

[13] *Ibid* at 315.

[14] *Rogerson Lumber Co v Four Seasons Chalet Ltd* (1980), 113 DLR (3d) 671 (Ont CA).

[15] *Royal Bank of Canada v Sparrow Electric Corp,* [1997] 1 SCR 411 [*Sparrow*].

[16] 2010 SCC 48 [*Radius*].

[17] *Ibid* at para 17, Charron J, referring to *Hall, supra* note 5. *Abraham v Canadian Admiral Corp (Receiver of)* (1998), 158 DLR (4th) 65 at paras 19–20 (Ont CA); *Rogerson Lumber Co v Four Seasons Chalet Ltd, supra* note 14; Ronald CC Cuming & Roderick J Wood, "Compatibility of Federal and Provincial Personal Property Security Law" (1986) 65 Can Bar Rev 267 at 276; William D Moull, "Security Under Sections 177 and 178 of the Bank Act" (1986) 65 Can Bar Rev 242 at 251.

[18] *Radius, supra* note 16 at para 20, Charron J, referring to Moull, preceding note.

[19] *Radius, supra* note 16 at para 20, Charron J. See also *Tailby v Official Receiver* (1888), 13 App Cas 523 (HL); *Holroyd v Marshall* (1862), 10 HL Cas 191.

property at the time the property is acquired,[20] but the expectation of that interest itself was recognized in equity.[21]

*III. The Bank's Acquired Interest in the Property*

Conceptually, the security interest involves a deemed transfer of title to the secured bank,[22] which distinguishes it from a *PPSA* security interest,[23] and the *Code civil du Québec* hypothec. The *Bank Act* does not contain a comprehensive property law framework. It thus has to rely on provincial law to complement its scheme,[24] and give meaning to the title fiction.

In Common Law provinces, the result of a transfer of title akin to a chattel mortage is that the debtor retains an equitable property right: the equity of redemption.[25] Because the debtor retains a recognized property right in the collateral, any *PPSA* security interest can still attach.[26]

In Québec, the bank must be considered to be the owner of the property. Doctrinal voices have argued for the "accessory rights theory;"[27] this theory explains that the bank's right is not one of ownership; rather, it as a type of – hypothecary – charge. This approach would clearly contradict the wording of the *Bank Act*.[28] This means that the bank must be considered to obtain ownership in the collateral. Apart from the fact that this means that the property must be allocated to the bank's patrimony – making it available to the bank's creditors – this also extinguishes any hypothec held by the bank in the same property. In Common Law, the debtor retains an equitable property right in the collateral to which a *PPSA* security interest can attach regardless of the identity of the creditor. In Civil Law, the conveyance of the property due to the *Bank Act* extinguishes the debtor's property right in the collateral. Where the hypothecary creditor is a third party, she is able to follow the hypothecary right into the new owner's (the bank's) hand, provided the condition of following

---

[20] *Radius, supra* note 16 at para 20, Charron J. See also *Tailby v Official Receiver,* preceding note; *Holroyd v Marshall,* preceding note; Ronald CC Cuming, Catherine E Walsh & Roderick J Wood, *Personal Property Security Law,* 2[d] edn (Toronto: Irwin Law, 2012) at 421–22.

[21] *Radius, supra* note 16 at para 20, Charron J. See also Royston M Goode, *Goode on Legal Problems of Credit and Security,* ed by Louise Gullifer, 5[th] edn (London: Sweet & Maxwell, 2013) at para 2.12.

[22] *Sparrow, supra* note 15; Poirier, *supra* note 5 at 313.

[23] Ronald CC Cuming, "Secured Creditors' Non-Statutory Remedies: Unfinished Business" (2012) 91:2 Can Bar Rev 243 at 252.

[24] Poirier, *supra* note 5 at 297–99.

[25] *Ibid* at 333. On the equity of redemption see Part III: § 12 A.I.3, "Chattel Mortgage".

[26] See Part III: § 12 C.I.2, "Rights in the Collateral".

[27] Poirier, *supra* note 5 at 342–43.

[28] *Ibid* at 343.

are met.[29] But if the bank was the hypothecary creditor, the union of ownership and hypothec means that the hypothec becomes extinguished.[30]

In addition to the title fiction, the bank also receives a "lien or claim" in the collateral. In practice, the deemed transfer of title is more important. The act also does not specify what exactly is meant by the word "lien," leaving the effect of this to provincial law, which is particularly problematic in case of Québec law, rendering it uncertain whether the "lien" can be transposed into a prior claim or a hypothec.[31]

### *IV. Bank Act Priority Rule*

In principle, the priority competition between a *Bank Act* security interest and a provincial security interest is governed by the *Bank Act* to the extent that the *Bank Act* contains rules for this type of priority competition. Furthermore, most provincial *PPSAs* contain a provision that excludes *Bank Act* security interests from the scope of the *PPSA,* but in Ontario, the *Personal Property Security Act* does not contain such a rule. In *Bank of Nova Scotia v International Harvester Credit Corp of Canada,*[32] the Court of Appeal held that this means that this the priority relationship between the *Bank Act* interest and the *PPSA* interest can be governed by the *PPSA* if the bank so elects. A bank can register its security interest pursuant to the *PPSA* framework, in which case it can elect to claim priority under either the *PPSA (Ont)* or under the *Bank Act.* Second, where a bank fails to perfect its *Bank Act* interest according to the *PPSA (Ont)* rules, the *PPSA (Ont)* priority and enforcement provisions do not apply. The resolution of priority disputes between the bank and *PPSA* security interests is governed by the *Bank Act.*

With regard to *PPSA* security interests acquired after the *Bank Act* interest, s 428 *Bank Act* gives priority to a *Bank Act* security over all after-acquired security interests. Any provincial rule providing otherwise is void.[33]

The competition between previously-acquired *PPSA* security interests and the *Bank Act* interest is resolved by ascertaining the effect of the title fiction and thus is a function of the rules of provincial property law,[34] which are subject to the recent amendments to the *Bank Act* discussed below.[35]

---

[29] See Part III: § 14 B.II.2, "Right to Follow".

[30] Poirier, *supra* note 5 at 341.

[31] *Ibid* at 314–15, note 111.

[32] (1990), 74 OR (2[d]) 738 (CA).

[33] *Bank of Montreal v Pulsar Ventures Inc* (1987), [1988] 1 WWR 250 (Sask CA); *Landry Pulpwood Co v Banque Canadienne Nationale* (1927), [1928] 1 DLR 493 (Can SCC); Poirier, *supra* note 5 at 321, note 148.

[34] See also Poirier, *supra* note 5 at 336–37.

[35] See Part IV: § 15 A.V.3, "Amendment to the Bank Act".

## *V. Priority under Provincial Property Law*

### *1. Common Law: Nemo Dat*

In two parallel cases – *Bank of Montreal v Innovation Credit Union* and *Radius* (both cases involved the same debtor but different *Bank Act* and *PPSA* creditors) – the Supreme Court of Canada addressed the relationship between the federal security interest and provincial secured transactions law and property law.

#### *a) Innovation Credit*

The facts of *Innovation Credit* were as follows. The debtor obtained a loan from the credit union (the *PPSA* creditor). To secure the loan, the debtor granted the *PPSA* creditor a security interest on all present and after-acquired property. The security agreement dated from October 7, 1991. The credit union registered its security interest on June 28, 2004. After the credit union had given the debtor the loan, the debtor obtained another loan from the Bank of Montreal (the *Bank Act* creditor), without disclosing the existence of the first loan and the security interest. In order to secure its loan, the *Bank Act* creditor took a security interest pursuant to the *Bank Act.* The collateral was largely the same property that the *PPSA* creditor had taken as collateral. When the debtor defaulted, the *Bank Act* creditor took the property, which was property acquired before the interests attached. The *PPSA* creditor sought a declaration that it had priority.

The applications judge ruled that in order to prevail over the *Bank Act* security interest, the *PPSA* security interest needed to have been obtained before the *Bank Act* security interest because s 428 *Bank Act* gives priority over all after-acquired security interests to a *Bank Act* security.[36] The judge ruled that a *PPSA* creditor only obtains a security interest after registration because priority by means of perfection is to be acquired through registration.[37] Since the *PPSA* creditor only registered after the *Bank Act* creditor received its security interest, the *Bank Act* creditor had priority under s 428 *Bank Act.* This result promotes two policy goals contained in the *PPSA:* first, it resolves conflicts between the

---

[36] *Innovation Credit Union v Bank of Montreal,* 2007 SKQB 471. The decision was commented on by Ronald CC Cuming, "Interface between the PPSA and Section 427 of the Bank Act: Desirable Policy vs. Hard Legal Analysis" (2008) 71 Sask L Rev 143.

[37] *Innovation Credit Union v Bank of Montreal,* preceding note at para 54, Zarzeczny: "This court's conclusion that registration (and consequently the notices provided by the registration systems of the Bank Act, and PPSA) establish priority ensures that lenders have notice of competing security interests and underwrite loan applications accordingly." *Bank of Montreal v Innovation Credit Union,* 2010 SCC 47 at para 9 [*Innovation Credit*].

*PPSA* and the *Bank Act;* second, it promotes "commercial and business lending efficacy and predictability."[38]

The Saskatchewan Court of Appeal overturned the Queen's Bench decision.[39] It held that the application judge erred in finding that the dispute was governed by s 428 *Bank Act.* Rather, a priority dispute between *Bank Act* creditor and *PPSA* creditor with a property right in the property in question was to be decided by s 427(2) *Bank Act* and s 435(2) *Bank Act.* These two rules provide that the *Bank Act* creditor takes the property as purchaser from the debtor. This means that the rule of *nemo dat quod non habet* applies. Because the property of the debtor was already subject to the granting of a security interest of the debtor to the *PPSA* creditor at the time he granted a security interest to the *Bank Act* creditor, the *Bank Act* creditor's security interest was subject to the *PPSA* creditor's security interest.

The Supreme Court confirmed the Court of Appeal's decision. The Court made reference to the fact that the concept of the *Bank Act* security interest pre-dates the *PPSA* significantly. Under the *Bank Act* concept, the creditor of a security interest takes the collateral upon receipt of the document as if she had received a bill of lading or warehouse receipt.[40] The recipient of such an instrument, in turn, confers to the bank such rights as the owner of the collateral has.[41]

From this, the Court concluded that the *Bank Act* leaves the resolution of conflicts between a *Bank Act* security interest and any security interest potentially acquired before the *Bank Act* security interest to general property rights principles.[42] The Court contrasted the property-based approach with the functional approach, which is used to resolve *PPSA* security interest conflicts. The functional approach is a result of the unification of the wide array of equitable and legal security interests under the old law. The Court then stressed how there is friction between the *Bank Act* conception of secured transactions and the one in the *PPSA,*[43] a friction that has not gone unnoticed by doctrine.[44] The Court noted that some legal scholars have called for an abolition of *Bank Act* security interests.[45] But the Court stressed that it has to apply the *lege lata* as it stands and to "resolve these difficulties as best as can be done on the basis of the

[38] *Innovation Credit,* preceding note at para 10.

[39] *Innovation Credit Union v Bank of Montreal,* 2009 SKCA 35.

[40] *Bank Act, supra* note 4, s 427(2).

[41] *Ibid,* s 435(2).

[42] *Innovation Credit, supra* note 37 at para 16, Charron J.

[43] *Ibid* at para 24, Charron J.

[44] Cuming, "Interface between the PPSA and Section 427 of the Bank Act", *supra* note 36; Poirier, *supra* note 5 at 395–400.

[45] Jacob S Ziegel, "Interaction of Personal Property Security Legislation and Security Interests under the Bank Act" (1986–1987) 12 CBLJ 73 at 91–95.

modern approach to statutory interpretation and in light of applicable constitutional principles."[46]

The Court then turned its analysis to the approach taken by the Court of Appeal in resolving the dispute. The Court of Appeal had identified three steps in resolving such a dispute:

"(1) set aside the *PPSA* from the analysis and determine the priority as if the *PPSA* did not exist; (2) determine the priority pursuant to [applicable provisions of the Bank Act] to the extent it is possible to do so; (3) where appropriate, apply the first-in-time priority rule."[47]

The Supreme Court pointed out that this three-step test is not entirely correct, although it did not render the Court of Appeal's decision materially incorrect.[48]

The Supreme Court agreed with the second step, as it conformed with its own case-law.[49] However, it clarified that the *PPSA* cannot be set aside entirely in such a priority dispute; rather, *their priority rules are not decisive* when the federal *Bank Act* comes into play.[50] This is because the *Bank Act* is federal legislation whose priority is not subject to provincial legislation, but rather determined by the *Bank Act* framework.[51]

The Court distinguished two priority disputes. In cases where a security interest is granted subsequent to the *Bank Act* security interest, s 428(1) *Bank Act* determines priority between the two competing security interests.[52] In a case such as the *Innovation Credit,* where there is a prior security interest which competes with the *Bank Act* security interest, priority is determined by reference to s 427(2) *Bank Act* and s 435(2) *Bank Act.* In the words of the Court, the question in this particular case was which

"proprietary rights were granted to the bank under [s 427(2) *Bank Act*]. As noted earlier and explained more fully below, the combined effect of [s 427(2) *Bank Act* and s 435(2) *Bank Act*] is that the bank can acquire no greater interest in the collateral than the debtor has at the relevant time."[53]

---

[46] *Innovation Credit, supra* note 37 at para 26, Charron J. Cf. *Bell ExpressVu Limited Partnership v Rex,* 2002 SCC 42 at para 26.

[47] *Innovation Credit Union v Bank of Montreal, supra* note 39 at 27, Jackson JA, referring to *Royal Bank of Canada v Agricultural Credit Corp of Saskatchewan* (1994), 115 DLR (4[th]) 569 at 586–87 (Sask CA). See also Ronald CC Cuming, "The Position Paper on Revised Bank Act Security: Rehabilitation of Canadian Personal Property Security Law or Curing the Illness by Killing the Patient" (1992) 20 CBLJ 336 at 340–42; Cuming & Wood, *supra* note 17 at 274, 276–77. See also *Royal Bank of Canada v Bank of Montreal* (1976), 67 DLR (3[d]) 755 (Sask CA).

[48] *Innovation Credit, supra* note 37 at para 27, Charron J.

[49] *Landry Pulpwood Co v Banque Canadienne Nationale, supra* note 33 at 500–1.

[50] *Innovation Credit, supra* note 37 at para 27, Charron J.

[51] *Ibid* at para 28, Charron J. See also *Hall, supra* note 5.

[52] *Innovation Credit, supra* note 37 at para 29, Charron J.

[53] *Ibid* at para 29, Charron J [emphasis added].

Going on, the Court elaborated that

> "[i]n determining what interest the debtor may have already conveyed to another creditor and, in such circumstances, what interest he or she had left to convey to the bank at the time of execution of the Bank Act security agreement, it becomes necessary to resort to the provincial property law, either at common law or under applicable provincial statutes. It is at this point that resorting to the *PPSA* becomes relevant."[54]

In determining what property is subject to the *Bank Act* security interest, provincial property law thus plays a complimentary role.[55] In other words, a bank can only take a security interest in such property as is left to the debtor under the applicable (provincial) property law. The Court drew an analogy to the decision in *Re Giffen*[56] on bankruptcy law. *Giffen* stands for the proposition that the content of rights passing from debtor to trustee in bankruptcy are determined by provincial property law, even though insolvency law is federal law.[57]

Applying these abstract considerations to the case, the Court held that the *PPSA* creditor obtained a valid, albeit unperfected, security interest.[58] The Court further repeated its stance from *Bank of Montreal v Hall*[59] that the effect of a *Bank Act* security interest is that the bank receives the security as a successor to the debtor.[60]

The Court held that the *PPSA* conveys a property right at the moment of perfection, unlike the floating charge which depends on a later event (the crystallization) before a proprietary interest is conveyed.[61] Consequently, the *PPSA* creditor held a property right in the property. Since there is no specific rule, the *nemo dat* rule applies between two competing legal interests[62] and the *PPSA* creditor's property right prevailed over the *Bank Act* security interest.[63]

---

[54] *Ibid* at para 30, Charron J [emphasis added].

[55] The interwoven nature of provincial property law and federal Bank Act security interest was already pointed out by Cuming & Wood, *supra* note 17 at 274. See also the previous edition of Ronald CC Cuming, Catherine E Walsh & Roderick J Wood, *Personal Property Security Law,* 1st edn (Toronto: Irwin Law, 2005) at 589 making this specific point already. The same discussion can now be found in Cuming, Walsh & Wood, *Personal Property Security Law, supra* note 20 at 697–98.

[56] [1998] 1 SCR 91.

[57] See Part IV: § 16 B.III.1, "Common Law Quasi-Security Devices and Deemed Security Interests in Bankruptcy".

[58] *Innovation Credit, supra* note 37 at paras 33–34, Charron J.

[59] *Supra* note 5.

[60] *Innovation Credit, supra* note 37 at para 38, Charron J. See also *Hall, supra* note 5 at 370; Moull, *supra* note 17 at 251.

[61] *Innovation Credit, supra* note 37 at para 45, Charron J. See also *Sparrow, supra* note 15 at 54.

[62] See Part III: § 12 C.IV, "Priority".

[63] *Innovation Credit, supra* note 37 at paras 51–52, Charron J.

The Court also dealt with a second argument from the bank – namely, that it should enjoy priority as a *bona fide* for value purchaser under s 20(3) *Personal Property Security Act.*[64] The Court rejected that argument because s 20(3) *PPSA (Sask)* is not applicable to creditors of a security agreement. The bank acquired its interest because it held a security interest. While the *Bank Act* security interest does not fall within the scope of the *PPSA (Sask),*[65] it is still a security interest under a security agreement within the meaning of the *PPSA (Sask).*[66]

*b) Radius Credit*

The facts of *Radius* differed from those of *Innovation Credit* in one respect: the collateral was acquired by the debtor (who was the same person) after he had granted the *PPSA* security interest and the *Bank Act* security interest. Just like in *Innovation Credit,* the *PPSA* security interest had been granted before the *Bank Act* security interest, but remained unperfected. The Court of Appeal had held that both security interests did not attach until the debtor acquired the property; but as discussed above, the Supreme Court later held that the time of creation of the *Bank Act* security interest is retroactively fixed to the time the agreement is delivered. The Court made reference to two prior decisions, *Royal Bank of Canada v Sparrow Electric Corp*[67] and *Banque nationale du Canada c William Neilson Ltd,*[68] the latter a decision by the Court of Appeal of Québec. The Québec court had held:

"Les droits de la banque dépendent du moment où la garantie est consentie. [...] De ces articles on doit conclure que les droits de la Banque sur les biens qui lui sont donnés en garantie sont acquis depuis la date de la convention dans la mesure où le cédant était alors ou est devenu propriétaire de ces biens. Dans ce cas, *la Banque est réputée détenir ses droits depuis la date de la convention sans égard aux différentes époques d'acquisition* des biens par le cédant."[69]

However, this did not help the *Bank Act* creditor because the *PPSA* creditor also acquired an – albeit unperfected – security interest in the after-acquired property at the time the security interest was created. The Supreme Court did not share Cuming's reservation regarding the intent of the legislature to confer an interest in after-acquired property.[70] Regarding the *PPSA* security interest,

---

[64] SS 1993, c P-6.2.

[65] *Ibid,* s 4(k).

[66] *Innovation Credit, supra* note 37 at paras 63–69, Charron J.

[67] *Supra* note 15.

[68] [1991] RJQ 712 (CA).

[69] *Ibid* at 3.1, Rousseau-Houle JA [emphasis added].

[70] *Radius, supra* note 16 at paras 24–27, Charron J. See Ronald CC Cuming, "Fitting a Square (Federal) Peg in a Round (Provincial) Hole: Rationalizing Section 427 Bank Act With Provincial Property Security Law" (2010) 73 Sask L Rev 1 at 16–19.

the Court held that the effect of the *PPSA* legislation is that "the Legislature created a statutory interest in after-acquired property, an interest which is correlative to an inchoate proprietary interest."[71] Since the *PPSA* security interest in after-acquired property is created when the security agreement is signed,[72] and no other priority rule than the first-in-time rule applies, the *PPSA* creditor's security interest prevailed over the *Bank Act* creditor's security interest.

*2. Civil Law: Absoluteness of Property Rights*

Had the law of Québec governed the security interest, the *nemo dat* rule would have not applied. Applying a conceptual criterion, two situations can be distinguished in *Innovation Credit*-style fact patterns. First, the *CcQ* creditor retains a right of ownership. Second, the *CcQ* creditor is granted a hypothec in the movable property. In both cases, the exercise of the *CcQ* creditor's right in the property *vis-à-vis* third parties – including the bank – depends on the proper registration, regardless of whether the transaction is hypothecary[73] or title-based.[74] As a result, the bank has priority over any hypothecary creditor or owner who fails to publish her right.[75] The same should apply in such cases where the vendor in possession of the property collateralizes the sold item. In that case, the purchaser's right of ownership cannot be exercised against third parties.[76]

As mentioned above, the result could be different where the *CcQ* creditor has a right to resolve the contract. This right need not be published and will retroactively re-vest ownership in the *CcQ* creditor, thus defeating the bank's interest.[77] On a law-and-economics basis, this priority can be defended on the basis that the vendor's priority is akin to a purchase-money security interest.

The different outcomes in Civil Law and Common Law is a function of the different approach to property rights in the two legal systems. In Civil Law, ownership is in principle absolute. Thus, even where there is a limited notion of relative ownership – that is, in title-based transactions and unperfected sales – relativity is limited to a dichotomy of two legal situations: the *inter partes* situation and the situation from the perspective of everybody else. In Common Law, on the other hand, relativity of title permeates the entire property law to such a degree that the bank cannot rely on having purchased the best title.

---

[71] *Radius, supra* note 16 at para 33, Charron J.

[72] *Ibid* at para 33, Charron J.

[73] See Part III: § 14 B.VI, "Opposability of the Hypothec".

[74] See also Part III: § 14 D, "Quasi-Security Devices in Civil Law".

[75] Poirier, *supra* note 5 at 350–53, 369–73.

[76] See Part II: § 4 F.III, "Consensualism in Québec Law".

[77] See Part III: § 14 C.II.1, "Prior Claim of a Supplier and the Right to Resolve the Contract". Cf. Poirier, *supra* note 5 at 351–53.

The *CcQ* creditor could be at an disadvantage where she duly registers a hypothec in after-acquired property before a *Bank Act* interest is created. In that case, the hypothec can only attach at the moment that the debtor acquires the property. The moment of creation of the *Bank Act* security interest in after-acquired property, on the other hand, is retroactively fixed to be the moment of creation of the security interest.[78] Poirier argues that in such cases, the *CcQ* hypothec will be lost, either because s 428(1) *Bank Act* gives the bank priority or because the debtor's ownership right is lost before the hypothec can attach.[79] The wording of art 2670 *CcQ* does not seem to allow a retroactive attachment of the hypothec, nor does the hypothec entail a *PPSA*-style inchoate security interest.

### *3. Amendment to the Bank Act*

The Supreme Court's decision in *Innovation Credit* and *Radius* revealed an undesirable result of the *Bank Act*'s reliance on provincial property law on the one hand and the incompleteness of the *PPSA's* approach of conceptual separation of general property law and *PPSA* priority on the other. But Crawford also identified a potential internal objection to the Court's decision.

> "Embracing *nemo dat* as the governing principle, the Court gives it extraordinary, unprecedented and unexamined force. It is assumed, rather than reasoned, that the creation of a security interest under provincial law deprives the customer of the power to create any valid competing interest. But a person who creates a security interest is still the 'owner' of the collateral, and that is all that section 427 requires to validate the grant of security under the *Bank Act*. And it is not self-evident that s. 427 intends to exalt *nemo dat* to extent that the Court does."[80]

This passage either ignores or completely misunderstands the meaning of the relativity of title in Common Law. While the debtor who creates a security interest is still the "owner" – or in Common Law terminology retains a title – this title is no longer unqualified. It has become subject of the security interest. The *Bank Act* creditor cannot receive better title than the debtor has because Common Law property does not operate with a notion of unqualified and absolute ownership.

Both *Radius* and *Innovation Credit* stood for the proposition that the creditor of a *PPSA* security interest in after-acquired property enjoys a legal property right in the property which will defeat a *Bank Act* security interest as long as the *PPSA* security interest attaches before the *Bank Act* security interest is cre-

---

[78] See Part IV: § 15 A.V.1.b), "Radius Credit".

[79] Poirier, *supra* note 5 at 373–74.

[80] Bradley Crawford, "In Defence of Secret Liens: How the Supreme Court Presses Parliament to Harmonize Section 427 of the Bank Act with the PPSAs" (2011) 26:2 Bank & Fin L Rev 305 at 310.

ated. Because the *Bank Act* creditor takes the property right as a regular purchaser, she cannot rely on her priority due to earlier registration. In response to this decision, Parliament has amended the *Bank Act.* s 428(1) *Bank Act* now states that the *Bank Act* security interest has "priority over all rights [...] of any person who had a security interest in that property that was unperfected at the time the bank acquired its security in the property." The amendment almost literally reflects Crawford's suggestion made after the decisions.[81]

Going further than Crawford's suggestion, s 425(1) *Bank Act* was amended to define the meaning of "perfection" in the context of the *Bank Act:*

> "'unperfected', in relation to a security interest, means that the security interest has not been registered in a public register maintained under the law under which the security interest is created, or has not been perfected or published by any other means recognized by that law, where the registration or other means of perfection or publication would have made the security interest effective against third parties or would have determined priorities in rank in respect of rights in, on or in respect of the property that is subject to the security interest;
>
> 'non parfaite' Se dit d'une sûreté qui n'a pas été enregistrée dans un registre public tenu en conformité avec la législation en vertu de laquelle la sûreté a été créée ou qui n'a pas été parfaite ou publiée d'une autre façon reconnue par cette législation de manière à la rendre opposable aux tiers ou à déterminer les droits de préférence dans le bien visé par la sûreté."

The problem with the *Bank Act* amendment is that it does not even achieve what it sets out to do. Under the *PPSA,* perfection requires attachment, and the security interest cannot attach before the debtor has a right in the collateral. Therefore, the debtor's security interest is not merely unperfected, it is non-existent with regard to not-yet purchased property.[82] It also seems doubtful that the rule defeats a title retention device. Because the *Bank Act* interest operates by applying the concept of "purchase" by the creditor, *nemo dat* could still apply where the *PPSA* creditor has retained title.[83] This conclusion is supported by the fact that the *Bank Act* definition of "security interest" is the same one as the one applied by the *Income Tax Act.* In such cases, the courts have consistently held that title retention does not constitute a security interest.[84] The rule

[81] *Ibid* at 313–14.

[82] A similar argument is made by Clayton D Bangsund, "Critical Examination of Recently Proposed Amendments to the Bank Act Security Provisions" (2012) 75:2 Sask L Rev 211 at 225–26. Cf. Roderick J Wood, "Bank Act-PPSA Interactions: Still Waiting for Solutions" (2012) 52:2 CBLJ 248 at 258–59.

[83] Bangsund, "Critical Examination of Recently Proposed Amendments to the Bank Act Security Provisions", preceding note at 231.

[84] *DaimlerChrysler Financial Services (debis) Canada Inc v Mega Pets Ltd,* 2002 BCCA 242, 212 DLR (4th) 41; *Canada (Deputy Attorney General) v Schwab Construction Ltd,* 2002

also does not explain how the "law under which the security interest is created" is to be determined.[85]

Bangsund argued that another problem with the amendment is that it does not address the problem of the *Bank Act* interest overruling a PMSI.[86] This is not entirely accurate. Because priority between a provincial security interest and a *BA* security interest is governed by general property law principles, this could easily be achieved by framing the PMSI in terms of a transaction in which the creditor has better title than the debtor.[87] The *PPSA* would re-characterize the transaction as far as priority between the PMSI and another *PPSA* security interest is concerned, but it would leave it intact as far as the priority competition between PMSI and *Bank Act* interest is concerned. The objection to this approach is that it seems unnecessary that the parties wanting to create a PMSI would need to engage in some kind of word magic to conceptualize the PMSI in a way that gives it priority. A more efficient way would be to coordinate between *Bank Act* and *PPSA*.

## B. Crown Privileges

### *I. The Drummond Decision*

In certain cases, monies owed to the Crown are paid not by the person owing the money (the liable debtor), but rather by somebody who, in turn, pays the liable debtor. These are called "source deductions."[88] In such cases, statutes can provide that the non-liable debtor is deemed to hold the monies in trust in favour of the Crown; these are Crown privileges. These cases include deductions deducted from wages for income tax liabilities,[89] pension contributions,[90] and employment insurance contributions.[91] While there are other statutory deemed trusts, s 67(2) *Bankruptcy and Insolvency Act* voids them in bankruptcy. But the deemed trusts for source deductions form a class of assets separate from the estate managed by the trustee in bankruptcy.[92]

---

SKCA 6; *Bank of Nova Scotia v Turyders Trucking Ltd* (2001), 32 CBR (4th) 14 (Ont Sup Ct J). See also Wood, "Bank Act-PPSA Interactions", *supra* note 82 at 260.

[85] Wood, "Bank Act-PPSA Interactions", *supra* note 82 at 259.

[86] Bangsund, "Critical Examination of Recently Proposed Amendments to the Bank Act Security Provisions", *supra* note 82 at 227–29.

[87] An option Bangsund acknowledges in a different context, see *ibid* at 231.

[88] *Century Services v Canada (AG),* 2010 SCC 60 at para 38, Deschamps J.

[89] *ITA, supra* note 7, s 227.

[90] *Canada Pension Plan,* RSC 1985, c C-8, s 23.

[91] *Employment Insurance Act,* SC 1996, c 23, s 86.

[92] *Bankruptcy and Insolvency Act,* RSC 1985, c B-3, s 67(3).

The deeemed-trust provisions create a particular interface between federal law and provincial property law (including secured transaction law). In *Sparrow,*[93] the Supreme Court of Canada held that the effect of a s 427 *Bank Act* and a *PPSA* security interest is to transfer title from debtor to the bank.[94] Because of this, the deemed trust could no longer attach to the debtor's title in the property, only to debtor's equity of redemption. Because of this, the security interest took priority over the Crown privilege. In the wake of this decision, Parliament amended the deemed trust provisions to clearly state that the Crown privilege also takes priority over any security interest.[95] "Security interest" is defined as follows:

"Section 224(1)(3) *ITA*

[...]

'security interest'

'garantie'

'security interest' means any interest in, or for civil law any right in, property that secures payment or performance of an obligation and includes an interest, or for civil law a right, created by or arising out of a debenture, mortgage, hypothec, lien, pledge, charge, deemed or actual trust, assignment or encumbrance of any kind whatever, however or whenever arising, created, deemed to arise or otherwise provided for;

[...]

[...]

'garantie'

'security interest'

'garantie' Intérêt ou, pour l'application du droit civil, droit sur un bien qui garantit l'exécution d'une obligation, notamment un paiement. Sont en particulier des garanties les intérêts ou, pour l'application du droit civil, les droits nés ou découlant de débentures, hypothèques, privilèges, nantissements, sûretés, fiducies réputées ou réelles, cessions et charges, quelle qu'en soit la nature, de quelque façon ou à quelque date qu'elles soient créées, réputées exister ou prévues par ailleurs.

[...]"

Under the *CcQ,* the same situation could not have arisen. In Civil Law, the effect of the deemed trust is that the Crown owns the monies, and no hypothec by the debtor's creditor can attach.[96]

The law of Crown privileges also gave the Supreme Court opportunity to expand on the notion of property rights as understood in federal law. In *Caisse populaire Desjardins de l'Est de Drummond v Canada,*[97] a Caisse populaire Desjardins gave credit to a debtor. The debtor deposited monies with the bank which – according to an agreement between the bank and the debtor – were not

[93] *Sparrow, supra* note 15.

[94] For a summary of *Sparrow* see Kevin Davis, "Priority of Crown Claims in Insolvency: Royal Bank of Canada v Sparrow Electric Corp. and Its Aftermath" (1998) 29:1 CBLJ 145.

[95] Cf. *Royal Bank of Canada v Tuxedo Transport Ltd* (1999), 64 BCLR (3d) 158 (BC SC).

[96] Cf. Alain Robichaud, "Les droits de la Couronne et les conflits avec les créanciers hypothécaires" in: Barreau du Québec, ed, *Développements récents sur l'hypothèque* (Cowansville, Québec: Éditions Yvon Blais, 1997) 55 at 76.

[97] 2009 SCC 29 [*Drummond*].

withdrawable and could only be used as a security for the benefit of the bank. Bank and debtor also agreed that the bank could withhold repayment of the monies until the credit was repaid and thus gave the bank a right to set-off the credit contract claims against the debtor's claims from the account. This triple arrangement is known as the "triple cocktail".[98] The debtor failed to make interest payments to the bank, but also to make certain salary deductions for its employees due to the Crown.

Due to the "deemed trust" framework of the *ITA,* the case revolved around the question whether the bank was a secured creditor – who could be subjected to the deemed trust – or whether it merely had an ordinary right to set-off its credit claims against the accounts debts. It has been argued that in such cases it is difficult to conceptualize the bank's right to set-off as a security interest in the bank account because it is difficult to view the bank having an interest in its own indebtedness,[99] but this has become accepted in Canadian Common Law.[100] The majority of the Supreme Court of Canada, in an opinion written by Rothstein J, held that because the *ITA* contains a definition of security interest in s 224(1.3) *ITA,* the question whether or not the property was subject to a security interest and thus the question of the bank's status as a secured creditor did not depend on the characterization of the interest in provincial law.[101] Rather, according to the broad functional definition of "security interest," the issue was to be determined by reference to the *ITA* alone.

At first glance, the decision poses a challenge if one requires that a security interest be a property right.[102] An easy way around this would have been to do without the necessity of the "security interest" within the meaning of s 224(1.3)

---

[98] See e.g. Clayton D Bangsund, "Set-Off & Security Interests" (2017) 50:1 UBCL Rev 1 at 24; Diccon Loxton, "One Flaw over the Cuckoos Nest: Making Sense of the 'Flawed Asset Arrangement' Example, Security Interest Definition and Set-Off Exclusion in the PPSA" (2011) 34:2 UNSWLJ 472 at 483.

[99] Cf. Roderick J Wood, "Journey to the Outer Limits of Secured Transactions Law" (2010) 48:3 CBLJ 482 at 490–93.

[100] *Transamerica Commercial Finance Corp, Canada v Royal Bank of Canada* (1990), 70 DLR (4th) 627 (Sask CA). For a detailed analysis of when the bank's interest crosses the security interest threshold see Bangsund, "Set-Off & Security Interests", *supra* note 98.

[101] *Drummond, supra* note 97 at para 10, Rothstein J.

[102] Ian J Binnie, "Comment on Caisse Populaire Desjardins De L'Est De Drummond v Canada" (2011) 26:2 Bank & Fin L Rev 327 at 332: "This obstacle is, in fact, a rather formidable one." (The author is not related to Binnie J of the Supreme Court of Canada who concurred with the majority decision of Rothstein J). Cf. Wood, "Journey to the Outer Limits of Secured Transactions Law", *supra* note 99 at 495.

*ITA* being a property right.[103] The Court did not adopt this approach.[104] As Deschamps J explained, the contract between bank and debtor modified the personal obligations. However, this did not amount to giving the bank a property right in its own indebtedness. She wrote "L'ajout d'un ou de plusieurs droits personnels n'a pas pour effet de créer un droit réel."[105] This sounds very much like a rejection of a Hohfeldian approach to property rights by Deschamps J. No matter how many sticks are added to the bundle, there is no threshold that allows us to now speak of a property right.

I would submit that while it is arguably difficult to conceptualize the right to set-off as being a property right, the same is not necessarily true of the other agreements between bank and debtor. The agreement to not assign the debt has no bearing on the obligation between bank and debtor. Rather, it defines the relationship between debtor and the bank account. Once again, it is important to keep the Civil Law distinction between right and object of right in mind.[106] The (property) right is the ownership of the personal obligation owed by the bank. The object of the right is the personal obligation. Just because the parties were connected by the personal obligation does not mean that they could not also enter into an agreement regarding the debtor's property right. The second-level question is whether they could do so with third-party effect or whether this would breach the *numerus clausus* principle. In regard to the latter question, it is important to remember that the *numerus clausus* principle in Québec law is not strict.[107] In this regard, I disagree with the majority of the Court.

"In this case, the issue is not whether the Caisse's interest in or right over Camvrac's property is one that conforms with the property security legislation of the provinces. This is because the deemed trust created by [s 227(4.1) *ITA*] and [s 86(2.1) *Employment Insurance Act*], which incorporate by reference the definition of 'security interest' in [s 224(1.3) *ITA*], applies '[n]otwithstanding … any enactment of a province' (see also [*DaimlerChrysler Financial Services (debis) Canada Inc v Mega Pets Ltd* at para 31])."[108]

---

[103] Cf. *Drummond, supra* note 97 at paras 83–91, Deschamps J [dissenting on the outcome].

[104] On the meaning of "interest" in the tax context see Martin Lamoureux, "The Income Tax Act, the Excise Tax Act and the Term Interest: An Interesting Case for Harmonization" in: Canada, Department of Justice & Association de planification fiscale et financière, eds, *Harmonization of Federal Legislation with Quebec Civil Law and Canadian Bijuralism: Collection of Studies in Tax Law* (Montréal: Association de planification fiscale et financière, 2002) 1. Lamoureux argued that the term "interest" has no meaning in Civil Law. Parliament added the words "or for civil law any right in" to the *ITA* security interest definition in 2013, see *Technical Tax Amendments Act,* 2013 SC, c 34, s 161.

[105] *Drummond, supra* note 97 at para 124, Deschamps J, dissenting.

[106] See Part II: § 4 D, "Right and Object of Right".

[107] See Part II: § 4 E, "Numerus Clausus in Civil Law".

[108] *Drummond, supra* note 97 at para 46, Rothstein J.

But because the issue is whether the secured creditor can be said to have a property right and there is no federal property law, provincial law still governs whether the creditor's right can be said to be a property right. It would not be one if the secured creditor's right violated the *numerus clausus*. In *Drummond,* this was not the case because under the decision in *Caisse populaire Desjardins de Val-Brillant c Blouin*[109], the creditor's right also conformed to the requirements of a hypothec with delivery in incorporeals.[110]

*II. Reaction to Drummond*

The reaction to *Drummond* is an example of how the vertical vector of bijuralism influences the provincial property laws. The Canadian *PPSAs* do not recognize control as means of perfecting a security interest in an account.[111] The recognition of certain interests in bank accounts thus poses a challenge for the *PPSA*. The *PPSAs* protect a bank's right in a bank account held by one of its customers to a limited extent. Ontario, Manitoba, Nunavut, and the Northwest Territories do recognize the priority of any right to set-off over a competing security interest.[112] Saskatechewan will soon follow suit.[113] However, one reading is that *Drummond* means that not only the flawed asset arrangement, but the entire triple cocktail including the right to set-off must be regarded as a *PPSA* security interest.[114] Consequently, where there is a triple cocktail, the entire arrangement including the right to set-off would be subject to the *PPSA* priority scheme. This jepoardizes a bank's potential to use a customer's bank account to secure lines of credit. While reform was announced in Ontario as far back as 2012,[115] no public progress has been made to allow perfection by control of a security interest in a bank account.[116] While this mechanism would

---

[109] 2003 SCC 31.

[110] *Drummond, supra* note 97 at paras 42–49, Rothstein J. See Part III: § 14 B.V.2.b)aa), "The Val-Brillant Decision".

[111] Anthony J Duggan, "Current Issues in Secured Transactions Law in Canada: An Ontario Perspective" in: Louise Gullifer & Orkun Akseli, eds, *Secured Transactions Law Reform: Principles, Policies and Practice* (Oxford, Portland: Hart, 2016) 95 at 104.

[112] *Personal Property Security Act,* CCSM, c P35, s 41(2); *Personal Property Security Act,* SNWT 1994, c 8, s 41(2); *Personal Property Security Act,* RSO 1990, c P.10, s 40(1.1).

[113] *Personal Property Security Amendment Act,* SS 2019, c 15.

[114] Duggan, "Current Issues in Secured Transactions Law in Canada", *supra* note 111 at 104–5; Catherine E Walsh, "Justifications for UCC Article 9's Treatment of Deposit Accounts: A Comparative Note" (2015) 4:1 Penn St J L & Int'l Aff 350 at 360.

[115] Ontario, Ministry of Government and Consumer Services, *Business Law Agenda: Priority Findings and Recommendations Report,* (2015) <https://www.ontariocanada.com/registry/showAttachment.do?postingId=18942&attachmentId=33251> accessed 3 September 2019 at 14.

[116] Duggan, "Current Issues in Secured Transactions Law in Canada", *supra* note 111 at 105.

restore the ability of the bank to easily take security in the bank account held by one of its customers, it should be noted that this is not universally seen as a positive thing. After all, perfecting security by control is a mechanism that sits outside the publicity principle embodied by the *PPSA* register.[117]

Unlike the *PPSA* jurisdictions, Québec has enacted provisions allowing perfection by control.[118] After *Val-Brillant,* the *CcQ* had been originally amended to only allow pledges over deposit accounts or other claims if they were negotiable instruments – securities – as defined under the *Loi sur le transfert de valeurs mobilières et l'obtention de titres intermédiés*[119] or financial assets in a securities account.[120] Given that the result of *Drummond* was a conceptualization of the triple cocktail as a security interest, there needed to be a special regime to facilitate the use of bank accounts as collateral. To achieve this, the Québec legislature has opted to introduce a special regime. A pledging of cash is achieved by taking control of monetary claims. Monetary claims in turn are defined in art 2713.1 *CcQ*. However a claim represented by a negotiable instrument, a claim that is a security or security entitlement within the meaning of the *LTVM* again are excluded from this definition because there already are special frameworks for these types of collateral.[121] The pledging of cash in this way gives the secured creditor a super-priority over all other secured creditors in relation to the same collateral, but they leave intact the superpriority of non-hypothecary interests created by statute such as the federal security interests.[122]

---

[117] Walsh, *supra* note 114 at 354–55.

[118] See Duggan, "Current Issues in Secured Transactions Law in Canada", *supra* note 111 at 105.

[119] *Loi sur le transfert de valeurs mobilières et l'obtention de titres intermédiés,* SQ 2008, c 20.

[120] See Sterling H Dietze, "My Cash and I: Cash Collateral Is Finally King in Quebec" (2016) 31:2 Bank & Fin L Rev 349 at 349–50.

[121] See *ibid* at 353.

[122] *Ibid* at 359–60.

# § 16 Property Rights in Insolvency

Debtors in distress can avail themselves of several options. The *Bankruptcy and Insolvency Act*[1] is the general insolvency and bankruptcy act. It contains rules on both creditor and debtor agreements leading to a reorganization as well as rules providing for the liquidation of the debtor's assets. The *Companies' Creditors Arrangement Act*[2] allows insolvent corporations owing their creditors in excess of $5 million to restructure their business and financial affairs. Finally, the *Winding-up and Restructuring Act*[3] provides a particular insolvency regime for certain companies, notably financial institutions. Because the *BIA* is the general liquidation framework and property rights play their most important role in liquidation rather than in debtor-creditor arranged restructuring, I focus on the *BIA*.

## A. Divestment of the Estate to the Trustee in Bankruptcy

### *I. Principle*

In *BIA* terminology "insolvency" denotes the inability of a debtor to fulfil all her obligations, while "bankruptcy" is the stage of liquidation after any agreement with the creditors has failed.[4] Bankruptcy divests the bankrupt of her property. According to s 71 *BIA*, "a bankrupt ceases to have any capacity to dispose of or otherwise deal with their property, which shall, subject to this Act and to the rights of secured creditors, immediately pass to and vest in the trustee."[5] This trustee is the "trustee in bankruptcy". She should not be confused with the trustee of a trust.

### *II. Insolvency of a Trust*

Due its nature as an ownerless patrimony, the Québec trust does not become subject to bankruptcy proceedings in either the trustee's or the beneficiary's

---

[1] RSC 1985, c B-3 [*BIA*].

[2] RSC 1985, c C-36.

[3] RSC 1985, c W-11.

[4] See *Century Services v Canada (AG),* 2010 SCC 60 at para 13, Deschamps J.

[5] English law takes a similar approach, see *Insolvency Act 1986,* 1986, c 45, s 306.

estate.[6] However, where the trustee goes bankrupt, the trustee's powers in relation to the trust property become vested in the trustee in bankruptcy.[7]

Bohémier argues that the absence of liability of the trustee and the impossibility of an insolvent trust patrimony leaves a lacuna in Canadian bankruptcy law that should be amended by allowing insolvency proceedings with regard to the trust patrimony,[8] but federal Parliament has not followed his suggestion.

A reverse problem occurs in Common Law: the bankruptcy of the trustee. Creditors of the trust cannot enforce their judgment against the trust itself. They can only rely on the trustee's right in the trust property to satisfy themselves. This raises the question what happens when trustee becomes bankrupt. When the Common Law trustee becomes bankrupt, the trust property does not form part of her estate. But the same is not true of the trustee's right in the trust property. Thus, trust creditors are in principle relegated to a *pari passu* sharing. To avoid this result, the trustee's right in the trust property should be made available in priority to the trust creditors who held debts relating to such property which became available to the bankrupt's estate.[9]

### *III. The Trustee's Title to the Property*

From a Civil Law perspective, the trustee should be considered to become the full owner of the debtor's property.[10] However, there is no provision in the *BIA* that specifically states that the debtor loses her ownership and the trustee becomes the new owner. The Superior Court of Québec held in one decision that the bankrupt remains owner of the property.[11] However, the Court of Appeal had already held in prior decisions that the trustee must be considered the owner of the property.[12] The Supreme Court left that question open, but

---

[6] Rainer Becker, *Die Fiducie von Québec und der Trust: Ein Vergleich mit verschiedenen Modellen fiduziarischer Rechtsfiguren im Civil Law* (Tübingen: Mohr Siebeck, 2007) at 365.

[7] Alain Vauclair & Martin-François Parent, "Harmonization of Federal Legislation with Quebec Civil Law: Some Examples from the Bankruptcy and Insolvency Act" in: Canada, Department of Justice, ed, *The Harmonization of Federal Legislation with the Civil Law of the Province of Quebec and Canadian Bijuralism: Second Publication* (Ottawa: Canada, Department of Justice, 2001) 1 at 24.

[8] Albert Bohémier, "Application of the Bankruptcy and Insolvency Act to the Trust of the Civil Code of Québec" (2003) 37:1 RJT 114.

[9] Lionel D Smith, "Trust and Patrimony" (2009) 28 ETPJ 332 at 338–42, referring to *Re Richardson,* [1911] 2 KB 705 (CA). Cf. Andrew S Burrows, *The Law of Restitution,* 3rd edn (Oxford: Oxford University Press, 2010) at 191–93 [Burrows, *Restitution*].

[10] Jacques Auger & Albert Bohémier, "The Status of the Trustee in Bankruptcy" (2003) 37:1 RJT 57 at 89; Vauclair & Parent, *supra* note 7 at 27–28.

[11] *Auger c Harvey,* [2000] RJQ 2075 at paras 26–31 (Sup Ct).

[12] *Droit de la famille - 3712,* [2000] RDF 589 (Queb CA); *Lefaivre c Côté,* [1976] CA 691.

stressed that the trustee's function cannot easily be described by using the term "ownership."

"The strict concept of ownership accounts poorly for the nature of the trustee's duties and the rights a trustee exercises over the bankrupt's property following the initial bankruptcy event. The trustee's rights are exercised only in relation to a patrimony whose content is legally defined in s. 67 B.I.A. This patrimony consists of only the property that could be liquidated for the benefit of the creditors. The trustee exercises certain statutory rights over this property that are in part similar to the rights of an owner. The trustee may dispose of the property of which he or she has seisin, but for a specific purpose, namely to pay the claims of the bankrupt's creditors. [...] The attribution and exercise of such powers do not correspond perfectly to alienation, so much so that some authors have expressed very strong criticism of the use of the assignee concept to describe the function of the trustee in bankruptcy (M. Cantin Cumyn, *Traité de droit civil: L'administration du bien d'autrui* (2000), at pp. 110–12."[13]

Furthermore, the Court held that the trustee does not have the rights an owner usually has under Civil Law because she cannot use the property as she sees fit.

"At any rate, the use of the concept of *dévolution* (vesting) in the French version of [s 71(2) *BIA*] does not eliminate the distinction between the two aspects of the trustee's role following the initial bankruptcy event. In *Mercure* v. *A. Marquette & Fils Inc.,* [1977] 1 S.C.R. 547, this Court clearly noted this distinction, which serves as a basis for characterizing the legal position of the trustee when exercising the powers and performing the obligations the law ascribes to trustees. [...] The trustee's legal position is therefore more akin to that of a third person in relation to the debtor. On the one hand, the trustee is subrogated to the bankrupt's rights in the exercise of his or her powers to hold and dispose of property of which he or she has been granted seisin. On the other hand, the law treats the trustee as the creditors' legal mandatary who will liquidate the property entrusted to him or her for the creditors' benefit. The dual nature of the trustee's duties does not therefore make it possible to regard the trustee as a third person in relation to the bankrupt, given all the powers conferred upon the trustee by law in order to preserve and liquidate the debtor's property."[14]

### *IV. The Equity of Redemption*

Section 130 *BIA* stipulates that if the trustee does not inform the creditor of her choice to redeem the property, she

---

[13] *Lefebvre (Syndic de); Tremblay (Syndic de),* 2004 SCC 63 at para 35, LeBel J.

[14] *Ibid* at para 36, LeBel J.

"is not entitled to exercise it, and the equity of redemption or any other interest in the property comprised in the security that is vested in the trustee shall vest in the creditor, and the amount of [the creditor's] claim shall be reduced by the amount at which the security has been valued.

n'a pas le droit de l'exercer; la faculté de réméré ou autre intérêt dans les biens compris dans la garantie qui est dévolue au syndic sont attribués au créancier, et le montant de sa réclamation est diminué du montant auquel la garantie a été évaluée."

Regarding real property, according to s 6(1) *Land Registration Reform Act;* s 6(3) *Land Registration Reform Act,* regarding land is no longer transferred to the mortgagee; rather the land is charged. Thus, the equity of redemption no longer means the right to demand re-conveyance of the title to the land, but the exercise of this right is still based on the fictional transfer of land to the mortgagee.[15] The *PPSA* did not similarly change the distribution of title, thus, an equity of redemption in its formal sense could still exist if the *PPSA* security interest is classified as a chattel mortgage. Furthermore, the *PPSA* continues to use the common law language of "redemption" when referring to the debtor's continued interest in the property.[16]

However, the trustee in bankruptcy of property subject to the *Code civil du Québec*[17] property law is already the owner of the property, and thus cannot redeem it; she consequently has no "equity of redemption." For that reason, the Drafting Commission intended to change that provision,[18] but this did not become law. In Civil Law, s 130 *BIA* can be interpreted to refer not to the equity of redemption, but to the repurchase of the security by the trustee.[19]

---

[15] *Scotia Mortgage Corporation v Davidson Estate,* [2009] OJ No 1781 at para 26 (Sup Ct J), Quigley J: "Prior to the Land Registration Reform Act, R.S.O. 1990, c. L.4, s. 1, s. 6(1), 6(3), a mortgagor who granted a mortgage charge to a lender as security for a mortgage debt transferred the legal estate to the creditor, subject to redemption and a re-conveyance upon payment of the debt. However, since the enactment of that legislation, a charge no longer operates to transfer the legal estate in mortgaged lands to the chargee. The legal estate is not transferred but the chargor and chargee are nonetheless entitled to all of the legal and equitable rights and remedies that would have been available to them if the chargor had transferred the land to the chargee by way of mortgage, subject to a proviso for redemption."

[16] See e.g. *Personal Property Security Act,* RSO 1990, c P.10 [*PPSA* (*Ont*)], s 66(1). On the equity of redemption see Part III: § 12 A.I.3, "Chattel Mortgage".

[17] SQ 1991, c 64.

[18] Canada, Department of Justice, Bijuralism & Drafting Support Services Group Legislative Service Branch, "Proposals for Harmonizing the Bankruptcy and Insolvency Act with Quebec Civil Law" (2003) 37:1 RJT 19 at 37.

[19] *Banque nationale du Canada c Restaurant Ocean Drive Inc (syndic),* [1996] JQ No 724 at para 10 (Sup Ct), Chaput JCS, "De son côté, la banque pouvait demander au syndic de choisir d'exercer son pouvoir de racheter sa garantie tel que le prévoit l'article 130. Elle ne l'a pas fait. La banque a plutôt décidé de réaliser sa garantie conformément à l'article 69.3(2) de la L.F.I. et aux dispositions applicables du droit civil provincial" Affirmed by

## B. Security Interests in Bankruptcy

According to s 71 *BIA,* the trustee in bankruptcy takes the estate subject to any security interests. The impact along the vertical vector of bijuralism of this rule on provincial property rights differs depending on whether the security interest in question is a general security interest of the type provided for by provincial law, a prior claim specific to Québec law, a title-based security device, or a Quistclose trust. I will look at each of these cases in turn.

### *I. General Security Interests in Bankruptcy*

This means that hypothecs and *PPSA* security interests will in principle be binding upon a trustee in bankruptcy. This rule can be viewed as a function of the *nemo dat quod non habet* rule.[20] There are two exceptions to this rule.

First, provincial *PPSA*s contain one important exception: an unperfected security interest is not binding on the trustee.[21] Provincial legislatures deemed it necessary to include this rule because the trustee is the successor of the debtor, not a *bona fide* third party purchaser.

In Québec, the question whether the trustee in bankruptcy has third-party status with regard to hypothecs has not been decided by the *CcQ,* but rather by the courts. This matters because if the trustee is a third party, the hypothec is not opposable without the requirements of opposability having to be met.[22] Under the *Code civil du Bas-Canada,* the Superior Court of Québec held in *Re Civano Construction Inc*[23] that the trustee in bankruptcy is not the successor to the ownership rights held by the debtor. In *Musée des Sciences Naturelles de Québec Inc (syndic) c Banque de Montréal*[24] the Court of Appeal of Québec held that publication of a hypothec is not necessary in the creditor-debtor relationship but that the trustee is a representative of the other creditors and thus a third party. The Court applied the same ratio in *Wilfrid Noêl & fils ltée c Bouchard.*[25]

A second exception to the continued effectiveness of security interests concerns the exercise of executory measures by the secured creditor. The trustee

---

*Banque nationale du Canada c Restaurant Ocean Drive Inc (syndic),* [1998] RJQ 1766, 164 DLR (4th) 117, 23 CBR (4th) 296, [1998] JQ No 1921 (CA) [leave to appeal refused].

[20] Ronald CC Cuming, "Secured Creditors' Non-Statutory Remedies: Unfinished Business" (2012) 91:2 Can Bar Rev 243 at 254.

[21] *PPSA (Ont), supra* note 16, s 20(1)(b).

[22] See Part III: § 14 B.VI, "Opposability of the Hypothec".

[23] (1961), [1962] CS 45.

[24] [1998] JQ No 814 (CA).

[25] [2000] JQ No 474 (CA).

in bankruptcy can make an order asking that the execution of the security interest be stayed.[26] However, this exception concerns the procedural aspects of the exercise of property rights rather than their substantive existence. It is thus outside the scope of this book.

### *II. Characterization of Prior Claims as a Credit Security*

#### *1. General*

As shown above,[27] prior claims under the new *CcQ* do not confer a real right of action. However, there are arguments for and against letting prior claims survive bankruptcy. For the survival of prior claims, the following could be argued. First, the trustee in bankruptcy is not a third-party acquirer of the patrimony of the debtor, but rather a successor of the bankrupt and a representative of all creditors.[28] In a way, it can be said that the trustee realizes the common pledge of all creditors. Prior claims before insolvency are opposable against all creditors and their common pledge. Thus, they should remain opposable against the trustee.[29] Second, the hypothec survives insolvency. Under the *CcQ,* a prior claim has priority over the hypothec. If the hypothec survives bankruptcy, so should prior claims.[30]

On the other hand, realization of a prior claim requires a personal action against the debtor, but s 69 *BIA* stays all proceedings against the debtor. The conditions for the realization of the prior claim can no longer be satisfied. *Before* the introduction of the *CcQ,* privileges under the *CcBC* were considered personal rights and thus the creditors were not considered secured creditors within the meaning of the *BIA.*[31] Prior claims are structurally similar to the old privileges. The old privileges were general privileges and did not attach to certain property. Under the *CcQ,* the same is true for the prior claims mentioned in art 2651(4) *CcQ;* art 2651(5) *CcQ.* Consequently, jurisprudence has decided that prior claims are not property rights. The creditor of a prior claim is thus not a secured creditor within the sense of the *BIA.*[32] This decision can also be

---

[26] *BIA, supra* note 1, s 69.3(2). See Jacques Deslauriers, "Utilisation de la Loi sur la faillite et l'insolvabilité par les créanciers garantis" in: Barreau du Québec, ed, *Développements récents sur l'hypothèque* (Cowansville, Québec: Éditions Yvon Blais, 1997) 21.

[27] See Part III: § 14 C, "Prior Claims".

[28] See Part IV: § 16 A.III, "The Trustee's Title to the Property".

[29] Louis Payette, *Les sûretés réelles dans le Code civil du Québec,* 5th edn (Cowansville, Québec: Éditions Yvon Blais, 2015) at para 207.

[30] *Ibid* at para 208.

[31] See Paul-Emile Bilodeau, *Précis de la faillite et de l'insolvabilité,* 2d edn (Brossard, Québec: CCH, 2004) at paras 229–41.

[32] *Château d'Amos ltée (Syndic),* [1999] RJQ 2612 (Sup Ct); *Québec Inc (Syndic de),* [1998] RDI 587 (Queb Sup Ct). See also with further references Payette, *supra* note 29 at para 210.

supported on the basis that the distribution logic of provincial property law and federal insolvency law need not be the same.

*2. State Claims*

In case of state claims, s 86(1) *BIA;* s 86(2) *BIA* provide the state with an equal priority as if they were entitled to a Crown privilege, provided the state registers the claims. While registration is not a necessary condition for a prior claim, art 3017 *CcQ* implies that the state can voluntarily register its prior claim.[33]

*3. Supplier Claims*

The *CcQ* abolished the bankruptcy-proof vendor's security right for the sales price. Contrary to Ziegel's suggestion,[34] s 81.1(1) *BIA* does not level the playing field between suppliers in Québec and elsewhere in Canada. Rather, it originally creates a preference in bankruptcy for all suppliers. The only difference is that even without s 81.1 *BIA,* a Québec supplier would have a right to resolve the entire contract. Due to the consensual nature of the transfer of property in Québec law,[35] this would re-vest ownership in the supplier. But in that case, the supplier would also lose her claim for the sales price. This might be undesirable if she has sold the property with a profit margin.

*4. Property Tax Claims*

As mentioned above,[36] there has been a revision to property tax prior claims. Under the old regime, the courts found that the municipal prior claim did not give the municipalities secured creditor status under the *BIA* because the prior claim contained neither a real right of action nor to a right to follow the property.

"La priorité ne constitue pas un droit réel et il n'y a pas de droit de suite sur le bien affecté. Ce droit de suite existe pour les taxes foncières, mais ce n'est pas en vertu de son statut de créance prioritaire, mais en vertu d'une disposition législative expresse, soit l'article 498 de la Loi sur les cités et villes. [...] De cette définition, n'est créancier garanti que celui détenant un droit réel sur les biens du débiteur et à défaut de procédure dans la Loi sur la faillite, le droit du Québec doit trouver application. Ainsi, le Code civil ne prévoit aucun recours par-

---

[33] Payette, *supra* note 29 at para 211, note 359 and paras 300–1.

[34] Jacob S Ziegel, "New and Old Challenges in Approaching Phase Three Amendments to Canada's Commercial Insolvency Laws" (2002) 37 CBLJ 75 at 102.

[35] See Part II: § 4 F.III, "Consensualism in Québec Law".

[36] See Part IV: § 16 B.II.4, "Property Tax Claims".

ticulier pour le créancier prioritaire, il doit utiliser les recours réservés aux créanciers ordinaires, compte tenu qu'il ne détient aucun droit réel sur l'immeuble. Les recours hypothécaires des articles 2748 et suivants ne lui sont pas disponibles."[37]

Article 2654.1 *CcQ* now allows the creditor to follow the property. The effect of the new art 2654.1 *CcQ* remains to be seen. On the one hand, it complements municipal prior claims with a right of following. On the other hand, *Hull (Ville de) c Tsang*[38] indicated that not only the absence of the right of following, but also the absence of a real right of action deriving from the prior claim is a reason not to qualify the prior claim creditor as a secured creditor within the meaning of the *BIA*. It would be up to federal Parliament to decide on a functional basis which characteristic of a prior claim should be enough to push it within the definition of security interest under the *BIA*.

### *III. Title-Based Security Devices in Bankruptcy*

The question as to whether property subject to a security based on title-allocation is property that becomes vested in the trustee has been the subject of decisions based on both Common Law and Civil Law. The outcome in these cases, however, varied. The federal legislature has already partly reacted to this difference.

#### *1. Common Law Quasi-Security Devices and Deemed Security Interests in Bankruptcy*

##### *a) Decision*

In Common Law Canada, the leading case on the question as to what extent property subject to a title-based security device becomes vested in the trustee is *Re Giffen.*[39] In that case, the debtor, Giffen, obtained a car from her employer under a long-term lease. Under s 1 *Personal Property Security Act,*[40] such a long-term lease is a deemed security interest. The employer, in turn, had leased the car from the respondent. The debtor then made an assignment in bankruptcy. The respondent seised the car and sold it. The trustee subsequently sought an order declaring that it was entitled to the proceeds of the sale because according to s 20(b)(i) *PPSA (BC),* an unperfected security interest (including a deemed security interest such as a long-term lease) is ineffective against the trustee in bankruptcy. In effect, the trustee claimed that the car formed part of the debtor's estate.

---

[37] *Hull (Ville de) c Tsang,* [1998] RDI 343 at 345 (Queb CM), Daoust J. See also *Château d'Amos ltée (Syndic), supra* note 32; *Lacoursière c Westmount (Ville de),* [1998] RJQ 1784 (Sup Ct); *Kostadinova Gantcheff (Syndic de),* [1996] RJQ 3030 (Sup Ct).

[38] Preceding note.

[39] [1998] 1 SCR 91 [*Giffen*].

[40] RSBC 1996, c 359 [*PPSA (BC)*].

In its decision, the Supreme Court of Canada stressed that the *PPSA* did away with traditional concepts of ownership, property, and estate.[41] Furthermore, the concept of "property" adopted in the *BIA* is rather broad. Under the definition in the *BIA,* a right to use and to possession under a long-term lease are property rights.[42] These rights passes to the trustee.[43] Section 20(b)(i) *PPSA (BC)* works to limit the effectiveness of the creditor's unperfected security interest. The creditor cannot exercise her security interest against the trustee, and since the trustee has a property right, she can take the car.[44] The Supreme Court held that the principle that the trustee in bankruptcy cannot succeed to property rights greater than the ones enjoyed by the debtor is modified by s 20(b)(i) *PPSA (BC).*[45]

Finally, the Supreme Court held that s 20(b)(i) *PPSA (BC)* does not disturb the distribution scheme of s 136 *BIA* because the content of what a "security interest" is for the purpose of the *BIA* is determined by provincial law.[46] Thus, insofar as provincial law decides to limit the effectiveness of a credit security in the event of insolvency, provincial law is at liberty to do so.

It should be noted that not all *PPSA* jurisdictions have adopted a s 20(b)(i) *PPSA (BC)*-style rule. For example, the *Personal Property Securities Act 1999* does not contain a comparable rule.[47] The *Personal Property Securities Act 2009* conceptualizes the ineffectiveness of the unperfected security interest as a re-vesting of the security interest in the grantor right before the bankruptcy.[48] This approach has difficulty explaining how the creditor's title is transferred to the bankrupt debtor when all that s 267 *PPSA (Cth) 2009* provides for is the revesting of the "security interest."[49]

### *b) Criticism*

The decision of the Supreme Court of Canada amounts to a recognition of a possessory right as a sufficient condition for considering the collateral to be part of the debtor's estate. This is a logical function of the notion of property rights in Common Law, where possession is a property right and there is more

---

[41] *Giffen, supra* note 39 at paras 25–28.

[42] *Ibid* at para 34, Iacobucci J.

[43] *Ibid* at para 35, Iacobucci J.

[44] *Ibid* at para 43, Iacobucci J.

[45] *Ibid* at paras 50–56, Iacobucci J.

[46] *Ibid* at para 60 ff.

[47] *Personal Property Securities Act 1999,* s 103. See Anthony J Duggan & Jacob S Ziegel, "Justice Iacobucci and the Canadian Law of Deemed Trusts and Chattel Security" (2007) 57 UTLJ 227 at 235.

[48] *Personal Property Securities Act 2009,* s 267. See *White v Spiers Earthworks Pty Ltd,* [2014] WASC 139.

[49] *White v Spiers Earthworks Pty Ltd,* preceding note does not address this question other than stating that it happens.

than one title.[50] I must disagree with the Supreme Court's statement that the *PPSA* did away with traditional concepts of ownership, property, and estate. Rather, the first two of these notions never existed at Common Law. The more important result of *Giffen* is not that possessory property rights vest in the trustee in bankruptcy, but rather that bankruptcy extinguishes title to better interests, such as the lessor's interest.

This result differs from other legal property rights. In general, the bankruptcy of the debtor does not mean that her possessory right becomes the best right in the world. For example, a trustee in bankruptcy will not be able to bring goods taken by the creditor back into the estate where the creditor can show a better right to the property. In principle, tort claims pass to the trustee as well. They are choses in action and thus form part of the debtor's estate.[51] Thus, the trustee in bankruptcy can bring a conversion claim against somebody who has taken something that was once in the debtor's possession, but she will fail where the taker has a better interest. In *Taylor v Plumer,*[52] a rogue converted bank notes and used them to acquire other monetary instruments. The original owner of the notes than brought the notes bank into his possession. The rogue then went bankrupt. An action by the trustee in bankruptcy for bringing the instruments into the bankrupt's estate failed because the Court held that the notes were the traceable proceeds of the original.

But as we have seen, *Giffen* stands for the proposition that the function of the *PPSA* is to extinguish the creditor's legal property right unless she has perfected it. The inclusion of deemed security interests in the *PPSA* extends this to property that is in essence not subject to a functional security interest because the interest is only a deemed security interest.[53] Bridge and others suggest that the policy underlying the decision is unfair. They argue that it may be fair to require owners to register their interest in competition against individual other creditors. The decision in *Giffen* – by putting the leased property in the estate of the debtor – amounts to a complete withdrawal of the creditor's title. This benefits third parties who did not expect such a windfall (notably unsecured creditors).[54] Against the argument that the lessor who fails to register only has herself to blame for the consequences, they argue that this begs the

---

[50] See Part II: § 5 G.II, "The Case for a Possession-Based Account of Personal Property".

[51] TC Williams, "Is a Right of Action in Tort a Chose in Action?" (1894) 10 LQR 143 at 146.

[52] (1815), 105 ER 721 (KB).

[53] See Michael G Bridge *et al,* "Formalism, Functionalism, and Understanding the Law of Secured Transactions" (1999) 44 McGill LJ 567 at 603. Cf. *Sprung Instant Structures Ltd v Caswan Environmental Services Services Inc,* [1997] 5 WWR 280 (Alta QB). For a historical and comparative account see Boris Kozolchyk, "Transfers of Personal Property by a Nonowner: Its Future in Light of Its Past" (1987) 61 Tul L Rev 1453. On deemed security interests see Part III: § 12 B.II, "The Functionalist Approach to Security Interests".

[54] Bridge *et al,* preceding note at 604.

question as to why somebody who did not want to convey ownership can be deprived of her ownership.[55]

One argument for the extinction of the creditor's title in deemed security interests is to say that the inclusion of true leases is efficient because it avoids legal uncertainty and thus in the end decreases transaction costs. However, in the context of a possible inclusion of long-term leases in the UCC, Mooney suggests that requiring a lessor of a true lease to register her interest would be economically inefficient because the cost associated with a filing regime for true leases surpasses the benefit associated with it.[56] By the inclusion of long-term leases within the scope of the *PPSA,* the provincial legislatures have decided against this argument and have decided that long-term leases are to be included. One may criticize this legislative choice – as Bridge and others do – but it is the current law as it was applied in *Giffen.*

### 2. Civil Law Quasi-Security Devices in Insolvency

#### a) Prior Cases

It was unclear whether the ratio of *Giffen* would be applied in Civil Law cases as well and there are several decisions that led up to decisions by the Supreme Court. Regarding the old s 2090 *CcBC* and s 2098 *CcBC,* the Court of Appeal had held that an unpublished right of ownership is effective against the trustee because the trustee is not a purchaser for value.[57] The Court later decided that this case law was no longer good authority for cases governed by the new *CcQ.*[58]

The Superior Court of Québec was not unanimous in its decisions regarding whether the conditions for the opposability of a hypothec[59] would have to be met in fact patterns comparable to the *Giffen* case in order to render the title-based transaction opposable against the trustee in bankruptcy. In several decisions, the Court held that in cases of conditional instalment sales, the seller lost her right of ownership if it was not published according to the provisions of

---

[55] *Ibid* at 604.

[56] Mooney, Jr, Charles W, "The Mystery and Myth of Ostensible Ownership and Article 9 Filing: A Critique of Proposals to Extend Filing Requirements to Leases" (1988) 39:3 Ala L Rev 683 at 706–24. See also Mooney, Jr, Charles W, "Filing Requirements For Personal Property Leases: A Comment and Response to Professor Ziegel" (1989–1990) 16 CBLJ 419. For a counter-argument see Jacob S Ziegel, "Should Canada Adopt an Article 2A Type Law on Personal Property Leasing?" (1989–1990) 16 CBLJ 369 at 391–97. See also Ronald CC Cuming, "An Article 2A For Canada?: A Comment on Professor Ziegel's Paper" [1989–1990] CBLJ 439 at 447–52.

[57] *Kowalski c Trust Général du Canada,* [1976] CA 93.

[58] *Re Bédard,* [2005] RJQ 1732 at para 53 (Sup Ct).

[59] See also Part III: § 14 D, "Quasi-Security Devices in Civil Law".

art 1749 *CcQ*.[60] In another decision, the Court held the opposite. While it maintained that the trustee was a third party, it held that she was not a third party to which art 1749 *CcQ* refers.[61] The Court of Appeal overturned this decision and held that the trustee needed to be treated as a third party purchaser.[62] The Court of Appeal decided similarly in *Massouris (syndic de)*[63] regarding long-term leases. These cases stood for the proposition that trustees had the status of third persons relative to the original owners of the property. This would have meant that the conditions for opposability of the creditor's ownership against third parties would have to be met.[64]

The judgments of the Court of Appeal were criticized in doctrine because they would amount to a modification of the rule in s 67 *BIA* stating that only the property owned by the debtor becomes part of the patrimony in bankruptcy since the debtor is not the owner of property that is subject to a title retention.[65]

*b) Lefebvre*

The question of the third party status of the trustee with regard to property owned by a creditor secured through a title-based transaction reached the Supreme Court of Canada. *Lefebvre (Syndic de); Tremblay (Syndic de)*[66] was an appeal in two similar cases. In both cases, the claimants leased their property to a debtor without registering their leases. Article 1852 *CcQ* requires that certain leases be registered and thus published in order for them to be effective against third parties.[67] The debtors in both cases went bankrupt before the appellants registered their respective rights. The appellants argued that the *CcQ* – unlike the *PPSAs* – does not provide that a right of ownership diminishes into a security interest and that *Giffen* is thus not good authority for the *CcQ* situation. The Supreme Court agreed with that view. It held that the trustee is not a third party in relation to the property for the purpose of art 1852 *CcQ* and that property leased but not owned by the debtor does not form part of the property vested in the trustee.

Duggan and Ziegel have criticized the Supreme Court of Canada's decision. According to their analysis, the situation in *Lefebvre (Syndic de); Tremblay (Syndic de)* was comparable to that in *Giffen*. They stress that the Supreme

[60] Cf. *Banque Royale du Canada c Mervis,* [2001] RJQ 1885 (Sup Ct), note 14.
[61] *Ibid.*
[62] *Banque Royale du Canada c Mervis,* [2002] RJQ 2268 (CA).
[63] *Massouris (syndic de),* [2002] JQ No 595 (CA).
[64] See Part III: § 14 D, "Quasi-Security Devices in Civil Law".
[65] Bilodeau, *supra* note 31 at para 275.
[66] *Supra* note 13.
[67] See Part III: § 14 D, "Quasi-Security Devices in Civil Law".

Court in *Giffen* had characterized the issue as one of priority, not property.[68] Thus, the question should not be whether the trustee or the creditor has a better right of ownership, but rather whether the creditor's right would have been enforceable against other creditors at the eve of bankruptcy.[69]

I argue that while this criticism might be valid as to how insolvency law should be, it ignores that the reasoning of the Supreme Court in *Giffen* also strongly relied on the possessory interest of the debtor that becomes vested in the trustee.[70] I quoted Ziegel's statement that the *PPSA* confers an equitable property right interest to the debtor of a title-allocation security earlier.[71] It appears that the Supreme Court embraced that view in *Giffen*. But this is not transferable to Civil Law. Furthermore, I have already addressed the fact that *Giffen* involved deemed security interests, not functional security interests. The long-term lease is not meant to secure credit; it is only treated as if it were a security interest. It is thus not even self-evident that the *Giffen* ratio should be given a wide scope. Maybe insolvency law should not be that way.

The *Giffen* approach cannot be applied to Civil Law because it has a rigid definition of "property":[72] there can be no ownership in something that has already been appropriated by another person. Thus in its subsequent decision in *Transport international pool inc c St-Georges, Hébert Inc*[73] – a case involving a long-term bail – the Court of Appeal for Québec achieved a result similar to *Lefebvre (Syndic de); Tremblay (Syndic de)*. It did so without having to make reference to the question of the third-party status of the trustee at all. The Court held that the right to vindicate one's own property is a fundamental function of ownership and not a right deriving from being the creditor of a security interest.[74] This reasoning was affirmed by *9089–3777 Québec inc c Fischer*[75] outside the insolvency context. As a result, the economically inefficient outcome of *Giffen*-type cases with regard to deemed security interests is avoided in Civil Law.

---

[68] *Giffen, supra* note 39 at para 54, Iacobucci J; Duggan & Ziegel, "Justice Iacobucci and the Canadian Law of Deemed Trusts and Chattel Security", *supra* note 47 at 233.

[69] Duggan & Ziegel, "Justice Iacobucci and the Canadian Law of Deemed Trusts and Chattel Security", *supra* note 47 at 234.

[70] See Part IV: § 16 B.III.1, "Common Law Quasi-Security Devices and Deemed Security Interests in Bankruptcy".

[71] See Part III: § 13 B, "The Debtor's Right in the Collateral and the Object of Attachment".

[72] See Part II: § 4 A, "Patrimony and Property".

[73] 2005 QCCA 28.

[74] See Part II: § 4 H, "Vindication of Property Rights".

[75] *9089–3777 Québec inc c Fischer*, 2012 QCCA 29.

### c) Ouellet

In *Ouellet (Syndic de),*[76] the Supreme Court held that property bought by the debtor as part of an instalment sale does not pass into the debtor's patrimony. Consequently, while the creditor must register her security to oppose it against third parties, the same does not apply *vis-à-vis* the trustee in bankruptcy because the latter only receives the patrimony of the bankrupt debtor. Property subject to an instalment sale never forms part of this patrimony.[77]

### d) Amendments to the Bankruptcy and Insolvency Act

In *Ouellet (Syndic de),* the Court noted that the result would have been different under the new *Federal Law-Civil Law Harmonization Act, No. 1.*[78]

"[I]t should be noted that amendments made to the *Bankruptcy and Insolvency Act* since the relevant time would have led to a different result had they been applicable to this case. The amendments made to this federal Act's definition of 'secured creditor' by ss. 25 to 28 of the *Federal Law—Civil Law Harmonization Act, No. 1,* S.C. 2001, c. 4, equate a reservation of ownership in an instalment sale with a security for the trustee's purposes. In the context of a bankruptcy, this right now is of no effect against the trustee if it is not published."[79]

The amendment referred to by LeBel J was made in s 2 *BIA,* which has been amended to change the definition of "secured creditor" and to encompass cases of title-based securities under the *CcQ.*

"Section 2 *BIA*

[...]

'secured creditor' means a person holding a mortgage, hypothec, pledge, charge or lien on or against the property of the debtor or any part of that property as security for a debt due or accruing due to the person from the debtor, or a person whose claim is based on, or secured by, a negotiable instrument held as collateral security and on which the debtor is only indirectly or secondarily liable, and includes

(a) a person who has a right of retention or a prior claim constituting a real right, within the meaning of the Civil Code of Québec or any other statute of the Province

[...]

'créancier garanti' Personne titulaire d'une hypothèque, d'un gage, d'une charge ou d'un privilège sur ou contre les biens du débiteur ou une partie de ses biens, à titre de garantie d'une dette échue ou à échoir, ou personne dont la réclamation est fondée sur un effet de commerce ou garantie par ce dernier, lequel effet de commerce est détenu comme garantie subsidiaire et dont le débiteur n'est responsable qu'indirectement ou secondairement. S'entend en outre :

a) de la personne titulaire, selon le Code civil du Québec ou les autres lois de la province de Québec, d'un droit de rétention ou d'une priorité constitutive de droit réel sur

[76] *Ouellet (Syndic de),* 2004 SCC 64.

[77] *Ibid* at para 14.

[78] SC 2001, c 4.

[79] *Ouellet (Syndic de), supra* note 76 at para 15, LeBel J.

of Quebec, on or against the property of the debtor or any part of that property, or

(b) any of

(i) the vendor of any property sold to the debtor under a conditional or instalment sale,

(ii) the purchaser of any property from the debtor subject to a right of redemption, or

(iii) the trustee of a trust constituted by the debtor to secure the performance of an obligation,

if the exercise of the person's rights is subject to the provisions of Book Six of the Civil Code of Québec entitled Prior Claims and Hypothecs that deal with the exercise of hypothecary rights;

[...]

ou contre les biens du débiteur ou une partie de ses biens;

b) lorsque l'exercice de ses droits est assujetti aux règles prévues pour l'exercice des droits hypothécaires au livre sixième du Code civil du Québec intitulé Des priorités et des hypothèques:

(i) de la personne qui vend un bien au débiteur, sous condition ou à tempérament,

(ii) de la personne qui achète un bien du débiteur avec faculté de rachat en faveur de celui-ci,

(iii) du fiduciaire d'une fiducie constituée par le débiteur afin de garantir l'exécution d'une obligation.

[...]"

The result of the amendment is that property subject to such a title-based device now passes to the trustee in bankruptcy. But this statutory definition has three problems.

First, according to art 1749 *CcQ,* the exercise of the creditor's rights is subject to the provisions that deal with the exercise of hypothecary rights if the creditor repossesses the property in case of the debtor's default. The reference in s 2 *BIA* to the *CcQ* is thus not entirely accurate. Possibly any instalment sale can potentially be subject to said provisions. Rather, the question one needs to ask is, "What event is the creditor reacting to?" Is her repossession a regular exercise of her right to ownership, or is she reacting to the debtor's default?

Second, art 1749 *CcQ* excludes instalment sales that are consumer contracts (which are defined in art 1384 *CcQ*). Thus, if the debtor is a consumer, the creditor is not a secured creditor, but an owner within the meaning of the *BIA*.[80] There is no insolvency law rationale for such a distinction.[81] Therefore, Grenon argues a better approach would have been to create a completely autonomous definition of "secured creditor" in the *BIA* that would have included any transaction that substantially secured credit.[82]

---

[80] See *Roy (Syndic de)*, 2006 QCCA 330.

[81] Aline Grenon, "La problématique entourant les « sûretés-proprietés » au Québec: Lefebvre (Syndic de); Tremblay (Syndic de) et Oulllet (Syndic de)" (2005) 35 RGD 285 at 320.

[82] *Ibid* at 315–20. This was one of the alternatives suggested in a pre-harmonization study, see Jacques Auger, Albert Bohémier & Roderick A Macdonald, "The Treatment of Creditors in the Bankruptcy and Insolvency Act and Security Mechanisms in the Civil Law of Québec"

Third, the definition in s 2 *BIA* only modifies the relationship between the trustee and the creditor, not the relationship between creditor and another creditor, even in cases where the debtor is insolvent.[83]

It should be noted that s 2 *BIA* does not completely eliminate the differences between *PPSAs* and *CcQ* property law. The ratio of *Lefebvre (Syndic de); Tremblay (Syndic de)* is still good authority in *Lefebvre (Syndic de); Tremblay (Syndic de)*-type cases. For example, *Transport international pool inc c St-Georges, Hébert Inc*[84] involved a long-term bail. Section 2 *BIA* only changes the characterization of other title-based devices in the *CcQ*. Long-term bails are excluded from the security interest characterization.

> "Cependant, puisque ni le Code civil ni aucune autre loi, dont la Loi sur la faillite et l'insolvabilité, n'édicte une présomption que les baux à long terme doivent être considérés comme des sûretés le défaut de publication ne fait pas perdre à l'appelante son statut et ses droits de propriété sur les remorques et les droits qui en découlent vis-à-vis la locataire."[85]

A function of the *PPSA* deemed security interests is that owners in long-term bail arrangements can lose their property if the debtor goes bankrupt. The *CcQ* does not have the same effect. This shows that Parliament decided to take a different approach to insolvency distribution than the provincial *PPSA* legislatures and saw no reason to extend the *PPSA* effect to *CcQ* property rights.

### *3. Bank Act Security Interest*

As discussed above, the *Bank Act*[86] security interest operates with a title fiction. The result of the title fiction is that the bank is deemed to own the collateral. In *Abraham v Canadian Admiral Corp (Receiver of),*[87] the Court of Appeal for Ontario held that this takes the collateral out of the estate managed by the trustee in bankruptcy.[88] Presumably this could mean that absent a rule akin to s 20(b)(i) *PPSA (BC),* the bank enjoys priority in bankruptcy even where its interest is not opposable against third parties because it is unperfected. While the reasoning in *Abraham v Canadian Admiral Corp (Receiver of)* can be criticized because it would have been possible to subsume the *Bank Act* title fiction under the term "mortgage" and s 2 *BIA* defines a security interest as including

---

in: Canada, Department of Justice, ed, *The Harmonization of Federal Legislation with the Québec Civil Law and Canadian Bijuralism* (Ottawa: Canada, Department of Justice, 1997) 911 at 986–87.

[83] See *Maschinenfabrik Rieter AG c Canadian Fidelity Mills Ltd*, 2005 QCCA 1033.

[84] *Supra* note 73.

[85] *Ibid* at para 59, Dalphond JCA.

[86] SC 1991, c 46.

[87] (1998), 158 DLR ($4^{th}$) 65 (Ont CA).

[88] *Ibid* at para 31, McKinlay JA.

a "mortgage," the same does not apply to Civil Law. Where property is governed by the *CcQ,* banks thus enjoy priority even where there interest is unpublished.

*4. The Creditor's Insolvency*

I have shown how the *CcQ* admission of hire-purchases can be used to create *PMSI*-like priority interests above.[89] However, in this scenario, the hypothecary creditor is potentially disadvantaged compared to her *PPSA* counterpart if she has to realize her hypothec and the titular creditor of the title-based security is bankrupt. As discussed above, the object of the hypothec is not the property itself, which is owned by the bankrupt vendor. Rather the hypothec attaches to the debtor's expectancy in the property. But once the vendor becomes bankrupt, the debtor's claim to have ownership transferred in the corporeal is relegated to a *pari passu* claim against the bankrupt estate. Thus the hypothecary creditor's right deriving from the hypothec in the debtor's claim suffers the same fate. Under the *PPSA* framework, on the other hand, the second-ranking *PPSA* creditor still enjoys priority in regards to the corporeal property because she has a property right in the property itself. This could be addressed at the level of insolvency law by allowing the hypothecary creditor to separate the hire-purchase property from the estate in return for outstanding payements.

*IV. Quistclose Trusts*

Quistclose trusts are trusts arising by operation of law. This class of trusts is named after the House of Lord's decision in *Barclays Bank Ltd v Quistclose Investment Ltd.*[90] A Quistclose-type trust arises where a creditor advances monies to the debtor for a specified purpose and the debtor becomes insolvent or divests herself of the monies in favour of a transferee taking with notice of the circumstances in which it was obtained by the debtor.[91] Quistclose-type

---

[89] See Part III: § 14 E.II.2, "Purchase Money Security Interests in the Code civil".

[90] *Barclays Bank Ltd v Quistclose Investment Ltd* (1968), [1970] AC 567 (HL) [*Quistclose Investment*].

[91] Michael G Bridge, "The Quistclose Trust in a World of Secured Transactions" (1992) 12:3 Oxford J Legal Stud 333 at 333 [Bridge, "Quistclose Trust"]. For a summary of the Canadian law on Quistclose trusts see Dennis R Klinck, "The Quistclose Trust in Canada" (1994) 23:1 CBLJ 45.

arrangements are considered to be outside of the scope of the *PPSA* framework.[92] Quistclose trusts are susceptible to an unjust enrichment analysis[93] or they can be classified as consensual trusts.[94] The Canadian position appears to be to treat them as trusts arising by operation of law.[95]

A formal argument for the exclusion of Quistclose trusts from the *pro rata* distribution is made by Denomme and Ziegel, who argue that the *PPSA* require that an equitable property right be transferred to the debtor.[96] Because the Quistclose trust is excluded from the *PPSA* and there is no special rule dealing with this scenario in the *BIA*, the creditor in a Quistclose-type arrangement can demand that the trust property be excluded from the bankrupt's estate.[97]

Outside bankruptcy, Quistclose trusts allow creditors to gain priority over secured creditors without giving notice. In *Canadian Pacific Air Lines Ltd v Canadian Imperial Bank of Commerce*,[98] for example, a travel agency held monies in trust for airlines. The monies were to be paid out when the accounting was done. The agency deposited the monies into its bank account and its bank, which was a general lender and had a security interest in the agency's account, made further advances on the assumption that the assets were held freely by the agency. The courts held that the airlines had priority because they held the status of being trust beneficiaries.[99] The airlines' priority is defensible in a secured transactions analysis because their status is akin to a purchase-money financer.[100] However, the function of the exclusion of Quistclose transactions from the *PPSA* framework is that the creditor receives priority without having to meet the publicity requirements of the *PPSA*. A secured creditor who wants to defeat the Quistclose creditor's interest must instead show that she – the secured creditor – is a *bona fide* purchaser for value without notice.

---

[92] Ronald CC Cuming, Catherine E Walsh & Roderick J Wood, *Personal Property Security Law*, 1st edn (Toronto: Irwin Law, 2005) at 83. The subsequent edition, Ronald CC Cuming, Catherine E Walsh & Roderick J Wood, *Personal Property Security Law*, 2d edn (Toronto: Irwin Law, 2012) at 141, removed the explicit reference to *Quistclose Investment*, *supra* note 90. See also Anthony J Duggan & Jacob S Ziegel, *Canadian Bankruptcy and Insolvency Law*, 2d edn (Toronto: Emond Montgomery Publications, 2009) at 183.

[93] See Part II: § 10 B.V, "The Principled Approach".

[94] Jamie Glister, "The Role of Trusts in the PPSA" (2011) 34:2 UNSWLJ 628 at 640–43.

[95] *Re Cliffs Over Maple Bay*, 2011 BCCA 180, reversing *Re Cliffs Over Maple Bay*, 2010 BCSC 389. Both decisions characterized the Quistclose trust as a resulting trust.

[96] Jacob S Ziegel & David L Denomme, *The Ontario Personal Property Security Act: Commentary and Analysis* (Aurora, Ont: Canada Law Book, 1994) at 63.

[97] Duggan & Ziegel, *Canadian Bankruptcy and Insolvency Law*, *supra* note 92 at 183.

[98] (1987), 61 OR (2d) 233 (HCJ).

[99] *Ibid*, affirmed by *Canadian Pacific Air Lines Ltd v Canadian Imperial Bank of Commerce* (1990), 71 OR (2d) 63 (CA).

[100] Bridge *et al*, *supra* note 53 at 613. See also Bridge, "Quistclose Trust", *supra* note 91 at 335.

Different treatment of Quistclose creditors and other secured creditors who fail to perfect their security interest also occurs in bankruptcy. The beneficiary of a Quistclose trust can demand that the trust property be excluded from the bankrupt's estate.[101] This example shows that the effectiveness of unregistered security devices in bankruptcy is not unknown to Common Law. Arguably the exclusion of Quistclose trusts from bankruptcy distribution is even less defensible than the exclusion of long-term leases under Québec law. The latter is not a functional security device, the former is.

## C. The Claimant's Non-Security Title in Insolvency

While the interaction between federal bankruptcy law and provincial property law may be due because of a security interest, it is also possible that a claimant claims a non-security interest in property administered by the trustee in bankruptcy. The resolution of a dispute between an owner and the trustee in bankruptcy is straightforward in Civil Law. The owner can vindicate her property. There is no judicial discretion.[102] The issue presents itself as being more complex in Common Law. If converted goods remain in the hands of the debtor and subsequently vest in the trustee in bankruptcy, the interest – even a mere possessory interest – held by the bankrupt passes to the trustee but the owner can make a claim against the trustee demanding that the converted goods be returned to her.[103] If the trustee refuses, she is herself liable in conversion.[104] Because of this, it is often argued that there is no insolvency law rationale requiring that the thief be treated as a constructive trustee.[105] This argument is also extended to other possessors who recognize the original owner's better interest.[106] The problem with this argument is that even outside bankruptcy the victim has no absolute claim to the property: a claim in conversion is discretionary regarding the remedy. Thus, absent a constructive trust, the owner would have no right to a restitutionary remedy as a matter of law. This problem

---

101 Duggan & Ziegel, *Canadian Bankruptcy and Insolvency Law, supra* note 92 at 182–83.

102 See Part II: § 4 H, "Vindication of Property Rights".

103 The procedure is set out in *BIA, supra* note 1, s 81.

104 See Robert Chambers, "Trust and Theft" in: Elise Bant & Matthew Harding, eds, *Exploring Private Law* (Cambridge: Cambridge University Press, 2010) 223 at 231; Michael Scott, "Conversion and Revendication" (1961) 5:1 Mal L Rev 40 at 50.

105 See e.g. Chambers, "Trust and Theft", preceding note at 231.

106 Jacob S Ziegel, "Unwelcome Intrusion of the Remedial Constructive Trust in Personal Property Security Law: Ellingsen (Trustee Of) v Hallmark Ford Sales Ltd" (2001) 34 CBLJ 460 at 468–70.

is nevertheless mitigated by the fact that it is unlikely that the trustee in bankruptcy would make herself personally liable for not restoring the claimant's property.

## D. Proprietary Restitution and Insolvency

In this section, I look at the impact of bankruptcy on property rights resulting from proprietary restitution. In Canada, according to s 67(1)(a) *BIA*, property available to the creditors of a bankrupt does not include any property held in trust by the debtor. This includes express trusts, statutory deemed trusts, constructive trusts, and resulting trusts.[107] This section makes extensive comparisons with American law because American law has developed a number of tools that allow one to tackle the problem of constructive trusts in insolvency. At the same time, I am mindful of the fact that American law has embraced the constructive trust as a pure remedy and rejected the approach of viewing it as an expression of a pre-existing interest in property.[108] In the first sub-section, I look at the meaning of the s 67(1)(a) *BIA* rule with regard to the *pari passu* sharing principle where proprietary restitution in the form of a constructive trust is involved. In the second sub-section, I look at how the law tries to cope with constructive trusts on insolvency distribution. In the third sub-section, I look at different models that attempt to postulate rules for when the constructive trust should be voidable in insolvency proceedings. In the fourth sub-section, I take a stand regarding the impact of proprietary restitution on the dissolution of intimate relations and insolvency. In the fifth sub-section, I offer my analysis of the treatment of equitable property rights arising from proprietary restitution in bankruptcy proceedings. I submit that the question whether or not proprietary restitution has any effects in bankruptcy proceedings is a question of insolvency law, not of restitution law, and thus should be addressed by Parliament. In doing so, Parliament should take into account that the provinces have jurisdiction over property rights and thus Parliament should only interfere in the provincial allocation of property rights in situations were the *pari passu* sharing principle is significantly disturbed.

### *I. Impact of the Constructive Trust*

The constructive trust results in the exclusion of the trust property from the bankrupt's estate to the disadvantage of other creditors.[109] The *Restatement,*

---

[107] *Bedard v Schell* (1987), 59 Sask R 71 at para 6 (QB), Gerein J; Duggan & Ziegel, *Canadian Bankruptcy and Insolvency Law, supra* note 92 at 181–83.

[108] See Part II: § 6 D.I.3, "American Law".

[109] Anthony J Duggan, "Proprietary Remedies in Insolvency: A Comparison of the Restatement (Third) of Restitution & Unjust Enrichment with English and Commonwealth

*Third, Restitution,* recognizes that the constructive trust plays an important role in shifting priorities between creditors,[110] and that the rights of a secured creditor are different depending on whether she is a *bona fide* purchaser of the property or not.[111] The constructive trust and other forms of proprietary restitution highlight the tension between two principles of insolvency law: the *pari passu* sharing principle and the property of the estate principle.[112] According to the former, all creditors have an equal claim to the bankrupt's estate. According to the latter, the estate only entails property held by the bankrupt. The constructive trust removes certain property from the estate.

This shrinking effect that proprietary restitution has becomes particularly pronounced where the constructive trust is seen as something merely remedial. If a constructive trust is too liberally recognized in cases of unjust enrichment, this leads to a result where in certain cases the actual owner of property loses her property when the debtor goes bankrupt,[113] whereas a creditor in unjust enrichment cases – who arguably has lesser title than the owner – retains her interest and succeeds in a claim against the trustee in bankruptcy.

In the United States, the argument has been made that – given the wide scope of constructive trusts – one should recognize the primary remedial nature of the constructive trust, and focus less on the constructive trust being analogous to an institutional express trust creating property rights.[114] On the other side of the debate, the property right nature of the constructive trust is stressed in the *Restatement, Third, Restitution.*[115] This again can be criticized as begging the question: saying that the restitution claimant in bankruptcy has priority in bankruptcy *because* she has a property right does not answer the question *why* she has a property right.[116]

Weintraub and Resnick formulate another criticism against the too-liberal application of the constructive trust. If a constructive trust is imposed for the

---

Law" (2011) 68:3 Wash & Lee L Rev 1229 at 1232; Emily L Sherwin, "Constructive Trusts in Bankruptcy" [1989] U Ill L Rev 297 at 297–98.

[110] American Law Institute, *Restatement of the Law, Third, Restitution* (St Paul, Minn: American Law Institute, 2011) at § 55, comment d [*Restatement 3$^{d}$, Restitution*].

[111] *Ibid* at § 55, comment d, illustration 6.

[112] Duggan, "Proprietary Remedies in Insolvency", *supra* note 109 at 1232.

[113] See *Giffen, supra* note 39. See See Part IV: § 16 B.III.1, "Common Law Quasi-Security Devices and Deemed Security Interests in Bankruptcy".

[114] John P Dawson, *Unjust Enrichment: A Comparative Analysis,* Reprint 1999 (Holmes Beach, Fla: Gaunt, 1999) at 26–33; Lacy, Jr, Frank, "Constructive Trusts and Equitable Liens in Iowa" (1954) 40 Iow L Rev 107 at 111–12; Sherwin, *supra* note 109 at 317.

[115] *Restatement 3$^{d}$, Restitution, supra* note 110 at § 55, comment d.

[116] Duggan, "Proprietary Remedies in Insolvency", *supra* note 109 at 1237.

benefit of a creditor who has not perfected her security interest (as in *Re Howard's Appliance Corp*[117]), then the constructive trust disturbs the security interest priority rules set out by *Article 9 UCC* (in Ontario, the *Personal Property Security Act*).[118]

To a certain extent, whether or not there is a problem with the constructive trust in bankruptcy is a function of the meaning ascribed to the term "remedial constructive trust" and the meaning of discretion.[119] Consequently, it is unclear to what extent the insolvency of the debtor influences the imposition of the trust.[120] In *Lac Minerals Ltd v International Corona Resources Ltd,*[121] the Supreme Court of Canada indicated *obiter dictum* that insolvency is a factor that favours imposition of the trust. In *Soulos v Korkontzilas,*[122] it indicated the contrary.

In the United States, it has occasionally been recognized that constructive trusts can arise by operation of law as well as by judicial decision.[123] If the former is the case, the trust is effective in bankruptcy[124] because it has attached before bankruptcy.

> "Although in *Omegas Group* we said that a constructive trust 'does not exist until a plaintiff obtains a judicial decision finding him to be entitled to a judgment 'impressing' defendant's property or assets with a constructive trust,' 16 F.3[d] at 1451, we recognized in *McCafferty* that a constructive trust can arise without a formal judicial decision under Ohio law."[125]

These decisions demonstrate that the question as to whether the constructive trust is remedial, semi-remedial, or institutional impact its application in bankruptcy cases. In the following two sub-sections, I look at the impact of proprietary restitution in bankruptcy cases in Canada and the United States.

---

[117] 874 F2[d] 88 (2[d] Cir 1989).

[118] Benjamin Weintraub & Alan N Resnick, "Bankruptcy Trustee's Strong-Arm Powers Balked by a Constructive Trust" (1989–1990) 22 Unif Comm Code LJ 367 at 373–74.

[119] See Part II: § 10 F.VI, "Certainty and Discretion in the Law of Proprietary Restitution".

[120] Albert H Oosterhoff *et al, Oosterhoff on Trusts,* 7[th] edn (Toronto: Carswell, 2009) at 740–41.

[121] [1989] 2 SCR 574.

[122] [1997] 2 SCR 217.

[123] *Re Morris,* 260 F3[d] 654 at 25 (6[th] Cir 2001), Batchelder J: "Under Ohio law, this contract is enforceable in equity, and because of the availability of equitable relief Morris had a duty to convey the property. Where such a duty exists, a constructive trust arises by operation of law."

[124] *Ibid* at 25, Batchelder J: "When we apply these principles, it is clear that a constructive trust in favor of Poss attached to the property prepetition."

[125] *Ibid* at 26, Batchelder J.

### 1. Canadian Law

#### a) Ellingsen

The facts of *Ellingsen (Trustee of) v Hallmark Ford Sales Ltd*[126] resemble those of *Giffen*. The defendant sold a truck to the debtor. The debtor undertook to conclude a conditional sales agreement between the debtor and a bank. However, he gained possession of the truck before the agreement was obtained. Then the debtor went bankrupt. The trustee in bankruptcy claimed that any security interest the defendant may have had was ineffective against the trustee pursuant to s 20(b)(i) *PPSA (BC)*.[127] He claimed that even if the defendant were entitled to a constructive trust, s 20(b)(i) *PPSA (BC)* provided juristic reason for the deprivation of the defendant.[128] The Court recognized a constructive trust in favour of the defendant.[129] It held – specifically referring to Paciocco[130] – that the defendant never meant to grant credit to the debtor.[131] Consequently, the other creditors were not unfairly deprived of the assets.[132] Chief Justice McEachern dissented and stated that in his view, s 20(b)(i) *PPSA (BC)* indeed provided juristic reasons for the enrichment of the estate.[133]

Ziegel attacks the decision for its application of the constructive trust doctrine. In his view, at common law, title never passed to Ellingsen because the purchase was not concluded. Canadian Common Law has no presumption of ownership for property in possession of the bankrupt, unlike earlier English law.[134] He agrees with the Court that registration of the vehicle under the BCMVA does not create a presumption of ownership for Ellingsen. Thus, the defendant had an action in detinue to receive the property back.[135]

"[P]roperty that is held in trust for a third party [...] is, on bankruptcy, delivered to that third party by the trustee in bankruptcy, and no other creditor has a claim on it, because it never was the property of the bankrupt, and the trustee only takes what the bankrupt owned. Again, a hypothetical example, in simple lay language, could be considered. If a third party takes furniture to a furniture repair establishment for repair and, prior to its redelivery to the customer, the repair company goes into bankruptcy without title to the furniture passing to the repair company, that would be, in simplistic terms, a trust relationship where the property

---

[126] 2000 BCCA 458 [*Ellingsen*].

[127] *PPSA (BC), supra* note 40.

[128] *Ellingsen, supra* note 126 at para 29.

[129] Unlike in *Giffen, supra* note 39.

[130] David M Paciocco, "The Remedial Constructive Trust: A Principled Basis for Priorities over Creditors" (1989) 68 Can Bar Rev 315.

[131] *Ellingsen, supra* note 126 at paras 32–34, Donald J.

[132] *Ibid* at para 37, Donald J.

[133] *Ibid* at paras 42–57, McEachern CJ dissenting.

[134] Ziegel, "Unwelcome Intrusion of the Remedial Constructive Trust in Personal Property Security Law", *supra* note 106 at 467 note 23.

[135] *Ibid* at 468–70. See also Anthony J Duggan, "Secured Transactions, Constructive Trusts and Insolvency" [2010] Ann Rev Insolvency L 619.

would remain owned by the third party and be delivered to the third party by the trustee in bankruptcy."[136]

One potential explanation for the Court's approach would be to say that while the deemed security interest provisions in the *PPSAs* subdue any property right held held by the debtor to the deemed security, this only applies where the parties have no intention about where the beneficial entitlement should lie; where they have have concrete assumptions about what should happen with the beneficial entitlement, there would still be room for recognizing the persistent property right held by the debtor. However, this approach would raise the follow-up issue as to why deference to the intention of parties should allow form-over-function approach to be frustrated.

### *b) Ascent*

In *Re Ascent Ltd,*[137] the following question was put before the court: "What is unjust enrichment, and can it form the basis of the use of the constructive trust in a commercial insolvency to provide an appropriate remedy?"[138]
In that case, C had a right to certain insurance premiums (valuing ca. $25 000), which Ascent was earlier ordered by the Court to set aside in trust for C. Ascent disregarded that order. Therefore – if the insurance premiums were to form part of the debtor's estate in bankruptcy – the estate would be enriched by $25 000 and C would have a claim against the estate valuing $25 000. In a regular bankruptcy case, where the claims outweigh the available estate, each unsecured creditor is thus be enriched as well because her ratio increases.

"As stated above, the result is that the Estate of Ascent has been augmented by the said sum. While I recognize that the debtor pool is also increased by like amount, mathematically the creditors are better off by the augmentation of the asset pool even though the debtor pool increases. This is not, as was argued at the hearing, a wash. Consider if there were unsecured claims totaling $100,000.00, and assets of $50,000.00 available to satisfy them. Clearly the creditors would be better off if there were $75,000.00 in assets to satisfy $125,000.00 in claims, as each creditor of the previous class will receive a slightly larger dividend when the extra $25,000.00 in assets is added to the Estate — obviously at the expense of the new $25,000.00 claimant also added to the debtor class. This is the case herein. The creditors are being enriched by the additional availability to them of the $24,374.00 that Ascent failed to set aside under the Hoy Order, and Cafo, which would otherwise receive all of those funds as trust funds, must now share with the other creditors — clearly to its detriment."[139]

The Court held that

---

[136] *Bank of Montreal v Dynex Petroleum Ltd* (1997), 1997 CanLII 14795 at para 25 (Alta QB), Rooke J.

[137] (2006), 18 CBR (5th) 269 (Ont Sup Ct J).

[138] *Ibid* at para 10, Nettie R.

[139] *Ibid* at para 15, Nettie R.

"in certain cases [it is] appropriate to do injustice to the [*BIA*] in order to do justice to commercial morality. After all, the cases are too numerous to cite wherein commercial morality is considered in insolvency settings. It is the clear role of the Bankruptcy Court to act as the arbiter of commercial morality, and I find no offence in equity intervening, even at the expense of the formulaic aspects of the [*BIA*] scheme of distribution."[140]

## 2. American Law

Many courts have recognized the existence of constructive trusts in bankruptcy cases.[141] Courts mostly treat the constructive trust as an equitable proprietary right, thus limiting the bankrupt's estate.[142]

Some courts recognize that a constructive trust conflicts with the equal-distribution policy in bankruptcy law and maintain it should be instituted cautiously.[143] A "constructive trust is fundamentally at odds with the general goals of the Bankruptcy Code."[144] This is true even though a federal court must apply the state law.[145] Thus, a constructive trust should be applied cautiously in bankruptcy cases.[146] Furthermore, courts have pointed out that the equities of bankruptcy are not the equities of the common law and that a bankruptcy court only has equitable jurisdiction as far as its bankruptcy jurisdiction extends.[147]

"The reluctance of Bankruptcy Courts to impose constructive trusts without a substantial reason to do so stems from the recognition that each unsecured creditor desires to have his particular claim elevated above the others. Imposition of a constructive trust clearly thwarts the policy of ratable distribution and should not be impressed cavalierly."[148]

---

[140] *Ibid* at para 17, Nettie R.

[141] See e.g. *Chiu v Wong,* 16 F3[d] 306 (8[th] Cir 1994). See also *Re Lett,* 238 BR 167 at 197 (WD Mo 1999), Venters J. See generally Andrew Kull, "Restitution in Bankruptcy: Reclamation and Constructive Trust" (1998) 72:3 Am Bankr LJ 265. For an extensive list of earlier cases see Sherwin, *supra* note 109 at 313–14.

[142] See e.g. *Re First Central Financial Corp,* 377 F3[d] 209 at 212 (2[d] Cir 2004), Parker J, recognizing this effect of a constructive trust; *Re Edison Bros, Inc,* 243 BR 231 at 235 (D Del Bankr 2000), Walrath J. *Re Columbia Gas Systems Inc,* 997 F2[d] 1039 at 1059 (3[d] Cir 1993), Cowen J: "[I]f [the debtor] holds the customer refunds in trust, as it asserts, these refunds are excluded from [the debtor]'s bankruptcy estate and are immediately payable to its customers." *Universal Bonding Ins Co v Gittens & Sprinkle Enterprises, Inc,* 960 F2[d] 366 at 372 (3[d] Cir 1992). See also Sherwin, *supra* note 109 at 315–16.

[143] *Re First Central Financial Corp,* preceding note at 217–18, Parker J.

[144] *Re Stotler & Co,* 144 BR 385 at 388 (ND Ill Bankr 1992), Aspen J.

[145] *Re First Central Financial Corp, supra* note 142 at 218, Parker J.

[146] *Re Haber Oil Co, Inc,* 12 F3[d] 426 at 535–36 (5[th] Cir 1994), King J.

[147] *Re Omegas Group, Inc,* 16 F3[d] 1443 at 1452–54 (6[th] Cir 1994), Batchelder J.

[148] *Re Behring Intern, Inc,* 61 BR 896 at 902 (ND Tex 1986), McGuire CJ.

### *II. Avoiding the Constructive Trust*

#### *1. Canadian Law*

##### *a) General Consideration*

In *Barnabe v Touhey,*[149] the Ontario Court of Appeal stated the following:

> "While a constructive trust, if appropriately established, could have the effect of the beneficiary of the trust receiving payment out of funds which would otherwise become part of the estate of a bankrupt divisible among his creditors, a constructive trust, otherwise unavailable, cannot be imposed for that purpose. This would amount to imposing what may be a fair result as between the constructive trustee and beneficiary, to the unfair detriment of all other creditors of the bankrupt."[150]

In *Baltman v Coopers & Lybrand Ltd (in re Melnitzer)*[151], the plaintiff had opened a line in credit in favour of Melnitzer due to fraudulent misrepresentation on the part of Mr. Melnitzer. Melnitzer then used the money to purchase artwork. Ms. Baltman, Melnitzer's wife, claimed the artwork as a gift. The bank claimed a constructive trust in the art. The Court held that there was no unjust enrichment.[152] *Obiter dictum,* the Court then identified why in equity the remedy of the constructive trust should be unavailable. One reason was that "the fact that an otherwise unsecured creditor is seeking, in effect, to 'jump the queue' over other unsecured creditors in the bankruptcy."[153]

In *Melchior v Cable Estate,*[154] the Supreme Court of British Columbia noted that "the authorities have expressed reservations as to the availability of a constructive trust where creditors and third party interests are affected."[155] While the Court held that no unjust enrichment had occurred it also reasoned that the interests of a *bona fide* lender without notice of the interest asserted by the plaintiff would be negatively affected by the constructive trust claimed by the defendant.[156]

These Canadian cases all show that the mere desire to avoid the bankruptcy distribution scheme is not sufficient reason to award a constructive trust, but they offer no principled guidance on deciding whether or not a constructive trust should be given effect in bankruptcy.

---

[149] (1995), 26 OR ($3^d$) 477 (CA).
[150] *Ibid* at 479, Bell J.
[151] (1996), 43 CBR ($3^d$) 33 (Ont Gen Div).
[152] *Ibid* at para 44, Killen J.
[153] *Ibid* at para 48, Killen J.
[154] 2007 BCSC 136.
[155] *Ibid* at para 68, Masuhara J.
[156] *Ibid* at para 93, Masuhara J.

*b) Awarding a Constructive Trust in Bankruptcy Court*

The award of an constructive trust for the first time in a bankruptcy court has been discussed in two cases: *Re Ascent Ltd*[157] and *Credifinance Securities Limited v DSLC Capital Corp.*[158] In both cases, it was held that a constructive trust could only be awarded for the first time in a bankruptcy court in extraordinary circumstances.[159] This is because it disturbs the *BIA* regime.

> "It also important to consider that imposition of a remedial constructive trust will take out of the hands of the Estate and the creditors the sum in dispute, and turn it over, in its entirety, to Cafo. This will clearly be a disruption of the scheme laid out in the BIA. This was the position of the Trustee at the hearing. I have considered this, but I have also considered *Brown* and the cases cited therein. I am satisfied that it is, in certain cases, appropriate to do injustice to the *BIA* in order to do justice to commercial morality. After all, the cases are too numerous to cite wherein commercial morality is considered in insolvency settings. It is the clear role of the Bankruptcy Court to act as the arbiter of commercial morality, and I find no offence in equity intervening, even at the expense of the formulaic aspects of the *BIA* scheme of distribution. It is simply not right for Ascent and its creditors to benefit from Ascent's failure to obey the Hoy Order, and then come to this Court to seek to retain such an unjust enrichment."[160]

A case can be made for obtaining a constructive trust in bankruptcy when the unsecured creditors would otherwise benefit from the immoral behaviour of their debtor and thus be unjustly enriched.[161] The approach adopted in these two cases resembles the unjust enrichment model adopted by some scholars.

*2. American Law*

American law has tackled the problem of the constructive trust on several levels. The first level is that of general bankruptcy law. The second level is the inherent equitable jurisdiction of bankruptcy courts. The third level is the law of tracing; technical tracing requirements limit the scope of the property to a constructive trust. The fourth level is again found in bankruptcy law; there is a statutory provision – s 544 *Bankruptcy Code*[162] – that can be used to limit the impact of a constructive trust.

---

[157] *Re Ascent Ltd, supra* note 137.

[158] *Credifinance Securities Limited v DSLC Capital Corp,* 2011 ONCA 160.

[159] *Ibid* at para 33, LaForme JA; *Re Ascent Ltd, supra* note 137 at para 17, Nettie R.

[160] *Re Ascent Ltd, supra* note 137 at para 17, Nettie R.

[161] *Credifinance Securities Limited v DSLC Capital Corp, supra* note 158 at para 36, LaForme JA; *Re Ascent Ltd, supra* note 137 at para 17, Nettie R.

[162] *Bankruptcy Code,* USC, c 11.

### *a) Bankruptcy Law Considerations*

In *Re Lett,*[163] the Court noted that case law is divided on the question whether a bankruptcy court can recognize a constructive trust.[164] It noted that in *Re Omegas Group, Inc,*[165] the Court of Appeal for the 6th Circuit had held that it had no jurisdiction to impose a constructive trust because s 523 *Bankruptcy Code* already deals with fraudulently-acquired property, and thus there is no room for equity in bankruptcy.[166] In *Re Unicom Computer Corp,*[167] the Court of Appeal for the 9th Circuit held that the state law constructive trust cannot be applied in a manner that is contrary to federal bankruptcy law.

"In reaching this conclusion we necessarily reject the BAP majority's holding that our opinion in *North American Coin & Currency, Ltd. (in re)* created an elaborate, multi-part test to determine whether and under what circumstances a constructive trust may be imposed on property of a debtor or of a bankruptcy estate. Our decision in *North American Coin & Currency, Ltd. (in re)* should not be read as saying more than what it actually says; *viz.,* that while state law must be the starting point in determining whether a constructive trust may arise in a federal bankruptcy case, that law must be applied in a manner not inconsistent with federal bankruptcy law."[168]

### *b) Equitable Limits*

In *Re North American Coin & Currency, Ltd,*[169] the Court emphasized that the constructive trust arises from state law, but because it is equitable, it can be awarded flexibly by bankruptcy courts.

"While we agree that any constructive trust that is given effect must be a creature of Arizona law, we cannot accept the proposition that the bankruptcy estate is automatically deprived of any funds that state law might find subject to a constructive trust. We refuted that proposition in *In re Esgro, Inc.,* 645 F.2d 794, 797 (9th Cir. 1981) and *Elliott v. Bumb,* 356 F.2d 749, 753 (9th Cir.), cert. denied, 385 U.S. 829, 87 S.Ct. 67, 17 L.Ed.2d 66 (1966), where we held that, because of countervailing policies behind the Bankruptcy Act, state law could not be permitted to impose a trust on commingled property of a bankrupt's estate. A constructive trust is not the same kind of interest in property as a joint tenancy or a remainder. It is a remedy, flexibly fashioned in equity to provide relief where a balancing of interests in the context of a particular case seems to call for it. See *Raestle v. Whitson,* 119 Ariz. 524, 582 P.2d 170 (1978)."[170]

---

[163] *Supra* note 141.
[164] *Ibid* at 197, Venters J..
[165] *Supra* note 147.
[166] *Ibid* at 1452–53, Batchelder J.
[167] 13 F3d 321 (9th Cir 1994).
[168] *Ibid.*
[169] 767 F2d 1573 (9th Cir 1984).
[170] *Ibid* at 1575, Canby J.

A guideline for the application of the constructive trust is whether equity requires that the creditor receive a benefit at the unsecured creditors' expense.[171]

*c) Limiting Through Tracing Requirements*

One way of limiting the scope of the preferential treatment resulting from the exclusion of the constructive trust property is to require strict tracing standards before the beneficiary is able to claim the debtor's assets as her property. This approach was favoured by the US Supreme Court in *Cunningham v Brown.*[172] As Sherwin notes, the tracing requirement for exercising the rights deriving from the trust under state law could be instituted by the Supreme Court, which has jurisdiction over federal law because it relates to the fund distribution scheme of the federal bankruptcy law.[173] However, the tracing requirement does not address the question, "Under what circumstances should a constructive trust be recognized?"

*d) Limiting Through Trustee's Long-Arm Power*

Another way of limiting the application of the constructive trust in bankruptcy cases is the extent of the estate in bankruptcy. The relevant provision is s 544 *Bankruptcy Code.*[174] Under s 544(a) *Bankruptcy Code,* the trustee takes the estate of the debtor as if he were a *bona fide* purchaser of the real property or as if holding a judgment lien or an execution order against all property ("long-arm power"). If the constructive trust property did not form any part of the debtor's estate to begin with, s 544(a) *Bankruptcy Code* could not have any effect. Section 541 *Bankruptcy Code* stipulates the extent of the estate. In particular, s 541(a) *Bankruptcy Code* states that property belonging to the trustee at the time of the commencement of bankruptcy proceedings[175] and interests acquired after the commencement of bankruptcy proceedings[176] form part of the estate. Section 541(d) *Bankruptcy Code,* in turn, stipulates that when additional property in which the debtor had already held legal title comes into the estate in a certain mode, the property does not lose any prior equitable interest attached to it. According to the cases decided, legislative intent was that the equitable title referred to in s 541(d) *Bankruptcy Code* include a constructive

---

[171] *Ibid* at 1577–78, Canby J.

[172] 265 US 1 (1924). For an overview of positive cases see Sherwin, *supra* note 109 at 319, note 95.

[173] Sherwin, *supra* note 109 at 320.

[174] See Douglas G Baird, *The Elements of Bankruptcy,* 6th edn (West Pub Co, 2014) at 102–3; Lionel D Smith, *The Law of Tracing* (Oxford: Clarendon Press, 1997) at 359.

[175] *Bankruptcy Code, supra* note 162, s 544(a)(1).

[176] *Ibid,* s 541(a)(7).

trust.[177] Thus, it was concluded that the trustee's estate cannot benefit from property the debtor did not own.[178] This view was not unequivocally shared in legal scholarship.[179]

Yet case law was divided on the question of whether the trustee could obtain full title under the old wording. The Court of Appeals for the 7th Circuit held that

> "allowing the estate to 'benefit from property that the debtor did not own' is exactly what the strong-arm powers are about: they give the trustee the status of a *bona fide* purchaser for value, so that the estate contains interests to which the debtor lacked good title. The estate gets what the debtor could convey under local law rather than only what the debtor owned under local law — a critical distinction."[180]

While s 541(d) *Bankruptcy Code* once referred to all modes of acquisition of interest in property enumerated in s 541(a) *Bankruptcy Code,* the provision was changed and no longer refers to acquisition of interests by virtue of the trustee's long-arm power. Thus, s 541(d) *Bankruptcy Code* no longer prevents the trustee from acquiring full title.[181] Since s 541(d) *Bankruptcy Code* now solely refers to s 541(a)(1) *Bankruptcy Code* and s 541(a)(2) *Bankruptcy Code,* the reconciliation of s 541(d) *Bankruptcy Code* and s 544 *Bankruptcy Code* clearly depends on an interpretation whereby the complete title the trustee acquires through the exercise of her long-arm power is not already part of the initial estate of the trustee.

An argument that can still be made against the application of the long-arm power against a constructive trust is to posit that s 544 *Bankruptcy Code* is not applicable in cases of constructive trusts at all. One analysis of the provision is to deem its purpose the avoidance of "secret" (unperfected) liens on estate

---

177 *Re Dameron,* 206 BR 394 at 399–400 (ED Va Bankr 1997), Douglas O'Tice J; *Re Columbia Gas Systems Inc, supra* note 142 at 1059, Cowen J: ["[I]f [the debtor] holds the customer refunds in trust, as it asserts, these refunds are excluded from [the debtor]'s bankruptcy estate and are immediately payable to its customers." With many references see Sherwin, *supra* note 109 at 315–16. See also Benjamin Weintraub & Alan N Resnick, "When Money Mistakenly Paid to the Debtor Is Transferred to Its Rightful Owner on the Eve of Bankruptcy - Voidable Preference or Constructive Trust?" (1994–1995) 27 Unif Comm Code LJ 103 at 105–6.

178 *Re Quality Holstein Leasing,* 752 F2d 1009 (5th Cir 1985).

179 See Sherwin, *supra* note 109 at 314–15 note 74.

180 *Belisle v Plunkett,* 877 F2d 512 at 516 (7th Cir 1989), Easterbrook J [emphasis added].

181 Regarding a resulting trust *Re Corzo,* 406 BR 154 at 159–60 (D Del Bankr 2008); *Re DVI, Inc,* 306 BR 496 at 502 (D Del Bankr 2004).

property.[182] It is argued that a secured creditor enjoys priority over any unsecured creditor without perfection.[183] By giving the trustee a status analogous to a secured creditor, this advantage of secured creditors is taken away from the unsecured creditors.[184] Thus, a secret lien would still be advantageous to a secured creditor outside bankruptcy and the avoidance of such a lien by the trustee is something that ordinary unsecured creditors could not do. This only confirms that secret liens are discouraged within bankruptcy proceedings. If the secret lien perspective is correct, this would speak against the application of the avoidance power in s 544 *Bankruptcy Code* to the constructive trust. The constructive trust beneficiary is not comparable to a secured creditor who willingly or negligently did not perfect her security interest.[185] Most noticeably, the beneficiary of a constructive trust is not necessarily a voluntary creditor.[186] On that analysis, s 544 *Bankruptcy Code* could not be used to bring full title to property subject to a constructive trust within the estate. This is the approach taken in the *Restatement, Third, Restitution.*[187]

Regardless of its applicability, the application of the trustee's long-arm power has one shortcoming. As far as personal property is concerned, it depends on state law allowing a creditor to void a constructive trust through a judgment lien or an execution order.[188] This is not the case in all American jurisdictions.[189] In fact, most American states rank the status of a judgment lien creditor below that of the beneficiary of a constructive trust;[190] a *bona fide* purchaser for value, on the other hand, usually enjoys priority over the beneficiary of a constructive trust.[191] Yet the trustee in bankruptcy enjoys *bona fide* purchaser status only in relation to real property, not personal property. Thus, even the existence of the long-arm power does not enable one to do away with the problem of the constructive trust in bankruptcy. It may even be undesirable

---

[182] Cf. *Restatement 3d, Restitution, supra* note 110 at 193; Sherwin, *supra* note 109 at 322–23.

[183] McCoid, II, John C, "Bankruptcy, the Avoiding Powers and Unperfected Security Interests" (1985) 59 Am Bankr LJ 175 at 192.

[184] *Ibid* at 192.

[185] Sherwin, *supra* note 109 at 323–24.

[186] *Ibid* at 323.

[187] *Restatement 3d, Restitution, supra* note 110 at 193.

[188] See Sherwin, *supra* note 109 at 324.

[189] See *Re DVI, Inc, supra* note 181 at 503, Walrath J. Noting that for the application of § 544 Bankruptcy Code, a characterization of a claim as a constructive trust is immaterial *Re Bullet Jet Charter, Inc,* 177 BR 593 at para 13 (ND Ill Bankr 1995), Schmetterer J.

[190] Amy M Hess, George G Bogert & George T Bogert, *The Law of Trusts and Trustees,* Revised second edition, 1995 replacement volume, as amended by 2009 cumulative supplement (St Paul, Minn: West Pub Co, 1995), § 887, p 242; Sherwin, *supra* note 109 at 324.

[191] Hess, Bogert & Bogert, preceding note, § 881, at 204 ff; Sherwin, *supra* note 109 at 324.

to avoid the structural problems facing the constructive trust by unconditionally reintegrating constructive trust property into the estate because there may be cases where it is desirable for the creditor to enjoy priority.

### *3. Conclusion*

This analysis has shown that American law has a wider arsenal that allows one to limit the impact of constructive trusts on bankruptcy distribution schemes. Nevertheless, American law still faces two shortcomings. First, whether or not the long-arm power allows the trustee in bankruptcy to bring the property subject to a constructive trust back into the estate relies on state law. This is due to the fact that the trustee in bankruptcy only allows *bona fide* purchaser status in relation to real property, not in relation to personal property. Second, the existence of a long-arm power does not answer when the long-arm power should be exercised. As I have submitted above, proprietary restitution plays an important role in securing property rights in Common Law, and undermining this security of property by always exercising a long-arm power would undermine this important normative economic goal. I address a number of theories that try to answer the question when security of property should yield to *pari passu* distribution in the next sub-section.

### *III. Different Approaches to the Problem of Constructive Trusts*

There are a number of models that try to formulate a test to determine when it is undesirable to give effect to a constructive trust in insolvency. Unlike the accounts of unjust enrichment and proprietary restitution above,[192] these models have a specific insolvency focus.

### *1. The Unjust Enrichment Model*

Sherwin bases her analysis of the constructive trust on the premise that the constructive trust is a remedy for unjust enrichment.[193] While it is acknowledged that the constructive trust developed as the equivalent of the express trust in cases of unjust enrichment,[194] Sherwin strongly opposes the idea that the beneficiary of a constructive trust should be considered to be the beneficial equitable owner.[195] Sherwin argues that the issue should not be when the unjust enrichment *vis-à-vis* the debtor occurred, but whether the estate, and consequently other unsecured creditors, are still unjustly enriched at the time the

---

[192] See Part II: § 10 B, "Explaining Proprietary Restitution".

[193] Sherwin, *supra* note 109 at 297.

[194] Dawson, *supra* note 114 at 26–28; George E Palmer, *The Law of Restitution* (Boston: Little, Brown & Co, 1978), § 1.3 at 9–12; Sherwin, *supra* note 109 at 301.

[195] Sherwin, *supra* note 109 at 311. Cf. *Re Foos,* 183 BR 149 (ND Ill Bankr 1995).

creditor seeks the remedy.[196] Preferential treatment over other unsecured creditors may not be warranted when the unjust enrichment takes place within the debtor-creditor relationship only.[197]

Sherwin requires there to be a relationship between the beneficiary's right to restitution and the potential trust property.[198] Sherwin notes that the accepted view – based on Scott – is that the beneficiary must be able to trace the initial trust property that equitably belonged to her to the debtor's present property.[199] This view has been accepted by jurisprudence.[200]

Sherwin criticizes the fact that – at the time of her writing – the limitations to the constructive trust thus far applied in the United States in bankruptcy cases did not address the fundamental issue, namely what the basis for preference of a creditor in unjust enrichment over other creditors is.[201] Sherwin requires three conditions be met in order for it to be appropriate that a constructive trust be given preference over other creditors' claims in bankruptcy:

(1) The special appeal of a claim based on unjust enrichment
(2) Identification of assets that represent the debtor's unjust enrichment in the bankrupt estate
(3) The claimants position as an unsecured creditor[202]

If one of these elements is absent, it may be appropriate to award the remedy of constructive trust outside of bankruptcy, but the trust should not be recognized in bankruptcy.[203] Sherwin contrasts her position with the view expressed in the first edition of the *Restatement, Second,*[204] since, in her view, the priority of the beneficiary over (unsecured) creditors should not be granted unconditionally.[205] Sherwin proposes to base the analysis of whether the beneficiary should enjoy priority over the creditors on whether the creditors would otherwise be unjustly enriched in relation to the beneficiary.[206]

In Sherwin's analysis, the constructive trust is restitution for unjust enrichment where the creditor can claim certain traceable property.[207] In her view, the

---

[196] Sherwin, *supra* note 109 at 326. See also Kull, *supra* note 141.

[197] Paciocco, *supra* note 130 at 418.

[198] Sherwin, *supra* note 109 at 307. Cf. James B Ames, "Following Misappropriated Property into Its Product" (1906) 19:7 Harv L Rev 511 at 514.

[199] Sherwin, *supra* note 109 at 308.

[200] *Ibid* at 308–9 note 51.

[201] *Ibid* at 298.

[202] *Ibid* at 298.

[203] *Ibid* at 298.

[204] American Law Institute, *Restatement of the Law, Second, Restitution, Draft No. 2* (Philadelphia: American Law Institute, 1984), § 202, comment e.

[205] Dawson, *supra* note 114 at 31; Sherwin, *supra* note 109 at 306.

[206] Sherwin, *supra* note 109 at 306.

[207] *Ibid* at 329–32.

application of a constructive trust in bankruptcy can be justified when the creditor has enriched the debtor's estate to the benefit of the unsecured creditors so that their enrichment is unjust *vis-à-vis* the creditor.[208] She acknowledges that this analysis in itself fails to explain why a constructive trust is awarded regardless of whether or not the creditor's traceable property has increases the estate of the debtor.[209] However, she claims, this can be explained by assuming that the addition of an increment requirement adds needless complexity to the application of a constructive trust.[210]

Sherwin recognizes that this interaction may give rise to questions of delimiting federal and state law.[211] However, her issues are partly based on concerns that state courts may be less considerate of federal law and federal court bankruptcy proceedings.[212] This concern should be less pressing in Canada with its unified court system.

Regarding the question of the beginning of the constructive trust, the unjust enrichment model focuses on the remedial character of the trust. Against the *ab initio* view, it is argued that a legal right cannot exist but be unenforceable.[213] However, different US jurisdictions have given several reasons to explain why a constructive trust can exist and be unenforceable at the same time.

"On the other hand, a constructive trust is a remedy which is inchoate prior to its imposition. Rather than being a determination of rights arising by law because of mistake or omission as is a resulting trust, a constructive trust is an equitable remedy."[214]

### 2. *The Assumption of Insolvency Risk Approach*

This approach looks at whether it is equitable to attribute the risk of insolvency to the creditor.[215] The inquiry is whether the creditor should resemble a secure

---

[208] *Ibid* at 332.

[209] *Ibid* at 333.

[210] *Ibid* at 332–33.

[211] *Ibid* at 298.

[212] *Ibid* at 298.

[213] *Ibid* at 312.

[214] *Re Markair, Inc,* 172 BR 638 at 641 (9th Cir 1994), Jones BJ [references ommitted].

[215] See Burrows, *Restitution, supra* note 9 at 134; Hanoch Dagan, "Restitution in Bankruptcy: Why All Involuntary Creditors Should Be Preferred" (2004) 78:3 Am Bankr LJ 247; Peter D Maddaugh & John D McCamus, *The Law of Restitution,* loose-leaf (Aurora, Ontario: Canada Law Book, 2004) at para 5.200.70; Craig Rotherham, "Tracing Misconceptions in Foskett v McKeown" [2003] RLR 57 at 64. Cf. William Swadling, "Policy Arguments for Proprietary Restitution" (2008) 28:4 LS 506 [Swadling, "Policy Arguments"].

or an unsecured creditor,[216] based on whether the creditor has assumed the risk of insolvency of the debtor.[217]

The requirements for a constructive trust under this view are outlined here. A secured creditor is somebody who has secured herself against the insolvency of the debtor. She has not assumed the risk of the debtor's insolvency. The enrichment of the debtor by subtraction from the creditor is the same as the giving of credit. The creditor usually has assumed the risk of insolvency when the basis for unjust enrichment is failure of consideration. Conversely, where the basis is not failure of consideration, the creditor has not assumed the risk of insolvency.[218]

The problem with this approach in the context of Canadian law is that insolvency law considerations fall within the realm of federal law. Swadling says that courts should not make a consequentialist argument when determining whether proprietary restitution should take place.[219] I do not concur with such a broad argument. It seems to be based on a purely formalist approach to the law. However, it becomes more forceful in the context of Canadian bijuralism. It is difficult to argue that the recognition of a constructive trust by provincial law should depend on its effect in federal insolvency law. As a result, I would argue that an assumption of insolvency approach is helpful in deciding whether a constructive trust should have effect in bankruptcy, but it cannot be of any guidance in determing whether the constructive trust exists outside bankruptcy.

The assumption of insolvency approach can also be defended *vis-à-vis* the non-priority of tort claimants. The difference between the unjust enrichment creditor and other involuntary creditors is that the unjust enrichment creditor has added value to the estate. There is a difference between the unjust enrichment creditor who enlarges the estate by addition of value and the tort creditor who at best enlarges it by absence of subtraction.

### *3. The Common-Pool Approach*

The common-pool approach or "relative entitlement" theory states that bankruptcy law should not encourage creditors, secured or unsecured, to put the debtor into bankruptcy. Thus, any law that improves the standing of a creditor in bankruptcy is bad law.[220] In the United States, an unsecured creditor who

---

[216] Andrew S Burrows, "Proprietary Restitution: Unmasking Unjust Enrichment" (2001) 117 LQR 412 at 423–28 [Burrows, "Unmasking"]; Burrows, *Restitution, supra* note 9 at 134; Oosterhoff *et al, supra* note 120 at 798–99.

[217] Burrows, *Restitution, supra* note 9 at 134. Cf. Paciocco, *supra* note 130 at 324–25.

[218] Burrows, "Unmasking", *supra* note 216 at 423–28; Burrows, *Restitution, supra* note 9 at 177–78.

[219] Swadling, "Policy Arguments", *supra* note 215 at 520–22.

[220] See Anthony J Duggan, "Constructive Trusts from a Law and Economics Perspective" (2005) 55 UTLJ 217 at 245–46.

becomes an execution creditor – after getting a judgment in her favour[221] – is better off than the beneficiary of a secret equitable interest, such as a constructive trust.[222] In Canada, on the other hand, the execution creditor does not trump the beneficiary of a constructive trust.[223] Thus, the unprotected unsecured creditor in Canada might have an incentive to put the debtor into bankruptcy if it allows her to avoid the constructive trust.

### *IV. Bankruptcy and Proprietary Remedies in Family Law Matters*

By receiving proprietary restitution on dissolution of intimate relationships, the claiming partner receives a strong position in bankruptcy. At first, this seems like a circumvention of federal insolvency policy. However, the interplay of provincial family law and federal insolvency law contains a precedent regarding in which the policy choices of provincial law are recognized and given effect by federal insolvency law.

In the event of a formal divorce of a marriage, some provinces use equalization payment schemes whereas others use division of property schemes. Under the former scheme, the less well-off spouse has a personal claim for an equalization payment, which allows her to participate in any increase in wealth made by the other spouse. Under the latter scheme, the less well-off spouse receives a property interest in the other spouse's property, but this interest can be bought by the better off spouse. As a result, both schemes can result in a payment being made from the better off spouse to the less-well off spouse.

The difference between the schemes becomes important where the better-off spouse goes bankrupt after the right of the other spouse comes into existence. If the matrimonial property law framework follows the equalization scheme, the claim becomes a claim against the bankrupt's estate and can be discharged at the end of bankruptcy. Where the matrimonial family law follows the property scheme, the bankruptcy leaves the spouse's right unaffected.[224]

In *Schreyer v Schreyer,* LeBel J criticized the unequal treatment of spouses depending on which scheme the provinces operate.[225] But as Leckey points out,

---

[221] But only then, see Kull, *supra* note 141 at 370.

[222] Baird, *supra* note 174 at 102–3; Duggan, "Constructive Trusts from a Law and Economics Perspective", *supra* note 220 at 245; Thomas H Jackson, *The Logic and Limits of Bankruptcy Law* (Cambridge, Mass: Harvard University Press, 1986) at 66.

[223] *Wickham v New Brunswick & Canada Railway Co* (1865), 3 Moo PCNS 416 (NB PC); Charles RB Dunlop, *Creditor-Debtor Law in Canada,* 2[d] edn (Toronto: Carswell, 1995) at 267–68 (personalty) and *ibid* at 355–56 (realty); Duggan, "Constructive Trusts from a Law and Economics Perspective", *supra* note 220 at 246.

[224] See *Schreyer v Schreyer,* 2011 SCC 35.

[225] *Ibid* at para 38, LeBel J: "[T]he possibility of mitigating the consequences of this litigation by means of a decision with respect to spousal support should not overshadow the problems created by the failure in the *BIA* to differentiate between equalization schemes and

the unequal treatment is a function of the separation of powers between Parliament and the provinces and a cry for uniformity is "insensitive to the dynamics of a federation and to provincial policy choices."[226] The general structure of the *BIA* and its distinction between proprietary and personal claims is supposed to be a toolkit which allows provincial law to have limited influence on bankruptcy priority decisions.[227] In other words, a completely uniform *BIA* would adopt a strictly functional approach to the classification of rights and claims and thus would not interact with provincial law at all. Parliament has rejected such a general approach and limited functional intervention to cases where it saw that the insolvency policy was threatened by provincial law. One example is the treatment of title-based security under Québec law in the *BIA*.[228] The Supreme Court of Canada also recognizes the complementarity of federal insolvency law and provincial law as regards equitable set-off.[229]

Similar to why the recognition of differences between property rights and equalization payment schemes is permissible, there is no inherent reason why the provincial Common Law should not be permitted to recognize proprietary restitution on the dissolution of intimate relationships that impact bankruptcy distribution. However, I should note that it is inappropriate to use the constructive trust to circumvent a provincial equalization scheme. Where a province operates an equalization payment scheme, equity should not intervene and recognize a constructive trust for the benefit of the less-well off spouse in the same property that was already accounted for when calculating the equalization payment.[230]

### *V. Analysis*

The constructive trust plays an important role in bankruptcy. If it were not for the constructive trust, the trustee in bankruptcy could elect to commit an act of conversion regarding the claimant's property. The constructive trust allows the claimant to secure the pre-existing property right even in bankruptcy. If the Common Law did not contain the constructive trust as a remedy for "unjust enrichment," this would need to be addressed on the bankruptcy law level. However, in the interest of fairness, the "unjust enrichment" could be restricted to cases where the Civil Law would recognize a right to vindicate. In other words, the facts of an unjust enrichment case should lead to the recognition of

---

division of property schemes. The best way to address the potentially inequitable impact of bankruptcy law on the division of family assets would be to amend the *BIA*."

[226] Robert Leckey, "Bankruptcy, Provincial Law, and the Family Farm" (2013) 91:2 Can Bar Rev 435 at 440.

[227] *Ibid* at 441.

[228] See Part IV: § 16 B.III.2.d), "Amendments to the Bankruptcy and Insolvency Act".

[229] See Part I: § 2 B.II.3.a), "Accepting Diversity".

[230] See *Thibodeau v Thibodeau,* 2011 ONCA 110.

a property right and the "unjust enrichment" is merely the retention of the property by the debtor without a right to do so.

I submit that the question of whether or not the constructive trust has effect in bankruptcy is a question of insolvency law, not a question of restitution law. With regard to the role of the constructive trust as a remedy for unjust enrichment, it is important to distinguish between its appropriateness against the defendant and its appropriateness against third party creditors.[231]

Duggan writes the following on the consequences of characterizing the constructive trust as a recognition of an inchoate property right:

> "[S]ince the constructive trust depends upon the establishment of a prior equitable claim, the courts have less room to maneuver depending on whether or not the defendant is bankrupt. Perhaps for this reason – and in contrast to the Restatement – English and Commonwealth law takes an all or nothing approach to the bankruptcy question. The cases proceed on the assumption that if constructive trust relief is available outside bankruptcy, it will be available inside bankruptcy, too, and on the same terms. This leads to a tail wagging the dog kind of debate, with some courts opposing proprietary remedies for breach of fiduciary obligations because of the potential bankruptcy implications, and others favoring them for deterrence reasons, even if the defendant is bankrupt."[232]

Unlike Duggan, who implies that Canada might be excluded from his analysis, I have submitted that the constructive trust in Canadian law is not merely remedial, but rather the expression of an underlying property right, although the requirements for this property right might still need fleshing out. In principle, I thus take an all-or-nothing approach to constructive trust relief as well. Whether or not the debtor is bankrupt should have no bearing on the question of the availability of proprietary restitution. Instead, Canadian insolvency law could be amended to give the trustee a long-arm power that allows the trustee in bankruptcy to add the trust property to the estate under certain conditions.

Tackling the problem of proprietary restitution and insolvency on the level of insolvency law has two further advantages. First, it treats cases in which the proprietary restitution claim is made during bankruptcy the same as cases in which the creditor has already obtained constructive trust relief. Thus, whether or not the trust property is available to unsecured creditors does not depend on the somewhat arbitrary point in time at which the trust beneficiary/creditor has brought her claim. Second, if the question whether or not proprietary restitution has effect in bankruptcy is characterized as one of restitution law rather than as one of insolvency law, this might create conflict-of-laws issues where the trust property has moved from a Common Law jurisdiction to Québec.[233] In

---

[231] John D McCamus, "Restitution on Dissolution of Marital and Other Intimate Relationships: Constructive Trust or Quantum Meruit" in: Jason W Neyers, Mitchell McInnes & Stephen G Pitel, eds, *Understanding Unjust Enrichment* (Oxford: Hart, 2004) 359 at 377.

[232] Duggan, "Proprietary Remedies in Insolvency", *supra* note 109 at 1260.

[233] See Part V: § 18 , "International Secured Transaction Law".

those cases, it might be unclear whether a Québec court would apply not only the rules according to which the trust was created while the property was outside Québec, but also the rules which would void it once it entered Québec. Making the avoidance rule belong to insolvency law, which is applicable throughout the Dominion, averts this problem.

Particularly if the constructive trust were available in cases that are not straightforward property vindication, the trustee could be given a long-arm power. There are two instances of a wider scope of proprietary restitution exceeding vindication I want to address. First, proprietary restitution has a wider scope than Civil Law vindication if one does not accept my submissions above[234] and considers a constructive trust to be available regardless of any pre-existing inchoate property right. This greatly expands the potential of the constructive trust to impact the *pro rata* distribution. Second, there is already a recognized instance where there is a notable difference between proprietary restitution and Civil Law vindication: tracing goes further than the property right does in Civil Law.

Civil Law does not generally recognize real subrogation in all cases. Thus, there is an uneven treatment where the property right is one in traced property. The claimant cannot not assert a property right in Civil Law, but she can in Common Law. At the same time, there are cases where the constructive trust impresses neither property that is a traceable substitute nor just the original property: proceeds. However, allowing an owner to recover more than just the original item of property is not unknown in Civil Law. Fruits in Civil Law pertain to the owner of the property who can vindicate them.[235] But I would argue that there is a difference between fruits of the property – which would have accrued to the owner had she been in possession – and proceeds of the property, which are foremost a function of the way the debtor has used the property in commerce.

Whether the constructive trust survives insolvency in its entirety, or whether there should be a long-arm power with regard to the constructive trust in proceeds is a question of insolvency policy and should be decided by federal Parliament. Equal treatment of property rights in Civil and Common Law would speak for a long-arm power with regard to the constructive trust in proceeds, but as we have seen, federal insolvency law recognizes different policy choices made by provincial law. The question should be whether it is economically efficient to allow a creditor to separate not only her original item of property from the bankrupt's estate, but also traceable proceeds. Where the value of the proceeds exceeds the value of the original item of property, there is no obvious

---

[234] See Part II: § 10 F, "Analysis of Proprietary Restitution".

[235] Pierre-Claude Lafond, *Précis de droit des biens,* 2[d] edn (Montréal: Éditions Thémis, 2007) at 2369, 2371.

economic rationale in allowing her to reclaim all the proceeds to the detriment of other unsecured creditors.

## E. Conclusion

The analysis of the interaction of federal bankruptcy law and provincial property law has shown that the two levels enjoy both conceptual autonomy and complementarity.

One example of conceptual autonomy is the divestment. The meaning of the divestment of the estate from the bankrupt debtor to the trustee in bankruptcy is not easily understood in Civil Law. Furthermore, conceptualising the divestment as a transfer of ownership raises problems with regard to the third-party status of the trustee in bankruptcy. She would either be a third-party purchaser or a successor. In the former case, a number of third-party ownership rights would become extinguished. In the latter case, she would be bound by unopposable hypothecs. Both results are undesirable. They can be avoided by viewing the divestment as a genuine insolvency law event. Its consequences should be foremost a function of insolvency law functionalism rather than of property law formalism.

The treatment of title-based security interests has shown that provincial property law is one example of complementarity. In principle, federal insolvency law recognizes the property rights allocations in provincial law. At the same time, a functional definition of "security interests" allows the federal legislature to intervene where the interplay between provincial property rights and the insolvency law framework leads to uneconomic results. This shows that it is possible to retain two property law systems – one of which derives from Civil Law – without ending up with an inefficient insolvency law. The question to what degree the retention of two property law systems can be made efficient where the two systems interact horizontally – rather than at the level of vertical interaction between federal and provincial law – is the topic of the next part of this book.

I submit that Parliament should take an approach to proprietary restitution in insolvency similar to its treatment of security interests. The mere fact that proprietary restitution favours the less well-off spouses of common law partnerships outside Québec over the less well-off spouses in Québec does not call for federal legislative intervention. This is a policy choice that is a genuine matter of provincial law. But – independent of the availability of proprietary restitution in dissolution-of-relationship cases – while the right of the creditor/trust beneficiary to separate the trust property from the estate should be recognized in principle, it should be limited where the rights enjoyed by the beneficiary exceed that which is needed to maintain the security of property rights entitlements. In this regard, it would be helpful if Canadian law introduced a long-arm power, which would allow the trustee to avail herself of the status of a *bona fide* purchaser of personal and real property.

The priority of Quistclose trusts, on the other hand, is defensible on the basis that resulting trust interest held by the beneficiary is a function of the limited transfer of property from the beneficiary to the debtor. The beneficiary transfers legal title to the debtor only so that the debtor can use it for a specific purpose. The same functional result can be achieved by giving the debtor a power over the beneficiary's property; in that case, the beneficiary would actually retain legal title to the property and not be a mere beneficiary.

Part V

# Horizontal Co-ordination

## § 17 International Property Law

In this chapter, I examine the provincial conflict of laws pertaining to property rights. I refer to this area of law as "international property law," but the reader should keep in mind that the provincial conflict of laws does not distinguish between inter-provincial and truly international conflicts of laws.[1] Provincial international property law has an important complimentary role to play. As I have discussed above,[2] the *Bankruptcy and Insolvency Act*[3] provides that, in principle, the trustee in bankruptcy takes the estate subject to security interests and other property rights. However, the *BIA* does not determine the law that governs which property rights exist in the property. This means that these questions are to be decided by the applicable conflict-of-laws rules of the bankruptcy forum. They are applicable because Parliament has not made use of its ancillary jurisdiction to legislate the conflict-of-laws questions related to bankruptcy.[4] In effect, this means that the provincial international property law of the bankruptcy court will determine the applicable law. This should also apply with regards to the *Bank Act.*[5]

In this chapter's first section, I look at the classification of property in the conflict of laws. In the second section, I look at the general *lex situs* rule, which provides that in principle, property rights are governed by the laws of the jurisdiction in which the property is located. In other words, international property law uses location as a connecting factor. In the third section, I look at the

---

[1] Cf. *Code civil du Québec,* SQ 1991, c 64, art 3077.

[2] Part IV: § 15, "Federal and Provincial Notions of Property and Security".

[3] RSC 1985, c B-3.

[4] Anthony J Duggan & Jacob S Ziegel, *Canadian Bankruptcy and Insolvency Law,* 2[d] edn (Toronto: Emond Montgomery Publications, 2009) at 825. On the relationship between the inherent jurisdiction of provincial law in conflict of laws questions relating to "civil rights and property" and Parliament's ancillary and paramount jurisdiction to legislate in ancillary conflict of laws questions connected with a subject matter within Parliament's jurisdiction see Jan Jakob Bornheim, "Same-Sex Marriage in Canadian Private International Law" (2013) 51:1 Alta L Rev 77 at 98–100.

[5] See Part IV: § 15 A.V.3, "Amendment to the Bank Act".

particular problems of a change in location. A change of location entails a change of applicable law by virtue of its significance as a connecting factor. In this chapter's fourth section, I look at the impact of the doctrine of vested rights on international property law. Finally, section five provides an overview of international trust law.

## A. Characterizing Property

In substantive law, Common Law jurisdictions divide a person's assets into real property and personal property.[6] The same distinction is not made in conflict of laws. Rather, for the purpose of conflict of laws, the distinction is drawn between movable and immovable property.[7] Whether a property is to be characterized as movable or immovable is determined by the *lex situs.*[8]

## B. The *Lex Situs* Rule

### *I. Common Law and the Lex Situs Rule*

#### *1. Principle*

The law applicable on immovables is the law of the *situs* of the property.[9] A court has no jurisdiction over immovables located outside the territory to whose government the court belongs.[10]

Historically, the Common Law followed the rule *mobilia personam sequuntur:* the laws of the domicile of the owner of the property governed personal property. The rule was most clearly stated in *Sill v Worswick:*[11]

"[I]t is a clear proposition, not only of the law of England, but of every country in the world, where law has the semblance of science, that personal property has no locality. The meaning

---

[6] See Part II: § 5 A, "Personal Property".

[7] See e.g. *Macdonald v Macdonald's Executrix,* [1932] SC (HL) 79 at 84 (Scot HL), Lord Tomlin, obiter; Lawrence Collins, Baron Collins of Mapesbury & Jonathan Harris, eds, *Dicey, Morris and Collins on the Conflict of Laws,* 15th edn (London: Sweet & Maxwell, 2012), vol 2 at paras 22.6–22.19; Stephen GA Pitel & Nicholas S Rafferty, *Conflict of Laws* (Toronto: Irwin Law, 2010) at 307.

[8] *Re Burke* (1927), [1928] 1 DLR 318 (Sask KB); *Re Berchtold* (1922), [1923] 1 Ch 192 (Ch D); Pitel & Rafferty, preceding note at 308.

[9] *Earl Nelson v Lord Bridport* (1846), 50 ER 215 (Ch).

[10] *Tezcan v Tezcan* (1987), 20 BCLR (2d) 253 (CA); *Henderson v The Bank of Hamilton* (1894), 23 SCR 716; *British South Africa Co v Companhia de Moçambique,* [1893] AC 602 (HL).

[11] (1791), 1 HBl 665 (Com Pl).

of that is, not that the personal property has no visible locality, but that it is subject to that law which governs the person of the owner."[12]

The question then became how to determine the domicile for the purpose of determining the law applicable on personal property.[13] The same rule applied in these cases was applied regarding secured transactions and bankruptcy as well.[14] The modern Common Law rule that succession to personal property is governed by the domicile of the deceased is a leftover of this rule.[15] Since the beginning of the twentieth century, the rule of *lex situs,* which had traditionally always applied to immovables has been applied to movable property as well.[16]

*2. Equitable Property Rights and the Lex Situs Rule*

The *lex situs* rule also applies to equitable property rights, at least as far as the action is an action *in rem* and the judgment cannot be executed *in personam.*[17] In *El Ajou v Dollar Land Holdings plc,*[18] Millet J stated that "[a]lthough equitable rights may found proprietary as well as personal claims, it has long been settled that they are classified as personal rights for the purpose of private international law."[19] But as Yeo points out,[20] Millet J interprets the following passage from *Ewing v Orr Ewing (No1):*[21]

"The Courts of Equity in England are, and always have been, Courts of conscience, operating in personam and not in rem; and in the exercise of this personal jurisdiction they have always been accustomed to compel the performance of contracts and trusts as to subjects which were not either locally or ratione domicilii within their jurisdiction. They have done so as to land, in Scotland, in Ireland, in the Colonies, in foreign countries."[22]

But we can assign a restricted meaning to his Lordship's words because he refers to *Penn v Lord Baltimore.*[23] *Penn v Lord Baltimore* only stands for the

---

[12] *Ibid* at 690.

[13] See *Marsh v Hutchinson* (1800), 126 ER 1249 (Com Pl); *Bruce v Bruce* (1790), 126 ER 1251 (HL).

[14] See e.g. *Phillips v Hunter* (1795), 2 HBl 402 at 406 (Com Pl). See also Ronald CC Cuming, Catherine E Walsh & Roderick J Wood, *Personal Property Security Law,* 2[d] edn (Toronto: Irwin Law, 2012) at 182.

[15] See *Marsh v Hutchinson, supra* note 13; *Bruce v Bruce, supra* note 13; Cuming, Walsh & Wood, *Personal Property Security Law,* preceding note at 182, note 9.

[16] *Winans v Attorney-General,* [1910] AC 27 (HL).

[17] *Henderson v The Bank of Hamilton, supra* note 10. Cf. *McNeil v Sharpe* (1915), 62 SCR 504. See also Tiong M Yeo, *Choice of Law for Equitable Doctrines* (Oxford: Oxford University Press, 2004) at paras 5.3–5.25.

[18] (1992), [1993] BCC 698 (Ch D).

[19] *Ibid* at 715, Millet J.

[20] Yeo, *supra* note 17 at paras 5.5–5.8.

[21] *Ewing v Orr Ewing (No1)* (1883), 9 App Cas 34 (HL).

[22] *Ibid* at 40, Selborne LC.

[23] (1750), 27 ER 1132 (Ch).

proposition that courts have jurisdiction to enforce equitable rights by actions *in personam.*[24] As the already-cited Canadian cases suggest, the proposition that all equitable rights are personal rights for the purpose of conflict of laws is unsustainable as a matter of Canadian law.[25] The better view is to reject it for English law as well. Panagopoulos argues that this is it at least true where the property right is created by a consensual transfer, but that a different analysis applies where the equitable property right is created through the operation of law.[26] He placed *Macmillan Inc v Bishopsgate Investment Trust Plc (No 3)*[27] in the former category.[28] I disagree – I submit that all cases of proprietary restitution are properly characterized as belonging to the law of property within the conflict of laws – but this is the topic of a later chapter.[29]

### *II. Civil Law and the Lex Situs Rule*

Québec law during the time of the *Code civil du Bas-Canada* generally followed the rule that the law of the owner's domicile governed movable property. It did not contain any specific rules regarding secured transactions in movables. Courts tended to characterize secured transactions and transfers of property as questions of contract law.[30] This led to a conflict between the law of secured transactions and the law of vindication.[31] Nowadays, art 3097 *Code civil du Québec* provides that property rights and their publicity are governed by the *lex situs,* except for goods in transit, which are governed by the law of the destination.

---

[24] A characterization accepted for European procedural law, see Case C-294/92 *Webb v Webb* [1994] QB 696. George Panagopoulos, *Restitution in Private International Law* (Oxford: Hart, 2000) at 72 acknowledges that the "assertion that equity acts in personam for the purposes of private international law" could be "a convenient common law nicety to give its courts greater jurisdiction." Pippa J Rogerson, "Equity, Rights in Rem and the Brussels Convention" (1994) 53 CLJ 462 points out that the jurisdictional analysis should not be transferred to characterization in the conflict of laws.

[25] *McNeil v Sharpe, supra* note 17; *Henderson v The Bank of Hamilton, supra* note 10; Pattarapas Tudsri, "Characterization of Proprietary Restitution in the Conflict of Laws" (2013) 44:2 Ottawa L Rev 261 at 283 rejecting it for the Common Law in general.

[26] Panagopoulos, *supra* note 24 at 75.

[27] (1995), [1996] 1 All ER 585 (CA Civ).

[28] Panagopoulos, *supra* note 24 at 75. On *Macmillan* see Part II: § 10 A.II.1.b), "Macmillan".

[29] See Part V: § 19 A, "Characterization of Proprietary Restitution".

[30] *Banque de Nouvelle-Écosse c Fournier,* [1985] CA 301; *Union Acceptance Corp Ltd c Guay,* [1960] BR 827; *Faubert c Brown* (1938), 76 CS 328; Claude Emanuelli, *Droit international privé québécois,* 3rd edn (Montréal: Wilson & Lafleur, 2011) at 514.

[31] Emanuelli, preceding note at 521.

## C. The *Conflit Mobile*

### *I. Principle*

#### *1. Scenarios of Conflits Mobiles*

The term *conflit mobile* describes cases in which the applicable property law changes because the factual element satisfying the connecting factor has changed; the term is occasionally used in Common Law, but it has been more thoroughly analysed in Continental Civil Law.[32] The analytical framework of Continental law is helpful because it allows me to clearly distinguish several fact patterns of *conflits mobiles.* Because international property law follows a *lex situs* principle, a *conflit mobile* will most often arise where movable property is moved between jurisdictions.

Two basic scenarios of a *conflit mobile* can be distinguished. First, a *conflit mobile* can arise where a purchaser has fully and effectively acquired a property right in one jurisdiction, and the item of property then moves to a second jurisdiction (*conflit mobile* type A).[33] Second, a *conflit mobile* can involve

---

[32] Janeen M Carruthers, *The Transfer of Property in the Conflict of Laws: Choice of Law Rules Concerning Inter Vivos Transfers of Property* (Oxford: Oxford University Press, 2005) at para 1.25; Emanuelli, *supra* note 30; Karl Kreuzer, "La propriété mobilière en droit international privé" in: Académie du droit international, ed, *Recueil des cours* (Leiden: Sijthoff, 1996) 9 56–65: 482–486; Pierre Mayer & Vincent Heuzé, *Droit international privé,* 11th edn (Paris: Librairie générale de droit et de jurisprudence, 2014) at 683–84; Marie-Laure Niboyet & de Geouffre de la Pradelle, Geráud, *Droit international privé,* 4th edn (Paris: Librairie générale de droit et de jurisprudence, 2013) at 85; Thomas von Plehwe in: *Nomos Kommentar BGB, vol 1, Allgemeiner Teil, EGBGB,* ed by Thomas Heidel; Rainer Hüßtege; Heinz-Peter Mansel; and Ulrich Noack (Baden-Baden: Nomos, 2012) Art 43 EGBGB at para 26; Janet Walker & Jean-Gabriel Castel, *Canadian Conflict of Laws,* 6th edn (LexisNexis Butterworths, 2005) at § 9.2.The term conflit mobile already appears in Hans Lewald, "Règles générales des conflits de lois: Contribution à la technique du droit international privé" in: Académie du droit international, ed, *Recueil des cours* (Leiden: Brill, 1939), vol 69, 1 at 95: "Si, en droit transitoire, l'appréciation juridique des faits dépend normalement de la loi contemporaine à ces faits, je n'oserais pas en dire autant en ce qui concerne *les conflits mobiles en droit international privé.* A mon avis, c'est l'interprétation de chaque règle de conflit qui doit nous fournir la solution." [Emphasis added].

[33] For a taxonomy of the conflit mobile see Kreuzer, preceding note at 58–65; Heinz-Peter Mansel in: Julius von Staudinger, *Kommentar zum Bürgerlichen Gesetzbuch mit Einführungsgesetz und Nebengesetzen, Internationales Sachenrecht,* ed by Dieter Henrich (Berlin: Sellier-de Gruyter, 2015) art 43 EGBGB, at paras 1226–30; Christiane Wendehorst in: *Münchener Kommentar zum Bürgerlichen Gesetzbuch, vol 11, Internationales Privatrecht II, Internationales Wirtschaftsrecht, Einführungsgesetz zum Bürgerlichen Gesetzbuch (Art. 25–248),* ed by Kurt Rebmann; Franz-Jürgen Säcker; and Roland Rixecker, 6th ed (Munich: CH Beck, 2015) art 43 EGBGB at paras 136–8.

cases in which a purchaser has started to acquire a property right, but the property moves between jurisdictions before the acquisition has fully taken place. This is an incomplete property transfer.

The second scenario can arise where the transfer of property itself involves several steps, or where third-party effect of the transfer of property depends on additional requirements that are not necessary for *inter partes* effect. The second scenario encompasses three sub-scenarios. These three scenarios can be distinguished from one another. First are cases where the transfer is incomplete from the point of view of *both the original jurisdiction and the destination* (*conflit mobile* type B). Second are cases where the transfer is incomplete from the point of view of the *destination,* but already complete from the point of view of the original jurisdiction (*conflit mobile* type C). Third are cases where the transfer is incomplete from the point of view of the *original jurisdiction* but complete from the point of view of the destination (*conflit mobile* type D).[34]

### *2. Recognition and Transposition of Property Rights*

Type A *conflits mobiles* in particular raise the question how property rights established under the old law are to be treated in the new jurisdiction. The *numerus clausus* principle posits that property rights wholly foreign to the recipient jurisdiction should not be recognized.[35] Lewald called the resulting process one of transposition:

> "Le transfert de la chose dans le territoire d'un autre Etat entraîne le changement de la législation compétente, de sorte que désormais la chose se trouve soumise au nouveau statut. Cependant, celui-ci recueille la chose avec les traits caractéristiques que lui a imprimés l'ancien statut. Les droits réels existant sur la chose ne s'éteignent pas, au contraire ils subsistent dans la mesure où ils sont compatibles avec le nouveau statut. Le sort de ces droits est moins un problème de conflit de lois qu'une question de droit comparé. Il n'y a aucune difficulté lorsque la nouvelle loi connaît la catégorie de droits réels envisagés. Le droit réel subsiste; il est simplement transposé dans la catégorie correspondante de la nouvelle loi."[36]

One can imagine three ways of coping with a foreign property right. These three mechanisms can be placed along a spectrum based on how intensely the modify the foreign property right:[37] first, the old property right is fully accepted

---

[34] Christiane Wendehorst in: *MüKo-BGB,* preceding note, Art. 43 EGBGB at paras 136–38.

[35] Cf. Carruthers, *supra* note 32 at para 3.45; Mansel in: von Staudinger, *supra* note 33, Art. 43 EGBGB at para 1279.

[36] Lewald, *supra* note 32 at 129.

[37] Gerhard Kegel & Klaus Schurig, *Internationales Privatrecht,* 9th edn (Munich: CH Beck, 2004) at 772–73, arguing for the *effet de purge;* Kreuzer, *supra* note 32 at 79–84; Mansel in: von Staudinger, *supra* note 33, Art. 43 EGBGB at paras 1247–65; von Plehwe in: *Nomos Kommentar BGB, supra* note 32, Art. 43 EGBGB at paras 30–31, 35.

in the recipient jurisdiction, but any exercise of rights deriving from the property right is restrained by the law of destination and only those discrete rights recognized in the recipient jurisdiction can be exercised (exercise control); second, the sticks – or incidents – of the property right making up the bundle of right are transposed into sticks corresponding to rights of and recognized by the recipient jurisdiction (weak transposition);[38] third, the functionally comparable property right of the recipient jurisdiction fully replaces the old property right (strong transposition or *effet de purge*).[39]

### *II. Common Law and the Conflit Mobile*

Case law authority indicates that the common law rule for a *conflit mobile* involving acquired property rights is to leave acquired property rights intact until a new transfer replaces them. The property right continues to be governed by the *lex originis i.e.lex situs* at the time of the acquisition of the property) until a right acquired according to the new *lex situs* displaces the old property right.[40] There is little authority that would allow one to locate the Common Law approach within the spectrum of transposition. Carruthers argues that the exercise of foreign property rights is limited "insofar as there exist difficulties of transposition of legal right or entitlement."[41] At the same time, she does not submit that the foreign property right as such is displaced. I would submit that case law – which speaks of the continued existence of the foreign property right – would place Common Law at the weak end of the spectrum. Foreign property rights are not transposed in the more limited sense of the word; rather, their exercise is subject to the *numerus clausus* of potential sticks of rights available at the current *situs*. This conforms to the *PPSA* rule on foreign-acquired security interests.[42]

---

[38] Mayer & Heuzé, *supra* note 32 at 685–86.

[39] Kegel & Schurig, *supra* note 37 at 772–73, arguing for the *effet de purge;* Bram Akkermans & Eveline Ramaekers, "Free Movement of Goods and Property Law" (2013) 19:2 Eur LJ 237 at 241.

[40] *Cammell & Others v Sewell & Others* (1860), 157 ER 1371 (Exch Ch). See also *Maden v Long* (1982), 41 BCLR 6 (BC SC); *Winkworth v Christie Manson & Woods Ltd & another* (1979), [1980] 1 Ch 496 (Ch D); *Century Credit Corporation v Richard,* [1962] OR 815 (CA); Collins, Baron Collins of Mapesbury & Harris, *supra* note 7 24 /pagemargin R:20–24. See furthermore Pierre A Lalive, *The Transfer of Chattels in the Conflict of Laws: A Comparative Study* (Oxford: Clarendon Press, 1955) at 175–84; JHC Morris, "The Transfer of Chattels in the Conflict of Laws" (1945) 22 Brit YB Int'l L 232; Pippa J Rogerson, "The Situs of Debts in the Conflict of Law: Illogical, Unnecessary and Misleading" (1990) 49 CLJ 441; Theodore JR Schilling, "Some European Decisions on Non-Possessory Security Rights in Private International Law" (1985) 34:1 ICLQ 87 at 94.

[41] Carruthers, *supra* note 32 at para 3.45.

[42] See Part V: § 18 A.I.3, "Change of Situs".

### *III. Civil Law and the Conflit Mobile*

Emanuelli submits that the exercise of acquired property rights is governed by Québec law, but their validity continues to be governed by the *lex originis.*[43]

## D. Vested Rights

The *conflit mobile* is often framed in terms of recognition of vested rights. Carruthers expresses the rule of vested rights as follows:

> "As a general rule, removal of an object across state borders should not undermine, per se, pre-existing, or vested, rights in the object, but this rule pertains only so long as there are no further dealings with the object in the new *situs.*"[44]

The purpose of this section is to look at the notion of vested rights and its impact on international property law.

### *I. Theory of Private International Law*

#### *1. Comity and Vested Rights*

The original theory of vested rights is an alternative to the theory of comity. Both theories are accounts for the necessity of private international law. "Comity" means extending something to another state in the expectation that the other state will reciprocate. In other words, courts of one state apply the laws of other jurisdictions – if the case is most closely connected to those jurisdictions – because the state expect other jurisdictions to reciprocate this favour.[45] Comity is an accepted principle of Canadian private international law:

"Comity" in the legal sense, is neither a matter of absolute obligation, on the one hand, nor of mere courtesy and good will, upon the other. But it is the recognition which one nation allows within its territory to the *legislative,* executive or judicial acts of another nation, having due regard both to international duty and convenience, and to the rights of its own citizens or of other persons who are under the protection of its laws.[46]

---

[43] Emanuelli, *supra* note 30 at 514.

[44] Carruthers, *supra* note 32 at para 105 [emphasis in original].

[45] Joseph Story, *Commentaries on the Conflict of Laws: Foreign and Domestic,* 3rd edn (Boston: Little, Brown & Co, 1846) at 39–40; Friedrich C von Savigny, *System des heutigen römischen Rechts* (Berlin: Veit & Comp, 1849), vol 8 at 26–27. See also Adrian Briggs, "Restitution Meets the Conflict of Laws" (1995) 3 RLR 94 at 82; Donald Earl Childress, III, "Comity as Conflict: Resituating International Comity as Conflict of Laws" (2010) 44 UC Davis L Rev 11 at 17–35.

[46] *Hilton v Guyot,* 159 US 113 at 163–64 (1895), Gray J [emphasis added], cited with approval in *R v Spencer* (1985), 21 DLR (4th) 756 at 759 (Can SCC), LaForest J.

> "The truth is that a system of law built on what a particular court considers to be the expectations of the parties or what it thinks is fair, without engaging in further probing about what it means by this, does not bear the hallmarks of a rational system of law. [...] On the international plane, the relevant underlying reality is the territorial limits of law under the international legal order. The underlying postulate of public international law is that generally each state has jurisdiction to make and apply law within its territorial limit. Absent a breach of some overriding norm, other states as a matter of 'comity' will ordinarily respect such actions and are hesitant to interfere with what another state chooses to do within those limits. *Moreover,* to accommodate the movement of people, wealth and skills across state lines, a byproduct of modern civilization, they will in great measure recognize the determination of legal issues in other states. And to promote the same values, they will open their national forums for the resolution of specific legal disputes arising in other jurisdictions consistent with the interests and internal values of the forum state. These are the realities that must be reflected and accommodated in private international law."[47]

The theory of vested rights differs from the comity theory.[48] In its general form, the theory holds that a person acquires rights under the laws of a certain jurisdiction. These rights vest in the person, so that other jurisdictions must give effect to them. The vested right theory was advanced as being the foundation of conflict of laws by Dicey.[49] However, the vested rights theory is not a complete rejection of comity. Rather, the two are linked. Rights vest because another sovereign has vested them in the party. Thus vested rights theorists refer to the principles of comity to support their theory.[50]

The origins of the vested rights theory can be traced back to intertemporal conflict of laws. Where a jurisdiction replaces one set of rules by another set of rules, the intertemporal doctrine of vested rights requires that the new enactment does not disturb acquired rights.[51]

A territorial approach to conflict of laws is a function of a vested rights approach,[52] but it is not a necessary condition. In other words: if the reason for

---

[47] *Tolofson v Jensen,* [1994] 3 SCR 1022 at 1046–47, LaForest J [emphasis added].

[48] See David MacClean, "De conflictu legum: Perspectives on Private International Law at the Turn of the Century" in: Académie du droit international, ed, *Recueil des cours* (Leiden: Sijthoff, 2000) 41 at 59–63, tracing the intellectual history of both theories.

[49] See Albert V Dicey, *A Digest of the Law of England with Reference to the Conflict of Laws,* 1st edn (London: Stevens and Sons & Sweet and Maxwell, 1896) and Albert V Dicey, "On Private International Law as a Branch of the Law of England" (1890) 6:1 LQR 1. See also Joseph H Beale, "Dicey's 'Conflict of Laws'" (1896) 10:3 Harv L Rev 168; Perry Dane, "Vested Rights, 'Vestedness,' and Choice of Law" (1987) 96:6 Yale LJ 1191 at 1194–96; Ralf Michaels, "EU Law as Private International Law?: Reconceptualising the Country-of-Origin Principle as Vested-Rights Theory" (2006) 2:2 J Priv Int'l L 195 at 214–16; Pitel & Rafferty, *supra* note 7 at 207.

[50] Alex Mills, "The Private History of International Law" (2006) 55:1 ICLQ 1 at 23 ff in particular 31.

[51] Ko S Sik, "The Concept of Acquired Rights in International Law: A Survey" [1977] Nethl Int'l L Rev 120 at 120–24.

[52] Dane, *supra* note 49 at 1195.

the application of foreign law is to give effect to rights acquired in a different territory, the method of conflict of laws necessarily requires one to locate the place at which the right was acquired. But vested rights are not the only imaginable reason why territory is chosen as the connecting factor.

The shortcoming of both the vested rights theory and the notion of comity is that they do not assist in the determination of the relevant jurisdiction.[53] Saying that a right needs to be recognized as a vested right begs the question because it presupposes that one knows which rights have been vested, which, in turn, requires one to have determined the applicable law.[54] The same problem cannot arise where the conflict of laws is intertemporal.

*2. Conflicts Revolution*

In the wake of American legal realism, a very different approach to conflict of laws developed.[55] Cook argued that conflict of laws is not the application of foreign law, but the adoption of foreign rules into domestic law. Therefore, the task of courts is not to identify the applicable foreign law through the application of a complex set of rules and the low-visibility process of characterization. The purpose of conflict of laws is to determine whether the foreign rule of decision could be incorporated into domestic law.[56]

Currie increased the emphasis on domestic policy by placing a stronger focus on policy and interest. He feared that giving effect to vested rights could allow courts to contravene the municipal jurisdiction's laws that are an expression of domestic policy choices.[57] The American conflicts revolution has not had much impact on Canadian law.[58]

---

[53] With regards to comity see *Davies v Collins,* 2011 NSCA 79 at para 34, Bryson J.

[54] RD Carswell, "The Doctrine of Vested Rights in Private International Law" [1959] CLJ 268 at 278–86.

[55] On the American conflicts revolution see e.g. Dane, *supra* note 49 at 1196–204; Albert A Ehrenzweig, "A Counter-Revolution in Conflicts Law?: From Beale to Cavers" (1966) 80:2 Harv L Rev 377; Gerhard Kegel, "Paternal Home and Dream Home: Traditional Conflict of Laws and the American Reformers" (1979) 27:4 Am J Comp L 615; Symeon C Symeonides, "Revolution and Counter-Revolution in American Conflics Law: Is There a Middle Ground?" (1985) 46:3 Ohio St LJ 549.

[56] Cook elaborated his theory of private international law in two main works, an article and a book, see Walter W Cook, "The Logical and Legal Bases of the Conflict of Laws" (1924) 33:5 Yale LJ 457 and Walter W Cook, *The Logical and Legal Bases of the Conflict of Laws* (Cambridge, Mass: Harvard University Press, 1942). See also Dane, *supra* note 49 at 1196–201.

[57] See e.g. Brainerd Currie, "Notes on Methods and Objectives in the Conflict of Laws" in: Brainerd Currie, *Selected Essays in the Conflict of Laws* (Durham: Duke University Press, 1963) 177 at 180–81.

[58] See e.g. Pitel & Rafferty, *supra* note 7 at 206–9.

### *3. Economic Analysis of International Property Law*

While the American conflict-of-laws revolution had no impact on Canadian law, it might trigger a critical evaluation as to whether the conflict-of-laws rule lead to a desirable policy result. The *lex situs* rule fares well in such an analysis. It is not only supported by judicial authority and doctrine, but also defensible in a law-and-economics analysis. Clear resource allocation requires that the same regime apply to all property and all property rights in the property as far as possible and feasible.[59]

## *II. Property Rights as Vested Rights*

As I have mentioned above, the Common Law usually conceptualizes the *conflit mobile* as a question of vested rights. The same applies to Québec Civil Law. This raises the question as to whether there is any substantive result that follows from this conceptualization. Some authors argue that the protection of vested rights requires that property rights created in the original jurisdiction be given effect after a change of *situs*.[60] In the European Union, the argument is made that the Member States must recognize property interests that have attached to property according to the law of one Member State (jurisdiction of origin).[61] Mansel goes further and submits that the principle of recognition of vested rights has an impact on the question of transposition: recognition of vested rights means that neither the property rights nor its incidents should be transposed into rights of the recipient jurisdiction; rather, the property law of

---

[59] See Daniel Klerman, "Jurisdiction, Choice of Law and Property" <https://papers.ssrn.com/sol3/papers.cfm?abstract_id=2422470> accessed 3 December 2017; James Y Stern, "Property, Exclusivity, and Jurisdiction" (2014) 100:1 Va L Rev 111.

[60] Carruthers, *supra* note 32 at para 3.45; Kreuzer, *supra* note 32 at 80; Hans Stoll in: Julius von Staudinger, *Kommentar zum Bürgerlichen Gesetzbuch mit Einführungsgesetz und Nebengesetzen, Internationales Sachenrecht,* ed by Jan Kropholler (Berlin: Sellier-de Gruyter, 1996) at para 121; Wendehorst in: *MüKo-BGB, supra* note 33, Art. 43 EGBGB at para 120. Cf. Mansel in: von Staudinger, *supra* note 33, Art. 43 EGBGB at paras 203–4; Sik, *supra* note 51 at 125.

[61] See Akkermans & Ramaekers, *supra* note 39; Jürgen Basedow, "Der kollisionsrechtliche Gehalt der Produktfreiheiten im europäischen Binnenmarkt: Favor offerentis" (1995) 59:1 RabelsZ 1 at 41–48; Heinz-Peter Mansel, "Anerkennung als Grundprinzip des Europäischen Rechtsraums: Zur Herausbildung eines europäischen Anerkennungs-Kollisionsrechts: Anerkennung statt Verweisung als neues Strukturprinzip des Europäischen internationalen Privatrechts?" (2006) 70 RabelsZ 651 at 731; Mansel in: von Staudinger, *supra* note 33, Art. 43 EGBGB at paras 166, 207, 1265; Michaels, "EU Law as Private International Law?", *supra* note 49; Niboyet & de Geouffre de la Pradelle, Geráud, *supra* note 32 at 85, 189. Cf. Wendehorst in: *MüKo-BGB, supra* note 33, Art. 43 EGBGB at paras 155–59.

the recipient jurisdiction should only act as a restraint on the exercise of the vested right.[62]

In this sense, the treatment of *conflits mobiles* in Canadian Common Law and Québec Civil Law can be seen as an expression of the recognition of vested rights. Allowing the recognition of property rights acquired under the laws of one Canadian jurisdiction in another Canadian jurisdiction as far as possible is also an expression of the first vector of bijuralism.

## E. International Trust Law

### *I. Common Law*

The common law international trust law is not clearly defined.[63] The general rule is to apply the law of the jurisdiction to which the trust is most closely connected and to allow for the application of different laws on different aspects of the trust or different trust property.[64] Whether the trust property is movable or immovable makes a difference.[65] In general, the law applicable on a trust interest in immovable property is the law of the *situs* of the property.[66]

### *II. The Hague Trusts Convention*

The *Hague Trusts Convention*[67] contains rules on international trust law.[68] Canada and the United Kingdom are both parties to the convention. In Canada, the

---

[62] Mansel in: von Staudinger, *supra* note 33, Art. 43 EGBGB at para 1265. Cf. Akkermans & Ramaekers, *supra* note 39.

[63] Pitel & Rafferty, *supra* note 7 at 377.

[64] *Ibid* at 377–78.

[65] *Ibid* at 377.

[66] Janet Walker, *Halsbury's Laws of Canada: Conflict of Laws* (Toronto: LexisNexis Butterworths, 2006) at HCF-241; Walker & Castel, *supra* note 32 at § 28.3.a.

[67] *Convention of 1 July 1985 on the Law Applicable to Trusts and on their Recognition.*

[68] On the convention in general see Alfred E von Overbeck, "Rapport explicatif" in: Conférence de la Haye de droit international prive, ed, *Actes et documents de la 14ème session* ('s-Gravenshage: Bureau permanent de la Conférence, 1980) 370. See also David Hayton, "The Hague Convention on the Law Applicable to Trusts and on Their Recognition" (1987) 36 ICLQ 260; Hein Kötz, "Die 15. Haager Konferenz und das Kollisionsrecht des trust" (1986) 50:3–4 RabelsZ 562; Pitel & Rafferty, *supra* note 7 at 371–76; Walker & Castel, *supra* note 32 at § 28.4. On recognition of trusts under the convention by Civil Law signatory states see Michele Graziadei, "Recognition of Common Law Trusts in Civil Law Jurisdictions under the Hague Trusts Convention with Particular Regard to the Italian Experience" in: Lionel D Smith, ed, *Re-imagining the Trust: Trusts in Civil Law* (Cambridge: Cambridge University Press, 2012) 29 [Graziadei, "Recognition"].

*Hague Trusts Convention* applies to all provinces except Ontario and Québec.[69] The United States have signed the *Hague Trusts Convention,* but have not ratified it in the last 23 years.

Article 6 *Hague Trusts Convention* and art 7 *Hague Trusts Convention* define the law applicable to a trust. According to art 6 *Hague Trusts Convention,* the law chosen by the settlor is applicable. Absent a choice of law the default rule of art 7 *Hague Trusts Convention* applies. The rule uses alternative connecting factors. Particularly noteworthy are the connecting factors asset *situs,* the objectives of the trust, and the places where they are to be fulfilled. art 7 *Hague Trusts Convention* mirrors the common law rule,[70] particularly the law in Ontario is the same.[71]

### *III. Québec Law*

#### *1. The Rule*

In Québec, the applicable law is determined by art 3207 *CcQ,* which is closely modelled on the *Hague Trusts Convention.*[72]

#### *2. Recognition of Trusts*

Article 11 *Hague Trusts Convention* provides that trusts created in accordance with the law specified by the *Hague Trusts Convention* chapter shall be recognized as trusts. This is read to be a rejection of splitting up and transposing the discrete rights arising from the trust into analogous institutions of the recognizing jurisdiction.[73] Instead, the trust is recognized as such, but the beneficiary can only avail herself of such rights as are known under the law of the recognizing jurisdiction.[74] The problem of splitting up the trust into discrete rights not only arises where a Common Law trust is to be recognized in a Civil Law jurisdiction. It also arises where a Civil Law trust is to be recognized by a different Civil Law jurisdiction that has taken a different approach to trust law.[75]

While Québec is not bound by the *Hague Trusts Convention,* the autonomous adoption of the same rules by the Québec legislature would favour the

---

[69] For further details regarding the applicability of the Hague Trusts Convention in Canada see Walker & Castel, *supra* note 32 at § 28.4.

[70] Collins, Baron Collins of Mapesbury & Harris, *supra* note 7 at para 29.21.

[71] *Branco v Veira* (1995), 8 ETR (2[d]) 49 (Ont Gen Div).

[72] See Emanuelli, *supra* note 30 at 528; Walker & Castel, *supra* note 32 at § 28.6.

[73] Cf. Graziadei, "Recognition", *supra* note 68 at 40.

[74] Emmanuel Gaillard & Donald T Trautman, "Trusts in Non-Trust Countries: Conflict of Laws and the Hague Convention on Trusts" (1987) 35:2 Am J Comp L 307 at 332–33.

[75] See Kurt Lipstein, *Private International Law: Trusts,* ed by Konrad Zweigert, Ulrich Drobnig, and Kurt Lipstein (International Encyclopedia of Comparative Law, III-23, Tübingen: Mohr Siebeck, 1994) at para 19.

operation of a rule similar to art 11 *Hague Trusts Convention* in Québec law. This then leads to the question which of the rights that the beneficiary of a trust under Common Law can avail herself can be exercised under Québec law.

### *a) Effects of the Trust*

For the purpose of this book – which is less concerned with the duties of the trustee in the management of the trust and more with the proprietary nature of the trust interest – the trust can be considered to confer three important rights to the beneficiary, which I shall refer to as "trust rights" for the remainder of this chapter:[76] first, provided certain conditions are met, the beneficiary can demand that title to the trust be transferred to her and that the trustee delivers the property to her; second, while the trustee can convey legal title the trust property in breach of trust, the beneficiary can follow the trust property into third-party hands unless the third party is equity's darling (*i.e.* a *bona fide* purchaser for value without notice); third, the beneficiary can trace her right in the trust property into traceable proceeds held by the trustee.

### *b) Comparable Rights in Québec Law*

Where the notion of a trust is wholly unknown in Civil Law jurisdictions, the notions of mandate, usufruct, and emphyteusis – among others – have been employed to either transpose the trust altogether or its discrete components.[77] I submit that these approaches are not necessary under Québec law.

#### *aa) Conveyance and Delivery of the Trust Property*

With regard to the first trust right – conveyance of legal title and specific performance – reception in Québec law is unproblematic. The notion that a creditor has a right to demand conveyance of ownership and specific delivery is at the heart of any sales contract, at least where the consensual effects of the transfer of property are delayed. Arguably, an outright sales contract, rather than a deferred sales contract provides an even closer analogy to the trustee-beneficiary relationship. After all, the function of consensualism and *bona fide* third-party protection is that a sales contract leads to a form of split ownership. Within the vendor-purchaser relationship, the purchaser has to be considered to be the owner of the property. Outside this relationship, the vendor has to be considered the owner of property.[78]

---

[76] See Part II: § 6 C, "The Trust Beneficiary's Right".

[77] Lipstein, *supra* note 75, at para 20.

[78] See Part II: § 4 F, "Acquisition of Ownership in Civil Law".

### *bb) Following*

With regard to the second trust right – following – Civil Law inalienability yields certain effects comparable to a Common Law trust.[79] This is particularly true with regard to Québec law. I have analysed the application and impact of the rules on alienability and power in the chapter on the Civil Law trust and come to the conclusion that inalienability confers a right of following to the beneficiary of the Civil Law trust.[80] The same should apply *mutatis mutandis* to the Common Law trust. The comparison of Common Law trusts with property subject to a restriction on alienability reveals the following.

First, trusts would fall into one of the categories of allowed restrictions on alienability: somebody could have an interest in a specific item of property, and it is this interest that needs to be protected.

Second, inalienable property does not form part of the *gage commun*. It is thus not part of the general patrimony; this makes it comparable to trust property, the only difference being that the recipient of inalienable property (the one who undertook to not alienate it) is still both the full titulary of that property and its owner.[81]

Third, the beneficiary of the restriction can do to two things: she can reverse the transfer and she can vindicate whatever right she has. The second option is a function of the wider concepts of property and possession in the *CcQ*. The knowing receipt claim that can be brought by the beneficiary of a constructive trust is thus functionally equivalent to the rights a beneficiary of a restriction has in Civil Law. The two notions are thus comparable.

### *cc) Tracing*

As argued above, the ability of the Common Law beneficiary to trace her property right into proceeds mirrors the Civil Law beneficiary's right to claim real subrogation with regards to the trust property improperly disposed of.[82]

### *dd) Publicity of the Trust*

The fact that the Common Law trust can be constituted without being entered into a registry is comparable to the constitution of a Québec trust.[83] It thus poses no challenge to the recognition of an equitable property right in Québec.

---

[79] Cf. John H Merryman, "Policy, Autonomy, and the Numerus Clausus in Italian and American Property Law" (1963) 12:2 Am J Comp L 224 at 231.

[80] See Part II: § 7 C.II.2.b), "Protection of the Trust Property".

[81] This is acknowledged by Michelle Cumyn, "Les restrictions à la liberté d'aliéner dans le Code civil du Québec" (1994) 39:4 McGill LJ 877 at 894.

[82] See Part II: § 7 C.II.2.b), "Protection of the Trust Property".

[83] See Part II: § 7 C.I, "Patrimony by Appropriation".

Where the trust is not made public, the inalienability argument could fail because restrictions on alienability need to be published, but this does not mean that the beneficiary should not be able to follow her property into third-party hands. Even where the Civil Law trust is not published, the beneficiary would be able to follow her property by virtue of the power model.[84] The same should apply to Common Law trusts given effect in Québec.

In the context of publicity, another issue arises. Québec Civil Law has no general *bona fide* purchaser rule.[85] This leads one to wonder whether a *bona fide* third party purchaser of property subject to a Common Law trust recognized in Québec could acquire the property. I would submit that this should be possible. After all, unlike the trustee of Civil Law trust property, the Common Law trustee has to be considered to be the owner of the property. The Civil Law trust rules on tracing and following are only used to support the claim that the exercise of the Common Law trust rights is compatible with Civil Law. A restriction on these rights should thus be possible.

---

[84] See Part II: § 7 C.II.2.b), "Protection of the Trust Property".

[85] Pierre-Claude Lafond, *Précis de droit des biens,* 2d edn (Montréal: Éditions Thémis, 2007) at para 2544.

# § 18 International Secured Transaction Law

## A. Conflict of Laws of Secured Transactions in Common Law

The *PPSAs* contain their own conflict-of-laws rules, which partly deviate from the principle of *lex situs.* As far as the *PPSAs* contain their own rules, reference to the common law rules of international property law is no longer appropriate.[1]

Depending on the kind of collateral and the specific issue, the *PPSAs* refer to different laws. The possible applicable laws are the law of the location of the collateral *(lex situs),* the law of the original location of the collateral *(lex originis),* the law of the destination of the collateral, *(lex destinati),* and the law of the domicile of the debtor *(lex domicilii).*

### *I. Lex Situs*

#### *1. Collateral Covered by the Lex Situs*

The *lex situs* covers two types of collateral. The first one is "goods,"[2] which are defined as all tangible personal property excluding "chattel paper, documents of title, instruments, money and investment property."[3] The category of collateral to which the *lex situs* applies is thus a "catch-all category." It covers all security interests in goods unless otherwise specified.

The second category of collateral contain instruments, a negotiable document of title, money and chattel paper. *Possessory* security interests in such collateral are governed by the *situs* of this collateral, rather than by the location

---

[1] Ronald CC Cuming, Catherine E Walsh & Roderick J Wood, *Personal Property Security Law,* 2[d] edn (Toronto: Irwin Law, 2012) at 184. See also *Holland v Chrysler Credit Canada Ltd,* [1992] AJ No 947 (QB), Funduk M: "The Act does not apply to transactions entered into in other jurisdictions where there is no connection in any way between that transaction and Alberta. The Act does not have an extra-territorial effect. Constitutionally it cannot have such an effect. […] That is the point that Advanced Diamond Drilling and counsel for the Applicant make. I think it is a valid point."

[2] *Personal Property Security Act,* RSO 1990, c P.10 [*PPSA (Ont)*], s 5(1)(a).

[3] *Ibid,* s 1(1).

of the property that forms the basis of the document.[4] The grace period of continued deemed perfection[5] does not apply to these instruments (s 6(2) *Personal Property Security Act* only refers to "security interests in goods").

*2. Scope of the Lex Situs*

Under the *PPSA, validity, perfection,* and *effects of perfection* (or non-perfection) are governed by the *lex situs.* In Ontario and other jurisdictions, the choice-of-law rule notably omits priority of the security interest.[6] In Saskatchewan, following the entering-into-force of amendments to the *Personal Property Security Act,* priority will be fully included within the scope of the *lex situs.*[7] This implements a recommendation by the CCPPSL Working Group.[8]

*3. Change of Situs*

*a) Conflit Mobile*

A change of *situs* entails a potential *conflit mobile.*[9] The relocation of the collateral at least partially changes the applicable secured transactions law. However currently, the *PPSAs* specify that *validity, perfection and effect of perfection* or non-perfection are immutably governed by the *lex situs* at the time of attachment.

The current *PPSAs* do not address which law governs priority disputes between the holders of security interests created according to the laws of two different jurisdictions. The CCPPSL Working Group recommends that the *PPSA*s be amended to specify that attachment be governed by the *lex situs* at the time of attachment, perfection and priority by the current *lex situs.*[10] Applying the *lex situs* at the time of creation to the attachment of a security interest, but perfection and priority according to the current *situs* would bring the

---

[4] *Ibid,* s 5(1).

[5] See Part V: § 18 A.I.3.b), "Continued Perfection".

[6] See Canadian Conference on Personal Property Security Law, Working Group (CCPPSL Working Group), *Report to the Canadian Conference on Personal Property Security Law on Proposals for Changes to the Personal Property Security Acts,* (2017) at 112–13.

[7] *Personal Property Security Amendment Act,* SS 2019, c 15 amends *Personal Property Security Act,* SS 1993, c P-6.2 [*PPSA (Sask)*], s 5.

[8] CCPPSL Working Group, *supra* note 6 at 113.

[9] See Part V: § 17 C, "The Conflit Mobile".

[10] CCPPSL Working Group, *supra* note 6 at 116.

*PPSAs* in line with art 91(2) *Model Law on Secured Transactions.*[11] This amendment has been accepted in Saskatchewan,[12] but not Ontario.[13]

Where the *PPSA* does not contain a choice-of-law rule relating to priority, the common law rules on international property law could still apply. At common law, an immutable comprehensive choice-of-law rule: attachment applies meaning that, perfection and priority are all governed by the original *lex situs;* the old priority rules would thus continue to govern priority conflicts between previously-acquired security interests.[14] In cases of a conflict between a security interest from another jurisdiction and the current jurisdiction, courts have applied the priority rules of the new jurisdiction,[15] but so far, courts have not decided what law is applicable in a priority dispute between security interests created according to two different jurisdictions in collateral now located in a third jurisdiction. Under the common law rule, the law of the jurisdiction where the last security interest was created should apply.[16]

*General Motors Acceptance Corp of Canada v Town & Country Chrysler Ltd*[17] discusses the relationship between a secured creditor and a purchaser. The Court found that the possibility of a purchase free of the security interest is governed by the current *lex situs,* and the law of the former *situs* governs the rights of the secured creditor *vis-à-vis* the purchaser.[18] The Court also indicated that the relationship between the *bona fide* purchaser or lessee during the grace period and the holder of a security interest deriving from another jurisdiction is governed by the *lex situs* at the time of the sale or lease, not by the *lex situs*

---

[11] UNCITRAL, *Model Law on Secured Transactions,* (UNCITRAL) <https://uncitral.un.org/en/texts/securityinterests/modellaw/secured_transactions> accessed 20 September 2019.

[12] *PPSA (Sask), supra* note 7, s 5 as amended by *Personal Property Security Amendment Act, supra* note 7.

[13] See *Schedule 49 to the Act to Implement Budget Measures and to Enact, Amend and Repeal Various Statutes,* SO 2019, c 7 [*Schedule 49, Ontario Budget Measures Act 2019*].

[14] CCPPSL Working Group, *supra* note 6 at 115; Cuming, Walsh & Wood, *Personal Property Security Law, supra* note 1 at 197–98.

15 *Holy Spirit Credit Union v McMullan (Trustee of),* [1994] MJ No 105 (QB); *Re Adair* (1980), 49 OR (2[d]) 583 (CA).

[16] Cuming, Walsh & Wood, *Personal Property Security Law, supra* note 1 at 198.

[17] (2005), 2005 CarswellOnt 1393 (Ont Sup Ct J).

[18] *Ibid* at para 52, Forget J: "In my opinion, the Defendants are correct in pointing out that GMAC's security interest in Ontario is derived from whatever security interest it held in Québec [...]. If there had been no security interest in Québec, GMAC would only have a claim on the Corvette as of January 24, 2000, and the Defendants would likely escape liability. In order to seek recovery against the Defendants, therefore, GMAC must argue that its claim in Ontario is a continuation of its already perfected security interest in Québec; GMAC can have no greater set of rights in Ontario than it would have in Québec, since it is only claiming a 'continuation' of its rights in Québec."

according to which the security interest originally attached.[19] In summary, purchase is an acquisition of an interest that can *potentially* destroy a prior property right that has to be qualified as a security interest. But the owner-creditor relationship continues to be governed by the original law proper to the security interest unless the security interest is *actually* displaced by a *bona fide* purchase.

All this indicates that the common law rule still applies in priority disputes between creditors of security interests that attached according to different prior *lege rei sitae*. This is justified for two reasons. First, the vested rights doctrine in private international law states that rights deriving from a security interest – including priority rights – should be governed by the law according to which the security interest was acquired.[20] Second, the current *lex situs* has no connection to a priority dispute between security interests that are otherwise solely governed by other *lege situs*.

### *b) Continued Perfection*

#### *aa) Basic Rule*

As the rules currently stands, the main impact of the *conflit mobile* is on perfection. While the *intra partes* effects of the security interest are commonly the same, each jurisdiction will have its own rules on perfection. Accordingly, the *PPSAs* contain specific rules on how to maintain perfection by registration after a change of *situs*.

Security interests in collateral brought *into* the jurisdiction continue to be perfected for a grace period. The grace period is the shortest of three alternatives. It is either sixty days after change of *situs*, fifteen days after the secured creditor is given notice of the relocation of the collateral, or the length of the period provided for by the jurisdiction in which the security interest *attached*.[21] If the security interest is never perfected after the lapse of the grace period, the security interest is deemed to have been unperfected even during the grace period. In other words, failure to perfect within the grace period removes perfection *ex tunc*. This was the result achieved under the old *PPSA (Ont)*.[22] It is generally accepted for all iterations of the *PPSA* now.[23]

---

[19] *Ibid* at paras 60–61.

[20] See Part V: § 17 D, "Vested Rights".

[21] *PPSA (Ont), supra* note 2, s 5(2).

[22] *Re Adair, supra* note 15; *Trans Canada Credit Corp Ltd v Bachand et al* (1980), 30 OR (2d) 405 (CA).

[23] *Re Kampman*, 2000 ABQB 705; *Associates Commercial Corp v Scotia Leasing Ltd* (1995), 24 BLR (2d) 310 (Ont Gen Div); *Royal Bank of Canada v Agricultural Credit Corp of Saskatchewan* (1994), 115 DLR (4th) 569 (Sask CA).

This leads to the question when collateral is deemed to have relocated for the purpose of this rule. Case law indicates that one should look at the reasonable understanding and expectations of third parties.[24] Goods that are typically immobile, such as household items, are deemed to have relocated if they cross the jurisdiction line.[25]

Mobile goods not subject to exceptions to the *lex situs* rule[26] must cross the border more than just temporarily in order for a change of *situs* to take place.[27] The mere fact that a privately-held car has crossed jurisdictional borders does not constitute a relocation;[28] the analysis changes if the car is brought into another province in the course of a move of residence.[29] This remains true even where the licence plate is not changed to the new province.[30]

*bb) The Good-Faith Purchaser Exception*

A buyer or lessee of the collateral without knowledge of the security interest who acquires her interest during the grace period will take the property free of the security interest.[31] This requires one to examine the concept of "knowledge" in the *PPSA* context.

The concept of "knowledge" in the *PPSA* follows an objective standard. Knowledge is determined by what the average person would have known, given the facts that were available to her.[32] This means that the creditor has to draw conclusions that a reasonable person would have drawn. This is general rule of the *PPSA* is also applicable outside its conflict-of-laws provisions. In a case that revolved around the question whether the secured creditor had had knowledge of a name change of the debtor – once the creditor has knowledge of the name change she is required to file a financing change statement[33] – the Ontario Superior Court of Justice imposed a higher standard of inquiry on the creditor. Where the creditor is also the debtor's landlord and can see the collateral displaying a new company name and receives invoices from the debtor displaying a new name, she can reasonably be expected to assume that the

[24] *Re Steed*, 2001 ABQB 157 at para 6; Cuming, Walsh & Wood, *Personal Property Security Law, supra* note 1 at 195.

[25] Cuming, Walsh & Wood, *Personal Property Security Law, supra* note 1 at 195.

[26] See Part V: § 18 A.II, "Lex Destinati".

[27] Cuming, Walsh & Wood, *Personal Property Security Law, supra* note 1 at 195–96.

[28] *Re Steed, supra* note 24 at para 7.

[29] *Ibid.*

[30] *Re Arseanau*, 2005 NSSC 26.

[31] *PPSA (Ont), supra* note 2, s 5(3).

[32] *Ibid*, s 69. On the *PPSA* concepts of knowledge and constructive notice see also Cuming, Walsh & Wood, *Personal Property Security Law, supra* note 1 at 55–63.

[33] *PPSA (Ont), supra* note 2, s 48(3).

debtor changed her legal name.[34] However, she is not required to draw too much inference from facts. The fact that bankruptcy proceedings were initiated against the debtor in another province does not mean that the creditor is assumed to have knowledge that the collateral has moved to that other province.[35]

Section 5(3) *PPSA (Ont)* differs from other provincial *PPSA*s[36] in one important respect. Other *PPSA*s do not require that the collateral be a consumer good in order for the buyer or lessee exception to apply, while the *PPSA (Ont)* requires just that. According to s 1(1) *PPSA (Ont),* the question whether property is a consumer good depends on the purpose for which it is used or acquired. Thus, a buyer who acquires collateral from the debtor in the course of a business would not be protected. However, if she then sells or leases the collateral to a consumer, the consumer will enjoy the protection of s 5(3) *PPSA (Ont)* by virtue of her being the successor of the party having the contract with the debtor.[37]

### *II. Lex Destinati*

There are cases where it is already foreseeable at the time of the conclusion of the security agreement that the collateral will be moved out of the jurisdiction in which it is currently located. In these cases the collateral is referred to as an "export good." According to the *PPSA,*[38] a security interest in export goods is not governed by the law of the current location, but rather by the law of its final destination, provided that the parties are aware of the export property of the collateral *at the time the security interest attaches,* and that the collateral is in fact relocated into that other jurisdiction within 30 days. The wording of the *PPSA* implies that the parties need to know not only that the collateral will be exported but also precisely what jurisdiction is the final destination. For instance, s 6(1) *PPSA (Ont)* provides:

"Section 6(1) *PPSA (Ont)*

(1) Subject to section 7, if the parties to a security agreement creating a security interest in goods in one jurisdiction understand at the time the security interest attaches that the goods will be kept in another jurisdiction and the goods are removed to *that other* jurisdiction, for purposes other than transportation through the other jurisdiction, within thirty days after the

---

[34] *HSBC Bank Canada v Expressway Concrete Supply Ltd* (1999), 1 BLR (3[d]) 147 (Ont Sup Ct J).

[35] *Searcy (Trustee of)* (1991), 61 BCLR (2[d]) 247 (SC).

[36] E.g. *Personal Property Security Act,* RSBC 1996, c 359, s 5(3).

[37] *General Motors Acceptance Corp of Canada v Town & Country Chrysler Ltd, supra* note 17 at para 61, affirmed by *General Motors Acceptance Corp of Canada v Town & Country Chrysler Ltd,* 2007 ONCA 904 (the appeal only dealt with the standard of review for the application of foreign law).

[38] See e.g. *PPSA (Ont), supra* note 2, s 6(1).

security interest attached, the validity, perfection and effect of perfection or non-perfection of the security interest shall be governed by the law of the other jurisdiction."[39]

The *PPSA* rule does not apply to any goods in transit not covered under the category of "export goods."[40]

The CCPPSL Working Group notes two problems with the *lex destinati* rule. First, it does not give a secured creditor the option to choose between the law of the current *situs* or the law of the destination. Second, similar to the rules on possessory and non-possessory security interests, it is overly wide in its temporal scope. The law of the original destination is used as an immutable connecting factor, meaning that perfection and priority will continue to be governed by the first *lex destinati* even after a further export away from the destination country.[41]

### *III. Lex Domicilii*

#### *1. Collateral Covered by the Lex Domicilii*

By virtue of s 7(1) *PPSA (Ont),* the *lex domicilii* applies to three basic types of collateral: security interests in mobile goods, non-possessory security interests in money and negotiable documents, and security interests in intangibles.[42] This list excludes investment property, which is the subject of its own rule. In Ontario and Saskatchewan, security interests in electronic chattel paper will be added to the list of collateral subject to the general *lex domicilii* rule once the respective amendments enter into force.[43]

##### *a) Mobile Goods*

The test for whether a good is a mobile good is done abstractly, not *in concreto.*[44] Goods that are used to transport goods or people are mobile goods. Furthermore, goods that are not moved as often, but that are used to complete certain tasks at varying locations are included as well (*e.g.* harvesting machinery).[45] The goods need to be either equipment, or inventory leased or held for

---

[39] *Ibid,* s 6(1) [Emphasis added].

[40] Cf. Cuming, Walsh & Wood, *Personal Property Security Law, supra* note 1 at 199–200.

[41] CCPPSL Working Group, *supra* note 6 at 129.

[42] *PPSA (Ont), supra* note 2, s 7(1).

[43] By virtue of the *Schedule 49, Ontario Budget Measures Act 2019, supra* note 13 and the *Personal Property Security Amendment Act, supra* note 7.

[44] See *Toronto-Dominion Bank v RNG Group Inc* (2002), 61 OR (3$^{d}$) 567 (Sup Ct J); *Trailmobile Canada Ltd v Kindersley Transport Ltd* (1986), 54 Sask R 1 (QB); *Westman Equipment Corporation v Royal Bank of Canada,* [1982] 5 WWR 475 (Man Co Ct); Cuming, Walsh & Wood, *Personal Property Security Law, supra* note 1 at 203.

[45] Cuming, Walsh & Wood, *Personal Property Security Law, supra* note 1 at 204.

lease by the debtor to others. These two conditions are alternatively, not cumulatively, applicable.[46]

If the collateral is a mobile good, the *lex domicilii* is not cumulatively applicable with the *lex situs;* rather, it is applied instead of it.[47]

*b) Non-Possessory Security Interests in Money and Negotiable Documents*

Unlike possessory security interests in money and negotiable documents,[48] non-possessory security interests in the same collateral are governed by the *lex domicilii.* This creates a potential conflict if there is a priority dispute between the creditors of a possessory and a non-possessory security interest respectively. Cuming, Walsh and Wood suggest that in these cases the law of the place where the possessory creditor took possession should govern the priority dispute rather than the law of the place where the collateral is *now* situated.[49] This confirms with this author's view on well-acquired rights.[50]

*c) Intangibles*

Pure intangibles have no evident physical *situs.* Thus, it is not self-evident that the *lex situs* should be applied to them. This leads to the question how the applicable law should be determined in cases of intangibles.[51]

In general choice-of-law rules, intangibles are dealt with by the *situs* rule. The *situs* of intangible is then determined by a close-connection test.[52] In the *PPSA* regime, the flexible close-connection test is replaced by a more rigid connecting factor, the domicile.

In the event of an assignment of an account, the approach found in modern statutory instruments is that the law applicable to the account itself should govern the rights the creditor has against the account debtor.[53] One possible option would thus be to apply the same law to validity, the perfection, the effect of perfection or non-perfection, and the priority of a security interest in an account.

---

[46] *Toronto-Dominion Bank v RNG Group Inc, supra* note 44 at 39; *Gimli Auto Ltd v BDO Dunwoody Ltd,* 1998 ABCA 154 at para 24; *Holland v Chrysler Credit Canada Ltd, supra* note 1; Cuming, Walsh & Wood, *Personal Property Security Law, supra* note 1 at 204.

[47] *Trailmobile Canada Ltd v Kindersley Transport Ltd, supra* note 44.

[48] See Part V: § 18 A.I.1, "Collateral Covered by the Lex Situs".

[49] Cuming, Walsh & Wood, *Personal Property Security Law, supra* note 1 at 205.

[50] See Part V: § 17 D, "Vested Rights".

[51] This is the explanation given by Cuming, Walsh & Wood, *Personal Property Security Law, supra* note 1 at 205–6.

[52] See *Tucowscom Co v Lojas Renner SA,* 2011 ONCA 548 at 69; *Canada v Folster* (1997), 148 DLR (4th) 314 at 319–20 (Can FCA); *Williams v Canada,* [1992] 1 SCR 877 at 891–93.

[53] Cuming, Walsh & Wood, *Personal Property Security Law, supra* note 1 at 205–6.

However, that would mean that for security interests held against a debtor with business activities in many different jurisdictions, many different laws would be applicable depending on the account collateralized. This would increase enforcement costs for the secured creditor, who would, in turn, charge a higher interest rate, and higher administration costs in insolvency, a cost born by all unsecured creditors. Such an approach would be inefficient. Consequently, the *PPSA* settled on the location, determined by the domicile, of the debtor of the security interest as the sole connecting factor.[54]

*2. Concept of Domicile*

In common law, the domicile of an economic enterprise is its principal place of business, a rule that has been codified in the *PPSA*.[55]

The *PPSAs* in their original form contain a cascade of subsidiary rules for determining the location of the debtor (location of business; if no place of business, then debtor's residence; if place of business in more than one jurisdiction, then location of the chief executive office). Problems in the application of this rule include determining whether a debtor operates a place of business, and a lack of definition of the term "chief executive officer." The official comment to *Article 9 UCC* defines chief executive office as "the place from which the debtor manages the main part of its business operations or other affairs. This is the place where persons dealing with the debtor would normally look for credit information."[56] There has also been case law addressing this issue in the United States;[57] however, it is still often problematic to ascertain when exactly a change of chief executive office took place.[58]

To address this problem, the *PPSA (Ont)* has introduced a new definition of the debtor's location. Saskatchewan will adopt similar rules.[59] In essence, the new Ontario rules distinguish between corporations (or limited partnerships) incorporated in Canada,[60] the US,[61] and elsewhere. For the first two categories, there is a strict head office determined by registration or constitution of the entity. In the latter case, an effective head quarter has to be determined by an

[54] *PPSA (Ont), supra* note 2, s 7(1).

[55] *Ibid,* s 7(3). See also Suzie Lanthier, *Les sûretés sur les valeurs mobilières: Le mouvement d'uniformisation d'origine américaine est-il transposable universellement?: Vers une approche québécoise à la question* (LL.M. Thesis, Université de Montréal, 2009) <http://hdl.handle.net/1866/3770> accessed 19 October 2017 at 109.

[56] Cited as in CCPPSL Working Group, *supra* note 6 at 82–83.

[57] See *Mellon Bank, NA v Metro Communications, Inc,* 945 F2$^{d}$ 635 at 642–43 (3$^{d}$ Cir 1991).

[58] See e.g. *Re Nemko, Inc,* 209 BR 590 (EDNY Bankr 1997) See CCPPSL Working Group, *supra* note 6 at 82–83.

[59] *Personal Property Security Amendment Act, supra* note 7.

[60] *PPSA (Ont), supra* note 2, ss 7(3)(c); (d).

[61] *Ibid,* ss 7(3)(e); (f).

assessment of facts.[62] All in all, the debtor-location rule uses a wide range of subsidiary and alternative connecting factors, which amount to 15 different ways of determining the location of the debtor. Of particular note is the option to determine the location of the debtor by reference to a choice-of-law clause in a partnership agreement where the debtor is an unlimited partnership.[63] In other words, the choice of law would not be obvious to the creditor. This violates the publicity policy of secured transactions law.[64] The choice-of-law option does not apply to limited partnerships or other corporations that come into existence by virtue of public registration. Saskatchewan will adopt a similar rule.[65]

*3. Scope of the Lex Domicilii*

In cases where the *lex domicilii* is applicable, the scope of the law is wider than the *lex situs.* The *lex domicilii* covers "validity, the perfection, the effect of perfection or non-perfection, and the priority" of a security interest.[66] Outside of Saskatchewan, the reference to priority is specific to the *lex domicilii.*

*PPSA* jurisdictions other than Ontario contain an exception to the scope of application of the *lex domicilii* in relation to the perfection requirement. They require a security interest to be registered in the respective jurisdiction if (1) the collateral is an account payable in that jurisdiction or a non-possessory security interest in chattel paper, a negotiable document of title, an instrument or money; (2) the collateral was located in that enacting jurisdiction at the time of attachment; and (3) the applicable law does not contain a registration system.[67] The CCPPSL Working Group recommends that requirement be scrapped; they argue it is not practically relevant, as all US states and Canadian jurisdictions have a registration system.[68]

For collateral which are subject to the *lex domicilii* rule in case of a non-possessory security, but the *lex situs* in case of a possessory security, the *PPSAs* use a different connecting factor to determine the law applicable to priority depending on whether the security interest is possessory or non-possessory (location of the debtor). This is problematic where the priority contest is one between a holder of a possessory and a non-possessory security.[69] To address the problem of a priority-contest between possessory and non-possessory security

---

[62] *Ibid,* s 7(3)(g).

[63] *Ibid,* s 7(3)(b).

[64] CCPPSL Working Group, *supra* note 6 at 90.

[65] Once the *Personal Property Security Amendment Act, supra* note 7, enters into force.

[66] *PPSA (Ont), supra* note 2, s 7(1).

[67] *PPSA (Sask), supra* note 7, s 7(4). However, in Saskatchewan, this requirement will be removed once the *Personal Property Security Amendment Act, supra* note 7 enters into force.

[68] CCPPSL Working Group, *supra* note 6 at 131–32.

[69] *Ibid* at 117–18.

interests, the CCPPSL Working Group recommends that priority always be governed by the *situs* of the collateral.[70]

*4. Change of Domicile*

Because the debtor's domicile determines the applicable secured transactions law, a change in domicile will result in a *conflit mobile.* Section 7(2) *PPSA (Ont)* contains a rule that is similar to the rule dealing with the change of *situs* and provides a grace period for re-perfection. However, the grace period rules differ depending on whether collateral *situs* or location of debtor are the connecting factor. In the former case, the grace period only applies when the collateral moves into the enacting jurisdiction. In the latter case, the forum state's grace period applies regardless of the rules of the debtor location jurisdiction.[71] Outside Ontario, a transfer of collateral to transferees outside the original jurisdiction will also trigger the re-registration requirements[72] Saskatchewan has made the proposal to delete the reregistration requirement. This is justified for two reasons. First, a creditor is not subject to a strict reregistration requirement where the debtor changes within the same jurisdiction. Second, failure to re-register the transferee as a new debtor does not unperfect the security interest, but only relegates below security interests correctly registered after the transfer (see e.g. s 51 *PPSA (Sask)*).[73]

The CCPPSL Working Group argues that the grace period of any given *PPSA* should only apply where the *conflit mobile* leads to the application of the respective *PPSA,* not where the *conflit mobile* ends the application of the respective *PPSA*. Thus, the rules in s 7 *PPSA (Ont)* for the debtor location rule and the rules relating to investment property in s 7.1 *PPSA (Ont)* should be accordingly amended to be unilateral grace period rules.[74]

*IV. Security Interests in Securities and the Conflict of Laws in the PPSA*

The *PPSAs* contain specific choice-of-law rules relating to "investment property." Investment property is defined as "a security, whether certificated or uncertificated, security entitlement, securities account, futures contract or futures account."[75] Section 7.1 *PPSA (Ont)* contains two subsections, s 7.1(1) *PPSA (Ont),* regarding validity of the security interest, and s 7.1(2) *PPSA (Ont),* regarding perfection, the effect of perfection or of non-perfection and priority. The *PPSA*s distinguish between attachment (immutable law determined at the

---

[70] *Ibid* at 118–19.

[71] CCPPSL Working Group, *supra* note 6 at 123.

[72] *Ibid* at 124.

[73] *Ibid* at 125.

[74] *Ibid* at 126.

[75] *PPSA (Ont), supra* note 2, s 1.

time of attachment) and perfection and priority (mutable current law). In addition, s 7.1(5) *PPSA (Ont)* contains certain exceptions regarding perfection.

The basic rule goes as follows: first, in case of a security interest in a certificated security, the law of the *situs* of the certificate is applicable; second, in case of an uncertificated security, the law of the issuer's jurisdiction governs the security interest – the issuer's jurisdiction is determined according to s 44(5) *Securities Transfer Act;* third, in case of a future's intermediary, the law of the location of the intermediary is applicable as well.

The difference between a future's intermediary and a security entitlement results from the fact that s 7.1(4) *PPSA (Ont)* contains its own definition of a future's intermediary. Yet the definition of the future intermediary's location and of the intermediary's location is exactly the same.

The exception mentioned at the beginning of this subsection relating to the general rules with regard to perfection is contained in s 7.1(5) *PPSA (Ont).* According to this subsection, the location of the debtor – determined in accordance with s 7(3) *PPSA (Ont)* – governs perfection where the security is to be registered or it is an uncertificated security – or more precisely: investment property granted by a broker or securities intermediary or future's contract or future's account granted by a future's intermediary – and the security interest's perfection depends on attachment.

## B. Conflict of Laws of Secured Transactions in Civil Law

Both *PPSA* and *UCC, Chapter 9* influenced the provisions in the *Code civil du Québec* on secured transactions and the conflict of laws.[76] Swiss law was a further influence.[77] The law of the *situs* of the immovable governs any property rights in immovable property. This is a function of art 3097 *CcQ*. Unlike movable property, there is no special provision dealing with security interests – as opposed to other property rights – in immovable property. Security in movables, on the other hand, is subject to a specific framework. art 3102 *CcQ* to art 3106 *CcQ* contain particular rules for movable security.

[76] See generally Michel Deschamps, "Les conflits de lois en droit des sûretés au Canada et aux Etats-Unis: Comparaison entre le Code civil du Québec, les PPSAs et le UCC" in: Norman A Saibil, ed, *Développements récents en droit bancaire* (Cowansville, Québec: Éditions Yvon Blais, 2003) 123 [Deschamps, "Conflits de lois"]; Janet Walker, *Halsbury's Laws of Canada: Conflict of Laws* (Toronto: LexisNexis Butterworths, 2006) HCF-235; Janet Walker & Jean-Gabriel Castel, *Canadian Conflict of Laws,* 6th edn (LexisNexis Butterworths, 2005), § 24.3 (e).

[77] Claude Emanuelli, *Droit international privé québécois,* 3rd edn (Montréal: Wilson & Lafleur, 2011) at 522.

### *I. Lex Situs*

#### *1. Principle*

The basic rule in art 3102 *CcQ* is similar to the *PPSA* rule. The law of the country in which the property is situated governs publications and effects of the security interest.

#### *2. Scope of the Lex Situs*

In *Schwartzman Distributing Inc c 9126–8359 Québec inc (Anthony Fruits & Vegetables Produce),*[78] the Court of Québec held that art 3102 *CcQ* is also applicable in cases of statutory security interests.

If a debtor creates a hypothec on all goods, the law of Québec does not govern collateral situated outside Québec or the security interest therein;[79] rather, the law of the other jurisdiction governs, unless one of the exception to the *lex situs* principle applies.

#### *3. Change of Situs*

##### *a) Conflit Mobile*

Just as in Common Law,[80] a change of *situs* entails a *conflit mobile,* but art 3102 *CcQ* avoids the *conflit mobile* for the creation and validity of a security interest by using an immutable connecting factor: these matters are always governed by the location of the property at the moment of creation. Perfection, in other words third-party effects, are governed by the law of the current *situs.*[81]

There is no specific rule regarding which law governs the effects of the security interest. Grenon argues that the effect of art 3102(2) *CcQ* is to limit the current *lex situs* to the effects of publication. The effects of the security right itself are instead governed by the same law that governs the validity of the security interest – that is the *lex situs* at the time of creation.[82]

##### *b) Continued Perfection*

Under art 3104 *CcQ,* a security interest continues it perfection if it is registered within a grace period. The grace period is the shortest of the following options:

---

[78] 2007 QCCQ 11288.

[79] Louis Payette, *Les sûretés réelles dans le Code civil du Québec,* 5th edn (Cowansville, Québec: Éditions Yvon Blais, 2015) at para 496.

[80] See Part V: § 18 A.I.3, "Change of Situs".

[81] CCPPSL Working Group, *supra* note 6 at 114.

[82] Emanuelli, *supra* note 77 at 522; Aline Grenon, "Major Differences between PPSA Legislation and Security over Movables in Quebec under the New Civil Code" (1996) 26 CBLJ 391 at 408 [Grenon, "Differences"].

30 days after relocation, 15 days after the secured creditor receives notice of the relocation, or the length of the grace period in the jurisdiction where the collateral was situated at the time of the *creation* of the security interest.

According to art 3104(3) *CcQ,* the buyer who buys the collateral in the ordinary course of the debtor's business will acquire the property free of any security interest. Any other exceptions do not apply.[83]

### *II. Lex Destinati*

Influenced by the UPPSA proposal,[84] the *CcQ* contains a more general rule on goods in transit (or, in Latin, *res in transitu*) rather than the narrower "export good" category employed in the *PPSA.* The *CcQ* contains two rules regarding goods in transit: a general rule for all property rights, and a second rule specifically for security interests. Comparing the wording of these rules with the wording of s 6(1) *PPSA (Ont)* discussed above,[85] one notices these differences.

"Article 3097 *CcQ*

(1) Real rights and their publication are governed by the law of the place where the property concerned is situated.

(2) However, real rights on property in transit are governed by the law of the country of their place of destination.

(1) Les droits réels ainsi que leur publicité sont régis par la loi du lieu de la situation du bien qui en fait l'objet.

(2) Cependant, les droits réels sur des biens en transit sont régis par la loi de l'État du lieu de leur destination."

"Article 3103 *CcQ*

Any movable that is not intended to remain in the country in which it is situated may be charged with a security according to the law of the country for which it is destined; the security may be published according to the law of that country, but publication has effect only if the property actually reaches the country within 30 days of the creation of the security.

Tout meuble qui n'est pas destiné à rester dans l'État où il se trouve peut être grevé d'une sûreté suivant la loi de l'État de sa destination; cette sûreté peut être publiée suivant la loi de cet État, mais la publicité n'a d'effet que si le bien y parvient effectivement dans les 30 jours de la constitution de la sûreté."

### *III. Lex Domicilii*

#### *1. Collateral Covered*

Article 3105 *CcQ* contains a choice-of-law rule leading to the application of the *lex domicilii* for certain collateral. The article applies to corporeal movables

[83] Cuming, Walsh & Wood, *Personal Property Security Law, supra* note 1 at 197.

[84] Uniform Law Conference of Canada, ed, *Proceedings of the 38th Annual Meeting* (Ottawa: Uniform Law Conference of Canada, 1971) at 181–217.

[85] See Part V: § 18 A.II, "Lex Destinati".

ordinarily used in more than one country or "incorporeal movables." Security interests in these movables are governed by the law of the country where the grantor was domiciled at the time of creation of the security.

According to art 3105(3) *CcQ,* the article does not apply to security interests in negotiable instruments or a "security published by the holding of the title exercised by the creditor." This exclusion leads to two questions.

First: Does the exception include negotiable instruments ordinarily used in more than one jurisdiction? I argue that the exception is meant to clarify that security interests in negotiable instruments are in fact security interests on corporeal property, and thus do not fall under the scope of the exception second alternative of art 3105(1) *CcQ*. Thus, security interests on negotiable instruments ordinarily used in more than one jurisdiction should still fall within the scope of art 3105 *CcQ*.

Second: Is a hypothec established by non-physical delivery of the hypothecated obligation excluded from the scope of art 3105 *CcQ?* This question goes back to the problems discussed in the context of the decision in *Caisse populaire Desjardins de Val-Brillant c Blouin.*[86] While the *Assemblée nationale* abolished most cases of possessory hypothecs with non-physical delivery, it is still possible to effect delivery of a life insurance claim.[87] Hypothecs in securities are subject to their own proper choice-of-law rules.[88]

### 2. *Change of Domicile*

The article contains not only a rule of private international law, but also a rule for intertemporal conflicts. According to art 3105(1) *CcQ, validity* of the security interest is governed by the domicile of the debtor at the time of creation, while publication and effects are governed by the current domicile. Because a change in domicile thus entails a change in applicable law, art 3106 *CcQ* mirrors the rule for the change of *situs.*

## *IV. Hypothecs in Securities and the Conflict of Laws in the Code civil*

Together with the new law on hypothecation of securities, a new choice-of-law framework for such security interests was introduced. It is contained in art 3108.1 *CcQ*-art 3108.8 *CcQ*. The law applicable on validity, publication, and effects of publication of a security interest on securities is determined by art 3108.8 *CcQ*. The rule contains subsidiarily applicable connecting factors.

---

[86] [2003] 1 SCR 666.

[87] See Part III: § 14 B.V.2.b), "Delivery of an Obligation".

[88] See Part V: § 18 B.IV, "Hypothecs in Securities and the Conflict of Laws in the Code civil".

In case of certificated securities, the law of the *situs* of the certificate is applicable.[89] In case of uncertificated securities, art 3108.8(2) *CcQ* refers to art 3108.2 *CcQ*. Article 3108.2 *CcQ,* in turn, governs the contractual obligations of the issuer of the security. It renders the law under which the issuer is constituted as applicable. Article 3108.2 *CcQ* allows a choice-of-law for the contractual obligation. Since the reference in art 3108.8(2) *CcQ* is meant to refer to the actual law applicable ("the law governing the matters listed in article 3108.2"), the combination of art 3108.8(2) *CcQ* and art 3108.2 *CcQ* allows for choice of law regarding the law applicable on the uncertificated security. Furthermore, because art 3108.8 *CcQ* refers not to art 3108.2 *CcQ,* but rather to the law governing the matters contained in art 3108.2 *CcQ,* art 3108.3 *CcQ* (the law governing sovereign securities – *i.e.* securities issued by a sovereign state – is determined by the issuer), and art 3108.4 *CcQ* (the law governing sovereign securities issued by the province of Québec and securities issued by issuers constituted under Québec law) are referenced as well.

Finally, in case of a security interest on security entitlements, the law governing security entitlements[90] is applicable. The law chosen in the entitlement contract in turn governs security entitlements. If no law is chosen, either the law of the location of the establishment maintaining the securities account, or, if no establishment is expressly specified, the law of the country in which the establishment identified in an account statement as the establishment serving the entitlement holder's account, or finally the law of the country in which the decision-making centre of the securities intermediary is located is applicable.[91]

According to the intertemporal rule of art 3108.8 *CcQ,* in case of the determination of the law applicable on the validity of a security interest on securities, the point in time taken into account is the time of the creation of the security. Regarding the publication and effects of publication, the law is variable in time. This mirrors the above-mentioned general rule for security interests and could result in *conflits mobiles.*

### *V. Hypothecs in Monetary Claims*

Together with the introduction of a specific perfection regime for hypothecs in monetary claims, the *CcQ* now also contains a special choice-of-law regime for these types of security interests in art 3106.1 *CcQ*.[92] This rule applies where the security interest is a pledge over a monetary claim relating to a credit balance of a financial account or an amount of money transferred to secure the

---

[89] *Code civil du Québec,* SQ 1991, c 64 [*CcQ*], art 3108.8(1).

[90] *Ibid,* art 3108.7.

[91] *Ibid,* art 3108.7.

[92] An analyis of these rule can be found in Sterling H Dietze, "My Cash and I: Cash Collateral Is Finally King in Quebec" (2016) 31:2 Bank & Fin L Rev 349 at 363–64.

performance of an obligation towards the creditor, a specific choice-of-law rule applies.

According to this rule, debtor and creditor can enter into a choice-of-law agreement specific to the security interest. Absent such an agreement, the security interest is governed by the law chosen for the underlying arrangement. If no such law is chosen, alternative connecting factors apply depending on whether the collateralized claim is the credit balance of a financial account or relates to an amount of money transferred to secure the performance of an obligation.

Where the monetary claim is a credit balance, the next default connecting factor is (1) the location of "the establishment expressly mentioned in the act governing the financial account as being the establishment where the account is maintained is located"; (2) absent an expressly mentioned establishment, the next connecting factor is the location of the "establishment identified in an account statement as the establishment serving the account holder's account"; the subsidiary default connecting factor is the location of "the decision-making centre of the person maintaining the account is located". Where the collateralized monetary claim is money transferred, the default connecting factor is the domicile of the money-holder, if it is a natural person, or the location of the decision-making centre of the money-holder.

## C. Analysis

An analysis of the choice-of-law rules reveals that there are a few areas in which the co-ordination between the legal systems within Canada is not quite as smooth as one would hope for in a system of efficient bijuralism. This analysis proceeds in two subsections. First, we look at some problems regarding the co-ordination of the choice-of-law rules. Second, we look at problems arising at the level of applying the applicable law from the jurisdiction determined according to the choice-of-law rules.

### *I. Co-ordination at the Choice-of-Law Level*

#### *1. Different Treatment of Goods in Transit*

The *CcQ* treats goods in transit differently than the *PPSAs* do. The differences between the *CcQ* and the *PPSA* concept are listed here. First, art 3103 *CcQ* does not make reference to the common understanding of the parties. Second, s 6(1) *PPSA (Ont)* literally only applies to cases where the goods are exported from one jurisdiction directly to the next one, whereas the collateral can cross several jurisdictions in case of art 3103 *CcQ* and yet the law of the destination will apply all the way through. Third, s 6(1) *PPSA (Ont)* requires that the collateral be moved to the other jurisdiction within 30 days in order for it to be *governed* by the *lex destinati.* Under the *CcQ,* the 30-days requirement only applies for the *publication* in the other country to take effect. Fourth, art 3103 *CcQ* provides for the security to be comprehensively governed by the law of the destination. Section 6 *PPSA (Ont),* on the other hand, does not include any statement about how priority between competing security interests is governed.

### 2. The Application of Lex Originis as a Recognition of Vested Rights

Civil Law and Common Law statutes differ with regard to the scope of the *lex originis.* While the Common Law position is understood to be that the *lex originis* governs effects of the security interest, the Civil Law position is less clear. Apart from the systematic argument that art 3102(2) *CcQ* can be read to be an exhaustive list of the scope of the current *lex situs,* a further argument for giving a broad scope to the *lex originis* is the desire to minimize the occurrence of *conflits mobiles.*[93] By giving the *lex originis* a wide scope, a change of *situs* will not result in a change of law. I submit that a further argument for the application of the *lex originis* is the recognition of vested rights. By applying the *lex originis,* Québec will recognize property rights acquired by the secured creditor in another Canadian jurisdiction. The ensuing predictability with regards to the contents and stability of property rights is also efficient from an economic standpoint. At the same time, a *numerus clausus*-based exercise control of the property rights[94] protects third-party interests.

### 3. The Different Meanings of Domicile

The debtor-location rules reveal a lack of bijural coordination at a general and a specific level. First, there is a disparity regarding the meaning of "domicile" between Common Law and Civil Law provinces. In most Common Law provinces, the domicile of a legal person is its principal place of business. This difference could have had a big impact because several Canadian financial institutions have their legal head offices in Montréal, Québec, but their principal places of business in Toronto, Ontario. This includes the Royal Bank of Canada and the Bank of Montreal. In case of securities held indirectly through security entitlements the use of domicile as connecting factor would have led to a divergence between the jurisdictions regarding the applicable law. The Québec legislature has avoided this result by abandoning domicile as a connecting factor for indirect security entitlements and instead using an approach that is similar to the "principal place of business" approach used in the Common Law provinces.

[93] Emanuelli, *supra* note 77 at 522.

[94] See Part V: § 17 C.I.2, "Recognition and Transposition of Property Rights".

Second, the new Ontario rules are not a full harmonization of the *PPSA (Ont)* with *Article 9 UCC,* nor with the *CcQ.*[95] They only correspond with s 9.307 *Article 9 UCC* if the debtor is an individual or registered organization under American law. In other cases, the "chief executive office" approach is maintained. The rules on US corprorations in s 7(3)(f) *PPSA (Ont)* were not updated in line with amendments to *Article 9 UCC,* defeating the purpose of horizontal co-ordination.[96]

The *CcQ* uses domicile as the connecting factor and refers to the registered head office, including in cases where the corporation is constituted under foreign laws. The use of choice-of-law clauses for determining the location of partnerships is unique to the *PPSA*. In relation to partnerships, the rules are also not co-ordinated with US or Québec law. While this will always occur where different choice-of-law systems use different connecting factor, this is particularly accute where the connecting factor is highly volatile, such as the one for partnerships that are subject to a more or less arbitrary choice by the partners.[97] Another issue concerns the use of the registered location as connecting factor when registration is the legal act that constitutes the debtor.[98] In Anglo-Canadian law, limited partnerships are created by registration, but unlimited partnerships are formed by agreement between the partners, with registration merely a compulsory requirement post-constitution. In Québec law, the position as to when partnerships form is unclear.[99] Section 7(3)(d) *PPSA (Ont)* are also not well-harmonized with federal law; as does not cover the entire range of entitities that can exist under federal law, such as corporations created by statute or, imaginably, order-in-council or royal warrant.[100]

### *4. The Tendency Towards Special Rules*

Both *CcQ* and the *PPSAs,* contain overly specific choice-of-law rules for certain classes of security interests. As a matter of policy, the choice-of-law rules for security interest in bank accounts in art 3106.1 *CcQ* are not very convincing because because they favour this type of creditor above everybody else. While other choice-of-law rules are based on publicity, the parties in an account pledge can choose the applicable law, or the applicable law might be the function of the account agreement not visible to third parties. The same criticism applies to the specific rules relating to the location of the debtor in the

---

[95] CCPPSL Working Group, *supra* note 6 at 86–87.

[96] CCPPSL Working Group, *supra* note 6 at 99–100.

[97] Cf. *ibid* at 90–91.

[98] *PPSA (Ont), supra* note 2, s 7(3)(c) in the case of partnerships, s 7(3)(d) in the case of corporations.

[99] CCPPSL Working Group, *supra* note 6 at 93.

[100] *Ibid* at 95.

*PPSAs.*[101] Because these special categories for which particular rules have been promulgated are not co-ordinated between the different legal systems, this throws a spanner in the works of horizontally co-ordinated bijuralism.

### *II. Co-ordination when Applying the Substantive Law*

#### *1. The Exclusion of Renvoi*

The *CcQ* includes a general exclusion of the doctrine of *renvoi* in art 3080 *CcQ*. Grenon argues that this means that if property is situated in a Common Law province but it is understood that it will be moved to Québec a Québec court would not apply Québec law; she submits that the law of Québec should apply by virtue of art 3082 *CcQ,* the patently closer connection rule.[102] I fail to see how this case is not already covered by art 3102 *CcQ,*which allows parties to create a security interest governed by the *lex destinatii* in collateral intended for export.

There is, however, a remaining difference. As I have shown above, the goods in transit rule differs between Common Law and Civil Law.[103] Furthermore, whereas Ontario excludes the possibility of a *renvoi,* other Common Law provinces permit it.[104] Unlike the *CcQ,* the rigid conflict-of-laws provisions of the *PPSA (Ont)* do not include a Savignian[105] "closest connection" exception. So even though both Québec and Ontario would apply the *lex destinatii* for goods intended for export to Ontario, an Ontario court would not apply the law of Ontario if the goods are currently situated in Québec and the requirements for the goods in transit exception are met under Québec law, but not Ontarian law. The Ontarian court could not derogate from this reference to Québec law. While the same is true for any other Canadian jurisdiction other than Québec, the effect of that rigidity is multiplied by the fact that the other jurisdictions have enacted similar *PPSAs* whereas the *CcQ* security regime differs significantly.

#### *2. Quasi-Security Devices*

The Court in *General Motors Acceptance Corp of Canada v Town & Country Chrysler Ltd* included foreign methods of security interest creation other than

---

[101] At least in Ontario and Saskatchewan, see Part V: § 18 A.IV, "Security Interests in Securities and the Conflict of Laws in the PPSA".

[102] Grenon, "Differences", *supra* note 82 at 409.

[103] See Part V: § 18 C.I.1, "Different Treatment of Goods in Transit".

[104] See Deschamps, "Conflits de lois", *supra* note 76 at 137–38; Michel Deschamps, "Les sûretés sur des titres détenus auprès d'un intermédiaire en droit canadien" (2005) 10 Unif L Rev 189 at 196.

[105] Friedrich C von Savigny, *System des heutigen römischen Rechts* (Berlin: Veit & Comp, 1849), vol 8 at 28.

attachment. That case dealt with collateral originally situated in Québec. The collateral was the subject of a conditional-sales agreement between seller and purchaser. The seller then assigned its right to GMAC. It is not explicitly mentioned in the judgment whether the seller also transferred its ownership in the collateral to GMAC as well. Since the right to revendicate is an outflow of the ownership itself and as such not assignable on its own,[106] it is safe to assume that GMAC also acquired ownership in the collateral. Subsequently, the collateral moved to Ontario and GMAC sought a motion to repossess the property. The Court held that the conditional-sales agreement is an attachment of a security interest for the purpose of s 5(3) *PPSA (Ont).*

In Québec, the conflict-of-laws provisions intentionally use a different terminology – "security" as opposed to "hypothec" – to signify that these provisions do not only cover the substantive hypothec under domestic Québec law but also quasi-security interests that are based on a title transaction.[107] The alternative suggestion treats a quasi-security device as a non-security. In this case, it would be subject to the general international property law rule. This could be supported on the basis that the starting point of characterization is the substantive law of the forum state;[108] the *CcQ* maintains a distinction between title-based quasi-security devices and hypothecs.[109]

Treating quasi-security devices as non-security transactions in property would mean that quasi-security devices would be subject to the general *lex situs* rule rather than the specialized international secured transactions law. Furthermore, we should recall that the *PPSAs* still allow a security interest to be created in the form of a quasi-security device. This does not have any impact on the conditions and effects of the security interest as long as the property remains within a *PPSA* jurisdiction and the forum is a *PPSA* jurisdiction. But if – from the perspective of Québec law – the general *lex situs* suddenly determines the applicable law for security interests in the form of a quasi-security device and Québec is the forum state, this could lead to situations in which the formal appearance of the security interests suddenly determines the applicable law – namely, when the *lex situs* differs from the law determined by the application of Québec international secured transaction law.

This result should be avoided in the interest of co-ordination between Québec Civil Law and the Canadian Common Law jurisdictions. Apart from the choice of the word "security" rather than "hypothec" – which could also be explained on the basis that the international secured transactions law in the

---

[106] See Part II: § 4 H.IV, "Assignability of the Right to Vindicate".

[107] Sandra Morin, "Le statut de la réserve de propriété en matière mobilière au Québec et en Ontario" (2008) 49:2 C de D 237 at 257; Payette, *supra* note 79 at paras 370–71.

[108] Deschamps, "Conflits de lois", *supra* note 76 at 143; Emanuelli, *supra* note 77 at 411–12; *CcQ, supra* note 89, art 3078. On the problem of characterization and alternative approaches see Ernst Rabel, "Das Problem der Qualifikation" (1931) 5 RabelsZ 241.

[109] Cf. Deschamps, "Conflits de lois", *supra* note 76 at 143–44.

*CcQ* is meant to encompass other forms of security, not just the hypothec identical to Québec law[110] – a broad interpretation of the word "security" that includes quasi-security devices is also defensible on the basis of the *lex fori* characterization approach.

While the *CcQ* maintains a distinction between quasi-security devices and hypothec, it does subject quasi-security devices to certain rules of the hypothecary framework; notably, quasi-security devices are only opposable against third parties if the conditions of opposability of the hypothec are met. The *CcQ* thus recognizes that quasi-securities are functionally similar to hypothecs. This should be maintained in private international law.

One could argue that there is a fundamental difference between quasi-securities and long-term leases; after all, they are treated differently in bankruptcy.[111] But I would submit that for the purpose of private international law, long-term leases should still be treated as security interests. First, the bankruptcy argument is not very forceful because Parliament's decision to maintain a distinction between long-term leases and other quasi-security interests under Québec law should have little bearing on the interpretation of provincial law. Second, international secured transactions law includes rules on publicity and it is here that Québec law – and the *PPSA* – decided to treat long-term leases similar to security interests in substantive law.

### *3. Conflits Mobiles*

Both Common Law and Civil Law contain rules dealing with *conflits mobiles* resulting from of a change of connecting factor. In each legal system, changes of either *situs* or domicile are treated alike and the creditor is given a grace period for re-perfection. The main difference is that the longest period is 60 days in Common Law and 30 days in Civil Law. In principle, the grace period is an easy way to allow security interests to survive a *conflit mobile.* However, the rules are not perfect. The two main means of perfection or opposability of a security interest are publication and possession. Given the fact that each province has adopted an electronic registry, it would be possible to prevent most *conflits mobiles* by adding a substantive rule to the *PPSAs* and the *CcQ* to the effect that the requirements for publication are met where the security interest is published in the registry of any Canadian jurisdiction, or by creating a uniform Canadian registry. In the former case, it would be beneficial if the provinces and territories at least provided a platform that would allow a meta-search so that third parties do not have to search the registries of eleven provinces and three territories.

---

[110] Aline Grenon, "Les sûretés mobilières en Ontario et le droit international privé" (1998) 2:1 RCLF 117 at 123.

[111] See Part IV: § 16 B.III.2, "Civil Law Quasi-Security Devices in Insolvency".

# § 19 International Proprietary Restitution Law

This chapter deals with the law applicable on proprietary restitution. As discussed above, there are two kinds of constructive trusts, the "institutional" and the "remedial" constructive trust. The former is the kind of trust recognized in England and Canada, the latter is the constructive trust reacting to "unjust enrichment" and is arguably known in Canada – but I have submitted that in Canadian law, proprietary restitution can be seen as a vindication of a pre-existing property right – and the United States. The question whether both kinds of trust are an expression of an underlying principle and whether the constructive trust is a vindication of property rights has implications for the characterization of the constructive trust in the conflict of laws as well.

In this chapter's first section I discuss the characterization of proprietary restitution. I come to the conclusion that proprietary restitution should *always* be properly qualified as being part of property law for choice-of-law purposes. The second section deals with the determination of the *situs* of property. The third section looks at the *conflit mobile* as applied to proprietary restitution, particularly where property moves from a Common Law jurisdiction to a Civil Law jurisdiction.

## A. Characterization of Proprietary Restitution

In this section, I look at the characterization of proprietary restitution. The characterization of proprietary restitution – and the question of applicable law – needs to be distinguished from the question of recognition of proprietary restitution already pronounced by a foreign court. As regards the latter question, a Canadian Common Law jurisdiction will recognize and enforce a constructive trust order pronounced by a foreign court where the property is found in this Canadian jurisdiction.[1] Regarding the scope of the choice-of-law rule, it is important to make one distinction. As explained above, unlike Civilian unjustified enrichment law, unjust enrichment law in the Common Law provinces

[1] *Bienstock v Adenyo Inc*, 2014 ONSC 4997, affirmed by *Bienstock v Adenyo Inc,* 2015 ONCA 310.

does not operate with a subsidiarity principle.[2] Instead of unjust enrichment being subsididary to a proprietary restitution claim, the cause of action is the same whether or not the claim is personal or proprietary. This means however that situations in which a proprietary restitution claim is made can also raise personal claims. This chapter is only concerned with determining the law applicable to the proprietary claim.

A preliminary question regarding choice of law for proprietary restitution is whether there can be a choice of law for equitable property rights at all. Historically, courts of equity would always apply the *lex fori* to equitable claims.[3] However, as Wass demonstrates, this is no longer the case in relation to equitable property rights.[4] Three cases demonstrate this principle. In *Macmillan Inc v Bishopsgate Investment Trust Plc (No 3),*[5] Millet J found that an equitable claim that is based on the claimant's persistent proprietary interest, one cannot escape the choice-of-process by applying the *lex fori* rather than the *lex causae.*[6] In *Martin v Secretary of State for Work and Pensions,*[7] the Court found that cases in which English law had been applied to determine the existence of a trust over property situated abroad,[8] this was not because equitable claims are always governed by the *lex fori,* but rather because the application of the specific choice-of-law rule lead to the application of English law.[9] In *Schumacher v Summergrove Estates Ltd,*[10] the Court found that a trust claim in relation to property in Ireland is governed by Irish law, even when the action is heard in a New Zealand court. Notably, the Court found that this was an application of the at-issue characterization approach taken by the Court of Appeal in *Macmillan Inc v Bishopsgate Investment Trust Plc (No 3).*[11]

---

[2] See Part II: § 9 A.I, "Québec Law of Unjustified Enrichment" and Part II: § 10 B, "Explaining Proprietary Restitution".

[3] See for example the case of *Penn v Lord Baltimore* (1750), 1 Ves Sen 444 (Engl and W Ch) relating to a boundary dispute in the British colonies, *i.e.* outside of the regular jurisdiction of English law. Regarding the historical position see also RW White, "Equitable Obligations in Private International Law: The Choice of Law" (1986) 11:1 Sydney L Rev 92 and Jack Wass, "The Court's in Personam Jurisdiction in Cases Involving Foreign Land" (2014) 63:1 ICLQ 103 at 107–9. See further Campbell McLachlan, "International Litigation and the Reworking of the Conflict of Laws" (2004) 120 LQR 580 at 601.

[4] Wass, preceding note at 109–10.

[5] (1993), [1995] 1 WLR 978 (Ch D).

[6] *Ibid* at 988–89.

[7] [2009] EWCA Civ 1289 [*Martin*].

[8] Case C-294/92 *Webb v Webb* [1994] QB 696 and *Lightning v Lightning Electrical Contractors Ltd,* [1998] NPC 71 (CA Civ).

[9] *Martin, supra* note 7 at para 29, Mummery LJ.

[10] [2014] 3 NZLR 599 (CA) [*Schumacher*].

[11] *Macmillan Inc v Bishopsgate Investment Trust Plc (No 3)* (1995), [1996] WLR 387 (CA Civ) [*Macmillan*]. See *Schumacher,* preceding note at para 32, Miller J.

With regard to the question of characterization Common Law takes a *lex fori* approach to characterization, as does Québec Civil Law.[12] The "enlightened *lex fori*" approach means that the categories of domestic substantive law are the starting point for characterization of legal issues, but they are modified insofar as it is necessary for conflict-of-laws purposes. The necessity to modify domestic categories will arise because legal categories are not identical throughout the world.[13] A characterization scheme solely based on domestic categories will thus run into the problem that it might be incompatible with foreign law. The connection might not render any law applicable or might result in the determination of a law that does not actually contain any rules for the fact pattern at hand.

There are three possibilities according to which proprietary restitution could be characterized: international trust law principles, international unjust enrichment principles, or international property law principles.

### *I. Trusts Approach*

#### *1. Hague Trusts Convention*

##### *a) Scope of the Hague Trusts Convention*

Article 3 *Hague Trusts Convention* specifies that *Hague Trusts Convention*[14] applies only to trusts created voluntarily and evidenced in writing. According to Hayton, the *Hague Trusts Convention* applies to resulting trusts, but not constructive trusts.[15] Other authors criticize that constructive trusts are to be excluded while resulting trusts are included.[16] Their argument is that this exclusion cannot be explained by the fact that one trust is voluntary whereas the other is not because there exist both involuntary resulting trusts, and constructive trusts that are the result of the intention of the parties.

---

[12] *Code civil du Québec,* SQ 1991, c 64, art 3078.

[13] Lawrence Collins, Baron Collins of Mapesbury & Jonathan Harris, eds, *Dicey, Morris and Collins on the Conflict of Laws,* 15th edn (London: Sweet & Maxwell, 2012), vol 1 at paras 2.8–2.14; Stephen GA Pitel & Nicholas S Rafferty, *Conflict of Laws* (Toronto: Irwin Law, 2010) at 215–17; Janet Walker & Jean-Gabriel Castel, *Canadian Conflict of Laws,* 6th edn (LexisNexis Butterworths, 2005) § 3.1. See also Kurt Lipstein, *Private International Law: Characterization,* ed by Konrad Zweigert, Ulrich Drobnig, and Kurt Lipstein (International Encyclopedia of Comparative Law, III-5, Tübingen: Mohr Siebeck, 1999) at 11–19.

[14] *Convention of 1 July 1985 on the Law Applicable to Trusts and on their Recognition* [*Hague Trusts Convention*].

[15] David Hayton, "The Hague Convention on the Law Applicable to Trusts and on Their Recognition" (1987) 36 ICLQ 260 at 263–64.

[16] See Jonathan Harris, *The Hague Trusts Convention: Scope, Application and Preliminary Issues* (Oxford: Hart, 2002) at 125–26; Maurizio Lupoi, *Trusts: A Comparative Study* (New York: Cambridge University Press, 2000) at 342.

Harris argues that to consider a presumptive resulting trust to be a voluntary creation would mean that one has to accept such a broad definition of "voluntary that it would be hard to maintain the exclusion of a great number of constructive trusts from the definition of voluntary trust."[17] This wide scope is exactly the result Lupoi wants to achieve. He argues that there are constructive trusts that come into existence because the settlor expressed her will at some point, but this expression was not sufficient to establish an express trust.[18]

Hayton's analysis is based on the assumption that the constructive trust is a personal remedy only, and has no value whatsoever if the debtor becomes bankrupt. Hayton also notes that the preparatory report[19] on the *Hague Trusts Convention* specifically excluded judicial trusts and thus constructive trusts that are awarded as a remedy. Hayton relates this limitation to art 2 *Hague Trusts Convention* and art 3 *Hague Trusts Convention,* which require that the trust be a legal relationships created by a person and that it be created voluntarily.[20]

*b) Recognition of Court-Declared Trusts*

Article 20 *Hague Trusts Convention* allows signatory countries to extend the scope of the *Hague Trusts Convention* to include judicially-declared trusts. Both the United Kingdom and Canada have extended the scope for their respective jurisdictions.[21] In the case of the United Kingdom, this conforms to the United Kingdom's responsibility to recognize any judicial decision by a competent jurisdiction under the *Brussels I Regulation.*[22]

Neither the United Kingdom nor Canada have made a declaration pursuant to art 21 *Hague Trusts Convention.* The *Hague Trusts Convention* is thus applicable regarding all foreign jurisdictions without a reciprocity requirement. Therefore, the United Kingdom recognizes judicial trusts declared in any EU member state. However, this extension pre-supposes that a foreign court already recognizes a constructive trust.

*c) The Connection*

According to art 6 *Hague Trusts Convention,* the law chosen by the settlor is the applicable trust law. This provision would obviously be inapplicable in

---

[17] Harris, preceding note at 126–27.

[18] Lupoi, *supra* note 16 at 342–45.

[19] Alfred E von Overbeck, "Rapport explicatif" in: Conférence de la Haye de droit international prive, ed, *Actes et documents de la 14ème session* ('s-Gravenshage: Bureau permanent de la Conférence, 1980) 370.

[20] Hayton, *supra* note 15 at 264.

[21] *Hague Trusts Convention, supra* note 14, Declarations, Reservations.

[22] *Regulation (EU) No 1215/2012 of the European Parliament and of the Council of 12 December 2012 on Jurisdiction and the Recognition and Enforcement of Judgments in Civil and Commercial Matters* [2012] OJ L 351/1.

most cases of proprietary restitution because there will be no settlor. The Convention's main connection would fail and a determination of the applicable law would have to rely on the closest connection rule of art 7 *Hague Trusts Convention.*

### *2. Common Law International Trust Law*

If one were to advance a trust approach to the characterization of constructive trusts, the common law rules – including the *Code civil du Québec* rules – on trusts[23] would still have a role to play. In those provinces where the *Hague Trusts Convention* is not applicable – or where it is not applicable in interprovincial cases – common law remains applicable.[24] Furthermore, even in the *Hague Trusts Convention* provinces, common law would have to determine the law applicable to constructive trusts if one were to conclude that constructive trusts are not included in the scope of the *Hague Trusts Convention.*[25]

## *II. Unjust Enrichment Approach*

### *1. Common Law*

Another analysis of proprietary restitution in the conflict of laws refers to the legal event creating the trust. If the trust reacts to unjust enrichment, then the law applicable on unjust enrichment should govern the remedial trust. Such an approach requires two premises to be true. First, that remedies are not governed by the *lex fori.* Second, that the legal event to which proprietary restitution is reacting is indeed unjust enrichment. Walker submits that a constructive trust is currently characterized as remedial rather than institutional for purposes of domestic law, but even if that were true, it would not mean that the characterization in substantive law needs to be followed for private international law purposes.[26] However, Walker wants to apply the unjust enrichment analysis as well.[27] Dicey, Morris and Collins took a similar approach before the entry into

---

[23] See Part V: § 17 E, "International Trust Law".

[24] For details see Walker & Castel, *supra* note 13 § 28.5.

[25] See Part V: § 17 E.II, "The Hague Trusts Convention".

[26] Walker & Castel, *supra* note 13 § 28.7 (b).

[27] *Ibid* § 28.7 (b). See also Kurt Lipstein, *Private International Law: Trusts,* ed by Konrad Zweigert, Ulrich Drobnig, and Kurt Lipstein (International Encyclopedia of Comparative Law, III-23, Tübingen: Mohr Siebeck, 1994) at para 23.3.

force of the *Rome II Regulation.*[28] There is some authority to that effect.[29] The unjust enrichment approach is adopted by Civilian doctrine as well.[30] This approach is influenced by a merely remedial look at the constructive trust, which is transferred to choice-of-law questions.[31]

### *2. Rome II Regulation*

In the European Union, the *Rome II Regulation* determines the law applicable to non-contractual obligations –including the law on unjust enrichment. The question to what extent constructive trusts are included within the scope of this regulation is relevant there as well. Given the fact that the sub-section of the regulation mentioning trusts (*i.e.* art 1(e) *Rome II Regulation*), draws on the *Hague Trusts Convention,*[32] a reference to the discussion in the context of *Rome II Regulation* may provide guidance.

According to art 1(e) *Rome II Regulation* "non-contractual obligations arising out of the relations between the settlors, trustees and beneficiaries of a trust created voluntarily" are excluded from the scope of the *Rome II Regulation.* The use of the word "settlor" in English suggests that the exclusion is only applicable in case of a formal trust because there would not necessarily be a settlor in cases of the constructive trust.

Dickinson argues that the exclusion does not reside on the formal criterion whether a trust arises by operation of law. Rather, the criterion should be whether the existence of the trust is the result of a voluntary act of the "settlor."[33] Thus, "common intention constructive trusts" (as they are discussed extensively in *Stack v Dowden*[34]) should be included in art 1(e) *Rome II Regulation,* and consequently excluded from the scope of the *Rome II Regulation* regulation. Based on that argument, the resulting trust is excluded from the scope of the *Rome II Regulation* as well.[35]

---

[28] *Regulation (EC) No 864/2007 of the European Parliament and of the Council of 11 July 2007 on the Law Applicable to Non-Contractual Obligations* [2007] OJ L177/40· See "Restitution" in: Lawrence Collins, ed, *Dicey, Morris and Collins on the Conflict of Laws,* 14th ed (London: Sweet & Maxwell, 2006) 1863 at para 34.44. See also George Panagopoulos, *Restitution in Private International Law* (Oxford: Hart, 2000) at 66–81.

[29] *Christopher v Zimmermann,* 2000 BCCA 532; *Barclay's Bank PLC v Inc Inc*, 1999 ABQB 110 at para 50, Coutu J.

[30] Claude Emanuelli, *Droit international privé québécois,* 3rd edn (Montréal: Wilson & Lafleur, 2011) at 529.

[31] See Pitel & Rafferty, *supra* note 13 at 289–90.

[32] Andrew Dickinson, *The Rome II Regulation: The Law Applicable to Non-Contractual Obligations* (Oxford: Oxford University Press, 2008) at para 3.184.

[33] *Ibid* at para 3.188.

[34] *Stack v Dowden,* [2007] UKHL 17, [2007] 2 AC 432, [2007] 2 WLR 831.

[35] Dickinson, *supra* note 32 at para 3.190.

On the other hand, Dickinson argues that constructive trusts that are "remedial constructive trusts" should be considered to fall under the scope of the *Rome II Regulation.*[36] Dickinson here refers to remedial constructive trusts currently not recognized in English law. However, Dickinson does not explain how far the constructive trust is supposed to fall within the scope of the *Rome II Regulation,* namely whether only the personal effects of the trust fall within the scope of the regulation or proprietary effects as well.[37] Dicey, Morris and Collins has adopted a similar approach.[38]

If the European Court of Justice applied its distinction between equitable rights and legal rights which it made as regards jurisdiction,[39] a legal action for trover or conversion[40] would be considered a property right, but their equitable counterpart – the constructive trust as a vindication of property rights – would be characterized as arising from the law of obligations. Given that in *OBG Ltd v Allan,*[41] the House of Lords held that an action for conversion is not available for intangible property – and thus an equitable vindication by means of a constructive trust is the only means available – this result is not very consistent with good bijuralism.

### *III. Property Law Approach*

#### *1. Distinguishing Personal and Proprietary Effects of Constructive Trusts*

The recent case *Johnston v Adam*[42] reiterates a very important distinction regarding the constructive trust – namely that it includes both personal and proprietary effects. While a court may have no jurisdiction regarding the latter, it may have jurisdiction regarding the former.[43] This is a distinction first recognized in *Catania v Giannattasio.*[44] In the former case, however, Justice Annis furthermore indicated that the property law effects of the recognition of a constructive trust are governed by the *situs* of the property.[45] It is important, however, to note that *Johnston v Adam* concerned immovable property. Because of

---

36 *Ibid* at para 3.192.

37 See Part V: § 19 A.III.1, "Distinguishing Personal and Proprietary Effects of Constructive Trusts".

38 Lawrence Collins, Baron Collins of Mapesbury & Jonathan Harris, eds, *Dicey, Morris and Collins on the Conflict of Laws,* 15th edn (London: Sweet & Maxwell, 2012), vol 2 at paras 30.80–30.87 [Collins, Baron Collins of Mapesbury & Harris, *Dicey, Morris & Collins*].

39 *Webb v Webb, supra* note 8. But see Pippa J Rogerson, "Equity, Rights in Rem and the Brussels Convention" (1994) 53 CLJ 462.

40 See *Fouldes v Willoughby* (1841), 151 ER 1153 (Ct Exch); *Cooper v Chitty* (1756), 97 ER 166 (KB).

41 (2007), [2008] 1 AC 1 (HL).

42 2011 ONSC 3808.

43 *Ibid* at paras 21–24, Annis J.

44 (1999), 174 DLR (4th) 170 (Ont CA).

45 *Johnston v Adam, supra* note 42 at para 25, Annis J.

the strong role of comity in international property law on immovables,[46] the reasoning cannot be simply applied to movable property.

A similar case was the basis of the decision in *Precious Metal Capital Corp v Smith.*[47] In that case, the applicant sought a declaration for a constructive trust interest in either real property or shares. Since the declaration of the constructive trust in the shares was subsidiary to the interest in the land and the Court recognized the interest in land, it did not have to decide whether the *in personam/ in rem* distinction between the personal and proprietary effects of the constructive trust first drawn in *Catania v Giannattasio* applies to personal property as well.

The separation of personal rights and property rights and their respective transfer can be explained by general conflict-of-laws principles. It is a well-established rule in common law that, regarding personal property; the law of the *situs* will govern the property rights regarding the property. Therefore, this law governs the conveyance as well, regardless of what law governs the causal obligation upon which the conveyance is based.[48]

In the realm of conflict of laws, there is thus a principle of separation between the statute that governs the causal personal obligations and the statute governing the conveyance of property.[49] If the latter statute considers the conveyance independent of the causal obligation, then cause and conveyance are abstract. Furthermore, the statute of conveyance can invalidate the conveyance where the rules on conveyance of the jurisdiction from which the statute of obligation is taken would not yield this result.

### 2. *Proprietary Characterization*

In *Macmillan,*[50] the plaintiff alleged its interest was superior to several banks' interest in certain shares and that the banks held the shares in constructive trust for the plaintiff because they had acquired them in breach of a trust agreement between the plaintiff and one defendant. On the question of the existence of a

---

[46] See Part V: § 17 B.I.1, "Principle".

[47] [2008] OJ No 1236 (Sup Ct J).

[48] See generally Collins, Baron Collins of Mapesbury & Harris, *Dicey, Morris & Collins, supra* note 38 at para 24.6; Pitel & Rafferty, *supra* note 13 at 78; Walker & Castel, *supra* note 13 § 24.1.

[49] See principally Gian C Venturini, *Private International Law: Property,* ed by Konrad Zweigert, Ulrich Drobnig, and Kurt Lipstein (International Encyclopedia of Comparative Law, III-21, Tübingen: Mohr Siebeck, 1976).

[50] *Supra* note 11.

constructive trust, either the *lex loci actus* or the *lex situs* could have been applied. The Court held that characterization should not be done on a per-legal-rule basis but that the issue in question needs to be characterized.[51]

Lord Justice Staughton identified three stages of determining the applicable law. First, the nature of the issue must be determined. This is what is called "characterization." Second, the conflict rule containing the connecting factor must be identified. Third, applying the connecting factor, the applicable law is to be identified.[52] Lord Justice Staughton embraced the approach of characterizing according to the content and purpose of the conflict-of-laws rule of the *lex fori,*[53] as did Auld LJ.[54]

Lord Justice Auld emphasised that characterization should not be constricted by the categories of the domestic substantive law alone.[55] He identified the issue at hand as being either one of a "receipt-based restitutionary claim or about property" and acknowledged that the former category may be alien to other legal systems.[56] Lord Justice Auld then characterized the constructive trust issue as one of property law in order to achieve international harmony.[57] Lord Justice Aldous concurred.[58]

Burrows indicates that proprietary restitution should be characterized as pertaining to international property law because of its functional equivalency to vindication.[59]

### *IV. Analysis*

The trust approach to the characterization of proprietary restitution should be rejected for a variety of reasons. One important reason is that proprietary restitution can take the form of a constructive trust, or an equitable lien. I have even argued that a number of resulting trust cases can be explained by an unjust enrichment account and they are thus substantially similar to other forms of proprietary restitution. A trust approach would treat all these legal replies arising from the same legal event differently. A trust approach could not be applied to equitable liens.

---

51 *Ibid* at 589. See also the analysis by Adrian Briggs, "Restitution Meets the Conflict of Laws" (1995) 3 RLR 94 and John Stevens, "Restitution or Property?: Priority and Title to Shares in the Conflict of Laws" (1996) 59:5 Modern L Rev 741.

52 *Macmillan, supra* note 11 at 589.

53 *Ibid* at 589–90.

54 *Ibid* at 604.

55 *Ibid* at 604.

56 *Ibid* at 604.

57 *Ibid* at 604.

58 *Ibid* at 615.

59 Andrew S Burrows, *The Law of Restitution,* 3rd edn (Oxford: Oxford University Press, 2010) at 720.

Because of the structure of international trust law, a trust characterization also requires there to be a certain degree of a meeting of minds between settlor and trustee. Yet this approach is unable to provide a clear guidance delimiting restitutionary trusts susceptible to a trust characterization and trusts which cannot be characterized as pertaining to international trust law because they do not meet the minimum threshold of a meeting of minds.

I also reject the unjust enrichment approach. At the level of substantive law, the Common Law has never developed a meaningful distinction between property law and the law of obligations.[60] At the same time, a clear delimitation of the two is required at the stage of conflict of laws. An unjust enrichment approach to proprietary restitution seems to be implicitly based on the fact that proprietary restitution can be described as responding to unjust enrichment in domestic law. But I submit that this is not a sufficient condition for an unjust enrichment approach to characterization.

I have described both Civil Law vindication[61] and Civil Law unjustified enrichment.[62] The conditions of unjustified enrichment are also present when the claimant brings a revendication action, and were it not for the subsidiarity principle, the vindication claim could easily be conceptualized as an unjustified enrichment claim. This is particularly true with regard to equity.

The unjust enrichment approach in conflict of laws is also not necessarily supported by case law. In support of her standpoint, Walker uses the case of *Frey v Heintzl Estate,*[63] in which the Supreme Court of British Columbia applied domestic law to a resulting and constructive trust.[64] In this case, the plaintiff claimed a constructive trust in real property in British Columbia that formed part of the deceased's estate, who had died domiciled in Germany. But the outcome of the case can be explained by a different analysis than an unjust enrichment one.

The Court stated that it has jurisdiction over real property in British Columbia.[65] As is common in Common Law jurisdictions, in certain cases, jurisdiction entails the application of the *lex fori.* This includes succession cases.[66]

---

[60] Pattarapas Tudsri, "Characterization of Proprietary Restitution in the Conflict of Laws" (2013) 44:2 Ottawa L Rev 261 at 264, referring to Andrew S Burrows, "Proprietary Restitution: Unmasking Unjust Enrichment" (2001) 117 LQR 412 at 412.

[61] See Part II: § 4 H, "Vindication of Property Rights".

[62] See Part II: § 9 A.I, "Québec Law of Unjustified Enrichment".

[63] [1988] BCJ No 223 (BC SC).

[64] Walker & Castel, *supra* note 13 § 28.7 (b), note 3.

[65] *Frey v Heintzl Estate, supra* note 63 at para 36.

[66] See Heinz Sonnenberger in: *Münchener Kommentar zum Bürgerlichen Gesetzbuch, vol 10, Internationales Privatrecht I:* Europäisches Kollisionsrecht, Einführungsgesetz zum Bürgerlichen Gesetzbuche (Art. 1–24), ed by Kurt Rebmann; Franz-Jürgen Säcker; and Roland Rixecker, 5th ed (Munich: CH Beck, 2010) Art 4 EGBGB at paras 42–55.

While the court only mentions its jurisdiction, it is in fact applying the substantive laws of British Columbia on succession in real property. In fact, as pointed out by the defendant,[67] if the Court had applied German law, there would have been no separate legal entity (the estate) that could have been sued. Instead, all property would have immediately passed to the heirs.[68] Furthermore, British Columbia law is applicable as the law of the *lex situs*. The trust can thus very well be considered to be a kind of vindication of property rights.

Within the European Union, an unjust enrichment would bring a number of proprietary restitution claims within the scope of the *Rome II Regulation*. While it is already doubtful whether this was legislative intent, this would be particularly worrisome as it would allow the parties to make a choice of law pursuant to art 14 *Rome II Regulation*.[69] Allowing parties to contract about property rights would undermine the *numerus clausus* and security of property rights.

Additionally, as is pointed out in *Macmillan*, the constructive trust is not a universal concept. If one were to take an unjust enrichment approach, Common Law jurisdictions might be alone in phrasing specific restitution in terms of unjust enrichment, while Civil Law jurisdictions might easily frame an action as one of a vindication of property rights and thus apply the *lex situs* on the claim. The outcome of a case would then depend on the forum, which is something that should be avoided because it is conducive to forum shopping. As well, in Civil Law countries, particularly the ones following a principle of separation and abstraction, the conveyance itself may be invalid. Thus, if one law is applied to the facts resulting in unjust enrichment and the *lex situs* to the passing of title, the conveyor/creditor may have an action for unjust enrichment, a resulting or constructive trust, and a *rei vindicatio* according to the *lex situs* available to her.

It is important to note that the property rights approach is not only sustainable for unjust enrichment by subtraction claims. Tudsri argues that proprietary restitution for wrongdoing can also be characterized as proprietary claims for conflict-of-laws purposes because, by employing a proper trust analysis, it is arguable that at the moment of wrongdoing, equity intervenes to create a property right.[70] This resembles my approach of viewing proprietary restitution claims as unjust enrichment claims based on the denial of an inchoate property right that was created for the benefit of the claimant.[71] Tudsri's argument is

---

[67] *Frey v Heintzl Estate, supra* note 63 at para 30.

[68] *Bürgerliches Gesetzbuch,* s 1922.

[69] Adeline Chong, "Choice of Law for Unjust Enrichment: Restitution and the Rome II Regulation" (2008) 57:4 ICLQ 863 at 895.

[70] Tudsri, *supra* note 60 at 284.

[71] See Part II: § 10 F, "Analysis of Proprietary Restitution".

thus of general validity for all cases of proprietary restitution, not just restitution for wrongdoing. Whether or not that inchoate property right is given effect in the form of a fully-vested equitable property right should be governed by the *lex situs* because of its third-party effects.[72] I agree with Tudsri that the question whether an inchoate property right arising in equity is given full third-party effect is not an ancillary question,[73] but the main question.[74] Whether or not the claimant can assert a property right is essential because of the third-party effect of fully-fledged property rights, particularly in insolvency.

From a conceptual standpoint, it is worth highlighting that there is a parallelism in the purpose of proprietary restitution in Common Law and vindication of property rights in Civil Law. As argued, equitable ownership is the entitlement to value, proprietary restitution is the vindication of this entitlement.[75] The problem from a Civilian law perspective is that Civil Law does not draw this distinction between value and possession entitlement. It is instead based on the notion that value will follow possession, and thus vindication of the monolithic legal right is the go-to proprietary remedy. But importantly, Civil Law ownership is not only concerned with possession but protects value as well.[76] It thus promotes a horizontal coordination of Civil Law and Common Law to characterize vindication claims and proprietary restitution claims equally.

## B. *Situs* of the Property

The proprietary characterization of unjust enrichment constructive trusts combined with the fact that the beneficiary, properly analysed, has no right in the trust property but a right in the right, or – provided one does not follow Smith[77] and conceptualizes the common law trust as a patrimony – a right in the patrimony, raises the question how to locate this right.

One view is to apply the *lex domicilii* of the trustee. This is the approach favoured by McFarlane, who views equitable rights as distinct from (legal) property rights.[78] In support of his approach, he points to *Re Anchor Line (Henderson Bros) Ltd.*[79] In that case, an English company granted a floating charge

[72] Tudsri, *supra* note 60 at 287.

[73] See Panagopoulos, *supra* note 28 at 79–81.

[74] Tudsri, *supra* note 60 at 288.

[75] See Part II: § 10 F, "Analysis of Proprietary Restitution".

[76] See Part II: § 4 D, "Right and Object of Right".

[77] Lionel D Smith, "Trust and Patrimony" (2009) 28 ETPJ 332. See Part II: § 8 E, "Theory of Equitable Property Rights".

[78] Ben McFarlane & Robert Stevens, "The Nature of Equitable Property" (2010) 4:1 J Equ 1 at 95–97. See also See Part II: § 8 E, "Theory of Equitable Property Rights".

[79] [1937] Ch 483 (Ch D).

– an equitable interest[80] – in land and in movable property in Scotland. Under Scots law at that time, this form of security did not exist. The company went into liquidation and funds representing the Scottish assets subsequently came into the liquidator's hands. Those funds were payable to B in accordance with the floating charge. It made no difference that the floating charge was invalid according to the *lex situs* of the jurisdiction where the movables were situated.[81] The problem with this approach is that the decisions were based on an understanding of equitable rights being foremost consensual undertakings and thus personal obligations, a classification even McFarlane rejects. A fortiori, this approach, which is already doubtful in relation to consensual equitable interests, does not seem to be transferable to non-consensual restitutionary constructive trusts.

I submit that the *situs* for the purpose of the application of the *lex situs* rule on proprietary restitution should be the *situs* of the property that is subject to the trust or equitable lien. Proprietary restitution creates equitable property rights that might be conceptually different from legal property rights, but their third-party effects are broadly similar. They allow the beneficiary to follow the property into a third party's hands and to exclude it from bankruptcy proceedings. In the interest of economic efficiency and publicity of property rights, they should thus be treated identically to legal property rights. This includes the determination of the *situs*.

## C. Proprietary Restitution and Change of *Situs*

For the reasons outlined above,[82] I am of the opinion that a constructive trust should be characterized as part of property law as far as private international law is concerned. If proprietary restitution needs to be recognized by a court of a jurisdiction in which proprietary restitution is not known, it will be recognized and might be claimed for the first time if the property is situated in a jurisdiction where the constructive trust is part of the law.

However, a situation could arise where the equitable property arose when the property was situated in a different jurisdiction, and the property was then transferred to a jurisdiction where proprietary restitution is not known. This is a *conflit mobile.*[83]

---

[80] See Part III: § 13 A, "Nature of the PPSA Security Interest".

[81] *Re Anchor Line (Henderson Bros) Ltd, supra* note 79, referring to *British South Africa Co v Companhia de Moçambique,* [1893] AC 602 (HL). Cf. *Webb v Webb, supra* note 8.

[82] See Part V: § 19 A, "Characterization of Proprietary Restitution".

[83] See Part V: § 17 C, "The Conflit Mobile".

## *I. Recognition of Proprietary Restitution in Civil Law*

### *1. Type A Conflit Mobile*

I have argued that the restitutionary constructive trust really consists of two steps: the creation of the causative inchoate property right (the event, or the first necessary condition with unjust enrichment being the second necessary conditions) and its recognition and vindication by means of a constructive trust (the response). Recognition of the restitutionary constructive trust arising in one jurisdiction (jurisdiction A) by another jurisdiction (jurisdiction B) would thus entail two steps. First, the event needs to be recognized. Second, the response needs to be recognized as well.

The recognition of the causative event is straightforward where it is legal title. It is arguably more complex where the constructive trust arises between spouses. Here, the constructive trust can be explained by realist reasoning as an expression of underlying values such as the equality of partners in a relationship, or by economic reasons, such as it being the result the parties would have bargained for if they had bargained about property rights arising from their relationship. This raises the question whether the recognition of the event is as straightforward in these cases. A realist, revolutionary approach to the conflict of laws might ask whether the values expressed by jurisdiction A should be given effect in jurisdiction B. But we find that the conflict of laws with regard to movable property is generally not concerned with events, only responses where the property right has already been acquired. This is particularly true where the international property law follows neither a principle of strong transposition, nor one of weak transposition, but only provides for an exercise control of foreign-acquired vested property rights.[84] This is the case in all Canadian jurisdictions, be they Common Law jurisdictions[85] or Civil Law jurisdictions.[86] The question regarding the recognition of equitable property rights in a type A *conflit mobile*[87] thus becomes one of the exercise of equitable property rights in Québec.

I have come to the conclusion that the *numerus clausus* principle in Québec operates in a liberal sense. An innominate property right is not void as a matter of principle, only if it violates principles of Québec property law.[88] Thus, it could be said that proprietary restitution does not violate the *numerus clausus* operating in Québec if it conforms to principles already found in Québec property law. I have analysed this in the section on the recognition of Common Law

[84] See Part V: § 17 C.I.2, "Recognition and Transposition of Property Rights".

[85] See Part V: § 17 C.II, "Common Law and the Conflit Mobile".

[86] See Part V: § 17 C.III, "Civil Law and the Conflit Mobile".

[87] See Part V: § 17 C.I.1, "Scenarios of Conflits Mobiles".

[88] See Part II: § 4 E, "Numerus Clausus in Civil Law".

trusts in Québec. Québec property law can accommodate Common Law equitable property rights.[89]

*2. Type B Conflit Mobile*

A type B *conflit mobile* arises where the creation of the property right is complete from the point of view of the original *lex situs* and incomplete from the point of view of the new *lex situs.*[90] Based on my account of proprietary restitution, such a scenario can arise where the claimant has an inchoate property right, but the retention of the property by the defendant is not yet unjust. In cases that involve defective transfers, retention of the inchoate property right and its maturation into a full equitable property right usually coincide. I address an exception below.[91] But, for example, in intimate relationship cases, this occurs where the relationship has not yet failed and thus provides a juristic reason for the defendant's interference with the claimant's inchoate property right. If the new *lex situs* is the law of Québec, the inchoate property right cannot mature into a full property right as a result of proprietary restitution because this form of restitution is unknown in Québec law. The inchoate property right itself is not something that Québec law can recognize or give any effect to because it is inchoate. This does not leave the claimant without a remedy, as she could avail herself of any of the regular remedies available to her under Québec law. This includes a personal unjustified enrichment claim.

*3. Type C Conflit Mobile*

In a type C *conflit mobile,* the acquisition of the property right is complete from the point of view of the old *lex situs,* but not from the point of view of the new *lex situs.*[92] A type C *conflit mobile* cannot arise where the property is moved from a Common Law jurisdiction to a Civil Law jurisdiction because Civil Law does not provide for equitable property rights. It cannot consider its creation to be incomplete. Rather, this type of *conflit mobile* can be solely phrased in terms of vested rights: Should the Civil Law jurisdiction give effect to the equitable property right fully acquired in a Common Law jurisdiction? My answer to this is given in the section on type A *conflits mobiles.* A type C *conflit mobile* is unlikely to arise if the only jurisdictions involved are Canadian Common Law jurisdictions because their law of proprietary restitution is for all purposes identical.

---

[89] See Part V: § 17 E.III.2, "Recognition of Trusts".
[90] See Part V: § 17 C.I.1, "Scenarios of Conflits Mobiles".
[91] See Part V: § 19 C.III, "Rescission".
[92] See Part V: § 17 C.I.1, "Scenarios of Conflits Mobiles".

### 4. Type D Conflit Mobile

In a type D *conflit mobile,* the acquisition of the property right is incomplete from the point of view of original and new *lex situs.*[93] From the point of view of the Civil Law jurisdiction, the situation is the same as the type B *conflit mobile* because Civil Law has no proprietary restitution. The situation is more complex where the property passes from one Common Law jurisdiction to another. There is little authority in Common Law on type D *conflits mobiles.* Two decisions from the German-English Mixed Claims Tribunal – a special tribunal set up after World War I to deal with commercial claims arising from the War – were based on the ratio that where a purchase of property fails under the law of one jurisdiction, the whole process has to be repeated in the new jurisdiction.[94] Applying the ratio of theses cases to proprietary restitution would mean that where the inchoate property right arose in one Common Law jurisdiction and the property moved into another Common Law jurisdiction, the inchoate property right could not be taken into account. This seems to be an undesirable result, particularly because each Canadian Common Law jurisdiction has the same substantive law as regards the creation of these inchoate property rights in intimate relationships. I thus submit that the Tribunal decisions should not be considered to be good authority. Instead, the fact that an inchoate property right already existed and thus certain steps necessary for proprietary restitution already occurred before the property moved jurisdictions should be taken into account when the new forum decides whether an equitable property right arises.

## II. Limits on Proprietary Restitution and the Conflit Mobile

The treatment of proprietary restitution also supports my submission that any limits on the availability of the constructive trust in bankruptcy should be a function of federal insolvency law, not provincial property law. This avoids a problem that is comparable to a *dépeçage.* The term *dépeçage* is used when the sets of substantive rules governing a factual situation are determined by different choice-of-law rules and the substantive rules are those of different jurisdictions; the combination of these different rules leads to a result that neither set

[93] See Part V: § 17 C.I.1, "Scenarios of Conflits Mobiles".

[94] See *Büsse v British Manufacturing Stationery Co* (1927), 7 Recueil des décisions des tribunaux arbitraux mixtes 345; George A Zaphiriou, *The Transfer of Chattels in Private International Law* (London: Athlone Press, University of London, 1956) at 170–72 provides a summary of *E Luttger and Co v. Ormninston and Glass Ltd and Busse v British Manufacturing Stationery Co.* See also Ernst Rabel & Ludwig Raiser, "Eine Entscheidung des deutsch-englischen gemischten Schiedsgerichts über den Versendungskauf" (1929) 3 RabelsZ 62.

of laws would achieve if it had governed the entire fact pattern.[95] The *conflit mobile* can result in a *dépeçage* in time, with different laws applying to different stages of a transaction. If any limits on the availability of proprietary restitution were part of the property law, they would apply where the property always remains in one jurisdiction. The beneficiary of proprietary restitution would thus not enjoy a priority in bankruptcy that is undesirable from a legal-policy standpoint. If the property had been in Québec the entire time, proprietary restitution would not have occurred. In certain cases, the claimant would have retained ownership and could have availed herself of proprietary actions, but these cases are already well-known to bankruptcy law. Where the property moves from Common Law to Civil Law, though, any limit that is characterized as pertaining to the law of proprietary restitution would not be attached to the property if its conditions were not yet met. This result could be avoided if federal Parliament addresses the impact of proprietary restitutions in the federal *Bankruptcy and Insolvency Act.*[96]

### *III. Rescission*

The characterization of proprietary restitution as pertaining to international property law raises a difficulty in cases of voidable transfers. The rescission of a contract will create a resulting trust where title to property does not automatically re-vest.[97] These resulting trusts are susceptible to an unjust enrichment analysis in substantive law because the transferee now holds title to property without juristic reason. She is unjustly enriched. This problem arises where the *situs* of the property changes between transfer of title and rescission. Rescission is a type B *conflit mobile.* The choice-of-law rules must react to a rescission that applies retroactively. I submit that the original *lex situs* — the *situs* at the time of the transfer — should govern. Where a transferor retroactively rescinds a transfer of property that took place in Ontario at a time when the item of property was already in Québec, but the effect of Ontario recession is to consider that the transfer never took place, the power to rescind and its consequences should be considered to be a right attached to the property. This right can then be exercised insofar as it does not contradict the *numerus clausus* at the *situs.* In other words, the Ontario power to rescind stays attached and can

---

[95] See generally the following: Emanuelli, *supra* note 30 at 400; Erik Jayme, "Betrachtungen zur dépeçage im internationalen Privatrecht" in: Hans-Joachim Musielak & Klaus Schurig, eds, *Festschrift für Gerhard Kegel zum 75. Geburtstag* (Stuttgart: Kohlhammer, 1987) 253; Paul Lagarde, "Le dépeçage dans le droit international privé des contrats" (1975) 11 Riv dir int priv proc 649; Willis LM Reese, "Dépeçage: A Common Phenomenon in Choice of Law" (1973) 73:1 Col L Rev 58. On Canadian Common Law jurisdictions regarding contracts see Walker & Castel, *supra* note 13 § 31.4 (a).

[96] RSC 1985, c B-3.

[97] Tudsri, *supra* note 60 at 294.

be exercised insofar as it conforms to the *CcQ* rules governing rescission. The same applies vice versa where the transfer took place in Québec and the item moves to Ontario. In that case, the rescission of the contract should re-vest ownership in the transferor. Because Civil Law ownership is unknown in Common Law, the transferor's rights are exercisable as if she were the beneficiary of a resulting trust while the property is in Ontario.

# Conclusion

The analysis of the interaction of different property law systems within the framework of Canadian bijuralism has shown that the retention of Civil Law plays an important role in the cultural identity of Québecers and in the integration of Québec in the Canadian confederation.

Within the Canadian confederation, three legal systems interact: provincial Common Law, Québec Civil Law, and federal law. This interaction takes place on two levels. First, there is a horizontal interaction between each provincial system of law, which becomes particularly notable where Civil Law interacts with Common Law. Second, there is a vertical interaction between provincial law and federal law. At the level of vertical interaction, the vertical division of power between the Dominion and the provinces means that the federal law / provincial law relationship is one of autonomy and complementarity. Federal law is autonomous because federal law defines its own legal concepts insofar as they are concepts pertaining to a matter of federal jurisdiction. Provincial law is complementary because federal law relies on provincial law to provide a general private law framework. This includes a reliance on provincial property law.

In the economic analysis of the law, the legal origin theory claims that Civil Law is inherently inferior to Common Law. This theory is not borne out by an analysis of the substantive rules of movable property law. Economic theory posits that property rights should be secure and clearly defined. This includes a *numerus clausus* of property rights. At the level of substantive law, Civil Law property rights in movable property are more secure than their Common Law counterparts because the framework for vindication of property is more straightforward.

Unlike Common Law, Civil Law has a clearly defined notion of ownership of movable property. Ownership is an institutional right. It is the most complete right in property in relation to everybody. Common Law, on the other hand, operates with a continuous spectrum of interests. The validity of these interests can differ in an infinite number of inter-personal relationships. In Civil Law, on the other hand, a property right is *a priori* good against everybody; occasionally, a limited exception is made. Where a property right – be it ownership, a hypothec, or another right – is not public, it is only valid *inter partes*. Therefore, everybody can say with certainty what relationship they have to an item of property.

Because Common Law has no vindication action and and because the personal property torts of Common Law protect possession rather than title or even "ownership," the unjust enrichment principle has a more important role to play in Common Law than unjustified enrichment does in Civil Law. The specific recovery of an item of property is also expressed in terms of an unjust enrichment action in Common Law, but it is an unjust enrichment action that results in proprietary, rather than personal, restitution. The importance of this taxonomy should not be over-emphasized, however. Functionally, proprietary restitution plays a role that vindication – including vindication of incorporeal property – plays in Civil Law. The fact that proprietary restitution, which includes a right in the proceeds, confers a wider right than Civil Law vindication, which usually does not entail an element of real subrogation, can be seen as a function of the different notion of property. Furthermore, even vindication in Civil Law can be understood to be a remedy for unjust enrichment, if the term is widely defined: "unjust enrichment" is possession without right.

Civil Law property fares better when it comes to avoidance of priority circles. These can arise in Common Law because its secured transactions law has not been fully integrated into its property law. This creates an uncertain relationship between proprietary restitution, which takes the form of an equitable property right, and security interests.

At the level of secured transactions law, Civil Law can integrate a modern secured transactions law framework into the general Civil Law property law. The Québec legislature has decided to maintain certain title-based transactions. This is due to the importance of ownership in Civil Law. Where the retention of title-based transactions for the purposes of provincial property law renders undesirable results in insolvency, federal Parliament can intervene under the *Bankruptcy and Insolvency Act.*[1] Parliament has chosen to do so with regard to quasi-security devices, but has not done so with regard to long-term leases. Common Law and Civil Law subject long-term leases of certain movable property to a publicity requirement, but only Common Law has decided to combine this publicity requirement with a rule that renders the lessor's title ineffective in insolvency. This is not uncontroversial because it is the opposite of functionalism. Parliament has decided that rendering unregistered long-term leases ineffective is not required in insolvency, but federal law respects the choice of Common Law jurisdictions in this matter.

The examples of the *Bank Act* security interest and Crown privileges have shown that it is difficult to create a uniform security interest that is valid in two

[1] RSC 1985, c B-3.

different legal systems without properly integrating it into the property law framework of each system.

On the level of conflict of laws, the co-existence of two different legal systems within one confederation requires that the greatest possible respect be given to property rights acquired in one of the legal systems. This is also economically efficient as long as the compatibility of the foreign property rights with the domestic legal system is guaranteed. By allowing parties to rely on their acquired rights after a change of *situs,* the conflict-of-laws rules increases security of property rights.

One acquired right parties can rely on is the equitable property right arising from proprietary restitution. I submit that proprietary restitution should be characterized as pertaining to property law. Whether or not the reader shares my submission on the substantive law level, this characterization should at least be done on the level of conflict of laws. Neither a trust law characterization nor an unjust enrichment characterization can provide a desirable framework for the determination of the applicable law. The property law characterization is necessary because proprietary restitution affects third parties' relationships with items of property. Québec Civil Law is well equipped to recognize proprietary restitution and give effect to it where the item of property has moved into Québec.

In conclusion, I submit that the example of Canadian bijuralism shows that the retention of two legal systems can be efficient. Neither legal system is inherently more efficient than the other, and both legal systems can interact on the first level of bijuralism. Where one legal system has an undesirable impact on the availability of property in bankruptcy, federal bankruptcy law can intervene by taking a functional approach.

# Bibliography

*Please note that cross-references in footnotes refer to the first citation within the chapter in which the cross-reference appears.*


Acemoglu, Daron and Simon Johnson, "Unbundling Institutions" (2005) 113:5 J Pol Econ 949–95

Acemoglu, Daron; Simon Johnson; and James A Robinson, "The Colonial Origins of Comparative Development: An Empirical Investigation" (2001) 91:5 Am Econ Rev 1369–401

Adler, Barry E, "Limits on Politics in Competitive Credit Markets" (1994) 80:8 Va L Rev 1879–85

Aghion, Philippe and Patrick Bolton, "An Incomplete Contracts Approach to Financial Contracting" (1992) 59:3 Rev Econ St 473–94

Akerlof, George A, "The Market for Lemons: Quality Uncertainty and the Market Mechanism" (1970) 84:3 Quart J Econ 488–500

Akkermans, Bram and Eveline Ramaekers, "Free Movement of Goods and Property Law" (2013) 19:2 Eur LJ 237–66

Allard, France, "The Supreme Court of Canada and Its Impact on the Expression of Bijuralism" in: Canada, Department of Justice, ed, *The Harmonization of Federal Legislation with the Civil Law of the Province of Quebec and Canadian Bijuralism: Second Publication* (Ottawa: Canada, Department of Justice, 2001) [Allard, "Expression"]

–, "Entre le droit civil et la common law: La propriété en quête de sens" in: Jean C Gémar & Nicholas Kasirer, eds, *Jurilinguistique: Entre langues et droits* (Montréal: Éditions Thémis, 2005) 193–223

American Law Institute, *Restatement of the Law, Second, Restitution, Draft No. 2* (Philadelphia: American Law Institute, 1984)

–, *Restatement of the Law, Third, Restitution, Draft No. 6* (Philadelphia: American Law Institute, 2008)

–, *Restatement of the Law, Third, Restitution* (St. Paul, Minn.: American Law Institute, 2011) [*Restatement 3^d^, Restitution*]

Ames, James Barr, "The Disseisin of Chattels (I)" (1889) 3:1 Harv L Rev 23–40 [Ames, "Chattel Disseisin I"]

–, "The Disseisin of Chattels (II): The Nature of Ownership" (1889) 3:7 Harv L Rev 313–28 [Ames, "Chattel Disseissin II"]

–, "The Disseisin of Chattels (III): Inalienability of Choses in Action" (1889) 3:8 Harv L Rev 337–46 [Ames, "Chattel Disseisin III"]

–, "The History of Trover" (1897) 11:5 Harv L Rev 277–89 [Ames, "Trover"]

–, "Following Misappropriated Property into Its Product" (1906) 19:7 Harv L Rev 511–22

Aristotle, *Nicomachean Ethics* (Indianapolis: Bobbs-Merrill, 1962)

Armour, John, "The Law and Economics Debate About Secured Lending: Lessons for European Lawmaking?" in: Horst Eidenmüller & Eva-Maria Kieninger, eds, *The Future of Secured Credit in Europe* (Berlin: Walter de Gruyter, 2008) 3–29

Ascheri, Mario, ed, *Ins Wasser geworfen und Ozeane durchquert: Festschrift für Knut Wolfgang Nörr* (Köln: Böhlau, 2003)

Aubry, Charles and Charles Frédéric Rau, *Cours de droit civil français: D'après la méthode de Zachariæ*, 4th edn (Paris: Marchal & Billard, 1873)

Auer, Marietta, *Der privatrechtliche Diskurs der Moderne* (Tübingen: Mohr Siebeck, 2014)

Auger, Jacques, "Le style civiliste et le droit des sûretés réelles" in: Nicholas Kasirer, ed, *Le droit civil: avant tout un style?* (Montréal: Éditions Thémis, 2003) 48–79

Auger, Jacques and Albert Bohémier, "The Status of the Trustee in Bankruptcy" (2003) 37:1 RJT 57–112

Auger, Jacques; Albert Bohémier; and Roderick Alexander Macdonald, "The Treatment of Creditors in the Bankruptcy and Insolvency Act and Security Mechanisms in the Civil Law of Québec" in: Canada, Department of Justice, ed, *The Harmonization of Federal Legislation with the Québec Civil Law and Canadian Bijuralism* (Ottawa: Canada, Department of Justice, 1997) 911

Austin, John, *Lectures on Jurisprudence: The Philosophy of Positive Law*, ed by Robert Campbell, 4th edn (London: J. Murray, 1873), vol 1

–, *Lectures on Jurisprudence: The Philosophy of Positive Law*, ed by Robert Campbell, 4th edn (London: J. Murray, 1873), vol 2

Avini, Avisheh, "The Origins of the Modern English Trust Revisited" (1996) 70:4 Tul L Rev 1139–63

Baird, Douglas G, *The Elements of Bankruptcy*, 6th edn (West Pub. Co, 2014)

Bangsund, Clayton Darryl, "Critical Examination of Recently Proposed Amendments to the Bank Act Security Provisions" (2012) 75:2 Sask L Rev 211–43

–, "Set-Off & Security Interests" (2017) 50:1 UBCL Rev 1–37

Bant, Elise and Matthew Harding, eds, *Exploring Private Law* (Cambridge: Cambridge University Press, 2010)

von Bar, Christian; Eric Clive; and Hans Schulte-Nölke, eds, *Principles, Definitions and Model Rules of European Private Law: Draft Common Frame of Reference (Outline Edition)* (München: Sellier, 2009)

Barkehall Thomas, Susan, "Thieves, Owners and the Problem of Title (I): Chattel" (2011) 5 J Equ 46

–, "Thieves, Owners and the Problem of Title (II): Money" (2012) 6 J Equ 33

Barker, Kit, "Understanding the Unjust Enrichment Principle in Private Law: A Study of the Concept and its Reasons" in: Jason W Neyers, Mitchell McInnes & Stephen G Pitel, eds, *Understanding Unjust Enrichment* (Oxford: Hart, 2004) 79–110

–, "The Nature of Responsibility for Gain: Gain, Harm, and Keeping the Lid on Pandora's Box" in: Robert Chambers, Charles C Mitchell & James E Penner, eds, *Philosophical Foundations of the Law of Unjust Enrichment* (Oxford: Oxford University Press, 2009) 146–80

Barkley, Tobias, "Trustees' Bare Legal Title: Concept or Misconception?" (2017) 26:1 Austral Prop LJ 44–64

Barreau du Québec, ed, *Développements récents sur l'hypothèque* (Service de la formation permanente, Cowansville, Québec: Éditions Yvon Blais, 1997)

Basedow, Jürgen, "Der kollisionsrechtliche Gehalt der Produktfreiheiten im europäischen Binnenmarkt: Favor offerentis" (1995) 59:1 RabelsZ 1–55

Battersby, Graham and AD Preston, "The Concepts of Property, Title and Owner Used in the Sale of Goods Act 1893" (1972) 35:3 Modern L Rev 268–88

Baudouin, Jean-Louis, "L'interprétation du Code civil québécois par la Cour suprême du Canada" (1975) 53 Can Bar Rev 715–37

Beale, Joseph H, "Dicey's 'Conflict of Laws'" (1896) 10:3 Harv L Rev 168–74

Beaulne, Jacques; Roxanne Guérard; and Michèle Lafontaine, eds, *Mélanges Ernest Caparros* (Montréal: Wilson & Lafleur, 2002)

Bebchuk, Lucian Arye and Jesse M Fried, "The Uneasy Case for the Priority of Secured Claims in Bankruptcy" (1996) 105:4 Yale LJ 857–934

–, "Uneasy Case for the Priority of Secured Claims in Bankruptcy: Further Thoughts and a Reply to Critics" (1996) 82:6 Cornell L Rev 1279–348

Bechmann, August, "Zur Lehre von der usucapio pro emtore" (1889) 75:2 AcP 281–302

Becker, Rainer, *Die Fiducie von Québec und der Trust: Ein Vergleich mit verschiedenen Modellen fiduziarischer Rechtsfiguren im Civil Law* (Tübingen: Mohr Siebeck, 2007)

Beck, Thorsten; Asli Demirgüç-Kunt; and Ross Levine, "Law, Endowments, and Finance" (2003) 70:2 J Financial Econ 137–81

Bekker, Ernst Immanuel, "Zweckvermögen, insbesondere Peculium, Handelsvermögen und Actiengesellschaft" [1861] ZHR 499

–, "Zur Lehre vom Rechtssubjekt: Genuß und Verfügung; Zwecksatzungen, Zweckvermögen und juristische Personen" (1873) 12 Jb Dogm 1–135

–, *System des heutigen Pandektenrechts* (Weimar: Hermann Böhlau, 1886), vol 1

Bélanger-Hardy, Louise and Aline Grenon, eds, *Éléments de common law et aperçu comparatif du droit civil québécois* (Scarborough, Ont.: Carswell, 1997)

Bentham, Jeremy, *Introduction to the Principles of Morals and Legislation*, 1st edn (London: T. Payne & Sons, 1789)

Bernadiba, Aurore, "La Loi sur le transfert des valeurs mobilieres et l'obtention des titres intermédiés: Ou les excès d'un régime d'exception en matière de sûretés mobilières" (2012) 53:2 C de D 303–48

Bertocchi, Graziella and Fabio Canova, "Did Colonization Matter for Growth?: An Empirical Exploration Into the Historical Causes of Africa's Underdevelopment" (2002) 46:10 Eur Econ Rev 1851–71

Bilodeau, Paul-Emile, *Précis de la faillite et de l'insolvabilité*, 2d edn (Brossard, Québec: CCH, 2004)

Binnie, Ian J, "Comment on Caisse Populaire Desjardins De L'Est De Drummond v Canada" (2011) 26:2 *Bank & Fin L Rev* 327–37

Bird, Joanna, "Choice of Laws Rule for Priority Disputes in Relation to Shares" [1996] LMCLQ 57–63

Birks, Peter, "English and Roman Learning in Moses V Macferlan" (1984) 37 Curr Legal Probs 1–28

–, "Restitution: A View of Scots Law" (1985) 38 Curr Legal Probs 57–82

–, "The Roman Law Concept of Dominium and the Idea of Absolute Ownership" (1985) 1 AJ 1–38

–, "Mixing and Tracing: Property and Restitution" (1992) 45 Curr Legal Probs 69–98

–, "Restitution and Resulting Trusts: Papers Presented at the First International Conference on Equity, the Faculty of Law, the Hebrew University of Jerusalem, June 1990" in: Stephen R Goldstein, ed, *Equity and Contemporary Legal Developments* (Jerusalem: Harry & Michael Sacher Institute for Legislative Research & Comparative Law, Hebrew University of Jerusalem, 1992) 335–73

–, "Equity in the Modern Law: An Excercise in Legal Taxonomy" (1996) 26 UWAL Rev 1–99
–, "Definition and Division: A Meditation on Institutes 3.13" in: Peter Birks, ed, *The Classification of Obligations* (Oxford: Clarendon Press, 1997) 1–35
–, "Property and Unjust Enrichment: Categorical Truths" [1997] NZL Rev 623–67
–, "Private Law" in: Peter Birks & Francis Rose, eds, *Restitution and Equity* (London: Mansfield Press, 2000), vol 1, 1–45
–, "Rights, Wrongs, and Remedies" (2000) 20 Oxford J Legal Stud 1–37
–, "Property, Unjust Enrichment, and Tracing" (2001) 54:1 Curr Legal Probs 231–54
–, "Unjust Enrichment and Wrongful Enrichment" (2001) 79 Tex L Rev 1767–94
–, "At the Expense of the Claimant: Direct and Indirect Enrichment in the English Law" in: David Johnston & Reinhard Zimmermann, eds, *Unjustified Enrichment: Key Issues in Comparative Perspective* (Cambridge: Cambridge University Press, 2002) 493–525
–, *Unjust Enrichment*, 2d edn (Oxford: Oxford University Press, 2005)
–, ed, *The Classification of Obligations* (Oxford: Clarendon Press, 1997)
Birks, Peter and Grant McLeod, "The Implied Contract Theory of Quasi-Contract: Civilian Opinion Current in the Century Before Blackstone" (1986) 6 Oxford J Legal Stud 46–85
Birks, Peter and Francis Rose, eds, *Restitution and Equity* (London: Mansfield Press, 2000), vol 1
Blackstone, William, *Of the Rights of Persons*, 1st edn (Commentaries on the Laws of England, vol 1, Oxford: Clarendon Press, 1765–1769)
Bohémier, Albert, "Application of the Bankruptcy and Insolvency Act to the Trust of the Civil Code of Québec" (2003) 37:1 RJT 114–46
Boodman, Martin, "The Myth of Harmonization of Laws" (1991) 39:4 Am J Comp L 699–724
Boodman, Martin and Roderick Alexander Macdonald, "How Far is Article 9 of the Uniform Commercial Code Exportable?: A Return to Sources" (1996) 27:2 CBLJ 249–77
Bordwell, Percy, "Property in Chattels (Part I): Property in the Trespasser" (1916) 29:4 Harv L Rev 374–94
–, "The Alienability of Non-Possessory Interests" (1940) 19:3 NCL Rev 279–303 [Bordwell, "Alienability"]
Bornheim, Jan Jakob, "Same-Sex Marriage in Canadian Private International Law" (2013) 51:1 Alta L Rev 77–100
–, "Die Wirkung relativer dinglicher Rechte nach deutschem internationalen Sachenrecht" (2015) 79:1 RabelsZ 36–71 [Bornheim, "Relative dingliche Rechte"]
Bouckaert, Boudewijn, "Divergences of the Law on Securities: A Law and Economics Approach" in: Ulrich Drobnig, Henricus J Snijders & Eric-Jan Zippro, eds, *Divergences of Property Law: An Obstacle to the Internal Market?* (Berlin: Sellier, 2006) 175–93
Boudreault, Marc, "Développements en droit des sûretés" in: Jacques Beaulne, Roxanne Guérard & Michèle Lafontaine, eds, *Mélanges Ernest Caparros* (Montréal: Wilson & Lafleur, 2002) 175–200
–, *Les sûretés*, 3rd edn (Montréal: Wilson & Lafleur, 2008)
Bouvier-Bangillon, Armand-Edmond, *De la tradition considérée comme mode translatif de propriété en droit romain et dans l'ancien droit français* (Paris: F. Pichon, 1877)
Bracton, Henry de, *On the Laws and Customs of England*, ed by George E. Woodbine (Cambridge, Mass.: Harvard University Press, 1968)
Brennan, David J, "Replevin and the Paradox of English Chattel Property" (2007) 36:4 Comm L World Rev 337–54

Breton, Albert and Anne Des Ormeaux, "Coevolution as an Influence in the Development of Legal Systems" in: Albert Breton & Michael J Trebilcock, eds, *Bijuralism: An Economic Approach* (Aldershot: Ashgate, 2006) 125–52

Breton, Albert and Michael J Trebilcock, "Introduction" in: Albert Breton & Michael J Trebilcock, eds, *Bijuralism: An Economic Approach* (Aldershot: Ashgate, 2006) 1–10

–, eds, *Bijuralism: An Economic Approach* (Aldershot: Ashgate, 2006)

Brickey, Kathleen F, "The Jurisprudence of Larceny: An Historical Inquiry and Interest Analysis" (1980) 33:5 Vand L Rev 1101–42

Bridge, Michael G, "The Quistclose Trust in a World of Secured Transactions" (1992) 12:3 Oxford J Legal Stud 333–61 [Bridge, "Quistclose Trust"]

–, "The Scope and Limits of Security Interests" in: Horst Eidenmüller & Eva-Maria Kieninger, eds, *The Future of Secured Credit in Europe* (Berlin: Walter de Gruyter, 2008) 180–214 [Bridge, "Scope and Limit of Security"]

Bridge, Michael G; Roderick Alexander Macdonald; Ralph L Simmonds; and Catherine E Walsh, "Formalism, Functionalism, and Understanding the Law of Secured Transactions" (1999) 44 McGill LJ 567–664

Brierley, John EC, "Quebec's Civil Law Codification: Viewed and Reviewed" (1968) 14:4 McGill LJ 521–89 [Brierley, "Codification"]

–, "The Co-Existence of Legal Systems in Quebec: «Free and Common Socage» in Canada's «pays de droit civil»" (1979) 20 C de D 277–87

–, "The Renewal of Quebec's Distinct Legal Culture: The New Civil Code of Quebec" (1992) 42:4 UTLJ 484–503

–, "The New Quebec Law of Trusts: The Adaption of Common Law Thoughts to Civil Law Concepts" in: H P Glenn, ed, *Droit québécois et droit français: Communauté, autonomie, concordance* (Cowansville, Québec: Éditions Yvon Blais, 1993) 383–97

–, "Regards sur le droit des biens dans le nouveau Code civil du Québec" (1995) 47:1 Rev Int Dr Comp 33–49 [Brierley, "Regards"]

Brierley, John EC; H Patrick Glenn; and Ethel Groffier, eds, *Mélanges Louis-Philippe Pigeon* (Montréal: Wilson & Lafleur, 1989)

Briggs, Adrian, "Restitution Meets the Conflict of Laws" (1995) 3 RLR 94–99

Brinkmann, Moritz, *Kreditsicherheiten an beweglichen Sachen und Forderungen: Eine materiell-, insolvenz- und kollisionsrechtliche Studie des Rechts der Mobiliarsicherheiten vor dem Hintergrund internationaler und europäischer Entwicklungen* (Jus Privatum, Tübingen: Mohr Siebeck, 2011)

Brinz, Alois, *Das Zweckvermögen*, 2[d] edn (Lehrbuch der Pandekten, 321, Erlangen: Andreas Deichert, 1879–1882)

Brown, Brendan F, "The Ecclesiastical Origin of the Use" (1935) 10:4 Notre Dame L Rev 353–66

Brown, Mark R and Andrew C Greenberg, "On Formally Undecidable Propositions of Law: Legal Indeterminacy and the Implications of Metamathematics" (1992) 43:6 Hastings LJ 1439–88

Brun, Henri, "Les origines du consensualisme en matière de transfert de proprieté et des mitigations apportées au principe par le droit civil québecois" (1967–1968) 9:2 C de D 273–86

Brunner, Otto; Werner Conze; and Reinhart Koselleck, eds, *Geschichtliche Grundbegriffe: Historisches Lexikon zur politisch-sozialen Sprache in Deutschland* (Stuttgart: Klett-Cotta, 1975), vol 2

Bryan, Michael, "The Receipt-Based Constructive Trust: A Case Study of Personal and Proprietary Restitution in the Supreme Court" (1999) 37 Alta L Rev 73–94

Bump, Orlando and James McIlvaine Gray, *A Treatise Upon Conveyances Made by Debtors to Defraud Creditors*, 4th edn (Washington, D.C.: W.H. Lowdermilk & Co, 1896)

Burns, Fiona R, "Giumelli v Giumelli Revisited: Equitable Estoppel, the Constructive Trust and Discretionary Remedialism" (2001) 22 Adel L Rev 123–56

–, "The Equitable Lien Rediscovered: A Remedy for the 21st Century" (2002) 25 UNSWLJ 1–32

Burrows, Andrew S, "Proprietary Restitution: Unmasking Unjust Enrichment" (2001) 117 LQR 412–30 [Burrows, "Unmasking"]

–, "We Do This at Common Law but That in Equity" (2002) 22:1 Oxford J Legal Stud 1–16

–, "The English Law of Restitution: A Ten Year Review" in: Jason W Neyers, Mitchell McInnes & Stephen G Pitel, eds, *Understanding Unjust Enrichment* (Oxford: Hart, 2004) 11–33

–, "Absence of Basis: The New Birksian Scheme" in: Andrew S Burrows & Alan Rodger, eds, *Mapping the Law: Essays in Memory of Peter Birks* (Oxford: Oxford University Press, 2006) 33–48

–, *The Law of Restitution*, 3rd edn (Oxford: Oxford University Press, 2010) [Burrows, *Restitution*]

Burrows, Andrew S and Alan Rodger, eds, *Mapping the Law: Essays in Memory of Peter Birks* (Oxford: Oxford University Press, 2006)

Calabresi, Guido, "Some Thoughts on Risk Distribution and the Law of Torts" (1961) 70:4 Yale LJ 499–553

Calabresi, Guido and A Douglas Melamed, "Property Rules, Liability Rules, and Inalienability: One View of the Cathedral" (1972) 85:6 Harv L Rev 1089–128

Calnan, Richard, *Proprietary Rights and Insolvency* (Oxford: Oxford University Press, 2010)

Canada, Department of Justice, ed, *The Harmonization of Federal Legislation with the Québec Civil Law and Canadian Bijuralism* (Ottawa: Canada, Department of Justice, 1997)

–, ed, *The Harmonization of Federal Legislation with the Civil Law of the Province of Quebec and Canadian Bijuralism: Second Publication* (Ottawa: Canada, Department of Justice, 2001)

Canada, Department of Justice, Bijuralism and Drafting Support Services Group Legislative Service Branch, "Proposals for Harmonizing the Bankruptcy and Insolvency Act with Quebec Civil Law" (2003) 37:1 RJT 19–55

Canada, Department of Justice and Association de planification fiscale et financière, eds, *Harmonization of Federal Legislation with Quebec Civil Law and Canadian Bijuralism: Collection of Studies in Tax Law* (Montréal: Association de planification fiscale et financière, 2002)

Canadian Conference on Personal Property Security Law, Working Group (CCPPSL Working Group), *Report to the Canadian Conference on Personal Property Security Law on Proposals for Changes to the Personal Property Security Acts*, (2017)

Cantin Cumyn, Madeleine, "De l'existence et du régime juridique des droits réels de jouissance innommés: Essai sur l'énumération limitative des droits réels" (1986) 46 R du B 3–56 [Cantin Cumyn, "Droits réels innommés"]

–, "Les personnes morales dans le droit privé du Québec" (1990) 31:4 C de D 1021–48

–, "Le droit privé des biens: À l'enseigne de la continuité" in: H P Glenn, ed, *Droit québécois et droit français: Communauté, autonomie, concordance* (Cowansville, Québec: Éditions Yvon Blais, 1993) 375–82

–, "L'origine de la fiducie québécoise" in: McGill University, Faculty of Law, ed, *Mélanges Paul-André Crepeau* (Cowansville, Québec: Éditions Yvon Blais, 1997) 199–219

Cantin Cumyn, Madeleine and Michelle Cumyn, "La notion des biens" in: Sylvio Normand, ed, *Mélanges offerts au Professeur François Frenette* (Québec: Les Presses de l'Université Laval, 2006) 127–50

Caparros, Ernest, ed, *Mélanges Germain Brière* (Collection Bleue, Montréal: Wilson & Lafleur, 1993)

Capitant, Henri, "Essai sur la subrogation réelle" (1919) 18 RTD 385

Carbonnier, Jean, *Droit civil* (Quadrige Manuels, Paris: Presses universitaires de France, 1964)

Caron, Yves, "The Trust in Quebec" (1980) 25 McGill LJ 421–44

Carruthers, Janeen M, *The Transfer of Property in the Conflict of Laws: Choice of Law Rules Concerning Inter Vivos Transfers of Property* (Oxford: Oxford University Press, 2005)

Carswell, RD, "The Doctrine of Vested Rights in Private International Law" [1959] CLJ 268–88

Chambers, Robert, "Constructive Trusts in Canada" (1999) 37 Alta L Rev 173–220

–, *An Introduction to Property Law in Australia*, 1st edn (Sydney: Thomson Law Books, 2001)

–, "Tracing and Unjust Enrichment" in: Jason W Neyers, Mitchell McInnes & Stephen G Pitel, eds, *Understanding Unjust Enrichment* (Oxford: Hart, 2004) 263–309

–, "Two Kinds of Enrichment" in: Robert Chambers, Charles C Mitchell & James E Penner, eds, *Philosophical Foundations of the Law of Unjust Enrichment* (Oxford: Oxford University Press, 2009) 242–78

–, "Trust and Theft" in: Elise Bant & Matthew Harding, eds, *Exploring Private Law* (Cambridge: Cambridge University Press, 2010) 223–46

–, "The End of Knowing Receipt" (2016) 2:1 CJCCL 1–32

Chambers, Robert; Charles Christopher James Mitchell; and James E Penner, eds, *Philosophical Foundations of the Law of Unjust Enrichment* (Oxford: Oxford University Press, 2009)

Charbonneau, Pierre, "Les patrimoines d'affectation: Vers un nouveau paradigme en droit quebecois du patrimoine" (1983) 85 R du N 491–530

Cheyne, William M, *Is the Thief a Trustee?: Principled Approaches to Proprietary Restitutionary Remedies* (University of Otago) <http://www.otago.ac.nz/law/research/journals/otago043955.pdf> accessed 6 November 2017

Childress, Donald Earl, III, "Comity as Conflict: Resituating International Comity as Conflict of Laws" (2010) 44 UC Davis L Rev 11–79

Chong, Adeline, "Choice of Law for Unjust Enrichment: Restitution and the Rome II Regulation" (2008) 57:4 ICLQ 863–98

Ciotola, Pierre and Antoine Leduc, "Arrêt Val-Brillant: Évolution ou régression de l'hypothèque mobilière avec dépossession, en droit civil quebecois" (2006) 40 RJT 5–74

Coase, Ronald H, "The Problem of Social Cost" (1960) 3 *JL & Econ* 1–44

Cohen, Neil B, "Internationalizing the Law of Secured Credit: Perspectives from the US Experience" (1999) 20:3 *U Pa J Int'l Econ L* 423–42

Cohn, Ernst J, "Precedents in Continental Law" (1935) 5:3 CLJ 366–70

Cokayne, George Eward, *Complete Peerage of England, Scotland, Ireland, Great Britain and the United Kingdom* (London: G. Bell & Sons, 1893)

Coke, Edward, *The First Part of the Institutes of the Laws of England: A Commentary Upon Littleton*, 1st edn (Philadelphia: Johnson & Warner, 1812), vol 1

Collins, Lawrence, ed, *Dicey, Morris and Collins on the Conflict of Laws*, 14th edn (London: Sweet & Maxwell, 2006)
Collins, Lawrence, Baron Collins of Mapesbury and Jonathan Harris, eds, *Dicey, Morris and Collins on the Conflict of Laws*, 15th edn (London: Sweet & Maxwell, 2012), vol 2
–, eds, *Dicey, Morris and Collins on the Conflict of Laws*, 15th edn (London: Sweet & Maxwell, 2012), vol 1
Conférence de la Haye de droit international prive, ed, *Actes et documents de la 14ème session* ('s-Gravenshage: Bureau permanent de la Conférence, 1980)
Cook, Walter Wheeler, "The Alienability of Choses in Action" (1916) 29:8 Harv L Rev 816–37
–, "The Logical and Legal Bases of the Conflict of Laws" (1924) 33:5 Yale LJ 457–88
–, *The Logical and Legal Bases of the Conflict of Laws* (Cambridge, Mass.: Harvard University Press, 1942)
Cope, Malcolm, *Constructive Trusts* (North Ryde, N.S.W.: Law Book, 1992)
Cortina, Jose R, "The Jus Emphyteuticarium and Trust: A Byzantine Solution for an Acadian Problem" (1981) 8:1 SUL Rev 95–132
Cotton, Barbara E, "The Equitable Lien: New Life in an Old Remedy" (1994) 16 *Advocates' Q* 385–409
Coupland, Reginald, *The Quebec Act: A Study in Statesmanship* (Oxford: Clarendon Press, 1925)
Cranston, Ross, ed, *Making Commercial Law: Essays in Honour of Roy Goode* (Oxford: Clarendon Press, 1997)
Crawford, Bradley, "In Defence of Secret Liens: How the Supreme Court Presses Parliament to Harmonize Section 427 of the Bank Act with the PPSAs" (2011) 26:2 *Bank & Fin L Rev* 305–14
Crépeau, Paul-André, "Les lendemains de la réforme du code civil" (1981) 59 Can Bar Rev 625–37 [Crépeau, "Lendemains"]
–, ed, *Rapport sur le code civil du Québec* (Québec: Éditeur officiel, 1978), vol 1
–, ed, *Rapport sur le code civil du Québec* (Québec: Éditeur officiel, 1978), vol 2
Culver, Keith, "Leaving the Hart-Dworkin Debate" (2001) 51:4 UTLJ 367–98
Cuming, Ronald CC, "An Article 2A For Canada?: A Comment on Professor Ziegel's Paper" [1989–1990] CBLJ 439–52
–, "The Position Paper on Revised Bank Act Security: Rehabilitation of Canadian Personal Property Security Law or Curing the Illness by Killing the Patient" (1992) 20 CBLJ 336–56
–, "Article 9 North of 49°: The Canadian PPS Acts and the Quebec Civil Code" (1995) 29 Loy L Rev 971–89
–, "The Internationalization of Secured Financing Law: The Spreading Influence of the Concepts UCC, Article 9 and Its Progeny" in: Ross Cranston, ed, *Making Commercial Law: Essays in Honour of Roy Goode* (Oxford: Clarendon Press, 1997) 499–523
–, "Interface between the PPSA and Section 427 of the Bank Act: Desirable Policy vs. Hard Legal Analysis" (2008) 71 Sask L Rev 143–52
–, "Fitting a Square (Federal) Peg in a Round (Provincial) Hole: Rationalizing Section 427 Bank Act With Provincial Property Security Law" (2010) 73 Sask L Rev 1–21
–, "Secured Creditors' Non-Statutory Remedies: Unfinished Business" (2012) 91:2 Can Bar Rev 243–74
Cuming, Ronald CC; Catherine E Walsh; and Roderick J Wood, *Personal Property Security Law*, 1st edn (Toronto: Irwin Law, 2005)
–, *Personal Property Security Law*, 2d edn (Toronto: Irwin Law, 2012)

Cuming, Ronald CC and Roderick J Wood, "Compatibility of Federal and Provincial Personal Property Security Law" (1986) 65 Can Bar Rev 267–302
Cumyn, Michelle, "Les restrictions à la liberté d'aliéner dans le Code civil du Québec" (1994) 39:4 McGill LJ 877–913
Cuniberti, Gilles, "The International Market for Contracts: The Most Attractive Contract Laws" (2014) 34:3 *Nw J Int'l L & Bus* 455–517
Currie, Brainerd, "Notes on Methods and Objectives in the Conflict of Laws" in: Brainerd Currie, *Selected Essays in the Conflict of Laws* (Durham: Duke University Press, 1963) 177
–, *Selected Essays in the Conflict of Laws* (Durham: Duke University Press, 1963)
Curwen, Nicholas, "General and Special Property in Goods" (2000) 20:2 LS 181–97
–, "The Remedy in Conversion: Confusing Property and Obligation" (2006) 26:4 LS 570–83
D'Amato, Anthony, "Can Legislatures Constrain Judicial Interpretation of Statutes?" (1989) 75:3 Va L Rev 561–603
Dagan, Hanoch, "The Craft of Property" (2003) 91:6 Cal L Rev 1517–71 [Dagan, "Craft"]
–, "Restitution in Bankruptcy: Why All Involuntary Creditors Should Be Preferred" (2004) 78:3 Am Bankr LJ 247–78
–, "The Realist Conception of Law" (2007) 57 UTLJ 607–60 [Dagan, "Realist Conception"]
–, "Restitution's Realism" in: Robert Chambers, Charles C Mitchell & James E Penner, eds, *Philosophical Foundations of the Law of Unjust Enrichment* (Oxford: Oxford University Press, 2009) 54–80
Dahan, Frederique and John Simpson, "Legal Efficiency of Secured Transactions Reform: Bridging the Gap Between Economic Analysis and Legal Reasoning" in: Frederique Dahan & John Simpson, eds, *Secured Transactions Reform and Access to Credit* (Cheltenham: Edward Elgar, 2009) 122–38
–, eds, *Secured Transactions Reform and Access to Credit* (Cheltenham: Edward Elgar, 2009)
Dam, Kenneth W, *The Law-Growth Nexus: The Rule of Law and Economic Development* (Washington, D.C.: Brookings Institution Press, 2006)
Dane, Perry, "Vested Rights, 'Vestedness,' and Choice of Law" (1987) 96:6 Yale LJ 1191–275
Daniels, Ronald J, "Should Provinces Compete?: The Case for a Competitive Corporate Market" (1991) 36:1 McGill LJ 130–90
Davidson, Nestor M, "Standardization and Pluralism in Property Law" (2008) 61:6 Vand L Rev 1597–666
Davies, Iwan, "Transferability and Sale of Goods" (1987) 7:1 LS 1–38
–, "The Reform of English Personal Property Security Law: Functionalism and Article 9 of the Uniform Commercial Code" (2004) 24 LS 295–321
Davis, Kevin, "Priority of Crown Claims in Insolvency: Royal Bank of Canada v Sparrow Electric Corp. and Its Aftermath" (1998) 29:1 CBLJ 145–60
Davis, Kevin E and Michael J Trebilcock, "The Relationship between Law and Development: Optimists versus Skeptics" (2008) 56:4 Am J Comp L 895–946
Davydenko, Sergei A and Julian R Franks, "Do Bankruptcy Codes Matter?: A Study of Defaults in France, Germany, and the UK" (2008) 63:2 J Fin 565–608
Dawson, John Philip, *Unjust Enrichment: A Comparative Analysis*, Reprint 1999 (Holmes Beach, Fla.: Gaunt, 1999)
Demolombe, Jean Charles Florent, *Traité des donations entre-vifs et des testaments*, 1st edn (Cours de Code Napoléon, Paris: A Durand & L Hachette, 1861)

Demsetz, Harold, "Toward a Theory of Property Rights" (1967) 57:2 Am Econ Rev 347–59

Department of Business Innovation and Skills, *A Better Deal for Consumers: Consultation on the Proposal to Ban the use of Bills of Sale for Consumer Lending* (London: Her Majesty's Stationery Office, 2009)

Deschamps, Michel, "Les conflits de lois en droit des sûretés au Canada et aux Etats-Unis: Comparaison entre le Code civil du Québec, les PPSAs et le UCC" in: Norman A Saibil, ed, *Développements récents en droit bancaire* (Cowansville, Québec: Éditions Yvon Blais, 2003) 123–48 [Deschamps, "Conflits de lois"]

–, "Les sûretés sur des titres détenus auprès d'un intermédiaire en droit canadien" (2005) 10 Unif L Rev 189–224

–, "Le nouveau régime québécois des sûretés sur les valeurs mobilières" (2009) 68 R du B 545–72

Descheemaeker, Eric, ed, *The Consequences of Possession* (Edinburgh: Edinburgh University Press, 2014)

Deslauriers, Jacques, "Utilisation de la Loi sur la faillite et l'insolvabilité par les créanciers garantis" in: Barreau du Québec, ed, *Développements récents sur l'hypothèque* (Cowansville, Québec: Éditions Yvon Blais, 1997) 21–53

DeVine, Stephen W, "Ecclesiastical Antecedents to Secular Jurisdiction over the Feoffment to the Uses to Be Declared in Testamentary Instructions" (1986) 30:4 Am J Legal Hist 295–321

Dewey, John, "Logical Method and Law" (1914) 10 Cornell LQ 17–27

Dicey, Albert Venn, "On Private International Law as a Branch of the Law of England" (1890) 6:1 LQR 1–21

–, *A Digest of the Law of England with Reference to the Conflict of Laws*, 1st edn (London: Stevens and Sons & Sweet and Maxwell, 1896)

Dickinson, Andrew, *The Rome II Regulation: The Law Applicable to Non-Contractual Obligations* (Oxford: Oxford University Press, 2008)

Dickson, Brice, "Unjust Enrichment Claims: A Comparative Overview" (1995) 54:1 CLJ 100–26

Dietze, Sterling H, "My Cash and I: Cash Collateral Is Finally King in Quebec" (2016) 31:2 *Bank & Fin L Rev* 349–70

Dion, Mario, "Evolution of Legal Systems: Bijuralism and International Trade" in: Canada, Department of Justice, ed, *The Harmonization of Federal Legislation with the Québec Civil Law and Canadian Bijuralism* (Ottawa: Canada, Department of Justice, 1997)

Djankov, Simeon; Rafael La Porta; Florencio Lopez-de-Silanes; and Andrei Shleifer, "Courts" (2003) 118 Quart J Econ 453–517

Djankov, Simeon; Caralee McLiesh; and Andrei Shleifer, "Private Credit in 129 Countries" (2007) 84:2 J Financial Econ 299–329

Doughty, Arthur George, "Appendix B" in: Arthur G Doughty, ed, *Report of the Public Archives for the Year 1918* (Ottawa: J de la Taché, 1920) 32–396

–, ed, *Report of the Work of the Public Archives for the Year 1913* (Ottawa: J. de la Taché, 1914)

–, ed, *Report of the Public Archives for the Year 1918* (Ottawa: J. de la Taché, 1920)

Driedger, Elmer A, *The Construction of Statutes*, 2d edn (Toronto: Butterworths, 1983)

Drobnig, Ulrich and Ole Böger, eds, *Proprietary Security in Movable Assets* (Principles of European Law, Berlin: Sellier-de Gruyter, 2015)

Drobnig, Ulrich; Henk J Snijders; and Eric-Jan Zippro, "Divergences of Property Law: An Obstacle to the Internal Market" in: Ulrich Drobnig, Henricus J Snijders & Eric-Jan

Zippro, eds, *Divergences of Property Law: An Obstacle to the Internal Market?* (Berlin: Sellier, 2006) 3–13
Drobnig, Ulrich; Henricus Joseph Snijders; and Eric-Jan Zippro, eds, *Divergences of Property Law: An Obstacle to the Internal Market?* (Berlin: Sellier, 2006)
Duggan, Anthony J, "Constructive Trusts from a Law and Economics Perspective" (2005) 55 UTLJ 217–52
–, "Secured Transactions, Constructive Trusts and Insolvency" [2010] Ann Rev Insolvency L 619
–, "Proprietary Remedies in Insolvency: A Comparison of the Restatement (Third) of Restitution & Unjust Enrichment with English and Commonwealth Law" (2011) 68:3 *Wash & Lee L Rev* 1229–70
–, "Current Issues in Secured Transactions Law in Canada: An Ontario Perspective" in: Louise Gullifer & Orkun Akseli, eds, *Secured Transactions Law Reform: Principles, Policies and Practice* (Oxford, Portland: Hart, 2016) 95–114
Duggan, Anthony J and Jacob S Ziegel, "Justice Iacobucci and the Canadian Law of Deemed Trusts and Chattel Security" (2007) 57 UTLJ 227–49
–, *Canadian Bankruptcy and Insolvency Law*, 2d edn (Toronto: Emond Montgomery Publications, 2009)
–, *Secured Transactions in Personal Property: Cases, Text and Materials*, 5th edn (Toronto: Emond Montgomery Publications, 2009)
Dunlop, Charles RB, *Creditor-Debtor Law in Canada*, 2d edn (Toronto: Carswell, 1995)
Durham, John George Lambton Earl of, *Lord Durham's Report on the Affairs of British North America*, ed by Charles Prestwood Lucas (Oxford: Clarendon Press, 1912), vol 2
–, *Lord Durham's Report on the Affairs of British North America*, ed by Charles Prestwood Lucas (Oxford: Clarendon Press, 1912), vol 1
–, *Lord Durham's Report on the Affairs of British North America*, ed by Charles Prestwood Lucas (Oxford: Clarendon Press, 1912), vol 3
Dworkin, Ronald M, "Hard Cases" (1975) 88:6 Harv L Rev 1057–109
–, *Taking Rights Seriously* (Cambridge, Mass.: Harvard University Press, 1978)
Edelman, James J, "Review: The Law and Ethics of Restitution" (2006) 69 Modern L Rev 131–35
–, "The Meaning of Loss and Enrichment" in: Robert Chambers, Charles C Mitchell & James E Penner, eds, *Philosophical Foundations of the Law of Unjust Enrichment* (Oxford: Oxford University Press, 2009) 211–41
Edgeworth, Brendan, "The Numerus Clausus Principle in Contemporary Australian Property Law" (2006) 32:2 Monash UL Rev 387–419
Eekelaar, John and John Bell, eds, *Oxford Essays in Jurisprudence: Third Series* (Oxford: Clarendon Press, 1987)
Ehrenzweig, Albert A, "A Counter-Revolution in Conflicts Law?: From Beale to Cavers" (1966) 80:2 Harv L Rev 377–401
Eidenmüller, Horst, *Effizienz als Rechtsprinzip: Möglichkeiten und Grenzen der ökonomischen Analyse des Rechts* (Tübingen: Mohr Siebeck, 1995)
Eidenmüller, Horst and Eva-Maria Kieninger, eds, *The Future of Secured Credit in Europe* (European Company and Financial Law Review Special Series, Berlin: Walter de Gruyter, 2008)
–, eds, *The Future of Secured Credit in Europe* (European Company and Financial Law Review Special Series, Berlin: Walter de Gruyter, 2008)
Elphinstone, Howard W, "What Is a Chose in Action" (1893) 9 LQR 311–15

Emanuelli, Claude, *Droit international privé québécois*, 3rd edn (Montréal: Wilson & Lafleur, 2011)
Emerich, Yaëll, "Faut-il condamner la proprieté des biens incorporels?: Reflexions autour de la proprieté des créances" (2005) 46:4 C de D 905–40 [Emerich, "Proprieté des biens incorporels"]
–, "Regard civiliste sur le droit des biens de la Common Law: Pour une conception transsystemique du droit de la propriété" (2008) 38:2 RGD 339–77 [Emerich, "Regard civiliste"]
–, "La nature juridique des sûretés réelles en droit civil et en Common Law: Une question de tradition juridique?" (2010) 44:1 RJT 95–140 [Emerich, "Sûretés réelles"]
–, "Why Protect Possession?" in: Eric Descheemaeker, ed, *The Consequences of Possession* (Edinburgh: Edinburgh University Press, 2014) 30–55 [Emerich, "Possession"]
Epstein, Richard A, "Possession as the Root of Title" (1978–1979) 13:4 Ga L Rev 1221–43
Evans-Jones, Robin, "Receptions of Law: Mixed Legal Systems and the Myth of the Genius of Scots Private Law" (1998) 114 LQR 228–49
–, ed, *The Civil Law Tradition in Scotland* (Edinburgh: Stair Society, 1995)
Evans-Jones, Robin and Phillip Hellwege, "Some Observations on the Taxonomy of Unjustified Enrichment in Scots Law" (1998) 2 Edin L Rev 180–217
Faure, Michael and Jan M Smits, eds, *Does Law Matter?: On Law and Economic Growth* (Ius commune europaeum, Cambridge: Intersentia, 2011)
Fenge, Anja, "Englisches Kreditsicherungsrecht versus schottisches Sachenrecht: Sharp v Thomson" (1999) 98 ZVglRWiss 410–20
Fine, J David, "Cause in the Quebec Law of Enrichment without Cause" (1973) 19:4 McGill LJ 453–76
Fleisig, Heywood, *The Power of Collateral* (Public Policy for the Private Sector, Washington, DC: World Bank, 1995)
–, "The Economics of Collateral and of Collateral Reform" in: Frederique Dahan & John Simpson, eds, *Secured Transactions Reform and Access to Credit* (Cheltenham: Edward Elgar, 2009) 81–109
Fleisig, Heywood; Mehnaz S Safavian; and Nuria de La Peña, *Reforming Collateral Laws to Expand Access to Finance* (Washington, D.C.: World Bank Publications, 2006)
Fleming, John G, *The Law of Torts*, 4th edn (Sydney: Law Book, 1971)
Fontenot, H Ward, "The Louisiana Judicial System and the Fusion of Cultures" (2003) 63:4 La L Rev 1149–60
Fortier, Mark, "Equity and Ideas: Coke, Ellesmere, and James I" (1998) 51 Renaissance Quarterly 1255–81
Fox, David, "Legal Title as a Ground of Restitutionary Liability" [2000] RLR 465–91
Fratcher, William F, "Uses of Uses" (1969) 34:1 Mo L Rev 39–66
Frenette, François, "Du droit de propriété: Certaines de ses dimensions méconnues" (1979) 20:3 C de D 439–47
–, "De l'hyopthèque: Réalité du droit et métamorphose de l'objet" (1998) 39:4 C de D 803–22
Fridman, Gerald HL, "Unjust Enrichment (Dis)Contented" in: Jason W Neyers, Mitchell McInnes & Stephen G Pitel, eds, *Understanding Unjust Enrichment* (Oxford: Hart, 2004) 35–45
Friedmann, Wolfgang, "Stare Decisis at Common Law and Under the Civil Code of Quebec" (1953) 31 Can Bar Rev 723–51
Füller, Jens Thomas, *Eigenständiges Sachenrecht?* (Jus Privatum, Tübingen: Mohr Siebeck, 2006)

Fuller, Lon L, "Positivism and Fidelity to Law: A Reply to Professor Hart" (1958) 71:4 Harv L Rev 630–72

Gaillard, Emmanuel and Donald T Trautman, "Trusts in Non-Trust Countries: Conflict of Laws and the Hague Convention on Trusts" (1987) 35:2 Am J Comp L 307–40

Garoupa, Nuno and Carlos Gómez Ligüerre, "Efficiency of the Common Law" in: Michael Faure & Jan M Smits, eds, *Does Law Matter?: On Law and Economic Growth* (Cambridge: Intersentia, 2011) 223–47

Gaudiosi, Monica M, "The Influence of the Islamic Law of Waqf on the Development of the Trust in England: The Case of Merton College" (1987–1988) 136:4 U Pa L Rev 1231–61

Gaudreault, Marie-Claude, "Canadian Legislative Bijuralism: An Expression of Legal Duality" (2006) 32:2 Comm L Bull 205–19

Gawkerere, Jean Paul, "Que reste-t-il du transfert consensuel de la propriété des biens meubles en droit canadien?: Considérations sur la codification d'un principe dans un système bijuridique" (2005) 46:3 C de D 671–716

Gémar, Jean C and Nicholas Kasirer, eds, *Jurilinguistique: Entre langues et droits* (Montréal: Éditions Thémis, 2005)

Gerecke, David G and Fraiba Jalal, "Amendments to PMSI Rules in Saskatchewan" (*Miller Thomson*, 12 February 2019) <https://www.millerthomson.com/en/publications/communiques-and-updates/financial-services-insolvency-communique/february-12–2019-fsi/amendments-to-pmsi-rules-in-saskatchewan/> accessed 13 May 2019

Giraud, Charles, "Précis de l'ancien droit coutumier français: Deuxième article" (1852) 13 *Bibliothèque de l'École des chartes* 1–22

–, "Précis de l'ancien droit coutumier français: Trosième et dernier article" (1852) 13 *Bibliothèque de l'École des chartes* 407–46

Glaeser, Edward L and Andrei Shleifer, "Legal Origins" (2002) 117:4 Quart J Econ 1193–229

Glenn, H Patrick, "Le droit comparé et la Cour suprême du Canada" in: John E Brierley, H P Glenn & Ethel Groffier, eds, *Mélanges Louis-Philippe Pigeon* (Montréal: Wilson & Lafleur, 1989) 197–214

–, ed, *Droit québécois et droit français: Communauté, autonomie, concordance* (Cowansville, Québec: Éditions Yvon Blais, 1993)

Glenn, Jane Matthews, "Mixed Jurisdictions in the Commonwealth Caribbean: Mixing, Unmixing, Remixing" in: Esin Örücü, ed, *Mixed Legal Systems at New Frontiers* (London: Wildy, Simmonds & Hill, 2010) 78–108

Glister, Jamie, "The Role of Trusts in the PPSA" (2011) 34:2 UNSWLJ 628–45

Gödel, Kurt, "Über formal unentscheidbare Sätze der Principia Mathematica und verwandter Systeme I" (1931) 38:1 MMP 173–98

Goff, Robert and Gareth H Jones, *The Law of Restitution*, 3rd edn (London: Sweet & Maxwell, 1986)

–, *The Law of Restitution*, ed by Gareth H. Jones, 7th edn (London: Sweet & Maxwell, 2007) [*Goff & Jones*7]

Goldstein, Stephen R, ed, *Equity and Contemporary Legal Developments* (Jerusalem: Harry & Michael Sacher Institute for Legislative Research & Comparative Law, Hebrew University of Jerusalem, 1992)

Goode, Royston Miles, *Goode on Legal Problems of Credit and Security*, ed by Louise Gullifer, 5th edn (London: Sweet & Maxwell, 2013) [*Goode on Security*]

Goodman, John C, "An Economic Theory of the Evolution of Common Law" (1978) 7:2 J Legal Stud 393–406

Gordley, James and Ugo Mattei, "Protecting Possession" (1996) 44 Am J Comp L 293–334
Grantham, Ross, "Doctrinal Bases for the Recognition of Proprietary Rights" (1996) 16 Oxford J Legal Stud 561–85
Grantham, Ross and Charles Rickett, "Property and Unjust Enrichment: Categorical Truths or Unnecessary Complexity?" [1997] NZL Rev 668–86
–, "Tracing and Property Rights: The Categorical Truth" (2000) 63:6 Modern L Rev 905–11
–, "Disgorgement for Unjust Enrichment?" (2003) 62:1 CLJ 159–80
–, "Property Rights as a Legally Significant Event" (2003) 62:3 CLJ 717–49 [Grantham & Rickett, "Property as Event"]
–, "Unjust Enrichment: Reason, Place and Content" in: Ross Grantham & Charles Rickett, eds, *Structure and Justification in Private Law: Essays for Peter Birks* (Oxford: Hart, 2008) 5–18
–, eds, *Structure and Justification in Private Law: Essays for Peter Birks* (Oxford: Hart, 2008)
Gray, Christopher B, "Patrimony" (1981) 22 C de D 81–157
Gray, Kevin J, "Property in Thin Air" (1991) 50:2 CLJ 252–307
Graziadei, Michele, "The Functionalist Heritage" in: Pierre Legrand & Roderick Munday, eds, *Comparative Legal Studies: Traditions and Transitions* (Cambridge: Cambridge University Press, 2003) 100–27
–, "Recognition of Common Law Trusts in Civil Law Jurisdictions under the Hague Trusts Convention with Particular Regard to the Italian Experience" in: Lionel D Smith, ed, *Re-imagining the Trust: Trusts in Civil Law* (Cambridge: Cambridge University Press, 2012) 29–82 [Graziadei, "Recognition"]
Grechenig, Kristoffel and Martin Gelter, "The Transatlantic Divergence in Legal Thought: American Law and Economics vs. German Doctrinalism" (2008) 31:1 *Hastings Int'l & Comp L Rev* 295–360
Greene, Jack, "By Their Laws Shall Ye Know Them: Law and Identity in Colonial British America" (2002) 33:2 The Journal of Interdisciplinary History 247–60
Green, Sarah, "To Have and Hold?: Conversion and Intangible Property" (2008) 71:1 Modern L Rev 114–20
Grenon, Aline, "Major Differences between PPSA Legislation and Security over Movables in Quebec under the New Civil Code" (1996) 26 CBLJ 391–421 [Grenon, "Differences"]
–, "Les sûretés mobilières en Ontario et le droit international privé" (1998) 2:1 RCLF 117–42
–, "La problématique entourant les « sûretés-proprietés » au Québec: Lefebvre (Syndic de); Tremblay (Syndic de) et Oulllet (Syndic de)" (2005) 35 RGD 285–322
–, "Le bijuridisme canadien à la croisée des chemins?: Réflexions sur l'incidence de l'article 8.1 de la Loi d'interprétation" (2011) 56:4 McGill LJ 775–820 [Grenon, "Croisée des chemins"]
Gretton, George L, "Constructive Trusts (Part I)" (1997) 1:3 Edin L Rev 281–316
–, "Trusts Without Equity" (2000) 49:3 ICLQ 599–620
–, "Proprietary Issues" in: David Johnston & Reinhard Zimmermann, eds, *Unjustified Enrichment: Key Issues in Comparative Perspective* (Cambridge: Cambridge University Press, 2002) 571–87
–, "Reception Without Integration?: Floating Charges and Mixed Systems" (2003) 78:1–2 Tul L Rev 307–32
–, "Ownership and Its Objects" (2007) 71:4 RabelsZ 802–51

Guest, Anthony Gordon, "Accession and Confusion in the Law of Hire-Purchase" (1964) 27 Modern L Rev 505–20
–, ed, *Oxford Essays in Jurisprudence* (Oxford: Oxford University Press, 1961)
Gullifer, Louise and Orkun Akseli, eds, *Secured Transactions Law Reform: Principles, Policies and Practice* (Oxford, Portland: Hart, 2016)
Häcker, Birke, *Consequences of Impaired Consent Transfers: A Structural Comparison of English and German Law* (Studien zum ausländischen und internationalen Privatrecht, Tübingen: Mohr Siebeck, 2009)
–, "Proprietary Restitution After Impaired Consent Transfers: A Generalised Power Model" (2009) 68:2 CLJ 324–60
–, "Causality and Abstraction in the Common Law" in: Elise Bant & Matthew Harding, eds, *Exploring Private Law* (Cambridge: Cambridge University Press, 2010) 200–22
–, "Das Trennungs- und Abstraktionsprinzip im englischen Recht: Dargestellt anhand der Übereignung" [2011] ZEuP 335–65
Hallebeek, Jan, "Transfer of Ownership: Traditionalism or Consensualism?" (2004) 45:1 Codicillus 6–16
Hansmann, Henry and Reinier Kraakman, "Property, Contract, and Verification: The Numerus Clausus Problem and the Divisibility of Rights" (2002) 31:S2 J Legal Stud 373–420
Hansmann, Henry and Ugo Mattei, "The Functions of Trust Law: A Comparative Legal and Economic Analysis" (1998) 73 NYUL Rev 434–79
Hardin, Garrettt, "The Tragedy of the Commons" (1968) 162:3859 Science 1243–48
Hargreaves, Anthony Dalzell, "Terminology and Title in Ejectment" (1940) 56:3 LQR 376–98
Harke, Jan Dirk, *Besonderes Schuldrecht* (Berlin: Springer, 2011)
DR Harris, "The Concept of Possession in English Law" in: Anthony G Guest, ed, *Oxford Essays in Jurisprudence* (Oxford: Oxford University Press, 1961) 69–106
J Harris, *The Hague Trusts Convention: Scope, Application and Preliminary Issues* (Oxford: Hart, 2002)
RC Harris, *The Seigneurial System in Early Canada: A Geographical Study*, Paperback (Kingston: McGill-Queen's University Press, 1984)
Harris, Steven L and Mooney, Jr, Charles W, "A Property-Based Theory of Security Interests: Taking Debtors' Choices Seriously" (1994) 80:8 Va L Rev 2021–72
Hart, HLA, "Positivism and the Separation of Law and Morals" (1958) 71:4 Harv L Rev 593–629
–, *The Concept of Law*, 2d edn (Oxford: Clarendon Press, 1997)
Hartkamp, AS, "Civil Code Revision in Quebec" (1977) 24 *Nethl Int'l L Rev* 614–16
Hart, Oliver; Rafael La Porta Drago; Florencio Lopez-de-Silanes; and John Moore, "A New Bankruptcy Procedure That Uses Multiple Auctions" (1997) 41 Eur Econ Rev 461–43
Hart, Oliver and John Moore, "A Theory of Debt Based on the Inalienability of Human Capital" (1994) 109 Quart J Econ 841–79
–, "Default and Renegotiation: A Dynamic Model of Debt" (1998) 113 Quart J Econ 1–41
Hawes, Cynthia, *Tortious Interference with Goods in New Zealand: The Law of Conversion, Detinue and Trespass* (Ph.D. Thesis, University of Canterbury, 2010) <http://ir.canterbury.ac.nz/handle/10092/3834> accessed 20 June 2016
Hayton, David, "The Hague Convention on the Law Applicable to Trusts and on Their Recognition" (1987) 36 ICLQ 260–82
Hedley, Steve, "Unjust Enrichment as the Basis of Restitution: An Overworked Concept" (1985) 5 LS 56–66

–, "Implied Contract and Restitution" (2004) 63:2 CLJ 435–55
Hegel, Georg Wilhelm Friedrich, *Grundlinien der Philosophie des Rechts* (Berlin: Nicolaische Buchhandlung, 1821)
Heirbaut, Dirk, "Feudal Law: The Real Ius Commune of Property in Europe, or: Should We Reintroduce Duplex Dominium?" (2003) 11:3 Eur Rev Priv L 301–20
Heller, Michael A, "The Tragedy of the Anticommons: Property in the Transition from Marx to Markets" (1998) 111:3 Harv L Rev 621–88
–, "The Boundaries of Private Property" (1999) 108:6 Yale LJ 1163–223
Henry, Peter Blair and Conrad Miller, "Institutions versus Policies: A Tale of Two Islands" (2009) 99 Am Econ Rev 261–67
Herman, Shael, "Utilitas Ecclesiae: The Canonical Conception of the Trust" (1996) 70:6 Tul L Rev 2239–78
Hess, Amy Morris; George Gleason Bogert; and George Taylor Bogert, *The Law of Trusts and Trustees*, Revised second edition, 1995 replacement volume, as amended by 2009 cumulative supplement (St. Paul, Minn.: West Pub. Co, 1995)
Hey, William, (attributed), "A View of the Civil Government and Administration of Justice in the Province of Canada While It Was Subject to the Crown of France" (1857) 1 LCJ 1–48
Hicks, John R, "The Foundations of Welfare Economics" (1939) 49:196 Econ J 696–712
Hillman, William C, "What's in a Name: The U.C.C. Filing System in the Courts" (1991) 44 Okla L Rev 151–60
Hohfeld, Wesley Newcomb, "Some Fundamental Legal Conceptions as Applied in Judicial Reasoning" (1913) 23:1 Yale LJ 16–59 [Hohfeld, "Fundamental Conceptions I"]
–, "Fundamental Legal Conceptions as Applied in Judicial Reasoning" (1917) 26:8 Yale LJ 710–70 [Hohfeld, "Fundamental Conceptions II"]
–, *Fundamental Legal Conceptions as Applied in Judicial Reasoning and Other Legal Essays*, ed by Walter Wheeler Cook (New Haven: Yale University Press, 1923)
–, "Some Fundamental Legal Conceptions as Applied in Judicial Reasoning (I)" in: Wesley N Hohfeld, *Fundamental Legal Conceptions as Applied in Judicial Reasoning and Other Legal Essays*, ed by Walter W Cook (New Haven: Yale University Press, 1923) 23
–, "Fundamental Legal Conceptions as Applied in Judicial Reasoning (II)" in: Wesley N Hohfeld, *Fundamental Legal Conceptions as Applied in Judicial Reasoning and Other Legal Essays*, ed by Walter W Cook (New Haven: Yale University Press, 1923) 65
Holdsworth, William Searle, "Terminology and Title in Ejectment: A Reply" (1940) 56:4 LQR 479–82
Holmes, Oliver Wendell, "The Path of the Law" (1897) 10:8 Harv L Rev 457–78 [Holmes, "Path"]
–, "Law in Science and Science in Law" (1899) 12:7 Harv L Rev 443–63
Honoré, Anthony Maurice, "Rights of Exclusion and Immunities Against Divesting" (1960) 34:3 Tul L Rev 453–68
–, "Ownership" in: Anthony G Guest, ed, *Oxford Essays in Jurisprudence* (Oxford: Oxford University Press, 1961) 107–47
Hudson, John, "The Case Against Secured Lending" (1995) 15:1 *Int'l Rev L & Econ* 47–63
Hunt, Chris DL, "Decline of Juristic Reasons: Unjust Enrichment and the Supreme Court of Canada" (2010) 43:1 UBCL Rev 173–92
UNCITRAL, *Model Law on Secured Transactions*, (UNCITRAL) <https://uncitral.un.org/en/texts/securityinterests/modellaw/secured_transactions> accessed 20 September 2019

Jackson, Thomas H, *The Logic and Limits of Bankruptcy Law* (Cambridge, Mass.: Harvard University Press, 1986)
Jackson, Thomas H and Anthony T Kronman, "Secured Financing and Priorities Among Creditors" (1979) 88 Yale LJ 1143–82
Jaffey, Peter, "Two Theories of Unjust Enrichment" in: Jason W Neyers, Mitchell McInnes & Stephen G Pitel, eds, *Understanding Unjust Enrichment* (Oxford: Hart, 2004) 139–64 [Jaffey, "Two Theories"]
–, "The Unjust Enrichment Fallacy and Private Law" (2013) 26 *Can JL & Juris* 115–36 [Jaffey, "Fallacy"]
Jayme, Erik, "Betrachtungen zur dépeçage im internationalen Privatrecht" in: Hans-Joachim Musielak & Klaus Schurig, eds, *Festschrift für Gerhard Kegel zum 75. Geburtstag* (Stuttgart: Kohlhammer, 1987) 253–68
Jenks, Edward, "A Blind Spot in English Law" (1933) 49 LQR 215–25
von Jhering, Rudolf, *Geist des römischen Rechtes*, 1st edn (Leipzig: Breitkopf & Härtel, 1865), vol 3.1
–, "Passive Wirkungen der Rechte: Ein Beitrag zur Theorie der Rechte" (1871) 10 Jher Jb 387–586
–, *Der Besitzwille* (Jena: Gustav Fischer, 1889)
Johnston, David and Reinhard Zimmermann, eds, *Unjustified Enrichment: Key Issues in Comparative Perspective* (Cambridge: Cambridge University Press, 2002)
Jones, Gareth, "Ultra Vires Swaps: The Common Law and Equitable Fall-Out" (1996) 55:3 CLJ 432–36
Jones, NG, "Uses and 'Automatic' Resulting Trusts of Freehold" (2013) 72:1 CLJ 91–114
Jörs, Paul; Wolfgang Kunkel; Leopold Wenger; Walter Selb; Heinrich Honsell; and Theo Mayer-Maly, *Römisches Recht*, 4th edn (Enzyklopädie der Rechts- und Staatswissenschaft Abteilung Rechtswissenschaft, Berlin: Springer, 1987)
*JurisClasseur: Civil Code* (Paris: LexisNexis, last update: 22 June 2012)
Kaldor, Nicholas, "Welfare Propositions of Economics and Interpersonal Comparisons of Utility" (1939) 49:195 Econ J 549–52
Kant, Immanuel, *Werke*, ed by Wilhelm Weischedel, 3rd edn (Darmstadt: Suhrkamp, 1971), vol 4
–, "Grundlegung zur Metaphysik der Sitten" in: Immanuel Kant, *Werke*, ed by Wilhelm Weischedel, 3rd ed (Darmstadt: Suhrkamp, 1971), vol 4, 58
–, "Metaphysik der Sitten: Rechtslehre" in: Immanuel Kant, *Werke*, ed by Wilhelm Weischedel, 3rd ed (Darmstadt: Suhrkamp, 1971), vol 4, 306 [Kant, "Rechtslehre"]
Kasirer, Nicholas, ed, *Le droit civil: avant tout un style?* (Montréal: Éditions Thémis, 2003)
Katz, Larissa, "Exclusion and Exclusivity in Property Law" (2008) 58:3 UTLJ 275–315
–, "The Concept of Ownership and the Relativity of Title" (2011) 2:1 Jurisprudence 191–203
Kegel, Gerhard, "Paternal Home and Dream Home: Traditional Conflict of Laws and the American Reformers" (1979) 27:4 Am J Comp L 615–34
Kegel, Gerhard and Klaus Schurig, *Internationales Privatrecht*, 9th edn (München: C.H. Beck, 2004)
Keller, Stefan and Stefan Wiprächtiger, eds, *Recht zwischen Dogmatik und Theorie: Marc Amstutz zum 50. Geburtstag* (Zürich, St. Gallen: Dike, 2012)
Kelsen, Hans, *Reine Rechtslehre*, 2d edn (Wien: Franz Deuticke, 1960)
Kennedy, Duncan, "Two Globalizations of Law & Legal Thought: 1850–1968" (2002) 36:3 Suffolk UL Rev 631–79

Kennedy, WPM and Gustave Lanctôt, eds, *Reports on the Laws of Quebec, 1767–1770* (Ottawa: F.A. Acland, 1931)

Kieninger, Eva-Maria, *Mobiliarsicherheiten im Europäischen Binnenmarkt* (Baden-Baden: Nomos, 1996)

–, "European Regulation of Security Rights" in: Ulrich Drobnig, Henricus J Snijders & Eric-Jan Zippro, eds, *Divergences of Property Law: An Obstacle to the Internal Market?* (Berlin: Sellier, 2006) 165–71

–, "Die Zukunft des deutschen und europäischen Mobiliarkreditsicherungsrechts" (2008) 208:2–3 AcP 182–226

–, ed, *Security Rights in Movable Property in European Private Law* (Cambridge: Cambridge University Press, 2004)

Kim, Kensie, "Mixed Systems in Legal Origins Analysis" (2010) 83:3 S Cal L Rev 693–729

Kiralfy, AKR, "The Problem of a Law of Property in Goods" (1949) 12 Modern L Rev 424–31

Kirchner, Christian, "The Difficult Reception of Law and Economics in Germany" (1991) 11:3 *Int'l Rev L & Econ* 277–92

Kitch, Edmund W, "The Fire of Truth: A Remembrance of Law and Economics at Chicago, 1932–1970" (1983) 26:1 *JL & Econ* 163–234

Klerman, Daniel, "Jurisdiction, Choice of Law and Property" <https://papers.ssrn.com/sol3/papers.cfm?abstract_id=2422470> accessed 3 December 2017

Klerman, Daniel; Paul G Mahoney; Holger Spamann; and Mark Weinstein, "Legal Origin or Colonial History?" (2011) 3:2 J Leg An 379–409

Klimchuk, Dennis, "The Normative Foundations of Unjust Enrichment" in: Robert Chambers, Charles C Mitchell & James E Penner, eds, *Philosophical Foundations of the Law of Unjust Enrichment* (Oxford: Oxford University Press, 2009) 81–99

Klinck, Dennis R, "The Quistclose Trust in Canada" (1994) 23:1 CBLJ 45–77

Klinck, Fabian, *Erwerb durch Übergabe an Dritte nach klassischem römischen Recht* (Berlin: Duncker & Humblot, 2004)

Kohler, Jürgen, "Vormerkbarkeit eines durch abredewidrige Veräußerung bedingten Rückerwerbsanspruchs" [1989] DNotZ 339–53

Kolish, Evelyn, *Nationalismes et conflits de droit: Le débat du droit privé au Québec, 1760–1840* (Cahiers du Québec Collection Histoire, LaSalle, Québec: Hurtubise HMH, 1994)

Kötz, Hein, "Die 15. Haager Konferenz und das Kollisionsrecht des trust" (1986) 50:3–4 RabelsZ 562–85

Kozolchyk, Boris, "Transfers of Personal Property by a Nonowner: Its Future in Light of Its Past" (1987) 61 Tul L Rev 1453–514

Krebs, Thomas, "In Defence of Unjust Factors" in: David Johnston & Reinhard Zimmermann, eds, *Unjustified Enrichment: Key Issues in Comparative Perspective* (Cambridge: Cambridge University Press, 2002) 76–100

Kreuzer, Karl, "La propriété mobilière en droit international privé" in: Académie du droit international, ed, *Recueil des cours* (Leiden: Sijthoff, 1996) 9–318

Kripke, Homer, "Law and Economics: Measuring the Economic Efficiency of Commercial Law in a Vacuum of Fact" (1985) 133:5 U Pa L Rev 929–85

Kruse, John, "Replevin: Repeal or Retain?" (2001) 23:1 Liv L Rev 95–115

Kuchinke, Kurt, ed, *Rechtsbewahrung und Rechtsentwicklung: Festschrift für Heinrich Lange zum 70. Geburtstag, 25. März 1970* (München: C.H. Beck, 1970)

Kull, Andrew, "Restitution in Bankruptcy: Reclamation and Constructive Trust" (1998) 72:3 Am Bankr LJ 265–302

L'Heureux, Jacques, "L'organisation judiciaire au Québec de 1764 à 1774" (1970) 1 RGD 266–331

La Peña, Nuria de, "Challenges in Implementing Secured Transactions Reform in Latin America" in: Frederique Dahan & John Simpson, eds, *Secured Transactions Reform and Access to Credit* (Cheltenham: Edward Elgar, 2009) 236–58

La Porta, Rafael; Florencio Lopez-de-Silanes; Cristian Pop-Eleches; and Andrei Shleifer, "Judicial Checks and Balances" (2004) 112 J Pol Econ 445–70

La Porta, Rafael; Florencio Lopez-de-Silanes; and Andrei Shleifer, "The Economic Consequences of Legal Origins" (2008) 46:2 J Econ Lit 285–332

La Porta, Rafael; Florencio Lopez-de-Silanes; Andrei Shleifer; and Robert W Vishny, "Legal Determinants of External Finance" (1997) 52:4 J Fin 1131–50

–, "Law and Finance" (1998) 106:6 J Pol Econ 1113–55 [La Porta et al., "Law and Finance"]

Lacy, Jr, Frank, "Constructive Trusts and Equitable Liens in Iowa" (1954) 40 Iow L Rev 107–56

Lafond, Pierre-Claude, *Précis de droit des biens*, 2[d] edn (Montréal: Éditions Thémis, 2007)

Lagarde, Paul, "Le dépeçage dans le droit international privé des contrats" (1975) 11 Riv dir int priv proc 649–77

Lalive, Pierre A, *The Transfer of Chattels in the Conflict of Laws: A Comparative Study* (Oxford: Clarendon Press, 1955)

Lametti, David and Audrey E Boctor, "Rewarding Ownership, Valuing Possessors: Making Sense of Articles 957–962 of the C.C.Q" in: Sylvio Normand, ed, *Mélanges offerts au Professeur François Frenette* (Québec: Les Presses de l'Université Laval, 2006) 151–94

Lamontagne, Denys-Claude, *Biens et propriété*, 6[th] edn (Cowansville, Québec: Éditions Yvon Blais, 2009)

Lamoureux, Martin, "The Income Tax Act, the Excise Tax Act and the Term Interest: An Interesting Case for Harmonization" in: Canada, Department of Justice & Association de planification fiscale et financière, eds, *Harmonization of Federal Legislation with Quebec Civil Law and Canadian Bijuralism: Collection of Studies in Tax Law* (Montréal: Association de planification fiscale et financière, 2002) ) 1–38

Langbein, John H, "The Contractarian Basis of the Law of Trusts" (1995) 105 Yale LJ 625–75

Langevin, Louise and Denise Pratte, "Du Code civil du Bas-Canada au nouveau Code civil du Québec: L'influence de la codification française" in: H P Glenn, ed, *Droit québécois et droit français: Communauté, autonomie, concordance* (Cowansville, Québec: Éditions Yvon Blais, 1993) 63–89

Lanthier, Suzie, *Les sûretés sur les valeurs mobilières: Le mouvement d'uniformisation d'origine américaine est-il transposable universellement?: Vers une approche québécoise à la question* (LL.M. Thesis, Université de Montréal, 2009) <http://hdl.handle.net/1866/3770> accessed 19 October 2017

Lavallée, Loius, "Bijuralism in the Supreme Court of Canada Judgments Since the Enactment of the Civil Code of Québec" in: Canada, Department of Justice, ed, *The Harmonization of Federal Legislation with the Civil Law of the Province of Quebec and Canadian Bijuralism: Second Publication* (Ottawa: Canada, Department of Justice, 2001) 1–29

Law Commission, *Company Security Interests: A Consultative Report* (LAW COM, vol 176, London: Her Majesty's Stationery Office, 2004)

Law Reform Commission of British Columbia, *Working Paper on Wrongful Interference with Goods* (Victoria: Law Reform Commission of British Columbia, 1992)

Lawson, Philip, *The Imperial Challenge: Quebec and Britain in the Age of the American Revolution* (Kingston: McGill-Queen's University Press, 1989) [Lawson, *Challenge*]
–, "A Perspective on British History and the Treatment of Québec" (1990) 3 Journal of Historical Sociology 253–71
Leckey, Robert, "Unjust Enrichment and De Facto Spouses" (2012) 114 R du N 475–500
–, "Bankruptcy, Provincial Law, and the Family Farm" (2013) 91:2 Can Bar Rev 435–53
Leeming, Mark, "The Comparative Distinctiveness of Equity" (2016) 2:2 CJCCL 403–20
Legrand, Pierre, "Civil Law Codification in Quebec: A Case of Decivilianization" (1993) 1 ZEuP 574
–, "Bureaucrats at Play: The New Quebec Civil Code" (1995) 10 Brit J of Can Stud 52
–, "Comparative Contraventions" (2005) 50 McGill LJ 669–83
Legrand, Pierre and Roderick Munday, eds, *Comparative Legal Studies: Traditions and Transitions* (Cambridge: Cambridge University Press, 2003)
Lepaulle, Pierre, *Traité théorique et pratique des trusts en droit interne, en droit fiscal et en droit international* (Paris: Rousseau, 1932)
–, "Trusts and the Civil Law" (1933) 15:1 *J Comp Leg Int'l L* 18–34
Levasseur, Alain A, "The Boundaries of Property Rights: La Notion de Biens" (2006) 54 Am J Comp L 145–65
Lewald, Hans, "Règles générales des conflits de lois: Contribution à la technique du droit international privé" in: Académie du droit international, ed, *Recueil des cours* (Leiden: Brill, 1939), vol 69, 1–148
Lewin, Jeff L, "Boomer and the American Law of Nuisance: Past, Present, and Future" (1989–1990) 54 Alb L Rev 189–299
Liebs, Rüdiger, "Die unbeschränkbare Verfügungsbefugnis" (1975) 175 AcP 1–43
Liew, Ying Khai, "The Secondary-Rights Approach to the 'Common Intention Constructive Trust'" [2015] Conveyancer 210–23
Lipstein, Kurt, "The Doctrine of Precedent in Continental Law with Special Reference to French and German Law" (1946) 28 *J Comp Leg Int'l L* 34–44
–, *Private International Law: Trusts*, ed by Konrad Zweigert, Ulrich Drobnig, and Kurt Lipstein (International Encyclopedia of Comparative Law, III-23, Tübingen: Mohr Siebeck, 1994) [Lipstein, *Trusts*]
–, *Private International Law: Characterization*, ed by Konrad Zweigert, Ulrich Drobnig, and Kurt Lipstein (International Encyclopedia of Comparative Law, III-5, Tübingen: Mohr Siebeck, 1999) [Lipstein, *Characterization*]
Listokin, Yair, "Is Secured Debt Used to Redistribute Value from Tort Claimants in Bankruptcy?: An Empirical Analysis" (2008) 57 Duke LJ 1037–79
Litman, MM, "The Emergence of Unjust Enrichment as a Cause of Action and the Remedy of Constructive Trust" (1987–1988) 26 Alta L Rev 407–70
Locke, John, *Two Treatises of Government*, ed by Thomas Hollis (London: A. Millar et al, 1764)
Longtin, Marie José, "Le style civiliste et la loi" in: Nicholas Kasirer, ed, *Le droit civil: avant tout un style?* (Montréal: Éditions Thémis, 2003) 185–205
Lopez-de-Silanes, Florencio, "Turning the Key to Credit: Credit Access and Credit Institutions" in: Frederique Dahan & John Simpson, eds, *Secured Transactions Reform and Access to Credit* (Cheltenham: Edward Elgar, 2009) 3–52
LoPucki, Lynn M, "The Unsecured Creditor's Bargain" (1994) 80:8 Va L Rev 1887–965
Loxton, Diccon, "One Flaw over the Cuckoos Nest: Making Sense of the 'Flawed Asset Arrangement' Example, Security Interest Definition and Set-Off Exclusion in the PPSA" (2011) 34:2 UNSWLJ 472–533

Lubetsky, Michael H, "Adding Epicycles: The Inconsistent Use Test in Adverse Possession Law" (2009) 47 OHLJ 497–552
Lupoi, Maurizio, *Trusts: A Comparative Study* (New York: Cambridge University Press, 2000)
MacClean, David, "De conflictu legum: Perspectives on Private International Law at the Turn of the Century" in: Académie du droit international, ed, *Recueil des cours* (Leiden: Sijthoff, 2000) 41–228
Macdonald, Roderick Alexander, "Enforcing Rights in Corporeal Moveables: Revendication and Its Surrogates (Part 1)" (1986) 31:4 McGill LJ 573–654 [Macdonald, "Enforcing Rights I"]
–, "Enforcing Rights in Corporeal Moveables: Revendication and Its Surrogates (Part 2)" (1986) 32:1 McGill LJ 1–95
–, "Change of Terminology? Change of Law?" (1992) 23 RGD 357–72 [Macdonald, "Change"]
–, "Faut-il s'assurer qu'on appelle un chat un chat?: Observations sur la méthodologie législative à travers l'énumération limitative des sûretés, «la présomption d'hypothèque» et le principe de «l'essence de l'opération»" in: Ernest Caparros, ed, *Mélanges Germain Brière* (Montréal: Wilson & Lafleur, 1993) 527–94
–, "Reconceiving the Symbols of Property: Universalities, Interests and Other Heresies" (1994) 39 McGill LJ 761–812 [Macdonald, "Symbols"]
–, "In Praise of the Hypothecary Charge" (2007) 7–8 DeCITA 287–308
MacDougall, Bruce, "The Debtor's Interest in Personal Property Under the PPSA" (1994) 33:1 Alta L Rev 80–115
MacLennan, Hugh, *Two Solitudes* (Toronto: Macmillan, 1945)
Maddaugh, Peter D and John D McCamus, *The Law of Restitution*, loose-leaf (Aurora, Ontario: Canada Law Book, 2004)
Mahoney, Paul G, "The Common Law and Economic Growth: Hayek Might Be Right" (2001) 30:2 J Legal Stud 503–25
Maitland, Frederic William, "The Seisin of Chattels" (1885) 1 LQR 314–41
–, "Mystery of Seisin" (1886) 2 LQR 481–96 [Maitland, "Mystery"]
–, "The Origin of Uses" (1894) 8:3 Harv L Rev 127–37
–, "Notes" in: Frederic W Maitland, ed, *Select Passages from the Works of Bracton and Azo* (London: Bernard Quaritch, 1895) 172–73
–, *Equity, Also the Forms of Action at Common Law: Two Courses of Lectures*, ed by A. H. Chaytor and W. J. Whittaker (Cambridge: Cambridge University Press, 1910)
–, "Lectures on Equity" in: Frederic W Maitland, *Equity, Also the Forms of Action at Common Law: Two Courses of Lectures*, AH Chaytor & WJ Whittaker (Cambridge: Cambridge University Press, 1910) 1
–, *Equity*, ed by A. H. Clayton and W. J. Whittaker (Cambridge: Cambridge University Press, 1936)
–, ed, *Select Passages from the Works of Bracton and Azo* (London: Bernard Quaritch, 1895)
Malaurie, Philippe and Laurent Aynès, *Les biens*, 4th edn (Paris: Defrénois, 2010)
Mansel, Heinz-Peter, "Anerkennung als Grundprinzip des Europäischen Rechtsraums: Zur Herausbildung eines europäischen Anerkennungs-Kollisionsrechts: Anerkennung statt Verweisung als neues Strukturprinzip des Europäischen internationalen Privatrechts?" (2006) 70 RabelsZ 651–731
Mathernová, Katarina, "The Slovak Secured Transactions Reform: Ingredients of a Successful Reform and Reflection on Its Achievements" in: Frederique Dahan & John

Simpson, eds, *Secured Transactions Reform and Access to Credit* (Cheltenham: Edward Elgar, 2009) 207–23

Mattei, Ugo, "Efficiency in Legal Transplants: An Essay in Comparative Law and Economics" (1994) 14:1 *Int'l Rev L & Econ* 3–19

Mayer, Pierre and Vincent Heuzé, *Droit international privé*, 11th edn (Paris: Librairie générale de droit et de jurisprudence, 2014)

McAuley, Michael, "Truth and Reconciliation: Notions of Property in Louisiana's Civil and Trust Codes" in: Lionel D Smith, ed, *Re-imagining the Trust: Trusts in Civil Law* (Cambridge: Cambridge University Press, 2012) 119–82

McCamus, John D, "Restitution on Dissolution of Marital and Other Intimate Relationships: Constructive Trust or Quantum Meruit" in: Jason W Neyers, Mitchell McInnes & Stephen G Pitel, eds, *Understanding Unjust Enrichment* (Oxford: Hart, 2004) 359–81

–, "Mistake, Forged Cheques and Unjust Enrichment: Three Cheers for B.M.P. Global" (2009) 48:2 CBLJ 76–101 [McCamus, "Three Cheers"]

McCoid, II, John C, "Bankruptcy, the Avoiding Powers and Unperfected Security Interests" (1985) 59 Am Bankr LJ 175–93

McCormack, Gerard, *Secured Credit and the Harmonisation of Law: The UNCITRAL Experience* (Cheltenham: Edward Elgar, 2011)

McFarlane, Ben, *The Structure of Property Law* (London: Bloomsbury Publishing, 2008)

McFarlane, Ben and Robert Stevens, "The Nature of Equitable Property" (2010) 4:1 J Equ 1–99

McGhee, John, *Snell's Equity*, 30th edn (London: Sweet & Maxwell, 2000)

McGill University, Faculty of Law, ed, *Mélanges Paul-André Crepeau* (Cowansville, Québec: Éditions Yvon Blais, 1997)

McGrath, Colm Peter and Helmut Koziol, "Is Style of Reasoning a Fundamental Difference Between the Common Law and the Civil Law?" (2014) 78:4 RabelsZ 709–49

McGrath, Noel, "Book Review: The Reform of UK Personal Property Security Law: Comparative Perspectives" (2011) 31 LS 159–72

McInnes, Mitchell, "The Canadian Principle of Unjust Enrichment: Comparative Insights Into the Law of Restitution" (1999) 37 Alta L Rev 1–37

–, "The Measure of Restitution" (2002) 52 UTLJ 163–220

–, "Interceptive Subtraction, Unjust Enrichment and Wrongs: A Reply to Professor Birks" (2003) 62:3 CLJ 697–716

–, "Making Sense of Unjust Enrichment: Unjust Enrichment after Garland v Consumers' Gas" (2004–2005) 42 Alta L Rev 399–427

–, "Taxonomic Lessons for the Supreme Court of Canada" in: Ross Grantham & Charles Rickett, eds, *Structure and Justification in Private Law: Essays for Peter Birks* (Oxford: Hart, 2008) 77–101

–, "Resisting Temptations to Justice" in: Robert Chambers, Charles C Mitchell & James E Penner, eds, *Philosophical Foundations of the Law of Unjust Enrichment* (Oxford: Oxford University Press, 2009) 100–45 [McInnes, "Resisting Temptations"]

–, "The Unitary Action in Unjust Enrichment" (2009) 48 CBLJ 102–24 [McInnes, "Unitary Action"]

–, "Garland's Unitary Test of Unjust Enrichment: A Response to Professor McCamus" (2011) 38:2 *Advocates' Q* 165–97 [McInnes, "Garland's Unitary Test"]

–, "The Reason to Reverse: Unjust Factors and Juristic Reason" (2012) 92 Boston UL Rev 1049–65 [McInnes, "Reason"]

McLachlan, Campbell, "International Litigation and the Reworking of the Conflict of Laws" (2004) 120 LQR 580–616

Mee, John, "Property Rights and Personal Relationships: Reflections on Reform" (2004) 24:3 LS 414–50

Meier, Sonja, *Irrtum und Zweckverfehlung: Die Rolle der Unjust-Gründe bei rechtsgrundlosen Leistungen im englischen Recht* (Studien zum ausländischen und internationalen Privatrecht, Tübingen: Mohr Siebeck, 1999)

–, "Unjust Factors and Legal Grounds" in: David Johnston & Reinhard Zimmermann, eds, *Unjustified Enrichment: Key Issues in Comparative Perspective* (Cambridge: Cambridge University Press, 2002) 37–75

–, "No Basis: A Comparative View" in: Andrew S Burrows & Alan Rodger, eds, *Mapping the Law: Essays in Memory of Peter Birks* (Oxford: Oxford University Press, 2006) 343–61

Mercier, Virginie, *L'apport du droit des valeurs mobilières à la théorie générale du droit des biens* (Presses Universitaires D'Aix Marseilles: Aix-en-Provence, 2005)

Merrett, Louise, "The Importance of Delivery and Possession in the Passing of Title" (2008) 67:2 CLJ 376–95

Merrill, Thomas W, "Property as Modularity" (2012) 125:1 Harv L Rev 151–63

Merrill, Thomas W and Henry E Smith, "Optimal Standardization in the Law of Property: The Numerus Clausus Principle" (2000) 110:1 Yale LJ 1–70

–, "What Happened to Property in Law and Economics?" (2001) 111:2 Yale LJ 357–98

Merryman, John Henry, "Policy, Autonomy, and the Numerus Clausus in Italian and American Property Law" (1963) 12:2 Am J Comp L 224–31 [Merryman, "Numerus Clausus"]

–, *The Civil Law Tradition: An Introduction to the Legal Systems of Western Europe and Latin America* (Stanford, Calif.: Stanford University Press, 1969)

–, "Ownership and Estate: Variations on a Theme by Lawson" (1974) 48 Tul L Rev 916–45

Michaels, Ralf, "EU Law as Private International Law?: Reconceptualising the Country-of-Origin Principle as Vested-Rights Theory" (2006) 2:2 *J Priv Int'l L* 195–242

–, "The Functionalism of Legal Origins" in: Michael Faure & Jan M Smits, eds, *Does Law Matter?: On Law and Economic Growth* (Cambridge: Intersentia, 2011) 21–39

Mignault, Pierre-Basile, "Les rapports entre le droit civil et la 'common law' au Canada, specialement dans la province de Québec" (1932) 11:4 R du D 201–11

–, "L'enrichissement sans cause" (1934–1935) 13 R du D 157–81

Miller, David L Carey, "Derivative Acquisition of Movables" in: Robin Evans-Jones, ed, *The Civil Law Tradition in Scotland* (Edinburgh: Stair Society, 1995) 128–56

–, "Transfer of Ownership" in: Kenneth G Reid & Reinhard Zimmermann, eds, *A History of Private Law in Scotland* (Oxford: Oxford University Press, 2000) 269–304

Millett, Peter, "Jones V Jones: Property or Unjust Enrichment" in: Andrew S Burrows & Alan Rodger, eds, *Mapping the Law: Essays in Memory of Peter Birks* (Oxford: Oxford University Press, 2006) 265–75

Mills, Alex, "The Private History of International Law" (2006) 55:1 ICLQ 1–50

Milsom, Stroud Francis Charles, "Sale of Goods in the Fifteenth Century" (1961) 77 LQR 257–84

Mitchell, Charles Christopher James, "Restitutionary Claims for Services: Identifying and Quantifying the Benefit" [2011] LMCLQ 504–27

Mitchell, Charles Christopher James; Paul Mitchell; and Stephen Watterson, *Goff & Jones: The Law of Unjust Enrichment*, 8th edn (London: Sweet & Maxwell, 2011)

–, Goff & Jones: *The Law of Unjust Enrichment*, 9th edn (London: Sweet & Maxwell, 2016) [*Goff & Jones*]

Modigliani, Franco and Merton H Miller, "The Cost of Capital, Corporation Finance and the Theory of Investment" (1958) 48:3 Am Econ Rev 261–97

Monaghan, Henry, "Constructive Trust and Equitable Lien: Status of the Conscious and the Innocent Wrongdoer in Equity" (1960–1961) 38 U Det LJ 10–33

Mooney, Jr, Charles W, "The Mystery and Myth of Ostensible Ownership and Article 9 Filing: A Critique of Proposals to Extend Filing Requirements to Leases" (1988) 39:3 Ala L Rev 683–790

–, "Filing Requirements For Personal Property Leases: A Comment and Response to Professor Ziegel" (1989–1990) 16 CBLJ 419–38

Morel, André, "Harmonizing Federal Legislation with the Civil Code of Québec: Why and Wherefore?" in: Canada, Department of Justice, ed, *The Harmonization of Federal Legislation with the Québec Civil Law and Canadian Bijuralism* (Ottawa: Canada, Department of Justice, 1997) 1–25

Morin, Michel, "Introduction historique au droit civil québécois" in: Louise Bélanger-Hardy & Aline Grenon, eds, *Éléments de common law et aperçu comparatif du droit civil québécois* (Scarborough, Ont: Carswell, 1997) 59–68

–, "Les changements de régimes juridiques consécutifs à la Conquête de 1760" (1997) 57 R du B 689–700 [Morin, "Changements"]

Morin, Sandra, "Le statut de la réserve de propriété en matière mobilière au Québec et en Ontario" (2008) 49:2 C de D 237–75

Morris, JHC, "The Transfer of Chattels in the Conflict of Laws" (1945) 22 *Brit YB Int'l L* 232–48

Moull, William D, "Security Under Sections 177 and 178 of the Bank Act" (1986) 65 Can Bar Rev 242–66

*Münchener Kommentar zum Bürgerlichen Gesetzbuch*, vol *6*, *§§ 854–1296 BGB, WEG, ErbbauRG*, ed by Kurt Rebmann; Franz-Jürgen Säcker; and Roland Rixecker, 6th edn (Munich: CH Beck, 2013)

–, vol *10*, *Internationales Privatrecht I*, ed by Kurt Rebmann; Franz-Jürgen Säcker; and Roland Rixecker, 5th edn (Munich: CH Beck, 2010)

*–, vol 11, Internationales Privatrecht II, Internationales Wirtschaftsrecht, Einführungsgesetz zum Bürgerlichen Gesetzbuch (Art. 25–248)*, ed by Kurt Rebmann; Franz-Jürgen Säcker; and Roland Rixecker, 6th edn (Munich: CH Beck, 2015)

Musielak, Hans-Joachim and Klaus Schurig, eds, *Festschrift für Gerhard Kegel zum 75. Geburtstag* (Stuttgart: Kohlhammer, 1987)

Neuberger, David, "Equity: The Soul and Spirit of All Law or a Roguish Thing?" (Paper presented to the University of New South Wales, Sydney, 4 August 2014)

Neumayer, Karl H, "Die sogenannte Vindikationszession (§ 931 BGB) im dogmatischen Spannungsfeld zwischen Übereignung und procuratio in rem" in: Kurt Kuchinke, ed, *Rechtsbewahrung und Rechtsentwicklung: Festschrift für Heinrich Lange zum 70. Geburtstag, 25. März 1970* (Munich: CH Beck, 1970) 305–24

Neyers, Jason W; Mitchell McInnes; and Stephen GA Pitel, eds, *Understanding Unjust Enrichment* (Oxford: Hart, 2004)

Niboyet, Marie-Laure and de Geouffre de la Pradelle, Geráud, *Droit international privé*, 4th edn (Paris: Librairie générale de droit et de jurisprudence, 2013)

Nicholls, GVV, "The Law Governing Conditional Sales in Canada" (1939) 21:1 J Comp Leg Int'l L 1–10

Noël, Jean-François, "Seigneurie et propriété urbaine sous l'Ancien Régime: Autour de la maison de Bertrand d'Argentré à Vitre" (1991) 38 *Revue d'histoire moderne et contemporaine* 177–204

Nolan, RC, "Equitable Property" (2006) 122 LQR 232

*Nomos Kommentar BGB*, vol *1*, *Allgemeiner Teil, EGBGB*, ed by Thomas Heidel, et al (Baden-Baden: Nomos, 2012)

Noreau, Pierre, ed, *Dans le regard d'autre - In the Eye of the Beholder* (Montréal: Éditions Thémis, 2007)

Normand, Sylvio, "Une relecture de l'arrêt Matamajaw Salmon Club" (1988) 29 C de D 807–13 [Normand, "Relecture"]

–, "La codification de 1866: Contexte et impact" in: H P Glenn, ed, *Droit québécois et droit français: Communauté, autonomie, concordance* (Cowansville, Québec: Éditions Yvon Blais, 1993) 43–62

–, "La notion de modalité de la propriété" in: Sylvio Normand, ed, *Mélanges offerts au Professeur François Frenette* (Québec: Les Presses de l'Université Laval, 2006) 255–81 [Normand, "Modalité"]

–, ed, *Mélanges offerts au Professeur François Frenette* (Québec: Les Presses de l'Université Laval, 2006)

North, Douglass C, *Structure and Change in Economic History*, 1st edn (New York: Norton, 1981)

Ogilvie, MH, "Privity of Contract and the Third Party Purchaser" (1987) 13:4 CBLJ 402–43

–, "The Tort of Conversion and the Collecting Bank" (2014) 91:3 Can Bar Rev 731–44 [Ogilvie, "Conversion"]

Ontario, Ministry of Government and Consumer Services, *Business Law Agenda: Priority Findings and Recommendations Report*, (2015) <https://www.ontariocanada.com/registry/showAttachment.do?postingId=18942&attachmentId=33251> accessed 3 September 2019

Oosterhoff, Albert H, "The Law of Mortmain: An Historical and Comparative Review" (1977) 27 UTLJ 257–334

Oosterhoff, Albert H; Robert Chambers; Mitchell McInnes; and Lionel D Smith, *Oosterhoff on Trusts*, 7th edn (Toronto: Carswell, 2009)

von Overbeck, Alfred E, "Rapport explicatif" in: Conférence de la Haye de droit international prive, ed, *Actes et documents de la 14ème session* ('s-Gravenshage: Bureau permanent de la Conférence, 1980) 370–415

Örücü, Esin, ed, *Mixed Legal Systems at New Frontiers* (JCL Studies in Comparative Law, London: Wildy, Simmonds & Hill, 2010)

Paciocco, David M, "The Remedial Constructive Trust: A Principled Basis for Priorities over Creditors" (1989) 68 Can Bar Rev 315–51

Paisley, Roderick RM, "Real Rights: Practical Problems and Dogmatic Rigidity" (2004) 9 Edin L Rev 267–97

Palmer, George E, *The Law of Restitution* (Boston: Little, Brown & Co., 1978)

Palmer, Vernon Valentine, "French Connection and the Spanish Perception: Historical Debates and Contemporary Evaluation of French Influence on Louisiana Civil Law" (2003) 63:4 La L Rev 1067–127

Panagopoulos, George, *Restitution in Private International Law* (Oxford: Hart, 2000)

Payette, Louis, *Les sûretés réelles dans le Code civil du Québec*, 5th edn (Cowansville, Québec: Éditions Yvon Blais, 2015)

Pearce, Robert and Jennifer Shearman, "The Pursuit of Proprietary Remedies for Breach of Fiduciary Duty" (2012) 24 Denn LJ 191–205

Penner, James E, "The Bundle of Rights Picture of Property" (1996) 43 UCLA L Rev 711–820 [Penner, "Bundle of Rights"]

–, "The (True) Nature of a Beneficiary's Equitable Proprietary Interest under a Trust" (2014) 27:2 *Can JL & Juris* 473–500 [Penner, "True Nature"]
Philbrick, Francis S, "Seisin and Possession as the Basis of Legal Title" (1938–1939) 24 Iow L Rev 268–308
Pistor, Katharina, "Rethinking the Law and Finance Paradigm" [2009] BYU L Rev 1647–70
Pitel, Stephen GA, "Characterisation of Unjust Enrichment in the Conflict of Laws" in: Jason W Neyers, Mitchell McInnes & Stephen G Pitel, eds, *Understanding Unjust Enrichment* (Oxford: Hart, 2004) 331–58
Pitel, Stephen GA and Nicholas S Rafferty, *Conflict of Laws* (Toronto: Irwin Law, 2010)
Plucknett, Theodore Frank Thomas, *A Concise History of the Common Law*, 5th edn (London: Butterworths, 1956)
Poirier, Marc-Alexandre, "Analysis of the Interaction Between Security Under Section 427 of the Bank Act and Provincial Law: A Bijural Perspective" (2003) 63 R du B 287–400
Pollock, Frederick, *The Expansion of the Common Law* (London: Stevens and Sons, 1904)
Pollock, Frederick and Robert Samuel Wright, *An Essay on Possession in the Common Law* (Oxford: Clarendon Press, 1888)
Posez, Alexis, "La subsidiarité de l'enrichissement sans cause: Étude de droit Français à la lumière du droit comparé" (2014) 91:2 Rev dr int dr comp 185–246
Posner, Richard A, "Utilitarianism, Economics, and Legal Theory" (1979) 8:1 J Legal Stud 103–40
–, "The Ethical and Political Basis of the Efficiency Norm in Common Law Adjudication" (1980) 8:3 Hofstra L Rev 487–508 [Posner, "Efficiency Norm"]
–, "The Value of Wealth: A Comment on Dworkin and Kronman" (1980) 9:2 J Legal Stud 243–52
–, "The Decline of Law as an Autonomous Discipline: 1962–1987" (1987) 100:4 Harv L Rev 761–80 [Posner, "Decline"]
–, *Law and Legal Theory in England and America* (Oxford: Clarendon Press, 1997)
–, "Bentham's Influence on the Law and Economics Movement" (1998) 51:1 Curr Legal Probs 425–39
–, *Economic Analysis of Law*, 7th edn (New York: Aspen Publishers, 2007)
Pound, Roscoe, "The Progress of the Law: 1918–1919 Equity" (1919–1920) 33 Harv L Rev 420–41
Priest, George L, "The Common Law Process and the Selection of Efficient Rules" (1977) 6:1 J Legal Stud 65–82
Pugh, Gordon, "Traditio in the Civil Law" (1962) 22:2 La L Rev 418–34
Quinn, Mary Ann, "Pratiques et théories de la coutume: Allodialité et conflits de droits dans la seigneurie de L'Isle-sous-Montréal au XVIIIe siècle" [1986] Études rurales 71–104
Rabel, Ernst, "Das Problem der Qualifikation" (1931) 5 RabelsZ 241–88
Rabel, Ernst and Ludwig Raiser, "Eine Entscheidung des deutsch-englischen gemischten Schiedsgerichts über den Versendungskauf" (1929) 3 RabelsZ 62–81
Radbruch, Gustav, "Gesetzliches Unrecht und übergesetzliches Recht" [1946] SJZ 105–8
Radin, Max, "Disseisin of Chattels: The Title of a Thief" (1922) 11:4 Cal L Rev 259–63
–, "Case Law and Stare Decisis: Concerning Präjudizienrecht in Amerika" (1933) 33:2 Col L Rev 199–212
Raffaele, Caterina, "Concepts and Remedies in the Law of Possession" (2004) 8 Edin L Rev 267–72
Rahmatian, Andreas, "A Comparison of German Moveable Property Law and English Personal Property Law" (2008) 3:1 J Comp L 197–248

Rank, Willem, "Harmonisation of National Security Rights" in: Ulrich Drobnig, Henricus J Snijders & Eric-Jan Zippro, eds, *Divergences of Property Law: An Obstacle to the Internal Market?* (Berlin: Sellier, 2006) 201–15

Reese, Willis LM, "Dépeçage: A Common Phenomenon in Choice of Law" (1973) 73:1 Col L Rev 58–75

Reid, Kenneth GC, "Unjustified Enrichment and Property Law" [1994] JRNS 167–99

–, "Obligations and Property: Exploring the Border" [1997] AJ 225–45

–, "Property Law: Sources and Doctrine" in: Kenneth G Reid & Reinhard Zimmermann, eds, *A History of Private Law in Scotland* (Oxford: Oxford University Press, 2000) 185–219

–, "The Idea of a Mixed Legal System" (2003) 78:1–2 Tul L Rev 5–40 [Reid, "Idea"]

Reid, Kenneth GC and Reinhard Zimmermann, eds, *A History of Private Law in Scotland* (Oxford: Oxford University Press, 2000)

Rémillard, Gil, "Présentation du projet de Code civil du Québec" (1991) 22 RGD 5–77

–, ed, *Code civil du Québec: commentaires du Ministre de la justice* (Montréal: Publications Dacfo, 1993)

Render, Meredith, "The Concept of Property" (2017) 78 Pittsburgh Law Review 437–92

Rheinstein, Max, "Traite Theorique Et Pratique Des Trusts by Pierre Lepaulle" (1934) 43:6 Yale LJ 1049–53

Riddell, William Renwick, "The First Court of Chancery in Canada" (1922) 2 Boston UL Rev 231–43

Robichaud, Alain, "Les droits de la Couronne et les conflits avec les créanciers hypothécaires" in: Barreau du Québec, ed, *Développements récents sur l'hypothèque* (Cowansville, Québec: Éditions Yvon Blais, 1997) 55–92

Roe, Mark J, "Legal Origins, Politics, and Modern Stock Markets" (2006) 120:2 Harv L Rev 460–527

Rogers, John M and Robert E Molzon, "Some Lessons About the Law from Self-Referential Problems in Mathematics" (1992) 90:5 Mich L Rev 992–1022

Rogerson, Pippa J, "The Situs of Debts in the Conflict of Law: Illogical, Unnecessary and Misleading" (1990) 49 CLJ 441–60

–, "Equity, Rights in Rem and the Brussels Convention" (1994) 53 CLJ 462–64

Rose, Carol M, "Possession as the Origin of Property" (1985) 52:1 U Chicago L Rev 73–88

–, "Crystals and Mud in Property Law" (1988) 40:3 Stan L Rev 577–610

Rosenthal, Leslie, "Economic Efficiency, Nuisance, and Sewage: New Lessons from Attorney-General v Council of the Borough of Birmingham" (2007) 36:1 J Legal Stud 27–62

Ross, Charles Stanley, "Shakespeare's Merry Wives and the Law of Fraudulent Conveyance" (1994) 25 Renaissance Drama 145–69

Rossier, Yves, "Etude comparée de certains aspects patrimoniaux de la fiducie" (1988) 34:4 McGill LJ 817–907

Rotherham, Craig, "Tracing Misconceptions in Foskett v McKeown" [2003] RLR 57–78

Roth, Wulf-Henning, "Secured Credit and the Internal Market: The Fundamental Freedoms and the EU's Mandate for Legislation" in: Horst Eidenmüller & Eva-Maria Kieninger, eds, *The Future of Secured Credit in Europe* (Berlin: Walter de Gruyter, 2008) 36–67

Rubin, Paul H, "Why Is the Common Law Efficient?" (1977) 6:1 J Legal Stud 51–64

Rudden, Bernard, "Economic Theory v Property Law: The Numerus Clausus Problem" in: John Eekelaar & John Bell, eds, *Oxford Essays in Jurisprudence: Third Series* (Oxford: Clarendon Press, 1987) 239–63 [Rudden, "Numerus Clausus"]

–, "Things as Thing and Things as Wealth" (1994) 14:1 Oxford J Legal Stud 81–97

Sachse, Harry R, "Report to the Louisiana Law Institute on Article Nine of the Uniform Commercial Code: Part I" (1967) 41:3 Tul L Rev 505–54

Safavian, Mehnaz S, "Firm-Level Evidence on Collateral and Access to Finance" in: Frederique Dahan & John Simpson, eds, *Secured Transactions Reform and Access to Credit* (Cheltenham: Edward Elgar, 2009) 110–21

Saibil, Norman A, ed, *Développements récents en droit bancaire* (Barreau du Québec, Service de formation permanente, Cowansville, Québec: Éditions Yvon Blais, 2003)

Salmond, John W, "Observations on Trover and Conversion" (1905) 21 LQR 43–54

Salmons, David, "Claims Against Third-Party Recipients of Trust Property" (2017) 76:2 CLJ 399–429

Sanders, Anne, "Cohabitants in Private Law: Trust, Frustration and Unjust Enrichment in England, Germany and Canada" (2013) 62:3 ICLQ 629–65

von Savigny, Friedrich Carl, *Vom Beruf unserer Zeit für Gesetzgebung und Rechtswissenschaft* (Heidelberg: Mohr, 1814)

–, *System des heutigen römischen Rechts* (Berlin: Veit & Comp, 1841), vol 5

–, *System des heutigen römischen Rechts* (Berlin: Veit & Comp, 1849), vol 8 [von Savigny, *System 8*]

–, *Das Recht des Besitzes*, ed by Adolf Friedrich Rudorff, 7th edn (Wien: Carl Gerold's Sohn, 1865)

Scavone, Robert M, "Stronger than Fictions: Canada Rethinks the Law of Securities Transfers in the Indirect Holding System" (2007) 45 CBLJ 67–93

Schilling, Theodore JR, "Some European Decisions on Non-Possessory Security Rights in Private International Law" (1985) 34:1 ICLQ 87–114

Schlesinger, Rudolf B, "The Past and Future of Comparative Law" (1995) 43:3 Am J Comp L 477–82

Schrage, Eltjo JH, "Notes on the Transfer of Property: Modus et Titulus Dominii Transferendi" (1992) 1 Fundamina 91–131

–, "Traditionibus et usucapionibus, non nudis pactis dominia rerum transferuntur: Die Wahl zwischen dem Konsens- und dem Traditionsprinzip in der Geschichte" in: Mario Ascheri, ed, *Ins Wasser geworfen und Ozeane durchquert: Festschrift für Knut Wolfgang Nörr* (Cologne: Böhlau, 2003) 913–58

Schwab, Dieter, "Eigentum" in: Otto Brunner, Werner Conze & Reinhart Koselleck, eds, *Geschichtliche Grundbegriffe: Historisches Lexikon zur politisch-sozialen Sprache in Deutschland* (Stuttgart: Klett-Cotta, 1975), vol 2, 65–115

Schwarcz, Steven L, "The Easy Case for the Priority of Secured Claims in Bankruptcy" (1997) 47:3 Duke LJ 425–89

Schwartz, Alan, "Security Interests and Bankruptcy Priorities: A Review of Current Theories" (1981) 10:1 J Legal Stud 1–37

–, "The Continuing Puzzle of Secured Debt" (1984) 37:5 Vand L Rev 1051–69

–, "A Theory of Loan Priorities" (1989) 18 J Legal Stud 209–62

–, "Taking the Analysis of Security Seriously" (1994) 80:8 Va L Rev 2073–87

Schwartz, Alan and Robert E Scott, "The Political Economy of Private Legislatures" (1995) 143:3 U Pa L Rev 595–654

Schwarzenbach, Sibyl, "Locke's Two Conceptions of Property" (1988) 14:2 *Soc Th & Pract* 141–72

Scott, Anthony, "Property Rights and Property Wrongs" (1983) 16:4 Can J Econ 555–73

Scott, Austin Wakeman, "The Nature of the Rights of the Cestui Que Trust" (1917) 17:4 Col L Rev 269–90

Scott, Michael, "Conversion and Revendication" (1961) 5:1 Mal L Rev 40–57

Scott, Robert E, "A Relational Theory of Secured Financing" (1986) 86:5 Col L Rev 901–77
–, "The Politics of Article 9" (1994) 80:8 Va L Rev 1783–851
Séguin, Maurice, "Le régime seigneurial au pays de Québec: 1760–1854" (1947) 1 *Revue d'histoire de l'Amérique française* 382–402 [Séguin, "Régime seigneurial I"]
–, "Le régime seigneurial au pays de Québec: 1760–1854" (1948) 1 *Revue d'histoire de l'Amérique française* 519–33
Seipp, David J, "The Concept of Property in the Early Common Law" (1994) 12 *Law & Hist R* 29–91
Sériaux, Alain, "La notion juridique de patrimoine: Brèves notations civilistes sur le verbe avoir" in: Ernest Caparros, ed, *Mélanges Germain Brière* (Montréal: Wilson & Lafleur, 1993) 312–23
Sherwin, Emily L, "Constructive Trusts in Bankruptcy" [1989] U Ill L Rev 297–365
Shortt, Adam and Arthur George Doughty, eds, *Documents Relating to the Constitutional History of Canada, 1759–1791*, 2d edn (Ottawa: J. de la Taché, 1918)
Siems, Mathias M, "Legal Origins: Reconciling Law and Finance and Comparative Law" (2007) 52:1 McGill LJ 55–81
–, "Measuring the Immeasurable: How to Turn Law into Numbers" in: Michael Faure & Jan M Smits, eds, *Does Law Matter?: On Law and Economic Growth* (Cambridge: Intersentia, 2011) 115–36
Sik, Ko Swan, "The Concept of Acquired Rights in International Law: A Survey" [1977] *Nethl Int'l L Rev* 120–42
Simmonds, Ralph L; George R Stewart; and David P Paciocco, *Study Paper on Wrongful Interference with Goods* (Toronto: Ontario Law Reform Commission, 1989)
Simpson, AWB, "The Introduction of the Action on the Case for Conversion" (1959) 75 LQR 364–80
Simpson, John and Frederique Dahan, "Mortgages in Transition Economies" in: Frederique Dahan & John Simpson, eds, *Secured Transactions Reform and Access to Credit* (Cheltenham: Edward Elgar, 2009) 172–204
HE Smith, "Property as the Law of Things" (2011) 125:7 Harv L Rev 1691–726
Smith, Lionel D, "The Province of the Law of Restitution" (1992) 71 Can Bar Rev 672–99
–, "Tracing in Taylor v Plumer: Equity in the Court of King's Bench" [1995] LMCLQ 240–68
–, *The Law of Tracing* (Oxford: Clarendon Press, 1997)
–, "W(h)ither Knowing Receipt" (1998) 114:3 LQR 394
–, "The Mystery of Juristic Reason" (2000) 12 Sup Ct L Rev 211–44 [Smith, "Mystery"]
–, "Unjust Enrichment, Property and the Structure of Trusts" (2000) 116 LQR 420–44
–, "Restitution: The Heart of Corrective Justice" (2001) 79:7 Tex L Rev 2115–75
–, "Property, Subsidiarity and Unjust Enrichment" in: David Johnston & Reinhard Zimmermann, eds, *Unjustified Enrichment: Key Issues in Comparative Perspective* (Cambridge: Cambridge University Press, 2002) 588–623
–, "Unravelling Proprietary Restitution" (2004) 40:3 CBLJ 317–38
–, "Tracing" in: Andrew S Burrows & Alan Rodger, eds, *Mapping the Law: Essays in Memory of Peter Birks* (Oxford: Oxford University Press, 2006) 119–39
–, "Demystifying Juristic Reasons" [2007] CBLJ 281–304 [Smith, "Demystifying"]
–, "Philosophical Foundations of Proprietary Remedies" in: Robert Chambers, Charles C Mitchell & James E Penner, eds, *Philosophical Foundations of the Law of Unjust Enrichment* (Oxford: Oxford University Press, 2009) 281–305
–, "Trust and Patrimony" (2009) 28 ETPJ 332–54

–, "Unauthorized Dispositions of Trust Property: Tracing in Quebec Law" (2013) 58:4 McGill LJ 795–810

–, ed, *Re-imagining the Trust: Trusts in Civil Law* (Cambridge: Cambridge University Press, 2012)

LD Smith; R Chambers; M McInnes; JW Neyers; and SGA Pitel, *The Law of Restitution in Canada* (Toronto: E. Montgomery Publications, 2004)

Smith, Stephen A, "Unjust Enrichment: Nearer to Tort Than Contract" in: Robert Chambers, Charles C Mitchell & James E Penner, eds, *Philosophical Foundations of the Law of Unjust Enrichment* (Oxford: Oxford University Press, 2009) 181–208

Snijders, Henk J, "Access to Civil Securities and Free Competition in the EU: A Plea for One European Security Right in Movables" in: Ulrich Drobnig, Henricus J Snijders & Eric-Jan Zippro, eds, *Divergences of Property Law: An Obstacle to the Internal Market?* (Berlin: Sellier, 2006) 153–71

Stagl, Jakob Fortunat, "Gutgläubiger Fahrniserwerb als „sofortige Ersitzung": Eine Neubestimmung der §§ 932 ff. BGB" (2011) 211:3–4 AcP 530–82

von Staudinger, Julius, *Kommentar zum Bürgerlichen Gesetzbuch mit Einführungsgesetz und Nebengesetzen, Buch 1. Allgemeiner Teil, §§ 134–138, Anh zu § 138: ProstG*, ed by Norbert Habermann (Berlin: Sellier-de Gruyter, 2011)

–, *Buch 2. Recht der Schuldverhältnisse, §§ 812 - 822 (Ungerechtfertigte Bereicherung)*, ed by Norbert Horn (Berlin: Sellier-de Gruyter, 2007)

–, *Buch 3. Sachenrecht, §§ 925–984; Anh zu §§ 929 ff (Eigentum 2)*, ed by Karl-Heinz Gursky (Berlin: Sellier-de Gruyter, 2011)

–, *Buch 3. Sachenrecht, §§ 985–1011*, ed by Karl-Heinz Gursky (Berlin: Sellier-de Gruyter, 2012)

–, *Internationales Sachenrecht*, ed by Jan Kropholler (Berlin: Sellier-de Gruyter, 1996)

–, *Internationales Sachenrecht*, ed by Dieter Henrich (Berlin: Sellier-de Gruyter, 2015)

Steinberg, Sylvan J (1955–1956) 30:1 Tul L Rev 153–56

Stern, James Y, "Property, Exclusivity, and Jurisdiction" (2014) 100:1 Va L Rev 111–81

Steven, Andrew JM, "Rights in Security over Moveables" in: Kenneth G Reid & Reinhard Zimmermann, eds, *A History of Private Law in Scotland* (Oxford: Oxford University Press, 2000) 333–62

Stevens, John, "Restitution or Property?: Priority and Title to Shares in the Conflict of Laws" (1996) 59:5 Modern L Rev 741–46

Stevens, Robert, "Three Enrichment Issues" in: Andrew S Burrows & Alan Rodger, eds, *Mapping the Law: Essays in Memory of Peter Birks* (Oxford: Oxford University Press, 2006) 49–64

–, "When and Why Does Unjustified Enrichment Justify the Recognition of Proprietary Rights?" (2012) 92:3 Boston UL Rev 919–37

Stevens, William S, "The Common Law Origins of the Infield Fly Rule" (1974–1975) 123 U Pa L Rev 1474–81

Stigler, George J, "The Economics of Information" (1961) 69 J Pol Econ 213–25

Stoffel, Walter A, ed, *Conflits et harmonisation: Mélanges en l'honneur d'Alfred E. von Overbeck à l'occasion de son 65ème anniversaire* (Fribourg: Édition universitaire, 1990)

Stone, Harlan F, "The Nature of the Rights of the 'Cestui Que Trust'" (1917) 17:6 Col L Rev 467–501

Story, Joseph, *Commentaries on the Conflict of Laws: Foreign and Domestic*, 3rd edn (Boston: Little, Brown & Co., 1846)

Stumbles, John GH, "The PPSA: The Extended Reach of the Definition of the PPSA Security Interest" (2011) 34:2 UNSWLJ 448–71

Swadling, William, "A Claim in Restitution?" [1996] LMCLQ 63–66
–, "Explaining Resulting Trusts" (2008) 124 LQR 72–102
–, "Ignorance and Unjust Enrichment: The Problem of Title" (2008) 28:4 Oxford J Legal Stud 627–58
–, "Policy Arguments for Proprietary Restitution" (2008) 28:4 LS 506–30 [Swadling, "Policy Arguments"]
–, "The Fiction of the Constructive Trust" (2011) 64:1 Curr Legal Probs 399–433
Sykes, Edward I, *The Law of Securities: An Account of the Law Pertaining to Securities over Real and Personal Property under the Laws of Australian Jurisdictions*, 5th edn (North Ryde, N.S.W.: Law Book, 1993)
Symeonides, Symeon C, "Revolution and Counter-Revolution in American Conflics Law: Is There a Middle Ground?" (1985) 46:3 Ohio St LJ 549–68
Tarrant, John, "Thieves as Trustees: In Defence of the Theft Principle" (2009) 3 J Equ 170
Tate, Joshua C, "Ownership and Possession in the Early Common Law" (2006) 48 Am J Legal Hist 280–313
Tetley, William, "Mixed Jurisdictions: Common Law vs. Civil Law (Codified and Uncodified)" (1999) 4 Unif L Rev 591–620, 877–907
Tettenborn, Andrew, "Reversionary Damage to Chattels" (1994) 53:2 CLJ 326–42
Theriot, Robert L, "An Examination of the Role of Delivery in the Transfer of Ownership and Risk in Sales under Louisiana Law" (1985–1986) 60:5 Tul L Rev 1035–60
Tilbury, Michael, "Remedy as Right" in: Ross Grantham & Charles Rickett, eds, *Structure and Justification in Private Law: Essays for Peter Birks* (Oxford: Hart, 2008) 421–40
Timm, Wolfram, "Außenwirkungen vertraglicher Verfügungsverbote?" (1989) 44:1 JZ 13–24
Townsend, Robert M, "Optimal Contracts and Competitive Markets with Costly State Verification" (1979) 21 J Econ Th 265–93
Trahan, John Randall, "The Continuing Influence of le Droit civil and el Derecho Civil in the Private Law of Louisiana" (2003) 63:4 La L Rev 1019–66
Trebilcock, Michael J, "The Lessons and Limits of Law and Economics" in: Pierre Noreau, ed, *Dans le regard d'autre - In the Eye of the Beholder* (Montréal: Éditions Thémis, 2007) 113–64
Trebilcock, Michael J and Paul-Erik Veel, "Property Rights and Development: The Contingent Case for Formalization" (2008) 30:2 *U Pa J Int'l L* 397–482
Trudel, Marcel, *The Seigneurial Regime* (Canadian Historical Association Booklets, Ottawa: Canadian Historical Association, 1963)
Tudsri, Pattarapas, "Characterization of Proprietary Restitution in the Conflict of Laws" (2013) 44:2 Ottawa L Rev 261–309
Ulen, Thomas S, "The Role of Law in Economic Growth and Development" in: Michael Faure & Jan M Smits, eds, *Does Law Matter?: On Law and Economic Growth* (Cambridge: Intersentia, 2011) 179–220
Ulpian, *Digests*
Uniform Law Conference of Canada, ed, *Proceedings of the 38th Annual Meeting* (Ottawa: Uniform Law Conference of Canada, 1971)
van Warmelo, Paul, *An Introduction to the Principles of Roman Civil Law* (Cape Town: Juta, 1976)
Vasey, Vincent, "Fideicommissa and Uses: The Clerical Connection Revisited" (1982) 41:1 Jurist 201–14
Vauclair, Alain and Martin-François Parent, "Harmonization of Federal Legislation with Quebec Civil Law: Some Examples from the Bankruptcy and Insolvency Act" in:

Canada, Department of Justice, ed, *The Harmonization of Federal Legislation with the Civil Law of the Province of Quebec and Canadian Bijuralism: Second Publication* (Ottawa: Canada, Department of Justice, 2001) 1–37

Venturini, Gian C, *Private International Law: Property*, ed by Konrad Zweigert, Ulrich Drobnig, and Kurt Lipstein (International Encyclopedia of Comparative Law, III-21, Tübingen: Mohr Siebeck, 1976)

Vincelette, Denis, "Définition et notion de la propriété: Plaidoyer pour la vraisemblance" (2001) 31:4 RGD 677–700

Virgo, Graham, *The Principles of the Law of Restitution*, 2^d edn (Oxford: Oxford University Press, 2006) [Virgo, *Restitution*^2]

–, "The Genetically Modified Constructive Trust" (2016) 2:2 CJCCL 579–607 [Virgo, "Genetically Modified"]

–, *The Principles of the Law of Restitution*, 3^rd edn (Oxford: Oxford University Press, 2016) [Virgo, *Restitution*]

Visscher, Fernand de, "Auctoritas et Mancipio" (1956) 22 SDHI 87–111

–, "Dualismo ed evoluzione della proprietà nella Roma repubblicana" (1957) 23 SDHI 26

Visser, Daniel, "The Absoluteness of Ownership: The South African Common Law in Perspective" (1985) 1 Acta Juridica 39–52

Wagner-Döbler, Roland, "Präjudizien in deutschen, englischen und US-amerikanischen Gerichtsentscheidungen: Ein quantitativer Vergleich" (1995) 59 RabelsZ 113–27

Wagner, Eberhard, "Rechtsgeschäftliche Unübertragbarkeit und § 137 S. 1 BGB" (1994) 194 AcP 451–78

Wagner, Gerhard, "Rudolph von Jherings Theorie des subjektiven Rechts und der berechtigenden Reflexwirkungen" (1993) 193:4 AcP 319–47

Walker, Janet, *Halsbury's Laws of Canada: Conflict of Laws* (Toronto: LexisNexis Butterworths, 2006)

Walker, Janet and Jean-Gabriel Castel, *Canadian Conflict of Laws*, 6^th edn (LexisNexis Butterworths, 2005)

Wallot, Jean-Pierre, "Le régime seigneurial et son abolition au Canada" (1969) 50:4 Can Historical R 367–93

Walsh, Catherine E, "Justifications for UCC Article 9's Treatment of Deposit Accounts: A Comparative Note" (2015) 4:1 *Penn St J L & Int'l Aff* 350–62

Ward, Roger K, "Bijuralism as an Assimilation Tool: Lord Durham's Assessment of the Louisiana Legal System" (2003) 63:4 La L Rev 1127–48

Warren, Elizabeth, "Making Policy with Imperfect Information: The Article 9 Full Priority Debates" (1997) 82:6 Cornell L Rev 1373–95

Wasserman, Howard M, "The Economics of the Infield Fly Rule" [2013] Utah L Rev 479–517

Wass, Jack, "The Court's in Personam Jurisdiction in Cases Involving Foreign Land" (2014) 63:1 ICLQ 103–35

Waters, Donovan WM, "The Nature of the Trust Beneficiary's Interest" (1967) 45:2 Can Bar Rev 219–83

–, "Matrimonial Property Disputes - Resulting and Constructive Trusts - Restitution" (1975) 53:2 Can Bar Rev 366–81

–, "Unification or Harmonization?: Experiences with the Trust Concept" in: Walter A Stoffel, ed, *Conflits et harmonisation: Mélanges en l'honneur d'Alfred E. von Overbeck à l'occasion de son 65ème anniversaire* (Fribourg: Édition universitaire, 1990) 591–609

–, "The Institution of the Trust in Civil and Common Law" in: Académie du droit international, ed, *Recueil des cours* (Leiden: Sijthoff, 1995) 113–453

–, “Resulting Trusts and the Canadian Remedial Constructive Trust: Reconciling the Two” (2013) 19:9 *T & T* 1–12 [Waters, “Reconciling”]
Watson, Alan, *Legal Transplants: An Approach to Comparative Law* (Edinburgh: Scottish Academic Press, 1974)
Watterson, Stephen, “Modelling Subrogation as an ‘Equitable Remedy’” (2016) 2:2 CJCCL 609–78
Watts, Peter, “Birks and Proprietary Claims, with Special Reference to Misrepresentation and to Ultra Vires Contracts” in: Ross Grantham & Charles Rickett, eds, *Structure and Justification in Private Law: Essays for Peter Birks* (Oxford: Hart, 2008) 361–78
Webb, Charlie, “Property, Unjust Enrichment, and Defective Transfers” in: Robert Chambers, Charles C Mitchell & James E Penner, eds, *Philosophical Foundations of the Law of Unjust Enrichment* (Oxford: Oxford University Press, 2009) 335–70
–, “The Myth of the Remedial Constructive Trust” (2016) 69:1 Curr Legal Probs 353–76 [Webb, “Myth”]
Weinrib, Ernest Joseph, “Corrective Justice in a Nutshell” (2002) 52 UTLJ 349–56
–, “Book Review: Restoring Restitution” (2005) 91 Va L Rev 861–78 [Weinrib, “Restoring”]
–, “Correctively Unjust Enrichment” in: Robert Chambers, Charles C Mitchell & James E Penner, eds, *Philosophical Foundations of the Law of Unjust Enrichment* (Oxford: Oxford University Press, 2009) 31–53 [Weinrib, “Correctively”]
–, *Corrective Justice* (Oxford: Oxford University Press, 2012)
–, *The Idea of Private Law*, 2d edn (Oxford: Oxford University Press, 2012)
Weintraub, Benjamin and Alan N Resnick, “Bankruptcy Trustee’s Strong-Arm Powers Balked by a Constructive Trust” (1989–1990) 22 Unif Comm Code LJ 367–74
–, “When Money Mistakenly Paid to the Debtor Is Transferred to Its Rightful Owner on the Eve of Bankruptcy - Voidable Preference or Constructive Trust?” (1994–1995) 27 Unif Comm Code LJ 103–7
White, RW, “Equitable Obligations in Private International Law: The Choice of Law” (1986) 11:1 Sydney L Rev 92
Wielsch, Dan, “Differenzierungen des Eigentums: Zur Entwicklung eines rechtlichen Grundbegriffs” in: Stefan Keller & Stefan Wiprächtiger, eds, *Recht zwischen Dogmatik und Theorie: Marc Amstutz zum 50. Geburtstag* (Zürich, St Gallen: Dike, 2012) 329–53
Williams, T Cyprian, “The Terms Real and Personal in English Law” (1888) 4 LQR 394–408 [Williams, “Real and Personal”]
–, “Is a Right of Action in Tort a Chose in Action?” (1894) 10 LQR 143–57 [Williams, “Right of Action”]
Windscheid, Bernhard, *Die Actio des römischen Civilrechts* (Düsseldorf: Julius Budeus, 1856)
Wong, Adrian, “An Introduction to Liens in Commercial Transactions” (1999) 20 Sing L Rev 134–58
Wong, Simone, “Constructive Trusts over the Family Home: Lessons to Be Learned from Other Commonwealth Jurisdictions?” (1998) 18:3 LS 369–90
Wood, Roderick J, “The Nature and Definition of Federal Security Interests” (2000) 34:1 CBLJ 65–113
–, “Circular Priorities in Secured Transactions Law” (2010) 47:4 Alta L Rev 823–52
–, “Journey to the Outer Limits of Secured Transactions Law” (2010) 48:3 CBLJ 482–97
–, “Bank Act-PPSA Interactions: Still Waiting for Solutions” (2012) 52:2 CBLJ 248–70
Wood, Roderick J and Michael I Wylie, “Non-Consensual Security Interests in Personal Property” (1992) 30:4 Alta L Rev 1055–99

World Bank (WB) and International Bank for Reconstruction and Development (IBRD), *World Development Report 2002: Building Institutions for Markets* (Oxford: Oxford University Press, 2002)
–, *Doing Business in 2004* (Oxford: Oxford University Press, 2004)
Worthington, Sarah, "Equitable Liens in Commercial Transactions" (1994) 53 CLJ 263–72
Xu, Guangdong, "The Role of Property Law in Economic Growth" in: Michael Faure & Jan M Smits, eds, *Does Law Matter?: On Law and Economic Growth* (Cambridge: Intersentia, 2011) 331–83
Yale, DEC, "The Revival of Equitable Estates in the Seventeenth Century: An Explanation by Lord Nottingham" (1957) 15:1 CLJ 72–86
Yaron, Reuven, "Reflections on usucapio" (1967) 35:2 Tijdschrift voor Rechtsgeschiedenis 191–229
Yeo, Tiong Min, *Choice of Law for Equitable Doctrines* (Oxford: Oxford University Press, 2004)
Zaccaria, Elena Christine, "The Nature of the Beneficiary's Right Under a Trust: proprietary Right, Purely Personal Right or Right Against a Right?" [2019] LQR 460–83
Zachariä, Karl Salomo, *Handbuch des französischen Civilrechts*, 3rd edn (Tübingen: Mohr, 1827)
Zaphiriou, George Aristotle, *The Transfer of Chattels in Private International Law* (London: Athlone Press, University of London, 1956)
Ziegel, Jacob S, "Interaction of Sales Law and the OPPSA, and Related Questions" (1982) 7 CBLJ 338–53
–, "Interaction of Personal Property Security Legislation and Security Interests under the Bank Act" (1986–1987) 12 CBLJ 73–95
–, "Should Canada Adopt an Article 2A Type Law on Personal Property Leasing?" (1989–1990) 16 CBLJ 369–418
–, "Personal Property Security and Bankruptcy: There Is No War!" (1993) 72:1 Can Bar Rev 44–53
–, "Harmonization of Private Laws in Federal Systems of Government: Canada, the USA, and Australia" in: Ross Cranston, ed, *Making Commercial Law: Essays in Honour of Roy Goode* (Oxford: Clarendon Press, 1997) 131–66
–, "Unwelcome Intrusion of the Remedial Constructive Trust in Personal Property Security Law: Ellingsen (Trustee Of) v Hallmark Ford Sales Ltd" (2001) 34 CBLJ 460–70
–, "New and Old Challenges in Approaching Phase Three Amendments to Canada's Commercial Insolvency Laws" (2002) 37 CBLJ 75–118
Ziegel, Jacob S and David L Denomme, *The Ontario Personal Property Security Act: Commentary and Analysis* (Aurora, Ont.: Canada Law Book, 1994)
Ziff, Bruce H, *Principles of Property Law*, 5th edn (Toronto: Carswell, 2010)
Zwalve, Willem J, "A Labyrinth of Creditors: A Short Introduction to the History of Security Interests in Goods" in: Eva-Maria Kieninger, ed, *Security Rights in Movable Property in European Private Law* (Cambridge: Cambridge University Press, 2004) 38–53
Zweigert, Konrad and Hein Kötz, *Einführung in die Rechtsvergleichung auf dem Gebiete des Privatrechts*, 3rd edn (Tübingen: Mohr Siebeck, 1996)
Zweigert, Konrad and Hans-Jürgen Puttfarken, "Statutory Interpretation: Civilian Style" (1969–1970) 44 Tul L Rev 704–19
Zweigert, Konrad and Kurt Siehr, "Jhering's Influence on the Development of Comparative Legal Method" (1971) 19 Am J Comp L 215–31

# Table of Cases

## Australia



## Canada

## European Union



## Germany



## Hong Kong



## New Zealand



## United Kingdom

## United States

## Other Jurisdictions

# Index